Japan Economic/Demographic Information

Geographic area:	145,856 sq. miles
Topography:	Four main islands—Honshu (mainland), Hokkaido, Kyushu and Shikoku
Government type:	Parliamentary democracy
Capital:	Tokyo
Population:	123,231,000
Population density:	844 per sq. mile, 76.7% urban
Agricultural products:	Rice, vegetables, fruits and sugar
Industrial products:	Metals, chemicals, textiles and electronics
Natural resources:	Fish, oil, natural gas, negligible amount of mineral resources
Literacy:	99%
Defense:	Less than 1% GNP
National budget:	$470 billion
Balance of payments:	+ $85 billion
Inflation:	0.7%
Gross National Product:	$2.1 trillion
Gross Domestic Product:	$1.6 trillion
International reserves: (less gold)	$98 billion
Gold reserves:	24.2 million fine troy ounces
Major imports:	Fuels, machinery, manufactured goods, raw materials and foodstuffs
Imports:	$187 billion
U.S.	20%
Middle East	26%
Southeast Asia	22%
European Community	6%
Major Exports:	Machinery, electrical equipment, motor vehicles, chemicals and manufactured goods
Exports:	$264 billion
U.S.	37%
Southeast Asia	23%
European Community	12%
Labor Profile:	
Agriculture, Forestry, Fishing	8.8%
Manufacturing	25.02%
Transport./Communications	5.91%
Construction	9.13%
Other	51.17%

AN INSTITUTIONAL INVESTOR PUBLICATION

INVEST JAPAN

The Structure, Performance and Opportunities of Japan's Stock, Bond and Fund Markets

WILLIAM T. ZIEMBA
SANDRA L. SCHWARTZ

PROBUS PUBLISHING COMPANY
Chicago, Illinois

This publication is designed to provide accurate and authoritative information in regard to the subject matter covered. It is sold with the understanding that the publisher is not engaged in rendering legal, accounting or other professional service.

Library of Congress Cataloging in Publication Data Available

ISBN 1-55738-234-4

Printed in the United States of America

BB

1   2   3   4   5   6   7   8   9   0

This book is dedicated to our daughter Rachel
who lived the Japanese experience with us.

INVEST JAPAN

Contents

PREFACE

Everywhere you look these days, in newspapers, magazines or on the TV news, there is talk of Japan and its financial markets. Obviously, the great wealth acquired in the 1980s by Japan and its giant companies has given the country vast economic power. The twenty one largest financial institutions in the world, ranked by capitalization, are Japanese. Even the tiny subsidiaries of the Japanese big four brokerage firms are in the top 20-35 U.S. brokerage firms. The top insurance companies each have $50+ billion in assets for a total of about $1 trillion. The Osaka stock exchange, the little sister of the Tokyo exchange, has a capitalization more than the London exchange while the Tokyo exchange rivals the New York exchange. Many of the richest individuals in the world are Japanese including many billionaires.

This book takes a broad view of the variables necessary to deal intelligently with stock, bond, and mutual fund investment in Japan including currency risk and hedging. A companion volume discusses futures, options and other derivative securities and stock hedging strategies. From 1949 to the end of 1989, land values and stock prices in Japan went up over 500 times in U.S. dollars. There's much discussion of the astronomical land prices in Japan, especially in Tokyo, and the high price earnings ratios of the stocks. Why did these prices get so high and can they stay there? Is a crash in stock or land prices inevitable or probable and to what extent and when? What is happening in Japanese finance now? Why were 1988 and 1989 such strong years for the Japanese stock market and what does the future look like? Where should one invest in Japan? Are there edges in the stock market and strategies that one should consider? How can you protect yourself against risks in the stock market and changes in the value of the yen? We address these and related questions to provide an up-to-date look at the investment potential and risks of Japan.

The steep fall in Japanese stock prices in 1990 is addressed in Chapter 7. The workings of the stock market, the various indices, and the performance over time of various measures of stock market activity are described. Data is provided in a form useable for future reference with much visual and tabular data to record useful information concerning Japanese financial markets. As much as possible we have tried to make the data current to the end of December 1990. Some data is current to the end of February 1991. Regarding specific investments, we discuss the present and probable future, provide sample portfolios, mutual fund suggestions and seasonal edge calendars.

Without implicating them in any way we thank our colleagues at the Yamaichi Research Institute and the University of Tsukuba for their helpful information and discussions on various aspects of Japanese culture, institutions, and investment strategies. It was Professor Keizo Nagatani of the University of British Columbia who, while visiting the University of Tsukuba on his sabbatical, suggested to Professor Rinya Shibakawa that he bring WTZ to Japan on the Yamaichi visiting professor chair program to help develop western style financial research and teaching in Japan. At the same time, SLS served as visiting Associate Professor of Economics and taught classes comparing U.S. and Japanese management for the information age and world debt. This allowed us to live the Japanese experience in daily life and in the financial markets.

This book is dedicated to our daughter Rachel who not only puts up with her father's academic globe-trotting but thrives on it. She had an extraordinarily pleasant experience in Japanese public school, Teshirogi Minami in Tsukuba, where she made friends, learned Japanese and learned about the Japanese culture.

We shall always treasure the wonderful treatment our family received during our stay in Japan in 1988-89. Every effort was made to make us feel comfortable and welcome. Our hosts did more for us than one would ever expect in a North American or European visit. The help through the maze of regulations and rules associated with university and business life was especially gratifying. Without their help it would have been hard to function. Atsuko Asano and Satoshi Nojiri were particularly helpful in this regard. We hope that this unique experience will be reflected positively in this book. Special thanks go to Yukio Okada, formerly the vice chairman of the Yamaichi Research Institute, the organizer of the Tsukuba professorships for his exceptionally kind and generous help during our visit. We would also like to thank other YRI colleagues particularly Shigeru Ishii, Asaji Komatsu, Hitoshi Shintani, and Hirokaza Yuihama for their generous help on many points concerning the Japanese financial system. While we learned much from our Yamaichi and Tsukuba colleagues, they are in a no way responsible for any of the statements, results and opinions stated in this book. Discussions with Professors Kiyoshi Kato, Kazuo Kishimoto, Hitosi Konno, and Katsushugi Sawaki have also been helpful. Jun Uno, of Nihon Keizai Shimbun, Inc, provided much valuable data and helpful information and comments on an earlier draft. Thanks also to his colleague Shizuya Kurata for supplying us with the Nikkei golf course membership data. Kazuhiko Fujiki of the Japan Real Estate Institute and his colleagues kindly supplied land price data. Thanks also go to Warren Bailey, David Myers, Julian Shaw, Doug Stone, Edward O. Thorp, Andy Turner and Peter Williamson for helpful discussions and comments on earlier drafts of the book. Special thanks go to Atsuko Asano, Bruno Vander Cruyssen and Nancy Thompson for their outstanding research assistance.

Continuing consulting and research related to Japanese financial markets with the Frank Russell Company, Edward O. Thorp and Associates and the Gordon Capital Corporation has been very beneficial to this book. Some chapters have also benefited from seminar and conference presentations at Cornell Univesity, Dartmouth College, New York University, the Vancouver ORSA/TIMS, the Osaka International TIMS, the Athens IFORS, the DAIS Group client conference, the Frank Russell client conference, the Operations Research Society of Japan, Tokyo and Nagoya branches, the Berkeley program in finance in the U.S. and in Asia and the Pacific Basin Finance conferences organized by the University of Rhode Island and the Taipex Foundation. Partial support of research activities on Japanese financial markets by the Social Sciences and Humanities Research Council of Canada and the Centre for International Business Research at the University of British Columbia is also gratefully acknowledged.

This book gives some sample recommendations that suggest that you seek out anomalies or security market regularities that arise because of the confluence of economic, institutional and psychological factors. The approach is then to use this edge to advantage in your investment approach. Markets and information change fast so you should be cautious in all investments and seek, but then carefully evaluate, professional advice.

William T. Ziemba
Sandra L. Schwartz

CHAPTER 1
THE STOCK MARKETS AND HOW THEY OPERATE

The Tokyo Stock Exchange (TSE) is a non-profit corporation established by member securities companies with their capital contribution. A stock exchange in Japan must be specially licensed and regulated by the Minister of Finance. The TSE was founded in 1878. The TSE in today's form was established April 1, 1949, during the occupation, under a new law. Figure 1.1 has historical highlights of the TSE from 1878 to 1990.

The TSE is located in a modern building with excellent facilities in the Nihonbashi section of Tokyo. Its modern earthquake-proof construction has given it the title *crash* proof! It is conveniently located next to a river so those who might jump out in any future crash will have a soft landing! The TSE is governed by a 24-member board of directors; the president and six officer-governors are in charge of daily operations. These people cannot be engaged in any other business. Some 900 are on the staff of the TSE and about 200 additional employees work for subsidiaries. The trading floor is very busy, about 2000 people work there.

TSE Membership is limited to securities companies licensed by the Minister of Finance. Regular members are ordinary broker-dealers, and *saitori* members are broker's brokers on the trade floors. There are 114 regular members and four *saitori*.

Equity securities and debt securities are listed on the TSE. Listed equity securities include domestic and foreign stocks. Domestic stocks are grouped into *first section stocks* and *second section stocks*. The former are those with a large number of shares issued, an extensive share distribution, and a good volume of trade. Newly-listed stocks are assigned to the second section; when they satisfy the requirements for a first section listing, they are assigned to it. See Tables 1.1 (a, b). Stocks in emerging companies are traded in the *over-the-counter-market*. ·Foreign stocks are assigned in the *foreign stock section*, see Table 1.1b. Debt securities, which include domestic, yen and foreign currency denominated foreign bonds, are assigned to the *bond section*.

1

Figure 1.1   Historical Highlights on the Tokyo Stock Exchange

May 15	1878	Tokyo Stock Exchange Co Ltd established
Jun 30	1943	Japan Securities Exchange , a quasi-governmental agency, organized by merger of all existing stock exchanges in Japan
Apr 16	1947	Japan Securities Exchange dissolved
Apr 1	1949	Tokyo Stock Exchange in the present form founded
Jun 1	1951	Margin transaction introduced
Apr 2	1956	Bond trading started
Oct 2	1961	Second section for stocks opened
Oct 1	1966	Government bonds listed for the first time after World War II
Jan 9	1967	Transaction in subscription rights to new shares started
Oct 2	1967	New auction process put into practice with abolition of *Baikai* trades (off-exchange trades by members reported as Exchange contracts.
Apr 1	1968	Licensing system for securities companies introduced in place of registration system
Jul 1	1969	Tokyo Stock Price Index inaugurated (Jan 4, 1968 = 100)
May 11	1970	Trading in convertible bonds started
Oct 15	1970	TSE joined in the International Federation of Stock Exchanges (FIBV)
Jul 19	1971	Book entry clearing system for stocks introduced
Apr 2	1973	Yen-based foreign bonds listed for the first time
Dec 18	1973	Foreign stock section opened
Sept 24	1974	Market information system (MIS) put into operation
Apr 1	1977	Ad valorem brokerage commission system introduced
Apr 2	1979	Block trading system for government bonds begun
Jan 23	1982	Computer assisted order routing & execution system (CORES) started for 440 inactive stocks
Apr 8	1982	TSE constitutional provisions against foreign membership deleted
Dec 28	1982	Special trading post abolished
Oct 1	1983	Computerized System for Transactions Collation (CSTC) put into full operation
Nov 1	1983	Criteria for stock listing amended
May 15	1984	Central Depository and Clearing of Securities Law promulgated
Dec 6	1984	New market building of TSE completed
Apr 6	1985	CORES expanded to include additional 750 issues
Apr 15	1985	Commission rates for block orders reduced
May 13	1985	Trading started in new market building
Oct 19	1985	Trading in government bond futures started
Feb 1	1986	10 securities companies including first six foreign companies, join the exchange
Feb 9	1987	NTT listed
Nov 2	1987	Book entry clearing system for convertible bonds introduced
Nov 4	1987	The number of regular members increased to 114 from 93
May 23	1988	22 securities companies including 16 foreign companies join the exchange
Jul 8	1988	Trading in 20-year government bond futures started
Sep 3	1988	Trading in stock index futures based on Topix started
Sep 3	1989	Trading in stock index futures options based on Topix started

Source: Tokyo Stock Exchange

Table 1.1a   Listing and Delisting Criteria for the TSE-I, April 1990

	Assignment of Listed Stock to First Section	Delisting
Application	All of the following criteria must be met	In case of falling under any of the following criteria
Number of shares listed	20 million shares or more	Less than 6 million shares
Number of shares held by *Special Few* as of each end of last 2 business years	70% or less of the number of shares listed	More than 70% of the number of shares listed (provisionally 80%)
Number of shareholders holding 1 unit or more (excluding *special few*) as of each end of last 2 business years	If the number of shares listed is: 1) less than 30 million shares, 3,000 or more 2) 30 million but less than 200 million shares, 3000 plus 100 for each 10 million shares in excess of first 20 million or more 3) 200 million but less than 220 million shares; 4800 or more 4) 220 million or more; 4800 plus 100 for each 20 million shares in excess of first 200 million shares or more	If the number of shares listed is: 1) less than 10 million shares; less than 500 2) 10 but less than 20 million shares; less than 750 3) 20 million shares or more, less than 1,000 plus 100 for each 10 million shares in excess of first 20 million shares, up to 2,000
Average monthly trading volume	For each period of last 6 months and preceding 6 months 1) TSE only; 200,000 shares or more 2) TSE and either of Osaka or Nagoya SEs; 200,000 shares or more on any of 2 SEs or 250,000 shares or more in total of 2 SEs 3) TSE, Osaka and Nagoya SEs; 200,000 shares or more on any of 3 SEs or 300,000 shares or more in total of 3 SEs	1) for last 1 year: less than 10,000 shares, or 2) no trades during last 3 months
Dividends	1) dividend records: ¥5 or more in cash per share for each of last 3 business years 2) dividend prospect: able to maintain ¥5 or more in cash per share after listing	No cash dividends paid for each of last 5 business years and excess liabilities continued for last 3 business years

Source: Tokyo Stock Exchange

Table 1.1b
Listing Details for Domestic and Foreign Securities for TSE-I and Foreign
Stock Section, April 1990

	Domestic Stock	Foreign Stocks
Application	All of the following criteria must be met	All of the following criteria must be met
Number of shares to be listed	If the issuer is based: 1) in or around Tokyo: 6 million shares or more 2) elsewhere: 20 million shares or more	If the stock is to be traded in a unit of: 1) 1000 shares: 20 million shares or more 2) 100 shares: 2 million shares or more 3) 50 shares: 1 million shares or more 4) 10 shares: 200,000 shares or more 5) 1 share: 20,000 shares or more
Number of shares held by *Special Few* (10 largest shareholders and those having special interest in the issue)	Provisional criteria 80% or less of the number of shares to be listed by the time of listing, and also 70% or less by the end of the first business year after listing	Not applicable. The stock is instead required to have a good liquidity in the home market.
Number of shareholders holding 1 unit or more (excluding *special few*)	If the number of shares listed is: 1) less than 10 million shares, 1,000 or more 2) 10 million but less than 20 million shares, 1500 or more 3) 20 million or more; 2000 plus 100 for each 10 million shares in excess of 20 million shares or more	Not applicable. The stock is instead required to have 1000 or more shareholders in Japan.
Time elapsed after incorporation	5 years or more with continuous business operation.	Not applicable. The stock is instead required to have 1000 or more shareholders in Japan.
Shareholders' equity	¥1 billion or more in total and ¥100 or more per share	¥10 billion or more in total.
Net profit before taxes	1) Annual total for each of last 3 business years: a. 1st business year ¥200 million or more b. 2nd business year, ¥300 million or more c. The last business year: ¥400 million or more 2) Per share amount: ¥15 or more for each of last 3 business years and ¥20 or more for last business year	Annual total for each of last 3 business years: ¥2 billion or more
Dividends	1) Dividend record: paid in cash for the business year ended within the latest year 2) Dividend prospect: able to maintain ¥5 or more in cash per share after listing	1) Dividend record: paid for each of last 3 business years ended within the latest year 2) Dividend prospect: able to pay continuously after listing.

Notes: (1) The TSE also has listing regulations for straight bonds, convertible bonds, bonds with warrants, etc
(2) All numerical criteria above are for a company which provides 1000 shares as the number of one "unit" of shares.

Source: Tokyo Stock Exchange

The TSE is a two-way, continuous pure auction market where buy and sell orders directly interact with one another. Figures 1.2 and 1.3 describe the manual and computer-aided order procedures, respectively. Trading occurs from 9 to 11 a.m. and from 1 to 3 p.m on Mondays to Fridays. The morning session is called the *zenba* and the afternoon the *goba*. Until the end of January 1989 there also was trading on the first, fourth, and (if there was one) fifth Saturday mornings of each month from 9 to 11 a.m. Regular member firms act as brokers and dealers in the exchange market while *saitori* members function solely as middlemen in transactions between regular members. *Saitori* members cannot trade for their own account, nor can they accept orders from the public.

Regular members may not:

1. Buy or sell at a new high or low for the day,
2. Buy or sell in the 15 minutes before closing,
3. Buy or sell issues for which equity-related financings have been officially announced.

Virtually all limit or market orders are placed by regular members with *saitori* members. *Saitori* members match orders in accordance with the auction principle, of price, priority and time precedence. The orders are settled in three days. See Figure 1.4 for details.

There are no responsible market-makers, such as the specialists on the New York Stock Exchange. Hence, the TSE has adopted the following measures to prevent short-term wild price fluctuations due to order imbalance:

1. When there is a major order imbalance in a listed stock, the exchange posts a *special bid quote* or a *special asked quote* at a slightly higher or lower price level than the last sale price, in order to solicit counter-orders and, at the same time, to allow bidders or offerers at the special quote to change their orders. The special bid or asked quote can be renewed upward or downward every five or more minutes within the price quotation spread set forth by the regulations of the Exchange, until sufficient orders come out for establishing equilibrium of demand and supply. See Table 1.2.
2. Another measure the TSE has been using to prevent wild swings in prices is the daily price limit. Any stock listed on the exchange cannot be traded at a price that exceeds the limit of price fluctuation from the

closing price of the stock on the previous day. See Table 1.3 for precise limits which average about 15%.

The TSE has been trying to maintain the quality of its market with the special quote system and the daily price limit. However, the procedures, without market makers, are not entirely satisfactory in times of extreme order imbalance. During many of the sharp declines in 1990 the system led to larger price declines as the offered price walked its way down.

Table 1.2 Price Quotation Spread

Last Sale Price	Upward or Downward in ¥
Less than ¥500	5
1,000	10
1,500	20
2,000	30
3,000	40
5,000	50
10,000	100
30,000	200
50,000	300
100,000	500
500,000	5,000
1,000,000	10,000
1,500,000	20,000
2,000,000	30,000
3,000,000	40,000
5,000,000	50,000
10,000,000	100,000
≥¥10,000,000	200,000

Table 1.3 Daily Price Limit

Previous day's Closing price	Upward or Downward in ¥
Less than ¥ 100	30
200	50
500	80
1,000	100
1,500	200
2,000	300
3,000	400
5,000	500
10,000	1000
30,000	2000
50,000	3000
100,000	5000
200,000	50000
500,000	80000
1,000,000	100000
1,500,000	200000
2,000,000	300000
3,000,000	400000
5,000,000	500000
10,000,000	1000000
≥¥10,000,000	2000000

Source: Tokyo Stock Exchange

Description of TSE Trading

The Tokyo Stock Exchange put its computer-assisted order routing and Execution System (CORES) into operation for 440 inactive stocks on January 23, 1982.

After a series of enhancements of the system capacity, most listed domestic and all foreign stocks are currently traded by the system, leaving only the 150 most active domestic stocks to the traditional open outcry trade method on the trading floor. CORES as shown in figures 1.2 and 1.3 is designed to replace manual works involved in the traditional, face-to-face trade method with key operations of computer terminals. No change in functions of exchange members has therefore been made with regard to transactions through CORES.

A regular member places an order through an order entry device which is installed in its main office. When the order is recorded in the central processing unit, an order acceptance notice is sent back to the order acceptance notice output device.

A *saitori* member watches an order book on the screen of the book display device and matches all sell and buy orders on the screen by key operation in accordance with the trading rules. CORES is designed to execute any orders automatically if such orders are to be executed at the same price as the last sale price. In addition, the *saitori* member may also give a narrow price range to CORES to enable the system to execute a trade automatically within the range.

When a transaction is completed, the result is immediately transmitted to the trade report output devices in the main offices of the regular members. The same information is also provided to the *saitori* member and the exchange.

Regular members learn the market information via the *book* inquiry device and the market information reporting device.

The exchange monitors the market and supervises transactions of each stock via the stock price and quote display board, which shows moment by moment development of trading, and the inquiry device which is used to find out trading details of individual stocks when necessary.

When a transaction is consummated, the trade price is automatically transmitted from CORES to the market information system of the exchange. Information vendors provide similar market data together with more pieces of information to their subscribers.

In addition to CORES, the exchange has developed CORES-F for futures trading. Trading through CORES-F in government bond futures has been effected since April 30, 1988, and Topix futures since its launch date, September 3, 1988.

The exchange has also developed CORES for convertible bond trading and CORES-o for Topix options trading, which began operating by mid-1989 and in the fall of 1989, respectively. These systems are described in Ziemba and Schwartz (1992).

Source: Adapted from TSE literature

Figure 1.2
Stock Trading Procedure on the Tokyo Stock Exchange for the Some 150
Stocks Traded Manually by Open Outcry

Trading Floor (19375 sq. ft)

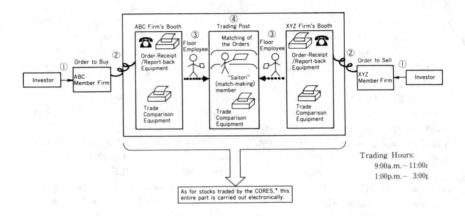

Trading Hours:
9:00a.m. — 11:00a
1:00p.m. — 3:00p

As for stocks traded by the CORES,* this
entire part is carried out electronically.

1. Investors place orders with member firms

2. The member firms then route the orders to their emplyees on the floor electronically (or by telephone).

3. The floor employees place the orders with a *saitori* member handling the stock at the trading post.

4. The *saitori* member matches the orders in accordance with the price priority and time precedence.

When executed, the orders are reported back to the investors by the same procedure in reverse.

(The above illustration shows the trading procedure for 150 manually traded domestic stocks)

* On the TSE all but about 150 listed stocks are electronically traded through the CORES

Source: Tokyo Stock Exchange

Figure 1.3　The CORES System on the TSE

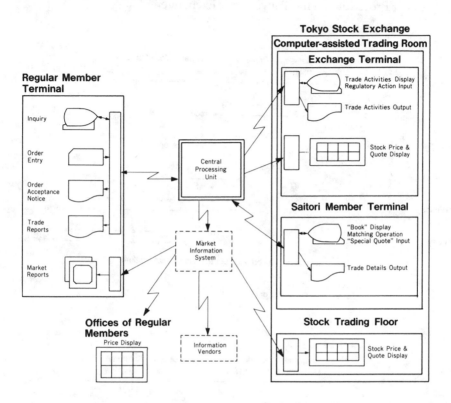

	Trading volume			Year-end number
	(A) Total (mils)	(B) CORES (mils)	B/A, %	of CORES issues
1984	103,741.8	4,441.2	4.3	414
1985	121,994.4	33,574.4	27.5	1,239
1986	198,008.8	47,602.7	24.0	1,255
1987	254,366.6	58,557.5	22.2	1,282
1988	282,853.1	73,783.5	26.1	1,540
1989	223,079.5	98,411.3	44.1	1,575

Source: Tokyo Stock Exchange

Figure 1.4
Settlement Procedure on the Tokyo Stock Exchange

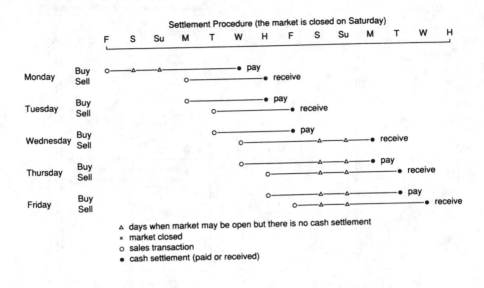

△ days when market may be open but there is no cash settlement
× market closed
○ sales transaction
● cash settlement (paid or received)

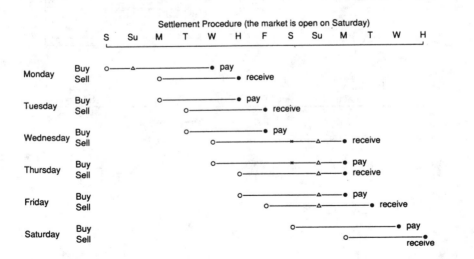

Source: Tokyo Stock Exchange and Ikeda (1985)

The commission rates for stocks, warrants, bonds, convertible and warrant bonds and foreign stocks and the securities and exchange taxes are shown in Table 1.4. There are no discount brokers in Japan so all *regular* customers pay the same rates regardless of the broker used. Brokers with working relationships may share the brokerage fees. Large institutional customers can negotiate additional discounts through methods similar to *soft dollars* used in the U.S. for other services. The tax reform law of 1988, which took effect on April 1, 1989, represents the most major overhaul of the tax system since the post-war reforms. The consumption tax shifts the burden. This has resulted in a lower securities transfer tax of 0.30% versus the previous 0.50% for traders other than securities companies. The latter now pay 0.12%.

Table 1.5 lists the number of companies and shares listed, shareholders' equity and market value currently on the eight stock exchanges in Japan year by year from 1949 to 1989. Table 1.6 lists the thirty leading companies on the TSE in 1988 in terms of number of shareholders, shareholder equity, and market value, and Table 1.7 lists the thirty leading companies in terms of trading volume and value. Both of these are as of the end of 1988.

Table 1.8 and Figure 1.5 have the twenty top capitalized firms as of December 6, 1989, in billions of yen and the total capitalization of the TSE-I on that data which exceeded ¥600 trillion for the 1159 first section companies. The ¥500 trillion mark was first reached on January 13, 1989. As of December 6, 1989, the NYSE's 1713 companies were worth about ¥420 trillion. Table 1.9 compares Japan's capitalization with the other Asian stock exchanges from 1989 to 1988.

Table 1.4   Brokerage Commission Rates as of March 1991

I. Shares and Warrants

Value traded	Commission rate	Plus Yen
up to ¥1 million	1.150%	-
over ¥1 million to 5 million	0.900%	2,000
over ¥5 million to 10 million	0.700%	12,500
over ¥10 million to 30 million	0.575%	25,000
over ¥30 million to 50 million	0.375%	85,000
over ¥50 million to 100 million	0.225%	160,000
over ¥100 million to 300 million	0.200%	185,000
over ¥300 million to 500 million	0.125%	410,000
over ¥500 million to ¥1 billion	0.100%	535,000
over ¥1 billion	0.075%	785,000

1. Brokerage commission on trading value less than ¥200,000 is ¥2,500.
2. The above rates include brokerage commission for preferred stocks, subscription rights and foreign stocks.
3. Shares are usually traded in blocks of 1000 unless they have unusually high par values. At about 2 million per share, NTT trades on a per share basis

II. Bonds

per ¥100 in par value traded

Type of bond/total par value	up to ¥5 M	¥5+ to 10M	¥10+to 50 M	¥50+to 100M	¥100+M to¥1B	over ¥1 B
Government bonds	¥0.40	¥0.35	¥0.30	¥0.25	¥0.10	¥0.05
Government guaranteed bonds, local gov bonds (foreign gov bonds and other bonds designated by the exchange)	0.60	0.50	0.40	0.30	0.15	0.10
Other bonds	0.80	0.65	0.50	0.35	0.20	0.15

III. Convertible bonds and warrant bonds

Value of convertible bonds and warrant bonds	Commission rate	Plus Yen
up to ¥1 million	1.00%	-
over ¥1 million to 5 million	0.90%	1,000
over ¥5 million to 10 million	0.70%	11,000
over ¥10 million to 30 million	0.55%	26,000
over ¥30 million to 50 million	0.40%	71,000
over ¥50 million to 100 million	0.25%	146,000
over ¥100 million to ¥1 billion	0.20%	196,000
over ¥1 billion	0.15%	696,000

Fractions falling short of one yen are discarded.

IV. Securities transfer tax (Payable by seller)

Securities	Other than securities company	Securities company
Shares and stock investment trust certificates	0.30%	0.12%
Straight bonds and bond investment trust certificates	0.03%	0.01%
Convertible bonds and bonds with warrants	0.16%	0.06%

V. Exchange transfer tax (% of trading value)*

Securities	Buyer	Seller
Government bond futures	0.001%	0.001%

• The exchange transfer tax is not imposed on stock index futures.

VI. Commission on foreign stock trades*

Transaction value	Commission rate	plus yen
up to ¥1 million	0.80%	-
over ¥1 million to 5 million	0.70%	1,000
over ¥5 million to 10 million	0.60%	4,000
over ¥10 million to 30 million	0.50%	9,000
over ¥30 million to 50 million	0.40%	19,000
over ¥50 million to 100 million	0.35%	34,000
over ¥100 million to ¥1 billion	0.30%	59,000
over ¥1 billion	0.25%	109,000

*For purchases, the transaction value includes the contract value in the local market, trade commission, tax and other levies. For sales, these fees are reduced.

Source: Tokyo Stock Exchange

Table 1.5
Number of Companies and Shares Listed, Shareholders Equity and
Market Value on all Stock Exchanges in Japan 1949-1989 in Billions

End of Year	Companies Listed		Shares Listed		Shareholders Equity		Market Value	
	Tokyo	All Japan	Tokyo	All Japan	Tokyo	All Japan*	Tokyo	All Japan
1949	529	681	2	2	...	...	122	129
1950	583	764	2	3	...	...	169	179
1951	554	729	3	3	...	...	257	273
1952	575	758	5	5	...	...	641	675
1953	587	784	7	7	...	...	847	894
1954	599	782	9	9	...	...	743	782
1955	596	783	10	11	...	...	1,058	1,102
1956	596	786	15	15	...	...	1,640	1,705
1957	602	789	19	19	...	...	1,675	1,746
1958	601	786	21	22	...	...	2,323	2,409
1959	603	792	26	26	...	...	3,777	3,929
1960	599	785	33	34	...	...	5,411	5,644
1961	1,007	1,265	50	50	...	...	6,140	6,430
1962	1,183	1,455	60	62	...	...	7,661	8,003
1963	1,258	1,574	69	72	...	...	7,428	7,718
1964	1,270	1,591	79	82	...	...	7,425	7,694
1965	1,255	1,577	80	83	...	...	8,511	8,805
1966	1,246	1,562	83	86	...	...	9,390	9,737
1967	1,248	1,561	88	92	...	...	9,271	9,639
1968	1,242	1,552	94	98	...	...	12,665	13,134
1969	1,250	1,556	103	107	...	...	18,353	19,030
1970	1,280	1,580	114	119	...	11,075	16,236	16,825
1971	1,303	1,606	122	127	...	13,018	22,715	23,520
1972	1,323	1,627	132	137	...	15,575	48,055	49,548
1973	1,372	1,680	144	150	14,104	18,116	38,556	40,034
1974	1,390	1,709	152	159	16,226	21,429	36,042	37,469
1975	1,398	1,713	166	173	17,122	23,413	43,245	44,780
1976	1,401	1,716	175	182	18,960	23,590	52,994	54,923
1977	1,407	1,724	186	193	20,463	27,694	51,574	53,638
1978	1,389	1,709	192	200	29,045	30,356	66,342	69,065
1979	1,398	1,723	199	207	32,380	33,783	69,303	72,024
1980	1,402	1,729	208	216	36,121	37,575	77,075	79,952
1981	1,412	1,745	222	231	41,138	42,794	91,906	94,862
1982	1,427	1,769	231	240	46,484	48,335	98,090	101,242
1983	1,441	1,789	240	249	51,287	53,304	126,746	131,231
1984	1,444	1,802	249	259	56,654	58,935	161,812	167,496
1985	1,476	1,829	259	268	62,496	65,082	190,127	196,222
1986	1,499	1,866	268	278	69,368	71,711	285,471	293,028
1987	1,532	1,912	281	291	79,817	79,879	336,707	345,604
1988	1,571	1,967	295	306	92,825	90,701	476,850	488,065
1989	1,597	2,019	314	324	110,732	104,407	611,152	630,122

*Excluding companies whose fiscal terms were changed during the year concerned.
Excluding foreign companies.

Source: Tokyo Stock Exchange

Table 1.6

The Thirty Leading Companies on the TSE in Terms of Shareholders, Equity and Market Value in 1989

Rank	Shareholders (thousands)		Shareholders Equity (¥ bils)		Market Value (¥ bils)	
1	Nippon Telegraph & Telephone	1,545	Nippon Telegraph & Telephone	3,815	Industrial Bank of Japan	15,002
2	Tokyo Electric Power	515	Toyota Motor	2,797	Sumitomo Bank	10,550
3	Nippon Steel	335	Matsushita Electric Ind	1,764	Fuji Bank	9,988
4	Kansai Electric Power	322	Nissan Motor	1,502	Dai-Ichi Kangyo Bank	9,214
5	Toshiba	307	Tokyo Electric Power	1,387	Mitsubishi Bank	9,164
6	Mitsubishi Heavy Ind	288	Fuji Bank	1,384	Tokyo Electric Power	8,128
7	Hitachi	275	Dai-Ichi Kangyo Bank	1,333	Sanwa Bank	8,093
8	Chubu Electric Power	239	Sumitomo Bank	1,295	Nippon Telegraph & Telephone	7,938
9	Mitsubishi Electric	195	Mitsubishi Bank	1,289	Toyota Motor	7,709
10	Tohoku Electric Power	176	Nomura Securities	1,207	Nomura Securities	6,736
11	Sumitomo Metal Industries	172	Sanwa Bank	1,170	Long-Term Credit Bank of Japan	6,542
12	Funuc	167	Industrial Bank of Japan	1,142	Nippon Steel	5,263
13	Kobe Steel	162	Hitachi	1,131	Tokai Bank	5,100
14	Fujitsu	160	Kansai Electric Power	999	Mitsui Bank	5,038
15	Sanyo Electric	157	Chubu Electric Power	859	Matsushita Electric Ind	4,806
16	Osaka Gas	146	Toshiba	804	Kansai Electric Power	4,765
17	Toray Industries	143	Fujitsu	754	Hitachi	4,642
18	Japan Air Lines	143	Daiwa Securities	752	Taiyo Kobe Bank	4,082
19	Matsushita Electric Ind	141	Sony	750	Toshiba	4,011
20	NKK	138	Tokai Bank	749	Mitsubishi Trust & Banking	3,965
21	Sony	131	Mitsui Bank	728	Bank of Tokyo	3,892
22	Shikoku Electric Power	121	Mitsubishi Trust & Banking	684	Mitsubishi Heavy Industries	3,843
23	NEC	118	NEC	677	Nissan Motor	3,677
24	Kyushu Electric Power	118	Long-Term Credit Bank of Japan	671	Chubu Electric Power	3,594
25	Tokyo Gas	112	Mitsubishi Heavy Industries	667	Sumitomo Trust & Banking	3,555
26	Asahi Chemical Ind	107	Nikko Securities	665	Seibu Railway	3,302
27	Kawasaki Steel	105	Nippon Steel	627	Tokio Marine & Fire Insurance	3,205
28	Sumitomo Chemical	104	Sumitomo Trust & Banking	625	Japan Air Lines	3,191
29	Nomura Securities	100	Bank of Tokyo	610	Tokyo Gas	3,190
30	Kirin Brewery	99	Sanyo Electric	609	Nippon Credit Bank	3,183

Note : Number of shareholders and shareholders' equity for business year ending between April 1988 and March 1989, and market value at the end of 1989.

Source: Tokyo Stock Exchange

Table 1.7
The Thirty Leading Companies on the TSE in Terms of Trading Volume
and Value in 1989

Rank	Stocks (mils of shares)	Volume	Rank	Stocks (¥ bils)	Value
1	Nippon Steel	5,103	1	Mitsubishi Heavy Industries	4,653
2	Sumitomo Metal Industries	4,379	2	Nippon Steel	4,478
3	Mitsubishi Heavy Industries	3,968	3	Sony	4,438
4	Toshiba	3,333	4	Toshiba	4,238
5	NKK	3,278	5	Tokyu	3,857
6	Kobe Steel	3,032	6	Sumitomo Metal Industries	3,730
7	Kawasaki Heavy Industries	2,671	7	Taisei	3,669
8	Kawasaki Steel	2,389	8	Fujita	3,120
9	Taisei	2,227	9	NKK	2,967
10	Fujita	1,817	10	Kawasaki Heavy Industries	2,869
11	Mitsubishi Electric	1,810	11	Mitsui Real Estate Development	2,712
12	Mitsui Engineering & Shipbuilding	1,805	12	Fuji Photo Film	2,683
13	Ishikawajima-Harima Heavy Ind	1,789	13	Shimizu	2,683
14	Marubeni	1,774	14	Sato Kogyo	2,648
15	Tokyu	1,575	15	Kobe Steel	2,567
16	Hitachi Zosen	1,522	16	Ohbayashi	2,535
17	Nisshin Steel	1,491	17	Kumagai Gumi	2,455
18	Ohbayashi	1,487	18	Ishikawajima-Harima Heavy Ind	2,277
19	Kumagai Gumi	1,479	19	Hitachi	2,275
20	Nippon Yusen	1,472	20	Kawasaki Steel	2,253
21	Sanyo Electric	1,465	21	Nisshin Steel	2,186
22	Hitachi	1,418	22	Nippon Telegraph & Telephone	2,103
23	Mitsubishi Metal	1,398	23	Nippon Oil	2,081
24	Sato Kogyo	1,301	24	Tokyo Electric Power	2,068
25	Shimizu	1,267	25	Mitsubishi Electric	2,040
26	Mitsui Mining ard Smelting	1,257	26	Ebara	1,935
27	Nippon Oil	1,231	27	Kajima	1,925
28	Nishimatsu Construction	1,221	28	Fanuc	1,841
29	Nissan Motor	1,211	29	Nissan Motor	1,807
30	Mitsui O.S.K. Lires	1,173	30	Nishimatsu Construction	1,804

Total trading volume of the 30 stocks (A)	61,342	A/B	Total trading value of the 30 stocks (C)	82,895	C/D
Total trading volume of all stocks (B)	222,599	27.6%	Total trading value of all stocks (D)	332,617	24.9%

Source: Tokyo Stock Exchange

Figure 1.5   Capitalization of TSE to December 6, 1989, in Trillions of Yen

Source: Tokyo Stock Exchange

Table 1.8
Market Value of the Twenty Largest Capitalized Firms in Japan as of December 6, 1989 in Billions of Yen

1	NTT	22,152.0	11	Long Term Credit Bank of Japan	6,131.3
2	Industrial Bank of Japan	14,108.8	12	Nippon Steel	5,574.9
3	Sumitomo Bank	10,718.2	13	Tokai Bank	5,114.8
4	Fuji Bank	9,630.4	14	Kansai Electric Power	5,050.2
5	Dai-Ichi Kangyo Bank	9,192.0	15	Matsushita Electric Industries	4,845.0
6	Mitsubishi Bank	8,999.7	16	Mitsui Bank	4,774.3
7	Tokyo Electric Power	8,455.7	17	Hitachi	4,670.7
8	Sanwa Bank	8,436.5	18	Toshiba	4,165.1
9	Toyota Motor	8,008.9	19	Mitsubishi Trust & Banking	4,080.2
10	Nomura Securities	7,400.9	20	Mitsubishi Heavy Industries	4,074.5

Source: Tokyo Stock Exchange

Table 1.9
Asian Stock Exchange Market Capitalizations, Millions of Dollars, 1980-88

	1980	1982	1984	1985	1986	1987	1988
Hong Kong	39,104	18,784	23,602	34,504	53,789	54,088	74,377
Indonesia	63	144	85	117	81	68	253
Japan	370,200	417,400	644,400	910,000	1,841,785	2,802,956	3,816,908
Malaysia	12,395	13,903	19,401	16,229	15,065	18,531	23,318
Philippines	3,478	1,981	834	669	2,008	2,948	4,280
Singapore	24,418	31,235	12,247	11,069	16,620	17,931	24,049
South Korea	3,829	4,408	6,223	7,381	13,924	32,905	94,238
Thailand	1,206	1,260	1,720	1,856	2,878	5,485	8,811

Source: Emerging Stock Markets Factbook, 1989

Table 1.10
Number of Member Companies and Shares Listed in Each Stock
Exchange, End of April 1990

Type of Member	Tokyo	Osaka	Nagoya	Kyoto	Hisro-shima	Fukuoka	Niigata	Sapporo
Regular	124	94	42	26	20	23	17	17
Japanese	(99)	(94)	(42)	(26)	(20)	(23)	(17)	(17)
Foreign	(25)	(-)	(-)	(-)	(-)	(-)	(-)	(-)
Special	-	-	1	1	1	1	1	1
Saitori & Nakadachi	4	1	1	-	-	-	-	-
Total	128	95	44	27	21	24	18	18

1. Saitori and Nakadachi members are specialized in matching orders placed by Regular members.
2. Special members are specialized in taking a position as a dealer on regional SEs and liquidating the position on major SEs.

(*) Including 10 new members (3 Japanese and 7 foreign) to be admitted in November 1990 or after.

	Tokyo		Osaka		Nagoya		Kyoto	Hiro shima	Fukuoka	Niigata	Sapporo
	I	II	I	II	I	II					
Listed companies	1161	436	822	295	423	112	235	193	242	199	191
Single Exchange	311	341	31	179	14	81	1	9	17	9	14
on 2 or more	850	95	791	116	409	31	234	184	225	190	177
8 SEs	95		95		95		95	95	95	95	95
7 SEs	24		24		23		18	19	23	20	17
6 SEs	32		32		29		19	20	26	17	17
5 SEs	31		31		29		12	7	18	14	13
4 SEs	55	1	54	1	72		18	7	17	17	12
3 SEs	240	11	241	12	143	8	42	23	27	10	8
2 SEs	373	83	314	103	48	23	30	13	19	17	15

Source: Tokyo Stock Exchange

THE JAPANESE STOCK EXCHANGES

There are eight stock exchanges in Japan - the Tokyo, Osaka, Nagoya, Kyoto, Hiroshima, Fukuoka, Niigata and Sapporo exchanges. The TSE has the bulk of the trades, about 86%, of the trading volume and value. Table 1.10 lists the number of members of each exchange. The number of foreign members is growing on the TSE, but foreign firms are not yet members of the other exchanges. Table 1.11 provides data on the minimum capital stock required for securities companies, while Table 1.12 shows the shareholders equity, number of companies, offices and workforce.

Table 1.11   Minimum Capital Stock Required for Securities Companies

Classification		Legal Minimum	MOF Guideline
Exchange Regular Member Company	1. Regular member of Tokyo or Osaka SE.	¥ 100 mil	¥300 mil
	2.Regular member of Nagoya SE.	¥ 50 mil	¥150 mil
	3.Regular member of any other SE.	¥30 mil	¥100 mil
Non-Member Company	1.Located in 23 wards of Tokyo or in Osaka City.	¥30 mil	¥70 mil
	2.Others	¥20 mil	¥70 mil
Company dealing solely with securities companies	1.Located in 23 wards of Tokyo or in Osaka	¥ 4 mil	
	2.Others	¥1 mil	
Underwriting Securities Co.	1. Managing underwriter also engaged in other securities business	¥3 bil	
	2. Managing underwriter specializing in underwriting.	¥1 bil	
	3. Others	¥200 mil	¥300 mil

Source: Tokyo Stock Exchange

Table 1.12
Securities Companies' Offices, Shareholders' Equity and Workforce. 1949-1989

Year	No. of Securities Companies (Main Offices) Members		Non-members	Total	All Offices	Shareholders' Equity (¥bils)	Workforce (thous)
1949	417	(32)	735	1,152	1,889	...	...
1950	317	(32)	641	958	1,601	...	...
1951	318	(32)	543	861	1,642	...	...
1952	327	(32)	500	827	1,794	...	...
1953	337	(33)	511	848	2,105	...	...
1954	309	(35)	468	777	1,997	...	32
1955	285	(35)	430	715	1,901	...	30
1956	273	(33)	396	669	1,846	...	31
1957	258	(34)	333	591	1,904	26	33
1958	247	(34)	314	561	1,984	27	34
1959	238	(34)	304	542	2,233	47	42
1960	233	(35)	320	553	2,537	70	58
1961	227	(37)	361	588	2,802	112	87
1962	224	(34)	374	598	2,928	117	99
1963	222	(34)	371	593	2,912	126	101
1964	212	(34)	320	532	2,542	102	87
1965	195	(34)	234	429	2,119	90	67
1966	193	(34)	211	404	2,041	119	66
1967	175	(22)	137	312	1,917	126	63
1968	172	(22)	105	277	1,849	149	62
1969	170	(22)	104	274	1,842	184	64
1970	168	(22)	102	270	1,851	229	67
1971	165	(22)	98	263	1,847	278	73
1972	162	(22)	100	262	1,864	347	80
1973	162	(22)	100	262	1,902	519	87
1974	161	(21)	99	260	1,905	528	87
1975	160	(21)	99	259	1,907	550	85
1976	160	(21)	100	260	1,938	654	85
1977	159	(21)	100	259	1,959	763	86
1978	157	(20)	101	258	2,006	924	86
1979	154	(20)	101	255	2,037	1,031	85
1980	154	(20)	101	255	2,081	1,101	85
1981	149	(18)	99	248	2,106	1,280	88
1982	148	(18)	100	248	2,120	1,331	90
1983	147	(18)	100	247	2,158	1,499	93
1984	138	(10)	99	237	2,217	1,792	101
1985	135	(8)	103	238	2,317	2,180	108
1986	139	(6)	110	249	2,451	2,948	117
1987	139	(6)	125	264	2,620	4,313	129
1988	158	(6)	109	267	2,808	5,309	141
1989	158	(6)	113	271	3,000	5,943	152

Notes: 1. Figures in parentheses indicate number of saitori and special members.
        2. Number of offices includes foreign securities companies branches in Japan.

Source: Tokyo Stock Exchange

THE INCREASE IN STOCK PRICES: 1949-1989

The Japanese stock market increased in value over 220 times from the end of 1949 to the end of December 1989. This is computed from the values of the Topix value-weighted index of some 1163 stocks (end of 1989 count), from the first section of the Tokyo Stock Exchange and the Nikkei Stock Average price-weighted index of 225 stocks and from the first section of the TSE. The increase has not been straight up; there have been many large falls as well, including two in 1990. Details about this growth appear in Chapter 2. The 1990 declines are discussed in Chapter 7. The Tokyo stock and bond markets now rival those in New York and have bypassed London in importance. The Tokyo Stock Exchange market capitalization at the end of 1988, was ¥462.9 trillion. This made it the world's largest stock exchange in volume dealing in one stock market. By late 1989 the capitalization was in the ¥550 trillion range. This figure exceeds corresponding figures in the New York and London markets. Some details appear in Tables 1.13 and 1.14b.

In 1988 the TSE has 86.1% of the volume and 85.8% of the value of Japanese stock exchanges. See Figure 1.6. Osaka, which is now larger in trading than London had 9.7% of the volume and 10.4% of the value. Nagoya had 3.7% and 3.4% respectively. The other five exchanges had only about 0.4% of the volume and value. The trading summary for a typical day on the TSE is shown below for August 17, 1988:

Closing Summary: Wednesday
Nikkei Average   28,178.86   (+282.31)

1st Section			2nd Section		
Stock price index	2,206.55	(0.87% +18.06)	Stock price index	2,941.27	(+0.24% +7.0?
Weighted average	1,251.10	(+10.81)	Weighted average	1,388.81	(+2.56)
Arithmetic average	1,339.08	(+3.98)	Arithmetic average	1,358.81	(+Y34.738)
Total market value	¥423,266.76B	(+Y3,656.27B)	Total market value	¥14,542.30B	(+Y34.738B)
Yield	0.50%	(+0.00%)	Yield	0.39%	(+0.00%)
Volume	850.00M		Volume	5.42M	

Osaka Stock
Futures 50	Sep	1,376.50 (+18.0)	Dec	1,375.00 (+13.0)	Mar 89	--
	Jun	--	Sep	--	Spot Av.	1.372.20 (+18.3)

In 1987, 1988 and 1989 over 600 stocks on the TSE increased in value by 30% or more, while less than 35 fell this much. In 1989, 1122 stocks increased by 30% or more and only 2 fell this much. Figure 1.7 shows

Invest Japan

these distributions for 1988 and 1989 and Table 1.14a lists the stocks that increased and decreased the most in 1989.

Table 1.13
Market Size of the World's Stock Exchanges, During or at the End of 1988

		Tokyo	New York	Toronto	U.K.	Frank-furt	Paris	Zurich
No. of Listed Companies								
	Domestic	1571	1604	1147	1993	238	459	161
	Foreign	112	77	67	587	219	217	219
No of listed Issues								
Stocks	Domestic	1576	2152	1584	1989	422	507	309
	Foreign	112	82	72	732	349	247	226
Bonds	Domestic	1197	2893	-	2491	5825	2406	1504
	Foreign	174	213	-	1933	958	61	840
Total Value (US $ million)								
	Stocks	3789035	2366106	241469	711527	221629	222893	140359
	Bonds	1135812	1561031	1036	558390	n.a.	364980	144614
Trading Value (US $ million)								
	Stocks	2234233	1356050	55402	361820	70682	69243	389452
	Bonds	699696	7702	-	526431	273431	574533	
Member Firms		114	555	78	389	122	45	29

		Amst'dam	Milan	Australia	Hong Kong	Singa-pore	Taiwan	Korea
No. of Listed Companies								
	Domestic	232	211	1393	282	132	163	502
	Foreign	228	-	36	22	-	-	
No of listed Issues								
Stocks	Domestic	209	317	2073	291	136	171	970
	Foreign	266	-	48	24	196	-	-
Bonds	Domestic	1147	1277	1819	8	114	218	5809
	Foreign	164	20	-	1			
Total Value (US $ million)								
	Stocks	103644	135417	182755	74407	53573	120102	94348
	Bonds	131410	414459	45048	520	93032	20045	49233
Trading Value (US $ million)								
	Stocks	30636	31705	38172	23635	6325	275491	79457
	Bonds	52171	16796	16540	56	251	35	11682
Member Firms		106	125	111	740	25	120	25

Source: Tokyo Stock Exchange

Table 1.14a   The TSE Stocks with the Greatest Changes in Value in 1989

Rank	Stocks	Rise from End of 1988, %	Rank	Stocks	Fall from End of 1988, %
1	Nikko	438.5	1	Mitsui Wtiarf	46.7
2	Shintom	413.3	2	Tokyo Rope Manufacturing	39.1
3	Utoku Express	341.1	3	Kokusai Kogyo	28.2
4	Toyo Sanso	334.6	4	Nichimo	28.1
5	Teikoku Hume Pipe	316.3	5	Nippon Felt	28.1
6	Oriental Photo Industrial	294.8	6	Inui Tatemono	23.7
7	S & B Shokuhn	252.0	7	Nippon Avionics	22.2
8	AIWA	244.4	8	Fujitsu Denso	19.3
9	Miyaji Construction & Engineering	242.9	9	Nippon Telegraph & Telephone	18.8
10	Kitanihon Spinning	240.0	10	Daiwa Motor Transportation	18.5
11	Omikenshi	238.9	11	Nichias	18.1
12	Kyosan Electric Wire	227.1	12	Aderans	16.1
13	Kagetsuenkanko	218.6	13	Taiheiyo Securities	15.6
14	Katakura Industri as	214.9	14	Mitsubishi Steel Mfg.	14.7
15	Konami Industry	211.7	15	Riken Vitamin	14.4
16	Amada Metrecs	209.0	16	Takakita	13.9
17	Tokyo Sokuhan	201.9	17	Yamanouchi Pharmaceutical	13.4
18	Seiren	198.8	18	Tosho Printing	13.3
19	Nippon Chemical Industrial	194.2	19	Kyowa Leather Cloth	13.2
20	Maruetsu	180.9	20	Tokyo Gas	12.7

Source: Tokyo Stock Exchange

Figure 1.6   Volume and Value Shares on Japan's Stock Exchanges in 1989

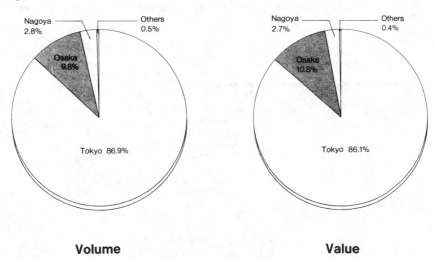

Source: Tokyo Stock Exchange

Table 1.14b
Stock Trading Volume and Value on All Stock Exchanges, in Japan, 1982-89 (Millions of shares, ¥ Billion)

	All Exchanges		Tokyo		Osaka		Nagoya	
	Volume	Value	Volume	Value	Volume	Value	Volume	Value
1982	91,241	42,668	78,474	36,571	9,179	4,576	2,564	1,148
1983	122,320	65,333	104,309	54,845	13,469	8,350	3,375	1,665
1984	124,346	83,122	103,737	67,974	16,247	12,448	3,331	2,097
1985	146,302	94,640	121,863	78,711	18,295	12,536	5,151	2,885
1986	238,354	193,059	197,699	159,836	29,028	25,181	10,394	7,307
1987	315,441	296,111	263,611	250,737	37,133	34,670	13,199	9,503
1988	328,311	322,757	282,637	285,521	31,690	34,504	12,485	11,349
1989	256,296	386,395	222,599	332,617	25,096	41,679	7,263	10,395

	Kyoto		Hiroshima		Fukuoka		Niigata		Sapporo	
	Vol	Value	Vol	Value	Vol	Value	Vol	Value	Vol	Value
1982	201	79	297	108	130	47	319	110	78	27
1983	244	104	331	149	149	61	341	120	102	39
1984	219	116	268	151	140	159	294	130	109	47
1985	245	123	156	82	152	93	329	155	110	55
1986	363	221	117	71	190	119	437	249	124	76
1987	444	367	160	138	236	195	512	376	143	125
1988	373	375	192	180	246	233	527	445	158	149
1989	331	443	189	235	267	330	397	475	151	221

Source: Tokyo Stock Exchange

Figure 1.7
Number of TSE Stocks that Increased or Decreased in Value in 1988 and 1989

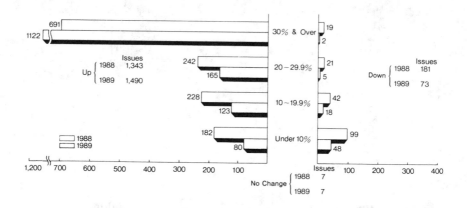

Source: Tokyo Stock Exchange

Table 1.15 and Figure 1.8 give the results and distribution of the profits of the domestic companies and shareholders equity (excluding financial and insurance companies) listed on the eight stock exchanges in Japan. Total liabilities and net worth of the companies was ¥250.2 trillion in 1988, up ¥11.2 trillion or 4.7% over the preceding year. Shareholders' equity was ¥68.6 trillion (up ¥6.1 trillion or 9.8%). Thus shareholders' equity ratio went up 1.2 percentage points to 27.4%. Current profits increased after a two-year decrease, up ¥1.2 trillion (13.8%) to ¥9.9 trillion. This has been attributed to profit increases in 18 industry groups including the steel industry. After-tax profits increased 18.4% to ¥4.5 trillion. The ratio of before interest current profits to total assets increased 0.1 percentage points to 6.5% in 1988. The ratio of after tax profits to shareholders' equity also increased 0.7 points to 7.0%. Cash dividends increased slightly to ¥1.7 trillion and the dividend payout ratio decreased 5.7 points to 37.1%.

Table 1.15
Profits and Dividend Payments of Firms Listed in Japan, Except Financial and Insurance Companies, 1982-89

		1982	1983	1984	1985	1986	1987	1988	1989
Number of Companies		1,607	1,629	1,643	1,658	1,672	1,661	1,620	1,666
Liabilities & net worth	(¥ trils.) A	190.3	197.1	208.0	222.1	225.8	239.1	250.2	282.8
Shareholders equity	(¥ trils.) B	38.0	42.1	46.7	51.7	56.7	62.5	68.6	80.2
Current profits	(¥ trils.) C	7.3	7.0	7.8	9.7	9.5	8.7	9.9	12.6
Financial expenses	(¥ trils.) D	7.3	7.2	7.2	7.0	6.9	6.4	5.7	6.0
After-tax profits	(¥ trils.) E	3.2	3.4	3.6	4.3	4.4	3.8	4.5	5.8
Cash dividends	(¥ trils.) F	1.3	1.3	1.4	1.5	1.6	1.6	1.7	1.9
Shareholders' equity ratio	(%) B/A	20.0	21.4	22.4	23.3	25.1	26.2	27.4	28.4
Ratio of current profits to Total assets	(%) C/A	8.0	7.4	7.4	7.7	7.4	6.4	6.5	6.9
Ratio of current profits to Shareholders equity	E/B	9.0	8.6	8.1	8.7	8.1	6.3	7.0	7.8
Ratio of dividends to Shareholders equity	F/B	3.6	3.3	3.2	3.1	2.9	2.7	2.6	2.6
Dividend payout ratio	F/E	39.6	38.8	39.4	35.3	35.7	42.8	37.1	33.0

Source: Tokyo Stock Exchange

Figure 1.8
Value of All Non-Financial Companies Listed on All Stock Exchanges,
1981-89, 1981=100

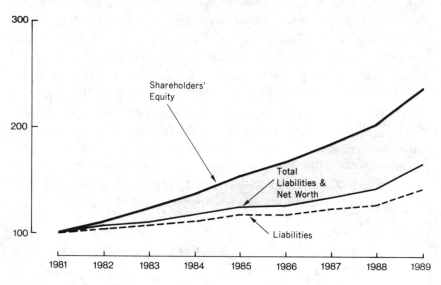

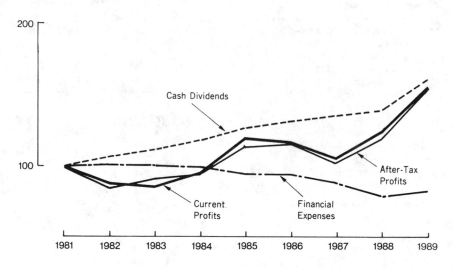

Source: Tokyo Stock Exchange

The Tokyo market has been dominated by a relatively small number of
gigantic banks and brokerage firms. These organizations are among the
largest in the world. The big four brokerage firms - Nomura, Daiwa,

Nikko and Yamaichi - control the bulk of the activity in Japanese securities. Together they have total equity in excess of $100 billion. Their actions move markets. Stocks they recommend increase in value and this market impact must be kept in mind.

In early 1991 there were 46 foreign security firms in Japan. The new entrants took the foreign membership to 22 seats on the TSE in May 1988, about 19.2 percent of the 114 member securities firms. The corresponding figure for the New York Stock Exchange is only 4% but the make-up of the market is very different from that of Tokyo. New York has 1,366 members, but they are individuals, not companies as on the TSE. In London, the figure is 22% of the exchange's 362 member securities firms. Both figures are as of March 1988, and are according to a report by the U.S. General Accounting Office in Washington.

Figure 1.9 and Table 1.16 show the relative growth of the Japanese stock market at the expense of the U.S. and the rest of the world, save Europe. While Japan's market capitalization in relative terms nearly tripled, the U.S. capitalization fell by over 40%. Since all of these markets rose in capitalization during these eight years, the absolute growth in Japan was extremely large. Data on the specifics year by year appear in Chapter 2.

Figure 1.9   Stock Market Capitalizations

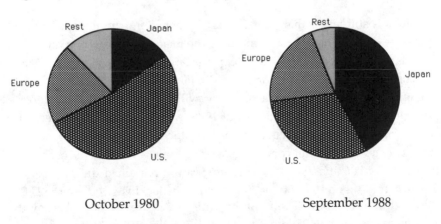

October 1980   September 1988

Source: Morgan Stanley Capital International

Table 1.16
Stock Market Capitalizations as a Percent of World Total , 20 Main
Markets

	Dec 1980	Sept 1988
Japan	15	42
U.S.	53	31
Europe	20	21
Rest of world	12	6

Table 1.16 simply counts up the values at current market prices of all the stocks on all the exchanges in the world. The widespread practice of cross holding of stocks in Japan and Germany, which amount to about 71% of all shares in Japan, overstates the true capitalization. If one deletes the effect of this double counting, then the real capitalization of the Japanese stock market is about 75% of that commonly stated. After an adjustment for this *mochiai* effect, McDonald (1989) found the end of 1988 market shares to be

	Unadjusted Morgan Stanley International Capital Values, %	Adjusted Values, %
U.S.	28.6	32.6
Japan	44.2	39.0
Europe	21.4	22.2
Other	5.8	6.2

So Japan is still larger than the U.S. but by not as much. Europe's share increases only slightly because many of the major European markets also have large cross holdings that are nearly as large as those in Japan.

Foreigners have less confidence in the Japanese stock market than the Japanese do. At a drop of a hat they will bail out if anything looks uncertain. For example, in the fall of 1988, with the Emperor gravely ill, some foreign investors scurried to sell stocks as the market moved gradually up but without conviction. Foreign sales exceeded purchases in 1984, 1985, 1986 and 1987. Foreigners' trading remained dull, probably because trading on Wall Street continued to be lackluster before the U.S. presidential election. Their buying interest centered on issues with hidden assets, such as Tokyo Gas, or large-capital shares in the steel and shipbuilding sectors, or brokerage houses with sharply improved earnings results, such as C. Itho & Co.

Estimates by a major brokerage house showed foreigners' stock trading in value surpassed ¥500 billion in the second week of September 1988 for the first time after a long interval. Major sales transactions by foreigners that week were: 9 million shares of NKK, 7 million shares of Nippon Steel, 4.5 million of Kawasaki Steel, 2.4 million of Oji Paper, 1.8 million of Toshiba, 700,000 of Tokuyama Sode, 500,000 each of Kobe Steel and Matsushita Electric Industrial and 400,000 each of Mitsubishi Heavy Industries and Hitachi, according to a large securities firm's survey. Stock market themes and future suggestions are discussed in Chapter 8.

MARGIN TRADING

Over 99.9% of the trading volume on the TSE is by *regular way* transactions, which are settled on the third business day following the day of the contract. However, some trades are made as *cash* transactions, settled on the contract day or the next business day, or as *when issued* transactions, settled in new shares after their issuance.

Margin trading is a transaction in which a securities company lends a customer money or securities needed for the settlement of the *regular way* transaction made on the stock exchange. It is allowed only on first section stocks and then for only some of the listed shares. Currently 576 of the first section stocks, about 51%, are eligible for margin trading.

When a contract is made under the margin trading system, the customer deposits guarantee money (*margin*) equivalent to the prescribed rate of the contract value with the securities company. Securities may be used in lieu of cash as the guarantee money. The securities have a margin which is a specified fraction of their current market value varying from 60 to 90%, see Table 1.17. Customers who purchase securities on margin pay interest to the securities company for the period of time until the money borrowed for his purchase is returned to the securities company. Generally margin must be repaid or rolled over within six months. Short sellers of borrowed securities receive interest until the securities are returned to the securities company. The interest rates for margin trades are based on the official discount rate. See Figure 1.10 for these rates from 1979-89.

Table 1.17 Margin Loan Value of Various Securities

Loan Value (%)			Loan value (%)		
Stocks	70	Listed issues	Foreign government bonds	85	Listed issues only
	60	OTC issues	Foreign local bonds	85	Listed issues only
Government bonds	95	Including short-term government bonds	World Bank bonds	90	INTL BK for Reconstruction & Development, JP¥BD
Local Government bonds	85	Excluding nonpublic offering bonds	Asian Development Bank bonds	90	Asian Development BK JP Á BD
Special bonds issued by corporations			Foreign special bonds	85	Listed issues only (Regulation was revised in August 1977)
Government guaranteed bonds	90	Excluding nonpublic offering bonds	Bond investment trusts	85	(Adopted in March 1986)
Other bonds	85	Discount bonds, interest-bearing bonds and others	Other investment trusts	70	Growth stock fund No. 1, New Large Capital stock fund, new large capital stock and bond fund, C.B. open fund,Universal fun, Index fund 225, International information and communication
Corporate bonds	85	Bonds issued by listed companies			
Convertible bonds	80				
Warrant Bonds	80				

Tax exempt securities are not eligible

Source: Yamaichi Securities

Major brokerage firms in Japan are very conservative in giving out margin. Indeed, according to the 1990 Yamaichi Securities booklet on the Japanese stock market the following types of customers are *not eligible* as potential margin investors:
1. *Women.*
2. *Anyone older than 70 or younger than 25.*
3. *Jobless.*
4. *Retired.*
5. *Pseudonymouns (trading under a fictitious name).*
6. *Anyone who refuses to send a trading report.*
7. *Living abroad.*
8. *Group investment.*
9. *Foreigners (excluding permanent residents).*

However, due to the strong demand from customers, investors who classify in any one of the first six categories may become eligible to engage in margin trading if admitted by the director after an initial interview by the head of the division or branch at which they have an account.

To engage in margin trading, investors must have a margin deposit in excess of ¥20 million in cash and total market value of eligible substitute securities in Yamaichi's custody. Permanent resident status in Japan is required to ensure effective communication between Yamaichi and the investor.

These rules are a reminder of Japanese society and how cultural norms often outweigh economic logic.

Figure 1.10
Interest Rates and Loan Values in Margin Transactions, 1980-89.

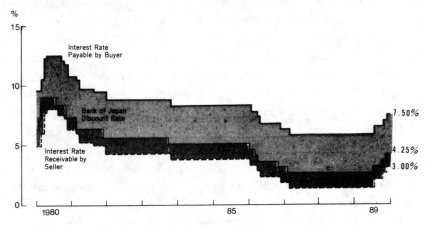

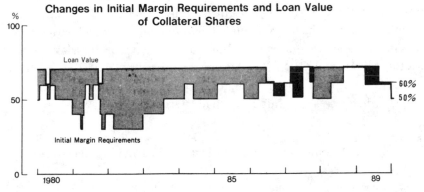

Source: Tokyo Stock Exchange

The Bank of Japan discount rate rose sharply from the spring of 1989 in an attempt to combat inflation which was initially caused by the 3% consumption tax and to contain the inflationary effects of a higher valued U.S. dollar. The fight against inflation led to a huge increase in interest rates from mid 1989 to late 1990. This in turn is strongly related to the 1990 stock market decline as discussed in Chapter 7. The discount rate of 2.50% was increased, in 1989, to 3.25% (May 31), 3.75% (October 11) and 4.25% (December 24) and then, in 1990, to 5.25% (March 20) and to 6.00% (August 30).

According to the TSE, margin transactions in 1986 totaled ¥55,825 billion, nearly double the previous year. Margin trading in *regular way* transactions went down 1.9 percentage points to 17.9%. See Table 1.18. Margin transactions accounted for 39.3% of the stock trading value by individual investors in 1988, dropping 8.1% from the previous year.

A special margin trading system for *designated stocks* was inaugurated on October 2, 1978. Margin transactions in the *designated stocks* can be made under either the general margin trading system or the special margin trading system. The new margin trading system calls for a trade to be made on the following conditions: the volume per transaction is 5,000 shares or more (as compared with 1,000 shares or more under the general margin trading system); the period of settlement is three months (six months under the general system); the brokerage commissions on offsetting transactions are 60% of the present general commission rates; the interest rate receivable by the seller is higher than that under the general system. As of the end of 1986, the following twelve issues are designated for this special margin trading system: Toray Industries, Asahi Chemical Industry, Nippon Oil, Sumitomo Electric Industries, NEC, Matsushita Electric Industrial, Mitsubishi Heavy Industries, Toyota Motor, Mitsui and Co., Tokio Marine and Fire Insurance, Heiwa Real Estate, and Nippon Yusen. In late 1989, margin debt on Japan's three major exchanges was slightly more than ¥8 trillion.

Table 1.18

Percentage of Transactions Done on Margin, Sales and Purchases, 1979-89

| | On margin | | Total | | | |
	(A) volume, bils shares	(B) value,¥ bils	(C) volume, bils shares	(D) value, ¥ bils	A/C	B/D
1979	48	17,765	190	66,822	25.3	26.6
1980	46	17,393	200	70,737	23.0	24.6
1981	50	24,732	212	96,510	23.6	25.6
1982	42	19,821	153	70,249	27.5	28.2
1983	51	25,962	200	101,596	25.5	25.6
1984	46	30,137	198	126,958	23.2	23.7
1985	45	29,852	236	150,790	19.1	19.8
1986	72	55,825	387	311,591	18.6	17.9
1987	87	74,345	518	490,636	16.8	15.2
1988	109	103,397	557	558,990	19.6	18.5
1989	71	100,554	436	651,212	16.2	15.4

Note: Figures for volume and value represent the total of sales and purchases

Source: Tokyo Stock Exchange

Weekend figures for the total open interest in margin transactions (total number of shares bought and carried on margin and total number of shares sold short and carried on margin) have been disclosed by the Tokyo, Osaka, and Nagoya stock exchanges since May 1969. Regarding open interest in individual stocks, weekend figures have been made public since October 1978 for all stocks qualified for money or stock loan from securities finance companies established under the Securities and Exchange Law. Daily disclosure of the open interest is made for each stock on which a margin trade restriction is imposed by the exchange. The open interest in each of the designated stock and the stocks that have come under the "guideline for watching a stock actively traded on margin" is made public every day. The daily disclosure reports the previous day's figures.

Table 1.19a indicates that in margin accounts, the short interest is typically about 10% of the long interest.

Table 1.19a
Open Interest in Margin Transactions, Total of Tokyo, Osaka and Nagoya Stock Exchanges

End of	Short interest Mils of shares (A)	¥ bil	Long interest Mils of shares (B)	¥ bil	Ratio B/A (times)
1978	410	125	3,205	1,126	7.8
1979	350	132	3,328	1,126	9.5
1980	359	164	3,265	1,394	9.1
1981	454	246	3,564	1,783	7.9
1982	608	319	3,521	1,840	5.8
1983	380	240	3,578	2,170	9.4
1984	457	301	3,974	2,851	8.7
1985	333	290	3,996	2,827	12.0
1986	463	494	4,543	4,200	9.8
1987	495	528	6,301	6,505	12.7
1988	511	587	6,193	7,230	12.1
1989	436	755	5,472	87,09	12.6

Source: Tokyo Stock Exchange

Table 1.19b provides data on the mix of sales and purchases of securities on the first section of the TSE from 1978 to 1987. There has been increasing volume by financial institutions, banks, and business corporations, while volume from individuals and foreigners has been dropping. In other categories, such as trading by securities companies and investment trusts, volume has held steady.

Table 1.19b
Sales and Purchases on the TSE-I by Various Customer Accounts from 31 Integrated Securities Companies, 1978-1987

Sales

Year	Total Accounts	Corps	Financial Institutions				Inv Trusts	Bus Corps	Other	Sec Corp	Indiv	For
			All	Ins Cos	Banks	Other						
1978	51,998	26.1	4.9	1.6	2.4	0.9	10.0	10.3	0.9	3.8	64.2	5.9
1979	51,488	28.5	6.4	1.4	4.0	1.0	9.8	11.1	1.2	4.1	62.2	5.2
1980	50,874	28.2	7.4	1.3	5.1	1.0	8.6	11.1	1.1	4.6	60.1	7.1
1981	56,272	24.8	6.4	1.0	4.4	1.0	6.7	10.3	1.4	3.8	58.3	13.1
1982	37,828	21.0	5.5	1.4	3.5	0.6	5.8	8.5	1.2	4.6	60.5	13.9
1983	52,918	19.7	4.6	0.9	3.2	0.5	5.3,	8.7	1.1	4.2	60.9	15.2
1984	55,820	21.5	5.9	1.0	4.3	0.6	4.9	9.8	0.9	3.9	54.6	20.0
1985	68,211	27.7	11.5	1.1	9.3	1.1	5.2	10.0	1.0	4.2	50.9	17.2
1986	118,883	38.1	17.4	0.9	14.9	1.6	5.6	13.8	1.3	3.4	43.0	15.5
1987	159,991	44.2	21.9	0.7	20.1	1.1	5.7	15.2	1.4	3.3	38.1	14.4

Purchases

Year	Total Accounts	Corps	Financial Institutions				Inv Trusts	Bus Corps	Other	Sec Corp	Indiv	For
			All	Ins Cos	Banks	Other						
1978	51,269	29.6	6.7	2.1	3.6	1.0	11.3	10.0	1.6	3.8	61.7	4.9
1979	50,696	31.2	8.5	1.9	5.7	0.9	9.9	10.9	1.9	4.3	59.8	4.7
1980	50,176	28.1	8.5	2.1	5.5	0.9	7.1	10.6	1.9	4.6	56.5	10.8
1981	54,665	26.9	8.2	1.8	5.3	1.1	6.4	10.2	2.1	3.6	55.4	14.1
1982	37,394	23.4	7.4	2.1	4.7	0.6	5.4	8 0	2.6	4.8	58.7	13.1
1983	52,604	20.4	6.1	1.6	3.9	0.6	4.6	7.7	2.0	4.2	57.2	18.2
1994	54,506	25.0	8.3	1.3	6.3	0.7	5.0	10.1	1.6	3.9	54.4	16.7
1985	66,164	31.4	14.0	1.0	11.8	1.2	6.0	9.9	1.5	4.3	49.6	14.7
1986	112,883	41.9	20.0	0.9	17.4	1.7	6.4	14.1	1.4	3.5	42.5	12.1
1987	150,934	48.0	24.2	0.8	22.3	1.1	6.9	15.5	1.4	3.5	38.6	9.9

Source: Tokyo Stock Exchange

FOREIGN STOCKBROKERS IN JAPAN

There are some forty-six foreign (*gaijin*) stock investment firms in Japan. Merrill Lynch was the first in 1961. Between them they hold 25 of the 115 seats on the TSE. Such a membership is essential to eliminate a third of the brokerage cost of trading and to have a chance to latch onto some of the lucrative institutional trading business. To not have a seat or an application pending is seen as lacking commitment to the Japanese market. There has been much expansion in recent years. Sixteen of the foreign firms became new members of the TSE in 1988. A seat on the TSE is expensive, about $2 million for fees and other start-up costs. Maintenance of the seat is about $7 million each year.

Is it worth it? The large Japanese firms, particularly the big four (Nomura, Daiwa, Nikko and Yamaichi), chalk up considerable earnings, the bulk of which they receive as commission income. These firms also have substantial underwriting and other fees and relatively modest income from trading for their own accounts. In contrast, the foreign firms are much more active in trading for their own accounts, including programmed arbitrage trading. However, they have a much harder time getting substantial commission income. In other words, they actually have to trade for profit, whereas the Japanese firms can make money on churning alone. Part of this lack of substantial business has been that the volume of trading from abroad is not very high and Japanese individuals and institutions simply prefer to trade with Japanese firms even if their performance recommendations are not as good. Statements such as, "You cannot get Japanese to buy Japanese stocks from foreigners," abound.[1]

Thus, on net, the foreign firms had posted losses on their Japanese operations. Because of high corporate tax rates and other accounting reasons, some of the profits the foreign firms have accrued appear on the ledgers of their home and other branches, leading to more paper losses in Japan. The losses have been quite substantial and could lead to a reduced foreign presence in Tokyo. For example, in the year ending in September 1988, the then 45 firms in total lost, after tax, some ¥24 billion on operating costs of ¥168 billion and revenues of ¥43.3 billion. Only six of the foreign firms made any profit at all. According to *The Economist* (January 14, 1989) the ten biggest losers were as shown in Table 1.20.

Glaringly apparent is the small amount of commission income, some ¥20.7 billion, which was hardly higher than the losses of ¥14.7 billion. All told, in 1988, the 45 firms had only about 2% of the total TSE trading volume except for programmed trading activities. Only Merrill Lynch, with five offices across Japan, has any significant retail business. If one had to break even only on commission income, then the typical reasonably sized firm would need to trade about 60 million shares a day,

---

[1]Performance is not the issue since the foreign firms provide competitive or even superior advice. It's custom. I recall one occasion when I was asked to give an interview to a Tokyo newspaper after a talk to a large number of Japanese brokers and researchers on U.S. stock market anomalies. The reporter repeatedly asked me questions about the Japanese financial markets, and we had a stimulating interview. The story was not printed. The editor may have thought, "What would a *gaijin* know about the Japanese stock market?"

or a 4% market share. In total, the foreign firms had a 6.2% market share
in 1989; see Table 1.21.

Table 1.20
Losses of Foreign Securities Firms in Japan, Year to September 1988

	Total Commission Income ,¥ billion	Net Loss ¥ billion
UBS-Philips & Drew	2.5	2.06
JP Morgan	0.7	1.96
Barclays de Zoete Wedd	1.6	1.84
County NatWest	2.2	1.83
Citicorp Vickers	4.1	1.44
Chase Manhattan	0.4	1.31
James Capel	2.1	1.20
Baring	4.9	1.08
Deutsche Bank	1.3	1.06
Morgan Grenfell	0.6	0.88
Total	20.4	14.66

Source: The Japan Bond Research Institute

Table 1.21
Trading Volume of Foreign Brokerage Firms in Japan, Millions of Shares,
1988

1	Salomon Brothers	3,755.58	12	County Natwest	871.68
2	Morgan Stanley	2,834.28	13	Prudential Bache	806.63
3	Baring	1,796.12	14	Smith Barney	791.21
4	Goldman Sachs	1,704.47	15	UBS Phillips & Drew	722.45
5	Merrill Lynch	1,659.34	16	Schroder	536.79
6	Jardine Fleming	1,626.15	17	SBCI	478.74
7	Shearson Lehman	1,324.65	18	Kleinwort Benson	452.61
8	First Boston	1,147.67	19	Dresdner	417.71
9	Citicorp Vickers	1,106.99	20	Kidder Peabody	381.87
10	S. G. Warburg	1,023.78	21	BD Capital	261.22
11	W.I. Carr	909.54	22	Sogen	232.19

Total   24,840 (6.2% Total TSE-I volume)

Source: *Japan Economic Journal*

Expenses are high, particularly rent on office space, rent subsidies to
employees, salaries and general overhead. For example, Britain's Barclays
de Zoete Wedd's quarters in the new Urbanner Building rents for ¥300,000
a square meter. This cost is more than a third of their entire overhead.

The profitable firms need to find other ways to break even or make
even modest profits. Successful trading for their own account is one such
avenue. Morgan Stanley, Salomon Brothers and Merrill Lynch are very

active in such trading and especially in lucrative programmed trading. So far, the Japanese big four investment companies have not been aggressive in programmed trading because there is still an aversion by the Japanese to making money this way. As one of my Yamaichi colleagues put it: *It's not a decent way to make money.* If they became aggressive in this type of trading, profits for the foreign firms would diminish or even dry up. This would probably force many of these firms out of Japan. The Japanese do not want this, particularly the bad publicity that would be generated at a time when there is pressure for them to open up their markets.

Salomon Brothers and Morgan Stanley had the highest trading volume of the foreign firms, about 0.94% and 0.75%, respectively. Both of them are around the 30th largest of all firms in Tokyo. Because much of this is arbitrage trading which boosts the total volume of the *gaijin* brokers to about 8% (and in late 1990 to about 10%), their real commission income is much less. Salomon Brothers made two thirds of all the profits of the 45 foreign houses, ¥1.2 billion. Their trading was very successful, bringing in nine times their commission income. They are the only financial firm (the 26th) among the 80 most profitable foreign firms in Japan. To put their earnings in perspective, each of the Japanese big four made at least ten times as much.

Table 1.22
Revenue and Pretax Income from Japanese Operations of Five Brokerage Firms, 1986-89

	1986	1987	1988	1989
Revenue (in millions of dollars converted from yen at recent rates)				
Salomon Brothers	$100.9	$167.9	$157.3	$158.0
Morgan Stanley	54.3	99.5	125.6	93.1
Merrill Lynch	76.9	98.8	92.4	54.3
Goldman Sachs	36.0	67.0	84.7	67.8
Credit Suisse-First Boston	20.5	39.5	55.7	48.7
Pretax Income (in millions of dollars converted from yen at recent rates)				
Salomon Brothers	34.8	47.5	31.3	53.6
Morgan Stanley	8.6	10.8	.4	5.8
Merrill Lynch	11.8	25.5	8.0	1.0
Goldman Sachs	1.1	9.3	3.7	12.8
Credit Suisse-First Boston	5.2	4.7	5.6	7.3

Source: *Asian Wall Street Journal*

Table 1.22 summarizes the volume of business and the pretax income for the most successful brokerage firms from 1984-1989. This shows the

Salomon Brothers dominance. Their Tokyo office has expanded greatly from 65 employees in 1986 to 550 in 1989. As of June 1989, their capitalization was $443 million. Table 1.23a shows the results for April to September 1989 and the previous six month period September 1988 to April 1989. This period was more favorable for most of the firms. Again, Salomon had a strong showing, although Baring had higher profits in each of the past two six-month periods. The steep decline in stock prices in 1990 was especially damaging to the Japanese brokerage firms. Trading was also down sharply for the foreign brokerage firms; however, the programmed trading and Nikkei put warrant hedging led to enormous profits for some of them. When the debacle clears we may see good profits but strained relations.

Table 1.23a
Business Results of Foreign Securities Houses, April-September 1989,
¥ Billion

Foreign securities firms	Operating revenue		Commission income		Trading profits		Net profits	
Salomon Brothers	16.5	(20.1)	11.7	(8.2)	2.41	(9.33)	0.67	(0.80)
Morgan Stanley	14.2	(13.2)	11.9	(11.6)	1.73	(1.22)	0.07	(- 0.80)
Goldman Sachs	9.1	(8.6)	8.8	(8.0)	- 0.53	(0.19)	0.54	(0.12)
CS First Boston	9.1	(6.9)	7.7	(5.8)	1.83	(1.33)	0.27	(0.13)
Baring	7.5	(5.0)	6.9	(4.8)	0.69	(0.21)	0.83	(0.98)
Merrill Lynch	6.8	(7.5)	7.2	(7.9)	- 0.32	(- 0.39)	0.14	(- 0.06)
Jardine Fleming	5.6	(4.7)	5.4	(4.3)	0.27	(0.41)	0.28	(0.05)
Shearson Lehman	4.9	(3.4)	3.6	(2.3)	1.17	(0.91)	0.51	(-1.05)
S.G. Warburg	3.3	(3.4)	3.5	(3.4)	- 0.09	(- 0.11)	0.10	(0.45)
Smith Barney	3.1	(2.6)	2.6	(1.7)	1.15	(1.84)	0.39	(-0.24)
Citicorp Vickers	3.0	(3.1)	2.1	(2.1)	0.99	(I. 1)	0.46	(-0.04)
Prudential Bache	3.0	(3.1)	2.9	(2.9)	9.05	0.05)	0.01	(-0.25)
County NatWest	2.4	(2.3)	1.7	(1.6)	0.85	(0.81)	- 0.11	(-0.56)
Kidder Peabody	2.3	(1.6)	2.0	(1.5)	0.28	(0.15)	0.50	(-0.32)
Schroder	2.3	(1.7)	1.6	(1.3)	0.88	(0.51)	0.27	(0.03)
Kleinwort Benson	2.2	(2.5)	2.4	(2.4)	-0.21	(0.07)	0.00	(0.16)
UBS Phillips & Drew	2.2	(1.9)	1.5	(1.6)	0.78	(0.42)	- 0.38	(-0.34)
SBCI	2.1	(2.3)	2.2	(1.8)	0.04	(0.51)	- 0.25	(0.03)
W.I. Carr	1.9	(2.0)	1.8	(1.9)	0.20	(0.22)	0.03	(0.00)
Sogen	1.5	(1.0)	0.4	(0.5)	1.28	(0.65)	- 0.12	(-0.05)
DB Capital	1.3	(1.0)	1.2	(1.0)	0.13	(0.06)	- 0.16	(-0.64)
Dresdner	0.7	(0.7)	0.4	(0.5)	0.24	(0.27)	- 0.14	(-0.02)

Note: - denotes losses. Figures in parentheses are business results of previous half-year term.
Source: Nikkei Newsletter on Bond & Money

   Some of these profits are shown in Table 1.23b for fiscal 1989 ending in March 1990. For ease of comparison, the previous six month values are in

( )s. The top earners were Salomon Brothers, Baring, Shearson Lehman and Merrill Lynch. The foreign brokers saw their share of trading rise to 8% in that year which saw declining values. They also doubled their pre-tax incomes. Japanese institutional clients account for much of their new business now that fund managers are being more closely watched for actual performance. In particular, the foreign brokers' analytical skills, including hedging and trading baskets of shares, are winning converts.

Table 1.23b
Business Results of Foreign Securities Houses in Tokyo, FY1989, ¥ Billion

Firm	Operating Revenues		Commission Income		Trading Profits		Recurring Pretax Profits		Net Profits	
Merrill Lynch	15.0	(7.5)	17.3	(7.9)	-2.17	(-0.39)	0.97	(-0.04)	0.94	(-0.06)
Citicorp Vickers	5.0	(3.1)	3.9	(2.1)	1.09	(1.10)	0.05	(- 0.01)	0.00	(-0.04)
Prudential Bache	5.4	(3.1)	5.1	(2.9)	-0.01	(- 0.05)	0.37	(0.02)	-0.13	0.25)
Smith Barney	6.6	(2.6)	6.1	(1.8)	1.67	(1.84)	1.44	(- 0.24)	0.29	(-0.24)
Jardine Fleming	11.6	(4.7)	11.3	(4.3)	0.28	(0.41)	1.30	(0.27)	0.11	(0.05)
Saloman Brothers	46.5	(20.1)	30.7	(8.2)	11.38	(9.33)	14.87	(7.62)	3.83	(0.80)
Kidder Peabody	6.3	(1.6)	4.6	(1.5)	0.75	(0.15)	1.35	(-0.30)	0.66	(- 0.32)
Goldman Sachs	19.9	(8.6)	18.9	(8.0)	1.12	(0.1 9)	1.88	(0.85)	0.39	(0.12)
Morgan Stanley	35.9	(13.2)	27.2	(11.6)	7.23	(1.22)	5.63	(0.82)	0.26	(-0.80)
S.G. Warburg	7.3	(3.4)	7.7	(3.4)	-0.07	(-0.11)	0.55	(0.53)	0.11	(0.45)
W.I. Carr	4.1	(2.0)	3.7	(1.9)	0.38	(0.22)	0.15	(0.16)	- 1.93	(0.00)
C.S. First Boston	13.5	(6.9)	10.8	(5.8)	3.44	(1.33)	1.18	(1.03)	- 0.76	(0.13)
Drexel Burnham	3.6	(1.6)	3.1	(1.4)	0.44	(0.19)	-0.17	(0.11)	-0.44	(0.00)
Kleinwort Benson	4.7	(2.5)	5.1	(2.4)	-0.38	(0.07)	0.22	(0.25)	0.04	(0.16)
Schroder	4.8	(1.7)	3.6	(1.3)	1.58	(0.51)	0.39	(0.16)	0.29	(0.03)
Cazanove	0.7	(0.3)	0.6	(0.3)	0.01	(0.00)	0.03	(-0.00)	0.00	(-0.00)
Hoare Govett	1.4	(0.4)	1.3	(0.4)	0.14	(-0.01)	0.10	(-0.27)	0.06	(-0.40)
DB Capital	4.2	(1.0)	4.0	(1.0)	0.23	(0.06)	1.12	(-0.61)	1.02	(-0.64)
Paine Webber	1.4	(0.6)	1.4	(0.6)	0.03	(0.01)	0.07	(0.09)	0.14	(0.08)
Shearson Lehman	12.6	(3.4)	10.8	(2.3)	1.48	(0.91)	1.63	(- 1.05)	1.59	(-1.05)
Baring	16.4	(5.0)	15.3	(4.8)	1.21	(0.21)	5.14	(1.20)	1.87	(0.98)
Dresdner	1.5	(0.7)	1.1	(0.5)	0.57	(0.27)	-0. 18	(-0.01)	-0.20	(- 0.02)
SBCI	4.5	(2.3)	4.1	(1.0)	0.63	(0.51)	0.25	(0.04)	0.23	(0-03)
County NatWest	5.3	(2.3)	3.6	(1.6)	1.95	(0.81)	0.11	(-0.55)	0.08	(- 0.56)
Sogen Securities	3.9	(1.0)	1.4	(0.5)	3.09	(0.65)	1.31	(0.14)	0.78	(-0.05)
UBS Phillips & Drew	4.7	(1.9)	3.6	(1.6)	1.20	(0.42)	- 0.09	(-0.33)	- 0.25	(-0.34)
DG Securities	0.4	(0.1)	0.2	(0.1)	0.17	(-0.05)	- 0.08	(-0.12)	- 0.09	(-0.12)
James Capel	6.4	(2.1)	5.7	(2.0)	0.56	(0. 15)	1.18	(-0.08)	0.91	(-0.09)

Note: - shows losses. Figures in parentheses are business results of previous half-year term.

Source: *Japan Economic Journal*

The 45 securities firms had pretax profits of ¥44 billion in the year ended March 31, 1990 up 180% from fiscal 1989. Net profits for these firms moved into the black for the first time. Profits rose largely from arbitrage and other derivative security trading and from commission income on stock transactions from abroad. Total commission income was up 43%

on the year. Operating revenues were up 25% to ¥295.2 billion. Cost control reduced the number of foreign securities houses with losses to 13, down from 27 the previous year. Total net profits for the 45 firms were ¥10.1 billion compared to losses of ¥4.3 billion in fiscal 1988. The April to September 1991 results are shown in Figure 1.23c for the firms that made profits. Total pretax recurring profits of the 46 foreign securities firms was ¥8.3 billion, down 47.4% from the same period in 1990. Salomon Brothers Asia Ltd had most of the profits, some ¥5.01 billion, up 39.2%. Most of this gain was from fees from arbitrage trading, profits and brokerage fees.

Table 1.23c
Business Results of Foreign Securities Houses in Tokyo, April to September 1990 in ¥Billion

Firms	Operating Revenues		Commission Income		Trading Profits		Recurring Pretax Profits		Net Profits	
Salomon Brothers	21.6	(16.5)	16.0	(11.7)	1.92	(2.41)	5.01	(3.60)	0.72	(0.67)
Sogen Securities	5.7	(1.5)	1.5	(0.4)	4.82	(1.28)	3.21	(0.34)	0.05	(-0.12)
Baring Securities	7.1	(7.5)	6.7	(6.9)	0.19	(0.69)	1.95	(2.47)	1.02	(0.83)
Goldman Sachs	11.5	(9.1)	11.1	(8.8)	-1.03	(-0.53)	1.59	(1.59)	0.63	(0.54)
DB Capital	2.8	(1.3)	2.5	(1.2)	0.09	(0.13)	1.09	(-0.16)	1.04	(-0.16)
BT Asia	4.0	(2.6)	3.4	(2.3)	0.01	(0.05)	1.07	(1.08)	0.40	(1.08)
Lehman Brothers	6.4	(4.9)	5.5	(3.6)	0.43	(1.17)	1.01	(0.61)	0.22	(0.51)
J.P. Morgan	3.2	(2.2)	3.0	(1.6)	0.05	(0.43)	1.00	(-0.55)	0.96	(-0.57)
Chase Manhattan	1.3	(0.7)	0.9	(0.2)	0.18	(0.32)	0.53	(-0.03)	0.52	(-0.03)
Smith Barney	2.8	(3.1)	3.6	(2.6)	-0.85	(1.15)	0.35	(0.75)	0.07	(0.39)

Note: - shows losses. Figures in parentheses are business results of a year earlier.

Source: *Japan Economic Journal*

    The future remains uncertain for these foreign securities firms operating in Japan. Despite the strong showing in 1989 and early 1990, largely from derivative securities trading, there is simply not enough business to go around unless they are able to break into the mainstream of the Japanese commission income market. They already have many Japanese employees and sales people plus many of the firms have superior execution and know how in various trading areas. However, with the fixed commission business so lucrative, it will not be easy to take this business away from the big four and the other Japanese security houses. Some firms, such as Hoare Govelt of London (100% owned by Security Pacific), are cutting back and there may be pull-outs. County Nat West, Deutsche Bank Capital, UBS-Phillips and Drew and others have been suffering considerable losses. Under normal circumstances many of these firms would simply sell their seats and leave Tokyo. But with all the trouble they went through, including help from their governments to get offices in Tokyo and seats on the TSE, the firms are holding out for better times and to maintain their world wide presence. The seats, which in 1990 were valued at $7-10 million, are hard to sell. The 1990 decline has made it more difficult for all firms since the total commission volume from non-arbitrage trading is down about 50% from 1989. In early 1991 the success and quick end of the Iraq war has improved the market and its volume.

FOREIGN INVESTMENT

Foreign investment in Japanese stocks turned negative in 1984. There continued to be more selling than buying each year until 1988 despite the large rises on the TSE and the increase in value of the yen against almost all currencies. In 1987 this disinvestment amounted to some 7.45 trillion yen. The total net selling of stocks from 1984 to the end of 1989 is quite remarkable and once again shows the great fear foreigners have of investing in Japan. Foreign buying of bonds has continued on a steady pace except for sizeable redemptions in 1986. After considerable buying in 1987, there was massive selling in 1988. Details appear in Figure 1.11 and Tables 1.24 and 1.25.

Figure 1.11   Foreign Investment in Japanese Securities, in Billions of Yen

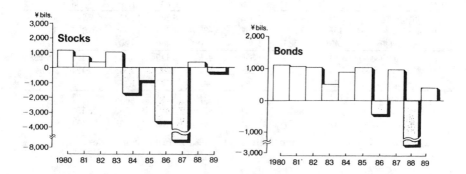

Source: Tokyo Stock Exchange

Foreigners are afforded nearly complete and free access to the Japanese stock market with a few exceptions. They are not allowed to purchase the domestic and international telephone companies, Nippon

Telephone and Telegraph and KDD. There is a limit of one-third foreign ownership in Japan Airlines and All Nippon Airways and a 20% limit on the Tokyo Broadcasting System and Nippon Television Network. These limits hardly affect foreign investment in Japan.

Table 1.24   Foreign Investment in Japanese Securities, ¥ Billions, 1979-89

	Stocks			Bonds		
	Purchases	Sales	Net Balance	Purchases	Sales	Net Balance
1979	1,104	1,235	-132	2,071	1,720	351
1980	2,873	1,688	1,185	3,601	2,352	1,249
1981	5,340	4,577	763	5,179	3,953	1,226
1982	4,000	3,620	380	6,971	5,846	1,125
1983	7,684	6,641	1,043	9,747	9,214	533
1984	8,441	10,158	-1,717	14,777	13,961	816
1985	9,381	10,161	-780	25,194	24,045	1,149
1986	17,027	20,617	-3,590	41,143	41,539	-396
1987	23,371	30,823	-7,452	43,909	42,916	993
1988	21,995	21,745	250	36,068	38,894	-2,826
1989	27,527	27,681	-154	34,426	33,934	492

Source: Ministry of Finance and the Tokyo Stock Exchange

Table 1.25   Foreign Investment on the TSE in ¥ Billions, 1982-89

	During	1982	1983	1984	1985	1986	1987	1988	1989
Total	Purchases	3,505	6,943	7,649	8,461	15,647	20,918	20,674	27,629
	Sales	3,342	6,206	9,583	9,276	19,408	27,841	20,562	29,406
	Net	416	737	-1,934	-815	-3,761	-6,924	1122	-1,777
United States	Purchase	549	931	1,021	1,213	2,288	3,179	2,988	5,110
	Sales	398	679	1,079	1,248	3,119	4,379	2,94294	4,692
	Net	151	151	-58	-35	-831	-1,200	46	418
Europe	Purchase	2,104	4,177	4,588	4,949	8,528	10,226	9,946	12,709
	Sales	2,133	3,791	6,052	5,639	10,978	14,534	10,357	14,382
	Net	243	385	-1,484	-690	-2,450	-4,309	-411	-1,673
Asia	Purchases	738	1,358	1,359	1,475	3,420	5,359	5,109	6,157
	Sales	714	1,316	1,543	1,517	3,792	6,545	5,124	6,644
	Net	24	42	-184	-42	-372	-1,186	-16	-487
Others	Purchases	114	477	701	824	1,411	2,154	2,631	3,653
	Sales	96	421	909	873	1,519	2,383	2,138	3,689
	Net	17	57	-208	-49	-108	-229	493	-36

Note: Calculated on the basis of reports from *integrated* securities companies.

Source: TSE

The total volume of foreign investment in Japanese stocks counting both purchases and sales, declined by ¥7,513 billion (15.4%) to ¥41,236 billion in 1988. Most of this decline was in foreign sales, with foreign purchases decreasing only slightly to ¥20,674 billion. For the first time since 1983, foreign investors became net *buyers* of Japanese stocks.

European investors were the largest net sellers with ¥411 billion, while U.S. investors made net purchases of ¥46 billion. Net sales by Asian investors decreased ¥16 billion from the preceding year. Other investors in other regions were the largest net buyers with ¥493 billion.

The Japanese do not really like much foreign ownership of their land and stocks. Among other reasons, they fear that a fall in prices elsewhere could cause foreign investors to sell in Japan, thus depressing prices. Indeed, the historical record is that foreigners have deserted the Tokyo market at the least sign of trouble. They were net sellers in the 1984-88 bull market and deserted the market in droves in the October 1987 crash. As we argue in Chapter 7, not only did they exit the market in 1990, they had a major effect on the decline. Until 1990 their net selling, in aggregate, has generally been a poor investment strategy. They have, however, been net buyers since the market bottomed out in October 1990. According to Roth (1989) in 1983 foreigners owned 6.3% of all Japanese stocks and accounted for at least 15% of the trades. They then owned high percentages of some major stocks. Roth's table comparing the 1983 and 1988 percentages owned of five major stocks shows how much this foreign ownership has dropped.

	1983	1988
Sony	47.3%	10.7%
Fanuc	37.1%	8.4%
TDK	32.0%	7.9%
Eisai	32.9%	8.6%
Murata Mfg	31.3%	13.7%

Other reasons for the lack of interest in foreign ownership are the fear of the ability to maintain total control over company affairs and the risk of leakage of secrets if foreigners are able to see company documents should they be powerful enough to demand this. The Boone Pickens/Koito affair discussed in Ziemba and Schwartz (1991) is a typical example of this.

SHARE OWNERSHIP IN LISTED COMPANIES

Figure 1.12 and Table 1.26 show the breakdown of share ownership on the Tokyo stock exchange until the end of 1989: (1) individual ownership has been consistently declining for the last 10 years to a record low of 22.4%; (2) foreign ownership continues to decline and at the end of 1989 was only 4.0%, and at the end of 1990 it was even lower at 3.5%; and (3) ownership

of financial institutions continues to be the largest investor group at 45.6%
and its percentage of total investment continues to rise sharply.

Figure 1.12   Change in Share Ownership on the TSE, 1950-89

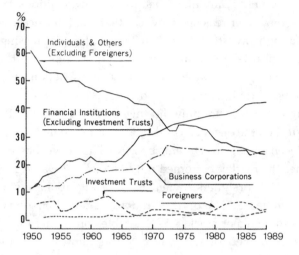

Source: Tokyo Stock Exchange

Table 1.26   Share ownership on the TSE, 1986-89

	1986	1987	1988	1989
Gov't and local gov't	0.8	0.9	0.8	0.7
Financial institutions	42.2	43.5	44.6	45.6
All banks	19.6	20.5	20.9	22.1
Investment trusts	1.3	1.8	2.4	3.1
Annuity trusts	0.7	0.9	1.0	1.0
Life insurance companies	13.5	13.3	13.2	13.1
Non-life insurance companies	4.5	4.4	4.3	4.2
Other financial institutions	2.6	2.6	2.8	2.1
Business corporations	24.1	24.5	24.9	24.9
Securities companies	2.0	2.5	2.5	2.5
Individuals and others	25.2	23.9	23.6	22.4
Foreigners	5.7	4.7	3.6	4.0
Total	100.0	100.0	100.0	100.0

Source: Tokyo Stock Exchange

FOREIGN STOCKS ON THE TSE

Trading in foreign stocks on the TSE began with six companies in December 1973. By 1976 there were 17 companies, but this fell to only ten by May 1984: it appeared this would not be a very viable activity. After this precarious start, both the number of entries and the volume grew dramatically through the end of 1987 with the increasing role of the yen as an international currency and the growing wealth of Japanese investors. The total number of foreign firms listed on the TSE stood at 112 at the end of 1990. In 1988 there were 26 newly listed companies and 2 dislistings. These stocks along with their December 1990 prices are listed in the appendix. Despite this growth, trading volume and value has fallen sharply since 1987. See Table 1.27 for details.

Table 1.27   Trading in Foreign Stocks on the TSE

	Trading Days	Number Listed at year end	Volume (1000s of shares) Total	Daily Average	Value (¥ mils) Total	Daily Average
1984	287	11	4,522	16	93,118	324
1985	285	21	131,424	461	853,336	2,994
1986	279	52	309,701	1110	1,151,863	4,129
1987	274	88	755,203	2756	3,469,228	12,661
1988	273	112	216,332	792	795,252	2,913
1989	249	119	480,193	1928	2,797,627	11,235

Source: Tokyo Stock Exchange

CROSS HOLDINGS AND INDUSTRIAL GROUPINGS

The objective of crossholding of shares is to protect each group company from outside control or threats, maintaining one another's status through interdependence

The majority of Japanese corporations are organized into great industrial or financial combinations called *zaibatsu*. The firms in industrial groups hold shares in each others' companies and jointly invest in new ventures and industries. These crossheld shares are held for business purposes and are never traded. For most companies in Japan, some 60% to 80% of the shares are crossheld or are nontrading shares held by insurance and other financial institutions. Table 5.7 provides averages by industry.

The *zaibatsu* can be organized horizontally - connecting a wide range of industries usually centered around a financial company such as a bank or trading company, or vertically - connecting various stages of production of a few or even one industry such as automobiles or iron and steel. The six most important *zaibatsu* are all organized horizontally and concentrate their activities on industrial Japan. They are the Mitsubishi, Mitsui, Sumitomo, Fuyo, DKB and Sanwa groups. Counting only the shares of the top ten shareholders of each company, at the end of fiscal 1987, about 22% of all shares in the 29 member Mitsubishi group were crossheld.

Until the end of WWII the Japanese economy was controlled by ten major *zaibatsu*: Mitsui, Mitsubishi, Sumitomo, Yasuda, Nissan, Asano, Furukawa, Okura, Nakajima and Nomura. These ten groups had more than a third of the market capitalization in the mid-1940s. Except for banks, the *zaibatsu* were split into smaller companies during the post-war occupation. But by the early 1950s, the old groups reformed into the current six. Their economic power was further strengthened in the 1960s through crossholding of shares. The Tokai group led by the Tokai Bank is a smaller but growing group which is also organized around a variety of industrial concerns. The Industrial Bank of Japan group is taking a purely financial approach by financing large co-operative projects, reviving financially distressed companies, and financing other large companies.

The largest vertical groupings are centered around iron and steel (Nippon Steel), automobiles (Nissan and Toyota), electrical and electronics (Hitachi and Matsushita), communications (NTT and KDD, the domestic and international phone companies, respectively), oil (Nippon Oil). These groups each have loose connections with the financial aspects of the major *zaibatsu*.

The closeness of the groups is determined in various ways through formation of councils of the presidents of the various companies, mutual appointment of key executives and intergroup financing. Though not identified as a decision-making body, presidential councils meet regularly to exchange views on the economic and financial environment, promising business ideas, R&D, maintenance of intragroup trademarks and company names, labor issues, and to make decisions on any joint investments in new industries, allocation of political contributions, public relations for the group, rehabilitation of financially troubled group companies and key personnel appointments. These groups have little formal legal authority and they are very careful to avoid any association with the prewar *zaibatsu* concept, insisting on the fostering of friendship and independence of all members. These groups help foster stability in Japan, making it easier to undertake long-term commitments, including R&D, and to take long-term risks, including market development.

There is some switching of loyalties, particularly in difficult times. The *endaka* or high yen shock beginning in late 1985, forced businesses to become more efficient and/or to move into new areas. This caused firms to link closer with their most powerful partners.

MOCHIAI, INTER-COMPANY SHAREHOLDING

Inter-company shareholding helps protect against hostile, outside takeovers and also helps to reinforce the long-term orientation of Japanese firms. These *mochiai* holdings maintain good business relations and are rarely, if ever, sold. For some time after WWII, nearly 70% of shares had been held by individual investors. However, since the late 60s, the share of individual investors has continually declined to its level of 22.6% at the end of 1989. Financial institutions owned 45.6%, business corporations, 24.9%, and trust banks a further 8.4%. Much of these holdings are *mochiai* and are never traded.

The average *mochiai* holdings for 1978 listed companies in Japan in 1989 was 71%. Figure 1.12 shows the change of ownership patterns on the TSE from 1958 to 1988. Table 5.13 shows the mochiai percentages for the largest companies in each of the 28 sectors of the TSE. These holdings are extremely high and vary from 73 to 95%. Tables 1.28 and 1.29 show the lowest and highest cross-held companies as of late 1985. These holdings are now larger.

This cross-holding leads to a considerable overstatement of the value of companies in Japan. The total capitalization of $3.85 trillion at the end of 1988 was really about $2.93 trillion, with some $924 billion being double counted *mochiai* holdings. McDonald(1989) has studied this effect. He used a sample of 75 major companies on the first section of the TSE that had about 53% of the section's capitalization. For these large capitalized companies, he counted the cross-holdings when they amounted to 0.05% or more. Analysis of these companies suggested that the real market capitalization in 1987-88 was about 76% of that reported, namely the sum of the capitalizations of the individual firms. Since small and unreported holdings were not counted and lower capitalized firms may have higher *mochiai* holdings, the total effect is probably somewhat higher than the sample's 24%. The size of Japan's market capitalization is such that the cross-holding bias is about the same as the entire six largest markets in continental Europe (Germany, France, Switzerland, Italy, Sweden and Spain) using end of 1989 valuations and exchange rates.

Recent legal changes have moved toward limiting the interdependence of shareholders. A 1982 law prohibited a subsidiary buying shares in its parent (a firm holding more than 50% of the outstanding shares of the subsidiary). In the case of cross-holdings, if a company owns more than 25% of another, that second company cannot exercise its voting rights on the first (thus the subsidiary cannot vote on the policies of the parent). This reduces the incentive to be affiliated but not wholly owned and increases the incentive for subsidiaries to actively seek to be bought (Pettway, Sicherman and Yamada (1989)).

Table 1.28
The 25 Companies with the Lowest Ratio of Stable Shareholders,
September 5, 1985

Rank	Company	Ratio
1	Heiwa Real Estate Co., Ltd.	7.13
2	Nankai Electric Railway Co., Ltd.	15.58
3	Teikoku Oil Co., Ltd.	15.68
4	Mitsui Mining and Smelting Co., Ltd.	17.85
5	Hankyu Corp.	18.08
6	Kirin Brewery Co., Ltd.	18.97
7	Seikia Sangyo Co., Ltd.	19.48
8	Fujiko Co., Ltd.	19.53
9	Kitakawa Iron Works Co., Ltd.	19.62
10	Toyo Terminal Mfg. Co., Ltd.	19.75
11	Noda Industrial Co., Ltd.	19.86
12	Nissan Chemical Industries, Ltd,	20.06
13	Nippon Steel Corp.	20.10
14	Nikkatsu Corp.	21.01
15	Kawasaki Steel Corp.	21.04
16	Sony Corp.	21.42
17	Miyairi Valve Mfg. Co., Ltd.	21-51
18	Unichika, Ltd.	21.59
19	Shinki Bus	21.60
20	Nippon Dream Kanko Co., Lid.	21.78
21	Ebara Corp.	21.80
22	Yamato Transport Co., Ltd.	22.03
23	Nippon Oil Co., Ltd.	22.40
24	Otori Semi Kogyo	22.48
25	Hitachi. Lt&	22.62

Source: Nikkei Sangyo Shimbum and Kanji Ishizumi (1988)

In Japan a foreign-owned firm is defined as one in which at least 50% of the equity is owned directly or indirectly by non-Japanese. The distribution of ownership among countries is shown in Table 1.30 (Ishizumi, 1988). As of March 1987, total cumulated foreign investment was $7 billion representing 2094 firms. In 1984 foreign capital investment represented 3.6% of the capital expenditures in Japan.

Table 1.29
The 10 Companies with the Highest Ratio of Stable Shareholders, September 5, 1985

Rank	Company	Ratio
1	Sanko Paper Mfg., Co. Ltd	86.86
2	Ohtsu Tim Co, Ltd	86.61
3	Toyo Bosuifu Mfg. Co, Ltd	85.28
4	Shin Nippon Drop Foreign Co, Lld	81.40
5	Tokyo Toyota Motor Corp	81.05
6	Zenisu Ryoko Concrete Co, Ltd	80.68
7	Fuji Steamship Co	79.96
8	Hosui	79.82
9	Ps Concrete Co.. Ltd.	79.73
10	Yurake Tochi Co.. Ltd.	79.71

Source: Nikkei Sangyo Shimbum and Kanji Ishizumi (1988)

Table 1.30
Distribution of Ownership of Foreign Firms in Japan, March 1987, Sample of 894 Firms

country	% of firms
U.S.	48.5
Germany	7.7
Britain	7.4
Switzerland	5.9
France	4.7
Asia	11.1

Source: Ishizumi (1988)

Kanji Ishizumi sets out the procedures for acquisitions in Japan. He emphasizes the importance of doing things the Japanese way and attempting to gain good-will and cooperation before making any move. For example, it is useful to gain agreement from the target firm's bank, to offer a mutually profitable business venture, to retain existing management, and to obtain cooperation from labor and other participants.

Table 1.31

Companies with M&A Potential based on Foreign Convertible Bonds

	PSCE Ratio (%)	Potential Shares (1000)	Nonconverted Unexercised Amount (¥ mil)
Osaka Oxygen Kogyo	48.04	40,331	11,220
Minebea Co, Ltd	42.93	93,821	65,718
Omjitsuya Co Ltd	39.38	22,935	15,521
Kenwood Corp	34.73	18,256	13,431
Gun San	33.86	11,698	4,288
Renown, Inc	23.96	37,565	27,568
Daishinpan Co, Ltd	22.85	8,845	6,609
Daido Sanso K.K.	22.48	10,070	2,537
Nakayama Steel Works, Ltd	21.91	17,183	7,744
Asics Corp, Ltd	21.32	28,058	12,438
Nioppon Shinpan Co, Ltd	21.15	52,930	33,619
Ryobi Ltd	20.51	24,974	10,123
Sanyo Electric Co, Ltd	20.25	6,922	8,908
Manuzen Co, Ltd	20.15	15,295	7,075
Durban Inc	19.58	9,493	4,908
Gun Ei Chemical	19.40	10,494	9,668
Asahi Ka Forging	19.12	6,999	2,421
Tsubakimoto Precision Product Co, Ltd	18.76	6,642	9,922
Takasago Thermal Engineering Co, Ltd	18.58	8,551	4,899
Fuji Tech	18.50	11,948	8,942
Zeto	18.10	3,638	2,263
Tokyu Department Store	17.96	28,862	13,889
Showa Line, Ltd	17.72	27,763	5,691
Pasco Corp	17.46	6,350	8,934
Daiichi Katei Dcnki Co, Ltd	17.26	11,879	7,828
Toshiba Plant	17.21	8,259	6,557
Osumi Howa	17.05	7,133	3,859
Han Wa Ko	16.93	29,101	20,567
Sonoike Took Mgf. Co, Ltd	16.59	9,771	10,668
Sankyo Seiki Mfg- Co, Ltd	16.56	11,649	15,111
Kayaba Industry Co, Ltd	16.55	23,770	7,241
Tokyu Store Co, Ltd	16-51	6,219	5,458
Silver Seiko Ltd	16.49	7,999	4,615
Yamamura Glass Co, Ltd	16.37	12,209	6,242
Iseki & Co, Ltd	16.06	26,049	10,075

Note: Potential share ratio is calculated based on the ratio of the potential share (non-converted convertible debenture and unexercised warrant) by issuing foreign bonds to the issued share (As of the end of July 1985).

Source: Nikkei Sangyo Shimbum and Kanji Ishizumi (1988)

One popular way to acquire a large stake in a company is to purchase stock from one of the major shareholders directly. Another way is to buy newly issued stock directly from the target company by private placement. In Japan, there are no laws protecting shareholders from dilution of their holdings by such private placement of new issues. These new issues have been offered at more than a 50% discount from the current market price, such as when Sony acquired Aiwa at ¥70 when the market closing price was ¥145.

By purchasing foreign convertible bonds, a would be acquirer can maintain secrecy because these are issued in bearer form. Some potential candidates are shown in Table 1.31. A related method is the purchase of newly issued convertible bonds from the company by private issue. Issuance of convertible bonds has also served to thwart takeover attempts.

For a foreign company to merge with a Japanese company it must first establish a subsidiary in Japan.

The sale of shares by the major holder can create a large tax liability. The same is true when a Japanese company sells all or part of its business. For example, the difference between the book value and the selling price is subject to capital gains tax and in consideration of the number of companies that carry land and other assets at original price, the unrealized capital gains liabilities are likely to be large. If a foreign company purchases assets at less than fair market value, this difference is considered a capital gain and taxable. Ishizumi's book provides valuable information and insight into the merger and acquisition process in Japan.

AMERICAN DEPOSITORY RECEIPTS

An ADR is a depository receipt issued by an American trust or other bank for a stock certificate held in a trust or other bank in Japan. ADRs can be sponsored by the bank which sees a need for the new investment vehicle or by the Japanese firm which wants a new trading vehicle for its shares. The creation, administration, exchange listing fees and SEC reporting costs are borne by the sponsor. The depository bank in the U.S. arranges for a Japanese custodian bank to hold the purchased shares. Then the bank issues ADR certificates on those shares in the U.S. The depository bank is then the intermediary for dividends and ownership transfers. The small fee for administering the dividend distributions is borne by the Japanese company if it is the sponsor, as it is for all NYSE and ASE listed ADRs. By such listing, one tracks these ADRs just like regular stocks including the possibility of using them for margin and other security.

On the surface it seems that there is no real difference between holding an ADR and the underlying shares in Japan. However, the ADR is denominated in *dollars*. Hence, although the underlying stock may rise or fall, the value of the ADR depends also on the currency changes involved.

Table 1.32 lists ADRs that traded in the U.S. on the New York, American or over-the-counter exchanges in early October 1989. The ADRs tend to have bid-ask spreads in the 1-2% range because of their thin trading. One ADR provides various amounts of shares of the underlying stock such as two shares in the case of Fuji Photo. For the other ADRs, the conversions are in ( ).

One would expect that the price in Japan converted to U.S. dollars would yield the price in New York. Kato, Linn and Schallheim (1987) studied this price parity using data from January 1, 1981, to December 31, 1984. They included all the stocks listed in the ISL Daily Stock Price Books where data on the ADRs can be found. They used closing prices in New York for comparison. Hence, there is a possible bias here with new news in the time between Tokyo's close and New York's open. They found that none of the Japanese firms showed significant differences in the mean or median of the daily price differences using a t-test. However, all of the ADRs, as might be expected, trade for prices that are below the stocks in Tokyo, as shown in Table 1.33. Kato, Linn and Schallheim investigated this further using non-parametric sign and signed-rank tests. For these tests the difference in prices is highly significant, as shown in Table 1.34.

Table 1.32 Japanese ADRs in New York (in dollars), Early October 1989

	Bid	Asked		Bid	Asked
Fuji Photo (2)	69	69.75	NEC (5)	65.125	65.75
Hitachi* (10)	110	112.25	Nissan Motors	21.75	22
Honda* (10)	27.25	27.625	Pioneer Electric*(2)	75.75	76.875
JAL (2)	248	249.5	Tokyo M&F (50)	74.5	75
Matsushita* (10)	165.5	169	Toyota (2)	36.5	36.875
Mitsui (10)	156	158.5			

other ADRs are:

Sony* (1)	Kubota* (20)
Canon (5)	Kyocera* (2)
Kirin (10)	TDK* (2)

* Means stock is listed on the NYSE

Investigating further, Kato et al found that the contemporaneous correlations are well below one, ranging from 0.239 to 0.895, see Table 1.34. The correlation of the ADR returns with the previous day Japanese returns was significantly greater than zero for all firms except Nissan

Motor. However, these correlations are much lower, ranging from 0.037 for Nissan to 0.284 for Honda. Finally the correlations between the ADR returns and the following day's return in Japan are very low, ranging from 0.004 to 0.081. Only two of these are significantly greater than zero with 95% confidence.

The conclusion for investors seems to be that ADRs, while easier to purchase and available in much smaller quantities than in Japan, have some significant problems when compared to owning the actual stock or a mutual fund composed of similar stocks. The ADRs do not correlate well and they trade for prices below the underlying stock. Moreover, they face currency risk and have large bid-ask spreads.

Table 1.33
Tests of differences between U.S. ADR and Japanese stock prices, January 1, 1981 to December 31, 1984

Company	Difference Mean (Median)	T-test (P(t))	Sign Probability	Wilcoxon Signed-Ranks Test Z-Value (P(Z))
Fuji Photo Film	-.0787 (-.0290)*	-.070 (.94)	.0005	-4.920 (.00)
Honda Motor	-.1164 (-.0538)	-.285 (.78)	.0016	-5.124 (.00)
Kirin Brewery	-.7087 (-.0736)	-.491 (.62)	.0000	-11.951 (.00)
Kubota, Ltd	-.0712 (-.0528)	-.558 (.58)	.0116	-3.706 (.00)
Matsushita Electric Industrial	-.0950 (-.0862)	-.144 (.88)	.0066	-3.645 (.00)
Nissan Motor	-.0640 (-.0148)	-.086 (.93)	.0079	-5.518 (.00)
Sony Corp	-.0317 (-0.301)	-.270 (.79)	.0000	-4.842 (.00)
Toyota Motor	-.1155 (-.0573)	-.128 (.90)	.0000	-10.926 (.00)

*P value for difference from zero hypothesis test.

Source: Kato, Linn and Schallheim (1987)

Table 1.34
Correlations between ADR and Japanese stock returns, January 1, 1981 to
December 31, 1984

Company	Same Day	Previous Day in Japan	Next Day in Japan
Fuji Photo Film	.793	.265	.015
	(.00)*	(.00)	(.66)
Honda Motor	.799	.284	.081
	(.00)	(.00)	(.02)
Kirin Brewery	.722	.239	.048
	(.00)	(.00)	(.16)
Kubota, Ltd	.239	.107	.047
	(.00)	(.00)	(.17)
Matsushita Electric Industrial	.766	.265	.004
	(.00)	(.00)	(.90)
Nissan Motor	.895	.037	.020
	(.00)	(.27)	(.56)
Sony Corp	.858	.136	.074
	(.00)	(.00)	(.03)
Toyota Motor	.546	.122	.063
	(.00)	(.00)	(.07)

*P value for difference from zero hypothesis test.

Source: Kato, Linn and Schallheim (1987)

CHAPTER 2
THE NIKKEI STOCK AVERAGE AND THE TOPIX INDICES

The Nikkei stock average (NSA) is a price weighted index, similar to the Dow Jones industrial average, computed on the value of 225 stocks traded in the first section of the Tokyo stock exchange. A list of the stocks in the NSA, by industry group, appears in Table 2.1. The index is tilted toward heavy industrials - consisting of chemical, steel and textile stocks - which have traditionally been the mainstay of the Japanese economy. Electronics and other recently developing industries are underweighted relative to their current capitalization and importance in the economy.

Table F4 in the appendix has more detail on the 225 component stocks such as their relative weights, trading volume, price earnings ratios, dividend yield, beta and prices as of March 30, 1990. On October 1, 1991, there will be more substantial changes in the NSA 225 membership to delete issues with low liquidity. Prices, as of January 4, 1991, for all stocks on the first, second and foreign stock sections of the TSE appear in appendix G.

The market value of the 225 Nikkei stocks amounts to about 50% of the market value of all stocks in the first section. These stocks account for about 75% of the trading volume on the first section of the TSE. The NSA is computed by adding the prices of all 225 stocks and a divisor that changes over time due to stock splits, rights issues, etc. The divisor at the end of December 1989 was 10.198. The index is calculated and reported at one-minute intervals during trading hours. Figure 2.1 a,b and Table 2.2 give the relative growth in value of the NSA since 1949 in yen and in U.S. dollars starting from 1¥ in 1949. The 1990 values give the highs and lows corresponding to the 21st and 22nd corrections which are discussed in Chapter 7. Additional data for the NSA appear in Appendix F.

Table 2.1   The 225 Stocks in the NSA Grouped by Major Industry

Industry	No.	Company Names
Fisheries	3	Kyukuyo, Nichiro, Gyopyo Suisan
Mining	3	Mitsui Mining, Sumitomo Coal Mining, Teikoku Oil
Construction	9	Taisei Ohbayashi, Simizu, Sato Kogyo, Tobishima, Fujita, Kajima, Tekken Construction, Toa, Daiwa House Industry
Foods	18	Nippon Flour Mills, Nisshin Flour Milling, Taito, Nippon Beet Sugar Mfg., Morinaga, Meiji Seika, Meiji Milk Products, Sapporo Breweries, Asahi Breweries, Kirin Brewery, Takara Shuzo, Godo Susei, Sanraku, Hohnen, The Nisshin Oil Mills, Kikkoman, Ajinomoto, Nichierei
Textiles	16	Katakura Industries, Toyobo, Kenebo, Unitika, Fuji Spinning, Nisshinbo Industries, Nitto Boseki, The Japan Wook Textile, DAito Woolen Spinning & Weaving, Teikoku Sen-i, Teijin, Toray Industries, Toho Rayon, Mitsubishi Rayon, Kuraray, Asahi Chemical Industry
Pulp and Paper	6	Sanyo-Kokusaku Pulp, Oji Paper, Honshu Paper, Jujo Paper, Mitsubishi Paper Mills, Hokuetsu Paper Mills
Chemicals	21	Mitsui Toatsu Chemicals, Showa Denko, Kumitomo Chemical, Mitsubishi Chemical Industries, Nissan Chemical Industries, Rasa Industries, Nippon Soda, Tosho, Toagosei Chemical Industry, Denki Kagaku Kogyo, Shin-Etsu Chemical, Nippon Carbide Industries, Nippon Chemical Industrial, Khyowa Hakko Kogyo, Japan Synthetic Chemical Industry, Ube Industries, Nippon Kayaku, Asahi Denka Kogyo, Nippon Oil and Fats, Fuji Photo Film, Konica
Pharmaceuticals	4	Sankyo, Takeda Chemical Industries, Yamanouchi Pharmaceutical, Dainippon Pharmaceutical
Oil Products	4	Nippon Oil, Showa Shell Seikiyu, Mitsubishi Oil, Tonen
Rubber Prods	2	The Yokohama Rubber, Bridgestone
Glass & Ceramics	12	Asahi Glass, Nippon Sheet Glass, Nihon Cement, Sumitomo Cement, Onoda Cement, Mitsubishi Mining & Cement, Tokai CArbon, Nippon Carbon, Noritake, Toto, NGK Insulators, Shinagawa Refractories
Iron & Steel	11	Nippon Steel, Kawasaki Steel, Nippon Kokan, Sumitomo Metal Industries, Kobe Steel, Nippon Stainless Steel, Nippon Metal Industry, Nippon Yakin Kogyo, Nippon Denko, The Japan Steel Works, Mitsubishi Steel Mfg.
Non-ferrous Metal and Met Prods	15	Nippon Light Metal, Mitsui Mining & Smelting, Toho Zinc, Mitsubishi Metal, Nippon Mining, Sumitomo Metal Mining, Dowa Mining, Furukawa, Shimura Kako, The Furukawa Electric, Sumitomo Electric Industries, Fujikura, Showa Electric Wire & Cable, Toyo Seikan, Tokyo Rope Mfg.
Machinery	11	Niigata Engineering, Okuma Machinery Works, Komatsu, Kubota, Ebara, Chiyoda, Nippon Piston Ring, Nippon Seiko, NTN Toyo Bearing, Koyo Seiko, Nachi-Fujikoshi
Electric Machinery	15	Hitachi, Toshiba, Mitsubishi Electric, Fuji Electric, Meidensha, NEC, Fujitsu, Oki Electric Industry, Matsushita Electric Industrial, Sharp, Sony, Sanyo Electric, Yokogawa Electric, Nippondenso, Yuasa Battery
Shipbuilding	5	Mitsui Engineering & Shipbuilding, Hitachi Zosen, Mitsubishi Heavy Industries, Kawasaki Heavy Industries, Ishikawajima-Harima Heavy Industries
Automobiles	7	Nissan Motor, Isuzu Motors, Toyota Motor, Hino Motors, Mazda Motor, Honda Motor, Suzuki Motor

Transport Equipment	1	Nippon Sharyo
Precision Instrument	4	Nikon, Canon, Ricoh, Citizen Watch
Other Products	3	Toppan Printing, Dai Nippon Printing, Yamaha
Trading Companies	6	C. Itoh, Marubeni, Mitsui, Sumitomo, Mitsubishi, Iwatani International
Retail	5	Mitsukoshi, Tokyu Department Store, Takashimaya, Matsuzakaya, Maruzen
Banking	8	The Kai-ichi Kangyo Bank, The Bank of Tokyo, The Mitsui Bank, The Mitsubishi Bank, The Fuji Bank, The Sumitomo Bank, The Mitsui Trust & Banking, The Mitsubishi Trust & Banking
Other Financial	2	Japan Securities Finance, Nippon Shinpan
Securities Companies	2	The Nikko Securities, The Nomura Securities
Nonlife Insurance	3	The Tokio Marine & Fire Insurance, Taisho Marine & Fire Insurance, The Yasuda Fire & Marine Insurance
Real Estate	3	Mitsui Real Estate Development, Mitsubishi Estate, Heiwa Real Estate
Rail & Bus Companies	6	Tobu Railway, Tokyu, Keihin Electric Express Railway, Odakyu Electric Railway, Keio Teito Electric Railway, Keisei Electric Raliway
Land Transport	1	Nippon Express
Marine Transport	6	Nippon Yusen, Mitsui O.S.K. Lines, Navix Line, Kawasaki Kisen, Showa Line
Air Transport	1	All Nippon Airways
Warehousing	2	Mitsubishi Warehouse & Transportation, The Mitsui Warehouse
Communication	1	Nippon Telegraph and Telephone
Electric Power	2	The Tokyo Electric Power, The Kansai Electric Power
Gas	2	Tokyo Gas, Osaka Gas
Services	5	Shochiku, Toho, Toei, Nikkatsu, Korakuen

Figure 2.1a
The Relative Growth of the NSA in Yen and U.S. Dollars, 1949-1970,
1949=1, Exchange Rate Fixed at 360¥ $ in this Period

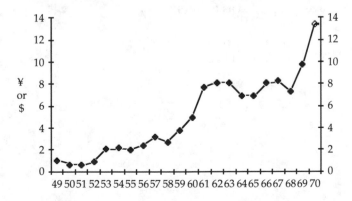

Figure 2.1b
The Relative Growth of the NSA in Yen and U.S. Dollars, 1970–February
1991, 1970=1

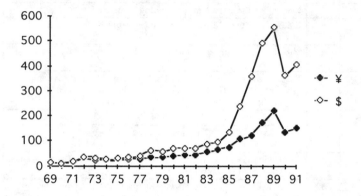

At the end of December 1989, the NSA was ¥38,915.87. This is a
theoretical number and should be distinguished from the real average
price in the market-place. The meaning of ¥38,915.87 is as follows.
Suppose one had bought one share of each of the 225 component stocks
listed on the Tokyo Stock Exchange at the time of the post-war inaugura-
tion of the exchange (May 16, 1949), then held them until the end of
December 1989 without putting additional funds into new shares issued
through rights offerings to shareholders. Instead one had reinvested the
value of every right evenly in the component stocks. The average price
would then have increased from ¥176.21 on the date of the original
investment, May 16, 1949, to ¥38,915.87, or 220.84 times, not counting
dividends and taxes. In dollar terms, the average increased a remarkable
553.04 times. The average is compiled as follows:

$$\text{Nikkei Stock Average} = \frac{\text{Sum of Prices of 225 Stocks}}{\text{Divisor}}$$

Table 2.2   NSA, Growth in Yen and U.S. Dollars, 1949-91 (February)

End of Year	NSA	Yen/$	Current Value of 1¥ invested in 1949 in ¥	1$ invested in 1949 in $
1949	109.9	360.00	0.62	0.62
1950	101.9	360.00	0.58	0.58
1951	166.1	360.00	0.94	0.94
1952	362.6	360.00	2.06	2.06
1953	377.9	360.00	2.14	2.14
1954	356.1	360.00	2.02	2.02
1955	425.7	360.00	2.42	2.42
1956	549.1	360.00	3.12	3.12
1957	474.5	360.00	2.69	2.69
1958	666.5	360.00	3.78	3.78
1959	874.9	360.00	4.97	4.97
1960	1356.7	360.00	7.70	7.70
1961	1432.6	360.00	8.13	8.13
1962	1420.4	360.00	8.06	8.06
1963	1225.1	360.00	6.95	6.95
1964	1216.5	360.00	6.90	6.90
1965	1417.8	360.00	8.05	8.05
1966	1452.1	360.00	8.24	8.24
1967	1283.5	360.00	7.28	7.28
1968	1714.9	360.00	9.73	9.73
1969	2359.0	360.00	13.39	13.39
1970	1987.1	360.00	11.28	11.28
1971	2713.7	314.80	15.40	17.61
1972	5207.9	302.00	29.56	35.23
1973	4306.8	280.00	24.44	31.42
1974	3817.2	300.95	21.66	25.91
1975	4358.6	305.15	24.74	29.18
1976	4990.8	292.80	28.32	34.82
1977	4865.6	240.00	27.61	41.42
1978	6001.8	194.60	34.06	63.01
1979	6569.5	239.70	37.28	55.99
1980	7116.4	203.00	40.39	71.62
1981	7681.8	219.90	43.59	71.37
1982	8016.7	235.00	45.50	69.69
1983	9893.8	232.20	56.15	87.05
1984	11542.6	251.10	65.50	93.91
1985	13113.3	200.50	74.42	133.62
1986	18701.3	160.05	106.13	238.72
1987	21564.0	123.00	122.38	358.18
1988	30159.0	125.85	171.15	489.59
1989	38915.9	143.76	220.84	553.04
1990	23848.7	135.40	135.34	359.83
(Feb)1991	26409.2	133.17	149.87	405.15

Originally, the divisor was 225 - the number of component stocks. Since 1949 the divisor has been adjusted whenever price changes resulting from factors other than those of market activity take place. The average is then not affected by such price changes. No adjustment is made for ex-dividends, including cash dividends or stock dividends. When a component stock goes ex-rights, the divisor is reduced.

$$\text{New divisor} = \frac{\text{day's divisor x [cum-rights final day's aggregated stock prices - sum equivalent to the drop in price by ex-rights]}}{\text{cum-rights final day's aggregated stock prices}}$$

Price pertaining to a right = sum-rights final day's stock price - theoretical stock price by ex-rights

$$\text{Theoretical stock price by ex-rights} = \text{cum-rights final day's stock price} + \frac{\text{paid-in capital x percentage of allotment for considerations}}{1 + \text{Percentage of allotments [equivalent to allotments for considerations + equivalent to allotments without considerations]}}$$

Figures 2.2 and 2.3 show the growth in the NSA in yen in the two subperiods 1949-68 and 1969-90. The total growth rates were similar; each period had a total gain of about 13 to 15 times (until the 1990 declines). Table 2.3 gives the year-by-year changes in the value of the NSA, along with its highs and lows.

Japanese stock markets have limited price changes, both up and down, to approximately 15% in any day. Hence the maximum daily fall in the index is essentially constrained to be 15%. On October 20, hours after the crash in New York the NSA fell 14.9%. But it bounced back 10.2% the following day. Since then it has recovered the late 1987 losses, reached new highs and had a steep correction in 1990. The record high through 1988 was 30,159 which was reached on the final day of trading in 1988 (December 28). In 1989 the market also closed the year at its high for the year, 38,916.

Figure 2.2   Growth in the NSA in Yen, 1949-1968

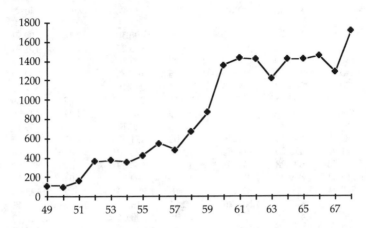

Source: TSE

Figure 2.3   Growth in the NSA in Yen, 1969-1991 (February)

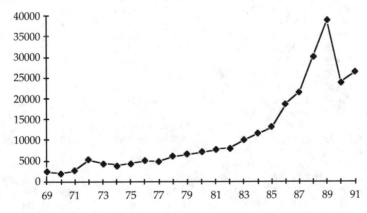

Table 2.4 has the ten largest absolute and percentage changes in the NSA until the end of 1989.   Table 2.5 updates the largest absolute and percentage changes for the violent market activity in 1990. Here the ten largest increases and decreases in the NSA index in absolute and percentage terms in 1990 are presented. Table 2.6 compares the yields, price earnings ratios and price to book values of ten peaks and valleys of the NSA average from 1949 to 1988. Finally, Table 2.7 lists the 20

Table 2.3
Average, Open, High, Low and Closing Values for the NSA, 1949-90

Year or Month	Average	Open	High	Date	Low	Date	Close
1949	149.95	176.21	176.89	9.01	98.50	12.14	109.91
1950	101.73	108.56	114.99	8.21	85.25	7.06	101.91
1951	136.10	102.10	170.32	10.27	102.10	1.04	166.06
1952	245.6'7	167.80	370.55	12.15	167.80	1.04	362.64
1953	390.91	364.89	474.43	2.04	295.18	4.01	377.95
1954	340.79	362.88	377.27	1.11	314.08	3.22	356.09
1955	374.00	361.10	425.69	12.28	345.89	4.27	425.69
1956	485.33	428.59	566.30	12.06	420.14	1.25	549.14
1957	535.57	549.45	595.46	5.04	471.53	12.27	474.55
1958	571.97	475.20	666.54	12.27	475.20	1.04	666.54
1959	821.52	671.28	976.93	11.30	664.69	1.09	874.88
1960	1,116.62	869.34	1,356.71	12.28	869.34	1.04	1,356.71
1961	1,548.94	1,366.74	1,829.74	7.18	1,258.00	12.19	1,432.60
1962	1,419.44	1,425.30	1,589.76	2.14	1,216.04	10.29	1,420.43
1963	1,440.61	1,418.25	1,634.37	4.05	1,200.64	12.18	1,225.10
1964	1,262.18	1,204.40	1,369.00	7.03	1,202.69	7.12	1,417.83
1965	1,203.16	1,227.11	1,417.83	12.28	1,020.49	7.12	1,417.83
1966	1,479.16	1,430.13	1,588.73	4.01	1,364.34	12.05	1,452.10
1967	1,412.01	1,441.35	1,506.27	3.01	1,250.14	12.11	1,283.47
1968	1,544 81	1,266.27	1,851.49	10.02	1,266.27	1.04	1,714.89
1969	1,956.16	1,733.64	2,358.96	12.27	1,733.64	1.04	2,358.96
1970	2,193.71	2,402.85	2,534.45	4.06	1,929.64	5.27	1,987.14
1971	2,385.72	2,001.34	2,740.98	8.14	1,981.74	1.06	2,713.74
1972	3,755.13	2,712.31	5,207.94	12.28	2,712.31	1.04	5,207.94
1973	4,759.25	5,232.86	5,359.74	1.24	3,958.57	12.18	4,306.80
1974	4,276.05	4,259.20	4,787.54	6.01	3,355.13	10.09	3,817.22
1975	4,243.05	3,777.40	4,564.52	5.12	3,627.04	1.10	4,358.60
1976	4,651.42	4,403.06	4,990.85	12.28	4,403.06	1.05	4,990.85
1977	5,029.69	4,998.85	5,287.65	9.05	4,597.26	11.24	4,865.60
1978	5,537.74	4,867.91	6,097.26	12.13	4,867.91	1.04	6,001.85
1979	6,272.33	6,041.57	6,590.69	9.29	5,925.87	4.10	6,569.47
1980	6,870.16	6,560.16	7,188.28	11.06	6,475.93	3.28	7,116.38
1981	7,510.73	7,150.95	8,019.14	8.17	6,956.52	3.13	7,681.84
1982	7,399.36	7,718.84	8,026.99	12.07	6,849.78	10.01	8,016.67
1983	8,808.71	8,021.40	9,893.82	12.28	7,803.18	1.25	9,893.82
1984	10,560.61	9,927.11	11,577.44	12.04	9,703.35	7.23	11,542.60
1985	12,556.63	11,558.06	13,128.94	12.17	11,545.16	1.05	13,113.32
1986	16,386.07	13,136.87	18,936.24	8.20	12,881.50	1.21	18,701.30
1987	23,176.03	18,820.55	26,646.43	10.14	18,544.05	1.13	21,564.00
1988	27,011.33	21,217.04	30,159.00	12.28	21,217.04	1.04	30,159.00
1989	34,042.79	30,243.66	38,915.87	12.29	30,183.79	1.05	38,915.87
1990 (J)	37,401.76	38,712.88	38,712.88	4	36,729.46	18	37,188.95
(F)	36,517.81	37,206.42	37,666.83	6	33,321.87	26	34,591.99

Source: Nihon Keizai Shimbum and Tokyo Stock Exchange

corrections of 10% or more in the NSA from 1949 to the end of 1989 plus the results concerning the 21st and 22nd corrections in 1990. The 21st and 22nd corrections in 1990 are discussed in Chapter 7.

Even though the market rose over 220 times in the forty years since 1949, the rise has not been straight up. Ten of these corrections were more than 20%, six were more than 25%, four were more than 30%, three were more than 35%, and one exceeded 50%. The market low close was 20,221.86 on October 1, 1990, down 48.0% from the end of the December 1989 peak. This decline was more severe than the first oil crisis in 1973/4 when the price of oil had quickly quintupled. At the end of 1990, the NSA closed at 23,848.71 down 38.7% on the year.

Table 2.4
The Ten Largest Daily Increases and Decreases in the NSA Index in Percentage and Absolute Terms to December 31, 1989

	% Increase	Date	Point Increase	Date
1	11.29	Dec 15 1949	2,037.32	Oct 21, 1987
2	9.30	Oct 21 1987	1,215.22	Jun 1, 1988
3	6.41	Apr 16 1953	906.42	Jul 2, 1987
4	6.31	Mar 6 1953	901.75	Nov 18, 1987
5	5.63	Jan 6, 1988	793.96	Mar 28,1989
6	5.51	Jul 15, 1950	731.15	Oct 10, 1987
7	5.39	Feb 13, 1950	632.40	Oct 27, 1987
8	5.32	Jun 26, 1972	604.54	Apr 14 1987
9	5.32	Jul 17, 1950	563.87	Oct 3, 1987
10	4.94	Feb 5, 1973	527.39	Oct 17, 1989

	% Decrease	Date	Point Decrease	Date
1	14.90	Oct 20, 1987	3,836.48	Oct 20, 1987
2	10.00	Mar 5, 1953	1,203.23	Oct 23, 1987
3	8.69	Apr 30, 1970	1161.19	Feb 21, 1989
4	7.68	Aug 16, 1971	1,096.22	Oct 26, 1987
5	6.97	Dec 14, 1949	935.87	Feb 23, 1989
6	6.73	Mar 30, 1953	831.32	Apr 27, 1987
7	6.61	Jun 24, 1972	731.91	Nov 10, 1987
8	5.93	Aug 19, 1971	666.41	Jan 15, 1989
9	5.41	Oct 9, 1974	658.28	May 20, 1987
10	5.03	Aug 23, 1971	653.36	Jan 12, 1989

Source: TSE

Table 2.5
Ten Largest Daily Increases and Decreases in the NSA Index in Absolute
and Percentage Terms in 1990

	% Increase	Date	Point Increase	Date
1	13.23%	Oct 2	2,675	Oct 2
2	5.39%	Aug 15	1,458	Mar 26
3	4.80%	Mar 26	1,439	Aug 15
4	4.67%	Sep 10	1,119	Apr 9
5	4.54%	Nov 13	1,119	Sep 10
6	4.30%	Dec 5	1,042	Nov 13
7	4.04%	Aug 27	1,029	Apr 6
8	3.82%	Apr 9	976	Aug 27
9	3.64%	Apr 6	969	Dec 5
10	3.51%	Oct 8	856	Aug 8

	% Decrease	Date	Point Decrease	Date
1	-6.60%	Apr 2	-1,978	Apr 2
2	-5.84%	Aug 23	-1,569	Feb 26
3	-4.74%	Sep 26	-1,473	Aug 23
4	-4.50%	Feb 26	-1,353	Mar 19
5	-4.22%	Aug 13	-1,161	Feb 21
6	-4.15%	Mar 19	-1,153	Aug 13
7	-4.13%	Aug 22	-1,108	Sep 26
8	-3.87%	Oct 11	-1,087	Aug 22
9	-3.84%	Aug 20	-1,059	Aug 20
10	-3.80%	Dec 2	-1,046	Mar 30

Source: TSE

Table 2.6
Fundamentals at Stock Peaks and Valleys (for the NSA 225)

Date	NSA	Yield	PER	PBR
At Peak of Stock Prices				
May 4, 1957	595.46	5.06	8.77	0.90
Jul 18, 1961	1,829.74	2.92	20.06	2.23
Apr 5, 1963	1,634.37	3.50	19.54	1.73
Apr 1, 1956	1,588.73	3.68	16.37	1.62
Apr 6, 1970	2,534.45	3.17	12.76	1.98
Jan 24, 1973	5,359.74	1.57	25.10	3.07
Aug 17, 1981	8,019.14	1.35	24.18	2.38
May 4, 1984	11,190.17	1.06	28.77	2.80
Aug 20, 1986	18,936.24	0.64	59.55	4.31
Oct 14, 1987	26,646.43	0.45	72.99	6.33
At Bottom of Stock Prices				
Dec 27, 1957	471.53	6.77	7.06	0.71
Oct 29, 1962	1,216.04	4.80	14.65	1.25
Jul 12, 1965	1,020.49	5.85	10.34	1.06
Dec 11, 1967	1,250.14	5.11	9.10	1.19
Dec 8, 1970	1,963.40	4.35	9.22	1.39
Oct 9, 1974.	3,355.13	3.00	13.87	1.57
Oct 11, 1982	6,849.78	1.64	20.94	1.88
Jul 23, 1984	9,703.35	1.23	23.47	2.28
Oct 22, 1986	15,819.55	0.76	51.41	3.66
Nov 11, 1987	21,036.76	0.57	56.98	5.12

Source: Yamaichi Research Institute.

Table 2.7a
The Twenty-two Corrections of 10% or More on the NSA, 1949 to 1990

Correction Number	Value at Peak	Value in Valley	Dates	% Decline	Duration (months)	Reasons for decline
1	176.89	85.25	9/1/49-7/6/50	-51.8	11	Korean war
2	474.43	295.18	3/4-4/1/53	-37.8	2	Stalin's death
3	366.69	321.79	5/6-6/3/53	-12.2	1	
4	595.46	471.53	5/4-12.27/57	-20.8	8	
5	1,829.74	1,258.00	7/18-12/19/61	-31.2	5	World wide recession
6	1,589.76	1,216.04	2/14-10/29/62	-23.5	9	World wide recession
7	1,634.37	1,200.64	4/5-12/18/63	-26.5	9	
8	1,369.00	1,020.49	7/3/64-7/12/65	-25.5	13	
9	1,588.73	1,364.34	4/1-12/15/66	-14.1	8	
10	1,506.27	1,250.14	3/1-12/11/76	-17.0	9	
11	2,534.45	1,929.64	4/6-5/27/70	-23.9	2	
12	2,740.98	2,227.25	8/14-10/20/71	-18.7	3	Dollar decline
13	5,359.74	3,355.13	1/24/73-10/9/74	-37.4	21	First oil crisis
14	4,564.52	3,814.02	5/12-9/29/75	-16.4	5	
15	5,287.65	4,597.26	9/5-11/24/77	-13.1	3	Second oil crisis
16	8,019.14	6,849.78	8/17/81-10/1/82	-14.6	14	World wide recession induced by high interest rates
17	11,190.17	9,703.35	5/4-7/23/84	-13.3	3	
18	18,936.24	15,819.58	8/20-10/22/86	-16.5	2	
19	25,929.42	22,702.74	6/17-7/22/87	-12.4	1	Overvalued PERs
20	26,646.43	21,036.76	10/14-11/11/87	-21.1	1	World wide crash
21	38,916	28,002	12/29/89-4/2/90	-28.0	3	Credit crunch, deregulation
22	33,293	20,222	7/17-10/1/90	-39.3	2.5	Credit crunch, Iraq oil crisis
Average				-23.4%	6.2	

Table 2.7b Comparing the 21st and 22nd Corrections

	High	Low	Change
21st Correction	38,916 Dec 28, 1989	28,002 April 2, 1990	-28.0%
Recovery	28,002	33,293 July 17, 1990	+15.9%
22nd Correction	33,293	20,222 Oct 1, 1990	-39.3%
Total Fall	38,916	20,222	-48.0%

THE TOPIX VALUE-WEIGHTED INDEX

The NSA suffers from the same criticisms as the Dow Jones Industrial Average. It is not a true representation of the real market because it has only small percentage of all the stocks on the TSE and, in addition, the price weighting scheme is not as representative a measure as the value-weighting scheme. In the words of the TSE,

Figure 2.4 The Topix Index, 1968-1989, January 4, 1968=100

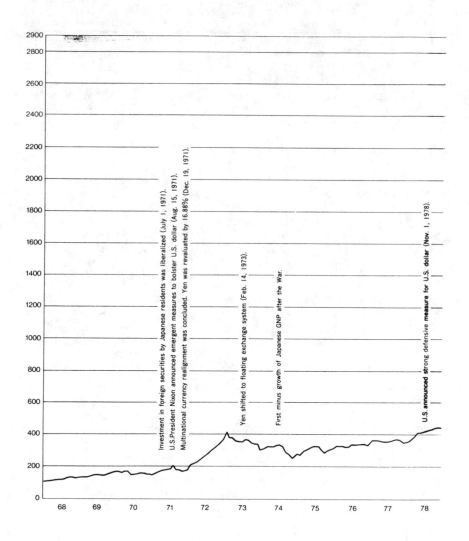

Source: TSE

Figure 2.4 (continued)

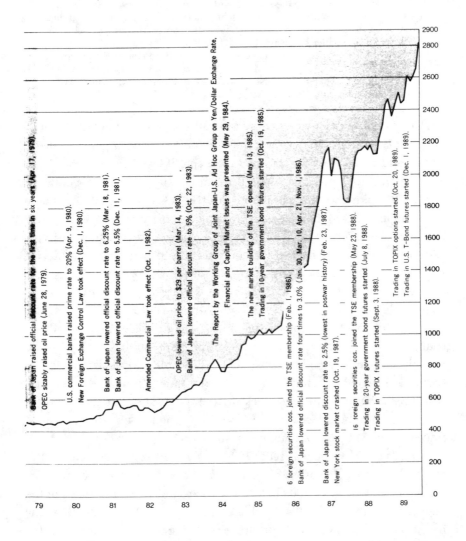

The Tokyo Stock Exchange stopped computing its Dow formula-based average and replaced it with Topix on July 1, 1969, as the Exchange found the average inappropriate for measuring the market for the following reasons: Firstly, investors are apt to confuse the average with the real price, despite the fact that the average is a theoretical arithmetic mean enlarged by applying a multiplier. Secondly, as the average is not weighted, it tends to be affected by price changes in a handful of smaller companies' stocks trading on high prices. Thirdly, as component stocks of the average have virtually been fixed since 1949, except for occasional substitutions caused by delistings and company mergers, the average does not reflect the change in industrial structure and therefore does not serve as an appropriate measure of the market as a whole.

Topix is the value-weighted average of the prices of all 1229 stocks (autumn 1990 count) on the first section of the TSE. The larger capitalized stocks tend to have higher prices. At the end of October 1989, the Topix average was 2693 points compared to an equally weighted average of about 1796 points; see the last column in Table 2.8. Compensation is made via an adjustment to the base value for any corporate activities that affect the current market value other than price changes, such as new listings, assignment of stocks from the second section to first section and vice versa, delisting, rights offering, public offerings, private placements, mergers, exercises of stock, subscription warrants, or conversion of convertible bonds or preferred stock into common stock.

In contrast to the actions above, a corporate decision that entails no change in the market value of shares of the company has nothing to do with the basic market value adjustment. Stock splits, capitalization issues (bonus issues), and stock dividends are thus eliminated from the adjustment, because the new stock price multiplied by the increased (or decreased) number of shares is theoretically the same as the old stock price multiplied by the old number of shares.

Topix's initial value was set at 100 on July 4, 1968, and its value at the end of December 1989 was 2867.97, a record close. For dates before 1968, the Topix traded below 100. In fact, it was around 10 near the start of the new phase of the TSE in 1949. Table 2.8 and Figures 2.4 and 2.5 show the index values for 1949 to 1990 along with highlights of stock market activity in the past two decades. Frequently, the year's minimum occurs early in January.

To maintain the continuity of the index, the base market value is adjusted to reflect price movements from auction market activity and eliminate the effects of other factors such as new listings, delistings and new share issues through public offerings or rights offering to shareholders. No adjustment is made for a stock split, a bonus issue, a stock dividend or a decrease in paid-in capital, because such corporate actions do not affect the current market value. The formula for the adjustment is:

$$\text{New base market value} = \text{Old base} \times \frac{\text{New market value}}{\text{Old market value}}$$

By doing so it is a better measure of overall market movements than the S&P 500 in the U.S. The corresponding index measure in the U.S. is the NYFE index. The Wilshire 5000, which is also value weighted, is broader than the Topix.

The Topix is computed and published, using the TSE's market information system, every 60 seconds. It is reported to securities companies across Japan and is available worldwide through computerized information networks. Data on the Topix are available on a daily closing basis from May 16, 1968. The subindices are available from January 4, 1968, the base date. Although the Topix and NSA 225 are quite different indices, they are closely related. The Tokyo stock exchange (1990) computed that the correlation between these two indices' daily rate of return was 0.9529 for the 861 days from January 4, 1986 to February 28, 1989. This calculation excluded the extremely violent falls and rises on October 20 and 21, 1987. The rates of return were computed via the log difference in prices, namely: $y_t = \log p_t - \log p_{t-1}$.

In addition to Topix, which covers all common stocks listed on the first section, the TSE computes and publishes the Topix sub-indices for each of 28 industry groups and three indices for large, medium and small size companies. Table 2.9 shows the rates of return for 1983 to 1988 for these 28 industry subgroups as well as for the large, medium and small capitalization stocks and in comparison with the NSA and Topix indices. Table 2.10 shows the increase by subindex on the TSE-I in 1988.

Figure 2.5 shows the trading volume on the TSE along with the year-by-year returns of small, medium, and large capitalized stocks. Figure 2.6 has these returns from 1979 to 1988. These small and large capitalized stocks had the highest returns which from 1979-88 were nearly indistinguishable over this period. The medium capitalized stocks had lower returns. Companies designated *large* have 200 million or more shares listed. *Medium* companies have 60-200 million shares listed, and *small* companies have less than 60 million shares listed.

Figure 2.5   Trading Volume on the TSE 1968-89

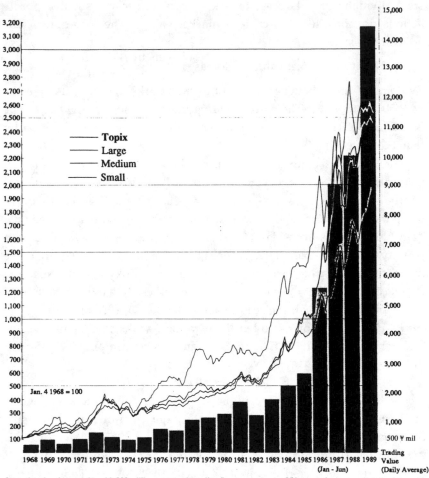

Large (stocks of companies with 200 million or more shares listed) . . . . 356 companies
Meduim (stocks of companies with 60 million or more shares but
     under 200 million shares listed) . . . . 453 companies
Small (stocks of companies with less than 60 million shares listed) . . . . 326 companies

Figure 2.6
Total Returns 1979-88 on Small, Medium and Large Capitalized Stocks on
the TSE-I

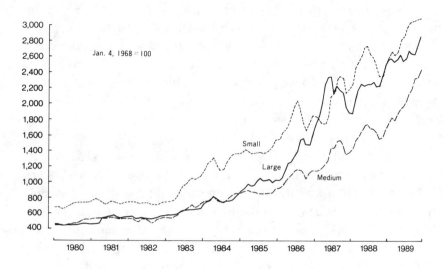

Source: TSE

As in the U.S., the large capitalized stocks were the main movers in
this bull market. Over longer periods, the small capitalized stocks outperformed the large capitalized stocks, particularly the very smallest
capitalized stocks and especially in the months of January and June.; see
Chapter 4. The small stocks that perform the best are those with low
capitalization not necessarily those with a low number of shares
outstanding. Overall, however, the large capitalization stocks
outperformed the small capitalized stocks in the 1983-89 period. But all
sectors participated in this huge rally. Table 2.11 shows the number of
companies, their market value, PER and yields by sector as of January 17,
1989.

The exchange also computes a value-weighted composite index called
the Second Section Stock Price Index, covering all common stocks listed
on its second section. The Topix sub-indices and the second section stock
price index are computed and reported six times a day - at 9:15 a.m., 10:00
a.m., 11:00 a.m., 1:15 p.m., 2:00 p.m. and 3:00 p.m.

Table 2.9 also has the beta values for the various industry and size subindices. Beta[1] measures the market risk of a stock and it estimates the stock's price movements when the market index (Topix in this case) changes. For example, the NSA had a beta of 0.86 in 1983-86. In this period its stocks move up and down 86% as fast as the Topix.

Banking, finance and insurance companies, and communication companies have high betas, above 1.50. They move up and down about 50% faster than the Topix does. Some industries, such as fisheries, forestry and construction are hardly affected by the market, and have betas close to zero. A few stocks even have negative betas because they tend to move counter to the market.

Tables 2.12 and 2.13 list the largest gains and losses in absolute and relative terms on the Topix to the end of December 1989. Tables 2.14 and 2.15 give the rates of return by year and over time with buy-and-hold strategies for all the stocks on the first and second section of the TSE. Tables 2.16 and 2.17 give the monthly returns by year for the first and second sections. Table 2.18 gives the rate of return with a yearly rebalancing scheme based on market capitalization by year and over time.

---

[1] Beta is the risk measure derived from the Sharpe-Lintner-Mossin Capital Asset Pricing Model see, e.g., Sharpe and Alexander (1990). It is defined as the covariance of the individual stock or portfolio in question with the market index, upon which the beta is defined, divided by the variance of return of the market index. For small changes in the market index, beta estimates the percentage change in the stock or portfolio that would result on average from a 1% move up or down in the market index. Research in the U.S. has called into question the real validity of the CAPM model. Studies by Ritter and Chopra (1989), Cadsby (1991) and others indicate that beta risk is only rewarded in January and then only for small stocks and at seasonaly anomalous periods of the year such as those discussed in Chapter 4. Similar studies have not been published in Japan. However, as a general guide, beta gives one a rough measure of how much the stock price will move when the TOPIX index changes. Beta and other valuation measures are discussed more fully in chapter 5.

Table 2.8 Tokyo Stock Price Index (Topix) 1949-1991

		High		Low		Arithmetic Average all TSE-I
	Year-End	Index	Date	Index	Date	Stocks for year*
1949	12.85	22.06	May 16	11.95	Dec 14	
1950	11.57	13.24	Aug 21	9.59	July 3	
1951	16.94	17.11	Oct 20	11.58	Jan 4	
1952	33.35	33.55	Nov 22	17.07	Jan 8	
1953	33.30	42.18	Feb 4	28.46	Apr 1	
1954	30.27	33.22	Jan 11	26.79	Nov 13	
1955	39.06	39.06	Dec 28	30.00	Mar 28	
1956	51.21	52.95	Dec 6	38.81	Jan 25	
1957	43.40	54.82	Jan 21	43.18	Dec 27	
1958	60.95	60.95	Dec 27	43.48	Jan 4	
1959	80.00	90.14	Nov 30	61.11	Jan 9	
1960	109.18	112.53	Nov 15	79.46	Jan 4	
1961	101.66	126.59	July 14	90.86	Dec 19	
1962	99.67	111.45	Feb 14	83.39	Oct 30	
1963	92.87	122.96	May 10	91.21	Dec 18	
1964	90.68	103.77	July 3	87.94	Nov 11	
1965	105.68	105.68	Dec 28	81.29	July 15	
1966	111.41	114.51	Mar 24	105.21	Jan 19	
1967	100.89	117.60	May 31	99.17	Dec 11	
1968	131.31	142.95	Oct 2	100.00	Jan 4	125.81
1969	179.30	179.30	Dec 27	132.62	Jan 4	171.65
1970	148.35	185.70	Apr 8	147.08	Dec 9	181.58
1971	199.45	209.00	Aug 14	148.05	Jan 6	184.70
1972	401.70	401.70	Dec 28	199.93	Jan 4	270.98
1973	306.44	422.48	Jan 24	284.69	Dec 18	309.10
1974	278.34	342.47	June 5	251.96	Oct 9	267.56
1975	323.43	333.11	July 2	268.24	Jan 10	268.95
1976	383.88	383.88	Dec.28	326.28	Jan 5	307.48
1977	364.08	390.93	Sept 29	350.49	Nov 24	320.77
1978	449.55	452.60	Dec13	364.04	Jan 4	365.68
1979	459.61	465.24	Sept 29	435.13	July 13	383.93
1980	494.10	497.96	Oct.20	449.01	Mar 10	382.92
1981	570.31	603.92	Aug.17	495.79	Jan 5	406.35
1982	593.72	593.72	Dec.28	511.52	Aug 17	381.98
1983	731.82	731.82	Dec 28	574.51	Jan. 25	463.29
1984	913.37	913.37	Dec.28	735.45	Jan 4	603.29
1985	1049.40	1058.35	July 27	916.93	Jan 4	682.47
1986	1556.37	1583.35	Aug 20	1025.85	Jan 21	866.18
1987	1725.83	2258.56	June 11	1557.46	Jan 13	1103.85
1988	2357.03	2357.03	Dec 28	1690.44	Jan 4	1294.17
1989	2867.97	2867.97	Dec 28	2364.33	Mar 27	1785.48
1990	1733.83	2867.70	Jan 4	1523.43	Oct 1	na
1991 (to Feb 27)	1935.37	1935.37	Feb 27	1647.56	Jan 16	na

*Not available before 1968

Source: Tokyo Stock Exchange

Table 2.9
Yearly Rates of Return and Beta Values for Industry Sub-Groups on the
TSE-I, 1983-1988

Category	1983.7 - 1988.6			1983.7-1985.1			1986.1-1988.6		
	Beta	R^2	ROR	Beta	R^2	ROR	Beta	R^2	ROR
Large	1.16	0.97	29.22	1.14	0.97	22.71	1.18	0.98	36.06
Medium	0.48	0.37	21.51	0.64	0.59	14.27	0.41	0.28	29.20
Small	0.37	0.17	23.49	0.71	0.49	20.74	0.23	0.07	26.30
Fish/forest	0.49	0.14	30.73	0.12	0.01	12.19	0.62	0.24	52.33
Mining	0.54	0.11	17.48	0.57	0.07	13.32	0.53	0.18	21.80
Construction	0.68	0.29	30.27	0.08	0.00	22.09	0.93	0.64	38.99
Foods	0.66	0.39	30.38	0.40	0.24	21.48	0.76	0.44	39.92
Textiles	0.74	0.39	24.81	0.83	0.38	22.62	0.71	0.41	27.05
Pulp & Paper	0.71	0.42	27.63	0.85	0.54	10.63	0.62	0.37	47.23
Chemicals	0.71	0.44	21.92	0.79	0.47	13.10	0.66	0.42	31.44
Oil & Coal	0.53	0.15	12.56	0.76	0.24	0.85	0.40	0.10	25.64
Rubber	0.65	0.31	29.23	0.43	0.16	7.71	0.71	0.37	55.04
Glass & Ceramics	0.73	0.55	27.46	1.01	0.63	22.88	0.61	0.54	32.21
Iron & Steel	0.96	0.36	32.07	0.96	0.58	2.59	0.91	0.30	70.01
Non-ferrous metals	0.87	0.48	15.96	1.33	0.57	9.34	0.67	0.48	22.97
Metal Products	0.45	0.13	32.38	0.69	0.29	28.39	0.34	0.07	36.50
Machinery	0.42	0.22	17.48	0.74	0.50	6.34	0.27	0.11	29.77
Electric appliances	0.45	0.09	11.04	0.88	0.32	3.99	0.25	0.03	18.56
Transport equipment	0.51	0.22	19.77	0.60	0.32	5.93	0.45	0.18	35.43
Precision Instruments	0.33	0.05	9.22	0.92	0.25	9.08	0.09	0.00	9.35
Other products	0.53	0.22	26.74	0.76	0.36	22.40	0.43	0.16	31.24
Commerce	0.66	0.54	23.51	0.64	0.68	15.05	0.66	0.49	32.59
Finance & insurance	1.70	0.76	42.59	1.73	0.66	44.78	1.71	0.83	40.43
Real estate	1.48	0.47	32.94	1.01	0.27	37.80	1.71	0.56	28.26
Land transportation	1.00	0.32	37.66	0.55	0.10	32.73	1.20	0.45	42.79
Marine transportation	0.85	0.26	19.82	0.22	0.03	-5.80	1.07	0.37	52.41
Air transportation	0.31	0.03	43.29	0.26	0.01	53.28	0.35	0.04	33.95
Warehousing	0.89	0.33	37.58	0.68	0.16	39.30	0.99	0.44	35.87
Communication	1.02	0.23	36.49	1.62	0.38	56.62	0.81	0.18	18.94
Elect power & gas	1.04	0.25	35.40	1.12	0.23	37.95	1.02	0.27	32.91
Services	0.54	0.21	32.39	0.66	0.25	34.12	0.50	0.19	30.69
Topix	1.00	1.00	27.18	1.00	1.00	20.66	1.00	1.00	34.05
NSA	0.84	0.86	25.64	0.84	0.86	16.92	0.83	0.86	35.00

Source: Tokyo Stock Exchange

Table 2.10   Increase in Industry Sub Indices, TSE-I, during 1989

| Industry | Stock Price Index | | Change from End of 1989 | |
| | End of 1988 | End of 1989 | Percent | Point |
Up	(A)	(B)	(B-A/A)	(B -A)
Mining	1,348.51	2,674.37	98.32	1,325.86
Marine Transportation	1,160.60	1,859.92	60.26	699.32
Machinery	1,218.92	1,947.72	59.79	728.80
Metal Products	1,692.95	2,701.25	59.56	1,008.30
Fishery & Forestry	1,215.04	1,864.97	53.49	649.93
Services	1,832.92	2,806.79	53.13	973.87
Warehousing & Harbor Transportation	2,549.96	3,877.33	52.05	1,327.37
Commerce	1,597.07	2,353.23	47.35	756.16
Construction	2,132.88	3,134.30	46.95	1,001.42
Rubber Products	1,589.80	2,206.28	38.78	616.48
Land Transportation	2,480.34	3,398.59	37.02	918.25
Textiles	1,292.95	1,764.84	36.50	471.89
Nonferrous Metals	1,689.74	2,299.21	36.07	609.47
Other Products	2,263.42	2,971.33	31.28	707.91
Oil & Coal Products	2,578.32	3,364.37	30.49	786.05
Precision Instruments	1,970.28	2,569.93	30.43	599.65
Glass & Ceramics Products	1,762.40	2,282.67	29.52	520.27
Foods	1,390.38	1,737.33	24.95	346.95
Chemicals	2,259.93	2,738.92	21.19	478.99
Air Transportation	3,039.66	3,656.31	20.29	616.65
Transportation Equipment	1,542.41	1,843.49	19.52	301.08
Electric Appliances	2,029.01	2,423.64	19.45	394.63
Real Estate	1,939.83	2,249.04	15.94	309.21
Finance & Insurance	8,700.23	10,085.33	15.92	1,385.10
Pulp & Paper	1,988.47	2,243.73	12.84	255.26
Iron & Steel	1,997.04	2,147.38	7.53	150.34
Down				
Communication	4,582.99	4,057.63	-11.46	-525.36
Electric Power & Gas	1,588.91	1,559.35	-1.86	-29.56

Source: Tokyo Stock Exchange

Table 2.11
Number of Companies, Market Value, PERs and Yields by Sector in the
Topix, January 17, 1989

Sector	Number of Companies	Market Value (¥ bil)	Prospective Weighted Average PER	Average Yield
Fishery	6	738	132.9	0.44
Mining	7	1,024	86.0	0.45
Construction	91	16,541	54.9	0.62
Foods	55	12,485	58.6	0.52
Textiles	43	8,219	58.4	0.61
Pulp & paper	19	4,401	46.5	0.51
Chemicals	122	32,822	49.9	0.49
Oil & coal products	9	4,928	60.1	0.63
Rubber products	9	2,145	37.5	0.72
Class & ceramics	31	7,425	51.5	0.48
Iron & steel	36	21,526	58.4	0.54
Non-ferrous metals	24	6,764	73.2	0.48
Metal products	22	2,599	40.8	0.41
Machinery	86	12,417	60.6	0.59
Electrical machinery	106	45,325	47.6	0.59
Transportation equip	50	28,364	47.3	0.59
Precision instruments	18	4,231	47.8	0.70
Other manufacturing	28	6,429	46.5	0.47
Commerce	125	29,999	58.1	0.55
Financial	128	149,964	51.1	0.32
Real estate	18	8,105	73.8	0.36
Land transportation	25	15,910	178.6	0.32
Shipping	14	3,287	-	0.15
Airlines	4	5,430	177.4	0.23
Warehousing	10	1,138	76.6	0.53
Communications	5	12,176	102.9	0.27
Electric power & gas	14	32,758	60.2	0.85
Services	25	3,909	86.1	0.34
Total (First Section)	1,130	481,057	55.8	0.48

Source: Tokyo Stock Exchange

Table 2.12

Largest Point Gains and Losses Topix Index to December 31, 1989

Rank	Biggest Gains (Points)	Date	Index after gain	Main Cause of Move
1	168.51	Oct 21, 1987	1,962.41	Backlash of the worldwide market crash
2	112.14	Jan 6, 1988	1,820.03	U.S. dollar recovered; accounting rules for the "Tokkin" were relaxed
3	81.16	July 24, 1987	1,999.35	Oil price declined
4	79.68	Apr 14, 1987	2,096.92	Rebound from sell-off
5	75.50	Nov 13, 1987	1,842.73	U.S. trade deficit decreased
6	64.41	Oct 30, 1987	1,867.18	Overseas market rise
7	58.13	Mar 28, 1989	2,422.46	Portfolio adjustment to New Year
8	52.57	Mar 27, 1987	1,922.08	Funds surplus
9	52.00	Sept 26, 1987	2,114.10	Selective strength grown
10	51.10	Apr 10, 1987	2,032.54	Rebound from sell-off

Rank	Biggest Losses (Points)	Date	Index after loss	Main Cause of Move
1	-307.27	Oct 20, 1987	1,793.90	Worldwide market crash
2	-94.52	Oct 23, 1987	1,894.97	Worldwide market crash
3	-88.07	Oct 26, 1987	1,818.25	Worldwide market crash
4	-78.06	Apr 27, 1987	2,050.92	Dollar rate tumbled
5	-67.19	May 30, 1987	2,054.91	New York stock market sharp decline
6	-65.74	June 22, 1987	2,109.07	Cautiousness of high stock prices
7	-57.48	July 20, 1987	1,939.21	Anxiety for interest rate hike
8	-56.62	Nov 10, 1987	1,779.58	Spurt of yen rate
9	-54.19	Sept 16, 1986	1,444.68	New York stock market sharp decline
10	-51.81	Oct 19, 1987	2,101.17	Spurt of yen rate

Source: Tokyo Stock Exchange

Table 2.13
Largest Percentage Gains and Losses Topix Index to December 31, 1989

Rank	Biggest Gains (%)	Date	Index after gain	Main Cause of Move
1	9.39	Oct 21, 1987	1,962.41	Backlash of the worldwide market crash
2	7.36	Dec 15, 1949	12.83	Heavy buying by life insurance companies and banks
3	6.57	Jan 6, 1988	1,820.03	U.S. dollar recovered and accounting rules for "Tokkin" were relaxed
4	6.39	Apr 16, 1953	32.79	Expectation of continued procurement by U.S. in Japan after Korean War
5	5.59	July 15, 1950	11.72	Korean War special procurement boom
6	5.38	Mar 6, 1953	34.06	Rebound from sharp fall caused by Stalin's serious illness
7	5.12	July 17, 1950	12.32	Korean War special procurement
8	4.55	July 12, 1950	10.57	Korean War special procurement
9	4.44	July 11, 1950	10.11	Korean War special procurement
10	4.27	Nov 13, 1987	1,842.73	U.S. trade deficit decreased

Rank	Biggest Gains (%)	Date	Index after loss	Main cause of Move
1	-14.62	Oct 20, 1987	1,793.90	New York stock market crashed
2	-8.75	Mar 5, 1953	32.32	Stalin seriously ill
3	-7.47	Apr 30, 1970	159.33	Worldwide stock market decline
4	-5.99	Mar 30, 1953	30.31	Korean War truce negotiation resumed
5	-5.90	Aug 16, 1971	196.66	Nixon announced "dollar defense" measures
6	-5.20	June 24, 1972	263.56	Pound Sterling value uncertain
7	-5.18	Aug 19, 1971	172.65	International money markets shaken
8	-4.75	Oct 23, 1987	1,894.97	Worldwide market crash chain
9	-4.62	Oct 26, 1987	1,818.25	Worldwide market crash chain
10	-4.33	July 19, 1963	109.53	U.S. Interest Equalization Tax announced

Source: Tokyo Stock Exchange

Table 2.14 First Section Market Rate of Return by Simple Buy and Hold Strategy Yearly Holding Periods,

Year Bought \ Sold	1953	1954	1955	1956	1957	1958	1959	1960	1961	1962	1963	1964	1965	1966	1967	1968	1969	1970
1952	57.1	14.9	17.7	24.7	23.2	21.3	25.8	28.9	31.5	28.3	25.5	21.5	19.7	20.5	19.5	19.7	20.5	20.1
1953	-	-15.4	2.5	16.9	17.1	15.6	21.5	25.3	28.7	25.2	22.4	18.4	16.6	17.6	16.7	16.9	17.9	17.7
1954	-	-	22.7	38.0	31.4	25.1	30.9	34.1	37.2	31.6	27.5	22.3	19.8	20.7	19.6	19.6	20.6	120.1
1955	-	-	-	52.1	35.0	25.4	32.8	36.8	40.4	33.5	28.5	22.6	19.7	20.5	19.4	19.5	20.5	19.8
1956	-	-	-	-	18.0	13.8	26.7	32.9	38.0	30.8	25.6	19.4	16.7	17.9	16.8	17.1	18.4	17.9
1957	-	-	-	-	-	8.5	30.7	37.8	43.0	33.2	26.8	19.6	16.6	18.0	16.7	17.0	18.3	17.8
1958	-	-	-	-	-	-	53.8	52.2	55.1	38.4	29.7	20.7	16.9	18.3	16.9	17.2	18.6	18.1
1959	-	-	-	-	-	-	-	43.1	53.3	32.6	23.8	14.7	11.8	13.7	12.8	13.3	14.9	14.9
1960	-	-	-	-	-	-	-	-	60.7	25.9	18.0	9.0	7.0	9.8	9.2	9.9	11.8	12.2
1961	-	-	-	-	-	-	-	-	-	-4.8	1.7	-2.9	-2.1	3.1	3.6	5.2	8.2	9.1
1962	-	-	-	-	-	-	-	-	-	-	10.5	-0.7	-0.7	5.6	5.7	7.0	9.9	10.7
1963	-	-	-	-	-	-	-	-	-	-	-	-13.0	-7.4	3.5	3.9	6.2	9.9	10.7
1964	-	-	-	-	-	-	-	-	-	-	-	-	-2.8	12.4	9.9	11.7	15.7	5.7
1965	-	-	-	-	-	-	-	-	-	-	-	-	-	28.4	16.9	17.3	21.5	20.4
1966	-	-	-	-	-	-	-	-	-	-	-	-	-	-	7.0	12.6	19.7	18.9
1967	-	-	-	-	-	-	-	-	-	-	-	-	-	-	-	17.9	26.8	22.9
1968	-	-	-	-	-	-	-	-	-	-	-	-	-	-	-	-	30.0	23.6
1969	-	-	-	-	-	-	-	-	-	-	-	-	-	-	-	-	-	17.4
1970	-	-	-	-	-	-	-	-	-	-	-	-	-	-	-	-	-	-
1971	-	-	-	-	-	-	-	-	-	-	-	-	-	-	-	-	-	-
1972	-	-	-	-	-	-	-	-	-	-	-	-	-	-	-	-	-	-
1973	-	-	-	-	-	-	-	-	-	-	-	-	-	-	-	-	-	-
1974	-	-	-	-	-	-	-	-	-	-	-	-	-	-	-	-	-	-
1975	-	-	-	-	-	-	-	-	-	-	-	-	-	-	-	-	-	-
1976	-	-	-	-	-	-	-	-	-	-	-	-	-	-	-	-	-	-
1977	-	-	-	-	-	-	-	-	-	-	-	-	-	-	-	-	-	-
1978	-	-	-	-	-	-	-	-	-	-	-	-	-	-	-	-	-	-
1979	-	-	-	-	-	-	-	-	-	-	-	-	-	-	-	-	-	-
1980	-	-	-	-	-	-	-	-	-	-	-	-	-	-	-	-	-	-
1981	-	-	-	-	-	-	-	-	-	-	-	-	-	-	-	-	-	-
1982	-	-	-	-	-	-	-	-	-	-	-	-	-	-	-	-	-	-
1983	-	-	-	-	-	-	-	-	-	-	-	-	-	-	-	-	-	-
1984	-	-	-	-	-	-	-	-	-	-	-	-	-	-	-	-	-	-
1985	-	-	-	-	-	-	-	-	-	-	-	-	-	-	-	-	-	-
1986	-	-	-	-	-	-	-	-	-	-	-	-	-	-	-	-	-	-

Table 2.14 (Concluded) 1971-1986

Year Bought \ Sold	1971	1972	1973	1974	1975	1976	1977	1978	1979	1980	1981	1982	1983	1984	1985	1986	1987
1952	19.9	21.6	21.0	19.4	18.8	18.6	18.4	18.4	18.0	17.5	17.4	16.9	17.1	17.3	17.5	17.9	18.5
1953	17.5	19.3	19.1	17.7	17.1	17.0	16.8	16.9	16.6	16.2	16.0	15.5	15.7	15.9	16.2	16.7	17.3
1954	19.6	21.4	21.3	19.6	18.9	18.7	18.4	18.4	18.1	17.6	17.4	16.8	16.9	17.2	17.4	17.8	18.3
1955	19.3	21.3	21.3	19.5	18.7	18.6	18.3	18.3	17.9	17.5	17.3	16.6	16.7	17.0	17.2	17.7	18.2
1956	17.5	19.7	19.7	18.0	17.3	17.2	17.0	17.0	16.7	16.3	16.1	15.5	15.7	16.0	16.3	16.9	17.5
1957	17.5	20.0	20.0	18.2	17.4	17.2	17.0	17.0	16.7	16.3	16.1	15.4	15.7	16.0	16.4	16.9	17.6
1958	17.8	20.6	20.8	18.7	17.7	17.5	17.2	17.2	16.9	16.4	16.2	15.4	15.8	16.1	16.4	17.0	17.7
1959	15.1	18.5	18.9	16.9	15.8	15.6	15.4	15.4	15.2	14.8	14.5	13.9	14.2	14.7	15.3	16.0	16.8
1960	12.9	17.0	17.6	15.6	14.4	14.1	14.0	14.1	14.0	13.7	13.4	12.9	13.1	13.8	14.5	15.3	16.2
1961	10.2	16.0	16.0	13.9	12.7	12.6	12.5	12.6	12.8	12.4	12.2	11.7	12.0	12.7	13.6	14.3	15.4
1962	11.7	17.1	18.3	15.8	14.3	14.0	13.7	13.8	13.8	13.6	13.2	12.5	12.8	13.5	14.3	15.0	16.0
1963	11.6	17.1	18.2	15.7	14.2	14.0	13.7	13.8	13.8	13.5	13.1	12.4	12.7	13.4	14.1	14.8	15.8
1964	15.8	21.3	21.8	18.7	16.8	16.5	16.0	16.1	15.8	15.4	14.8	14.0	14.2	14.8	15.5	16.2	17.1
1965	19.0	24.9	25.1	21.3	19.0	18.5	17.8	17.8	17.4	16.8	16.1	15.1	15.3	15.9	16.5	17.1	18.0
1966	17.3	24.5	25.0	20.8	18.2	17.6	16.9	17.2	16.7	16.1	15.4	14.1	14.7	15.5	16.1	16.8	17.8
1967	20.5	28.5	28.1	22.8	19.8	19.0	18.1	18.1	17.5	16.8	15.9	14.8	15.2	15.9	16.5	17.3	18.3
1968	20.7	31.6	30.8	24.1	20.2	19.3	18.2	18.2	17.6	16.9	15.8	14.5	14.9	15.7	16.4	17.3	18.4
1969	17.0	33.7	32.9	24.4	19.6	18.6	17.6	17.7	17.2	16.4	15.0	13.7	14.1	15.0	15.7	16.8	17.8
1970	14.9	40.9	36.8	25.2	19.6	18.8	17.6	17.8	17.1	16.1	14.9	13.4	14.1	15.1	15.7	16.8	17.8
1971	-	69.6	48.6	29.2	20.8	20.0	18.3	18.5	17.7	16.6	15.2	13.6	14.5	15.6	16.0	16.9	17.8
1972	-	-	25.7	11.5	7.9	10.5	10.7	12.4	12.2	11.6	10.9	9.6	11.1	12.5	12.9	14.1	15.1
1973	-	-	-	-1.4	1.4	7.5	8.6	11.2	10.8	10.1	9.7	8.4	10.2	11.8	12.3	13.7	14.8
1974	-	-	-	-	5.1	13.2	12.8	15.0	13.5	12.2	11.5	9.8	11.6	13.2	13.6	15.2	16.3
1975	-	-	-	-	-	20.4	16.2	18.2	16.1	14.1	12.7	10.6	12.5	14.4	14.9	16.3	17.6
1976	-	-	-	-	-	-	11.2	17.0	15.0	12.9	11.0	9.0	11.1	13.3	14.3	16.0	17.6
1977	-	-	-	-	-	-	-	22.5	17.2	13.8	11.2	8.7	11.2	13.7	14.7	16.5	18.2
1978	-	-	-	-	-	-	-	-	12.1	9.8	8.0	5.6	9.1	12.3	13.7	15.9	17.9
1979	-	-	-	-	-	-	-	-	-	6.1	5.9	3.5	8.3	12.2	13.9	16.7	18.9
1980	-	-	-	-	-	-	-	-	-	-	6.3	2.6	9.3	13.9	15.8	19.0	21.3
1981	-	-	-	-	-	-	-	-	-	-	-	-1.1	10.3	16.1	18.4	21.9	24.3
1982	-	-	-	-	-	-	-	-	-	-	-	-	22.7	25.5	25.4	28.2	29.8
1983	-	-	-	-	-	-	-	-	-	-	-	-	-	26.5	27.2	30.9	32.6
1984	-	-	-	-	-	-	-	-	-	-	-	-	-	-	-27.3	33.6	35.0
1985	-	-	-	-	-	-	-	-	-	-	-	-	-	-	-	37.2	36.7
1986	-	-	-	-	-	-	-	-	-	-	-	-	-	-	-	-	33.2

Source: Japan Securities Research Institute (1988)

Table 2.15   Second Section Market Rate of Return Buy and Hold Strategy

Year \ Bought	Sold 1976	1977	1978	1979	1980	1981	1982	1983	1984	1985	1986	1987
1975	37.8	28.1	30.4	27.7	20.7	17.9	14.7	17.3	20.9	19.8	19.8	19.7
1976	-	17.4	26.8	24.9	17.1	14.2	11.3	14.4	18.6	17.9	18.3	18.4
1977	-	-	36.5	29.3	17.5	14.0	10.5	14.3	19.1	18.3	18.6	18.6
1978	-	-	-	21.7	8.6	6.7	4.4	10.0	16.1	15.8	16.6	16.8
1979	-	-	-	-	-4.6	-1.4	-1.3	6.6	14.1	14.2	15.7	16.4
1980	-	-	-	-	-	1.3	0.2	10.4	18.8	18.3	19.6	19.9
1981	-	-	-	-	-	-	-1.0	14.4	24.2	23.0	24.0	23.8
1982	-	-	-	-	-	-	-	31.5	38.4	32.2	30.8	29.2
1983	-	-	-	-	-	-	-	-	40.9	32.4	31.0	29.5
1984	-	-	-	-	-	-	-	-	-	24.0	28.2	27.9
1985	-	-	-	-	-	-	-	-	-	-	28.4	27.3
1986	-	-	-	-	-	-	-	-	-	-	-	22.0

Source: Japan Securities Research Institute (1988)

Finally to compare the results of various investment strategies, Figure 2.7 shows the growth from the end of 1970 to the end of 1988 for all TSE-I stocks, all TSE-II stocks, all TSE-I small capitalized stocks, S&P 500 stocks and small capitalized NYSE stocks (small capitalized is defined as the bottom quintile). Starting with $1 at the end of 1970, Hamao and Ibbotson (1989) computed that the S&P 500 grew to $6.51 by the end of 1988, small capitalized U.S. stocks to $14.18, TSE-II stocks to $27.15, TSE-I stocks to $61.36, and TSE-I small capitalized stocks to an eye-popping $130.22! In all cases dividends are included but taxes are not.

The yearly geometric mean total return and standard deviations in percent for these returns in U.S. dollars were as follows:

Quantity	Geometric Mean	Standard Deviation
TSE-I	25.70	33.40
S&P 500	10.97	16.52
TSE-II	13.36	26.89
TSE-I smallest quintile	31.06	42.04
NYSE small quintile	15.87	23.71
U.S. Treasury Bills	7.61	2.75
U.S. inflation	6.36	3.49
Yearly increase, yen over U.S. dollar	5.97	13.76

Table 2.16 First Section Market Rate Return by Month, 1952–1987

Year	Jan	Feb	Mar	Apr	May	Jun	Jul	Aug	Sep	Oct	Nov	Dec	VWI	EWI	Size Effect	Dividend Return, %
1952	13.2	-3.9	1.5	12.9	11.2	9.2	3.8	2.1	8.1	12.3	12.2	1.3	-	-	-5.6	17.4
1953	21.9	-11.0	-17.0	5.8	-4.5	4.2	9.4	4.9	12.0	-4.3	-2.2	-8.1	56.7	51.1	-8.5	-111.7
1954	-6.3	-0.4	-5.6	5.5	-6.2	7.1	-4.7	2.2	2.2	-6.0	1.0	9.3	-6.9	-15.4	1.7	36.5
1955	3.2	1.6	-1.3	-0.9	1.9	1.4	5.2	6.6	2.7	6.7	-2.9	9.1	24.4	22.7	4.3	17.3
1956	0.2	3.6	5.7	3.8	4.7	2.4	0.8	-1.1	1.3	3.8	10.7	-0.9	47.8	52.1	1.8	42.7
1957	3.8	0.0	3.3	0.7	-10.8	0.0	-6.4	7.6	2.0	-3.7	-3.1	-2.5	16.2	18.0	-7.3	43.7
1958	9.4	0.6	1.9	4.3	1.5	4.0	-2.4	4.3	0.9	4.8	3.7	6.7	15.8	8.5	-3.2	11.2
1959	4.6	3.2	9.1	-2.8	9.1	0.8	4.4	2.6	6.7	4.8	3.5	-11.4	57.0	53.8	4.0	12.6
1960	6.9	3.7	8.5	4.5	-10.7	10.9	0.8	6.3	5.7	-0.1	1.2	3.1	39.	43.1	35.0	17.7
1961	6.4	0.4	3.5	0.9	-0.7	4.7	-1.4	-8.6	-3.2	-12.6	0.6	8.2	25.7	60.7	-0.6	-93.6
1962	5.3	-2.3	-3.0	-3.4	-0.6	5.6	-1.3	0.7	-7.9	-3.4	17.2	-0.8	-4.8	-4.8	-8.6	29.2
1963	4.4	3.5	12.9	1.3	-1.5	0.0	-11.8	-2.9	-2.6	3.1	-5.1	2.3	19.1	10.5	-9.1	-133.7
1964	8.3	-4.5	-1.0	-0.2	8.2	3.2	-2.3	-2.5	-1.6	0.8	0.0	5.3	-3.9	-13.0	-8.5	102.2
1965	4.5	-0.5	-4.7	3.0	-5.3	-1.3	3.7	11.9	0.7	-0.4	7.3	4.9	5.7	-2.8	0.1	19.8
1966	2.4	1.9	5.0	-0.7	-2.1	-0.4	2.5	-.2	-0.3	3.7	-2.0	0.0	28.3	28.4	0.9	81.3
1967	2.0	1.4	-0.7	-0.1	5.2	-0.7	-0.6	-8.1	-0.3	-5.7	-5.7	6.2	6.1	7.0	1.8	32.3
1968	2.7	1.9	2.8	4.6	1.8	4.8	5.4	9.8	9.8	2.2	-1.0	-0.3	16.1	17.9	-7.3	13.2
1969	5.7	-2.0	7.2	2.3	8.0	-2.7	-5.0	7.8	7.8	2.3	4.8	8.2	37.3	30.0	5.1	33.2
1970	-1.9	1.5	5.5	-13.0	-2.5	1.6	1.6	-1.8	-2.1	-5.2	-4.2	7.5	12.3	17.4	-4.9	22.1
1971	5.0	6.1	8.1	5.4	0.3	7.8	2.2	-13.0	5.1	2.0	6.4	2.0	19.8	14.9	-2.5	5.0
1972	5.8	6.3	7.2	5.1	8.6	4.2	8.5	2.1	6.0	0.7	11.7	-5.5	72.1	69.6	5.0	7.8
1973	0.7	-3.3	2.1	-10.5	0.7	1.4	5.8	-3.1	-4.9	0.7	-7.6	-3.0	30.3	25.7	-4.6	-18.3
1974	5.5	0.6	-0.6	3.3	3.6	-2.3	-3.9	-8.1	-3.9	-8.0	10.0	1.8	-11.4	-1.4	-10.8	40.9
1975	3.8	8.6	4.6	3.6	-0.4	2.7	-4.2	2.8	0.7	8.9	0.4	11.2	5.9	5.1	-0.8	14.8
1976	6.0	-0.5	0.8	0.5	1.3	3.3	-2.7	4.8	1.1	-1.6	-1.6	-1.0	16.1	20.4	4.3	18.4
1977	-2.3	2.0	-1.0	1.4	-0.6	-0.2	-1.4	0.2	3.1	-3.6	-2.1	1.8	11.7	11.2	-0.5	14.4
1978	5.0	2.5	5.1	0.5	0.1	1.8	1.5	3.1	3.0	-3.4	0.9	2.2	15.0	22.5	7.5	18.2
1979	3.0	-3.0	1.0	0.5	-0.5	-0.4	-0.5	2.1	2.7	1.6	0.4	2.9	10.8	12.1	1.3	21.8
1980	1.8	0.1	3.0	3.0	-0.1	1.1	-0.4	1.8	-6.1	0.5	-0.5	2.7	8.5	6.1	-2.4	9.2
1981	3.2	-0.4	-2.1	5.9	0.1	4.7	1.1	-0.4	-0.6	3.6	0.4	2.9	21.0	6.3	-14.7	85.9
1982	2.2	-4.8	5.4	2.4	0.1	-1.3	-1.5	-6.1	2.4	3.6	0.4	2.7	2.1	-1.1	6.3	7.8
1983	-0.9	0.7	-3.0	2.4	3.1	3.1	1.5	-0.1	1.2	4.6	6.6	6.5	23.0	22.7	-3.2	5.2
1984	6.2	-0.1	12.8	-1.0	-10.0	2.6	-4.0	7.0	1.3	0.0	1.8	4.3	29.4	26.4	-0.3	4.7
1985	2.0	5.0	2.7	-3.2	3.1	3.2	-3.4	2.4	-1.6	-7.2	-1.7	4.1	27.0	27.3	-3.0	2.7
1986	-0.7	4.8	16.5	-1.1	4.0	4.4	5.2	8.2	-0.6	-10.3	7.1	3.3	40.1	37.2	-2.9	1.7
1987	13.0	1.3	4.6	11.1	3.3	-5.0	-1.2	6.9	-0.6	-10.3	-3.5	-6.5	46.1	33.2	-12.9	1.7
Arithmetic Averages	4.3	0.6	2.8	1.5	0.6	2.4	0.1	0.7	1.3	0.4	1.8	1.4	18.6	20.7	1.0	12.2

Source: Japan Securities Research Institute (1988)

Table 2.17 Second Section Market Rate of Return by Month, 1974-1987

	J	F	M	A	M	J	J	A	S	O	N	D	VWI	Size EWI Effect	%Ret on Div
1974	-	-	-	-	-	-	-	-	-7.8	3.0	1.3	-	-	-	--
1975	2.3	3.8	2.3	4.3	2.4	1.8	-2.7	-2.2	-2.3	2.8	1.8	3.9	--	-	--
1976	7.4	6.3	7.2	0.5	2.7	2.2	1.0	5.1	-1.1	1.7	-4.5	4.0	41.0	37.8 -3.2	5.3
1977	5.9	0.2	0.0	-0.5	3.3	-2.2	-4.0	0.5	-0.2	-4.9	-3.2	2.2	12.0	17.4 5.4	14.3
1978	9.2	5.3	4.6	2.5	1.9	4.6	8.7	10.6	5.9	1.5	-0.4	1.1	37.9	36.5 -1.4	6.6
1979	5.7	-1.2	0.0	-6.1	-3.0	1.0	-2.9	6.6	-0.7	-7.4	0.3	1.9	19.4	21.7 2.3	96.9
1980	1.1	-2.0	-2.3	0.8	1.2	1.6	1.8	1.1	2.2	0.2	2.7	5.3	1.3	-4.6 -5.9	6.4
1981	7.2	-1.5	-0.9	-1.6	-2.6	5.2	-0.2	-0.9	-5.8	-0.8	1.4	1.4	20.0	1.3 -18.7	33.7
1982	3.2	-4.3	-5.4	1.6	2.5	0.0	-1.5	-1.6	0.6	-1.1	4.8	4.0	-3.6	-1.0 2.6	2.3
1983	1.3	2.4	7.7	12.1	8.9	1.1	10.4	6.3	-1.7	0.6	2.8	7.2	53.4	31.5 -21.9	2.0
1984	7.6	5.0	4.6	-5.7	-7.3	-0.4	-1.5	13.5	5.1	43.1	-0.8	-2.3	43.2	40.9 -2.3	8.8
1985	3.7	2.0	-3.2	-2.8	-2.4	-0.5	-6.5	4.4	-0.2	3.9	3.3	2.0	8.2	24.0 15.8	3.5
1986	4.9	0.6	0.8	5.0	4.0	4.5	-2.0	-3.7	-8.5	-01.5	6.2	0.0	19.6	28.4 8.8	3.2
1987	-0.5	1.4	-2.5	-1.1	12.8	5.2	5.0	7.5	0.7	-10.8	-1.6	-0.8	17.6	22.0 4.4	3.2
Arithmetic Averages: by Month															
	4.5	1.4	1.0	0.7	1.9	1.9	0.4	3.6	-0.5	-1.4	1.1	2.2	22.5	21.3 -1.2	10.0

Source: Japan Securities Research Institute (1988)

Table 2.18
Average Compound Rates of Return in Percent by Value Weighting with Yearly Rebalancing of the TSE-I

Year\ Bought	Sold 1978	1979	1980	1981	1982	1983	1984	1985	1986	1987
1979	10.8	-	-	-	-	-	-	-	-	-
1980	9.6	8.5	-	-	-	-	-	-	-	-
1981	13.3	14.6	21.0	-	-	-	-	-	-	-
1982	10.4	10.3	11.2	2.1	-	-	-	-	-	-
1983	12.8	13.3	15.0	12.1	23.0	-	-	-	-	-
1984	15.4	16.4	18.4	17.6	26.1	29.4	-	-	-	-
1985	17.0	18.1	20.1	19.9	26.4	28.2	27.0	-	-	-
1986	19.7	21.0	23.2	23.6	29.7	32.0	33.3	40.0	-	-
1987	22.7	23.9	26.3	27.1	32.9	35.4	37.5	43.1	46.1	-
1988(p)	21.2	22.4	24.3	24.7	29.0	30.2	30.4	31.6	27.5	11.3

Source: Japan Securities Research Institute (1988)

The average rate of return per year for Japanese stocks in U.S. dollars has been higher that of U.S. stocks. From 1949 to 1989, U.S. stocks returned about 12% per year in total returns from asset value gains and dividends. Japanese stocks returned about 14.5% in yen and 24.0% in U.S. dollars. From 1977 to 1985 the difference was 13.3% vs. 7.58% in U.S. dollars. In both countries, small capitalized stocks had higher returns than larger capitalized stocks.

Figure 2.7
Growth of $1 Invested in Japanese Small Capitalized, TSE-I, TSE-II, U.S.
Small Capitalized and S&P 500 Stocks, 1971-88

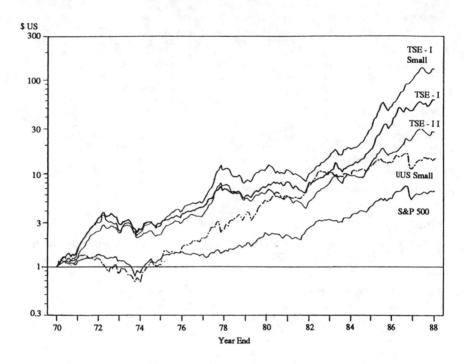

Source: Hamao and Ibbotson (1989)

THE OVER-THE-COUNTER-MARKET

The over-the-counter-market is the fastest growing stock market in Japan.
Its size now rivals NASDAQ in the U.S. as shown in Figure 2.8b. At the
end of 1990 there were about 275 issues traded. The OTC was a stellar
performer in the first half of 1990. While the NSA declined, the OTC
increased sharply. There are plans for about 90 new issues in 1990. An
automated quotation system is expected in 1991. The weighted PER is
86.4 versus 50 on the TSE-I, but many OTC companies are growing at an
annual rate of 20-30%. Institutional investors are taking a growing
interest in the OTC. The index which was 100 at the beginning of 1990
was over 140 by June 1 for a 40%+ gain as shown in Figure 2.8a. The TSE-

II has also done well in 1990. In total there were modest gains with a substantial recovery after the April lows.

Figure 2.8   The Over-the-Counter-Market
a. Market comparison, 1990=100   b. OTC trading volume

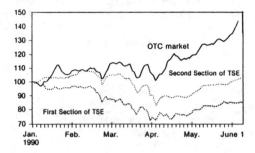
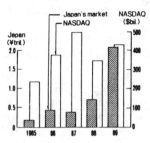

Source: Yamaichi Research Institute

Source: Nihon Tento Shoken, NASDAQ

THE RELATIONSHIP ACROSS MARKETS

The Tokyo market is the first to open each day, followed by London and then New York. Figure 2.9 shows the times of trading. Between London and New York, there is a one hour overlap when both markets are open.[2]

Figure 2.10 shows the effect of the New York market on the Tokyo market via the correlations of Topix's close to open returns on the previous day (close to close) returns in New York from 1975 to 1989. The correlation is quite strong and has been fairly steady, at about 0.6, since 1985. This measure uses a 140-day moving average. The effect of Tokyo's market on New York's is less, averaging about 0.10.

Hamao, Masulis and Ng (1990) have studied the short-term relationship of the volatility and returns of securities traded in London, New York and Tokyo. They found that volatility surprises in New York and London have a significant effect on Tokyo's volatility. The reverse does not seem to occur, although it did during the crash of October 1987. They also found, for all three markets, that the close-to-close previous day's return significantly affects the opening price - the close-to-open return in the next market.

---

[2]Japan does not go on daylight savings time so the hours would need to be adjusted but still no overlaps are created with either London or New York.

Figure 2.9   The Trading Day in Tokyo, London and New York

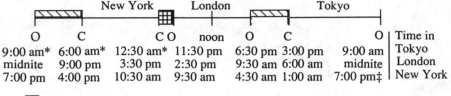

	New York			London		
O	C	C O	noon	O	C	O
9:00 am*	6:00 am*	12:30 am*	11:30 pm	6:30 pm	3:00 pm	9:00 am
midnite	9:00 pm	3:30 pm	2:30 pm	9:30 am	6:00 am	midnite
7:00 pm	4:00 pm	10:30 am	9:30 am	4:30 am	1:00 am	7:00 pm‡

Time in
Tokyo
London
New York

◩ neither market open   ‡previous day in New York
▦ overlap New York/London   *next day in Tokyo

Market in:	New York Time Open	Close	London Time Open	Close	Tokyo Time Open	Close
New York	9:30 am	4:00 pm	2:30 pm	9:00 pm	11:30 pm	6:00 am
London	4:30 am	10:30 am	9:30 am	3:30 pm	6:30 pm	12:30 am
Tokyo	7:00 pm	1:00 am	12:00 am	6:00 am	9:00 am	3:00 pm

Table 2.19
Correlations Between the Tokyo, New York and Other Stock Markets,
Monthly Returns in U.S. dollars, April 1982-March 1987.

Return in US$	%	NY	Tky	Lon	Tor	Fr	Syd	Paris	Zur	HK	Mil	Ams	Sin
New York	21.10	1.00	0.27	0.46	0.72	0.15	0.19	0.28	0.35	-0.05	0.22	0.27	0.27
Tokyo	42.10		1.00	0.39	0.21	0.38	0.07	0.59	0.43	0.02	0.42	0.40	0.12
London	20.10			1.00	0.50	0.33	0.41	0.57	0.55	0.17	0.28	0.31	0.18
Toronto	17.40				1.00	0.11	0.35	0.38	0.44	-0.03	0.22	0.29	0.15
Frankfurt	27.00					1.00	0.12	0.48	0.74	0.22	0.41	0.62	-0.07
Sydney	19.70						1.00	0.18	0.32	0.18	0.08	0.07	0.21
Paris	32.80							1.00	0.56	0.19	0.53	0.50	-0.01
Zurich	24.10								1.00	0.19	0.37	0.70	0.06
Hong Kong	11.80									1.00	0.29	0.20	0.10
Milan	29.10										1.00	0.52	0.05
Amsterdam	35.60											1.00	0.09
Singapore	7.70												1.00

Note: Correlation coefficient between each stock market return in US$ calculated from
the most recent 60 monthly returns.

Source: *TSE Quarterly Review* (**Daiwa Securities Research Institute**)

The monthly correlation between the returns in Tokyo and a number
of other markets for the periods April 1982 to March 1987 and June 1981 to
September 1987 are shown in Tables 2.19 and 2.20, respectively. During
this period, the Tokyo market had the highest gain in U.S. dollar terms.
Figure 2.11 shows the returns of the S&P 500 index in dollars and in yen.
In yen the S&P500 had no gains at all in this seven year period. Its
correlations are positive with all the other country indices. The linkage
with the European markets, such as those in London, Paris, Milan, Zurich
and Amsterdam, is higher than that in North America.

Table 2.20
Correlation Coefficients of Monthly Percentage Changes in Major Stock Market Indices, Local Currencies, June 1981 to September 1987

	Australia	Austria	Belgium	Canada	Denmark	France	Germany	Hong Kong	Ireland	Italy	Japan	Malaysia	Mexico	Netherlands	New Zealand	Norway	Singapore	South Africa	Spain	Sweden	Switzerland	U.K.
Austria	0.219																					
Belgium	0.190	0.222																				
Canada	0.568	0.250	0.215																			
Denmark	0.217	-0.062	0.219	0.301																		
France	0.180	0.263	0.355	0.351	0.241																	
Germany	0.145	0.406	0.315	0.194	0.215	0.327																
Hong Kong	0.321	0.174	0.129	0.236	0.120	0.201	0.304															
Ireland	0.349	0.202	0.361	0.490	0.367	0.374	0.067	0.320														
Italy	0.209	0.224	0.307	0.321	0.150	0.459	0.257	0.216	0.275													
Japan	0.162	-0.025	0.223	0.294	0.106	0.361	0.147	0.137	0.163	0.241												
Malaysia	0.329	-0.013	0.096	0.274	0.151	-0.134	-0.020	0.159	0.082	-0.119	0.109											
Mexico	0.220	0.018	0.104	0.114	-0.174	-0.009	0.002	0.149	0.113	0.114	-0.021	0.231										
Netherlands	0.294	0.232	0.344	0.545	0.341	0.344	0.511	0.395	0.373	0.344	0.333	0.151	0.0386									
New Zealand	0.389	0.290	0.275	0.230	0.148	0.247	0.318	0.352	0.314	0.142	-0.111	0.136	0.231	0.239								
Norway	0.335	0.009	0.233	0.381	0.324	0.231	0.173	0.356	0.306	0.042	0.156	0.262	0.050	0.405	0.201							
Singapore	0.374	0.030	0.133	0.320	0.133	-0.085	0.037	0.219	0.102	-0.038	0.066	0.891	0.202	0.196	0.212	0.290						
South Africa	0.279	0.159	0.143	0.385	-0.113	0.267	0.007	-0.095	0.024	0.093	0.225	-0.013	0.260	0.058	0.038	0.156	-0.056					
Spain	0.147	0.018	0.050	0.190	0.019	0.255	0.147	0.193	0.175	0.290	0.248	-0.071	0.059	0.170	0.095	0.075	0.056	-0.088				
Sweden	0.327	0.161	0.158	0.371	0.131	0.159	0.227	0.196	0.122	0.330	0.115	0.103	0.000	0.324	0.136	0.237	0.180	0.070	0.181			
Switzerland	0.334	0.401	0.276	0.551	0.283	0.307	0.675	0.379	0.290	0.267	0.130	0.099	0.026	0.370	0.397	0.331	0.157	0.112	0.192	0.334		
U.K.	0.377	0.073	0.381	0.500	0.218	0.332	0.263	0.431	0.477	0.328	0.354	0.193	0.068	0.534	0.014	0.313	0.250	0.168	0.209	0.339	0.435	
U.S.	0.328	0.138	0.250	0.720	0.351	0.390	0.209	0.114	0.300	0.224	0.326	0.347	0.063	0.475	0.003	0.356	0.377	0.218	0.214	0.299	0.300	0.513

Source: Roll (1988)

Figure 2.10
Running 140 Day Correlation, Tokyo Topix, Close-to-Open, with New
York Close-to-Close, 1975-1989

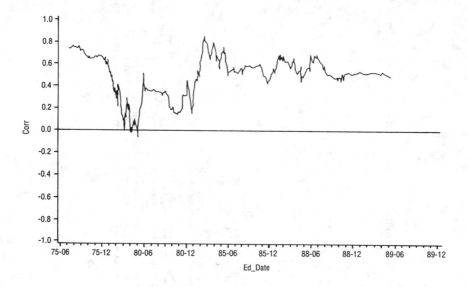

Source: Yamaichi Research Institute

Figure 2.11   The S&P 500 Index in Dollar, Yen, Pounds and Marks, 1983-1989

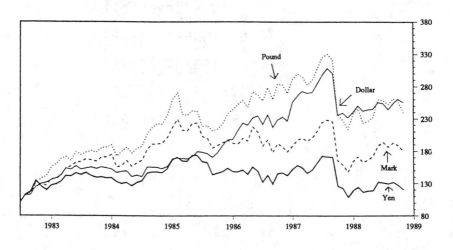

Source: First Boston

THE DAILY CORRELATION OF THE TOPIX INDEX: 1949-88

Kishimoto (1990) has studied the daily price movements of the Topix spot index for the period May 16, 1949 to May 31, 1988. Besides the total 39 year period, he has considered sub-periods, such as the four decades. He aims to demonstrate that there is positive dependence in stock price changes. Assuming only that the daily price distributions are symmetric allowing heteroscedasticity, he demonstrates that successive days do have price changes that are dependent.

Figure 2.12a compares a random investment in stock with an investment that buys long or sells short in the index when the previous day so suggests using a 1% filter rule. Using a distance measure, the difference between these curves shows, with over 99% confidence, that there is positive dependence for filter sizes smaller than 3.6%. This does not necessarily mean that profitable trading strategies exist based solely on these dependencies. The latter probably exist for traders with trading costs in the 0.1 to 0.3% range for a one way transaction. See Kishimoto (1990) for additional tests of this form.

Kishimoto found that the daily return distributions have a fat tail with a larger number of no changes, and more wide changes up and down than a normal distribution would predict, as shown in Figure 2.12b. Mandelbrot (1963), (1965), Fama and Roll (1971), Officer (1972), Blattberg and Gonedes (1974), Hsu, Miller and Wichern (1974), Kon (1984), Harris (1986), Hall, Brorsen and Irwin (1989) among others have found similar distributions in U.S. stock price data. Sakakibara et al (1988), Tse (1991), and Ikeda and Kanazaki (1991) have investigated these distributions. Tse found that the returns are best explained as the mixture of a sum of normal distributions and there is evidence against infinite variance stable distributions. Ikeda and Kanazaki found most support for a mixed jump log-normal diffusion process. Both found strong evidence against a normal distribution hypothesis with constant variance. Sakakibara et al (1988) find some support for the normal distribution in small subperiods, but again, the evidence is against this hypothesis over longer periods. Kishimoto did not specifically test distributional hypotheses in a formal fashion; but, his evidence is consistent with the others. Since we have strong evidence of stochastically varying volatility as discussed later in this chapter, the normality assumption is tenuous at best and the mixture

of normal or lognormals hypotheses despite their complexity are probably
the best models to utilize to analyze Japanese stock price movements.

Figure 2.12a   Topix Daily Data 1949-1988
Significance Level 1:

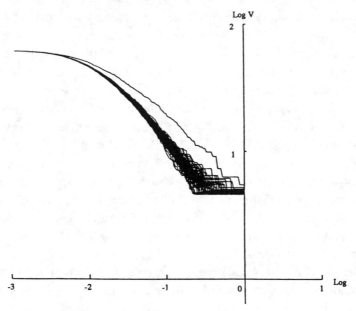

Source: Kishimoto (1990).

Figure 2.12b   Normal and Fat Tailed Distributions

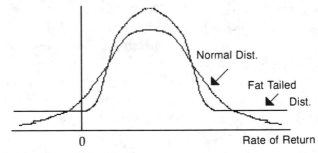

This makes statistical tests based on normal distributions inaccurate,
hence leading Kishimoto to his non-parametric approaches.

Table 2.21 shows the one-day serial correlations over time along with
the average daily rates of return and the daily standard deviation of

returns. Volatility has been fairly constant, with 1949 to 1959 being the highest and the last ten years (1979 to 1988) next. The mean daily rates of return, however, are much different. The strongest period was the last one, 1979-88, and 1959-69 was the weakest. All the periods have been strongly positive until 1990.

Table 2.21
One Day Rates of Return and Serial Correlation of Returns for Various Periods During 1949-1988 for the Topix Index

	1949-59	1959-69	1969-79	1979-88	1949-69	1969-88	1949-88
Number of Days	3019	3006	2898	2547	6026	5445	11,471
Daily mean Rate of return	0.04020%	0.02497%	0.03618%	0.06106%	0.03262%	0.04782%	0.03983%
Daily standard Deviation of Return	0.9103%	0.7168%	0.7075%	0.8059%	0.8192%	0.7551%	0.7895%
One day serial Correlation of returns	0.2681	0.1500	0.2104	0.09988	0.2227	0.1520	0.1923
% of Next Days' Advances or declines explained	7.16	2.25	4.42	1.00	4.96	2.31	3.70

Source: Kishimoto (1990)

As in the United States, there is a strong one-day serial correlation of the daily stock price changes in Japan. When prices go up on one day they tend, on average, to increase the next day. They will display a similar pattern when they fall. A perfect correlation would be P_j, the correlation coefficient, equal to +1 if prices move the same direction and -1 if they are perfect opposites. Thus, the daily return on one day, if positive or negative, will tell you exactly if the next day will be positive or negative. Of course, stock prices are not that predictable. During the full 39 years, the one day correlation was 0.1923, so $(0.1923)^2$ or about 3.70% of the next day's advances or declines are explained.

Over time the daily correlations are falling so that the market is becoming more random. From 0.2681 in 1949-59, the correlation became 0.1500 in 1959-69, 0.2104 in 1969-79 and only 0.09988 in 1979-88. Overall for the 39 years it was 0.1923.

The two and three day serial correlations are smaller than the daily correlations because it is less likely that the price change on Day 1 will affect Day 3 or 4 as it would Day 2.

	1949-69	1969-88	1949-88
Number of two-dayperiods in sample	3013	2723	5736
Two-day meanrate of return	0.06505%	0.09562%	0.07966%
Two-day standard deviation of return	1.275%	1.166%	1.2240%
Two-day serial correlation of returns	0.1223	0.03120	0.08328

The three-day correlations and other data are:

	1949-69	1969-88	1949-88
Number of Three-Day Periods	2009	1815	3824
Three-day meanrate of return	0.09756%	0.1428%	0.1193%
Three-day standard deviation of return	1.624%	1.453%	1.522%
Three-day serial correlation of returns	0.1102	0.0532	0.1051

The weekly correlations are even lower.

	1949-69	1969-88	1949-88
Number of weeks	1042	988	2030
Weekly mean ROR	0.001885%	0.002627%	0.2856%
Weekly standard deviation of return	0.02499%	0.02105%	2.316%
Weekly serial correlation of returns	0.1568	-0.224758	0.02856

THE DAILY CORRELATION OF THE NSA AND TOPIX INDICES: 1984-89

Brenner, Subrahmanyam and Uno (1990) studied the daily correlation of the NSA and Topix indices from 1984-89. Like Kishimoto they find strong statistically significant positive one-day serial correlation up to 1988. However, the one-day autocorrelation is not significant from September 1988 to November 1989 for either the NSA or Topix indices. This period coincides with the introduction of NSA and Topix futures contracts in Japan on September 3, 1988. These contracts are discussed in Ziemba and Schwartz (1992). Table 2.22 shows the results for three separate periods:

- January 1984 to August 1986 when there were no futures contracts on the NSA or Topix;

- September 1986 to August 1988 when there was only one such contract for the whole period, the NSA futures contract on the SIMEX and one futures contract, the Osaka 50, which traded for part of this period (September 1987 to August 1988). The Osaka 50 is highly correlated with the NSA and Topix; and

- September 1988 to November 1989 when all four futures contracts were trading.

Table 2.22

Mean and Standard Deviations of the First, Second and Third Order Serial Correlation Coefficients of the NSA and Topix Spot and Near Term Futures Contracts, 1984-89

Period		NSA Spot	NSA Futures SIMEX	OSE	Topix Spot	Futures
Jan 1984-Aug 1986						
One day	mean	0.108*	-	-	0.212*	-
	st dev	0.203	-	-	0.196	-
Two day	mean	-0.028	-	-	-0.053	-
	st dev	0.179	-	-	0.233	-
Three day	mean	-0.116*	-	-	-0.106*	-
	st dev	0.165	-	-	0.162	-
Sample size		32	-	-	32	-
Sep 1986-Aug 1988 [excluding October and November 1987]						
One day	mean	0.132*	0.055	-	0.183*	-
	st dev	0.197	0.200	-	0.193	-
Two day	mean	-0.052	-0.008	-	-0.034	-
	st dev	0.173	0.158	-	0.209	-
Three day	mean	-0.096	-0.100	-	-0.083	-
	st dev	0.196	0.169	-	0.196	-
Sample size		22	22	-	22	-
Sep 1988-Nov 1989						
One day	mean	-0.010	0.030	0.035	0.116	0.011
	st dev	0.206	0.226	0.203	0.192	0.215
Two day	mean	-0.004	0.028	-0.035	0.017	-0.040
	st dev	0.219	0.204	0.247	0.240	0.182
Three day	mean	0.032	-0.071	-0.030	0.031	0.016
	st dev	0.141	0.137	0.116	0.129	0.136
Sample size		15	15	15	15	15

Source: Brenner, Subrahmanyam and Uno (1990)

As of September 1989, options contracts on the NSA 225 have also been trading. They are discussed in Ziemba and Schwartz (1992).

The first order serial correlations are 0.108 and 0.212 for the NSA and Topix spot indices in the first period, January 1984 to August 1986. In the second period, September 1986 to August 1988, they were 0.132 and 0.183, respectively. All of these correlations are significantly different from zero at the 10% level. These values are consistent with and similar to Kishimoto's results. The two and three day serial correlations are all negative in these two periods. Only the three day serial correlations in the first period are significantly different from zero at the 10% level. These results over the shorter periods are in contrast with Kishimoto's results. He found small but positive two and three day serial correlations in the twenty year period 1969 to 1988.

In the new period, September 1988 to November 1989, Brenner et al (1990) found that none of the serial correlations for one to three days for the spot and future NSA and Topix contracts were significant at the 1% level. The one day NSA spot even has a negative serial correlation.

OTHER JAPANESE STOCK MARKET INDICES

There are a number of other indices of Japanese stocks in addition to the NSA, Topix, and their subindices. In this section, we record some detail about several of these indices. The Osaka 50 is discussed in Ziemba and Schwartz (1992). The NSA, while having popular stocks, does not have as large capitalized stocks as the other indices because it is price, not value weighted. At the moment there are no small stock indices in Japan based on capitalization. The TSE's small stock index is based on shares outstanding and is not a good measure for small stocks.

Average Company Size billions of ¥

Nikkei 225	1.34
Osaka 50	2.15
Topix	2.46
FT Japan	2.75
Capital Intl Japan	3.17

According to BARRA, the industry mixes of the various indices as of June 30, 1988, in percent , were as follows:

Topix		FT Japan		Capital Intl Japan	
City banks	19.83	City banks	23.86	City banks	23.48
Energy utilities	5.69	Energy utilities	6.95	Energy utilities	6.71
Automobiles	4.56	Automobiles	5.07	Automobiles	5.05
Secutities firms	4.47	Securities firms	4.47	Securities firms	4.90
Chemicals	4.02	Steel	4.12	Steel	4.65
Computers	3.91	Chemicals	4.02	Drugs	4.17
Steel	3.89	Computers	3.98	Chemicals	3.99

Nikei 225		Osaka 50		Russell/Salomon	
Food	9.17	Chemicals	9.44	City banks	18.13
City banks	7.57	Food	9.29	Energy utilities	9.14
Chemicals	5.98	Photography	5.63	Securities firms	8.14
Textiles	5.83	Electronics	5.41	Automobiles	6.26
Nonferrous metals	5.73	Textiles	5.30	Nonferrous metals	5.75
Glass & ceramics	4.56	City banks	5.23	Electric machinery	4.81
Drugs	4.32	Automobiles	4.98	Consumer electric	4.28

VOLATILITY OF THE NIKKEI AND TOPIX STOCK AVERAGES

The price movements over time of the NSA are quite variable. Not only is the volatility, as measured by the standard deviation, quite high, but also the volatility level itself is extremely non-stationary. In recent years several factors might have affected this volatility, including much greater use of computerized trading, linkages across markets, deregulation leading to more open markets and numerous derivative securities, and greater economic uncertainty because of the world debt, creditor and trade imbalance situations, as well as the Iraq oil crisis that began in August 1990.

Figure 2.13 shows the yearly volatility[3] for each month from May 1949 to April 1989. Volatility peaked in October 1987 at 73.5%. It averaged around 13% but often exceeded 20%. Figure 2.14 is a histogram of the volatility levels. The bulk of the mass is in the 6-11% range with another large mass in the 13-17% range. There is a considerable mass in the 21-30% and over 31% ranges. On average, there seems to be mean reversion since the volatility is falling versus the last month when it is high (the ☐ areas) and rising when it is low (the ⧵ areas).

---

[3]These annualized values were estimated using the formula $\sigma = \sqrt{\dfrac{250}{20} \sum_{i=1}^{20} r_i^2}$ where

$r_i = 100 \ln\left[\dfrac{NSA_t}{NSA_{t+1}}\right]$ in the last 20 trading days of the month and NSA_t, is the NSA on day t assuming there are 250 trading days in the year as there now are approximately. These estimates were made by Jun Uno of Nihon Keizai Shinbum, Inc.

Figure 2.13
NSA Historical Volatility Monthly Averages of Daily Data Annualized
May 1949-April 1989

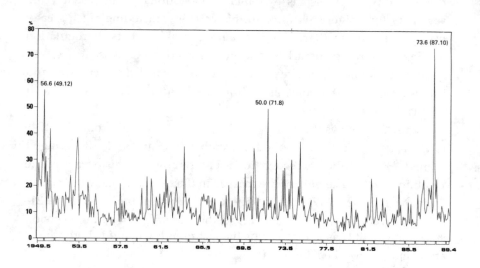

Source: Jun Uno, Nihon Keizai Shinbum, Inc.

Figure 2.14
Histogram of NSA Historical Volatility, Monthly Averages of Daily Data
Annualized, May 1949 to April 1989,
☐ indicated that volatility fell in next month and ◩ that it rose

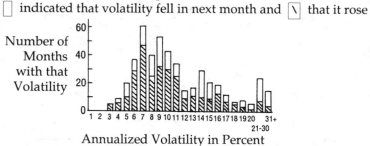

Number of Months with that Volatility

Annualized Volatility in Percent

Source: Jun Uno, Nihon Keizai Shinbum, Inc.

Table 2.23 shows how the volatility of the NSA and the Topix have
changed over time in five year intervals and varied with the average

monthly annualized return. The Nagoya Stock Exchange computed the estimates for 1983 to 1988 shown in Table 2.24.

Table 2.23
Volatility of the NSA and Topix Averages in Five Year Periods 1949-89

Period	NSA	Topix	Annualized Average Monthly Return
1949-53	20.0	16.5	15.3
1954-58	9.7	8.5	12.3
1949-63	13.4	12.2	14.5
1964-68	11.1	8.7	7.9
1969-73	14.4	11.9	20.4
1974-78	9.8	7.8	7.7
1979-83	8.5	7.3	10.4
1984-88	12.7	13.1	23.8
Average	12.5	10.8	14.0

Source: Jun Uno, Nihon Keizai Shinbum, Inc.

Figure 2.15 contains estimates made by Warren Bailey and reported in Bailey and Ziemba (1991) of the daily percent standard deviation of the NSA for January 1977 to December 1985. Each point on the graph is the estimated standard deviation for daily returns in the specified month. As with Uno's calculations, there are no overlapping data in these estimates.

To convert to yearly volatilities one multiples these values by $\sqrt{250}$. As a comparison, the volatilities of various financial instruments appears in Table 2.25.

Table 2.24   Annualized Volatility of the NSA and Topix Indices

Year	Average Annualized Volatility of the NSA	Average Annualized Volatility of the Topix
1983	8.2	7.3
1984	10.9	10.7
1985	9.2	8.9
1986	14.4	15.0
1987	25.7	26.4
1988	12.7	13.7
Total	13.5	13.7

Source: Nagoya Stock Exchange

Figure 2.15 Daily Volatility of the NSA by Month, 1977-1985

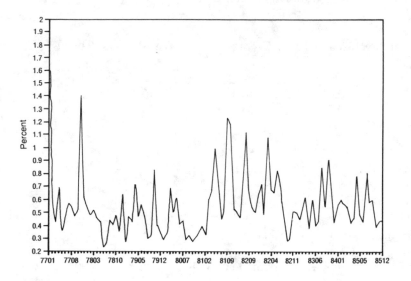

Source: Bailey and Ziemba (1991)

Table 2.25 Daily Volatility of Various Financial Instruments in 1988-1989

	1ST HALF '89	1ST HALF '88
DJ Industrial Average	0.7987%	1.3732%
Japanese yen*	0.7385%	0.8121%
British pound*	0.7361%	0.7420%
S&P 500	0.7305%	1.2883%
West German mark*	0.6859%	0.6974%
Shearson Long-Term T-Bond	0.5344%	0.6578%
CRB Futures Index	0.5118%	0.6801%
Nasdaq composite	0.4895%	0.7409%
Amex Index	0.4198%	0.7682%
Salomon Mortgage-Backed	0.3350%	0.2350%
Merrill Lynch Corporate Master	0.2963%	0.2830%
Bond Buyer Muni	0.2581%	0.8493%
ML High Yield (junk bonds)	0.1363%	0.1043%

*Based on late New York trading

Volatility varied greatly month by month

Source: *Asian Wall Street Journal*, July 7, 1989

RETURNS, VOLATILITIES AND SERIAL CORRELATIONS IN U.S. FUNDS

Bailey and Stulz (1990) estimated the mean returns for the NSA for the period January 1977 to December 1985 in U.S. dollars. The mean return is 13.30% and is nearly double the mean return on the S&P 500 during this period which was 7.58%. They also estimated the mean volatility of both of these indices using daily, weekly and monthly data. Although the results vary slightly, the S&P 500's volatility was in the 13-14% range and the NSA's was in the 18-19% range. These differences can be interpreted as violations of the efficient market hypothesis. See Lo and McKinlay (1988) on this point.

In U.S. funds, the daily serial correlation of the S&P 500 was 0.106 which was highly significant. However, the NSA daily correlation was an insignificant -0.003%. Bailey and Stulz also computed similar returns, volatilities and autocorrelations for other Pacific Basin countries. These results are shown in Table 2.26. Further autocorrelations appear in Bailey, Stulz and Yen (1989). Among other things, they found that infrequent trading induces positive serial correlation in the index.

Table 2.26
Mean Percentage Returns, Standard Deviations and First-Order Autocorrelations for the Pacific Basin Indices and the S&P 500 in U.S. Dollars, January 1977 to December 1985

| Index | Mean | Annualized Standard Deviations using data from returns computed: | | | Autocorrelation coefficient |
		Daily	Weekly	Monthly	
Japan NSA	13.30	18.37	18.30	18.68	-0.003
U.S. S&P500	7.58	13.34	14.29	13.00	0.106*
Australia, All Ordinaries	6.95	16.17	18.73	22.02	0.163*
Hong Kong, Hang Seng	10.55	30.60	32.72	37.18	0.038
Malaysia, Industrials and Commercials	5.88	20.92	21.90	26.72	0.056
Philippines, Manila Mining	-27.40	25.10	29.70	31.68	0.158*
Singapore, All-Shares	16.27	20.89	16.27	22.11	-0.196*
S. Korea, Composite	6.23	18.51	19.75	17.32	0.085*
Taiwan, Weighted Index	10.28	16.06	20.43	21.99	0.003
Thailand, Book Club	1.25	16.06	18.93	20.29	0.241*

* denotes first order autocorrelation coefficient ρ exceeds two standard deviations. ρ is computed using daily data.

Source: Bailey, Stulz and Yu (1989)

VOLATILITIES OF THE NSA AND TOPIX INDICES, 1984-91

Brenner, Subrahmanyam and Uno (1990) have investigated the volatility of the NSA and Topix indices and futures contracts based on these indices for 1984-89. We also add to their results the monthly volatilities of the cash indices for the twelve months of 1990, which included two steep market corrections, and the first two months of 1991.

The U.S. evidence suggests that volatility drops once futures contracts are introduced. Brenner et al find this in the period up to November 1989. December 1989 also had low volatility. However, the 21st correction starting on the first day of January 1990 led to a new era of high volatility that rivals that in October 1987 and other highly volatile periods shown in Figure 2.13. Table 2.27 shows their results separated into the three subperiods, as in Table 2.22, with the highly volatile period October 20 to November 30, 1987 eliminated from the second period.

Table 2.27
Mean Returns and Volatilities* on the NSA and Topix Index Spot and
Futures Contracts, January 1984 to November 1989

		NSA Futures		Topix	
Period	NSA Spot	SIMEX	OSE	Spot	Futures
Jan 1984-Aug 1986					
daily mean return	0.08%			0.10%	
daily volatility	0.66%			0.66%	
yearly volatility	10.4%			10.4%	
Sample size	764			764	
Sep 1986-Aug 1988 [excluding October and November 1987]					
daily mean return	0.10	0.08		0.10	
daily volatility	1.00	1.13		1.08	
yearly volatility	15.8%	17.9%		17.1%	
Sample size	485	475		485	
Sep 1988-Nov 1989					
daily mean return	0.10%	0.10%	0.08	0.09	0.08
daily volatility	0.58%	0.52%	0.49	0.58	0.58
yearly volatility	9.2%	8.2%	7.7%	9.2%	9.2%
Sample size	307	302	300	307	300

*The daily volatilities are the standard deviation of the log of the day by day price relatives, $\ln(P_t/P_{t-1})$ for the spot and futures contracts. The annual volatilities are the daily volatilities times $\sqrt{250}$ assuming that there are 250 trading days per year

Source: Brenner, Subrahmanyam and Uno (1990)

To update to February 1991, we computed the daily and annualized volatilities for the NSA spot for the months December 1989, January to December 1990 and January and February 1991. These values appear in Table 2.28. These volatilities are not only much larger than in the previous six years (except for the omitted October 1987 data) but they were also increasing during the 21st correction that ended in early April 1990 and the 22nd correction from July to October 1990.

Figure 2.16 shows the month-by-month daily volatilities of the NSA from January 1984 to December 1990. The volatilities range from 0.3% in February 1986 to 1.8% in October 1987 to its peak of 3.31% in October 1990. This range of volatility of nearly ten times is much greater than the roughly 2.5 times range for the S&P 500 found by Schwert (1989) for the bulk of this period.

Table 2.28
Daily and Annualized Volatilities by Month for the NSA Spot, December 1989 to February 1991

Month	Daily Volatility	Annualized Volatility	Sample Size
December	0.41%	6.47%	18
January	0.92%	14.58%	19
February	1.68%	26.53%	18
March	2.01%	31.75%	21
April	2.44%	38.61%	20
May	0.91%	14.35%	21
June	0.99%	15.61%	20
July	1.40%	22.12%	21
August	3.10%	49.07%	22
September	2.21%	34.98%	18
October	3.31%	52.40%	22
November	1.84%	29.12%	19
December	1.84%	29.15%	19
January	1.69%	26.74%	21
February	1.21%	19.20%	19

Figure 2.16a
Volatility of the Natural Logarithm of Daily Price-Relative of the NSA
Index, by Month, January 1984 to November 1989.

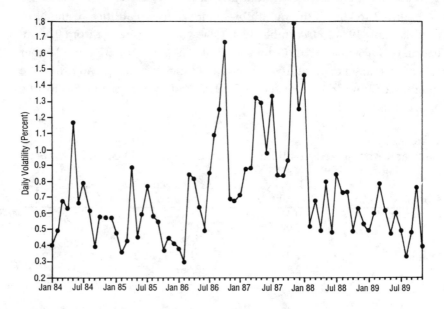

Source: Brenner et al (1990)

Figure 2.16b
Volatility of the Natural Logarithm of Daily Price-Relative of the NSA
Index, by Month, December 1989 to February 1991

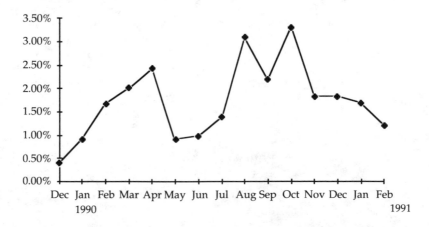

ARE VOLATILITIES HIGHER WHEN MARKETS ARE OPEN?

Table 2.29, compiled by Bailey (1989), investigates whether volatilities are higher when markets are open using data on the NSA from September 1986 to March 1987. French and Roll (1987) found that the volatility of U.S. common stock returns is, on average, greater when the stock markets are open than when they are closed overnight or across weekends and holidays. Bailey found that similar effects prevail in Japanese stock markets. Weekday close-to-close returns span a twenty-four hour period while weekend close-to-close returns span a period of two to three days. Therefore, the weekend close-to-close standard deviation should be larger than that of the weekday close-to-close by a factor of $\sqrt{2}$ to $\sqrt{3}$ if the index volatility is the same. However, the weekend close-to-close is only 1% higher than the weekday for the NSA. Hence, price volatility in Japan is greater when the markets are open.

The NSA opening prices further illustrate this point. The open-to-close spans six hours, while the close-to-open spans eighteen hours on weekdays and two to three days on weekends. With identical volatility across periods, the close-to-open standard deviation should be larger than the open-to-close by a factor of at least $\sqrt{3}$ instead of the 11% that was found. Table 2.29 also presents summary statistics on returns measured close-to-open over the weekend only. Given a forty-eight to seventy-two hour market closure, the weekend close-to-open standard deviation should be many times larger than the weekday open-to-close instead of the 6.5% found.

Barclay, Litzenberger and Warner (1990) investigated weekend effects in Japanese financial markets that supplements Bailey's results. They were specifically concerned with the effects of Saturday trading. As of February 1989 there is no more Saturday trading in Japan.

As discussed in Chapter 3, having Saturday trading has a major effect on the mean return on the following Monday and Tuesday as well as the previous Friday. Barclay et al found that when the exchange is open on Saturday the weekend variance is about 60% higher than when it is closed. However, weekly variances are not affected by whether or not the previous week ended with Saturday trading.

Table 2.29
Summary Statistics for Daily Stock Index Returns for 153 Trading Days,
September 3, 1986 to March 31, 1987, of the NSA

Daily return index	Mean	Standard deviation
close to close		
daily	0.001007	0.01017
Mon to Fri or Sat*	0.002133	0.009898
Fri or Sat to Mon	-0.003767	0.01008
Tuesday	-0.0009497	0.01063
close to open		
daily	0.0000445	0.001138
weekend only	0.0000964	0.000649
open to close		
daily	0.0008900	0.009942
Mon to Fri	0.0006478	0.01005
Saturday	0.003295	0.00879
Correlation (p-test) of close		
to close returns	0.195	0.016

• Fri or Sat uses Saturday price on Saturdays when market is open, Friday otherwise.

Source: Bailey (1989)

The increase in weekend volume and variance caused by Saturday
trading is offset by lower volume and variance on surrounding days.
These results are consistent with the view that Saturday trading changes
the timing of trades. This is consistent again with the mean return results
discussed in Chapter 3.

The variance seems to be caused by private information revealed
through trading. U.S. stocks traded on the TSE or Japanese stocks traded
on the NYSE have increased trading hours. But the trading of stock on a
foreign exchange is typically light relative to domestic volume. The
increased trading hours are not associated with an increase in stock return
variance. Hence a substantial volume is required for private information
to be incorporated into stock prices. There is no causal relation between
trading hours and stock return variance.

Table 2.30
Variance of Returns and Trading Volume for the Topix by Day of Week,
January 1973 to July 1987

Day of Week	Ratio of Return Variance to Average Weekday Return Variance	Ratio of Trading Volume to Average Weekday Trading Volume
Monday	1.01	0.78
Tuesday	0.94	0.91
Wednesday	0.95	1.04
Thursday	1.04	1.01
Friday	1.02	1.04
Saturday	0.57	0.63
One Day Holiday	1.42	0.84
Year-end Six Day Holiday	0.75	0.56

Monday is based on Saturday close to Monday close for weeks when the exchange was open on Saturday and Friday close to Monday close on other weeks. Tuesday through Saturday returns are one day close to close returns. The average weekday return variance was .000044. The average weekday volume was 393,129 shares.

Source: Barclay, Litzenberger and Warner (1990)

Barclay et al used data from January 1973 to July 1987. During that period, the TSE was open 545 Saturdays and closed on 204. The Saturday trading was in the morning session only so one would expect its volume to be about half of that of the regular day's, and it was. The return variance was 57% of a normal week day return variance and the trading volume was 63% of normal. Table 2.30 shows this and the other days of the week, plus holidays and the year-end six day break. Saturday trading does not affect the total weekly volume (Wednesday close to Wednesday close) even though the combined Saturday/Monday average trading volume is 71% above that of Monday's trading volume if the previous Saturday is closed. The volume is just shifted around. The higher weekend variance with Saturday trading is offset by lower Monday to Wednesday variances. Table 2.31 shows this and related results.

Table 2.31
Ratio of Return Variances and Trading Volumes for the Topix for Periods
near Saturdays When the Exchange is Open Relative to Periods Near
Saturdays When the Exchange is Closed, January 1973 to July 1987

Day of Week	Ratio of Variances	Ratio of Volume
Periods Including Saturdays		
Friday to Monday	1.63[a]	1.71[a]
Friday to Tuesday	0.95	1.30[a]
Friday to Wednesday	0.68	1.14[b]
Wednesday to Wednesday	0.78	1.06
Periods Preceding Saturdays		
Thursday	1.34	0.93
Friday	1.22	0.92
Wednesday to Friday	1.26	0.95
Periods Following Saturdays		
Tuesday	0.67[c]	0.93
Wednesday	0.75[d]	0.94
Monday to Wednesday	0.65[c]	0.93

[a] one tailed test significantly greater than 1.0 at .01 level
[b] one tailed test significantly greater than 1.0 at .05 level
[c] one tailed test significantly less than 1.0 at .01 level
[d] one tailed test significantly less than 1.0 at .05 level

Source: Barclay, Litzenberger and Warner (1990)

LAND PRICES ARE ASTRONOMICAL

> *Tsukamoto Sozan Building in Ginza 2-Chome in central Tokyo is
> the most expensive land in the country with one square meter
> priced at ¥37.7 million or about $279,000 U.S. at the (December
> 1990) exchange rate of about ¥135 per U.S. dollar.*

Some 120 million people live in Japan in an area of about 378,000 km², about the size of Montana or California. Most of the land is mountainous or used for agriculture. Only 4% of the land is used to house all these people, an area about the size of Connecticut. Some 67% of the land is forested. A further 14.5% is in agriculture. Moors, rivers and roads amount to 0.8%, 3.5% and 2.9% respectively. Table 2.32 gives this break-down. Hence, with high incomes, crowded conditions, and an intense desire to invest at home, land prices in the most desirable locations have escalated beyond belief. Almost 30 million people, or a quarter of the population, lives in the greater Tokyo area.

Table 2.32   Land Use in Japan (1986)

Agriculture	14.5
Woodlands	66.9
Moors	0.8
Rivers	3.5
Roads	2.9
Dwellings	4.0
Other	7.4
Total	100.0
Total Area	377.8 (1000 km^2)

Source: National Land Agency, Japan

Much of the housing is owned by the large corporations, and their employees receive subsidized rent. However, fully 60% of families (55% in Tokyo) own their own home, and many individuals invest in raw land or in apartments that they rent. Figures 2.17 (a, b) give indices of land prices for industrial, residential, commercial and all land in the six largest cities and throughout the country for 1955 to 1990. The six largest cities are Tokyo, Yokohama, Nagoya, Kyoto, Osaka and Kobe. The country wide indices are based on 140 cities. The data are appraisal based. Simple averages of samples of ten lots in each city form the indices which were normalized at 100 as of March 31, 1980. The sampling procedure separates land into high, medium and low grades reflecting location, social circumstances, yield, etc. The sampling procedure selects lots randomly and equally from each of these three classes. Table D1 in the appendix has the detailed data series. Data on agricultural and forest land also apears in Appendix D.

Since 1955, land prices have escalated astronomically. In the largest cities land prices have outpaced the CPI by twenty times since 1955. Unstated real estate assets of Japanese corporations grew by $2.8 trillion from 1986 to 1988, about equal to the size of the GNP. Meanwhile stock values grew 300%. While there have been twenty-two corrections of 10% or more in the stock market from 1949 to 1990, only once did land prices fall and that was only about 5-8% (depending on the area and type of land) in the first OPEC oil crisis of 1973/74. Even then, land prices started rising almost immediately after.

Figure 2.17
Land Price Indices for Industrial, Residential, Commercial and All Land
and Annual Rates of Price Change for All Land, 1955-90

a. In the six largest cities
(semi log scale)

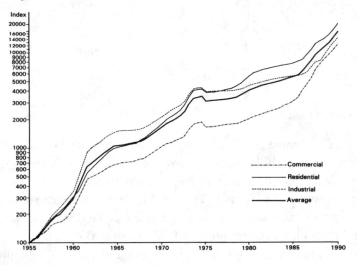

Average annual rates of price change % (6 cities)

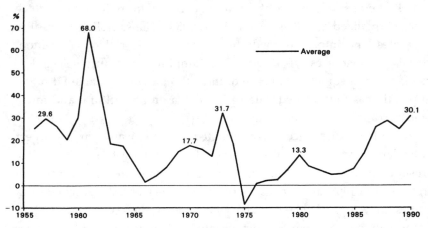

b. In the entire country (140 cities) (semi log scale)

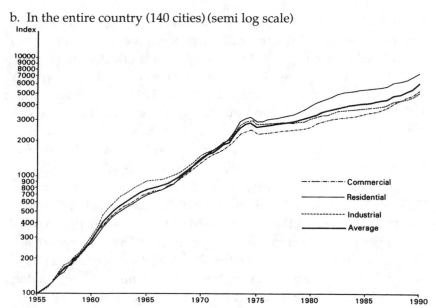

Average annual rates of price change % (140 cities)

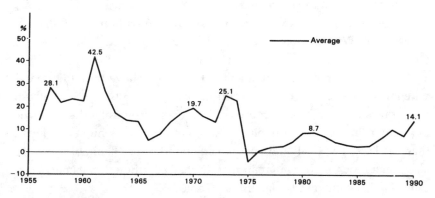

Source: Japan Real Estate Institute

In the Ginza district of Tokyo each square meter of land is worth over $200,000 U.S. Choice downtown land goes for the equivalent of nearly a billion an acre. At neighborhood land prices, the value of the land under the Emperor's palace in Tokyo equals that of California or of Canada.

The total land value in Japan in 1990 was about 4.1 times that of the whole United States. Japanese land was worth some ¥2180 trillion as of the end of 1989. This compares with a value of ¥1050 trillion at the end of 1985. Using an exchange rate of ¥143.76 per dollar at the end of 1989, this translates into a land value of $15.16 trillion. As of September 1990, all land had an index of 203.1, up 16.2% from September 1989. With an end of 1990 exchange rate of 135.40, total Japanese land values were in the $18.7 trillion range in late 1990. The average acre of land in Japan is worth fully 100 times the average acre in the U.S. So even though the U.S. has about 25 times more land than Japan, its current total value is less than a fourth as much. Essentially half the world's land value at current, 1987-90, prices is accounted for by Japanese land! It also accounts for about 20% of the total asset value in the world. Simple houses in Tokyo rent for more than $10,000 per month and cost in the millions. Office space for sale in Tokyo's financial district costs nearly $75,000 per square foot. Appendix D has additional data to supplement this section.

In 1988, Tokyo's land value alone was about $7.7 trillion, or about half the land value of the whole country. To understand how much this is, we can do a simple experiment. Let's borrow on it up to 80% of its value, as many banks in Japan would gladly do on particular plots of land. We could then have almost enough to purchase all the land in the U.S. for $3.7 trillion and all the stock on the New York, American, and NASDAQ over-the-counter stock exchanges for about $2.6 trillion in an all-cash transaction! With the loans available in mid 1989 at 5.7% variable and 6% fixed rates, it might be a good purchase.

Land turnover is very small as the Japanese believe in holding land whenever possible. This is reinforced by the tax system which encourages the purchase of more land and discourages land sales. The population in per unit of habitable area is thirty times higher in Japan than the U.S. The GNP and energy consumption per habitable area are also much much higher in Japan than in the U.S. (though the energy per unit GNP is much lower in Japan), see Table 2.33.

Land in Tokyo as of January 1988 cost 30 to 100 times more than in major cities in other countries. In Tokyo's Setagaya district, land was 99 times more expensive than a similar plot in Los Angeles, 50 times that in San Francisco and Sydney and 30 times that in London and Frankfurt. Tokyo was the only place where land averaged ¥1 million a square meter. The cost per meter was ¥1.08 million in Setagaya versus ¥18,900 in Los Angeles, ¥27,800 in Sydney, ¥35,900 in London, ¥227,000 in Osaka, ¥262,000 in Taipei and ¥489,000 in Paris; see Figure 2.18. As of January 1990, the maximum prices per square meter for residential lots were recorded by Sanban-cho in Tokyo at ¥12.3 million, and Temma in Osaka at ¥2.4 million.

Another comparison is the amount of land that can be purchased with one year's average salary. It's 4.4 square meters for a Setagaya worker, 48.4 for a Londoner, 197.8 for a Los Angeles worker and 309.9 for a worker in Auckland.

Table 2.33 Comparison of Fundamentals, Japan and the U.S., 1989

	Japan	U.S.	Japan as % of U.S.
Population, millions	120	239	50.21
Total area (1000 sq km)	377	9373	4.02
Habitable area (1000 sq km)	80	4786	1.67
Population per habitable area (pop/sq km)	1500	50	3000.00
GNP per habitable area (million $/sq km)	16.90	0.80	2112.50
Energy consumption (tons oil equivalent/sq km)	4650	390	1192.38

Source: Daiwa Securities America, Inc

According to the 1988 White Paper on National Land Use, land prices throughout the country in yen per square meter were 69,900 in Japan versus 5900 in the U.S., 6300 in the U.K., and 9400 in Germany. The cost of land is reflected in the amount of park area in square meters per capita: London has the most at 30.2 followed by New York at 19.2 and Paris with 12.2 compared with only 2.2 in Tokyo.

Table 2.34 shows the rents in Tokyo in mid 1989. Extreme demand leads to the high occupancy rates and the huge deposits in addition to the extremely high rents. Both are measured in *tsubo* an area of $3.3m^2$ or about $35ft^2$.

The average price of a condominium purchased by salaried workers in metropolitan Tokyo rose 63% to ¥42.20 million in three years, while the price of a new detached house rose 53% to ¥55.24 million. The average age of condominium buyers rose 1.5 years to 39.2. Meanwhile, the average floor area of houses rose 10 square meters, to 115.2, with the move further from the center of Tokyo and further from train and bus stations.

Table 2.34 Rental Office Situation by Area in Tokyo, Mid 1989

District	Average Deposit ¥/tsubo	Average Rent ¥/tsubo	Average Real Rent ¥/tsubo	Rate of Increase, %	Newly Supplied tsubo	Occupancy Rate, %	Comment
Marunouchi, Otemachi & Yurakucho	1,109,800	58,850	64,810	9.30	0	100.0	Newcomers may find it difficult to enter. Large-scale buildings will be provided in the 1990s.
Uchisiwaicho, Kasumigasaki & Nagatacho	997,100	49,450	54,150	18.56	145	99.9	Little tenant mobility. Supplies are expected to increase in Nagatacho.
Kojimachi, Hirakawacho & Klocho	654,000	30,260	36,820	11.68	8,065	98.4	Demand-supply situation has been stable. A few high-rise buildings are planned.
Bancho	633,600	28,910	33,460	11.83	4,816	95.2	The market is fluid with foreign companies coming here.
Muromachi, Honcho	983,500	38,120	44,220	22.86	5,084	99.6	Demand is so high that new supplies are not enough.
Nihonbashi, Yaesu & Kyobashi	829,000	32,700	40,540	14.39	4,732	99.5	It is difficult to find vacant rooms and offices. Little tenant mobility.
Ginza	781,500	32,190	38,990	27.25	7,868	97.1	Supplies are scarce, creating a *landlord's market*.
Shinbashi, Nishi-Shinbashi	736,700	31,770	34,280	20.01	8,348	99.1	Most buildings are small. Demand for mid-size building is very strong.
Hamamatsucho, Shibakoen	610,600	24,440	28,040	9.39	10,531	99.7	Supplies increased, but demand is unlikely to rise as fast .
Shibaura,Kaigan	434,400	19,630	21,800	21.92	15,198	95.8	There are many large-scale development projects for the area.
Shiba, Mita	588,600	24,470	27,460	4.55	9,768	98.5	Rents differ widely depending on building size and facilities.
Roppongi	793,100	32,050	36,170	19.31	1,046	92.1	Office buildings, social buildings and residential buildings are mixed in the district.
Akasaka	1,053,700	42,720	48,620	15.38	4,476	98.9	Demand-supply situation has been stable. Small scale office spaces are plentiful.
Aoyama	1,175,100	47,590	53,460	18.42	1,422	99.0	Rents are so high that many prospective tenants tend to seek offices in other districts.
Nishi-Shinjuku	518,200	21,400	27,410	8.99	4,587	99.4	The head office buildings of the Tokyo Metropolitan Government will be relocated here in March 1991.
Nishi-Ikebukuro, Ikebukuro	303,300	13,210	15,770	7.76	4,652	95.5	A construction boom here is likely to cause oversupplies.
Shibuya	496,400	23,280	26,240	13.03	6,422	98.5	Rents differ widely depending on whether buildings are new and where they are located.

The average rent is the average of all rents for old and new building. One *tsubo* 3.3 m^2.

Source: 89 IDSS Office Market Report prepared by Ikoma Data Service System, a subsidary of Ikoma Corp. in the *Japan Times*

Figure 2.18
Land Prices Around the World, Cost Per Square Meter in U.S. dollars,
January 1989

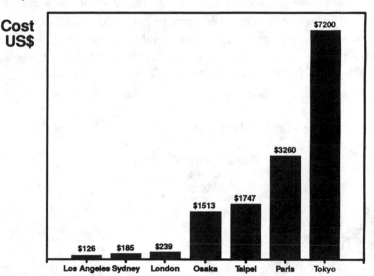

Source: Japanese Association of Real Estate Appraisal

Land for all purposes is scarce. A recent concern is for grave sites.
The situation is so tight for land near the major cities that lotteries are
held to sell abandoned grave sites. At a recent lottery some 14,000 people
in Tokyo vied for 750 plots. Across Japan, families must travel hours to
visit graves of relatives. It is hard to get people to move to Tsukuba
because newcomers are not allowed to establish graves in the area.
Japanese graves are easily movable being above ground and a small area
can house a family. The Buddhist temple we visited in Tokyo is
encouraging people to move their relatives' remains to a suburban site.

In Tokyo someone has introduced tomb-like lockers in multi-story
buildings, calling them grave apartment buildings, or *haka manshon*, to
end life as it was lived. This still costs ¥7-900,000. An average downtown
plot costs ¥3 million and the gravestone about ¥1.5 million, but it serves
the whole family.

Many others are introducing sites in the countryside. An active
business has evolved recruiting potential customers who flock on
weekends in buses to search for desirable grave sites for the family. For
$17,000, one can have a communal family site in a high-rise graveyard

terraced plot. A cemetery in the mountains two hours from Tokyo is
running one-day free tours to the grounds. These plots cost ¥300,000 to
¥4.4 million. One can see it evolving: an entire resort area built near
cemeteries so families can come and pay respects on holidays.

Across Japan land prices vary considerably as shown by the map in
Figure 2.19a. As of early 1989 Tokyo was at 100 (¥507,300/m²), Osaka at
62 and Nagoya at 27. Figure 2.19b shows the land value by region in
Japan and the heavy concentration in metropolitan and greater Tokyo.

Figure 2.19a   Housing Land Price Index

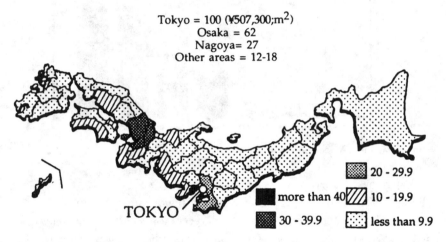

Source: Japanese Real Estate Institute

Tokyo's land prices have been leveling off, and Japanese investment
in land in the U.S., Australia, Hong Kong and other countries is
expanding at a huge rate. For example, some 70% of the new hotels in
Hawaii are Japanese owned, as are large portions of Los Angeles and
New York. See Ziemba and Schwartz (1991) for more on this investment
outside Japan. Still, with the bulk of the property controlled by the major
companies and the government, and with the tax structure and the
incentives favoring land holding and buying by individuals and
institutions, the prices may well stay at these lofty levels.

Figure 2.19b   Land Value by Region in Japan

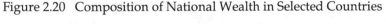

¥ trillion

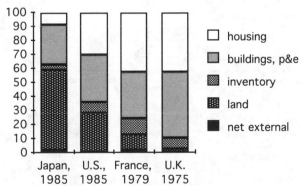

Source: Economic Planning Agency reported in Canaway (1990)

Figure 2.20   Composition of National Wealth in Selected Countries

Source: Economic Planning Agency, Japan

If there is to be a major stock market crash in Japan, it may start with or be linked to land values. Figure 2.20 shows that as of 1985 a staggering 57% of the national wealth of Japan was land! The current percentage may be even higher. The early 1989 value of national land was about ¥1.637 quadrillion; the stock market was worth only about one third as much, some ¥519 trillion.

Figure 2.21
Year by Year Land Price Changes in Various Major Cities, Areas and
Prefectures, 1981 to 1989

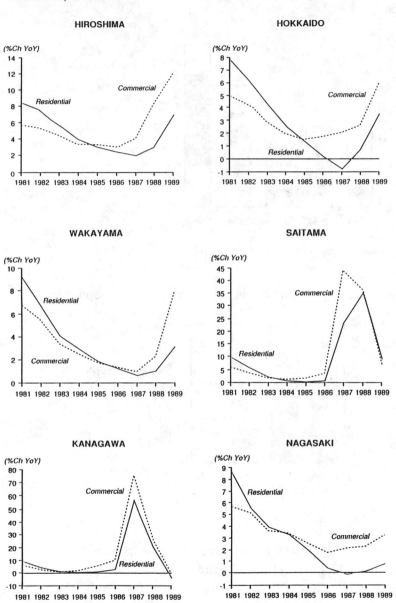

Source: Economic Planning Agency reported in Canaway (1990)

Figure 2.21 concluded

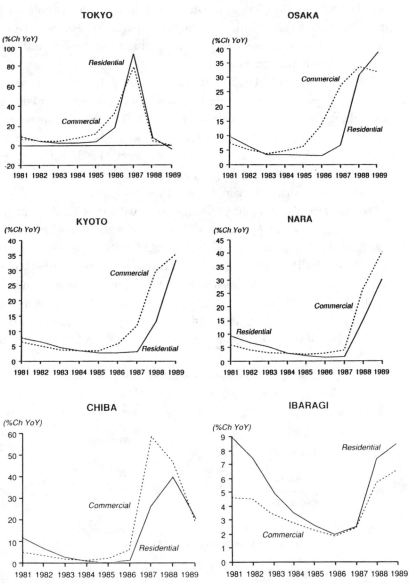

Until mid 1990, banks were still eager to make real estate loans. They were then told by the Bank of Japan to limit lending for speculative real estate purchases that would put further upward pressure on prices. Specifically, they were requested to increase their loan base by only about 3% to 5% in each quarter.

Although Tokyo's land values may have leveled off at least temporarily, prices in the suburbs of Tokyo, and in other major cities and their suburbs, continue to increase. Figure 2.21 shows the year by year price index changes from 1981 to 1989 in Tokyo, Osaka and eight other areas of the country for residential and commercial land. Although price increases vary considerably by area and time, it is rare for prices to fall. In difficult times, prices remain flat and then rise later.

Overall, Japan's land and buildings were valued at ¥2.51 quadrillion at the end of 1987, up 20.2% from 1986. This was the highest increase since fiscal 1973 when land prices increased 26.3%. In that year the prices were fanned by the archipelago reconstruction of then Prime Minister Kakuei Tanaka. Table 2.35 gives some data on this for the year ending in July 1988. Price increases are all over the map. How accurate these increases are in the thin markets in these areas is not known. But the increases are all positive! Some increases are small, yet others are 100% or more.

Not all studies show increasing land prices in all areas in 1988. A survey of land prices for July to October 1988 by the National Land Agency found the following price changes in percent:

	residential	commercial
Tokyo	-2.1	-0.7
central wards*	-3.7	
Kanagawa	-2.4	-0.2
Saitama	0.9	1.5
Chiba	2.6	2.9

*Including Minato, Chuo and Bunkyo; all commercial
property was down except in south Tama

According to a survey by the Tokyo Metropolitan government, land prices throughout Tokyo continue to decline, though not enough to erase the drastic increase of 1987. Residential prices in central wards such as Minato, Chuo and Bunkyo were down an average of 3.7 percent as of October 1, 1988. Prices were also declining in all commercial districts except for south Tama; although, residential land prices in south and west Tama were slightly higher.

Table 2.35
Yearly Land Price Increases in Japan in Percent, July 1987 and July 1988

	1986-87	1987-88
Overall	9.7	7.4
City Land		
Tokyo	57.5	22.6
Osaka	7.9	27.0
Nagoya	3.0	12.8
Suburb Land		
Chiba Prefecture	23.3	34.0
Saitama Prefecture	22.1	33.8
Osaka Prefecture	10.2	30.6
Tokyo Commercial Land	85.7	7.9
Housing Land		
Saitama Prefecture	21.9	33.9
Chiba Prefecture	21.2	33.0
Osaka Prefecture	6.7	30.9
Nara Prefecture		12.5
Hyogo Prefecture		14.1
Nagoya	4.7	29.8
Tokyo		4.5
Tama Area of Tokyo	90.0	11.8
Toride, Ushiku, Figishiri,		
Southern Ibaraki Prefecture		19
Central Kyoto		500-800
Kobe		500-800
Osaka		400
Yokahama		
Kyoto Prefecture		108
Outside the Largest Three Cities		2.1
Commercial Land		
Sapporo		17.3
Sendai		26.6
Shizukoa Prefecture		20.9
Hamamatsu		
Soka		64.8
Kisarazu Chiba Prefecture		108.9
Imai-Chiba Prefecture		231
Kisaruzu, 2-Chrome, Chiba Pref.		225
Soka, Koshigaya, Iruma, Niiza		49-50

Source: Japan Times, October 1, 1988, based on data from the National Land Agency.

According to a survey by the Tokyo Metropolitan government, land prices throughout Tokyo continue to decline, though not enough to erase the drastic increase of 1987. Residential prices in central wards such as

Minato, Chuo and Bunkyo were down an average of 3.7 percent as of October 1, 1988. Prices were also declining in all commercial districts except for south Tama; although, residential land prices in south and west Tama were slightly higher.

On December 1, 1988, a price survey was conducted by MRD, an affiliate of Misawa Homes Co., on housing lots of 130 square meters or more in 439 locations in Tokyo and in the prefectures of Kanagawa, Chiba, Saitama, and Ibaraki. The survey found that the average price increase from December 1987 to December 1988 was only 8.4%, down from 73.5% in the previous one-year period.

The decline was attributed to strengthened surveillance by the government under the National Land Utilization Law, banks' self-restraint in providing funds to land dealers, and slower demand for new housing. Land prices turned downward in areas where they had been surging previously, such as Tokyo and Kanagawa. They fell 8% and 6.2%, respectively, in these areas, both record year-to-year declines. But land prices still posted sharp rises in regions that were relatively lower in previous years. The average price rose by a record 41.3% in Ibaraki, 38.8% in Chiba and 7.6% in Saitama.

The drops are small and probably are in the range of the error of measurement, especially with the thin markets. However, a November 21, 1988, report in Barron's by Maggie Mahar signals a more dramatic danger. Could the prices drop enough to create a panic? Both *Diamond*, Japan's most widely read business magazine, and *Toyo Keizai*, a major business magazine, described land price declines in late 1988 in the order of 25% or more in Tokyo.

Alan Woodhull of Merrill Lynch's Tokyo office said:

> The property market isn't really a market at all; it's part of a carefully managed economy. And because government controls are so firm what looks like a house of cards is actually a house of bricks, an economy set in concrete. After adjusting for Japan's low interest rates and low inflation, the real return on Tokyo real estate is comparable to the real return in Manhattan. In other words, Tokyo's real estate is overpriced and poised for a plunge only if you see one coming in New York.

Over the long run, it seems that the government will attempt to slowly let the air out of the bubble with gradual tax and land regulation changes and the encouragment of bank self-restraint. The current rules encourage selling very small pieces of land to pay for inheritance taxes. These taxes are not really very high because land is assessed at only about 40% of its value and the first ¥30 million of capital gains is tax exempt. Moreover, if the land is sold for public use (parks, highways, etc.), the first ¥50 million of the gain is tax exempt.

The new land reform measure passed in December 1990, an attempt to hold prices down by taxing land, provides for only a slight tax. Starting in 1992 there will be a 0.2% tax which will rise to 0.3% in 1993. Since the tax is based on official evaluations which are about 50-60% of actual values, the tax rates are quite minimal. Also, small (less than 1000 square meters) and low valued (less than ¥30,000 per square meter) plots are not taxed at all. Nor is land owned by local and national governments and private land used for public purposes.

There are more than one million separate owners of Tokyo's commercial and residential land and 40% of these properties are $10m^2$ or less. It is hard to use this land for large apartment and commercial buildings. Putting together enough land in one place is very difficult, because virtually all of the small shopkeepers and people living in ramshackle houses worth millions prefer not to sell.

The drops in land prices in Tokyo, if they are real, may be a small correction - the conventional wisdom of the Japanese - or possibly the start of a deeper problem. Currently only about 2% of Tokyo's land changes hands each year. With such a small amount sold there are many buyers, so there is a strong tendency for prices to stay sky high.[1] Because the debt held on land is so high, a real drop of 25% overall would cause considerable problems. Of total bank loans in mid 1990, about 23% are to real estate but other loans may be effectively collatoralized by stocks or other assets that have large land components. However, there would likely be no real crack in the armor unless prices fell about 50%. Until then the drops would be considered temporary aberrations. The more than 25% drops mentioned in these articles are probably also based on a very thin market with few transactions. The Japan Real Estate Institute appraisal based data shown in Figure 2.17 and in Appendix D show no such decline.

---

[1]In North America, high prices tend to induce people to put their house on the market, take their capital gains, and move elsewhere; in Japan, people are not as mobile.

The degree of leveraging is so high that many people and institutions would be forced into bankruptcy should their loans be called in. One of the measures to cool off the overheated market has been a lowering of lending activity by the banks for what they feel are speculative land transactions. This measure was forced on the banks by the government in July 1987. Bankruptcies among real estate firms are also on the rise, up 36% in 1987, while the average bankruptcy rate for all firms was up only 14%. Figure 2.22 shows the volume of real estate loans. Of particular interest is its variability and predictive power for leveling off periods. Moreover, rents (see Figure 2.23) are rising slower than land prices; hence, one expects increases in valuation to provide profits. That is, the short-run losses that are fully tax deductible will be made up by long-term gains, which are taxed at much lower rates.

Figure 2.22   Figure 2.23
Real Estate Loans in Japan   Residential Land Prices vs Rents

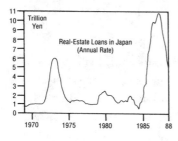

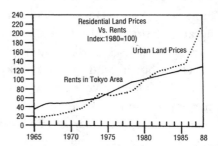

Source: Japan Real Estate Institute,
Management and Coordination Agency

In 1989, prices in Tokyo were flat.[2] On average they fell 0.3% and were down for the second consecutive year. In western Tokyo, Tama residential area prices fell by as much as 14.3% to counterbalance 1988s rises there. However prices rose sharply in Tokyo's suburbs. The area near Narita airport saw rises in the 67-79% range. Saitama and Ibaraki prefectures had rises of over 10% and Yamanashi prefecture west of Tokyo rose 30%. There the gain was largely in response to the proposed building of a state of the art linear magnetic railway.

---

[2]*Japan Times*, April 2, 1990, based on National Land Agency data.

In Nagano Prefecture in central Japan, prices rose about 10%. There, a campaign to stage the 1996 Winter Olympics added to the price pressure as well as improved access to Tokyo.

The big increase, though, was in Osaka where a new international airport in Osaka Bay and related traffic networks are being built. The average increase in 1989 for residential property was a whopping 56.1%. Commercial land was up 46.3% which was a record increase among the land agency's annual surveys beginning in 1970. The average price of housing land in Osaka was ¥476,000 or 2.78 times that of 1983. Osaka has nearly caught up with Tokyo. New condominiums now cost about ¥50 million, about 90% of those in Tokyo. These condos, like many speculative investments, peaked in March 1990 and have since fallen. Part of the fall was caused by selling by investors with stock market margin calls. While golf courses, also a speculative investment, had a similar fall, there was no decline in overall land prices.

By prefecture, prices of residential land rose 61.8% in Kyoto, 58.6% in Osaka, 50.2% in Nara, and 38.6% in Hyogo. Across the country the average increase in 1989 was 17%. As in the past, government authorities have attempted to provide rules to slow the price increases. However, these rules do not seem to be working and are often simply sidestepped by the parties involved. The prices have simply risen to the market clearing level.

Prices have become so high that mortgages are becoming longer and longer. Some have reached 100 years, which allows homeowners to stretch payments over several generations. The total payment then becomes quite large. Using mid 1990 interest rates in the 8.4% range, a $500,000 house costs $4.2 million in payments over the 100 years.[3]

Peter Boone (1989) developed several models in an attempt to rationalize the high land values in Japan from an economic point of view. He found that if Japan's GNP growth exceeds that in the U.S. by about 2% per year forever, then land prices 100 times higher in Japan than in the U.S. are consistent with the economic model. He also developed the following simple model for the relative land price in Japan versus that in the U.S.:

---

[3]These are almost interest only loans.

$$\text{Relative land price in Japan} = \frac{\text{Land value}}{\text{Rents}} \times \frac{\text{Rents}}{\text{GNP}} \times \frac{\text{GNP}}{\text{Land}}$$

$$= \frac{1}{a} \times 1 \times b,$$

where **a** is essentially the ratio of rents in Japan for comparable properties which are known to be 0.25 to 0.50 in the U.S., **b** is the GNP to land estimate which ranges from 20-30 (Table 2.33 estimates this at 21 in 1989), and rents/GNP= 1 is consistent with the Cobb-Douglas production model that Boone assumes. Using the following a's and b's gives the relative land prices in the range 40 to 120 which brackets the actual ratio of 100:

a	b	Relative land price
1/2	20	40
1/3	20	60
1/3	20	60
1/4	30	120

It is more than likely that prices in Tokyo will remain flat and prices in outlying areas and other major cities will continue to creep up. Too much is at stake. If land prices in Tokyo crash, the Japanese economic miracle would be over. It is likely that the world's shrewdest businessmen and government would not let that happen if at all possible. In Chapter 7 we discuss the risks for the stock and land markets and the possibility of a future bursting of the bubble.

LAND AND STOCK PRICES IN JAPAN

In this section we look at the relationship between land prices and stock prices and land returns and stock returns. The evidence points very strongly to the proposition that stock prices lead land prices.

Figure 2.17 and Table D1 in the appendix show index values for commercial, residential, industrial and all land in the six largest cities and in the entire country from 1955 to 1990. There is a remarkable correlation between the level of the stock market as measured by the NSA and the level of land prices. The closest relationship is with commercial land. Presumably commercial land prices and stock prices are driven by the same economic factors and move in tandem.

Figure 2.24 shows the remarkable correlation between the level of the NSA and the level of land values. Commercial land values explain 97.5% of the variation in prices in the NSA with a semi-annual model.

Moreover, earnings explain *nothing* once commercial land or land in the six biggest cities is considered; see Ziemba (1991b).

Figure 2.24
Level of the NSA versus Commercial, Land Prices, Semi-Annual Data, 1955-88*

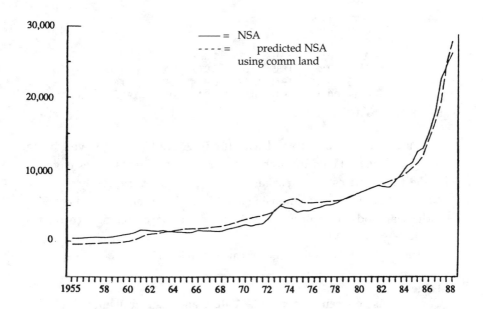

NSA = -818.629 + 75.225 Commercial Land Index
      (-5.19)   (50.7)
    has an adjusted R^2 of 0.975, a Durban-Watson statistic of 0.468, an auto-correlation
    of 0.759, and an sum of squared errors of 891.2, where the t-statistics are in ( ) .

Source: Ziemba (1991b)

Using the semiannual data, one obtains the correlation matrix in Table 2.36 for the NSA stock index, and land price indices, for all land, all commercial land, housing land, industrial use land and these latter four indices in the six largest cities.

Table 2.36
Contemporaneous Correlations of the NSA with Various Land Indices,
Semiannual Data, 1955-88

| | NSA | Land Indices Throughout Japan | | | | Land Indices in 6 Largest Cities | | | |
| | | ALL | COML | HOUSE | INDL | ALL | COML | HOUSE | INDL |
	1	2	3	4	5	6	7	8	9
1	1.000								
2	0.858	1.000							
3	0.857	0.998	1.000						
4	0.874	0.995	0.989	1.000					
5	0.820	0.996	0.997	0.984	1.000				
6	0.963	0.958	0.960	0.961	0.938	1.000			
7	0.988	0.879	0.885	0.885	0.850	0.978	1.000		
8	0.956	0.965	0.962	0.974	0.942	0.996	0.964	1.000	
9	0.889	0.991	0.995	0.981	0.987	0.978	0.919	0.975	1.000

Source: Ziemba (1991b)

All the correlations of land with the NSA are high, the lowest being
0.82 for industrial land throughout Japan. The six largest cities have the
highest land prices and their land values correlate very highly with the
NSA. All land is at 0.963, housing at 0.956 and commercial land at 0.988.
Industrial land, much of which is lower priced large acreage, correlates
less well with the NSA.

The lag behind correlations appear in Table 2.37.

Table 2.37
Correlations Between Current NSA Values and Lagged Behind Land
Values, Semiannual Data, 1955-88

| | Current | Land Indices Throughout Japan Six Months Before | | | | Land Indices in 6 Largest Cities Six Months Before | | | |
| | NSA | ALL | COML | HOUSE | INDL | ALL | COML | HOUSE | INDL |
	1	2	3	4	5	6	7	8	9
1	1.000								
2	0.853	1.000							
3	0.847	0.998	1.000						
4	0.873	0.995	0.988	1.000					
5	0.816	0.996	0.998	0.983	1.000				
6	0.945	0.970	0.969	0.973	0.953	1.000			
7	0.978	0.905	0.906	0.911	0.881	0.980	1.000		
8	0.940	0.972	0.966	0.982	0.951	0.996	0.968	1.000	
9	0.868	0.993	0.996	0.982	0.992	0.980	0.929	0.974	
1.000									

Source: Ziemba (1991b)

Finally, lagging forward, the current NSA and the six month future
land index values are shown in Table 2.38.

Table 2.38
Correlations of the Current NSA index with Six Month Later Land
Indices, Semiannual Data 1955-88

| | Current NSA | Land Indices Throughout Japan Six Months Before | | | | Land Indices in 6 Largest Cities Six Months Before | | | |
| | | ALL | COML | HOUSE | INDL | ALL | COML | HOUSE | INDL |
	1	2	3	4	5	6	7	8	9
1	1.000								
2	0.863	1.000							
3	0.868	0.998	1.000						
4	0.875	0.996	0.989	1.000					
5	0.824	0.996	0.996	0.984	1.000				
6	0.976	0.946	0.951	0.948	0.923	1.000			
7	0.993	0.860	0.871	0.864	0.827	0.978	1.000		
8	0.966	0.960	0.960	0.968	0.935	0.995	0.960	1.000	
9	0.915	0.984	0.990	0.975	0.977	0.979	0.923	0.978	1.000

Source: Ziemba (1991b)

These correlations are higher than the lag behinds and contemporaneous correlations and suggest that the NSA's current value predicts land values in the future better than the reverse. The correlation with commercial land six months later in the six largest cities is an astounding 0.993, or an R^2 of 0.986 for a regression fit. Hence, the level of the NSA explains nearly 99% of the level of commercial land prices in Japan's six largest cities in the past 34 years. See Ziemba (1991b) for more on these correlations. See Canaway (1990) for studies that also suggest that stock prices increases lead land price increases by about eleven months.

A major conclusion of this study is that the single best predictor of stock price levels in Japan is the price of commercial land in the six largest cities and vice versa. These two economic series are simply very closely related and over periods of several years nearly fully explain one another.

Using index values is fraught with econometric difficulties. To get a deeper understanding of the relationship between land and stock prices in Japan, Stone and Ziemba (1990) focused on rates of return and an analysis of returns in various subperiods. Figure 2.25 shows that despite the astronomical land prices, the stock market, as measured by the Topix, has actually gone up much more since 1971.

Figure 2.25   Land and Stock Index Values, 1971-1989

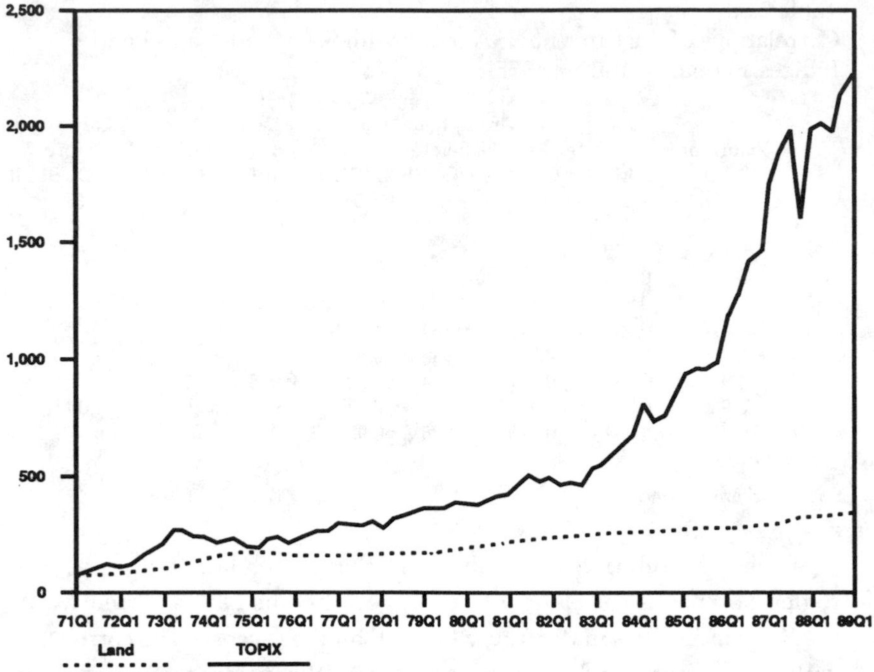

Source: Stone and Ziemba (1990)

Table 2.39   Comparison of Growth of Value of Japanese Land Indices

	National			
	All	Comm	Resid	Indus
Number of times increase 1955:1 to 1990:2,	65.5	59.6	81.2	56.7
Number of times increase 1955:1 to 1970:2	15.1	14.5	15.5	15.8
Number of times increase 1970:2 to 1990:2	4.3	4.1	5.2	3.6
	Six Largest Cities			
	All	Comm	Resid	Indus
Number of times increase 1955:1 to 1990:2,	178.8	127.7	219.1	150.8
Number of times increase 1955:1 to 1970:2,	18.7	11.0	20.2	23.6
Number of times increase 1970:2 to 1990:2	9.6	11.6	10.8	6.4

Table 2.39 summarizes the land price increases from 1955 to 1989 and from 1971 to 1989. Since 1955 land is up 100-175 times in the six largest

cities, while stocks were up 109 times. However, the big rise in land prices relative to stock prices was *prior* to 1971. Since 1971 land is up 5 to 10 times in the six largest cities and 3 to 4 times overall. Meanwhile stocks were up about twenty times. Land has had only one correction; the 5-8% decline after the 1973/74 oil crisis. Stocks, on the other hand, had twenty corrections of ten percent or more up to 1989 plus the two steep declines in 1990.

However, as shown in Figure 2.26, stocks returns were much more variable than land returns during 1971 to 1989.

Figure 2.26   Land and Stock Index Values, Quarterly, 1971-1989

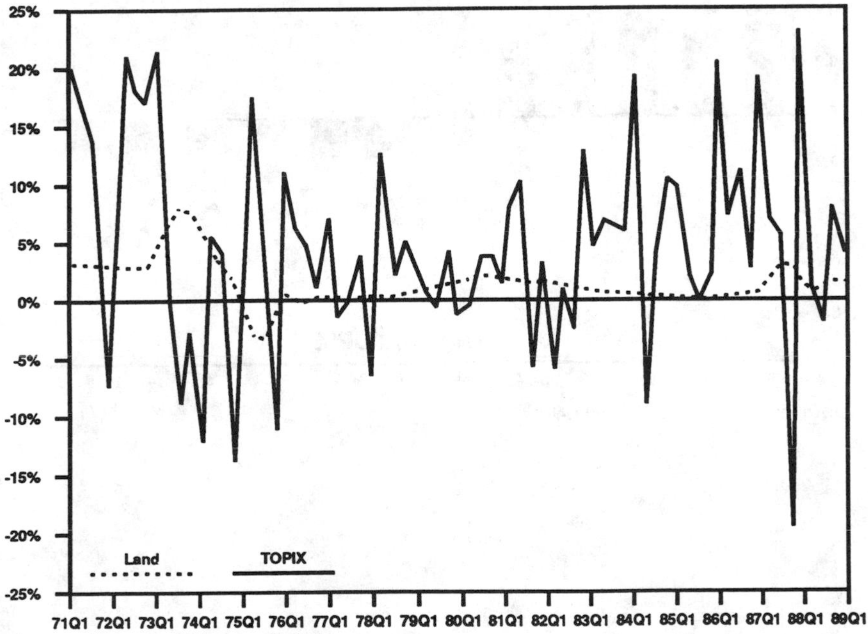

Source: Stone and Ziemba (1990)

Figure 2.27a and Table 2.40 provide strong evidence that stock returns lead land returns and not the reverse. Comparing Topix returns with national and all land returns, there is a negative correlation with spot returns. However, with Topix returns lagged six, twelve or eighteen months, there is a strong and consistent positive correlation with all forms of land. Six-cities land correlates higher than all land in short periods. However, over twelve to eighteen month periods, the correlation is similar, around 40% and if anything, overall land returns

are affected more by previous stock returns than six-cities land. The
latter simply reacts faster.[4] The comparison of the Russell 1000 stock
index, in Figure 2.27b, with the Russell-NCREIF property index shows
that there is no such strong effect in U.S. markets.

Figure 2.27a
Cross-Correlations Topix and National Land, All, 1971:1-1989:1

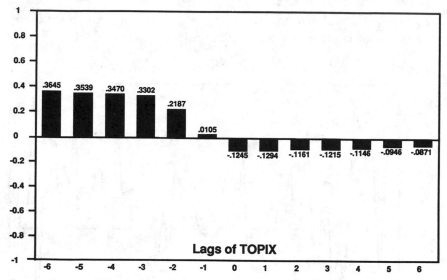

Source: Stone and Ziemba (1990)

---

[4]Stone and Ziemba (1990) provide a formal test using the Granger-Sims causality test
with lags of order four for all land returns versus Topix returns from 1972Q1 to 1987Q2.
The results were:

Null Hypothesis	$F(4,53)$	pValue
H1: Topix returns do not lead all land returns	8.857	0.000149
H2: All land returns do not lead Topix returns	1.722	0.15872

Hence H1 is strongly rejected, that is, stock price returns do lead land price returns.
Moreover, H2 cannot be rejected, so land price returns do not lead stock price returns.

Figure 2.27b
Cross-Correlations Russell 1000® Index and Russell-NCREIF Property
Index, 1971:1-1989:1

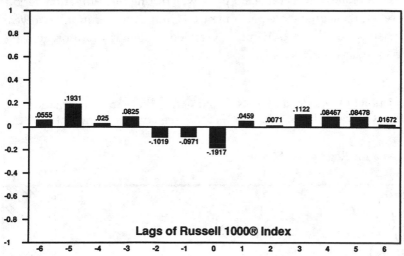

Source: Stone and Ziemba (1990)

Table 2.40
Correlations of Land Returns & Topix Returns, 1971:1 to 1989:1

	No Lags	6 mos lag	12 mos lag	18 mos lag
National Land				
All	-0.124	0.221	0.357	0.416
Commercial	-0.088	0.237	0.377	0.459
Industrial	-0.102	0.188	0.327	0.357
Housing	-0.157	0.216	0.363	0.424
Six City Land				
All	-0.040	.0338	0.374	0.388
Commercial	-0.005	0.297	0.310	0.369
Industrial	-0.063	0.315	0.319	0.399
Housing	-0.063	0.350	0.387	0.332

Source: Stone and Ziemba (1990)

Stone and Ziemba estimated econometric models that use past stock price returns in an attempt to predict current overall land price returns. The three classes of models estimated were:

a. A dynamic regression model with autoregressive terms.

b. A Box-Jenkins model.

c. An autogressive conditional heteroscedastic model.

Figure 2.28 shows the results of these models in the sample estimation period, 1972:2 to 1989:1, and in the forecast period, 1989:2 to 1990:3. The models all follow the actual land price well during the estimation period. However, their predictive performance is much weaker in the two year forecast period. The dynamic regression model with autoregressive terms predicts the best.

Figure 2.28
Prediction of Land Price Models In and Out of the Sample Estimation Period, Quarterly Data, 1972:3 to 1989:1 and a Forecast Period of 1989:2 to 1990:3

a. Dynamic Regression Model

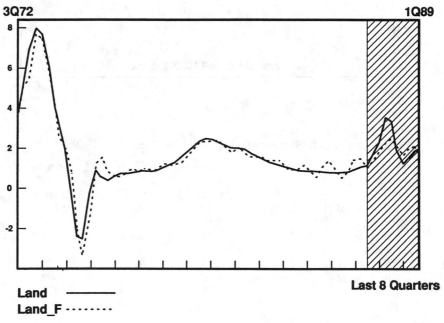

b. Box Jenkins Model*

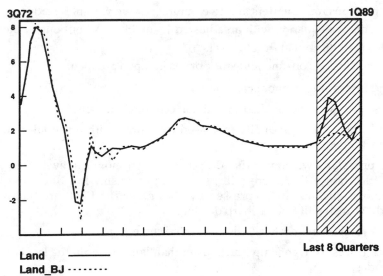

*The equation used was an Arima (2,2,1) ,namely

$$y_t - y_{t-2} = 0.2616 y_{t-1} - 0.61376\, y_{t-2} - 0.8129\, \varepsilon_{t-1} + \varepsilon_t.$$

c: ARCH Model

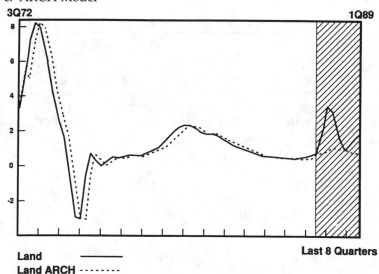

Source: Stone and Ziemba (1990)

This model is summarized in Table 2.41. Using lagged Topix returns for the previous four quarters and two autoregressive variables leads to a good predictive equation with an adjusted R^2 of 95%. All but one of the variables is significant at the 5% level.

The conclusions on land and stock prices in Japan are then:

1. Land prices are astronomical in Japan.

2. These prices can be justified by rational economic models.

3. Land prices have gradually increased over time with essentially no corrections.

4. The prevailing wisdom is that despite their astronomical levels there is little chance that there will be a gigantic crash. But dissenting opinions, such as that expressed by *The Economist* (1990) are that a credit crunch will force a sharp decline.

5. Stock returns are more volatile with more corrections.

6. Stock prices have gone up much faster than land prices in the last two decades.

7. Stock returns lead land returns.

Table 2.41
The Dynamic Regression Model to Predict Land Price Changes Using Past Stock Price Returns

Variable	Coefficient	Standard Error	t-Statistic	Significance
Constant	0.9689	0.4041	2.3980	0.0160
Topix (-4)	0.0128	0.0072	1.7880	0.0740
Topix (-3)	0.0355	0.0108	3.2910	0.0010
Topix (-2)	0.0398	0.0108	3.6650	0.0001
Topix (-1)	0.0161	0.0070	2.2920	0.0220
Auto (-1)	1.6509	0.0833	19.7970	0.0001
Auto (-2)	-0.8001	0.0832	-9.6160	0.0001

R2	0.954
Adjusted R2	0.949
Akaike Criterion (AIC)	0.464
Schwarz Criterion (BIC)	0.526
Durbin Watson	1.605
RMS Error	0.411

Source: Stone and Ziemba (1990)

GOLF COURSE MEMBERSHIP RETURNS AND STOCK RETURNS

The value of golf courses in Japan alone are worth more than the entire Australian stock market. Actually, with the phenomenal increase in land prices in 1988 and 1989, the enormous growth in the number of courses in Japan, and the sharp fall in the Australian dollar, the golf courses win out easily. The Australian stock market's value at some A$250 billion is well below the sum of the golf course memberships in Japan at the more than 400 courses. Valuations of golf courses consist of land values, memberships, greens fees and the like. Golf is extremely popular in Japan. It provides the opportunity to relax, to spend time in pleasant surroundings away from the city and to conduct business and to make and cement friendships. Memberships in good courses cost about $500,000 and, in the best courses, up to ¥100 million, some $7.4 million at the end of 1990 exchange rate of ¥135 per dollar. With hundreds of memberships and high greens fees for guests, the sums are staggering.

The Narita area has many golf courses. On the flight into Tokyo, one sees at least four major courses plus several others under construction. WTZ was invited by his boss to join in a round of golf at a good quality course near Narita airport. The invitation to play golf with the *boss* is a multi-event process. First, there is at least one practice session - the guest couldn't be an embarrassment and this one had only played once in the last twenty years. (In high school, he did play occasionally and was a caddy, but that was thirty years ago.) A colleague and his wife came out for us on a Sunday, and both of us and our daughter and an American visitor were all also treated to the golf practice. WTZ was even treated to a special leather golf glove.

The driving range itself is interesting. Remember land is at a premium and driving ranges are easy to spot. The plots of land are completely covered on the sides and top with green netting. They are double or even triple decked and covered so you can play in the rain. Running them is extremely profitable because they do not use much land, are easy to maintain, and serve hundreds of customers paying high fees each day. They are constantly full of golfers practicing before the next time they play on a course.

Another event was buying WTZ a pair of golf shoes. His colleague found a store that had Western sizes and picked us up on a Sunday afternoon to take us into Tokyo. There, after much practice including photos of his swing, the necessary equipment was secured, including a bag to hold everything.

Then came the game itself at a lovely course near Narita airport with three sets of nine holes. After the drive to the course, the ritual included a morning tea, purchase of golf balls, a drink break after five holes, one set of holes and then lunch, followed by the next set with the snack break after the fourteenth hole, a hot tub bath at the end, and an hour long ride home. The caddies -*the best in the world* as they are called - were 60-70 year old women decked out in hats and rain jackets. They really know the course, the irons to use, and the roll of the green. It's easy to understand the enthusiasm for golf. On the course, it felt like being in beautiful British Columbia.

The day cost ¥30,000 in greens fees for each person except the leader who paid ¥6000 because a company colleague had a membership. Incidently, in 1989, the membership was worth about $400,000. The cost of playing golf for the day for the four of us was around $2000. Although the firm's executives often have access to company memberships, the rank and file employee who strives for success in the company still must pay over ¥25,000 each time he or she plays just for greens fees not to mention all the other expenses associated with the sport. This along with practice sessions and equipment can amount to more than $1000 each month.

Indices of golf course membership in various parts of Japan have been computed by the Nihon Keizei Shimbum, Inc., since January 1982 when they were set at 100. Table 2.42 gives the Nikkei Golf Membership indices as of May 13, 1989 along with the change in the index in absolute and percentage terms for the previous week and the index four, twenty five and fifty weeks earlier. The index is updated at the end of each week by Nikkei from interviews with the six major golf membership dealers who deal in the top 400 clubs. The brokers supply the current bid and ask prices of each club and the index is the arithmetic average of these. When there are no bid or ask prices, statistical substitution is used to adjust the index to maintain continuity.

$$I \quad = \quad \frac{1}{2} \sum_{i=1}^{400} \frac{Bid_i + Ask_i}{400} \, .$$

There are some 700 membership dealers in Tokyo and over 1000 in total. Members own a share of the golf course land, the expected appreciation of value along with the popularity of the club influences its price. According to *The Economist*,

> ... there is the unquantifiable prestige of being able to rub golf-bags with Japan's elite in business and politics - a source, if the recent Recruit share-trading scandal is any indication, of invaluable information with which to make the sort of stockmarket killings that make even Japan's golf-club memberships look cheap.

Tokyo had increased from 100 to 425.14 on May 13, 1989 a very large increase. But other areas have had much sharper price rises: Osaka was at 924.60, Kyoto at 1139.81, and Wakagama prefecture at 1678.35.

Figure 2.29 compares the Nikkei Golf Membership index for the whole country and for Tokyo with that of the NSA, the price weighted index of 225 TSE-I from 1982-90:1. The index initially peaked on February 22, 1987, at 552.26, up some 450% since 1982, and it has consistently out-performed the stock market. As *The Economist* mentions, it may lead the stock market:

> The Golf Membership Index fell in June (stocks in October), up in September (stocks in January); down in November (stocks kept going up in March, oops!); and up in February (stocks in August).

The index in Tokyo has mirrored the NSA quite closely, except in the period just prior to the 1987 stock market crash and in 1990, coinciding with the 21st and 22nd stock market corrections. After the stock market crash in October 1987, memberships were sold to cover stock losses and to meet margin calls. Prices collapsed for most of the courses except the most prestigious clubs such as Tokyo's Koganei whose price stayed at ¥340 million ($2.4 million) and the very cheap clubs whose membership sold for less than ¥5 million. The NSA and Tokyo golf indices were then in balance until 1990 and into 1991.

Figure 2.29
The NSA Index versus the Nikkei Golf Membership Index, 1981:4-1991:1

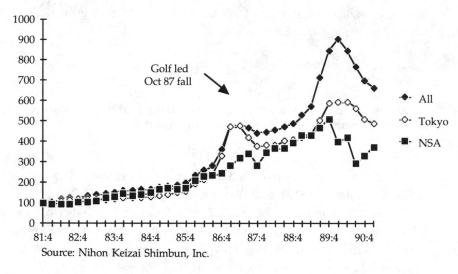

Source: Nihon Keizai Shimbun, Inc.

Figure 2.30a
Nikkei Golf Course Membership Indices for All, Western and Eastern
Japan versus the NSA, 1981:4-91:1

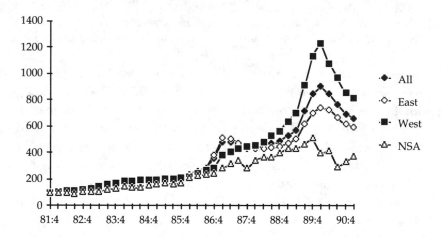

Source: Nihon Keizai Shimbun, Inc.

Figure 2.30b
Golf Course Membership Indices for Tokyo, Osaka, Kyoto, Nara and
Wakayama versus the NSA, 1981:4-91:1

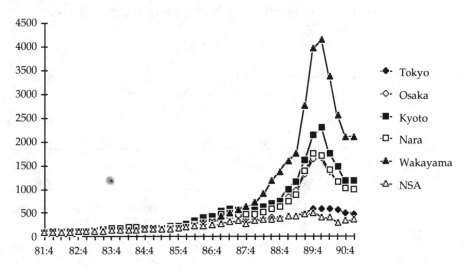

Source: Nihon Keizai Shimbun, Inc.

Figure 2.31
Golf Course Membership Indices for Tokyo, Osaka, Kyoto, Nara,
Wakayama and All Japan versus the NSA, 1986:1-91:1

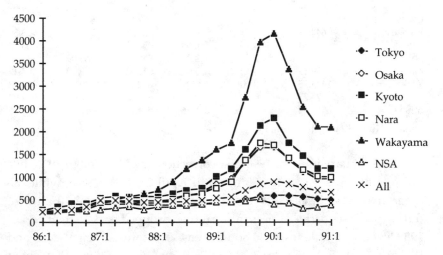

Source: Nihon Keizai Shimbun, Inc.

Figure 2.31 considers the 1986 to 1991 period when the golf memberships exploded, outpacing the NSA, which also rose sharply in absolute and PER terms, see Figure 5.1. There is clearly a gap to be filled here to bring the golf membership index, particularly for Tokyo, back into line with the NSA.

Table 2.42
Golf Course Membership Indices for May 13, 1989 and for 4, 25 and 50 Weeks Earlier, January 1982 = 100 for Various Parts of Japan

Area	Index May 13,' 89	Absolute change in week	% change in week	Index Value -4 weeks	-25 weeks	-50 weeks
all	544.90	6.27	1.16	533.18	480.47	452.12
eastern	480.97	5.32	1.12	470.26	442.25	435.79
western	670.15	8.22	1.24	656.59	548.88	470.50
East:						
Tokyo	425.14	3.89	0.92	413.81	406.09	384.40
Kanagawa	395.33	2.43	0.62	391.77	354.16	355.10
Chiba	527.25	5.19	0.99	522.23	506.33	513.12
Saitama	380.58	2.10	0.55	374.77	374.92	371.75
Ibaraki	574.98	6.91	1.22	562.12	537.45	536.71
Tochigi	616.95	9.10	1.50	596.34	563.89	585.00
Gunma	896.21	10.94	1.24	873.83	785.46	721.83
Shizukoka	851.67	17.13	2.05	815.84	708.89	675.79
other	888.65	26.58	3.08	822.34	652.33	584.50
West:						
Aichi	473.97	0.19	0.04	473.29	476.72	475.44
Gifu	530.58	1.17	0.22	528.53	521.06	519.75
Mie	683.46	0.00	0.00	687.30	658.62	624.87
Osaka	924.60	10.62	1.16	887.07	639.77	480.09
Hyogo	642.16	0.21	0.03	635.49	502.78	403.50
Kyoto	1139.81	84.75	8.03	1050.97	748.18	600.88
Shiga	880.06	17.58	2.04	843.56	663.09	531.28
Nara	839.11	24.43	3.00	812.55	619.50	498.42
Wakayama	1678.35	0.00	0.00	1642.96	1329.38	816.33
Kyusho	625.77	0.00	0.00	619.56	574.62	544.94
others	564.64	7.05	1.26	544.73	467.34	395.76

Source: Nihon Keizai Shimbum, Inc.

In the January to April 1990 21st correction, the NSA fell to 392 while Tokyo golf courses rose to 588 up until April 21, 1990. Meanwhile, all other areas rose in early 1990 with many increases in the 10% range during the first quarter. Prices in April then dropped back to their end of 1989 levels or a little lower in some areas. Kyoto was then at 2065 and Wakayama at 3554. Figures 2.29 and 2.30 (a,b) display this. They show that all the golf course membership indices have consistently risen except during the 1987 crash and from April to December 1990. Most areas rose much faster than in Tokyo or the NSA before the 1990 decline.

Figure 2.32   Correlation of Topix and Tokyo Golf Course Values

Variance of Input = 124.731
Number of Observations = 29

Gross Correlations

```
LAG COVARIANCE  CORRELATION -1 9 8 7 6 5 4 3 2 1 0 1 2 3 4 5 6 7 8 9 1
 -8    20.2348    0.20387                            *###
 -7   -15.6733   -0.15791                 .   ###
 -6   -17.5775   -0.17709                 .  ####
 -5    -8.41506  -0.08478                 .   ##
 -4    18.9397    0.19082                 .      ####
 -3     4.25956   0.04292                 .      #
 -2     4.00803   0.04119                 .      #
 -1     4.8322    0.04868                 .      #
  0    35.1953    0.35459                 .      ########
  1    25.3228    0.25513                 .      #####
  2     1.79558   0.01809                 .      #
  3   -29.8133   -0.30037              .  #####
  4    12.4909    0.12585                 .    ###
  5     9.26027   0.09330                 .   ##
  6   -17.7073   -0.17840              .   ####
  7   -23.3906   -0.23566              .  #####
  8     9.99565   0.10071                 .    ##
          .' MARKS TWO STANDARD ERRORS
```

OBS	period	TSERET	TOOKOOLF	OBS	period	TSERET	TOOKOOLF
1	82QI	-5.637	3.861	16	85Q4	2.515	5.512
2	82Q2	1.188	5.181	17	86Q1	20.896	24.994
3	82Q3	-2.063	3.044	18	86Q2	7.453	9.683
4	82Q4	13.487	4.901	19	86Q3	11.670	12.676
5	83Q1	4.938	0.867	20	86Q4	2.743	36.866
6	83Q2	7.126	-2.287	21	87Q1	19.577	42.353
7	83Q3	6.555	-1.799	22	87Q2	7.350	1.037
6	83Q4	6.180	3.281	23	87Q3	5.805	-11.872
9	84Q1	19.670	3.311	24	87Q4	-19.483	-8.769
10	84Q2	-8.721	2.668	25	88Q1	23.813	-1.382
11	84Q3	4.225	0.166	26	88Q2	1.490	1.444
12	84Q4	10.061	1.899	27	88Q3	-1.755	6.054
13	85QI	9.860	6.203	28	88Q4	8.332	0.586
14	85Q2	2.892	3.604	29	89Q1	4.294	2.833
15	85Q3	0.068	4.318				

Source: Stone and Ziemba (1990)

In 1989, the index finally reached and surpassed the February 1987 levels with the July 1, 1989, index at 573.74. Table D3 in the appendix gives the golf course indices for all courses, eastern and western Japan, Tokyo, Osaka, Kyoto, Nara and Wakayama prefecture by quarter from January 1982 to March 1991.

The NSA peaked at 510 at the end of 1989 with Tokyo golf then at 588. Other areas, where golf memberships were catching up with Tokyo, were much higher. Osaka, for example, was at 1646, Kyoto at 2134, Nara at

1742 and Wakayama at an astounding 3967. After the peak in April 1990, there was a substantial decline during the rest of the year.

Stone and Ziemba (1990) looked into the causality more carefully using quarterly data on price changes from 1982 to 1990. Their results do not lead to the conclusion that the golf course indices lead the stock market. However, the golf course indices do seem to lead other forms of land price appreciation.

Using lead and lag correlations for the eight quarters before and after a given period, Stone and Ziemba found no clear pattern of potential causality between the golf course returns and the stock market returns as measured by the Topix. As shown in Figure 2.32, none of these correlations is significantly different from zero at the 5% level.

An equation to attempt to predict Topix returns is

$$\text{Topix Ret}_t = 5.397 + 0.3741 \text{ TokGolf}_{t-2} - 0.6937 \text{ Golf}_{t-3} + 0.4678 \text{ Golf}_{t-4}$$
$$\phantom{\text{Topix Ret}_t = } (2.872) \quad (2.270) \qquad\qquad (-3.540) \qquad\qquad (2.828)$$

$R^2 = 0.385$, R^2 adj $= 0.297$, and $N = 23$.

This equation was fit up to the end of the first quarter of 1989. Using the equation to predict the Topix returns for the next six quarters gave the following results:

Period	Predicted TSEret	Actual	Golf2	Golf3	Golf4
June 1989	2.09	-0.68	0.59	6.05	1.44
Sept 1989	6.05	10.46	2.83	0.59	6.05
Dec 1989	4.62	6.74	3.18	2.83	0.59
Mar 1990	9.49	-22.59	16.84	3.18	2.83
June 1990	-0.07	5.20	16.62	16.84	3.18
Sept 1990	-5.90	-32.96	0.61	16.62	16.84

The 1989 predictions are reasonable but the model gave poor results in 1990.

While the proposition that golf course returns lead stock returns is dubious, Stone and Ziemba did find that Tokyo golf does seem to lead national land prices. First, as shown in Figure 2.33 many of the lead and lag correlations are significant at the 5% level and there seems to be a clear causality: golf course membership returns lead land returns.

Figure 2.33
Lead and Lag Correlations, Tokyo Golf and National Land Returns for 29
Quarters from 1982:1 to 1989:1

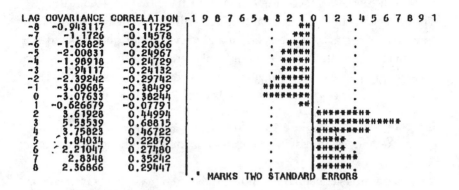

```
LAG  COVARIANCE  CORRELATION -1 9 8 7 6 5 4 3 2 1 0 1 2 3 4 5 6 7 8 9 1
 -8   -0.943117    -0.11725                    .      ##
 -7    -1.1726     -0.14578                    .     ###
 -6    -1.63825    -0.20366                    .   ####
 -5    -2.00831    -0.24967                    .  ######
 -4    -1.98918    -0.24729                    . ######
 -3    -1.94117    -0.24132                    . #####
 -2    -2.39242    -0.29742                    .#######
 -1    -3.09685    -0.38499                  ########
  0    -3.07633    -0.38244                  ########
  1   -0.626679    -0.07791                    .  ##
  2    3.61928     0.44994                    .       #########
  3    5.53539     0.68815                    .       ##################
  4    3.75823     0.46722                    .       ##########
  5    1.84034     0.22879                    .       #####
  6    2.21047     0.27480                    .       ######
  7    2.8348      0.35242                    .       ########
  8    2.36866     0.29447                    .       ######
                                .* MARKS TWO STANDARD ERRORS
```

Source: Stone and Ziemba (1990)

Stone and Ziemba provided two equations to predict national land returns from lagged Tokyo golf. The first equation has an adjusted R^2 of 0.478 but has a high auto correlation of errors. It is highly significant that Tokyo golf returns lagged three quarters.

National
Land$_t$ = 0.911 + 0.0457 TokGolf$_{t-3}$ - 0.0169 Golf$_{t-6}$
     (6.02)   (4.59)   (1.678)

$R^2 = 0.522$, R^2 adj $= 0.478$, and first order autocorrelation $= 0.694$ which is high.

Using a lagged error term to eliminate the autocorrelation problem yields the equation

National
Land$_t$ = 1.18 + 0.0344 TokGolf$_{t-3}$ - 0.00309 Golf$_{t-6}$ - 0.875 ε_{t-1}
     (2.55)   (5.62)   (0.499)   (-7.27)

$R^2 = 0.613$, total $R^2 = 0.861$. Tokyo golf lagged three quarters and lagged errors are highly significant and provide a good predictive equation.

There have been substantial declines in the golf course membership indices in 1990. Land itself has not fallen. The NSA has had a steep decline. If the past is a guide there will be downward pressure on land prices which will tend to make them flat until conditions improve for them to rise again.

CAN PROFESSIONAL FUND MANAGERS BEAT THE MARKET AVERAGES?

The evidence is that professional managers all over the world have a hard time beating the market averages. In a given year, only about 25% to 40% of managers actually beat a buy-and-hold strategy of holding the index. Over longer periods, say 5-10 years, the percentage is even lower. There are a number of reasons for this. For example, from U.S. research:

- The market averages stay fully invested at all times, never missing market moves nor paying commissions for stock changes and market timing.

- When funds get behind the index, they often make hasty moves to try to catch up and, more often than not, this puts them further behind.

- Portfolio managers have a tendency to window dress at reporting times, adding to turnover and commissions.

- Since the managers collectively more or less *are* the market (with individual investors forming less and less of the market each year) the indices, on average, beat half of the fund managers. Then with commissions, fees, and these other reasons, only the 25% to 40% typically beat the market averages (which does quite well with a lot less work).

- The fund managers take fees; the averages work for free.

- The fund managers' goals may get in the way of the fund's best interests. This is the the so-called agency problem.

- Portfolio managers tend to follow each other's moves. They tend to move the market which gains the full amount, and they can easily be a little behind.

A portfolio trustee suggested the following four reasons the high commissions of active trading often lead to poorer performance than the market indices. First, commissions are higher in active portfolios because the turnover is greater. Second, the bid-ask spreads are larger for many smaller international securities that an active manager would buy. Third, exchange taxes can be as large as 1% on both buys and sells. Fourth, active managers usually hold a small number of large positions so they have market impact on getting in and out.

Table 2.43
Sector Median Returns of Hong Kong Based Funds Compared with
Market Averages, January 1 to November 30, 1988

Class of Fund	Median Return, %	Reference Market Average	% Change	Number of Funds Outperforming Market Average
Japanese equity funds	19.1	TSE Index	34.9	4 of 30
Hong Kong equity funds	24.4	Hang Seng index	20.8	9 of 15
Australian equity funds	23.1	All-Ordinaries index	43.3	1 of 11
Singapore/Malaysian equity funds	25.8	FT Actuaries Singapore	25.9	3 of 7
Asean equity funds	41.4	FT Actuaries HK & Singapore	27.7	11 of 13
Far East equity funds	22.1	FT Actuaries Pacific	35.1	3 of 20
US equity funds	7.6	S&P Composite	14.0	5 of 25
British equity funds	6.8	FT All Shares Index	10.9	4 of 19
European equity funds	13.0	FT Actuaries Europe	13.9	7 of 15
International managed funds	9.4	FT Actuaries World	23.1	0 of 6
British gilt funds	1.0	FT All Stock Bond index	5.0	1 of 6
			(28.7%)	48 of 167

Source: *Far Eastern Economic Review*

   Table 2.43 gives such results for 1988 for 167 funds based in Hong
Kong with investments in various parts of the world. Only 48, or 28.7%,
actually beat the benchmark indices. ASEAN equity funds did do well,
averaging 41.4% returns versus the market's 27.7%, and 11 of the 13 funds
beat this measure. But Japanese equity funds did not fare so well.
Indeed only 4 out of 30 funds beat the TSE index of 34.9% and their
average return was 19.1%, more than 15 points below the Topix.

GAINS FROM DIVERSIFICATION IN JAPANESE STOCKS BY U.S. INVESTORS
It is beyond the scope of this book to fully cover the gains possible from
international diversification of portfolios. An excellent survey of this
literature up to 1986 appears in Solnik (1988). In this section, we briefly
discuss this topic using the results in Bailey and Stulz (1990). This study
did not use any currency hedging strategies. Such procedures as
outlined in Chapter 6 would strengthen the results, particularly the
strong results in favor of Japan. The Bailey Stulz data are from January
1977 to December 1985. Table 2.44 shows the daily correlations of the
NSA and other Pacific Basin stock markets with the S&P 500.

Table 2.44
Correlations of Pacific Basin Index Returns with that of the S&P 500 in
U.S. Dollars, January 1977 to December 1985

	Daily Serial Correlation	Correlations with the S&P 500 Returns Computed		
		Daily	Weekly	Monthly
Japan NSA	0.086*	0.179*	0.256*	0.263*
Australia, All Ordinaries	0.085	0.292*	0.300*	0.368*
Hong Kong, Hang Seng	0.110*	0.184*	0.251*	0.156*
Malaysia, Industrials and Commercials	0.044	0.185*	0.180*	0.229*
Philippines, Manila Mining	0.037	0.102*	0.216*	0.258
Singapore, All-Shares	0.046	0.188*	0.196*	0.292*
S. Korea, Composite	-0.031	-0.018	-0.076	0.080
Taiwan, Weighted Index	0.050*	0.064*	0.184*	0.278*
Thailand, Book Club	-0.004	0.001	-0.120	-0.128

*Denotes that the correlation coefficient is significantly different from zero at
the 0.05 level.

Source: Bailey and Stulz (1990)

Because of time differences, it is not possible to optimally match the
returns on consistent days. However, since New York closes before the
other markets open on the next (t+1) day, those correlations are the most
relevant for the daily data. The results for the two ways of computing the
daily correlations in Table 2.44 also present further evidence that the New
York markets lead the Asian markets and that this correlation is much
larger than the effect of the Asian markets on the U.S. markets. A further
conclusion from Table 2.44 is that the longer the measurement interval,
the more closely the Pacific Basin markets move with the U.S. securities.
Bailey and Stulz utilized the raw results. Further research will
investigate the interesting question of how new returns are generated in
each market net of that which could be predicted based on the general
correlations and the prior movements in New York on the previous day.

Figure 2.34
Efficient Frontier from 1977 to 1985 in Annualized U.S. Returns Using the
S&P 500 and Pacific Basin Indices*

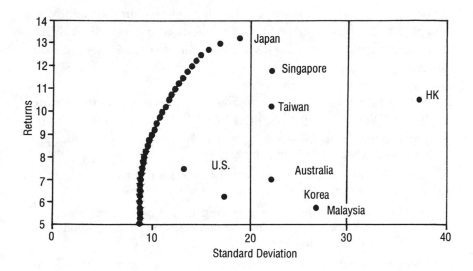

*The Philippines and Thailand are not shown here because their average returns are too low to fit in the figure.

Source: Bailey and Stulz (1990)

Bailey and Stulz computed an efficient frontier in mean-standard deviation space utilizing the S&P 500 and the other Asian stock market indices all computed in U.S. funds. Shown in Figure 2.34, the results indicate that none of the pure country indices appears on the efficient frontier except Japan in the monthly case. The S&P 500 is well inside the frontiers suggesting a strong advantage to international diversification of U.S. portfolios. Such an investor can reduce portfolio standard deviation to about 6% with diversification from about 13% for the S&P 500 without changing the mean return. This is for daily returns. With monthly returns, the reduction in risk is from 13% to 9%. These results show that the gains from international diversification are larger the shorter the time period chosen.

INTERNATIONAL DIVERSIFICATION BY U.S. INVESTORS

Foreign investment by U.S. pension plans and other tax-exempt institutions was about $60 billion in 1988 versus only $3 billion in 1980. This is still only about 3% of their total assets. With Japan alone amounting to 30-40% of the world's stock market capitalization until 1990 and offering extremely high returns, one questions the wisdom of such a low international exposure. Reasons for the low investment abroad include:

- The comfort factor: pension boards and investment companies are more comfortable with what they think they know - the U.S. market.

- Regulations: most tax-exempt plans have limits on asset allocation classes such as 10% in foreign investments.

- Fear: there is fear involved with having one's resources invested abroad because of possible currency and repatriation changes.

- Transactions costs: the cost of investing abroad both in terms of costs of currency exchange, taxes, transaction costs, and management fees exceeds that of U.S. investments.

- Prejudice: some pension trustees perceive investment abroad and particularly in Japan as giving help to a competitor.

- Lack of knowledge: less is known about foreign investment and its advantages and disadvantages.

- Currency risk: foreign investment naturally involves currency risk, so that the total return is the return in local currency plus the currency gain or loss.

How much should one invest abroad? This is a deep and difficult problem. References to relevant studies appear at the end of this section. The evidence seems to overwhelmingly suggest that it should be significantly more than 3%.

Jorion (1989) studied the wisdom of foreign investment for U.S. investors during the eleven year period 1978-1988. Table 2.45 shows the performance, in U.S. funds, of U.S. stocks and bonds as well as foreign stocks and bonds both unhedged or hedged against currency changes. The various classes of investments were measured by the following indices with all dividends and coupons reinvested:

U.S. stocks   S&P 500
U.S. bonds   Salomon Brothers U.S. Government Bond Index
Foreign stocks   Morgan Stanley EAFE Index (Europe, Australia,
                       Far East)
Foreign bonds   Salomon Brothers Non-Dollar Bonds Index.

Table 2.45   Performance of asset classes: January 1978 - December 1988

	U.S. Stocks	Bonds	Foreign Stocks	Bonds	Hedged Foreign Stocks	Bonds
Average return	15.8	9.7	22.9	12.6	20.9	11.3
Volatility	16.5	11.2	17.2	13.7	13.1	6.8
Correlations with						
U.S. stocks	1.00					
bonds	0.29	1.00				
Foreign stocks	0.43	0.23	1.00			
bonds	0.05	0.42	0.66	1.00		
Hedged stocks	0.59	0.12	0.76	0.09	1.00	
bonds	0.19	0.53	0.34	0.58	0.24	1.00
60/40 U.S. mix	0.93	0.62	0.44	0.20	0.53	0.35
Beta with						
60/40 mix	1.28	0.58	0.63	0.22	0.58	0.20
U.S. stocks	1.00	0.20	0.45	0.04	0.47	0.08
U.S. bonds	0.43	1.00	0.35	0.51	0.14	0.32

Source Jorion (1989)

Hedging was done month by month on a rolling basis, with the foreign investment sold at the beginning of the month and the account closed at the end of the month. The returns were value weighted month by month to construct the hedged indices. This hedging procedure is not perfect because it does not consider intra-month portfolio value changes. However, nearly all of the currency risk is eliminated. For currencies with lower interest rates than the U.S., such as Japan, the hedge improves the return. Conversely, for currencies with higher interest rates than the U.S. such as Canada, the hedge lowers the return. For more details on currency hedging, consult Chapter 6. The returns are compared to the common portfolio mix of U.S. pension plans of 60% stocks and 40% bonds.

The conclusions are:

•   Foreign stocks had the highest returns. They outperformed the U.S. market by 7.1 percentage points per year on average, 22.9% versus 15.8%.

- The Solnik-Noetzlin (1982) study shows that foreign stocks also outperformed U.S. stocks in 1970-80.

- The volatility of foreign stocks was slightly higher than U.S. stocks, 17.2% vs. 16.5% in terms of annualized standard deviation.

- Hedged foreign stocks had a slightly lower mean return of 10.9% but significantly lower volatility of 13.1%. The mean-variance of these stocks dominate U.S. stocks with a mean that is 5.1 percentage points higher and a standard deviation that is 3.4 percentage points lower.

- Hedged versus unhedged foreign stocks have a trade off of about twice as much risk avoided per unit of mean return lost.

- Foreign bonds also had higher mean returns than U.S. bonds with slightly higher risk. However, when hedged, the mean-variance of foreign bonds dominate the U.S. bonds. Their mean return of 11.3% was 1.6 percentage points higher than the U.S. bonds and their risk at 6.8% was 4.4 percentage points lower.

- The correlations (Table 2.45) between U.S. and foreign stocks and bonds, 0.43 and 0.42, respectively, are low; hence they diversify a U.S. portfolio well.

Figure 2.35   Portfolio Volatility with Foreign Bonds, 1978-1988

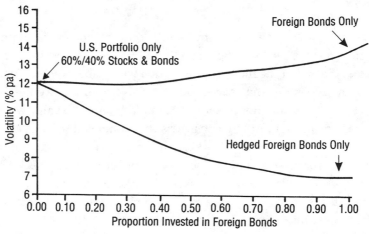

Source: Jorion (1989)

When hedged, foreign bonds strongly lower total portfolio risk as shown in Figure 2.35.

- The more funds placed into hedged foreign bonds, the lower is the total risk.

- The beta values relative to the 60/40 mix, U.S. stocks or U.S. bonds is quite low for foreign stocks and bonds - hedged or unhedged - again suggesting the diversification potential.

- Hedging increases the correlation with U.S. assets, because most exchange rate movements are unrelated to movements in U.S. asset prices and are diversifiable.

Taking into account both lower volatility and higher correlation, hedging barely reduced the systematic risk over the period studied. For foreign bonds, the reduction in volatility from 13.7% to 6.8% is accompanied by an increase in the correlations with the 60/40 U.S. mix from 0.20 to 0.35. Hedging only reduced the beta risk from 0.22 to 0.20. For foreign stocks, hedging reduced the beta from 0.63 to 0.58.

Figure 2.36 shows the asset allocation of a U.S. portfolio with unhedged foreign stocks and bonds.

Figure 2.36
Asset Allocation U.S. Portfolio and with Unhedged Foreign Assets but No Hedged Foreign Assets, 1978-1988

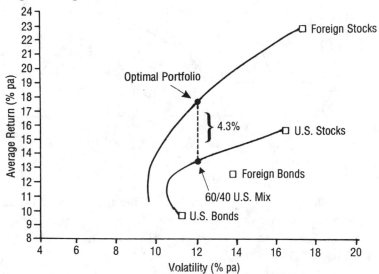

- With unhedged foreign assets, U.S. stocks, U.S. bonds and the 60/40 mix are all on a curve dominated by the optimal portfolio. Foreign stocks are on the efficient frontier. Foreign bonds are dominated by both the U.S. and the world efficient frontiers.

- In comparison with the 60/40 mix, moving to a globally diversified portfolio on the efficient frontier adds 4.3% per year to the return with the same risk.

Adding the hedged foreign stocks and hedged foreign bonds gives an even higher efficient frontier shown in Figure 2.37. The 60/40 mix can be improved by a further 2.5% to provide an additional 6.8% total mean return difference with the same level of risk. The curve in the middle is the efficient frontier without hedged foreign assets.

Figure 2.37   Efficient Frontier with Hedged Foreign Assets, 1978-1988

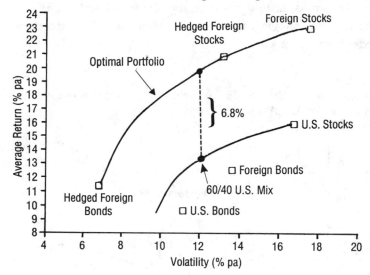

Source: Jorion (1989)

Table 2.46 computes the optimal weights in the various asset classes using a mean-variance approximation to the growth optimal portfolio (namely the portfolio strategy that maximizes wealth over a long period, see Ziemba and Hausch, 1987).

One concludes that:

- Without hedged assets 52% of the portfolio is in foreign stocks, 32% in U.S. bonds, and only 16% in U.S. stocks with no foreign bonds.

- With hedged assets, the optimal portfolio contains *no* U.S. stocks or bonds nor any foreign unhedged stocks. The portfolio contains 9% unhedged foreign bonds, 29% hedged foreign bonds and 62% hedged foreign stocks. Hedged foreign stocks improve the return and foreign bonds partially hedged reduce the risk.

- Jorion (1989) also considered weak and strong subperiods. It is optimal to have large amounts of foreign assets hedged or unhedged in all periods.

- Even if one sets the mean returns equal for U.S. and foreign stocks at 15%, and U.S. and foreign bonds at 10%, and assuming hedging loses 2%, there are still large amounts of foreign stocks and bonds in the optimal portfolio because of diversification.

- Table 2.47 gives the results of limiting each of the four foreign portfolio classes to 10%.

Table 2.46
Asset Allocation with No Limits on Foreign Investments, in Percent

	U.S.		Foreign		Hedged Foreign	
	Stocks	Bonds	Stocks	Bonds	Stocks	Bonds
78/88 actual	15.8	9.7	22.9	12.6	20.9	11.3
Optimal Portfolio						
no hedge	16.0	32.0	52.0	0	-	-
hedging	0	0	0	9.0	62.0	29.0
Subperiods						
78/80 Weak Dollar -						
actual	18.5	6.6	19.9	9.3	15.9	6.0
Optimal Portfolio						
no hedge	43.0	0	57.0	0	-	-
hedging	13.0	0	17.0	0	70.0	0
81/84 Strong Dollar-						
actual	1.2	6.0	8.5	2.8	21.2	16.5
Optimal Portfolio						
no hedge	14.0	76.0	10.0	0	-	-
hedging	0	0	0	0	13.0	87.0
85/88 Weak Dollar -						
actual	18.3	13.2	39.4	24.9	24.4	10.2
Optimal Portfolio						
no hedge	0	7.0	71.0	22.0	-	-
hedging	0	7.0	71.0	22.0	0	0
Hypothetical						
expected returns	15.0	10.0	15.0	10.0	13.0	8.0
Optimal Portfolio						
no hedge	37.0	34.0	0	29.0	-	-
hedging	15.0	17.0	0	9.0	28.0	31.0

Source: Jorion (1989)

- The 60/40 mix would have returned 13.4%, with volatility of 12.0%.

- Adding foreign stocks and bonds improves the performance. Investing 10% in foreign stocks and 10% in foreign bonds increases the return to 14.4% and lowers the risk to 11.1%.

- Hedging and 10% in both foreign stocks and bonds gives a return of 14.0% and a risk of 10.8%.

Table 2.47   Asset Allocation with Limited Foreign Investment

| Percentage invested in | | | | | | Portfolio Performance 1987 | |
| U.S. | | Foreign | | Hedged Foreign | | | |
Stocks	Bonds	Stocks	Bonds	Stocks	Bonds	Return	Risk
60	40	-	-	-	-	13.4	12.0
55	35	10	0	-	-	14.4	11.7
55	35	0	10	-	-	13.3	11.2
50	30	10	10	-	-	14.4	11.1
55	35	-	-	10	0	14.2	11.6
55	35	-	-	0	10	13.2	11.1
50	30	-	-	10	10	14.0	10.8

Source: Jorion (1989)

CONCLUSIONS[5]
- International diversification has historically provided benefits both in terms of higher return and lower risk.

- Allocating 10-20% of a U.S. portfolio to foreign assets lowers total portfolio risk with or without hedging.

- Foreign bonds should be a larger part of foreign portfolios than the 17% of total foreign assets as of the end of 1987. A mix in the 40-50% range is preferable.

- Foreign investments can also be viewed as hedges against imported inflation, as the economy becomes more open and influenced from outside.

- Hedging must be considered carefully and its effect or gain depends upon the percent of foreign investments and where they are located.

- *Caveat*: This study does not use rolling asset distributions, as in practice, so the results are biased in the direction of those assets that in fact did well ex post rather than ex ante.

---

[5]Additional studies on this important question of optimal international diversification are: Jorion (1990ab, 1985), Giovannini and Jorion (1989), Glen (1989), Mulvey (1989), Eun and Resnick (1988), Solnik (1988), Adler and Dumas (1983), Solnik and Noetzlin (1982), Levy and Sarnat (1970), and Grubel (1968).

The 1970s were similar to the 1980s as shown by the study of Solnik and Noetzlin (1982). Figure 2.38 summarizes their findings. U.S. stocks and bonds were much dominated by portfolios formed using foreign stocks and bonds.

Figure 2.38
Efficient Frontier in U.S. Funds, December 1970 to December 1980

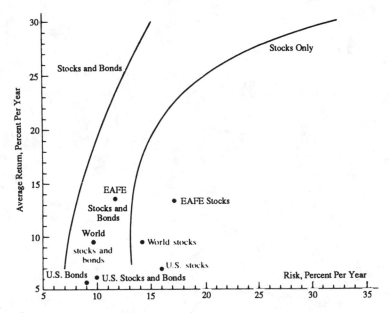

Source: Solnik and Noetzlin (1982)

French and Poterba (1991) have estimated the equity portfolio weights for U.S., Japanese and British investors as of December 1989. As shown in Table 2.48, U.S. investors have 94% at home, Japanese investors 98% and British investors 82%. The U.S. had 1.3% in Japanese and 5.9% in British investments.

Table 2.48
Equity Portfolio Weights for U.S., Japanese and U.K. Investors as of
December 1989

	Portfolio Weights		
	U.S.	Japan	U.K
United States	93.8	1.3	5.9
Japan	3.1	98.1	4.8
United Kingdom	1.1	0.2	82.0
France	0.5	0.1	3.2
Germany	0.5	0.1	3.5
Canada	1.0	0.1	0.6

Source: French and Poterba (1991)

CHAPTER 3
DAY OF THE WEEK EFFECTS IN JAPANESE STOCKS

Many of the anomalies in the U.S. markets also occur in Japan. Although literature on Japanese stock market anomalies is just starting to be written, we do have some good independent studies of intra-day and day of the week, small firm, and January and monthly effects, as well as the development of data bases and arbitrage pricing equations. This chapter, which is based on Kato, Schwartz and Ziemba (1989), is concerned with the day of the week effect. Other anomalies are discussed in Chapter 4.

EVIDENCE FROM THE 1970S AND 1980S

Using data from January 5, 1970, to April 30, 1983, on the Nikkei Stock Average (NSA), Topix and the S&P 500, Jaffe and Westerfield (1985b) found that there was a substantial day of the week effect. This is detailed in Table 3.1.

Table 3.1
Returns in Percent on Stock Indexes in the U.S. and Japan by Day of Week, 1970-83

	Mon	Tues	Wed	Thurs	Fri	Sat	All Days
U.S S&P 500 1970-83							
mean	-0.129	.020	.097	.032	.078		.021
std. dev.	1.015	.883	.924	.823	.827		.889
Japan NSA 1970-83							
mean	-.020	-.090	.150	.026	.063	.115	.038
std. dev.	.876	.788	.815	.875	.788	.668	.817
Japan Topix 1970-83							
mean	-.014	-.064	.124	.026	.057	.099	.035
std. dev.	.701	.684	.671	.741	.626	.530	.672

Returns are computed as $r_t = [(V_t/V_{t-1})-1] \bullet 100$, where V_t is the value of the index at the end of day t.

Source: Jaffe and Westerfield (1985b).

The U.S. results indicate typically sharp average losses on Mondays, with large gains on Wednesdays and Fridays, and modest gains on Tuesdays and Thursdays. In Japan, there are small losses on Mondays and more substantial losses on Tuesdays. In sum Japan's Tuesday losses are more or less in the ballpark of Monday's U.S. losses. One would suspect that these losses would be highly correlated, especially since Japan's trading day starts, depending on the season, 16 or 17 hours before New York's. But, this was not the case during 1970-83; the correlation between Monday's return in New York and Tuesday's return in Japan was only 0.076 for the NSA and 0.004 for the Topix.

Corresponding to the Wednesday and Friday high mean returns in the U.S. are large average gains in Japan on Wednesdays and Saturdays. These gains are about three times the average daily gain of 0.038% and 0.035% on the NSA and Topix, respectively. Jaffe and Westerfield looked at leads and lags of up to five days throughout the week. The lead and lag effects are minuscule with the lead +1 correlation being 0.072 and 0.086, respectively, for the NSA and Topix. The same day correlations are larger, being 0.163 and 0.154, respectively. Still it is a minor relationship during this time period.

More recent studies of the day of the week effect in Japan were done by Ikeda (1985, 1988) (in Japanese), Kato and Schallheim (1985), Kato, Schwartz and Ziemba (1989) and Kato (1990a,b). Some of these results are summarized in Table 3.2. These studies are based on the Topix index, which had 1,229 securities as of autumn 1990, consisting of a value weighted average of the entire first section of the TSE, for January 1, 1977 to December 31, 1986, and April 4, 1978 to June 18, 1987, respectively. Kato also split his data into subperiods from April 4, 1978, to December 31, 1981, and from January 1, 1982, to June 18, 1987. In general, these results are consistent with and reinforce those of Jaffe and Westerfield.

Kato (1990a) tested but did not report results from the NSA because they were similar to his Topix findings. Monday is more or less even, Tuesday is quite negative, Wednesday and Saturday are strongly positive, and Thursday and Friday are moderately positive. One change in Kato's study is that Thursdays became very positive during 1982-1987, and in this later period they nearly rival Wednesday and Saturday. The distribution of returns is weighted a bit more to the right on Monday and Wednesday to Saturday, and to the left on Tuesday than a normal distribution would be. The visual display of Kato's (1990a) data is in Figure 3.1.

Table 3.2   Returns in Percent for the Topix Stock Index by Day of Week

	Mon	Tues	Wed	Thurs	Fri	Sat	All Days
Jan. 1, 1977-Dec. 31, 1986*							
mean	.039	-.110	.153	.028	.082	.138	.052
t-value***	1.61	-4.21	6.11	0.95	3.36	6.08	4.88
April 4, 1978-June 18, 1987**							
mean	.0039	-.0902	.1449	.0648	.1049	.1397	.0581
t-value	0.13	-3.08	4.95	2.22	3.60	4.11	4.72
April 4, 1978-Dec. 31, 1981**							
mean	.0007	-.0852	.1283	-.0273	.0834	.0957	.0302
t-value	0.02	-2.58	3.89	-.83	2.54	2.54	2.17
Jan. 1, 1982-June 18, 1987**							
mean	.0061	-.0935	.1561	.1279	.1195	.1707	.0771
t-value	0.14	-2.15	3.58	2.92	2.74	3.33	4.19

*Ikeda (1988)

**Kato (1990a)

*** All returns are significantly different from zero at the 5% level, except all Monday results and Thursdays during 1978 to 1981.

Kato (1990a) also investigated the intra-day and close-to-open effects. Data on the Topix for each 15 minute period of trading are publicly available in Japan in the Japanese Securities newspaper, Nihon Shoken Shimbun. During the period of this study, trading occured from 9-11 a.m. and 1-3 p.m. on weekdays and 9-11 a.m. on Saturdays. Historically, there was trading on all Saturdays until the end of 1972. Then until July 1983, the market was closed on the third Saturday, and the second Saturday was closed from August 1983-July 1986. There was then trading on the first and fourth Saturdays in the month and the fifth if there was one. Saturday trading stopped altogether at the end of January 1989.

Figure 3.1   Histograms of Returns of the Topix, in Percent, 1978-1987

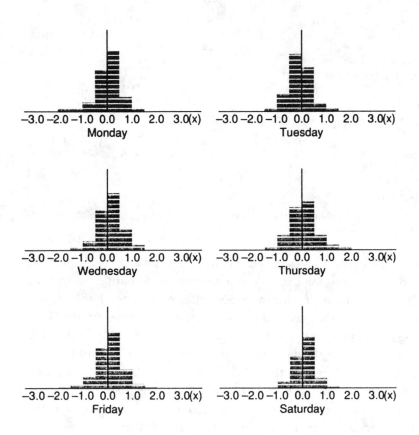

Source: Kato (1990a)

Figure 3.2
Cumulative Mean Intra-day Returns in Percent for the Topix, January 1,
1982-June 18, 1987

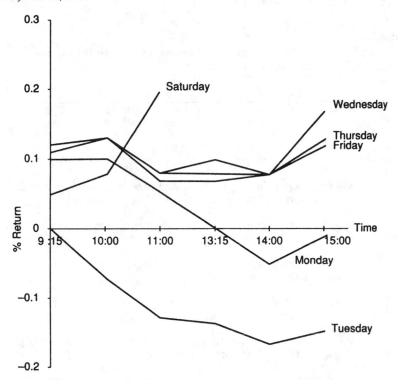

Source: Kato (1990a)

The average inter-day effects are depicted in Figure 3.2 for the period January 1, 1982 to June 18, 1987. All days have an initial surge, except for Tuesdays; Wednesdays to Fridays are then roughly flat until they have a kick at the end of the day, similar to what Harris (1986) found on the NYSE. Mondays lose their initial gains and drift negatively except for the final kick, which puts them about even. Tuesdays have a pattern similar to Monday but without the early gains. They close down about -0.15%, despite the final kick. Saturdays are very positive throughout the day. They open up and continue increasing until the final bell. Interestingly, the non-trading periods are all positive; gains occur during the night and the market opens up, even on Tuesdays.

Table 3.3 shows Kato's results including the intra-day returns using the previous close to open as the starting point. Except for Mondays, which are strongly negative, not much happens during the lunch break; although, Kato's data for this period has 15 minutes of trading in it, so the conclusion is a little muddled.

Table 3.3
Trading, Non-trading, and Intra-day Returns in Percent for the Topix, January 1, 1982, to June 18, 1987

Period	Statistic	Mon	Tues	Wed	Thurs	Fri	Sat	All Days	F
Close to Close	Mean	-0.0213	-0.1331	0.1792	0.1201	0.1212	0.1983	0.0723	6.88**
	t-Value	(-0.41)	(-2.60)	(3.52)	(2.35)	(2.38)	(3.28)	(3.35)	
Close to Open*	Mean	0.1002	0.0013	0.1177	0.1211	0.1134	0.0487	0.0855	23.58**
	t-Value	(5.08)	(0.07)	(6.11)	(6.26)	(5.88)	(2.13)	(10.47)	
Open to Close	Mean	-0.1217	-0.1344	0.0611	-0.0017	0.0069	0.1490	-0.0135	4.54**
	t-Value	(-2.73)	(-3.07)	(1.41)	(-0.04)	(0.16)	(2.89)	(-0.74)	
9:15- 10 a.m.	Mean	-0.0040	-0.0671	0.0114	0.0065	0.0237	0.0278	-0.0016	3.67**
	t-Value	(-0.24)	(-4.13)	(0.70)	(0.40)	(1.47)	(1.45)	(-0.23)	
10:00- 11 a.m.	Mean	-0.0543	-0.0589	-0.0457	-0.0546	-0.0627	0.1210	-0.0330	10.46**
	t-Value	(-0.26)	(-2.90)	(-2.26)	(-2.69)	(-3.11)	(5.05)	(-3.84)	
11:00- 1:15 p.m.	Mean	-0.0514	-0.0097	0.0232	0.0029	0.0019		-0.0070	4.47**
	t-Value	(-4.22)	(-0.81)	(1.95)	(0.24)	(-0.16)		(-1.295)	
1:15- 2:00 p.m.	Mean	-0.0516	-0.0251	-0.0160	-0.0035	0.0070		-0.0175	3.24**
	t-Value	(-3.44)	(-1.71)	(-1.09)	(-0.24)	(0.48)		(-2.65)	
2:00- 3:00 p.m.	Mean	0.0387	0.0215	0.0885	0.0466	0.0407		0.0473	8.55**
	t-Value	(2.12)	(1.20)	(4.97)	(2.62)	(2.29)		(5.90)	

* The market opens at 9 a.m. Kato's close to open is from the previous day's close to 9:15, a period when most stocks have opened.

** These F statistics all indicate that the regression model used to fit these returns, namely

$$R_t = \sum_{k=1}^{6} B_k D_{kt} + E_t,$$

where $D_{1t} = 1$ for Mondays, $D_{2t} = 1$ for Tuesdays, ..., $D_{6t} = 1$ for Saturdays, and zero otherwise, is significant at the 1% level.

Source: Kato (1990a)

The effects of Saturday trading are very interesting. First, Saturdays were extremely positive. Second, Saturdays were even more positive if the previous week had Saturday trading during the first week of the month in the sample period. See Table 3.4. Third, Mondays were negative if the previous Saturday was closed (the third and fourth weeks) and even more negative if the third had no Saturday trading. However, Mondays were positive if the previous Saturday had trading and especially so if the second week of the month week had no Saturday trading.

Table 3.4
Effects of Saturday Trading on the Topix, April 4, 1978, to June 18, 1987, Mean Daily Returns in Percent

Week	Trading Ends This Week	Last Week	Mon	Tues	Wed	Thur	Fri	Sat	F	Sample Size
1st,5th A1	Sat	Sat	0.0198	-0.1072	0.1790	0.0581	0.0605	0.1678	8.67**	1406
4th A2	Sat	Fri	-0.1008	-0.1102	0.1074	0.0306	0.1582	0.0793	2.53*	649
2nd B1	Fri	Sat	0.1135	-0.0649	0.0980	0.0933	0.1341		4.05**	539
3rd B2	Fri	Fri	-0.3489	0.1931	0.2479	0.2609	0.2193		0.46	58
	All Weeks		0.0039	-0.0902	0.1449	0.0648	0.1049	0.1397		
Sample Size			449	464	464	465	467	343		2652

* and ** indicates significance at the 1% and 5% levels, respectively

Source: Kato 1990a

Before we continue analyzing this data, let's pause to see if this makes any sense. We know from U.S. and Japanese data, see Chapter 2, that there is strong one-day serial correlation of returns. Hence, if Saturday were positive (and we need it to be open to be so), then Monday likely would be positive and we could have the usual negative Tuesday. If Saturday is closed, the Friday will be stronger than usual. In Chapter 4 we consider Fridays as special preholidays, a possible reason for their strength. Somehow the long weekend, as in the U.S., gives traders more time to think about selling. With Monday so negative, Tuesday can be positive but only in weeks that end with Friday trading. For weeks ending with Saturday trading, the loss would be more or less split between Monday and Tuesday.

When the anomalous effect does not materialize as expected, plan for it to be pushed around a little. The Friday-Friday weeks have the most negative Monday following the first Friday, and then the rest of the week is very strong. Is it the sight of a positive Tuesday giving the market life? We do not know, but the effect seems to be there. Kato's data cover more than nine years with differing rules on Saturday trading, and this may also affect the results.

Figure 3.3
Cumulative Mean Intra-day Returns by Four Groups Classified by Saturday Trading, Topix, 1983-87

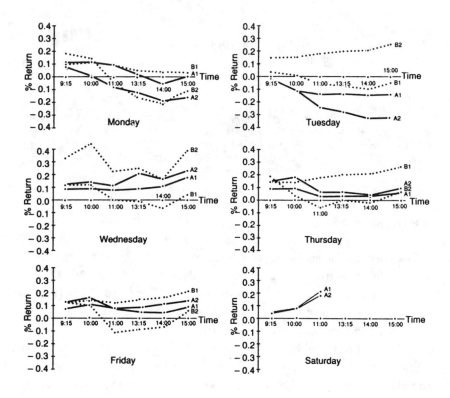

Source: Kato, Schwartz and Ziemba (1989)

Table 3.4 lists the weeks of the month corresponding to the trading data rules for this period, so that one can data snoop some more. Kato (1990a) also plots the intra-day patterns by day of the week using the 1982-1987 data; they have similar interpretations. See Figure 3.3. Kato has a little more information on this, namely the effect of the New York Dow on the Tokyo Topix. He analyzed this with and without Saturday to explain, in particular, the switching of the negative Tuesdays to Mondays when there is no Saturday trading. This is discussed below.

Ikeda (1985, 1988) and Kato (1990a) discuss the settlement hypothesis as a possible explanation of the day of the week effect. The idea is that on certain days, the time one has to pay for stock or receive money for sales is different, and thus there should be a premium for the additional interest fore-gone or earned from this process. The delivery of securities and receipt of payment takes place on the third business day (which cannot be a Saturday) after the transaction. Figure 1.4 has the rules for this settlement.

The results found by Kato and Ikeda, similar to those in North America, are mixed. The settlement hypothesis is a partial explanation of the day of the week phenomenon. However, the average returns on Tuesdays are negative except they are strongly positive in the third week, which has no Saturday trading, following a week without Saturday trading which is inconsistent with this theory. If we let **R** be the rate of return on the stock in question and **i** be the cost of capital, then the differences in return across days of the week, with and without Saturday trading, should be as follows - assuming there are no holidays in this period:

	Mon	Tues	Weds	Thurs	Fri	Sat
Saturday trading	2R+i	R+i	R+3i	R	R+i	R+i
No Saturday trading	3R+i	R+i	R+3i	R+i	R+i	--

Hence the returns should be highest on Mondays and Wednesdays with or without Saturday trading. The returns should be the same on Tuesdays, Thursdays in weeks without Saturday trading, Fridays and Saturdays. One very important implication of the settlement rules is that in weeks with Saturday trading, stocks can be purchased on Wednesdays and sold on Thursdays, and have settlement on the same day, namely the following Monday. This is widely believed to have a positive effect on Wednesdays, something that is consistent with the data. The law governing this was enacted in 1978. [1]

As we can see from the previous results, some of this is consistent with the facts, but it is far from a proper explanation of the day of the week phenomenon. See Ikeda (1988) for some calculations adjusting the returns

---

[1] It is titled *maigetsu no daini doyoubi igai o doyoubi ni kansuru gyoumukitei shinyooutorihiki ayobi taishaku tarkhiki kitei narabini jutakukeiyaku junsoku no tokurei* translated rules for business concerning Saturdays other then the second Saturday of each month; trust business and loan business rule; and special rules of the embellishment of trust contracts.

for this theory. He concludes that once adjustment for these settlement differences are made, the day of the week differences are less anomalous than before in a statistical sense.

Since the day of the week effect casts doubt upon the homogeneity of the return generating process across the week, Ikeda (1988) suggests considering not only the mean but also higher moments of the return distribution for each day of the week. Examining the skewness and kurtosis and testing the *stability under addition property*, he rejects a stable paretian hypothesis. When the interval used for calculating returns was extended from a day to a week, from a week to two weeks, from two weeks to a month, etc., the kurtosis and skewness become less significant. The use of a mixture of normal distributions (or subordinated stochastic process) then describes the return generating process for Japanese stocks. He applied a model relating this mix of normals to the information generating process to the day of the week effect. See also Tse (1991) and Ikeda and Kanazaki (1991) for additional work on this.

THE CORRELATION WITH THE NEW YORK STOCK EXCHANGE

Kato (1990a) re-examined the earlier study by Jaffe and Westerfield (1985b) on the correlation between the New York and Tokyo markets with his more recent data. For 1980 to 1987, he found much higher correlations, namely 53.6%, between the previous day's return in New York and the close-to-open returns in Tokyo, using the Dow Jones industrial average in New York and the NSA in Tokyo. This is not surprising since the two markets have grown to watch the other's movements very closely.

The previous day's return in New York is the most relevant information leading into Tokyo's opening. The reverse effect, namely the correlation between Tokyo's close-to-close and New York's close-to-open on the next trading day is only 11%. Hence, Tokyo's effect on New York is less than New York's effect on Tokyo. Other correlations are smaller for each directional effect, but still statistically significant. Kato's results are summarized in Table 3.5. Because these data cover a relatively long period, 1980-87, one would expect many changes in these correlations over time. Additional results on this appear in Hamao, Masulis and Ng (1990, 1991).

Table 3.5
Correlation Coefficients between the Dow Jones Industrial Average and
the NSA, 1980-87

	New York		Tokyo (t=0)		
			C-O	O-C	C-C
New York's Effect (t=-1)		Close-to-Open	0.3306	0.2817	0.3721
on Tokyo		Open-to-Close	0.3823	0.1091	0.2453
		Close-to-Close	0.5363	0.2551	0.4313
Tokyo's Effect (t=0)		Close-to-Open	0.1556	0.0565	0.1096
on New York				(0.0138)	
		Open-to-Close	-0.0057	0.0591	0.0484
			(0.8031)		(0.0348)
		Close-to-Close	0.0887	0.0929	0.1145

All coefficients are significant at 1% or lower except those with p values in ( )'s. The only effect that is statistically zero is open-to-close in New York on t=0 versus close-to-open in Tokyo on t=0 which had a small negative correlation.

Source: Kato, 1990a.

The trading or non-trading on Saturday, coupled with the effects of New York trading on Tokyo, provide a method to investigate more fully why there are such different Monday and Tuesday effects in these two circumstances. To investigate this Kato (1990a) ran the following regression:

$$R_{Tt} - R_{NY,t-1} = \sum_{K=1}^{6} \beta_k D_{kt} + \varepsilon_t$$

where $R_{T,t}$ is the return in Tokyo on day t and $R_{NY,t-1}$ is the return in New York on the previous day, the β's are the coefficients, the D_{kt}'s are "dummy" variables to pick up the day of the week effects. That is, if t is a Tuesday then $D_{1t}=0$, $D_{2t}=1$, $D_{3t}=...=D_{6t}=0$, etc., and ε_t is the error in this equation. He found that when there is Saturday trading, the F-statistic for the fit is 0.32, which is not significant even at the 10% level.

However, when there is no Saturday trading, the F-statistic is 3.48, which is significant at the 1% level. This fit is caused mainly because of the low Monday return on the NSA relative to the high return on Friday's New York Dow. When there is Saturday trading and Monday is excluded from Tokyo's data, that is in New York trading takes place on MTWThF and in Tokyo is TWThFS - then we cannot reject the hypothesis that the weekly patterns of both markets are identical.

In particular, the low Monday in New York matches the low Tuesday in Tokyo, and the high Friday in New York matches the high Saturday in Tokyo. The other days are correspondingly similar. Hence, whatever reasons are the true causes for the day of the week effect in New York, they are probably similar to those in Tokyo. Perhaps in weeks with Saturday trading, investors do not have enough time to vacation and contemplate their portfolios leading to Monday sales, so the fall is on Tuesday. This idea is considered in the next section.

A TEST OF MILLER'S WEEKEND HYPOTHESIS[2]

Miller (1988) has argued that the weekend effect in U.S. security markets can be explained by a tendency for self-initiated sell orders to exceed self-initiated buy orders over the weekend, while broker-initiated buy trades result in a surplus of buying during the remainder of the week. This causes security prices to fall over the weekend and during the day on Monday as market makers sell back stock that they purchased supporting the market on its open. Prices then move higher during the week because of broker induced buying. The days of the week variation is higher for small capitalized than for large capitalized firms because of the larger bid-ask spreads and the thin trading in these generally low price securities. Keim and Smirlock (1987) document this for U.S. markets and Stoll and Whaley (1986) document the bid-ask spreads.

Miller's idea is predicated on the fact that people are simply too busy to think much about stocks during the week. If they do anything, it's more often than not to buy upon the recommendation of a broker. Brokers have a vested interest in purchases. It projects a positive image. First, they do not have to find people who own stock and suggest they sell it. Second, they receive two commissions for the purchase (usually recommended by the broker) and the sale (usually initiated by the stock owner). Groth, Lewellen, Sohlarbaum and Lease (1979) surveyed 6,000 recommendations. Some 87% were purchase and only 13% were sale recommendations. Over the weekend individual investors have more time to think about their holdings, and this reflection, on average, leads to more selling than buying. Individuals, on balance, are net sellers of stock.

Figure 3.4 from Ritter (1988) details this with data on individual orders at Merrill Lynch from 1971-1985 during January and the rest of the year. This figure also shows the strong turn of the year effect for U.S. small stocks on trading days -1 to +4. Table 3.6 shows that individual investors have been net sellers in Japan as well as the U.S. for the period 1981-89.

---

[2]This section was adapted from Ziemba (1990a).

Figure 3.4
Mean Buy/Sell Ratios and the Excess Return on Small Stocks by Trading
Day in January and the Rest of the Year, 1971-85

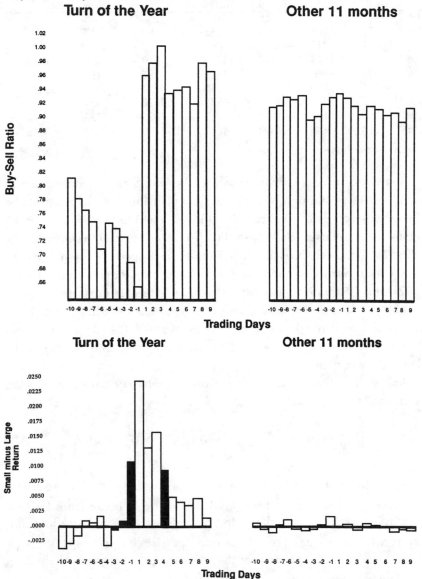

Source: Ritter (1988)

Table 3.6
Net Purchases (Sales) of Stocks in Billions of Yen (February) by Various
Investor Groups, 1981-1989

	Individuals			Financial Institutions	Industrial Corps	Investment Trusts	Foreigners
	Total	Cash	Margin				
1981	-425	na	na	417	287	-95	110
1982	-330	na	na	422	82	17	181
1983	-862	-1417	555	769	27	-69	726
1984	-55	-1228	1173	1479	319	324	-1922
1985	-942	-1586	643	1825	283	468	-869
1986	-1762	-3109	1327	4568	754	1057	-3787
1987	-1307	-3350	2043	6274	1150	1811	-7196
1988	-3288	-5102	1814	4365	626	1730	77
1989	113	-4485	4599	4683	-1150	-2192	3348

Source: Yamaichi Research Institute

Individual investors' portfolios are also much more concentrated in small stocks. Although Miller's story is plausible, he did not test the theory with real data. Ziemba (1990a) investigated this hypothesis for the Japanese market using daily NSA data from May 16, 1949 to December 28, 1988. The data were broken into 475 ten year sub-periods beginning with May 1949 to April 1958 and ending with January 1979 to December 1988.

Ziemba (1989, 1991a) has studied holiday effects in Japanese spot and futures markets and found strong and significant positive preholiday effects and negative post holiday effects over the 1949-89 period. This research is discussed in Chapter 4. Hence it is appropriate to separate the day of the week effects.

For each of the 475 ten year periods Ziemba (1990a) estimated the equation

$$R_t = \sum_{j=1}^{6} \hat{\gamma}_j \cdot day_j + \sum_{j=1\,2\,3\,6} \hat{b}_j \cdot before_j + \sum_{j=1\,2\,3\,6} \hat{a}_j \cdot after_j \qquad (1)$$

In (1) the coefficients a_j refer to the single trading days that are after a $j=1$ (one), $j=2$ (two), $j=3$ (three), and $j=6$ (six) day break from trading holiday or weekend. Similarly, the b_j's refer to the single trading day before a 1, 2, 3 or 6 day break from trading. Hence equation (1) gives as coefficients γ_j for the six days of the week the pure effects of these days separate from the holiday and weekend effects.

Figure 3.5 gives the mean returns by day of the week estimated from equation (1) after adjusting for pre and post holiday effects by year from

1949 to 1988. Each ten year period is plotted at its final month. For example, May 1949 to April 1958 is plotted as of April 1958. Hence there are 475 such points for Monday, Tuesday to Saturday in the estimate of γ_1 to γ_6 in equation (1) for that ten year period. The 475 points represent partially overlapping periods over the more than 39 years of data. Figure 3.6 shows the test of hypotheses by day of the week that the daily return is not zero for each of the months in the years of the sample May 1949 to December 1988. Most of the time the daily return is not zero at the 5% significance level.

A test of a hypothesis along the lines of Miller's is shown in Figure 3.7 with P-statistics in Figure 3.8. Case A1 is the one day weekends following weeks with Saturday trading and A2 is the two day weekends. The coefficients $\hat{a}_1$ and $\hat{a}_2$ are again from equation (1) for each of the 475 ten year overlapping periods. The supposition is that the average returns on the A2 days should be lower than those on the A1 days. Figure 3.7 confirms this, showing Monday's average daily returns for the 475 ten year periods. P-values for the hypothesis that the return on Monday is not zero using a two-sided test appear in Figure 3.8.

Sales efforts are intensified before holidays and weekends, and this results in high returns on the preholidays, Fridays and Saturdays. Figure 3.9 shows that the daily rise before two-day holidays and weekends is larger than for one day breaks from trading using the $\hat{b}_1$ and $\hat{b}_2$ coefficients. Figure 3.10 gives the P-values for the sample period 1954-89.

Figure 3.5
Day of the Week Effects by Ten Year Period Ending in the Plotted Month
for Periods Ending in April 1958 to December 1988 with Holiday and
Weekend Effects Separated Out

Source: Ziemba (1990a)

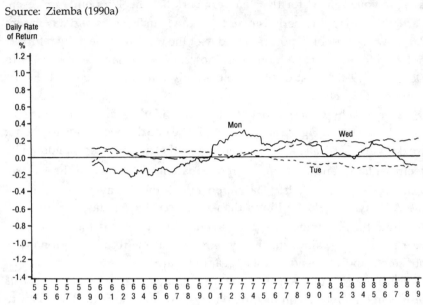

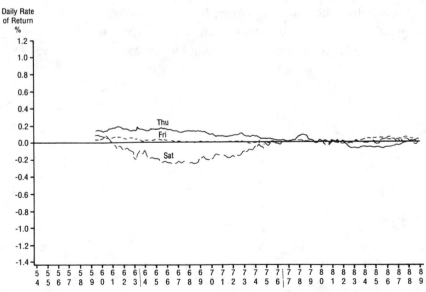

Figure 3.6
P-Statistics for Hypothesis that Daily Return is not equal to Zero (Two-sided Test) for Figure 3.5

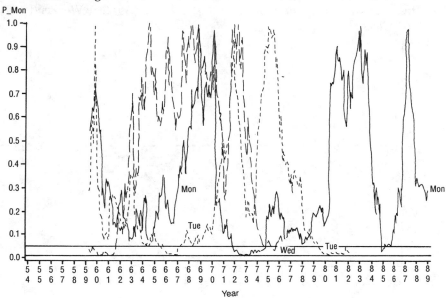

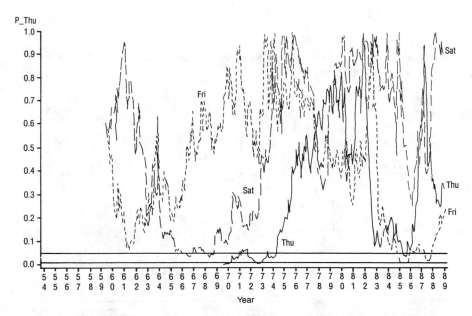

Source: Ziemba (1990a)

Figure 3.7
Mean Daily Rates of Return on Mondays, Net of Holiday and Weekend
Effects, on the NSA, 1960-89 for One (A1) and Two (A2) Day Weekends,
1960-1989

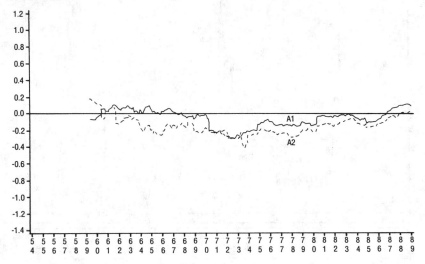

Source: Ziemba (1990a)

Figure 3.8
P-Values for the Hypothesis of Non-zero Returns on Monday Using a
Two-sided Test for Figure 3.7

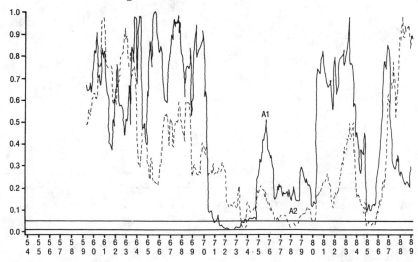

Source: Ziemba (1990a)

Figure 3.9
Mean Daily Rates of Return on Preholiday and Pre-weekend Trading
Days for One (B1) and Two (B2) Day Trading Breaks, NSA for the 475 Ten
Year Periods, 1949-1988

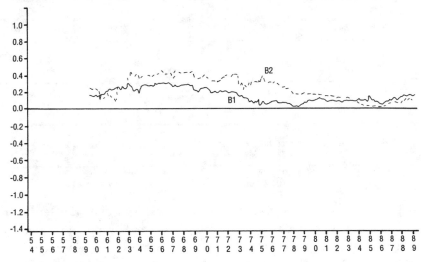

Source: Ziemba (1990a)

Figure 3.10
P-Values for the Hypothesis that the Returns on the Preholiday and Pre-
weekend are not Zero with a Two-tail Test for Figure 3.9

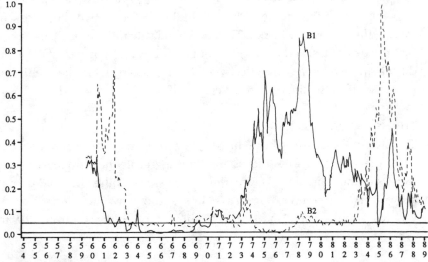

Source: Ziemba (1990a)

Table 3.7
Estimated Coefficient Values for Equation (1) for the Four Decade Periods

	bmon	btue	bwed	bthu	bfri	bsat	bB1	bB2	bA1	bA2	bA1-bA2	bB1-bB2
1949-59												
est	-1.083	-0.0356	0.0935	0.1466	0.0433	0.0797	0.1504	.2329	-0.0555	0.1718	-0.22704***	-0.0825***
t-stat	-0.708	-0.732	1.9310	3.0260	0.8930	0.5230	1.0230	.9410	-03760	0.7020	-44.881	16.171
Sign.												
1960-69												
est	-0.0333	0.0629	-0.0063	0.1149***	0.0104	-0.1682	0.2256	.3611	-0.0106	0.1710	0.1604	0.1355
t-stat	-0.283	1.611	-0.1610	2.9550	0.2660	-1.4440	2.0180	1.762	-0.0940	-0.8470	37.953	37.953
Sign.												
1970-79												
est	0.1551	-0.0900**	0.1713***	0.0122	0.03807	0.0259	0.0901	.1673*	-0.1576*	-0.2322**	0.074**	0.0772***
t-stat	1.5570	-2.340	4.4510	0.318	0.925	0.2500	0.2500	1.888	-1.6530	-2.0430	27.076	31.652
Sign.												
1980-88												
est	-0.113	-0.1067***	0.2157***	0.0450	0.0621	0.0554	0.1046	.1004	0.1163	0.0266	0.0898***	-0.0043
t-stat	-1.095	-2.7590	5.5980	1.1650	1.394	0.5280	1.0470	1.253	1.1790	0.2290	29.7240	-1.6830
Sign.												

*, **, or *** indicate that the coefficient is not equal to zero at the 10%, 5% or 1% level, respectively

The calculations discussed above are averages over the ten year periods, but these periods are overlapping. To avoid overlapping, Ziemba (1990a) considered equation (1) for the decades of the 1950s (including 1949), the 1960s, the 1970s and the 1980s. Table 3.7 describes the results.

The next to last column has the coefficient $b_{A1}-b_{A2}$ corresponding to the hypothesis that the two-day breaks yield lower returns. This was indeed the case and significantly so except during the 1950s. Similarly, the last column has the coefficient $b_{B1}-b_{B2}$ corresponding to the hypothesis that the market return is higher before a two-day break in trading than a one-day break. The results indicate this was the case in the first three decades, and the coefficient is significantly positive. However, during the last decade, this effect was slightly negative, but the coefficient is not significantly different from zero.

THE FULL EVIDENCE: 1949-88

The studies discussed above utilize data from the 1970s and 1980s to study the day of the week effects and they aggregate the results over large subsets of these periods. Hence, the results are smoothed out and do not show yearly differences. Figures 3.11abc and d show the effects year by year for both the Topix and the NSA indices for the 40 years from 1949 to 1988.

Figure 3.11 Mean Return by the Day of the Week

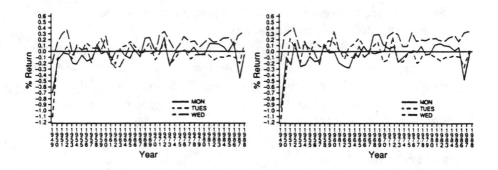

a: Mean Return on Monday, Tuesday and Wednesday on the Topix Index, 1949-1988

b: Mean Return on Thursday, Friday and Saturday on the Topix Index, 1949-1988

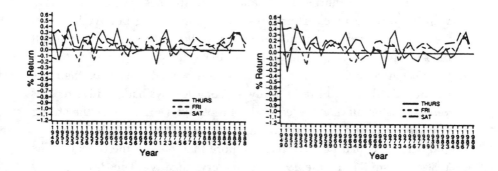

c: Mean Return on Monday, Tuesday and Wednesday on the NSA Index, 1949-88

d: Mean Return on Thursday, Friday and Saturday on the NSA Index, 1949-88

Source: Kato, Schwartz and Ziemba (1989)

There is considerable variation over time, but in general the previous results of low or negative Monday and Tuesday returns and high Wednesday to Saturday returns are supported. Tuesday was consistently negative from 1973 to 1987. Tuesdays were slightly positive in 1988. Mondays are negative or slightly positive throughout the whole forty years. Wednesdays became positive in 1970 and have remained positive during each of the past nineteen years at levels of about 0.2% per day. Thursdays show great variation over the entire sample period with wide swings in average returns from year to year switching from highly positive to negative returns and back to positive returns in short periods. Recently they have been more positive.

On the Topix, each year since 1983 shows positive average returns reaching levels of 0.2% to 0.3% per day in 1986 and 1987. For the NSA, the returns on Thursday are not positive until 1985. Since then, they have been very positive and they have provided average gains in every year on both indices since 1974. Saturdays are even more positive, with gains throughout the forty year sample period except for a brief period in the mid-1960s on the NSA.

Table 3.8 investigates the returns during the past four decades in the NSA by day of the week. The conclusions are that: (a) Mondays and Tuesdays were negative in the 1950s, with Wednesday, Thursday and Saturday having progressively higher returns. Saturdays returned over four times the average daily returns and provided gains nearly two-thirds of the time; (b) In the 1960s, Mondays were still negative but Tuesdays were slightly positive. Thursdays were again strong but Wednesdays were essentially even. Saturdays had gains, but only 50% higher than all days compared to 350+% higher in the 1950s; (c) Mondays and Tuesdays were negative in the 1970s with Tuesdays now switching to be the more negative day by a 7 to 1 ratio. Only 44% of Tuesdays had positive returns versus 55% on all days. Wednesdays replaced Thursdays as the strong mid-week day and Saturdays were again very strong. Both Wednesdays and Saturdays had positive returns more than 60% of the time; (d) The 1980s are similar to the 1970s with very negative Tuesdays, mildly negative Mondays, stronger Thursdays (than the 70s), as well as stronger Fridays. Wednesdays again were the strongest days, returning 0.215% on average and providing positive returns 63.3% of the time. Saturdays were very positive, returning 0.16% per day and were positive 63.6% of the time. The NSA results are, not surprisingly, quite similar to the Topix results for the 1970s and 1980s discussed earlier.

Obviously many of the anomalies affect one another and interact. Kato (1990a) has investigated the interaction of the January and small firm effects by days of the week to attempt to isolate the separate influences of these anomalies using Topix data from January 4, 1976, to June 8, 1987. His results are detailed in Tables 3.9 and 3.10 and Figure 3.12. Kato found that the strong days - Wednesday, Friday and Saturday - have positive gains during the day. These essentially nullify the losses on the weak days - Monday, Tuesday and Thursday. Only on the very strongest days - Wednesday and Saturday - are there positive returns during the day for all levels of capitalized stocks outside of January.

Table 3.8   Returns by Day of the Week by the NSA, by Decade, 1949-1988

	Day	Sample Size	% Mean Return	t- Statistic	Percent Positive Returns
1949-1959					
1	All	3193	.0565*	2.85	53.6
2	Mon	531	-.1545*	-3.08	43.3
3	Tue	531	-.0284	-0.59	50.3
4	Wed	534	.0957	1.87	53.0
5	Thu	531	.1488*	2.68	56.9
6	Fri	535	.0467	0.98	53.3
7	Sat	531	.2302**	6.76	65.5
1960-1969					
1	All	3000	.0368*	2.32	52.8
2	Mon	501	-.0396	-1.01	50.5
3	Tue	499	.0643	1.69	50.5
4	Wed	501	.0004	0.01	50.7
5	Thu	501	.1221*	2.82	56.7
6	Fri	495	.0160	0.40	51.9
7	Sat	503	.0575	1.93	56.7
1970-1979					
1	All	2892	.0391*	2.46	52.3
2	Mon	488	-.0135	-0.33	54.1
3	Tue	502	-.0968*	-2.67	44.4
4	Wed	494	.1702**	4.47	61.7
5	Thu	499	.0091	0.21	54.5
6	Fri	496	.0660	1.75	55.6
7	Sat	413	.1136**	3.29	62.5
1980-1988					
1	All	2444	.0625**	3.75	56.0
2	Mon	417	-.0135	-0.36	57.3
3	Tue	427	-.1183*	-2.40	43.8
4	Wed	431	.2151**	5.14	63.3
5	Thu	428	.0606	1.61	52.3
6	Fri	433	.0944*	2.56	58.0
7	Sat	308	.1601**	4.74	63.6

** indicates significance at the 1% level and * at the 5% level in this and Tables 3.9 to 3.11

Source: Kato, Schwartz and Ziemba (1989)

All the gains are at night and there are positive returns on every trading day. Moreover, the small capitalization stocks make their major gains

Invest in Japan

then. Then, in total, we have the advantage of the small stocks over the big stocks day by day in the close-to-close returns on every day of the week regardless if the day is positive like Wednesday or Saturday or negative as on Tuesdays.

Table 3.9
Mean Portfolio Close-to-Close, Close-to-Open and Open-to-Close Returns by Day of the Week and Firm Size on the Topix, January 4, 1974-June 18, 1987

	Firm Size	Mon	Tues	Wed	Thurs	Fri	Sat	F's
Close	All firms	0.0544	-0.0406	0.2188	0.0604	0.1119	0.1489	30.67**
to	Smallest	0.1249	0.0240	0.2803	0.1157	0.1583	0.2059	51.73**
Close	2	0.0855	-0.0277	0.2325	0.574	0.1348	0.1674	34.15**
	3	0.0519	-0.0472	0.2114	0.0287	0.1297	0.1590	27.80**
	4	0.0500	-0.0491	0.1899	0.0321	0.1067	0.1459	24.10**
	Largest	0.0340	-0.0672	0.1591	0.0357	0.1053	0.1447	17.41**
	F's	10.20**	4.00**	83.32**	7.20**	31.23**	61.86**	
	N	3,225	3,350	3,350	3,340	3,360	2,460	
Close	All Firms	0.1776	0.0483	0.1176	0.1510	0.1252	0.0532	116.95**
to	Smallest	0.2616	0.1030	0.1844	0.2084	0.1673	0.1381	191.77**
Open	2	0.2324	0.0805	0.1537	0.1942	0.1577	0.0961	174.54**
	3	0.2039	0.0679	0.1325	0.1639	0.1509	0.0813	144.77**
	4	0.1661	0.0393	0.0952	0.1207	0.1106	0.0409	87.02**
	Largest	0.0959	-0.0113	0.0425	0.0793	0.0707	0.0022	23.25**
	F's	234.77**	33.92**	127.10**	197.06**	102.22**	43.91**	
	N	3,225	3,350	3,350	3,340	3,360	2,460	
Open	All Firms	-0.1234	-0.0889	0.1008	-0.0908	-0.0134	0.0952	30.25**
to	Smallest	-0.1367	-0.0792	0.0952	-0.0929	-0.0093	0.0676	28.98**
Close	2	-0.1469	-0.1082	0.0783	-0.1368	-0.0230	0.0711	35.23**
	3	-0.1519	-0.1151	0.0785	-0.1352	-0.0214	0.0775	33.57**
	4	-0.1160	-0.0884	0.0944	-0.0888	-0.0040	0.1048	25.27**
	Largest	-0.0621	-0.0559	0.1164	-0.0440	0.0346	0.1422	18.13**
	F's	50.21**	23.84**	25.11**	34.00**	1.50	46.07**	
	N	3,225	3,350	3,350	3,340	3,360	2,460	

Source: Kato (1990a)

Table 3.10

Mean Returns in Percent for Trading and Non-Trading Periods on the Topix, January 4, 1974-June 8-1987

JANUARY RETURNS

Firm Size	Mon	Tues	Wed	Thurs	Fri	Satu	All Days	F's
Open to Close Returns:								
Smallest	0.4450	0.2976	0.4416	0.3970	0.4198	0.1402	0.3801	25.88**
2	0.3118	0.2056	0.3664	0.2870	0.3500	0.2138	0.2932	15.66**
3	0.1972	0.1559	0.3066	0.2270	0.3252	0.1596	0.2326	9.85**
4	0.1293	0.1113	0.2759	0.1518	0.2455	0.1392	0.1779	6.42**
Largest	0.0592	-0.0225	0.2499	0.0415	0.2791	0.1321	0.1242	4.56**
Close to Open Returns:								
Smallest	0.4003	0.2353	0.2929	0.2713	0.2827	0.1522	0.2781	48.58**
2	0.3523	0.1687	0.2220	0.2365	0.2162	0.1396	0.2263	39.82**
3	0.2829	0.1568	0.1685	0.1987	0.2097	0.1101	0.1914	26.98**
4	0.2085	0.1284	0.1381	0.1565	0.1587	0.3417	0.1432	16.88**
Largest	0.1281	0.0358	0.0879	0.0793	0.1529	0.0361	0.0893	5.96**
Open to Close Returns:								
Smallest	0.0440	0.0618	0.1481	0.1250	0.1364	0.0875	0.1015	4.33*
2	-0.0408	0.0367	0.1439	0.0500	0.1335	0.0738	0.0665	2.51*
3	-0.0858	-0.0010	0.1377	0.0280	0.1152	0.0493	0.0410	1.99
4	-0.0794	-0.0172	0.1374	-0.0050	0.0867	0.0973	0.0345	2.08
Largest	-0.0691	-0.0572	0.1617	-0.0380	0.1259	0.0957	0.0348	2.65*

ALL MONTHS BUT JANUARY

	Mon	Tues	Wed	Thurs	Fri	Satu	All Days	F's
Close to Close Total Returns:								
Smallest	0.0962	0.0005	0.2661	0.0914	0.1350	0.2030	0.1290	39.72**
2	0.0652	-0.0477	0.2208	0.0377	0.1156	0.1634	0.0894	26.98**
3	0.0389	-0.0646	0.2030	0.0116	0.1122	0.1589	0.0731	23.19**
4	0.0429	-0.0629	0.1824	0.0218	0.0943	0.1465	0.0675	10.46**
Largest	0.0317	-0.0711	0.1512	0.0352	0.0898	0.1457	0.0602	14.47**
Close to Open Returns:								
Smallest	0.2492	0.0916	0.1749	0.2030	0.1570	0.1369	0.1697	158.46**
2	0.2217	0.0729	0.1477	0.1906	0.1524	0.0924	0.1482	145.83**
3	0.1968	0.0603	0.1293	0.1609	0.1457	0.0788	0.1304	123.10**
4	0.1623	0.0316	0.0915	0.1176	0.1063	0.0408	0.0936	73.87**
Largest	0.0930	-0.0153	0.0385	0.0793	0.0633	0.0007	0.0447	19.36**
Open to Close Returns:								
Smallest	-0.1529	-0.0913	0.0906	-0.1117	-0.0223	0.0659	-0.0409	32.17**
2	-0.1564	-0.1207	0.0725	-0.1529	-0.0370	0.0708	-0.0590	37.66**
3	-0.1578	-0.1249	0.0733	-0.1493	-0.0335	0.0799	-0.0574	34.60**
4	-0.1194	-0.0946	0.0906	-0.0960	-0.0120	0.1055	-0.0262	24.33**
Largest	-0.0615	-0.0558	0.1124	-0.0445	0.0265	0.1462	0.0153	16.17**

Source: Kato (1990a)

Figure 3.12
Mean Returns by Day of the Week, Close-to-Close, Close-to-Open and
Open-to-Close, Topix, 1974-1987

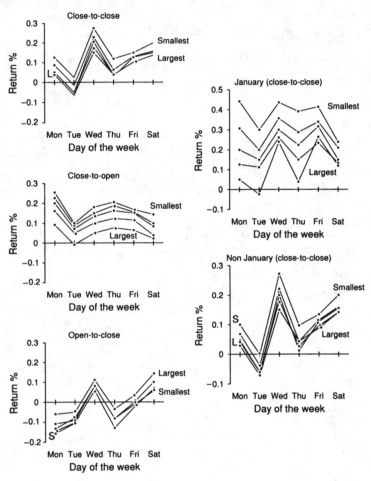

Source: Kato, Schwartz and Ziemba (1989)

WHY DO THE ANOMALIES OCCUR?
There is little discussion neither here nor elsewhere with convincing
reasons why this anomalous day of the week effect as well as other
security market regularities occur. Indeed even in the books on anomalies
such as Coulson (1987), Dimson (1988), Hirsch (1986), and Ziemba (1991e),
the authors are fairly silent on this point. Connolly (1988a,b) argues with
much data and strong statistical tools that the day of the week effect in the

U.S. is not as clear cut as previously believed and may not have even existed until recently in U.S. security markets.

The main reason anomalies are anomalies is that we cannot explain them. Cash flows, institutional constraints and practices and investors' psychological trading habits are clearly involved though. The various anomalies have pestered hard-line financial economists to such an extent that they are now quite fashionable, and such results can now be published and are encouraged in the most prestigious journals in the field. The anomalies, of course, do seem to violate traditional equilibrium models of asset behavior over time. They do have causes that are not understood. Some thoughts along these lines regarding day of the week effects appear below. The rigorous testing of the validity and percent explained by the various hypotheses will entail considerable effort and statistical ingenuity. Initial research on this appears in Hiraki, Aggarwal and Rao (1988) and Ziemba (1990ac). The main results in the latter papers are presented here and in Chapter 4.

Some possible reasons for day of the week anomalies:

1. Negative Tuesdays with Saturday trading.

   - Investors are more likely to sell if they have a weekend to think it over.
   - Sales representatives have a more difficult time getting buy orders after Saturday, especially with a rise on Saturday.
   - You must sell on Tuesday if you need money on Friday because of the three day business settlement rules because there are no Saturday settlements.
   - There is a lag from New York's Monday fall via the correlation effect.
   - It takes time to get into the market again in the new week.

2. Negative Mondays after Saturdays closed.

   - Investors are more likely to sell if they have a weekend to think it over.
   - It takes time to get into the market again in the new week.
   - Sales on Monday provide receipts before the end of the week.
   - Dealers have a more difficult time soliciting buy orders.
   - Individuals are net sellers especially of small capitalized stocks. Their sell orders accumulate over the weekend and outweigh the buy orders of brokers recommendations because brokers are not soliciting orders on the weekend. Hence, contrary to the other days

of the week, there is net selling on Monday; see Miller (1988), Ziemba (1990a) and the discussion earlier in this chapter.

3. Positive Wednesdays.

    • According to the settlement hypothesis, Wednesdays should be very strong.

    • Some brokerage dealers buy on Wednesday then sell on Thursday in weeks with Saturday trading. The settlement for both is on Monday. Since transaction costs are almost zero and Wednesdays are typically strong, this can be a profitable strategy. This is the only day brokers can use this strategy.

4. All gains overnight.

    • Orders are collected after the close of trading for execution at the open by salespeople's push with a bias towards buy orders.

    • There is cross selling late in the day to recover funds to match purchases made on the open.

    • Speculative purchases are made at the open expecting the market to rise, then there is covering at the end of the day for these trades.

FUTURES MARKETS EFFECTS

Ziemba (1989) investigated seasonality effects in Japanese futures markets including days of the week effects using the SIMEX NSA 225 and Osaka Kubusaki 50 contracts for the period September 1986 to September 1988 when there was still Saturday trading.

The spot effect of weak Mondays and Tuesdays and strong Wednesday to Saturday is continuing. Wednesdays are the strongest days followed by Thursdays and Saturdays in the spot market. The Simex futures in Singapore look just like the spot market in Tokyo except in the Wednesday to Thursday period. Possibly this market is following rather than leading, although other evidence suggests the leading hypothesis.

The futures seem to rise and fall with the spot. The Osaka 50 seems to anticipate the days of the week effect. Saturdays hardly rise at all in the futures markets despite the spot gains, thus anticipating Monday's fall. Then these futures fall on Monday to anticipate a further fall on Tuesday. They then rise on Tuesday to anticipate the gains on Wednesday, Thursday, Friday and Saturday. They are then flat until they fall the next Monday. Figures 3.13 and 3.14 show the results with specific data in Table 3.11.

Figure 3.13
Days of the Week Effects in the NSA Spot Market and the Osaka 50 Spot
Market in Tokyo and the Kabusaki 50 Futures in Osaka, June 6, 1987 to
September 20, 1988

Mean Daily
Return, %

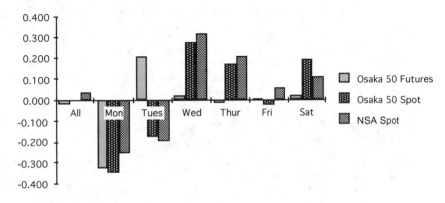

Source: Ziemba (1989)

Figure 3.14
Days of the Week Effects in the NSA Spot Market in Tokyo and the SIMEX
Futures Markets in Singapore, September 3, 1986 to September 19, 1988

Mean Daily
Return, %

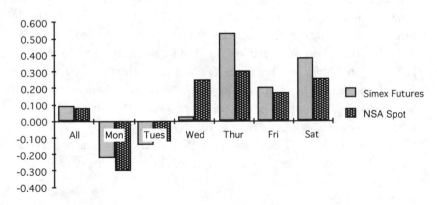

Source: Ziemba (1989)

Table 3.11
Days of the Week Effects in the NSA Spot Market and the Osaka 50 Spot
Market in Tokyo and the Osaka 50 Kabusaki Futures in Osaka, June 6,
1987 to September 20, 1988

| | *Osaka 50 Futures* | | | | *Osaka 50 Spot* | | | |
Day	Sample Size	Mean Return	t-Statistic	% Positive	Sample Size	Mean Return	t-Statistic	% Positive
All	352	-0.020	-0.30	49.4	353	0.000	0.00	52.1
Mon	65	-0.329*	-2.35	38.5	65	-0.347*	-2.50	38.5
Tues	62	0.205	1.20	54.8	63	-0.173	-0.62	60.3
Wed	64	0.018	0.10	51.6	64	0.275	1.15	53.1
Thur	63	-0.012	-0.09	50.8	63	0.173	1.31	55.6
Fri	64	0.007	0.04	46.9	64	-0.025	-0.15	46.9
Sat	34	0.018	0.08	58.8	34	0.190	0.90	64.7

| | *NSA Spot* | | |
Day	Sample Size	Mean Return	t-Statistic	% Positive
All	353	0.033	0.45	56.4
Mon	65	-0.254	-1.93	46.1
Tues	63	-0.196	-0.75	52.4
Wed	64	0.318	1.57	59.4
Thur	63	0.204	1.79	63.5
Fri	64	0.059	0.39	56.3
Sat	34	0.107	0.62	64.7

Source: Ziemba (1989)

EFFECTS OF THE END OF SATURDAY TRADING AFTER JANUARY 1989
In this section, we update the futures market effects of the now four
contracts trading in Japanese stocks and the ending of Saturday trading.
First, let us look at the historical record. Table 3.12 has the mean daily
returns for Monday to Saturday for the years 1949 to 1988 for the NSA.
This can then be compared to the 1989 results for the four months
February to May also shown in Table 3.12. January 1989 which had
Saturday trading is included in the 1988 data. One sees negative
Mondays, -0.14%, positive Tuesdays, +0.17%, strongly positive
Wednesdays, +0.38%, mildly negative Thursdays, -0.03% and positive
Fridays, +0.14%. The Tuesday and Wednesday returns are virtually
identical to those in 1988. By month, the daily returns in 1989 are shown
in Table 3.13.

Table 3.12   Rates of Return by Trading Day of the Week, NSA, 1949-1989

Year	Mon	Tue	Wed	Thur	Fri	Sat
1949	-0.96858	-1.1334	0.13444	0.51476	0.00984	0.39546
1950	-0.08109	-0.1939	0.30202	-0.36615	-0.12054	0.39734
1951	-0.23387	0.2204	0.35465	0.13887	0.12967	0.41701
1952	0.17340	0.0060	0.40003	0.47695	0.13975	0.38640
1953	-0.27173	-0.1950	0.04650	0.22266	0.00675	0.35440
1954	-0.23529	0.1886	0.12228	0.03390	-0.23510	0.03500
1955	-0.09790	-0.0705	0.03622	0.18753	0.14861	0.17078
1956	-0.17909	0.1677	0.0004 6	0.28270	0.16599	0.07507
1957	-0.14937	0.0896	-0.23254	-0.06802	0.03652	0.04877
1958	0.10106	0.0413	0.12134	0.14379	0.05611	0.22162
1959	-0.04561	0.1992	-0.04121	0.20620	0.15405	0.09553
1960	-0.01443	0.1365	0.33907	0.16152	0.07947	0.18995
1961	0.21145	0.0176	0.05182	0.12591	0.10133	0.17307
1962	-0.25996	-0.1565	-0.01362	0.35992	0.10339	0.03026
1963	-0.29152	0.0511	-0.08649	0.08292	-0.12440	0.10472
1964	-0.05277	0.1096	-0.13307	0.23528	-0.16215	-0.00195
1965	-0.10752	0.2200	0.12047	0.20506	0.03884	-0.13646
1966	0.08037	0.0932	-0.11947	0.02637	0.03226	-0.04254
1967	-0.05495	-0.0258	-0.02109	-0.04238	-0.03267	-0.05620
1968	0.25866	0.0542	-0.05242	0.05789	0.09969	0.18039
1969	0.27643	0.1474	0.00286	0.00899	0.03368	0.201.61
1970	0.09106	-0.1995	-0.02519	-0.30148	-0.00874	0.12779
1971	0.03956	-0.1471	0.25582	0.23019	0.18375	0.11595
1972	0.10196	0.2368	0.32006	0.40248	0.13386	0.12675
1973	-0.22595	-0.2234	0.25474	0.05318	0.17124	-0.03056
1974	-0.12548	-0.1840	0.05868	-0.09719	0.05679	0.08327
1975	-0.03127	-0.0679	-0.06605	0.01172	0.14125	0.20692
1976	0.01550	-0.0141	0.31121	-0.10018	0.03938	0.05405
1977	-0.03566	-0.2196	0.14179	-0.13912	0.1 2663	0.10975
1978	0.07585	-0.0854	0.16724	0.04268	0.10084	0.16885
1979	-0.06830	-0.0703	0.15524	-0.02806	0.07636	0.16556
1980	-0.06839	-0.0862	0.19476	-0.05717	0.09943	0.08742
1981	0.10139	-0.1217	0.21006	-0.10076	0.05283	0.03723
1982	0.11709	-0.1788	0.16707	-0.06945	0.00329	0.08908
1983	0.08321	-0.1077	0.16294	0.11906	0.04757	0.16731
1984	0.06557	-0.1120	0.21406	-0.09870	0.12090	0.18003
1985	0.00S62	-0.1007	0.24714	-0.02232	-0.01878	0.18694
1986	0.06199	-0.1299	0.12734	0.21705	0.21813	0.34803
1987	-0.50150	-0. 2701	0.29796	0.38858	0.29169	0.26276
1988	-0.05051	0.1702	0.38630	0.07590	0.02910	0.14237
1989	-0.14124	0.1743	0.37747	-0.03053	0.13605	

Source: Yamaichi Research Institute

Table 3.13: Daily Returns by Month, January to May 1989

January	February	March	April	May
0.2318	0.0683	0.1226	0.1333	.0849

Table 3.14 and Figure 3.15 show this more clearly along with the returns of the NSA and Topix futures contracts.

Table 3.14
Days of the Week Effects1988 and 1989 for the NSA Spot, NSA Futures and Topix Futures

1988	Mon	Tues	Wed	Thur	Fri	Sat
ROR	-0.052050	0.280860	0.441083	-0.149260	0.138297	0.040710
FUT-N	0.026710	0.322562	0.191266	-0.014940	0.133797	0.027935
FUT-T	0.056370	0.333585	0.183224	0.036930	0.151995	-0.018845
1989						
ROR	-0.141240	0.174340	0.377468	-0.030530	0.136055	
FUT-N	-0.022010	0.255222	0.169690	0.039840	-0.002527	
FUT-T	-0.045920	0.159982	0.074796	-0.047990	-0.042898	

Figure 3.15
Days of the Week Effects, 1988 and 1989 for the NSA Spot, NSA Futures and Topix Futures

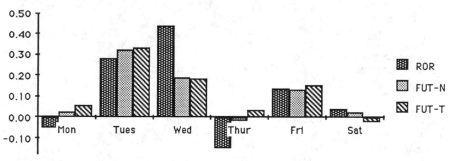

Days of the Week Effects, Sept 88 – Jan 89

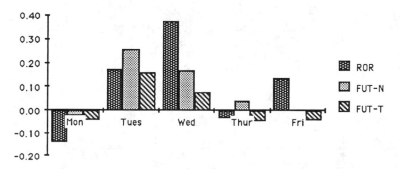

Days of the Week Effects, Feb 89 –May 89

There is much anticipation of the spot effects in the futures markets. Also, Wednesday's high returns continue despite the fact that buying Wednesday selling Thursday with each closing on Monday trades can no longer be made. The effects are then much closer to those in the U.S. markets with weak Mondays and strong Wednesdays and Fridays, except that Tuesdays are stronger than in the U.S. and Thursdays weaker.

In Chapter 10 we discuss the seasonality calendars and give estimates for the future to rank all the days on a scale of +4 (best) to -4 (worst). These rankings reflect all the anomalies such as holidays, turn of the month and year discussed in Chapter 4.

CHAPTER 4
MONTHLY, SIZE, TURN OF THE MONTH AND YEAR, HOLIDAY, AND GOLDEN WEEK EFFECTS IN JAPANESE STOCKS

Research in English on Japanese anomalies is quite recent, partly because there is a lack of interest in such studies by the big Japanese brokerage firms, which are unaware and suspicious of their potential use. Also, these firms do not like to publish research findings, even in Japanese. Recently, however, U.S. and Japanese researchers have been studying these markets. The thrust has been mainly to ascertain the similarities and differences with the results in U.S. markets. The U.S. literature on seasonal regularities is voluminous. Surveys and lists of references appear in Schwert (1983), Keim (1986), Jacobs and Levy (1988) and in the books by Dimson (1988) and Ziemba (1991e).

We begin our study of seasonal regularities with a survey of recent January, monthly, and size effect literature based on data for subsets of the 1949-88 periods for the first section of the TSE. Since the first section of the TSE has about 86% of the trading values and volume of all the stock exchanges in Japan, its study provides a good measure of the whole market. At the end of 1989, the first section of the TSE had a capitalization of about ¥550 trillion, about $4 trillion, which was more than the value of all the stock exchanges in the U.S. Much of this chapter is based on Ziemba (1991a).

THE JANUARY AND MONTHLY EFFECTS

There seems to be a January effect in Japan similar to that in the U.S., Canada and many other countries. In Japan, the effect is not based on tax loss selling. For individuals, there had been no taxes on capital gains or credits on losses. Current taxes are discussed in Appendix H but they are low. Corporations must pay taxes on capital gains, but each firm can choose its own tax year and the majority are in March, not at the turn of the year.

In addition to excess gains in January, particularly for small stocks, there are excess gains in June for small stocks. Part of the reason for these gains seems to be the large semi-annual bonuses paid by most Japanese companies in December and June. The precise dates vary, but typically these bonuses are paid early in the month. For example, the big brokerage firms pay these bonuses near the beginning of the month. These bonuses, which are steeped in tradition, can amount to as much as three months' salary. They provide a great measure of flexibility to the Japanese corporation facing economic swings. Employees purchase gifts - called *ochugen* in the summer and *oseibo* in the winter - and collectively invest some of their considerable savings in the stock market and this boosts prices.

Earnings forecasts may also be a factor. Corporate officers often make their earnings forecasts in May and financial analysts make theirs in March, June, September and December, see Kunimura (1984). The bonuses are likely part but not all of the explanation for the June effect. Australia, for example, has a January and a June effect yet it has no taxes due for the end of December period and no bonuses in June, see Guletiken and Guletiken (1983), Brown, Kleidon and Marsh (1983) and Haugen and Lakonishok (1988).

Kato and Schallheim (1985) studied monthly returns in Japan during the twenty-nine year period, 1952 to 1980. The number of firms with clear data ranged from 529 in 1964 to 844 in 1980. Those firms that were delisted or had other data irregularities had monthly effects similar to those firms in the sample. Equally and value weighted indices, EWI and VWI, were constructed from the Nissho Monthly Stock Price file (1952-80) and the Nikkei Needs Financial Data file (1964-81). They found a small firm effect: the average monthly return for the EWI was 0.42% higher than the VWI. This yearly edge of $(1.0042)^{12} -1 = 5.16\%$ is similar to that found in the U.S. in this period.

However, only the post 1964 period exhibits the small firm effect in Japan. This is similar to the U.S. (see, e.g. Ziemba, 1991e, for precise results and references) and, in the case of Japan, coincides with the opening up of the Japanese economy to foreign investors. There was a strong January seasonal effect in both the equally and value weighted indices of 7.08% and 4.48%, respectively, relative to the other months. The mean return difference was larger for the 1952-63 period, 8.27% and 5.99%, respectively, then in the 1964-80 period, which gained 6.24% and 3.41%, for the EWI and VWI, respectively. From 1964 to 1980, Kato and Schallheim found the mean return differences in January returns to be size dependent. For the equally weighted index, the excess gain in January relative to the other months ranged from 8.68% for the smallest decile firms and 3.18% for the largest decile firms with the other decile firms being:

Largest	2	3	4	5	6	7	8	9	Smallest
3.18	3.82	4.42	6.25	6.12	7.16	8.15	8.20	8.55	8.68

For the value weighted index, the January versus the rest of the year mean return differences were:

Largest	2	3	4	5	6	7	8	9	Smallest
-0.98	-0.19	0.61	1.19	2.18	3.34	4.05	4.38	4.87	5.16

These are similar to the U.S. Value Line-S&P 500 futures spread gains in January, see Clark and Ziemba (1988), Vander Cruyssen and Ziemba (1991) and Ziemba (1991e). Kato and Schallheim computed the mean return difference between the equally and value weighted indices by portfolio size. This is not the best measure for the small versus large firm spread but one that gleans the effect. The spread in January excess returns relative to the CAPM market model using equally and value weighted indices were:

	Largest	2	3	4	5	6	7	8	9	Smallest
EW	-2.48	-2.01	-1.44	-0.84	-0.52	0.53	1.08	1.40	1.82	2.02
VW	-0.98	-0.19	0.61	1.49	2.18	3.34	4.05	4.38	4.87	5.16

The monthly size effect is shown in Figure 4.1 using the mean monthly returns. Kato and Schallheim also found elements of the June effect. Both January and June have significantly higher returns than the other months for small firms. However, the medium and large firms effect is not significant, and it is dependent on the market index used.

A similar but more recent study by Horimoto (1988), also using monthly return data, is described in Tables 4.1 and 4.2 for all the stocks on the first section of the TSE from January 1965 to December 1987 using an equally weighted index. Table 4.1 indicates that the smallest decile stocks gained 9.53% in January on average, which is 7.21% more than the largest decile stocks. The smallest stocks also gained 4.34% more, on average, than the largest stocks in June. March and December are relatively strong months for the big stocks probably because of window dressing and corporate dividend and reporting effects. By month the highest average returns on the TSE were in January, followed in order by March, December and June.

Table 4.1
Monthly Mean Returns in Percent of Ten Size Deciles on the TSE-I by
Month 1965-87

	Jan	Feb	Mar	Apr	May	Jun	Jul	Aug	Sep	Oct	Nov	Dec	Mean	St Dev Stocks	St Dev Decile
Suallest															
1	9.538	2.108	1.289	1.305	2.536	5.308	2.759	1.543	-0.426	1.135	1.081	2.625	2.567	6.107	2.591
2	7.704	2.379	2.064	0.622	1.818	4.436	2.155	0.859	-0.261	0.568	1.013	2.350	2.148	5.186	2.126
3	6.993	1.796	1.908	0.697	1.876	3.963	2.374	0.881	0.229	0.327	1.036	2.140	2.012	5.005	1.979
4	6.303	1.561	2.882	0.790	1.042	3.403	0.670	0.877	-0.270	0.545	0.131	2.102	1.729	4.843	1.774
5	5.931	2.002	3.162	0.691	1.250	2.603	1.126	1.315	0.258	0.224	0.860	2.052	1.789	4.811	1.596
6	4.866	1.938	3.194	0.795	1.350	2.390	0.816	1.289	-0.001	-0.365	1.255	2.098	1.635	4.513	1.419
7	4.596	1.706	3.315	0.875	0.800	2.506	0.327	1.388	0.580	0.000	0.998	1.759	1.563	4.422	1.338
8	3.232	1.373	3.527	0.934	0.619	1.454	0.232	1.457	0.830	-0.104	1.215	1.906	1.390	4.100	1.085
9	2.850	1.446	3.663	0.551	0.714	1.291	0.290	0.739	0.742	-0.156	1.579	2.567	3.356	4.351	1.141
10	2.332	0.774	3.763	0.934	0.899	0.966	0.461	1.213	1.129	-0.430	1.295	3.142	1.373	4.808	1.163
Largest															
Mean	5.435	1.709	2.877	0.818	1.290	2.831	1.121	1.156	0.281	0.174	1.113	2.274	1.757	4.915	1.610

Source: Adapted from Horimoto (1988)

Table 4.2
Standard Deviations of Ten Size Deciles on the TSE-I by Month 1965-87

	Jan	Feb	Mar	Apr	May	Jun	Jul	Aug	Sep	Oct	Nov	Dec	St Dev Stocks	St Dev Decile
Smallest														
1	4.752	3.897	4.298	6.024	7.443	5.197	5.334	8.000	4.849	6.643	5.391	4.941	5.564	1.244
2	3.747	3.604	4.269	5.063	5.912	4.399	4.392	6.829	4.400	5.350	5.546	3.945	4.780	0.958
3	3.513	3.073	4.053	4.647	5.381	4.840	3.944	7.276	4.322	5.642	4.991	4.152	4.645	1.115
4	2.335	2.516	4.431	5.279	5.101	4.002	3.659	7.470	3.940	5.169	5.332	3.630	4.447	1.336
5	3.107	3.130	4.023	5.047	5.199	3.255	3.923	7.704	5.080	5.090	5.553	3.876	4.484	1.320
6	2.530	3.405	3.530	4.720	4.501	3.272	3.475	6.838	4.149	5.334	5.276	3.830	4.238	1.173
7	2.349	3.232	3.804	5.546	4.592	3.270	3.685	6.808	3.750	4.835	4.771	3.269	4.159	1.213
8	2.478	3.275	3.765	4.463	4.266	2.753	3.559	6.073	3.932	4.919	4.677	3.239	3.933	0.996
9	2.107	3.632	3.191	4.609	4.501	2.511	3.861	6.204	3.305	4.751	5.275	3.109	4.147	1.179
10	3.777	3.896	5.465	5.568	3.964	2.779	4.757	5.862	4.265	5.249	5.860	4.748	4.693	0.966
Largest														
Mean	3.120	3.367	4.283	5.097	5.076	3.628	4.039	6.906	4.082	5.288	5.266	3.944	4.508	1.150

Source: Adapted from Horimoto (1988)

There seem to be two windows of opportunity for small stock buyers. The period January to February has an edge of about 8.6% and the April to July period has one of about 8.2%. Small stocks are not in favor by the big four securities companies and they have not encouraged their clients to bid up these prices to close these rather large differences in small versus large firm average returns.

The data also show clearly the observation that September and October are typically weak months for all stocks. Risks in small stocks are higher than in big stocks as measured by the standard deviations shown in Table 4.2. However, the risks in January and June are lower than most other months and below the mean monthly standard deviation. Also, they are not much higher than the average standard deviations by month for all ten of the deciles.

Moreover, small firms in Japan have extremely low beta values. Some of the smallness is probably due to thin trading and the bias that this gives to beta estimates that are not computed using the Dimson or Scholes-Williams estimation methods. However, using these methods still yield low beta estimates. For the five year period July 1983 to June 1988, the average beta for the NSA (relative to the TOPIX's 1.00) estimated by the TSE was 0.84, for the largest capitalized stocks it was 1.16, for the medium capitalized stocks 0.48 and for the smallest stocks only 0.37. For this study, small firms were defined to be those with less than 60 million shares outstanding, medium sized firms with 60 to 200 million shares and large firms more than 200 million shares.

This is not as good a measure of smallness as capitalization, the usual measure. The Topix index is a value weighted average of all, some 1229, stocks on the first section of the TSE. The NSA is a price weighted average of 225 well known stocks. Its value is computed like the DJIA by adding the values and dividing by the current divisor. More details on these indices appear in Chapter 2. These results are shown in Figure 4.2 and can be compared with the Kato and Schallheim (1985) results for the earlier period shown in Figure 4.1. Figure 4.3 shows the monthly small firm minus large firm return differences.

Figure 4.1   Mean Monthly Returns on the Ten Size Portfolio, 1964-80

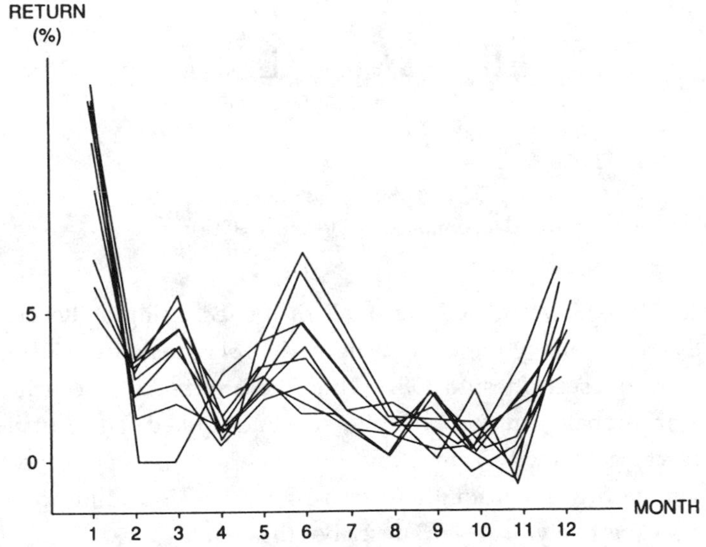

Source: Kato and Schallheim (1985)

Figure 4.2   TSE Stocks Mean Returns by Month and Decile Size, 1965-87

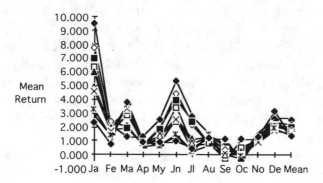

Source: Constructed from data compiled by Horimoto (1988)

Figure 4.3
TSE Stocks Mean Return Differences by Month and Decile Size, 1965-87

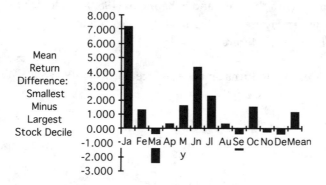

Source: Constructed from data compiled by Horimoto (1988)

Kato (1990a) investigated the small firm effect using daily returns on all TSE stocks, namely the value-weighted Topix index, from 1974, when there were 806 securities, to 1987, when there were 1,069 securities. He used yearly rebalancing on portfolio size and ranked the securities into five size categories with 1 denoting the smallest stocks and 5 the largest. The average firm sizes for these groups were ¥773 million to ¥32,689 million , respectively. Table 4.3 describes the results.

Table 4.3   Topix Mean Returns for Size Related Portfolios, 1974-1987

Firm Size	Average Market Value ¥ million	Mean Return Close to Close	Close to Open	Open to Close
Smallest	773	0.1492	0.1784	-0.0295
2	1,716	0.1058	0.1545	-0.0489
3	3,275	0.0859	0.1354	-0.0495
4	6,554	0.0764	0.0976	-0.0213
Largest	32,689	0.0653	0.0483	0.0168

Source: Kato (1990a)

Small stocks outgain the big stocks by a two to one margin and the gain is monotonic in size. So the usual size effect was present in Japan during 1974-87. As in the U.S., the yearly size effect was not present during 1983-87. However, even in this period, small firms do have much higher absolute and risk-adjusted returns in January and June. Interestingly, all the gains occur in the non-trading period at night as the close-to-open returns are statistically at least as high as the total, that is, close-to-close returns. The returns during the day provide no gains at all and, in fact, are slightly negative except for the highest capitalized stocks.

Table 4.4
Average Monthly Returns on a Portfolio Containing All the Stocks in the Sample, Over the Period January 1955-December 1985

Average Monthly Return Over	Sample Size	Equally-Weighted Portfolio Average Return	t- Statistic	Value-Weighted Portfolio Average Return	t- Statistic
All months	372	1.60%*	6.40	1.84%*	7.55
All Months but January	341	1.24%*	4.75	1.61%*	6.22
January	31	5.58%*	13.17	4.36%*	9.85
February	31	1.00%	1.85	0.99%	1.73
March	31	2.90%*	3.77	3.85%*	4.48
April	31	0.51%	0.57	1.01%	1.23
May	31	0.18%	0.20	0.86%	0.91
June	31	2.51%*	4.59	2.43%*	4.09
July	31	0.65%	0.75	0.44%	0.51
August	31	0.92%	0.85	1.05%	1.09
September	31	0.13%	0.17	1.28%*	1.85
October	31	0.52%	0.48	0.49%	0.56
November	31	1.81%	1.76	2.42%*	2.27
December	31	2.48%*	3.02	2.87%*	3.25

* indicates that the average return is significantly different from zero at the 5% level.

Source: Hawawini (1991)

This finding is somewhat akin to Keim and Stambaugh's (1987) results for U.S. stocks. They found that the major gain in the Value Line small stock index was mostly at night but there were large gains during the day for the large capitalized S&P 500 index. See Kato (1990a) for an analysis of these effects by day of the week in January and other months and chapter 3 for some plausible reasons for this behavior.

Additional insight has been provided by Hawawini (1988, 1991) who is the Yamaichi Professor of Finance at INSEAD in Fontainebleau, France. His study used monthly data for the thirty-one years from January 1955 to December 1985. The firms he considered are traded on the TSE-I. There were 373 firms that traded continuously during this entire period and 566 that traded in the second half, January 1970-December 1985. The effect across months appears in Table 4.4.

January has the highest returns for small stocks (the equally-weighted index) averaging 5.58% per month. The big stocks (the value weighted index) do nearly as well, returning 4.36% per month. June and December, the bonus months, also have high returns, in the 2.5% range, as does March, namely 2.90% and 3.85% for the small and big stocks, respectively.

Table 4.5
TSE Investment Strategies Returns, January 1955 to December 1985

Strategy	Arithmetic Mean	Geometric Mean	Standard Deviation with Arithmetic Mean
Topix	18%	17%	18%
Bottom quintile on TSE-I	28%	22%	38%
Bottom quintile in January & Topix Rest of Year	22%	21%	14%

Source: Hawawani (1991)

The January effect and the excess gains of small stocks over big stocks is very beta dependent. The small stocks do much better than the big stocks, and more so the higher the β is. The smallest stocks with the highest β's return 12.40% in January versus only 1.14% for the largest stocks with the lowest β's. Table 4.6 shows this effect, which is analogous to that observed on U.S. stocks. See, for example, Ritter and Chopra (1989). A strategy to exploit this is to invest in small stocks in January, especially those with high betas, and then if transactions costs are small to move into big stocks for the rest of the year. For the period 1975 to 1984, without transactions costs, returns in U.S. dollars are listed in Table 4.5.

More on strategies of this type appear in the section on a small stock experiment at the end of this chapter.

Table 4.6
Risk and Return Characteristics of the Largest and Smallest Size Portfolios Partitioned into Four Sub-Portfolios Ranked by Decreasing Magnitude of their Beta Coefficient Risk, TSE January 1955-December 1985

Average Portfolio	Sub-Portfolios Ranked by Risk		Average Monthly Return	
Size (¥ mil)	Risk (Beta)	Size (¥ mill)	All Year	January
¥164,716	1.44	158,275	1.29%	6.20%
Largest	0.89	179,708	0.77%	3.33%
Quintile	0.57	160,110	0.61%	2.74%
	0.21	160,772	0.69%	1.14%
¥4942	1.97	5,406	2.02%	12.40%
Smallest	1.37	4,776	1.34%	8.16%
Quintile	0.97	4,710	1.35%	5.75%
	0.43	4,876	1.42%	2.51%

All beta coefficients and mean returns are significantly different from zero at the 5% level.

Source: Hawawini (1991)

The strategy of being in small stocks in January and big stocks in the rest of the year has lower risk than even big stocks throughout the year and nearly as high mean returns as being in small stocks all the time.

THE MONTHLY EFFECT ON THE NSA AND TOPIX MARKET INDICES 1949-88
The monthly returns on the NSA from 1949 to September 1988 are given in Table 4.7 and Figure 4.4. January has by far the highest returns, and all months are positive except for September which is just slightly negative. With January excluded, one cannot reject the hypothesis of equal mean returns in all months. January has significantly higher returns than the other months. The market increased 60.7% of the days compared to 54.3% in all months (including January). The other months have similar behavior, with September and October being the weaker months. Even then, more days rise than fall.

Table 4.7
Mean Daily Return, Standard Deviation, and Percent Positive Returns by
Month of the NSA, 1949-1988

Month	Sample Size	% Mean Return	t- Statistic	% Positive Returns
All days	11529	.0482**	5.56	54.3
January	885	.1816**	5.80	60.7
February	905	.0549	1.87	56.7
March	986	.0457	1.50	55.0
April	947	.0623*	2.10	54.2
May	956	.0074	0.27	53.1
June	1011	.0641*	2.39	56.8
July	1043	.0083	0.27	52.3
August	1038	.0790*	2.96	55.2
September	931	-.0059	-0.22	51.6
October	998	.0088	0.24	50.9
November	910	.0371	1.27	52.4
December	919	.0470	1.37	53.8

* and ** in this and succeeding tables indicates that the mean return is significantly
different from zero at the 5% and 1% levels, respectively

Source: Ziemba (1991)

Figure 4.4   NSA Mean Daily Return by Month 1949-1988

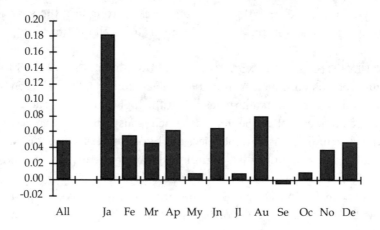

To investigate the changing patterns, Tables 4.8-4.11 and Figures 4.5-4.8 consider the past four decades. The main differences are:

1. During the 1950s, August was very strong, surpassing even January, while December was slightly negative, and March was significantly negative. Both January and August had gains about 60% of the days, while March had losses on more days than gains.

2. In the 1960s Januarys were very strong, with average returns of about 0.21% per day, and the market advanced about 63% of the time. Once January was over, the market had a reasonable showing in the first half and then fell in the second half of the year but managed to close positively in December. The bonus month of June was positive with the market rising about 57% of the time. The July-November period was very weak.

3. In the 1970s January again had the highest returns and again June and December had strong returns. The second half of the year, July-November was again weak, with net losses in this period, although the market did manage to close higher on more than half of the days. February and March were strong and had returns above December and nearly as high as January. The market was up about 60% in these months, similar to January's performance.

4. In the 1980s January again had the highest return but only marginally above March. July was weak also, as was the September-October period. Other months – April, August, November and December – had strong returns.

5. In terms of decades, the 1950, 1960, 1970 and 1980 returned 0.056%, 0.037%, 0.039%, and 0.062% respectively, for an average gain over the thirty-nine years of 0.048% per day.

Table 4.8
Mean Daily Return, Standard Deviation, and Percent Positive Returns by
Month of the NSA, 1949-1959

Month	Sample Size	% Mean Return	t-Statistic	% Positive Returns
All Days	3193	0.0565*	2.85	53.6
January	232	0.1990*	2.33	59.9
February	239	0.0495	0.60	57.2
March	256	-0.1284	-1.59	47.7
April	247	0.1446*	2.13	52.2
May	262	0.0142	0.27	50.7
June	283	0.0192	0.34	54.4
July	291	0.0897	1.06	54.4
August	292	0.2482**	5.31	59.6
September	273	0.0330	0.67	55.3
October	292	0.0481	0.85	52.1
November	262	0.0031	0.05	48.1
December	264	-0.0460	-0.51	52.3

Source: Ziemba (1991a)

Figure 4.5   NSA Mean Daily Return by Month 1949-1959

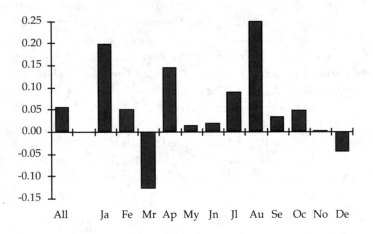

Table 4.9
Mean Daily Return, Standard Deviation, and Percent Positive Returns by
Month of the NSA, 1960-1969

Month	Sample Size	% Mean Return	t-Statistic	% Positive Returns
All Days	3000	0.0368*	2.33	52.8
January	232	0.2170**	4.56	62.9
February	241	0.0271	0.62	52.7
March	258	0.0483	0.81	51.6
April	248	0.0465	0.95	51.6
May	246	-0.0128	-0.23	53.3
June	257	0.0906	1.56	56.8
July	265	-0.0592	-1.05	51.3
August	267	0.0139	0.29	48.7
September	246	-0.0362	-0.66	47.6
October	260	-0.0135	-0.22	49.2
November	240	0.0448	0.74	52.9
December	240	0.0965	1.72	56.7

Source: Ziemba (1991a)

Figure 4.6   NSA Mean Daily Return by Month 1960-1969

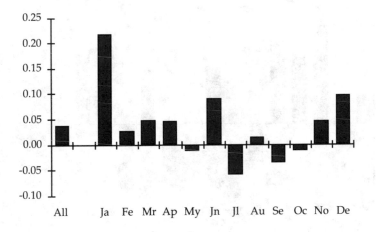

Table 4.10
Mean Daily Return, Standard Deviation, and Percent Positive Returns by
Month of the NSA, 1970-1979

Month	Sample Size	% Mean Return	t- Statistic	% Positive Returns
All Days	2892	0.0391*	2.46	55.3
January	224	0.1370*	2.47	59.4
February	225	0.1075	1.94	59.1
March	252	0.1158*	2.87	60.3
April	239	-0.0555	-0.84	51.9
May	240	0.0219	0.42	56.7
June	251	0.0794	1.51	57.8
July	258	0.0193	0.49	52.3
August	259	-0.0686	-1.01	55.2
September	232	0.0749	0.15	51.3
October	249	-0.0915	-0.15	49.8
November	230	0.0335	0.63	54.3
December	233	0.0977	1.66	55.4

Source: Ziemba (1991a)

Figure 4.7 NSA Mean Daily Return by Month 1970-1979

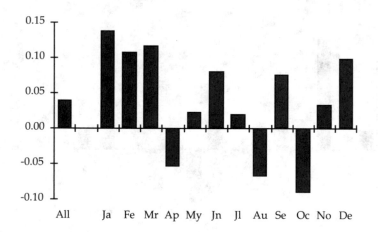

Table 4.11
Mean Daily Return, Standard Deviation, and Percent Positive Returns by
Month of the NSA, 1980-1988

Month	Sample Size	% Mean Return	t-Statistic	% Positive Returns
All Days	2444	0.0625**	3.748	56.1
January	197	0.1658**	3.410	60.4
February	200	0.0361	0.981	58.5
March	220	0.1648**	3.270	61.8
April	213	0.1175*	2.379	62.4
May	208	0.0060	0.108	51.9
June	220	0.0738	1.807	58.6
July	229	-0.0292	-0.570	50.2
August	220	0.1074*	2.410	57.3
September	180	-0.0406	-0.677	51.7
October	197	0.0027	0.023	52.8
November	178	0.0814	1.395	55.6
December	182	0.0516	1.173	50.0

Source: Ziemba (1991a)

Figure 4.8   NSA Mean Daily Return by Month 1980-1988

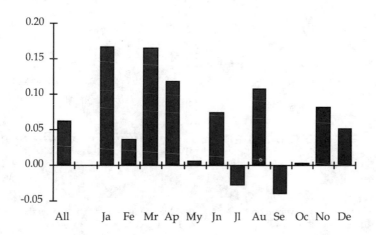

Figures 4.9 and 4.10 provide the monthly returns year by year on both
the Topix and the NSA from 1949 to 1988. These results are obviously
more variable than the aggregated results discussed above, but in general
similar conclusions are drawn.

Figure 4.9   Mean Return by Month of the Year

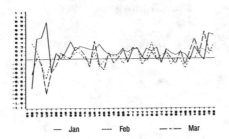

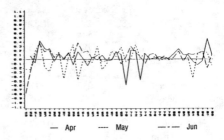

a: Mean Return January to March on the Topix   b: Mean Return April to June on the Topix
Index, 1949-1988   Index, 1949-1988

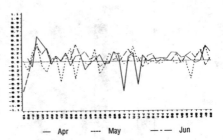

c: Mean Return January to March on the NSA   d: Mean Return April to June on the NSA
Index, 1949-1988   Index, 1949-1988

Source: Ziemba (1991a)

Figure 4.10 Mean Return by the Month of the Year

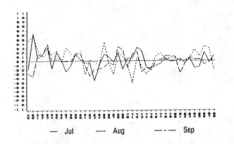

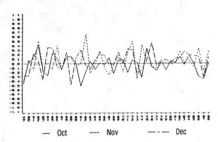

a: Mean Return July to September on the
Topix Index, 1949-1988

b: Mean Return October to December on the
Topix Index, 1949-1988

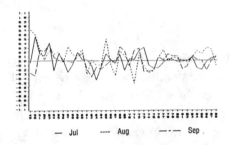

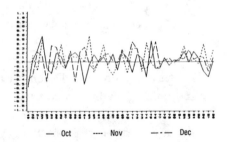

c: Mean Return July to September on the NSA
Index, 1949-1988

d: Mean Return October to December on the
NSA Index, 1949-1988

Source: Ziemba (1991a)

THE BUY/SELL RATIO AND THE MONTHLY EFFECT[1]
Table 3.6 gives the net purchases (sales) by individuals, financial
institutions, industrial corporations, investment trusts, and foreigners for
1981 to February 1989. Individuals have been net sellers throughout this

---

[1]This section was adapted from Ziemba (1990c).

period. Tables 4.12-4.15 describe how various investor groups' buy/sell ratios changed by month during 1975 to 1988 and how these changes correlate with the actual returns on the NSA, the Topix and a small stock index of the bottom 300 stocks in the TSE-I.

Table 4.12
Rates of Return and Buy/Sell Ratios for Various Investor Groups for the Topix, NSA and Smallest 300 Stocks on the TSE-I, by Month, January 1975 to December 1988*

| | Daily Geom Mean ROR | | | Mean Buy/Sell | | | | |
	Smallest 300	Topix	NSA	Total	Members	Corporations	Individuals	Foreigners
Jan	0.2934	0.1474	0.1333	1.0122	1.1086	1.0566	0.9506	1.014
Feb	0.1247	0.0734	0.0587	1.0083	1.0718	1.0833	0.9504	1.090
Mar	0.0056	0.1222	0.1088	1.0055	1.0570	1.0288	0.9777	1.052
Apr	0.1416	0.0871	0.1164	1.0163	1.1051	1.1374	0.9505	0.990
May	0.1206	0.0083	0.0021	1.0108	1.0863	1.1815	0.9411	0.983
Jun	0.1518	0.0655	0.0686	1.0123	1.0820	1.1935	0.9381	0.932
Jul	0.0617	-0.0057	-0.0283	1.0089	1.0680	1.1929	0.9430	0.973
Aug	0.0229	0.0611	0.0580	1.0104	1.0859	1.0872	0.9553	1.006
Sep	0.0615	-0.0306	-0.0303	1.0080	1.0332	1.1194	0.9686	1.013
Oct	0.0097	-0.0350	-0.0040	1.0092	1.1010	1.1575	0.9550	0.843
Nov	0.0913	0.0648	0.0704	1.0097	1.0979	1.1533	0.9377	0.884
Dec	0.0506	0.1393	0.0986	1.0128	1.0973	1.1635	0.9158	0.899

*The first week of the month starts if it contains the 1st trading day of the month.

The data in Table 4.12 for the NSA indicates that individuals are net sellers and more so in December than in any other month. They still sell more than they buy in January, but there is a difference of about 0.035% between December and January. Foreigners are net sellers, particularly in the last quarter of the year; though, they are net buyers in the first quarter. Except for the securities companies which sell and buy nearly equal amounts in almost every month, the other investor groups are net buyers in all months.

Table 4.13 has the correlations of the NSA returns with the buy/sell ratios of various investor groups. Table 4.14 has the same correlations but relative to the Topix. Members and foreigners were the most astute investors in terms of market timing. Corporations and nonmember securities firms had poor market timing in all twelve months. Individuals did not fare much better, but the three months where their buy/sell ratios did positively correlate to the returns on the NSA were at the turn of the year plus February.

The Topix correlations with the buy/sell ratios are similar. However, the correlations of the returns of the small stocks with the buy/sell ratios shown in Table 4.15 are quite different. In particular, individuals have high positive correlations of their buy/sell ratios with the returns in December and January, as would be expected from the small firm effect.

Table 4.13
Correlations of the Buy/Sell Ratios with the NSA Returns for the Various Investor Groups, by Week for Various Months of the Year

	Total	Members	Corps	Indivs	Fors	Sec Firms
Jan	0.3871	-0.0296	-0.4589	0.0400	0.2965	-0.331
Feb	0.2066	0.0386	-0.3118	0.1002	0.3404	-0.439
Mar	0.3700	0.1926	-0.1125	-0.2556	0.2441	-0.447
Apr	0.2141	0.4007	-0.3260	-0.1574	0.0435	-0.369
May	0.4167	0.3687	-0.3775	-0.3049	0.1549	-0.303
Jun	0.2257	0.1379	-0.1931	-0.1222	0.1617	-0.258
Jul	0.1914	0.2643	-0.3602	-0.0303	0.0533	-0.012
Aug	0.1275	0.2721	-0.2515	-0.3903	0.0757	-0.261
Sep	-0.0531	0.1156	-0.4770	-0.1434	0.1502	-0.081
Oct	0.4585	0.2105	-0.2823	-0.4195	0.4722	-0.393
Nov	0.1731	0.3151	-0.4544	-0.0179	0.2832	-0.219
Dec	0.2120	0.1851	-0.1819	0.2492	0.0185	-0.116

Table 4.14
Correlations of the Buy/Sell Ratios with the Topix Returns for the Various Investor Groups by Week for Various Months of the Year

	Total	Members	Corps	Indivs	Fors	Sec Firms
Jan	0.2692	0.0045	-0.4200	-0.0849	0.2292	-0.2713
Feb	0.1846	-0.0050	-0.3801	0.1244	0.3895	-0.4150
Mar	0.3329	0.2287	-0.1208	-0.2637	0.2004	-0.4039
Apr	0.0953	0.2737	-0.2568	-0.2285	0.0615	-0.2780
May	0.4446	0.3377	-0.3698	-0.3394	0.2361	-0.3567
Jun	0.2769	0.2092	-0.2604	-0.2394	0.2411	-0.2321
Jul	0.0610	0.3234	-0.3463	-0.1563	0.0154	0.0579
Aug	0.1180	0.3120	-0.2603	-0.4622	0.1163	-0.1608
Sep	0.0078	0.1523	-0.4358	-0.2299	0.1671	-0.0905
Oct	0.4433	0.2331	-0.2587	-0.4610	0.4748	-0.3320
Nov	0.2060	0.2104	-0.4014	-0.0588	0.2561	-0.2064
Dec	0.1598	0.1594	-0.1248	0.2017	0.0223	-0.0645

Table 4.15
Correlations of the Buy/Sell Ratios with Returns for the 300 Smallest
Capitalized Stocks on the TSE-I by Investor Group by Week for Various
Months of the Year

	Total	Members	Corps	Indivs	Fors	Sec Firms
Jan	0.3429	0.1799	-0.3601	0.3020	0.0744	-0.1495
Feb	0.1768	0.0289	-0.2538	0.0702	0.2423	-0.4323
Mar	0.2743	0.1148	-0.0085	-0.0679	0.0798	-0.2195
Apr	0.3395	0.3047	-0.1133	-0.1222	0.0468	-0.4086
May	0.2929	0.4041	-0.2248	-0.4181	0.0274	-0.2559
Jun	0.0432	0.2582	-0.1179	-0.1276	-0.0179	-0.1839
Jul	0.2259	0.1969	-0.1837	-0.1824	0.1982	-0.1061
Aug	0.0685	-0.1661	0.0143	-0.1845	-0.0202	-0.1072
Sep	-0.0056	0.1356	-0.3660	-0.0247	0.1215	-0.2033
Oct	0.3540	0.2262	-0.1137	-0.4335	0.2550	-0.3700
Nov	-0.0261	0.4544	-0.4382	-0.0767	0.1876	-0.3103
Dec	0.4154	0.1105	-0.1658	0.5285	-0.1512	-0.2382

MUTUAL FUND RECEIPTS BY MONTH

Investment trusts began operations in Japan in July 1951. Most of the
funds invested in these trusts were by individuals with additional
investments by institutions. The total fund receipts by investment trust-
mutual funds by month in millions of yen for the years 1952 to 1987 are
shown in Table 4.16. The data show regular growth in savings month by
month with peaks in December and June. These contributions correspond
to the time when the semi-annual bonuses are received. The funds are
then invested in the stock market in December and January and June by
the mutual fund managers.

The individuals who go directly to the market with their savings tend
to invest in January and June but given that the turn of the month and
year effects start in the previous month - see the next section - some of this
investment shows up in December. Much of this investment is made
through door to door sales visits of security house representatives to
homemakers. This activity is very high in December and partially leads to
the strong returns in December for the large capitalized stocks that the
fund managers like to purchase.

Table 4.16
Mutual Fund Receipts by Month, in Millions of Yen, 1952-1987

	January	February	March	April	May	June	July	August	September	October	November	December	Total
1952	5.00	2,000	1,750	1,100	2,000	2,703	3,705	2,223	3,900	2,100	3,500	8,165	33,644
1953	3,500	5,150	4,950	2,500	3,700	3,000	6,300	3,000	4,450	5,782	7,950	9,700	59,982
1954	0	3,500	3,350	3,600	1,120	2,100	2,209	1,100	2,250	1,400	1,820	1,670	24,110
1955	710	2,115	1,000	1,375	2,100	964	1,365	2,755	3,170	2,169	3,480	5,120	26,382
1956	4,000	4,040	3,700	3,850	4,120	4,050	4,117	4,369	4,016	5,470	4,020	5,680	51,432
1957	7,253	5,918	6,892	6,635	6,332	5,550	6,323	6,907	7,409	7,576	6,468	7,530	92,545
1958	6,121	6,491	10,099	11,200	10,201	9,621	8,968	4,757	7,409	8,210	9,670	13,484	106,413
1959	10,372	11,430	11,663	12,340	12,908	17,958	14,588	16,495	17,211	17,597	17,289	22,631	182,181
1960	22,662	17,737	14,007	16,031	16,672	33,003	23,338	25,170	24,061	31,135	36,417	101,718	362,067
1961	88,915	111,628	70,636	90,433	58,303	105,960	58,957	68,059	45,337	35,141	22,500	76,247	832,695
1962	40,749	35,596	32,780	27,710	25,050	38,840	53,850	69,620	52,055	26,414	21,828	45,856	430,936
1963	33,605	27,371	53,813	37,413	41,926	43,952	56,318	31,975	29,153	29,483	29,363	27,328	441,730
1964	91,224	25,404	19,583	62,430	22,093	24,337	92,226	23,866	31,344	17,709	18,003	21,446	452,491
1965	31,266	25,640	21,938	27,404	23,724	24,277	31,863	26,830	27,473	28,270	22,899	25,913	317,495
1966	28,042	24,667	24,405	24,594	22,835	24,630	29,593	26,665	23,405	23,737	20,613	25,263	291,451
1967	43,386	10,825	19,044	35,078	32,523	24,718	29,329	31,312	22,207	24,234	20,359	33,314	336,051
1968	37,446	28,189	20,165	28,826	28,909	33,559	44,687	33,244	49,498	35,927	36,975	56,588	442,633
1969	50,690	39,966	35,303	50,191	53,457	63,752	55,588	46,737	49,022	54,988	57,561	81,077	611,330
1970	57,006	49,120	49,092	51,403	49,721	54,493	51,635	41,982	16,911	44,915	36,975	69,064	602,331
1971	50,933	43,250	45,102	51,053	62,911	74,902	58,005	50,297	43,328	47,503	51,591	73,178	652,708
1972	75,685	58,744	69,710	60,394	81,281	80,155	92,038	81,218	72,708	90,866	85,200	129,703	963,874
1973	104,027	72,392	73,235	71,083	76,038	86,936	87,093	67,208	63,990	66,262	68,180	121,225	958,366
1974	91,997	88,488	68,961	73,818	83,366	119,050	131,111	87,076	72,932	88,074	70,723	144,686	1,120,283
1975	98,668	105,006	92,422	100,851	84,811	102,011	191,269	82,993	115,043	85,141	77,991	195,280	1,338,120
1976	93,731	86,911	91,245	100,622	111,042	114,077	157,316	109,021	101,676	151,328	96,029	264,933	1,538,585
1977	122,565	119,353	170,432	175,278	187,081	162,261	194,933	157,390	128,507	170,367	161,570	257,117	2,076,854
1978	140,839	148,905	135,604	240,751	173,043	200,157	231,114	120,615	186,622	151,710	143,102	279,255	2,150,677
1979	174,449	172,769	165,677	182,380	131,461	220,819	214,571	133,280	165,238	141,375	123,740	250,940	2,070,732
1980	127,962	128,084	130,402	140,078	200,203	233,855	223,002	165,495	175,761	165,744	171,520	265,387	2,136,421
1981	168,062	196,310	216,092	231,471	210,435	266,017	254,496	253,415	262,417	497,754	917,473	480,125	3,959,667
1982	287,399	273,342	333,976	603,658	310,131	573,043	591,311	353,033	683,371	468,233	619,784	923,392	6,145,018
1983	625,188	699,022	818,304	960,760	1,010,230	1,680,550	1,815,875	1,561,386	1,623,122	1,984,895	1,685,003	2,326,851	10,951,294
1984	1,995,297	2,226,827	2,727,311	3,200,302	2,424,220	2,110,609	1,750,466	1,728,631	1,912,985	2,032,492	2,369,303	2,723,680	27,366,198
1985	2,143,673	2,122,150	2,082,137	1,530,693	1,080,810	1,784,253	1,065,338	1,394,397	1,443,967	1,518,009	1,158,408	1,921,674	20,454,518
1986	1,356,327	1,486,851	2,166,203	2,319,096	2,040,400	2,643,201	2,992,968	3,055,907	2,884,779	2,697,098	2,128,395	1,921,338	29,377,167
1987	2,789,995	2,992,744	3,044,237	3,401,112	3,777,670	4,007,460	3,810,422	3,208,153	3,036,344	3,406,620	1,921,098	2,818,910	98,931,765
Total	11,006,972	11,464,799	13,520,548	14,118,911	13,138,404	16,082,201	14,033,268	13,133,182	13,434,915	14,165,724	12,252,897	17,838,621	163,799,471
	6.72%	7.00%	8.20%	8.62%	8.02%	9.21%	8.93%	8.02%	8.20%	8.69%	7.48%	10.89%	100.00%

Source: Investment Trusts Association

THE TURN-OF-THE-MONTH EFFECT
In the United States the returns on trading days -1 to +4 of each month
dominate the other days, particularly for small stocks. We call this the
turn-of-the-month effect. The return in this period, coupled with that in
the second week of the month, roughly trading days +5 to +8 or +10,
essentially amounts to *all* the gains in the spot stock market in the period
of the 1960s, 70s and 80s. See Ariel (1987) for spot data for the period
1963-82 and Sick and Ziemba (1991) for futures data for 1982-91. This
literature is summarized in Ziemba (1991e).

The rest of the month is essentially noise and at best provides zero
returns. The reason or reasons for this effect are not fully known, but part
of the story is likely that people receive their salaries on or around the -1
day and they receive their stock account statements so they have funds to
invest in stocks. There are also the portfolio balancing and renewal
effects. When would one expect the turn-of-the-month to be in Japan?
Most companies pay their salaries on the 25th of the month. Does the
turn-of-the-month start then and is it similar to that in the U.S.?

Figure 4.11 displays the daily return over the 27 possible trading days
each month in Japan for the NSA, 1949-1988. There seem to be higher
returns in Japan's turn-of-the-month: -5 to +2, a seven-day trading period.
Each of these days has returns of 0.10% or more on average and these
returns are all significant. The -1 day is especially strong, as it is in the
U.S., with returns over 0.22%, making its effect about as strong as a pre-
holiday, namely providing returns about five times as large as on a typical
trading day. The first half of the month effect also seems present, being
the days -5 to +7, a twelve-day trading period. The fifteen-day period +8
to +17 and -10 to -6 amounts to a second half of the month which has
returns that are, at best, noise. These returns are negative, on average.
The hypothesis that these returns are less than or equal to zero cannot be
rejected at the 5% level.

Figure 4.11
Rates of Return by Trading Day-of-the-Month, NSA, 1949-1988

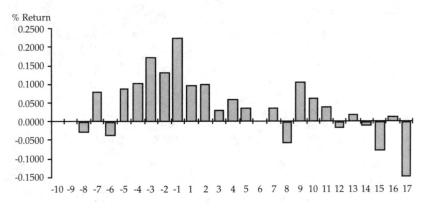

Source: Ziemba (1991a)

It is difficult to align the days correctly, because each month in Japan is slightly different. For example, for this sample period, Saturdays traded on the first, fourth and fifth (if there was one) week of the month. Table 4.17 shows the -5 to +2 and -5 to +7 periods more clearly. These periods have the highest returns. The remainder of the month, starting either on day +8 or possibly on +12, is noise and provides zero or negative returns. This is striking, since the average day during these thirty-nine years had returns of nearly 0.05% per day.

The data for Figure 4.12 appears in Table 4.17. If we let day +22 be in our turn-of-the-month, then the -5 to +7 periods (of which there are 22) return 1.142%, on average or more than 1% a month. For the +8 to +21 periods (+8 to +17 and -10 to -6 in the other counting), the returns, though slightly positive, are insignificant from zero and return only 0.0482%, on average. This is only 1 in 23.7 times as much as in the turn of the month.

Table 4.17 Turn-of-the-Month Data, 1949-1988

Trading Day	Sample Size	Mean Return, %	Maximum Return, %	Minimum Return, %	t-Statistic
-5	471	.0899*	3.650	-2.578	2.75
-4	471	.1041*	5.321	-2.853	2.65
-3	471	.1733**	4.118	-4.216	3.82
-2	471	.1334**	4.555	-6.734	3.18
-1	471	.2255**	2.750	-8.686	5.36
1	471	.0980*	4.501	-3.987	2.43
2	471	.1006*	3.673	-4.849	2.47
3	471	.0307	5.633	-4.368	0.72
4	471	.0592	11.149	-9.997	1.15
5	471	.0358	6.307	-10.649	0.81
6	471	-.0005	4..41	-3.899	-0.01
7	471	.0357	3.471	-4.600	0.09
8	471	-.0585	4.554	-8.218	-1.34
9	471	.1065*	6.877	-4.716	2.46
10	471	.0620	4.795	-4.399	1.58
11	471	.0395	5.394	-4.025	1.05
12	471	-.0196	4.681	-6.970	-0.50
13	471	.0115	11.289	-7.680	0.24
14	471	-.0042	6.408	-3.542	-0.10
15	471	-.0306	6.138	-14.901	-0.54
16	471	.0716	9.888	-7.493	1.35
17	471	-.0498	4.716	-4.253	-1.20
18	429	-.0207	3.582	-4.930	-0.49
19	350	.0162	3.924	-5.032	0.36
20	229	-.0286	4.604	-4.705	-0.48
21	118	-.0476	3.600	-6.610	-0.46
22	39	.0562	2.008	-1.732	0.45

		trading days	
1st Half	22-7	1.1142	
2nd Half	8-21	0.0482	

Source: Ziemba (1991a)

Figure 4.12 NSA Rates of Return by Trading Day-of-the-Month, 1949-1988

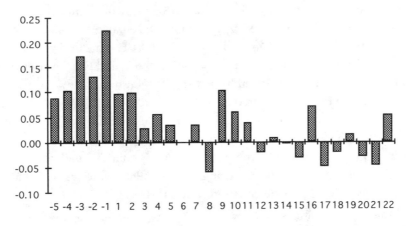

Source: Ziemba (1991a)

Discussions with experienced brokerage executives provided the following list of possible reasons for the turn of the month effect. To test these hypotheses rigorously would require considerable statistical ingenuity and data collection effort. Our purpose here is to record possible explanations for the use of future researchers.

- Most salaries are paid on days 20 to 25 of the month with the 25th being especially popular.
- Buying pressure begins on the 25th.
- There is portfolio window dressing on day -1.
- Security firms can invest for their own accounts in amounts based on their capitalization. Since their capitalization usually rises each month and is computed at the end of the month, there is buying as early as on day -3 to account for this (because of the three day settlement process on the TSE). Buying is done as soon as possible.
- Large brokerage firms have a sales push that lasts 7 to 10 days and this starts on day -3.
- Employment stock holding plans and mutual funds receive money in this period to invest, starting around day -3.
- People buy mutual funds with their pay which they receive on calendar days 15 to 25 of the month. These funds are then invested in stocks with a lag, so most of the buying occurs on days -5 to +2.
- For low liquidity stocks, buying occurs over several days by dealing in different accounts to minimize price pressure effects.

HOLIDAY EFFECTS

There seems to be a holiday effect in Japanese securities similar to that in U.S. securities as documented by Ariel (1991); see also Lakonishok and Smidt (1989), Ziemba (1991e) and Zweig (1986). The mean return of all days on the NSA from 1949 to 1988 is 0.048% per day. On the pre-holidays, the return is about five times as high: 0.246% per day. Moreover, the risk as measured by the standard deviation is also lower: 0.794% versus 0.979% per day, respectively. As in the U.S. there are no abnormal gains on the days around holidays except for the pre-holiday trading day. For example, the days following holidays had returns of 0.0067% per day on the NSA during 1949 to 1988, which is less than a typical day. The regression equation shows this:

$$R = \underset{(3.745)}{0.0352} + \underset{(1.491)}{0.0799\text{Day}_{-3}} + \underset{(0.424)}{0.0222\text{Day}_{-2}} + \underset{(3.709)}{0.1894\text{Day}_{-1}} - \underset{(-1.334)}{0.0663\text{Day}_{+1}} + \underset{(0.023)}{0.00114\text{Day}_{+2}}$$

where R is the daily return and the effects of trading days -3 to +2 are separated out using 0,1 variables for these coefficients. Hence, only the pre-holiday with a mean return of 0.1894% per day, in addition to the typical return of 0.0352%, is statistically significant with a t-statistic of 3.709.

These are the holidays in Japan:

January 1	*Shogatsu*	New Year's Day
January 15	*Seijin-no-hi*	Coming of Age Day
February 11	*Kenkoku-kinenbi*	National Founding Day
March 21	*Shunbun-no-hi*	Vernal Equinox Day
April 29	*Midori-no-hi*	Greenery Day
May 3	*Kenpo-kinenbi*	Constitution Memorial Day
May 5	*Kodomo-no-hi*	Children's Day or Boys' Festival
September 15	*Keiro-no-hi*	Respect for the Aged Day
September 23	*Shunbun-no-hi*	The Equinox
October 10	*Taiku-no-hi*	Health Sports Day
November 3	*Bunka-no-hi*	Culture Day
November 23	*Kinro-kansha-no-hi*	Labor Thanksgiving Day
December 23	*Tenno-tanjobi*	Emperor's Birthday (new holiday)

If we lump Fridays without Saturday trading and Saturdays in as *special pre-holidays*, then the average return over the thirty-nine years is still 0.156% per day and the trading day after special and regular holidays has negative returns namely -0.048%. This, of course, is mostly the effects of the negative Mondays. See Kato (1990a) or Kato, Schwartz and Ziemba

(1989). In Japan, Tuesdays are negative, on average, except when there was Saturday trading the previous week. In that case, Monday was strongly negative, on average. These results are summarized in Table 4.18 and Figure 4.13.

Table 4.18 Holiday Effects on the NSA, 1949-1988

Day	Sample Size	Minimum Return, %	Maximum Return, %	Mean Return, %	Standard Dev%	t-Statistic
Pre-holiday	408	-5.4069	3.0631	0.2461**	0.7943	6.26
Non Pre-holiday	7143	-14.9009	11.2893	0.0489**	0.9786	4.22
Days after holidays	408	-8.6856	4.7122	0.0068	0.9893	0.14
Pre-holidays plus Fridays and Saturdays Preceeding Market Closing	2268	-6.6101	6.8765	0.1561**	0.7242	10.27
Days after holidays and weekends	2268	-8.6856	5.3938	-0.0480	0.9473	-2.41

Source: Ziemba (1991a)

Figure 4.13
Mean Daily Return in Percent NSA, by Type of Day 1949-88
PH (Pre holiday), NPH (Non Pre Holiday), AH (After Holiday), EPH (Pre Holiday plus Fridays and Saturdays Preceding Market Closings), and AHW (After Holidays and Week Ends)

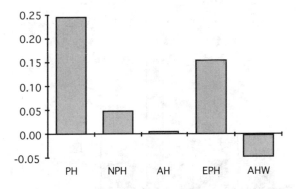

Table 4.19 and Figure 4.14 shows that pre-holidays improve every day of the week. Lakonishok and Smidt (1989) found similar results in their 90 year Dow Jones industrial average study. Even Mondays and Tuesdays are positive if they are pre-holidays. Wednesdays, Thursdays, Friday and

Saturdays have extremely high returns if they are pre-holidays. These
days have positive returns about 70% of the time.

Table 4.19
Mean Daily Return, Standard Deviation and Percent Positive Returns on
Pre-holidays by Days of the Week of the NSA, 1949-1988

	Sample Size	Mean Return,%	t-Statistic	Positive Returns,%
All Mondays	1937	-0.0589*	-2.73	50.9
All Tuesdays	1959	-0.0419*	-1.93	47.4
All Wednesdays	1960	0.1164**	5.30	56.9
All Thursdays	1959	0.0871**	3.77	55.1
All Fridays	1959	0.0544*	2.62	54.6
All Saturdays	1755	0.1409**	8.38	61.9
Mon. Before Holidays	59	0.3106**	3.10	76.3
Tues. Before Holidays	59	0.0103	0.10	57.6
Weds. Before Holidays	58	0.1600	1.17	69.0
Thurs. Before Holidays	60	0.1868*	2.82	73.3
Fri. Before Holidays	71	0.3821**	4.05	74.6
Sat. Before Holidays	101	0.2758**	4.44	64.4
1	256	0.2097**	4.58	62.5
2	1703	0.0310	1.36	53.4
3	18	0.2648	1.38	77.8
4	56	0.1895*	2.53	66.1

1=Fridays before a no-trading Saturday; 2=Fridays before a trading Saturday; 3=Fridays
before no-trading Saturday and no-trading Monday; 4=Saturdays before no-trading
Monday (Saturdays before a Monday holiday.

Source: Ziemba (1991a)

Figure 4.14   The Effect of Pre-Holiday on the Days of the Week

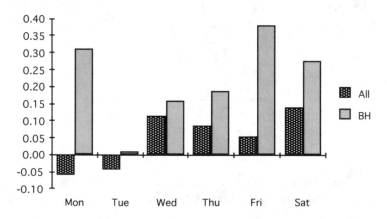

Table 4.20 shows the effect of the pre-holidays as separate from the day-of-the-week effects. The regression estimates show that the pre-holiday effect is the largest, being about 0.246% per day. Mondays and Tuesdays are negative as expected. These estimates use the entire thirty-nine years of the NSA. In this period, returns on Wednesdays are slightly less than those on Saturdays. These two days return the bulk of the week's return. All the coefficients are significant at the 5% level. The standard deviations are coincidentally extremely close for all days of the week except for the preholidays.

Table 4.20
Day of the Week and Pre-Holiday Effects on the NSA, 1949-1988

Effect	Mean Return, %	t-Statistic
Monday	-0.0705**	-3.29
Tuesday	-0.0435*	-2.04
Wednesday	0.1151**	5.40
Thursday	0.0807**	3.79
Friday	0.0420*	1.97
Saturday	0.1327**	5.81
Pre-holiday	0.2461**	5.35

Source: Ziemba (1991a)

Table 4.21
NSA Mean Daily Return, Standard Deviation on Pre-holidays, 1949-1988

Holiday	Advances	Mean Return, %	Minimum Return, %	Maximum Return, %	t Statistic
January 1	32/39	.2457*	-3.38	1.269	2.01
January 15	32/39	.4711**	-2.04	1.947	4.11
February 11	15/22	.3011*	-0.42	1.810	2.65
March 21	21/39	.0687	-1.50	1.912	0.69
April 29	25/39	.2272	-2.96	2.731	1.71
May 3	31/39	.4989**	-0.74	3.063	4.65
May 5	30/39	.3884**	-0.66	2.188	3.92
September 15	14/22	.0154	-2.48	0.670	0.10
September 23	27/39	.2341*	-0.92	1.310	3.00
October 10	12/22	-.2487	-5.41	1.256	-0.81
November 3	24/39	.2987*	-1.27	2.770	2.15
November 23	25/39	.2414	-2.18	2.585	1.55
December 23					

Source: Ziemba (1991a)

Are some pre-holidays better than others? Table 4.21 investigates this for the twelve holidays. Most of the pre-holidays have high returns. The exceptions are September 15, which is just barely positive and October 10, which is negative. This is not surprising as the earlier research showed very poor returns in September and October over the years in both Japan and the U.S. The death of Emperor Showa early in 1989 has led to his birthday April 29, a current holiday, being renamed Greenery Day. Emperor Akihito's birthday, December 23, becomes a new holiday so there are now thirteen holidays.

THE GOLDEN WEEK EFFECT

In late April and early May there are three holidays in a one-week period referred to as *Golden Week*. The holidays are on April 29, May 3 and May 5. Hence, we would expect that April 28, May 2 and May 4 would have strong returns. Also, as with the Christmas holiday period, as

Table 4.22   NSA Mean Return per Day Around Golden Week, 1949-1988

Date	Sample Size	% Mean Return	t-Statistic
April 20	32	-.1285	-0.73
April 21	32	-.0234	-0.18
April 22	33	.0476	0.34
April 23	34	-.0024	-0.01
April 24	33	.1133	1.23
April 25	34	.1339	0.92
April 26	33	.2922*	2.10
April 27	33	.1277	0.74
April 28	34	.2148	1.41
April 30	31	-.1418	-0.47
May 01	33	.4312*	2.69
May 02	34	.5359**	4.47
May 04	30	.3255*	2.96
May 06	31	-.0976	-0.60
May 07	34	.0903	0.87
May 08	33	-.1326	-0.79
May 09	33	-.1174	-0.91
May 10	32	-.0350	-0.23
May 11	32	.0282	0.28
May 12	33	-.0701	-0.70
May 13	33	-.1336	-1.02
May 14	33	-.2421	-1.75
May 15	31	-.2111	-1.70
May 16	32	-.0635	-0.50
May 17	32	-.2209	-1.39
May 18	33	-.3210*	-2.20
May 19	34	-.2898	-1.47
May 20	32	.0081	0.06
May 21	32	.3553	1.57

Source: Ziemba (1991a)

Lakonishok and Smidt (1989) found for the DJIA in the U.S., other days in this period are likely to have large returns as well. The results for the NSA 1949-1988 data displayed in Table 4.22 and Figure 4.15 show that the three pre-holidays do indeed have high returns. April 28 returns, on average, 0.215%, May 2 a whopping 0.536% and May 4, 0.326%. May 1, a +1 day, and a -2 pre-holiday, returns an extremely high 0.431%.

The post-holiday day is poor; not surprisingly, it returns a negative 0.142%. It is an exception to the observed fact that the -1 day of the month is extremely positive. It is not for May in Japan! But, with the movement for more vacations, has come a three day holiday from May 3-5. The high returns on May 4 are now gone and the -1 day of May will probably have better returns as a consequence. It did in 1989 and 1990.

Figure 4.15
Mean Return Per Day Around the Time of Golden Week, NSA 1949-1988

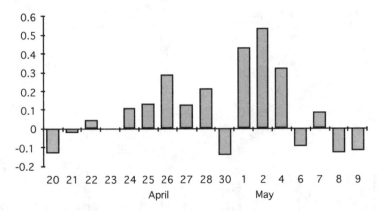

Source: Ziemba (1991a)

THE TURN-OF-THE-YEAR EFFECT
Based on our discussion of the turn-of-the-month effect, one would expect the turn-of-the-year effect to begin around day -5 and run to the middle of January. The data shown in Table 4.23 and Figure 4.16 indicate that the effect seems to start on day -7 when the mean return is 0.142% per day. The effect then has positive returns on every trading day until +14. Many of the days have phenomenal average returns: -4 is 0.468%, -3 is 0.441%, -1 is 0.246%, +3 is 0.381%, +5 is 0.407%, +7 is 0.255%, +9 is 0.401%, +10 is 0.274%, +11 is 0.224%, and +14 is 0.218%. This is with the thirty-nine years of NSA data from 1949-1988. There are no small firm indices readily

available in Japan. It seems quite likely, given the results discussed earlier, that the small firms would have even higher returns. The cumulative average return on these twenty-one trading days averages about 3%.

Table 4.23
Mean Rates of Return for the Thirty-Nine Turn-of-the Years, NSA by Trading Day, 1949-1988

Trading Day	Mean Return, %	t-Statistic	Trading Day	Mean Return, %	t-Statistic
-15	.0292	0.24	1	.0369	0.22
-14	-.0603	-0.38	2	.1539	0.91
-13	-.2631	-1.29	3	.3812*	1.92
-12	.2210	0.72	4	.2460	1.46
-11	-.1036	-0.90	5	.4067*	2.74
-10	.0202	0.09	6	.0856	0.68
-9	-.1197	-0.54	7	.2546	1.51
-8	.0347	0.17	8	.0985	0.74
-7	.1413	0.76	9	.4007*	2.91
-6	.1738	1.31	10	.2736*	2.50
-5	.1303	1.08	11	.2243	1.95
-4	.4683**	4.48	12	.0375	0.32
-3	.4413*	2.49	13	.1101	0.98
-2	.0613	0.39	14	.2180*	2.04
-1	.2457*	2.01	15	-.0334	-0.14

Source: Ziemba (1991a)

Figure 4.16
Mean Rates of Return for the Thirty-Nine Turns of the Year by Trading Day, NSA 1949-1988

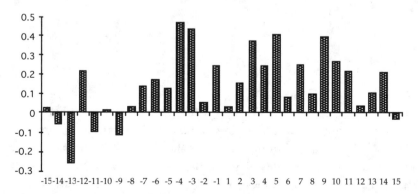

Source: Ziemba (1991a)

The -1 day, the final trading day of the year, is the start of the U.S. turn-of-the-month effect. How important is it in Japan? Its return, by itself, is about 0.198% per day, or more than four times the average day's return of about 0.0476%. We have the following regression equation model:

		Mean Return %	t-Statistic	p-Statistic
b_0	Typical Day	0.0476**	5.47	.0001
b_1	-1's	0.1981	1.32	.1856

where

$$b_1 = \begin{cases} 1 \text{ for -1 day of the month} \\ 0 \text{ otherwise} \end{cases}$$

The following regression model separates out the -1 day of the year effect, from the -1 day of each other month from the pre-holiday effect. The results show that each of these three effects is quite similar in size, returning about 0.2% per day. At least one third of the total mean returns amounts to -1's and pre-holidays which is similar to what Lakonishok and Smidt (1989) found for the Dow Jones industrial average over the ninety years from 1897 to 1986.

		Mean Return	t-Statistic	p-Statistic
b_0	Typical day	0.0341**	3.78	.0002
b_1	-1 of the year	0.2116	1.42	.1568
b_2	-1 of the month	0.1822**	3.95	.001
b_3	Pre-holidays	0.2121**	4.30	.0001

$$b_1 = \begin{cases} 1 \text{ for last trading day of December} \\ 0 \text{ otherwise} \end{cases}$$

$$b_2 = \begin{cases} 1 \text{ for -1 day of the month except for January and preholidays} \\ 0 \text{ otherwise} \end{cases}$$

$$b_3 = \begin{cases} 1 \text{ preholidays except -1 day of year} \\ 0 \text{ otherwise} \end{cases}$$

These various anomalies along with those in Chapter 3 are tested in Chapter 10 on the 1988, January 1989, February to September 1989, and 1990 data to see how well they suggest a ranking of the days. That chapter also ranks the days for 1991-92.

WHY DO THE ANOMALIES OCCUR?

To continue our discussion begun in Chapter 3, on possible reasons for the various anomalies, we list the following plausible explanations:

Pre-holidays

- The effect is similar to the strong Saturday returns before Sundays off. Fridays are strong when there is no Saturday trading.
- A speed or market momentum idea to get in the market before it rises because one thinks the market will continue rising after the holiday; plus, there is one free day.
- The settlement hypothesis idea that one saves another day's interest before you have to pay for a stock purchase.
- There is a self-fulfilling prophesy for those who know about the holiday effect.

Turn of the month effect

- Most salaries are paid during the period of the 20th -25th day of the month, with the 25th being especially popular.
- Buying pressure begins on the 25th.
- There is portfolio window dressing on day -1.
- Security firms can invest for their own accounts on amounts based on their capitalization. Since their capitalization usually rises each month and is computed at the end of the month, there is buying on day -3 to account for this. Buying is done as soon as possible.
- Large brokerage firms have a sales push that lasts 7 to 10 days and this starts on day -3.
- Employment stock holding plans and mutual funds receive money in this period to invest, starting around day -3.
- People buy mutual funds with their pay, which they receive on calendar days 15 to 25 of the month; the funds then invest in stocks with a lag, so most of the buying occurs on days -5 to +2.
- For low liquidity stocks, buying occurs over several days by dealing in accounts to minimize price pressure effects.

A TEST WITH REAL YEN[2]

In December 1988 a private investor, the president of a small Japanese company, provided real money - a ¥30 million stake - to test the small stock anomalies. The arrangement was to buy the stocks at the December 1988 turn of the year and then sell them at the end of July 1989. Stocks were selected from the 300 smallest stocks on the TSE-I. These are known to have high mean returns, low betas, and not particularly high standard

---

[2]Without implicating them, I would like to thank my YRI colleagues, Shigeru Ishii and Asaji Komatsu for their help in researching and keeping track of this experiment. Discussions with Professor Kiyoshi Kato and his paper, Kato (1990b) , were also helpful.

deviation risk. U.S. evidence provided by Professor Donald Keim for the 1960s to the early 1980s demonstrates that the very smallest stocks have the greatest risk adjusted returns in January. The typical effect is shown in Figure 4.17. This idea is the basis for many small capitalized funds such as those run in various countries by Dimension Fund Advisors with considerable success. There is also much evidence about how these stocks' returns should move relative to the NSA and Topix indices throughout the year.

To rank stocks in the universe, a selection model was developed based on anomalous and fundamental factors. The selection model rates the smallest 300 stocks from 1 to 300 and it was developed and then tested on data from 1975 to 1988. The small stocks are then grouped into the best 10, 25, 50, 100, 150, 200, 250 and all 300 small stocks. The portfolios are then rebalanced once a year at the end of December. The best stocks did extraordinarily well during this period (see Figure 4.18).

Knowing that January is the strongest month for small stocks makes it an advantageous time to make the revisions. During the fourteen year period, the NSA and Topix increased 15.8% and 16.4% per year, respectively, for a total gain of about eight times the original investment. Only in 1977 did they have a loss. Table 4.24 details this year by year. Since 1983 these returns have been very high. The results for 1989 were also strong, with these indices up about 29%.

Figure 4.17
Risk adjusted return of U.S. stocks by market capitalization in millions of
dollars in January

Average return
above T-bill

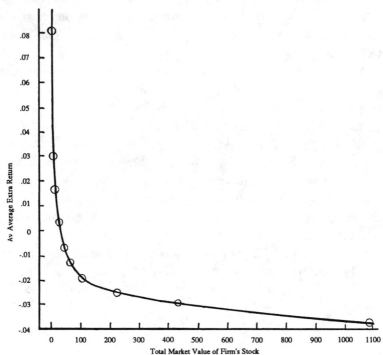

Source: Keim (1987)

Figure 4.18
Growth of 1¥ from 1974 to 1988 for Portfolios 10, 25, 50, 100, 150, 20, 250
and 300, Topix and NSA

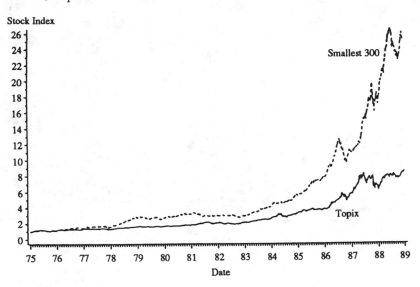

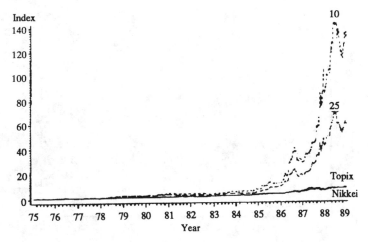

Figure 4.18 continued

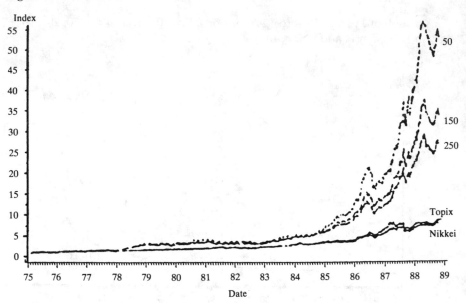

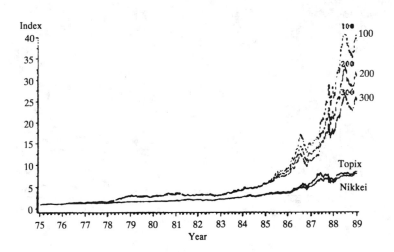

Table 4.24
Rates of Return by Year and Summary Statistics for Yearly Rebalancing
for the 10, 25, 50, 100, 150, 200, 250 and 300 Smallest Capitalized Stocks on
the TSE-I versus the NSA and Topix, 1974-1988

Year	10	25	50	100	150	200	250	300	NSA	Topix
1975	-2.67	11.03	11.60	7.05	12.45	13.76	14.21	14.69	15.39	17.17
1976	8.46	16.67	17.00	22.94	23.65	23.22	25.17	26.34	13.35	17.65
1977	8.94	10.70	20.33	16.96	16.06	15.55	14.18	12.35	-2.67	-5.22
1978	106.14	94.97	92.17	91.24	83.39	77.34	72.12	70.06	23.29	23.49
1979	10.84	-3.83	0.83	-2.16	-0.26	-1.52	-1.51	-1.98	8.74	1.49
1980	67.74	37.55	25.65	22.23	17.48	19.53	18.62	17.54	8.48	7.69
1981	-12.19	-12.95	-11.23	-10.86	-8.48	-7.65	-7.05	-7.33	7.42	15.03
1982	-9.44	-6.76	-6.86	-3.24	-2.15	-2.37	-1.83	-2.05	3.86	3.73
1983	41.80	32.59	42.71	42.45	36.61	38.34	40.94	41.02	23.34	23.49
1984	30.81	26.92	29.85	26.67	30.45	31.86	31.35	30.34	16.27	24.19
1985	71.30	85.54	68.80	61.58	54.46	49.69	45.29	41.91	13.46	14.45
1986	134.24	89.15	64.00	56.55	50.15	45.84	42.80	39.73	42.36	48.35
1987	198.16	120.83	91.15	76.14	68.99	65.69	60.42	55.81	14.58	9.56
1988	59.05	51.43	59.04	54.05	51.98	51.08	46.91	47.69	42.15	39.43
geometric mean	41.79	33.96	32.79	29.98	28.65	27.74	26.55	25.90	15.80	16.39
symmetric SD*	28.80	22.71	23.60	22.87	16.95	16.29	15.42	15.30	7.18	8.67
mean Beta	0.34	0.40	0.42	0.42	0.45	0.46	0.48	0.50	1.04	1.00
Risk adjusted**	25.20	23.65	23.61	22.87	22.91	22.44	21.79	21.22	14.77	14.89
Total Return for 1¥ in 1975										
	132.71	59.92	53.02	39.28	34.03	30.83	27.02	25.14	7.79	8.12

*Since the small stock portfolios have many years with very high returns, see Figure 4.21, the ordinary standard deviation is not a very meaningful measure since one is then penalized for doing well. To symmetrize the standard deviation, we define it as $\sqrt{2}$ times the one sided standard deviation when the return is below the geometric mean.

†These utility values are computed via the formula: mean - variance/risk tolerance, using a risk tolerance of 100, which is that for a U.S. investor fully invested in stocks. See Kallberg and Ziemba (1983) or Sharpe (1987) for analyses that show the generality of this approach.

The smallest stocks performed even better with the 10, 25 and 50 stock portfolios having mean geometric returns well over 30% per year. Since 1983, these stocks have had phenomenal returns. See Table 4.24 for specific results including the year by year rates of return for the various portfolios along with their sample statistics. Figure 4.18 has the cumulative returns for the various small stock portfolios for the 14 years. The ending values are given in Table 4.24. The 300 small stock universe nearly tripled the indices returning ¥25 for each yen invested. The portfolios 10, 25, ... , and 250 did even better. For example, the smallest 50 stock portfolio returned ¥53 for each yen invested in 1974. In the year of the stock market crash, these stocks had a huge increase and after the

crash, were up about 100% depending on the portfolio size. Figure 4.19
shows the returns in 1987 as well as the other years from 1974 to 1988.

Figure 4.19
Year by Year Returns for Yearly Rebalancing for the 10, 25, 50, 100, 150,
200, 250 and 300 Smallest Stocks on the TSE-I versus the NSA and Topix,
1974 to 1988

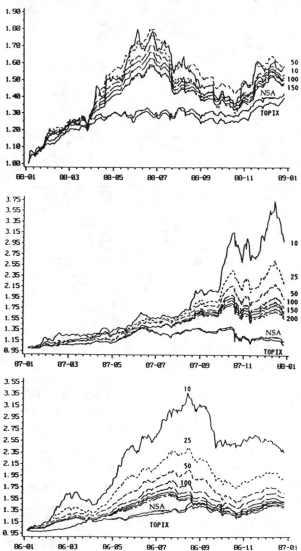

Figure 4.19 continued

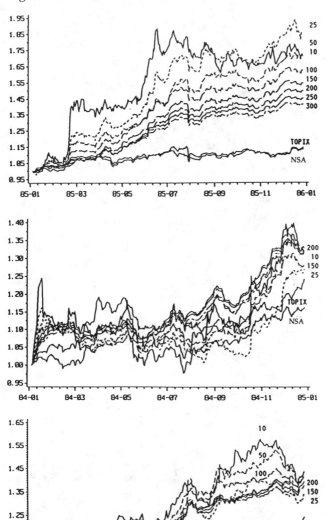

Figure 4.19 continued

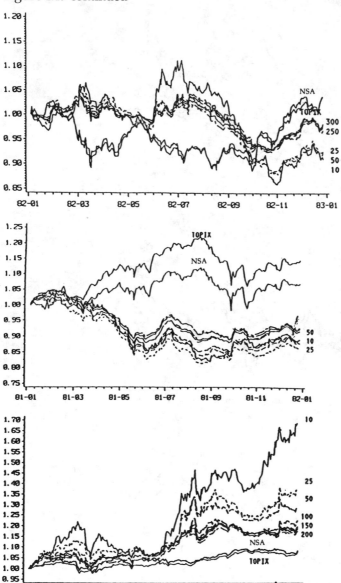

Figure 4.21
Number of Years with Various Returns for 50, and 100 Small Stock
Strategies Versus the NSA and Topix

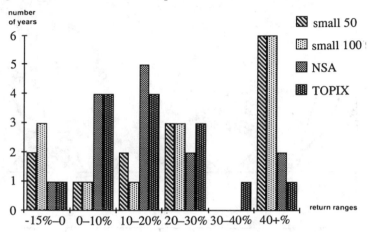

Two or three thousand shares of each of the fifteen stocks, were purchased. After commissions, the total investment was ¥30,498,500. Table E.1 in the appendix has the daily returns from late December 1988 until the end of July 1989. Since orders were low, about 1.2% commission for each purchase was charged. By the end of December, we were essentially behind by the commission. The NSA without commission was then up 0.36% from the day all the positions were in place and 2.36% from the day the yen were in the account.

Figure 4.22
Mean Daily Returns by Month in Percent for Various Portfolios Versus the
Topix, Data in Mean Daily Returns, 1975-88

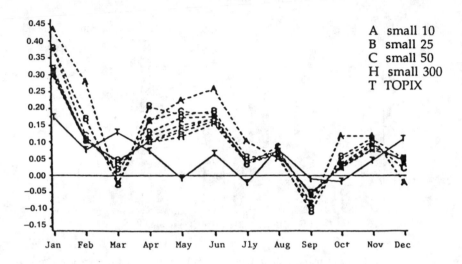

A small 10
B small 25
C small 50
H small 300
T TOPIX

One expects the big stocks to outperform the small stocks in December,
and that is what happened. One expects the small stocks to do extremely
well in January and to also perform well in February relative to the big
stocks. That was the outcome. Our portfolio was up about 13% at the end
of January vs 7% for the NSA. February was fairly flat for both portfolios.

One expects the small stock portfolio to underperform in March and it
did. In 1989 small stocks underperformed by more than usual. So, by the
end of March, the NSA had caught up. The April-July period is usually
strong for the small stocks, and this was the case. The period from the
beginning of April to the end of Golden Week in May was very strong for
the small stock portfolio and it moved to about 20% ahead and 5% above
the NSA. June, traditionally the second strongest month for small stocks
was clouded by the Beijing influence and the general market apathy. Still,
the small stocks outperformed the indices by staying nearly even while
the latter fell.

Table 4.26   Purchase of Stocks for ¥30 Million Portfolio, December 1988

	Code	Name	Industry	Date	Price	Shares	Total Paid	Commission	Cost
1	2604	Yoshihara Oil	Food	Dec 27	830	3000	2,490,000	26,900	2,516,900
2	3524	Nitto Seimo Co.	Textiles	Dec 23	630	1000	630,000	7,560	637,560
				Dec 26	630	2000	1,260,000	14,600	1,274,600
3	4210	Toyo Chemical	Chemicals	Dec 27	799	1000	799,000	8,653	807,653
				Dec 27	800	1000	800,000	8,664	808,664
				Dec 27	808	1000	808,000	8,753	816,753
4	4614	Toa Paint	Chemicals	Dec 22	870	2000	1,740,000	19,400	1,759,400
5	5263	Daido Concrete	Glass & Cer	Dec 20	769	2000	1,538,000	17,380	1,555,380
6	5544	Yahagi Iron	Iron & steel	Dec 20	659	3000	1,977,000	21,770	1,998,770
7	6378	Kimira Chem Plants	Gen machinery	Dec 20	685	3000	2,055,000	22,550	2,077,550
8	6590	Shibaura Eng Works	Elec machinery	Dec 21	850	2000	1,700,000	19,000	1,719,000
9	6901	Sawafuji Elec	Elec machinery	Dec 27	875	1000	875,000	9,415	884,415
				Dec 27	875	1000	875,000	9,415	884,415
				Dec 27	880	1000	880,000	9,470	889,470
10	7104	Fuji Car Mfg	Trans equip	Dec 27	770	2000	1,540,000	16,733	1,556,733
				Dec 27	770	1000	770,000	8,367	778,367
11	7961	Nissan Nihrin Kogyo	Misc manuf	Dec 20	634	1000	1,902,000	21,020	1,923,020
12	8042	Nihon Matai	Commerce	Dec 21	900	1000	900,000	10,800	910,800
				Dec 23	900	1000	900,000	10,800	910,800
13	8065	Sato Shoji	Commerce	Dec 12	920	2000	1,840,000	20,400	1,860,400
14	8099	Yuasa Trading	Commerce	Dec 21	655	1000	655,000	7,216	662,216
				Dec 21	655	2000	1,310,000	14,434	1,324,434
15	8122	OSG Corp	Commerce	Dec 27	960	2000	1,920,000	21,200	1,941,200
			Total				30,164,000	334,500	30,498,500

My agreement with the YRI client was to end the experiment at the end of July.[3] I placed limit orders through the August turn of the month and got good execution on most of the stocks. Because of the agreement some stocks had to be sold at their market price to complete the experiment. So the 23-24% gain based on closing prices during the first part of August yielded a gross return of 21.92%. After the two way commission plus the 1% capital gains tax, the net gain was 18.84%, see Table 4.27. The NSA returned 17.42% which does not include any commissions or taxes. An index portfolio would, on final sale, have to pay the 1% tax for Japanese residents. On the final day August 10, the NSA was at 34,719.80 and our portfolio at 37,163, or up 23.2% versus 17.42% (the gain from the day the funds were placed in the account - NSA at 29,597.81 - until the close out day). With a larger scale and less pressure to exit, more of the 5.8% advantage could have been kept.

---

[3]It was my opinion that the market had yet to see its high and that the client should not cash out yet. However, the decision was made to liquidate as the original arrangement specified.

Exit execution loss	$\cong$	1.2%
Round trip commission	$\approx$	2.1%
Taxes	$\approx$	1.0%

5.8%-4.3%=1.5%

Table 4.27
Results of the Small Stock Portfolio Versus the NSA, Late July to Early
August 1989

date	15 Stock Portfolio Equivalent Value	Gross Gain of 15 Stock Portfolio	NSA Gain
July 25	36,193,000	20.0	16.8
July 26	36,720,000	21.7	16.8
July 27	36,974,000	22.6	17.6
July 28	37,365,000	23.9	17.4
July 31	37,481,000	24.3	18.2
August 1	37,221,000	23.4	18.0
August 2	37,228,000	23.4	18.0
August 3	37,256,000	23.5	17.6
August 4	37,232,000	23.4	17.5
August 7	37,095,000	23.0	17.1
August 8	37,460,000	24.2	17.6
August 9	37,145,000	23.1	17.9
August 10	37,163,000	23.2	17.4

The experiment was a success and the client, YRI, and we were pleased. The June effect did not occur. I believe that it was delayed because of the uncertainty caused by the China massacres and the internal domestic leadership problem. The money from the June bonuses was simply parked for later use. Hence, I continued to watch and monitor this portfolio. The June effect did materialize during October's turn of the month. The small stock portfolio then moved to 39.0% versus 20.1% for the NSA for an edge of 18.9%. At the end of 1989 the portfolio was up 60.1% versus 31.5% for the NSA for an edge of 28.6%. I did not revise the portfolio at the end of the year. However, you can find the best 50 model stocks as of January 1, 1991 in the small stock sample portfolio in Chapter 8. The best 15 as of then are the top 15 in this list. It is advised that the portfolio be revised as general conditions and valuations of individual stocks change.

In 1990, the January-February edge of the small stocks over the big stocks materialized as per script. By the end of February 1990, the edge was 47.9 percentage points with the small stock portfolio up 65.8% and the NSA up 17.9%. The NSA was hit hard in early 1990 as discussed in

Chapter 7. The small stock portfolio held up and kept rising. As of March 9, 1990, the portfolio was up 74.1% versus 12.7% for the NSA for an edge of 61.4%. The unfavorable March period and bad investment climate finally hit the small stocks, and in mid March they fell very sharply. The small stocks had a poor performance for the rest of 1990. There was a parallel with the golf course membership indices which also performed very poorly in this period; see the discussion in Chapter 2. The small stock portfolio ended 1990 down 8.3% versus December 1988 which was 11.1% better than the -19.4% return on the NSA.

For the second year in a row, March was a very bad time to be in small stocks. They bottomed out in the first week of April and then began to make their April to July run. As of April 19, they were up 23.3% from December 1988 versus 1.2% for the NSA. On August 10, they were 39.4% above the NSA.

Table 4.28 shows the month by month results from December 1988 to the end of December 1990 for the small stock portfolio and the NSA. Table 4.29 compares this return for the small stock portfolio and the NSA via the *script* or what we expect to happen according to the anomalous behavior as shown in Figure 4.22. Table 4.28 shows the prices of the individual stocks at various points. The strong gains in the portfolio, until the sharp decline in mid March 1990, were obtained across the board with all stocks up in the year plus period. In December 1990 many of the stocks were close to their December 1988 levels. The script guided and was fairly consistent with the results. The low beta of the portfolio is seen in the daily performance in Table E.1 in the appendix. Days like June 15, 1989 when the portfolio rose over 1% when the NSA fell 498.90 show the effect. The portfolio does seem to rise before and fall after holidays, as expected.

Table 4.28
Small Stock Portfolio versus the NSA, December 1988 to December 1990

code	name	industry	purchase Dec	1989 Feb	Mar	Apr	May	Jun	Jul	Aug	Sep	Oct	Nov	Dec
1 2604	Yoshihara Oil Mill	Foods	830	970	880	980	920	890	900	898	916	940	960	1170
2 3524	Nitto Seimo Co.	Textiles	630	726	666	795	780	705	740	724	762	1230	1150	1140
3 4210	Toyo Chemical	Chem	802	840	904	940	890	820	809	946	960	999	1030	1070
4 4614	Toa Paint	Chem	870	960	1010	1080	995	930	1050	990	1080	1270	1500	1410
5 5263	Daido Concrete	Glass & Cer	769	916	1060	1006	1020	920	1030	1020	1200	1140	1220	1160
6 5544	Yahagi Iron	Iron & Steel	659	825	810	907	905	850	886	840	818	839	890	926
7 6378	Kimura Chem Plants	Gen Mach	685	761	760	894	919	908	919	951	990	965	1090	1250
8 6590	Shibaura Eng Works	Elec Mach	850	980	939	962	980	1070	1070	1030	1090	1150	1160	1270
9 6901	Sawafuji Elec	Elec Mach	878	820	821	918	909	870	910	910	919	1170	1140	1180
10 7104	Fuji Car Mfg	Trans Equip	770	810	780	845	879	919	880	884	891	930	1010	1380
11 7961	Nissan Nihrin Kogyo	Misc Manu	634	640	611	739	731	668	730	701	691	963	835	930
12 8042	Nihon Matai	Commerce	900	949	905	980	962	1260	1280	1150	1100	1060	1170	1180
13 8065	Sato Shoji	Commerce	920	1160	1190	1250	1230	1200	1300	1310	1430	1630	1196	1900
14 8099	Yuasa Trading	Commerce	655	740	686	770	790	721	761	734	776	823	876	1490
15 8122	OSG Corp	Commerce	960	1064	991	973	1209	1109	1300	1345	1536	1609	1660	1610
	Portfolio value		30167	33454	32944	35866	35961	35031	36665	36454	38041	42295	42755	48668
	% increase			9.7%	8.0%	17.7%	18.0%	14.9%	20.3%	19.6%	24.9%	39.0%	40.5%	60.1%
	NSA value		29598	31986	32839	33713	34267	32949	34954	34431	35637	35544	37269	38916
	% increase			8.5%	11.5%	14.4%	16.3%	11.8%	17.8%	17.8%	20.4%	20.1%	25.9%	31.5%
	excess over NSA		-1.2%	1.2%	-3.4%	3.3%	1.7%	3.1%	2.6%	1.9%	4.5%	18.9%	14.6%	28.6%

code	name	industry	1990 Jan	Feb	Mar 9	Mar 23	Mar 26	Mar 30	Apr 2	Apr 5	Apr 19	May 14	Jun 1	Jun 22	Jul 4
1 2604	Yoshihara Oil Mill	Foods	1330	1170	1170	900	880	870	821	559	729	750	939	920	895
2 3524	Nitto Seimo Co.	Textiles	1240	1190	1230	885	880	860	800	628	733	730	960	950	970
3 4210	Toyo Chemical	Chem	1190	1130	1160	900	915	977	887	670	790	780	950	930	991
4 4614	Toa Paint	Chem	1420	1470	1550	1140	1120	1200	1080	923	1020	1000	1240	1270	1370
5 5263	Daido Concrete	Glass & Cer	1160	1150	1330	979	1070	1040	952	829	920	925	1420	1120	1250
6 5544	Yahagi Iron	Iron & Steel	900	1020	1000	680	729	745	680	488	625	635	770	680	720
7 6378	Kimura Chem Plants	Gen Mach	1300	1300	1280	989	1030	1030	928	724	885	1000	1140	1020	980
8 6590	Shibaura Eng Works	Elec Mach	1460	1490	1310	1220	1340	1200	1100	940	1040	1020	1110	1230	1200
9 6901	Sawafuji Elec	Elec Mach	1330	1300	1330	910	966	1050	960	834	930	1000	1050	1160	1130
10 7104	Fuji Car Mfg	Trans Equip	1260	1200	1470	1120	1260	1160	1070	930	1230	1130	1220	1360	980
11 7961	Nissan Nihrin Kogyo	Misc Manu	1010	1000	1200	860	909	955	905	703	768	810	1100	970	1230
12 8042	Nihon Matai	Commerce	1240	1300	1440	1200	1240	1250	1150	879	1050	995	1240	1308	980
13 8065	Sato Shoji	Commerce	1890	1920	1870	1900	1750	1940	1820	1730	1900	1870	1810	1730	1800
14 8099	Yuasa Trading	Commerce	1690	1530	1600	750	816	801	730	580	810	780	1030	900	870
15 8122	OSG Corp	Commerce	1610	1600	1780	1540	1650	1550	1500	1420	1600	1480	1582	1850	1370
	Portfolio value		51310	50380	52880	39940	41495	41704	38547	31790	37560	37425	44281	43686	42238
	% increase		68.9%	65.8%	74.1%	31.2%	36.4%	37.0%	26.6%	4.2%	23.3%	22.9%	45.6%	43.6%	38.8%
	NSA value		37189	34891	33368	30372	31840	29980	28002	28249	29945	29689	32042	31694	32446
	% increase		25.6%	17.9%	12.7%	2.6%	7.6%	1.3%	-5.4%	-4.6%	1.2%	0.3%	8.3%	7.1%	9.6%
	excess over NSA		43.2%	47.9%	61.4%	28.6%	28.8%	35.8%	32.0%	8.7%	22.1%	22.6%	37.3%	36.5%	29.2%

code	name	industry	1990 Aug 10	1990 Sep 6	1990 Sep 28	1990 Oct 31	1990 Nov 30	1990 Dec 28
1 2604	Yoshihara Oil Mill	Foods	884	679	590	771	560	615
2 3524	Nitto Seimo Co.	Textiles	780	645	520	805	1100	1190
3 4210	Toyo Chemical	Chem	798	680	520	671	500	538
4 4614	Toa Paint	Chem	1500	1250	561	1050	799	713
5 5263	Daido Concrete	Glass & Cer	1000	770	680	1030	685	725
6 5544	Yahagi Iron	Iron & Steel	710	620	580	581	498	780
7 6378	Kimura Chem Plants	Gen Mach	845	680	455	711	530	500
8 6590	Shibaura Eng Works	Elec Mach	1100	930	730	825	750	730
9 6901	Sawafuji Elec	Elec Mach	1030	880	705	790	640	566
10 7104	Fuji Car Mfg	Trans Equip	1200	915	830	930	720	789
11 7961	Nissan Nihrin Kogyo	Misc Manu	757	559	509	665	481	493
12 8042	Nihon Matai	Commerce	1140	975	925	934	799	785
13 8065	Sato Shoji	Commerce	1820	1470	1200	1210	999	1000
14 8099	Yuasa Trading	Commerce	820	600	500	706	500	503
15 8122	OSG Corp	Commerce	1750	1680	1550	1450	1350	1100
	Portfolio value		40092	32924	26919	32888	27351	28028
	% increase		31.7%	7.9%	-12.0%	7.8%	-10.5%	-8.3%
	NSA value		27329	23811	20984	25194	22455	23848
	% increase		-7.7%	-19.6%	-29.1%	-14.9%	-24.1%	-19.4%
	excess over NSA		39.4%	27.5%	17.1%	22.7%	13.6%	11.1%

Table 4.29
Script versus *Reality* for Small Stock Portfolio, December 1988-December 1990

Month	The Script	The Result
1988 December	Big stocks have edge, end of year portfolio rebalancing	Yes, the portfolio was 3.5% behind (1.2% commission +2.3% relative loss)
1989 January	Small stocks have large edge, Dec bonuses plus January effect	Yes, at end of month up 13% vs 7% for NSA
February	Small edge for small stocks	No, market flat for both portfolios, but NSA gains about 2% relative to portfolio
March	Edge for big stocks (end of fiscal year adjustments)	Yes, even stronger than usual, NSA catches up and moves ahead by 3%
April to May GoldenWeek	Strong for small stocks	Yes, portfolio up 18% versus 14% for NSA
rest of May	Weak	Yes, portfolio up 18% vs 16% for NSA
June	Usually extremely strong for small stocks	Yes, relatively, NSA fell to 12% vs. portfolio at 15%
July	Strong for small stocks	Yes, portfolio up 20% vs. 18% for NSA
August	Flat	Yes, both portfolios about even
September	Weak	No, portfolio gains 5% to +25% vs 20% for NSA
October	Weak	Yes, general market flat. But portfolio gains 14% to +39% vs. 20% for NSA at the October turn of the month. Bonus money held till China and PM problems resolved.
November	General market picks up, small stocks have small edge	Yes, portfolio continues to advance more than NSA which also increases, total increase on Dec 2 was 50.5% vs 26% for the NSA , 10% of increase at turn of month.
December	Big stocks have edge, end of year portfolio rebalancing	No, general market is very strong, the NSA closes at 38,915.87 up 29.04% on the year; the small stock portfolio closed the year up 58%
1990 January	Small stocks have large edge, Dec bonuses plus January effect	Yes, portfolio up about 9% in Jan, meanwhile the NSA falls to 37,189 down 6%. As of Friday Jan 12 , the portfolio was up 63.4% vs 26.9% for the NSA. At the end of the month it was up 68.9% vs 25.6% for the NSA or 43.2 % higher.
February	Small edge for small stocks	Yes, small stocks fall 3% but NSA falls 8%.
March	Edge for big stocks (end of fiscal year adjustments)	Yes, again very strong relatively for big stocks. Small stocks held up despite large NSA declines till mid month then they fell sharply. As of March 30 , portfolio was down considerably but still up 37% vs NSA which was only up 1% over these 15 months, for a 36% excess.
April to May Golden Week	Strong for small stocks	No and yes. The turn of the month saw a sharp decline in the NSA and an even sharper decline in the small stocks. The small stocks then seem to have bottomed out and as of May 1, they were up 22.9% vs 0.3% for the NSA for an excess of 22.6%.

Rest of May	Weak	No, market continued recovery. Small stocks outperformed large stocks as expected.
June	Extremely strong for small stocks	No, the market measured by the NSA was flat and the small stocks fell.
July	Strong for small stocks	Yes, the NSA fell sharply while the small stocks slightly increased.
August	Flat	Yes, both indices fell about the same amount.
September	Weak	Yes, both the NSA and small stocks fell. The small stocks fell more and on September 6 they were up 7.9% since December 1988 versus a loss of 19.6% for the NSA for an edge of 27.5%.
October	Weak	No, the 22nd correction ended on October 1 and October 2 saw a gain on the NSA of 2675 points, some 13.2%. The month closed up for both the NSA and small stocks. Relative to the small stocks, the NSA gained.
November	General market picks up, small stocks have edge.	No, the NSA fell 9.2% and the small stocks fell 18.3%.
December	Big stocks have edge, end of year portfolio rebalancing.	Yes, small stocks rose 2.2% and the NSA 4.7%. The year ended down 43.4% for the small stocks and down 38.7% so the big stocks out performed the small stocks in 1990. However, during the small stocks periods of advantage, namely January and February and April to July, the small stocks did substantially outperform the NSA.

The small stock portfolio performed poorly in 1990 compared to the NSA after peaking at 61.4% on March 9, 1990. The end of 1990 edge was only 11.1%. However, the small stocks performed much better than the NSA in the periods that they normally do, in January and February and then again in April to July. Investors who were in these stocks in these periods made profits even without hedging against the NSA. In managing a real portfolio, one would also adjust periodically, using a pricing model to sell overpriced stocks and using valuation models, such as those discussed in Chapter 5, to buy underpriced stocks.

CHAPTER 5
VALUATION TECHNIQUES

In the fall of 1969, when I first invested in Japanese stocks, and the Nikkei index was well below ¥2,000, I was assured that the market had "topped out." In the next three years, the index proceeded to rise about 2 1/2 times while the yen strengthened from 360 to 306 to the U.S. dollar. Since the spring of 1981 when I first published my studies on Japanese ratios, I have been steadily warned of stratospheric P/E ratios and an impending market collapse. The investment world is littered with those "sophisticated professionals" who underweighted or shorted Japan. Rather than seriously analyze what was wrong with their predictions, they seemed to angrily resent the Japanese stock market and almost seemed to wish the Japanese market would collapse to prove that they were always correct.

Paul Aron (1988b)

PRICE EARNINGS RATIOS

High price earnings ratios (PERs) send frights into most foreign investors with the very mention of Japanese stocks. Japanese PERs are among the highest in the world and much higher than those in the U.S., Canada, Britain, West Germany and other major industrial countries; see Figures 5.1 to 5.4. Tables 5.1 to 5.4 and the earlier Table 2.11 show these PERs and also price to book values, earnings per share, stockholders' equity per share, total market values, weighted average stock prices for corresponding periods and industries. The price earnings ratio is calculated by dividing the price per share by the annual after-tax profit per share. The price to book value ratio (PBR) is calculated by dividing the price per share by shareholders equity (net assets) per share. The reasons for the high PERs include:

- Hidden assets such as land and securities carried at book value that can be a tenth or even less of its current market value.

- Japan's different accounting methods underestimate earnings.

- Japanese interest rates are typically lower than those in the U.S.

- Most shares in Japan are held for business purposes and are rarely, if ever, traded.

- Confidence in the long-term prospects for the Japanese economy with low inflation and high growth rates of both the GNP and the real

245

money supply, leads to investors feeling that the future growth will be strong and stock prices will rise.

Table 5.1
Average PER and PBR along with EPS and Stockholders Equity per Share for TSE-I and II, 1971-1989

End of	1st Section				2nd Section			
Year	PER	PBR	EPS	Equity PS	PER	PBR	EPS	Equity PS
1971	14.9	1.8	13.5	111.5	12.9	1.3	12.3	121.7
1972	25.5	2.8	13.2	120.4	20.8	2.3	12.8	116.1
1973	13.3	1.9	19.6	136.9	12.2	1.6	16.7	127.1
1974	13.0	1.6	18.1	146.8	10.1	1.4	17.8	128.6
1975	27.0	1.9	10.3	146.4	31.2	1.6	6.4	125.6
1976	46.3	2.3	7.2	145.1	113.3	2.2	2.4	124.0
1977	24.2	2.0	12.3	148.8	37.3	2.0	6.5	121.0
1978	34.3	2.5	11.8	162.3	56.5	3.2	7.2	126.9
1979	23.3	2.2	16.0	169.4	25.3	2.5	14.8	150.2
1980	20.4	2.2	19.5	181.0	21.4	2.4	18.6	165.7
1981	21.1	2.1	19.0	194.7	21.8	2.1	17.4	177.1
1982	25.8	2.0	15.4	203.8	21.7	1.9	17.8	198.9
1983	34.7	2.5	15.6	217.0	45.0	3.1	14.3	207.8
1984	37.9	2.8	17.3	234.0	53.3	3.4	13.4	207.7
1985	35.2	2.9	20.5	251.9	39.0	3.1	19.8	247.9
1986	47.3	3.4	19.8	274.9	48.3	3.2	17.6	267.3
1987	58.3	3.7	18.5	289.2	58.5	3.7	18.6	294.3
1988	58.4	4.2	22.8	320.6	56.2	4.0	23.3	325.4
1989	70.6	5.4	26.9	351.9	57.4	5.2	32.0	356.4

• Earnings per share and stockholders' equity per share are the yen value per share with par value of ¥50 until October 1982 when it was redefined as a *unit of shares* divided by 1000.

• Data is updated on the basis of the latest after-tax profits and stockholders' equity on the beginning of the third month following a closing date.

• PER and PBR are computed on the current number of outstanding shares.

Source: TSE

When recalculated following U.S. accounting standards, earnings in Japan have been found to be understated by 53.5%. This makes the PER about 27.2 rather than the 50.8 reported by the Morgan Stanley Capital International Perspective (MSCIP) on August 31, 1988. Moreover, when earnings are recalculated according to the U.S. GAAP and capitalized on the same basis, the average PER was then 15.5 versus 11.3 for U.S. firms. As of August 31, 1989, Japanese earnings per share were understated by 58.0% with an adjusted PER of 28.7 versus the 49.6 reported by the MSCIP. Adjusting for the differences in the required rates of return give PERs of 17.5 for Japan versus 13.5 for the U.S. One can see that even with common standards, Japanese corporations earn less profit per unit of market value than U.S. counterparts but the difference is not 3 or 4 to 1 as are the standard PERs.

Japanese companies issue financial statements semi-annually for the parent-company's earnings but only annually on a consolidated basis. U.S. companies can file two reports - one to stockholders maximizing EPS and one to government revenue collectors minimizing them. In Japan, pre-tax income reported to stockholders can be lower than taxable income reported to the goverment due to government limitations on deductions for entertainment and other expenses. However, in general, the two reports are similar and tend to minimize earnings and, hence, taxes.

Table 5.2
Average PER and PBR along with EPS and Stockholders Equity per Share by Size and Industry for the TSE I and II, December 1989

| | First Section | | | | | Second Section | | | |
	#	PER	PBR	EPS	Equity PS	#	PER	PBR	EPS	Equity PS
Composite	1,161	70.6	5.4	26.9	351.9	436	57.4	5.2	32.0	356.4
By size of company										
Large	366	68.3	5.5	24.5	306.6		-	-	-	-
Medium	466	69.9	5.4	27.4	355.6	-	-	-		-
Small	329	73.6	5.4	28.9	397.2					-
By type of industry										
Fishery, Forestry	6	319.1	8.7	3.8	141.8	1	67.2	4.0	70.0	1,183.53
Mining	7	99.4	6.1	17.6	289.5	2	119.4	4.8	8.8	219.5
Construction	92	70.7	5.4	26.8	351.5	25	58.1	6.3	28.2	260.6
Foods	55	66.0	4.7	26.5	376.0	22	65.7	4.8	25.1	344.8
Textiles	43	103.3	6.0	15.4	232.0	15	87.8	5.7	13.6	209.6
Pulp & Paper	20	58.9	5.1	23.7	274.4	6	65.2	6.8	16.9	163.2
Chemicals	124	68.0	5.0	24.1	299.8	36	48.8	4.9	35.0	347.1
Oil & Coal Products	9	54.7	6.3	29.4	265.2	3	51.2	4.1	24.4	304.6
Rubber Products	9	71.5	5.9	19.7	238.4	8	98.2	6.5	11.2	171.4
Glass & Ceramic Prod	31	72.1	5.0	24.0	292.2	14	77 .5	5.9	18.2	240.9
Iron & Steel	36	48.0	6.6	30.9	230.9	15	45.1	7.0	25.1	161.4
Nonferrous Metals	24	97.9	6.0	13.6	202.2	11	84.8	7.6	14.9	167.4
Metal Products	24	58.4	5.4	37.4	397.9	15	56.4	4.8	37.6	440.7
Machinery	91	81.6	5.3	22.5	350.2	47	44.3	5.5	35.2	284.2
Electric Appliances	109	65.6	4.3	32.8	499.4	60	67.2	4.5	26.8	399.9
Transportation Equip	51	75.4	4.0	19.1	310.6	23	35.1	4.4	39.4	316.4
Precision Instruments	20	76.1	3.9	20.3	394.5	14	70.3	5.0	23.2	327.2
Other Prcducts	29	67.1	5.5	37.8	461.4	11	78.7	4.6	31.2	531.0
Commerce	130	79.3	5.7	31.7	443.0	45	49.3	4.0	49.0	610.8
Finance & Insurance	137	49.9	5.0	37.7	378.7	11	28.5	5.0	84.2	483.3
Real Estate	18	77.6	6.2	28.2	353.1	4	87.8	14.3	88.0	540.8
Land Transportation	25	173.2	10.6	11.5	189.1	8	88.3	7.2	22.6	278.3
Marine Transport	13	275.6	20.1	5.2	72.6	10	81.2	12.6	16.2	104.6
Air Transportation	4	126.3	5.0	16.1	411.6	1	138-8	7.7	16.1	289.4
Warehousing & Harbo Transport	10	97.9	8.3	17.8	209.8	9	115.7	10.2	14.9	169.5
Communication	5	67.3	5.0	42.0	569.3	-	-	-	-	-
Electric Power & Gas	14	61.1	5.1	10.6	128.7	1	40.6	4.6	32.0	285.5
Services	25	112.0	7.4	27.6	418.0	19	86.0	5.3	36.1	585.1

PER and PBR by size of companies are available only for the TSE-I

Source: TSE

Table 5.3 Average Price Earnings Ratios of the NSA 225, 1968-1990 (April)

	Total Market Value		Based on Estimated Earnings						Based on Results			
	Total Market Value	Wt Av	Av	High	Date	Low	Date	Yr or Mon End	Yr or Mon End	High	Date	Low	Date
	¥100 mil	¥	times	times		times		times	times	times		times	
1968	116,506	107.46	10.43	12.28	10.02	9.19	1.04	10.74	11.48	13.42	10.02	10.05	1.04
1969	167,167	131.65	11.43	12.45	12.27	10.70	3.04	12.45	12.67	13.78	i 1.27	10.80	8.08
1970	150,913	137.42	10.67	12.93	4.02	9.16	5.27	9.32	14.30	13.81	3.31	9.45	12.8
1971	214,998	145.49	12.25	15.21	12.28	9.30	1.06	15.21	12.57	15.39	12.28	9.46	1.06
1972	459,502	225.89	20.51	25.01	12.28	15.20	1.04	25.01	11.40	28.28	12.28	15.41	1.40
1973	365,071	279.31	19.23	25.32	1.29	13.28	12.18	4.41	14.96	28.57	1.29	13.71	12.18
1974	344,195	229.23	16.21	18.02	3.26.	13.79	1 10	6.62	14.87	16.90	6.01	12.22	10.90
1975	414,682	217.41	22.15	26.60	12.27	15.83	1.10	26.60	10.48	21.64	7.01	15.05	1.10
1976	507,510	232.14	23.38	27.84	1.26	18.41	12.14	19.24	10.62	28.15	12.28	22.32	1.05
1977	493,502	244.71	20.22	22.22	9.05	18.85	11.24	20.93	12.57	28.47	1.26	17.89	11.07
1978	627,038	264.09	23.02	24.04	12.13	20.91	1.04	22.31	12.03	26.81	12.13	19.10	1.04
1979	659,093	281.27	20.15	22.71	1.31	17.64	10.04	18.78	5.77	26.81	2.01	21.87	10.26
1980	732,207	293.00	19.09	20.05	7.03	17.56	3.27	9.68	8.06	24.07	1.30	21.05	7.70
1981	879,775	333.39	22.50	24.62	11.26	19.92	1.05	23.09	16.44	24.33	8.17	21.43	9.28
1982	936,046	321.62	21.88	26.42	11.29	19.02	6.10	26.08	16.24	27.44	12 28	20.51	3.17
1983	1,195,052	373.17	26.84	28.84	12 05	24.76	6.08	28.76	15.39	29.02	5.09	24.11	6.02
1984	1,548,424	472.54	27.41	30.56	3.31	23.47	7.23	28.99	17.97	33.12	12.27	26.98	5.31
1985	1,826,967	574.95	31.92	34.83	2.28	28.30	1.05	34.83	18.46	35.37	3.28	30.08	11.19
1986	2,770,563	757.23	49.80	64.01	12.24	33.54	1.21	63.33	15.72	51.79	9.29	30.04	1.23
1987	3,254,779	1,115.93	70.04	80.15	5.15	56.62	12.26	56.74	15.50	92.28	10 14	50.75	1.13
1988	4,628,963	1,211.85	63.75	67.10	3.30	55.15	1.04	65.40	19.53	85.68	5.02	66.61	1.04
1989	5,909,087	1,444.10	65.98	71.96	12.29	60.89	6.15	71.96	23.48	80.35	5.08	60.72	10.16
90.01	5,633,504	1,546.71	68.64	70.95	4	67.35	18	68.71	24.70	66.79	4	62.39	18
90.02	5,292,732	1,502.00	67.24	69.33	6	61.47	26	63.81	24.60	63.79	2	56.43	26
90.03	4,580,056	1,343.33	60.32	63.59	9	55.75	30	55.75	24.21	57.42	11	49.05	22
90.04	4,574,151	1,202.75	51.75	53.86	91	49.51	2	52.31	25.44	52.56	9	47.38	2

Source: Yamaichi Research Institute

Table 5.4   Price/Earnings Ratios around the World, 1974-1989 (November)

	World	Japan	USA	Canada	UK	Germ	France	Neth	Switze rland	Austra lia	Hong Kong	Singap ore
1974	8.8	14.7	9.8	9.1	5.3	10.2	8.6	4.4	7.3	9.5	12.9	17.9
1975	10.0	18.6	11.1	8.8	7.8	12.2	8.5	8.6	9.0	9.3	13.1	14.0
1976	12.7	23.1	12.2	10.0	9.7	13.0	20.6	10.8	11.6	12.3	18.6	18.3
1977	10.5	19.0	9.8	8.8	8.9	9.6	12.4	5.9	10.8	9.9	13.9	16.0
1978	10.0	18.3	8.8	8.7	8.3	10.1	13.7	6.8	10.2	10.1	13.2	17.4
1979	9.0	18.9	7.7	8.9	7.2	9.7	14.1	5.5	12.9	10.1	11.8	17.3
1980	8.5	18.4	8.1	8.7	5.6	8.1	7.5	3.6	12.3	10.3	16.2	20.0
1981	9.2	17.4	8.3	9.0	7.6	8.3	5.5	5.0	11.1	11.9	17.0	22.4
1982	9.5	18.8	8.2	11.9	8.6	9.7	11.0	5.1	9.7	10.1	9.1	20.0
1983	13.7	23.2	12.3	34.4	10.6	13.5	76.4	6.4	11.2	13.8	8.0	25.9
1984	12.1	26.1	10.1	19.4	10.4	13.8	47.7	6.4	11.1	11.4	10.1	23.9
1985	13.3	26.6	11.7	15.4	11.4	14.1	14.0	7.1	11.4	11.5	14.6	21.2
1986	17.1	36.2	14.3	16.1	13.2	15.2	18.4	9.2	13.5	1.0	15.7	27.1
1987	21.8	57.6	17.1	22.8	14.7	13.5	16.3	11.2	18.0	15.1	15.5	36.0
1988	18.4	55.8	12.7	12.0	11.3	13.3	10.8	9.9	13.7	11.8	11.4	23.6
1989	18.9	51.4	13.8	13.3	11.0	16.0	11.8	9.4	16.7	11.3	10	19.6
Mean	12.7	27.8	11.0	13.6	9.5	11.9	18.6	7.2	11.9	10.6	13.2	21.3
SD	4.2	14.4	2.7	7.0	2.6	2.5	18.2	2.4	2.7	3.0	3.0	5.3

Source: Morgan Stanley Capital International Perspective

Figure 5.1
Price/Earnings Multiples of Japan, U.S., Canada and UK, 1974-1989

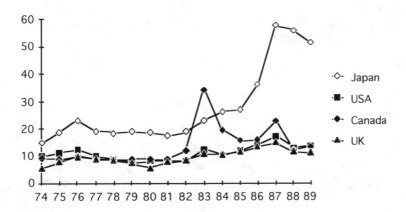

Source: Morgan Stanley/Guardian International Statistics

Figure 5.2a
Price/Earnings Multiples of Germany, France, Netherlands and
Switzerland Compared with Japan, 1974-1989

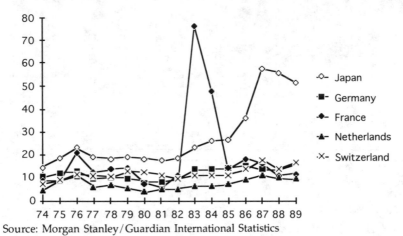

Source: Morgan Stanley/Guardian International Statistics

Figure 5.2b
Price/Earnings Multiples of Australia, Hong Kong, and Singapore
Compared with Japan, 1974-1989

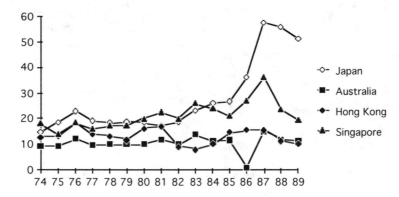

Source: Morgan Stanley/Guardian International Statistics

Figure 5.3
Price/Earnings Ratios versus Long Term Government Bond Yields in
Japan, 1980-1991 (February)

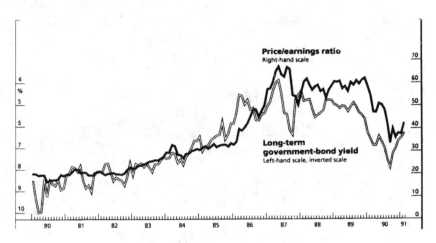

Source: Lifestream, reported in *The Economist*

Figure 5.4
Distribution of PERs and PBRs for the TSE-I and TSE-II, December 1989

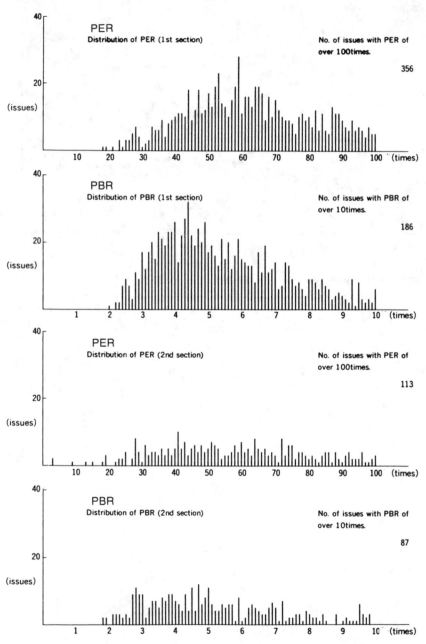

Source: Tokyo Stock Exchange

Paul Aron, vice chairman emeritus of Daiwa Securities in New York, has computed adjusted Japanese PERs on a continuing basis since 1981. He found that the Japanese PERs when measured on common grounds have been roughly comparable to those in the U.S. in the 1980s, as shown in Table 5.5. The boxed values indicate overvalued markets measured by these adjusted PERs. The values up to August 31, 1989 are in Aron (1989). The values since then are simple adjustments we made using differing interest rates and earnings gains. See Aron (1990) for an update of his calculations to the end of August 1990.

Table 5.5 U.S. and Japanese PER from Paul Aron Reports with Updating

Date	U.S. PER	Japan, adj PER	NSA
Apr 26, 1981	9.1	4.0	7548
Oct 19, 1984	10.0	11.5	10929
Apr 17, 1986	13.7	13.5	15827
May 26, 1987	17.4	17.4	24533
Sept 11, 1987	20.3	18.1	24829
Dec 31, 1987	14.4	14.5	21533
May 31, 1988	13.1	15.4	26963
Aug 30, 1988	11.3	15.5	27679
Aug 31, 1989	13.5	17.5	34808
Dec 31, 1989	13.5	23.9	38915
Mar 30, 1990	15.5	19.7	29980
June 30, 1990	17.0	20.1	31940
Sept 30, 1990	13.6	15.2	20983
Oct 1, 1990	14.3	13.5	20022
Oct 2, 1990	14.3	15.4	22896
Dec 28, 1990	13.8	14.8	23849
Feb 22, 1991	16.2	14.9	25903

Source: Aron (1989b) with updating

The values for periods after August 1989 use the following assumptions:

	Interest Rates		Earnings Gain
	U.S	Japan	over Aug 89
Dec 1989	8.2	6.4	5%
Mar 1990	8.4	7.4	10%
June 1990	8.2	7.0	12%
Sept 1990	8.2	7.75	8%
Oct 1, 1990	8.1	7.5	8%
Oct 2, 1990	8.1	7.5	8%
Dec 28, 1990	7.6	6.5	8%
Feb 22, 1990	7.6	6.0	8%

Hence, despite a slight decrease in interest rates and a small increase in earnings, the rise from the 30,000 range at the end of March 1990 to the 32,000 range at the end of June resulted in the market's adjusted PER rising to 20.1. Thus, the market in June 1990, was still pricey and vulnerable if interest rates were to rise again or business conditions falter.

Indeed as discussed in Chapter 7, the market did fall. Finally in late September, the NSA fell to such an extent that even with higher interest rates than in June, the market was fairly valued. This was the first time in 1990 that the market was not overvalued by this measure. On October 2, 1990, the adjusted PERs were about 13.5 which was a major buy signal.

These values also pointed to the overvalued securities all over the world in the fall of 1987 that led to the October crash.[1] The May 1987 estimate of 17.4 for Japan also clued in the June 1987 correction, see Table 2.7. The August 31, 1989 valuation of 17.5 also clued in the correction in January-April 1990. This increased to a very high 23.9 as of the end of December 1989. Even after the fall of the NSA in the first quarter of 1990, the end of March 1990 adjusted PER was still quite high at 19.7. The 21st correction ended in early April 1990 when the market began to firm. Still, at the end of June 1990, the adjusted PER was 20.1, which was well in the danger zone for another possible correction should some event trigger a new decline. The Iraq invasion of Kuwait and the subsequent oil crisis was the trigger and the market fell sharply. As of early October 1990 when the 22nd correction ended, the PERs were finally not overvalued. These corrections are discussed in Chapter 7.

Aron's calculation of the adjusted Japanese PER is computed as follows, see Aron (1989) for further details. As of August 31, 1989, the stated PER was 49.6. Various earnings and accounting adjustments lower the PER to 28.73 with the following adjustments:

---

[1]An analysis and survey of studies concerning the crash around the world appears in Ziemba (1991e).

2.02	Stated earnings per ¥100 of equity	$\dfrac{100}{2.02} = 49.6$	Raw PER
↓			
+0.04	Timing of earnings		
↓			
+0.15	Differences with MSCIP		
↓			
+0.12	Reserves		
↓			
+0.16	Consolidation		
↓			
+1.10	Accounting and depreciation		
↓			
= 3.48	Adjusted earnings per ¥100 of equity	$\dfrac{100}{3.48} = 28.73$	Adjusted PER

In August 1989, the capitalization rates assumed were 8.2% in the U.S. and 5.0% in Japan for a ratio of 1.64. Then 28.73/1.64 = 17.52, as shown in Table 5.5. These values were already in the high area since the 17.4 and 18.1 values in May and September 1987, which are boxed predated corrections. The PERs at other times were computed in the following simple way:

$$\text{Dec } 1989 \quad \frac{17.5}{1.12}\left(\frac{38916}{34808}\right)\frac{8.2/5.0}{8.2/6.4} \quad = \quad 23.9$$

$$\text{Mar } 1990 \quad \frac{17.5}{1.10}\left(\frac{29980}{34808}\right)\frac{8.2/5.0}{8.4/7.4} \quad = \quad 19.7$$

$$\text{Jun } 1990 \quad \frac{17.5}{1.12}\left(\frac{31940}{34808}\right)\frac{8.2/5.0}{8.2/7.0} \quad = \quad 20.1$$

$$\text{Sept } 1990 \quad \frac{17.5}{1.08}\left(\frac{20022}{34808}\right)\frac{8.2/5.0}{8.1/7.75} \quad = \quad 13.5$$

$$\text{Oct 1 } 1990 \quad \frac{17.5}{1.08}\left(\frac{20983}{34808}\right)\frac{8.2/5.0}{8.2/7.75} \quad = \quad 15.2$$

$$\text{Oct 2 } 1990 \quad \frac{17.5}{1.08}\left(\frac{22896}{34808}\right)\frac{8.2/5.0}{8.1/7.5} \quad = \quad 15.4$$

$$\text{Dec } 1990 \quad \frac{17.5}{1.08}\left(\frac{23849}{34808}\right)\frac{8.2/5.0}{7.6/7.5} \quad = \quad 14.8$$

$$\text{Feb } 1991 \quad \frac{17.5}{1.08}\left(\frac{25903}{34808}\right)\frac{8.2/5.0}{7.6/6.0} \quad = \quad 14.9$$

Table 5.6 provides details on stock supply from 1985 to 1989, government bond yields, margin purchases, consolidated PERs, and continued price to cash flow computed by Goldman Sachs. For a study of 727 companies on the TSE, Aron (1988b) found that parent company EPS was understated by 20.3% for fiscal year 1987. Table 5.7 shows Aron's adjustment of five non-life insurance stocks. The mean PER of 66.1 adjusts down to 29.0. Table 5.8 shows the role of hidden assets for a wide range of companies as of March 1989.

Table 5.6
Stock Supply, Bond Yields, Individual Purchases, Consolidated PERs and Price to Cash Flow Estimates by Goldman Sachs, 1985-1989

Year	Stock Supply, ¥ billions	Government Bond Yield	Net Margin Purchases, Annualized ¥ bil	PER (consol)	Price/Cash Flow Ratio (consol)
1985	4,286.6	5.87%	¥ 643	39.6	13.0
1986	5,530.3	5.42	1,327	52.0	14.8
1987	16,587.1	5.07	2,043	41.1	11.8
1988	18,750.1	4.59	1,814	37.8	10.7
1989e	20,000.0	5.00	4,599	33.2	9.4

Table 5.7
Adjustment of PERs of Five Non-Life Insurance Stocks Earnings Per Share as of March 31, 1988

	A Price ¥	B PER MSCIP	C=A/B EPS MSCIP ¥	D EPS US GAAP ¥	E=D/C Under- valuation %	F=A/D PER US GAAP	G Unrealized prifit, P/S ¥
Nippon Fire	952	48.5	19.59	37.69	192.39	24.1	2,178
Sumitomo M&F	1,150	54.9	20.95	38.30	182.82	31.1	1,975
Taisho M&F	1,070	88.2	12.13	42.21	347.98	27.0	1,734
Tokio M&F	1,940	78.4	24.74	51.79	209.34	39.2	2,107
Yasuda M&F	1,020	60.7	16.80	44.43	264.45	23.6	1,770
Averages	1,226	66.1	18.84	42.88	239.40	29.0	1,952

Source: Aron (1988b)

Scheineman (1988, 1989) has criticized Aron's calculations as being too optimistic. However, our experience has been that they do seem to signal over-valuation quite well, as we have seen above. This is discussed in the context of the 21st and 22nd corrections in 1990 in Chapter 7, but one gleans much from Table 5.5. Aron (1990) provides his latest updates. Alternative calculations have also been made by French and Poterba (1990) for non-financial companies as measured by the Nomura Research

Table 5.8 Hidden Assets of a Group of Japanese Stocks and their effect on PERs as of March 31, 1989

	A	B	C	D	E	F	G	H	J	K	L	M	N	O	P	Q	R
Honda	7267	1690	99.5	Mar-88	17.0	173	1517	936.9	178149	190.15	1	98.5	15.4	119	118.8	12.9	20.9
Toyota	7203	2390	120.0E	Jun-87	19.9	741	1649	2666.2	2215464	830.94	2.5	117.5	14	134.9	132.4	12.5	15.0
Kirin	2503	2320	39.2	Jan-88	59.2	297	2023	904.2	300075	331.87	1	38.2	53	35.7	34.7	58.3	-4.5
Mitsubishi chem	4010	1160	18.7	Jan-88	62.0	89	1071	1320.0	164704	124.78	0.4	18.3	58.4	na	na	na	na
NTT	9432	2400000	15592.0	Mar-88	153.9	160894	2239106	15600.0	na	na	na	na	na	17308	na	na	20.0
Fujitsu	6702	1490	20.4	Mar-88	73.0	487	1003	1703.5	863976	507.18	1.5	18.9	53.1	45.9	44.4	22.6	87.6
NEC	6701	2100	17.3	Mar-88	121.4	433	1667	1468.5	691800	471.15	1.4	15.9	104.9	38.5	37.1	45	124.7
Sony	6759	5230	148.9	Mar-68	35.1	610	4620	238.9	182684	764.69	2.3	146.6	31.5	219.2	216.9	21.3	53.2
Shiseido	4911	1670	32.7	Nov-87	51.1	411	1259	275.7	127466	462.34	1.4	31.3	40.2	25.4	24	52.4	-22.3
Nomura	6604	4380	148.9	Sep-87	29.6	na	na	1856.8	na	na	na	na	na	122.4	na	na	-16.2
Sumitomo Bank	8316	3780	42.5E	Mar-86	88.9	1436	2344	2471.9	na	na	na	na	na	na	na	na	6.0
Tokio Marine	8751	2070	24.7	Mar-58	83.8	2107	-37	1456.4	na	24.54	1.2	23.5	na	26.1	na	na	5.6
Hitachi	6501	1410	44.1	Mar-88	32.0	286	1124	2939.7	883973	300.70	0.9	43.2	26	55.3	54.4	20.7	27.9
Mitsubishi Elec	6503	746	10.8	Mar-88	69.1	262	484	2060.1	597981	290.27	0.9	9.9	48.7	19.2	18.3	26.5	80.1
Toshiba	6502	787	20.4	Mar-88	38.6	139	648	2971.8	455042	153.12	0.5	19.9	32.5	29.6	29.1	22.3	46.6
Kracera	6971	5410	140.6	Mar-88	38.5	294	5116	153.7	55327	359.97	1.1	139.5	36.7	176.2	175.1	29.2	25.7
Green Cross	4522	2230	17.4	Dec-87	128.2	63	2167	206.1	15867	76.99	0.2	17.2	126.2	16.6	16.6	130.8	na
Takeda	4502	3040	43.9	Mar-88	69.2	383	2657	666.4	308743	356.35	1.1	42.8	62	46.2	45.1	58.9	5.4
Mitsui R.E.	8801	2090	39.2	Mar-88	53.3	366	1724	686.1	270305	393.97	1.2	38	45.3	45	43.8	39.3	14.9
Ito Takado	8264	4300	119.8	Feb-88	35.9	1626	2674	360.2	604176	1679.31	3	114.8	23.3	134.4	129.4	20.7	12.2
Nippon Steel	5401	487	5.7E	Mar-88	85.4	200	287	15867.0	1506140	226.94	0.7	5	57.2	14.3	13.6	21.1	135.0
Nisshin Steel	5407	818	13.9E	Mar-88	58.8	255	563	897.6	252063	280.82	0.8	13.1	43.1	27.3	26.5	21.3	76.7
Toray	3402	810	21.6	Mar-88	37.5	239	571	1332.2	334600	251.16	0.8	20.8	27.4	22.4	21.6	26.4	3.6
Mitsubishi Corp	6058	1360	20.3	Mar-88	67.0	740	620	1533.3	1284603	837.80	2.5	17.8	34.9	22.2	19.7	31.5	9.1
Sumitomo Elec	5802	1430	28.0	Mar-88	58.2	319	1111	677.6	368486	543.81	1.6	26.4	42.1	30.9	29.3	38	11.8

A Code
B Price, ¥
C Latest fiscal year EPS, ¥, E=estimate
D Fiscal year end
E PER = B/C
F Hidden assets/share, unrealized securities gain 3/31/88
G Price less hidden assets, B-F
H Shares outstanding in millions
J Market value of securities held, ¥ millions

K Market value per share, ¥ (J/H)
L Dividends on MV/S (K/H)
M EPS less dividends received (C-L)
N Adj PER based on M (G/M)
O EPS, next fiscal year estimated, ¥
P EPS, nest fiscal year, ¥
Q PER, next fiscal year
R Net income growth, 1988/89

Institute 350 index. They used adjustments for three Japanese accounting practices that are very different from those in the U.S.:

1. Reporting consolidated versus parent-company earnings.
2. Reserve accounts that permit Japanese firms to deduct significant amounts from reported earnings in advance of future expenses.
3. Depreciation practices.

The first adjustment is made because Japanese firms report parent firm unconsolidated earnings rather than consolidated earnings that include the net income of subsidiaries and of other firms in which the firm has more than a 20% stake. Since unconsolidated earnings reflect the dividends received from subsidiaries but not their undistributed profits, this leads to a systematic upward bias in PERs for Japan relative to those in the U.S. Aron corrected for this using ratios of consolidated to unconsolidated returns.[2] French and Poterba, following Ando and Auerbach (1990) and Ueda (1990), do so using a cross holding adjustment.

It is assumed that parent unconsolidated earnings are overstated by intercorporate dividend receipts, but prices are more overstated because they capitalize future intercorporate dividends plus undistributed earnings of subsidiaries.

The adjusted PER is then

$$PER_{adj} = \left(\frac{1\text{-}s\ a}{1\text{-}s\ a\ d}\right)PER$$

where s is the share of the total market the non-financials own, a is the market value of all traded shares divided by the market value of non-financial companies, and d is the fraction of earnings paid in dividends.

They assume that the market value of non-financial corporations is the value of outstanding equity minus the value of shares held on corporate account. Intercorporate dividends are subtracted from the reported earnings of parent firms.

Table 5.9 shows French and Poterba's calculations for 1975 to 1988 for the NRI 350. The NRI 350 is a large capitalized index. For more on it, see the section on Elton and Gruber's factor model later in this chapter. The cross-holding adjustment lowers the PER by 20-30%. This is consistent

---

[2]The main difficulty with this approach is that Japanese firms have considerable discretion regarding their consolidated earnings reports, hence some earnings may not be included in consolidated earnings.

with alternative calculations by McDonald (1989) and Kobayashi (1990), discussed in Chapter 1 and in the next section. In 1988 the Japanese payout ratio was 0.28, **sa** was 0.407 leading to an adjustment factor of 0.669. This reduces the NRI 350's PER from 54.3 to 36.3. Since cross-holdings have increased from 1975 to 1988, this adjustment factor has lowered the relative PERs over time.

Table 5.9   Adjusted Price-Earnings Ratios, Japan and U.S. 1975-1988

	Japan NRI 350								U.S. S&P500	
		Cross Holding			Depreciation Adjustment					
	unadj		interim	Reserves	Method 1		Method 2		Unadj	Adj
Year	PER	Factor	PER	Factor	Factor	PER	Factor	PER	PER	PER
1975	25.2	0.784	19.8	0.98	.599	11.5	.905	17.2	11.8	11.0
1976	22.0	0.824	18.1	0.97	.655	11.6	.920	16.1	11.2	10.1
1977	19.3	0.797	15.4	0.97	.684	10.2	.926	13.7	9.1	8.1
1978	21.5	0.792	17.0	0.97	.704	11.7	.931	15.3	8.2	7.5
1979	16.6	0.778	12.9	0.97	.717	9.0	.935	11.7	7.5	6.8
1980	17.9	0.770	13.8	0.97	.755	10.1	.947	12.6	9.6	8.7
1981	24.9	0.764	19.0	0.97	.702	13.0	.932	17.1	8.2	7.6
1982	23.7	0.769	18.2	0.97	.700	12.4	.931	16.3	11.9	11.1
1983	29.4	0.795	23.4	0.97	.692	15.8	.936	21.1	12.6	11.9
1984	26.3	0.734	19.3	0.97	.711	13.3	.943	17.5	10.4	9.4
1985	29.4	0.694	20.4	0.97	.668	13.3	.924	18.2	15.4	14.2
1986	58.6	0.695	40.7	0.98	.624	24.8	.908	35.7	18.7	17.5
1987	50.4	0.665	33.5	0.97	.660	21.5	.920	29.8	14.1	12.9
1988	54.3	0.669	36.3	0.97*	.660*	23.2	.920*	32.1	12.9	11.7

*Estimated using 1987 values.

Source: French and Poterba (1990)

The special reserve adjustment accounts for the fact that firms may set aside funds in the given year to provide for future expenses such as product returns, repairs, payments on guarantees, losses on accounts and retirement payments. Aron's adjustment is that the difference in earnings because of this effect is the net reserve contribution net of taxes. Marginal tax rates are in the 50-55% range. The effect of these reserves is to over-state earnings by 2-3% so the adjustment is fairly minor.

Japanese firms must use the same depreciation policy for tax and for financial reporting purposes; hence, they usually choose to minimize taxes. Double-declining balance depreciation is used by almost all firms.

This procedure, along with the fact that most Japanese firms are growing rapidly, yields lower reported returns for Japanese as compared to U.S. firms. Aron corrects for this using the assumption that the ratio of depreciation to cash earnings is the same in Japan as in the U.S. French and Poterba argue that this approach overstates Japanese earnings because Japanese firms are more capital intensive than U.S. firms. They instead use two methods. The first, which yields results close to Aron's, computes the straight-line depreciation that Japanese firms would have reported if all of their assets were used. This is an upper bound on the true effect; and its use, French and Poterba argue, overstates true earnings and understates true PERs.

The annual double-declining balance rate is:

$d = 1-(0.1)^{1/L}$

where L is the asset life in years. This depreciation rate is approximately equal to $2/L$ which is double that of straight-line depreciation. This leads to an over reporting of earnings of 52% in 1987 and similarly in other years. Then for 1988 the PER of the NRI350 which began at 54.3 and was 36.3 after the cross-holding adjustment, becomes 23.2.

French and Poterba argue that this method of converting accelerated to straight-line depreciation is accurate if all Japanese assets were new. Hence, this estimate overstates the actual difference because the depreciable amount for the straight-line method is constant but that for the double declining falls as the asset ages. Their approach leads to the correction formula for the amount of earnings under reported of

$(1-t) [\{1 - (1 - e^{-gL}) (2D+g)\} / sDgL]$

where t is the marginal tax rate, g is the growth rate of investments, L is the age at which half the asset is used up, and D is the depreciation rate.

As shown in Table 5.9, this yields much lower effects of depreciation rates in the 0.9 to 0.95 range rather than the 0.6 to 0.75 for the other method. Hence, 1988's adjusted PER is 23.2 versus 32.1 for the first depreciation method. The last two columns in Table 5.9 give French and Poterba's estimates for the S&P 500. After similar adjustments, the U.S. PERs fall about 10% from their reported values. After the accounting corrections, French and Poterba's adjusted Japanese PERs:

1. Are about the same as Aron's if one uses the first depreciation method.

2. Are much higher than those in the U.S. using the second depreciation method.

3. Became much more out of whack when the PERs in Japan doubled in 1986 from 29.4 to 58.6 for the NRI 350.

We are then left with the required rate of return adjustments. Aron simply uses the ratio of T-bill risk free interest rates.[3] As a first approximation, this is an appropriate strategy, and the answers obtained have given considerable insights, particularly regarding overpriced market declines.

French and Poterba, following Ando and Auerbach (1988), argue that inflation is the main reason for differences in accounting and economic earnings. Since depreciation is computed using the historical costs of assets, the true depreciation deductions are understated and profits are overstated. The bias is larger the higher is inflation. Secondly, by not distinguishing between the real and nominal cost of debt, earnings are understated and again the bias is inflation related. Reported earnings are based on nominal interest rates even though the economic cost of borrowing is measured by the real interest rate. The higher debt-equity ratios of Japanese versus U.S. firms makes this overstatement more important for Japanese than for U.S. earnings. Finally, inflation yields profits for inventories held and assets sold. Nominal but not real appreciation of inventories is listed as profit, and so are the revenues from appreciated assets.

For the period 1967-83, the reported Japanese PERs averaged 15.4 and the U.S. PERs 10.6. Ando and Auerbach's corrected values are 10.9 for Japan and 11.8 for the U.S. The U.S. and Japan differ because of leverage and depreciation rate differences but the values are quite close. This is consistent with Aron's results until the doubling in 1985. After 1985's doubling of PERs, the Ando and Auerbach and French and Poterba results deviate from Aron's. There are two possible explanations for the discrepancies. Growth opportunities account for a larger share of value in Japan than in the U.S. and this percent increased around 1985. Second, the required return on equity in Japan is lower than in the U.S. and the difference magnified around 1985. French and Poterba utilize Miller and Modigliani's (1961) valuation methods with the following characteristics: there is a constant discount rate **i**; firms can invest **K**% of each year's earn-

---

[3]Actually he uses the yield on 10 year government bonds priced on the secondary market as a proxy for the riskless asset. He also adjusts this rate to account for the fact that Japanese purchase foreign bonds as well. This leads to an interest rate that is weighted 32.27% times the U.S. bond rate and 67.73% times the Japanese bond rate. Since the bond yield is hardly risk free and these weightings are subject to change we have used the T-bill rates in Table 5.5 for the December 1989 to February 1991 calculations.

ings to provide returns of **R**. The remaining earnings are paid in dividends, **D,** and earnings grow at the rate of **g=KR**. If such returns are available forever, then

$$PER = \quad (1\text{-}K)\frac{P}{D} = \frac{1\text{-}K}{i\text{-}KR} = \frac{1\text{-}K}{i\text{-}g}.$$

If these returns are only available for T years, then

$$PER = \quad 1\text{+}KT\frac{R\text{-}i}{i} = \frac{1 + T(g\text{-}Ki)}{i}.$$

French and Poterba used their 1985 and 1986 adjusted PERs (depreciation method 2) to compute the implied growth rates **g** that would be consistent with Miller and Modigliani's models and various required rates of return **i**. Table 5.10 shows these calculations. The estimated value of **i-g** was 2.25% in 1985 and 1.37% in 1986. Hence, the doubling of the PERs in 1986 can be explained by an increase in the perpetual growth rate and/or a decrease in the required return of 0.88%. Hence, the hair trigger model just like many of the other models discussed later in this chapter and in Chapter 7 can explain the facts. Using the finite horizon model with a growth rate of 4.5% and a ten year horizon implies that the required rate of return in 1985 was 6%.

This model has more trouble explaining the facts, but it can do it with reasonably believable parameter changes. A modified model that lets the growth rate vary in a specified way over an infinite horizon might be preferable. In any event, doubling the PERs in 1986 with the required return still at 6% requires an increase in the expected annual growth rate from 4.5% to 14.48% which is unrealistic. Alternatively, with the growth rate remaining at 4.5% the PERs are consistent if the required return were to drop from 6% to 3.55%. With a 25 year horizon - unrealistic in our view because of the ageing population among other reasons. The implied return with expected growth constant at 4.5% must fall from 6.5% to 4.5%. Hence, the doubling of the PERs in 1986, even with French and Poterba's high PER calculations, can be explained with a reduction in required returns and/or an increase in the expected growth rate that totals more than 2%.

Table 5.10
The Implied Difference Between the Required Return i and the Growth
Rate **g** in Two Scenarios for Japan and U.S., 1985 and 1986

Assuming perpetual growth opportunities:

		i-g	PER	K
Japan	1985	2.25	18.2	0.59
	1986	1.37	35.7	0.51
U.S.	1985	3.59	14.2	0.49
	1986	3.20	17.5	0.44

The Implied Growth Rate Assuming Supernormal Investment
Opportunities of Various Durations, T:

T				Required Return, t				
	3.0	3.5	4.0	4.5	5.0	5.5	6.0	6.5	7.0
Japan 1985									
10	-2.77	-1.56	-0.36	0.84	2.05	3.25	4.46	5.67	6.87
25	-0.05	0.61	1.27	1.93	2.59	3.25	3.91	4.57	5.23
∞	0.75	1.25	1.75	2.25	2.75	3.25	3.75	4.25	4.75
Japan, 1986									
10	2.24	4.28	6.32	8.36	10.40	12.44	14.48	16.52	18.56
25	1.81	2.78	3.75	4.72	5.69	6.66	7.63	8.60	9.57
∞	1.63	2.13	2.63	3.13	3.63	4.13	4.63	5.13	5.63
U.S., 1985									
10	-4.27	-3.31	-2.36	-1.41	-0.45	0.50	1.46	2.41	3.37
25	-0.83	-0.30	0.23	0.76	1.29	1.82	2.35	2.88	3.41
∞	-0.59	-0.09	0.41	0.91	1.41	1.91	2.41	2.91	3.41
U.S., 1986									
10	-3.43	-2.33	-1.24	-0.15	0.95	2.05	3.14	4.23	5.33
25	-0.58	-0.01	0.56	1.13	1.70	2.27	2.84	3.41	3.98
∞	-0.20	0.30	0.80	1.30	1.80	2.30	2.80	3.30	3.80

Source: French and Poterba (1990)

Which if either of these effects is a plausible explanation of the 1986
rise in PERs? After investigation of growth estimates by major forecasting
firms, French and Poterba reject a substantial increase in growth rates as
the key explanation. The ten year growth forecasts for Japan listed in
Table 5.11 computed from the Data Resources/Nikkei Japanese Review
are fairly constant in the 3.8-4.3% range. If anything, the evidence is that
growth rates declined rather than increased in 1986.

Table 5.11
Expected Annual Growth Rates and Nominal and Real Yields on Long-term Government Bonds, the U.S. and Japan, 1980-88

| | Expected Long-term Growth | | | Before-tax Yields | | | |
| | U.S. | Japan | | Nominal | | Real | |
	10-yr	5-yr	10-yr	U.S.	Japan	U.S.	Japan
1982	3.2	4.6		10.32	7.81	4.0	2.4
1983	3.2		3.8	11.43	7.42	5.6	4.2
1984	2.9	3.7	4.0	11.51	6.85	6.1	4.4
1985	2.9	4.0	4.3	9.05	6.32	4.4	4.1
1986	2.6	3.6		7.26	5.51	2.6	2.9
1987	2.3	3.3		8.91	5.15	3.9	3.3
1988	2.3	3.9	3.9	9.18	4.80	4.1	3.0

Source: French and Poterba (1990)

Hence, required returns through lower interest rates and lower inflationary explanations is the prime candidate to explain the 1986 PER doubling. Required equity returns in the U.S. and Japan might differ for reasons like the following:

1. Expectations of long term real exchange rate changes (such as the rise in the yen from 1985-1988).

2. Perceived risks from foreign equity investments lead to large differences between expected returns in home versus away markets (such as the returns in Japan and other foreign markets in the 1970s and 1980s as discussed in Chapter 2 in the section on international diversification).

3. Taxation differences (such as withholding taxes on dividends due to foreign investors; both the U.S. and Japan have taxation rates in the 15-20% range).

Nominal and real interest rates did drop in Japan in 1985. Indeed, the simple Nomura regression model, discussed in Chapters 7 and 10, clearly shows this effect on stock prices. Table 5.11 has French and Poterba's estimates which show that real Japanese interest rates fell 1.2% from 4.1% to 2.9% in 1986. Also, Table 5.11 indicates that real Japanese interest rates have been consistently below those in the U.S. The finite horizon Miller-Modigliani growth model with a twenty five year horizon, a growth rate of 4.5% and a real interest rate decline of 1.25%, implies that the adjusted PERs should have increased from 19.2 in 1985 to 27.7 in 1986. This is lower then French and Poterba's estimate of 35.7 using the second depreciation method but higher than the 24.8 from their first depreciation method. Hence, the evidence comes back to vindicate Aron's approach quite well. However, using a clever real interest rate correction rather than the ratio of nominal interest rates would probably be an improvement.

Table 5.12
PER Units Per Unit of Growth Using GNP as a Proxy for Earnings Growth

August 1989	U.S.	Japan
a Riskless rate-yield of 10 year central government bonds	8.2%	5.0%
b Earnings yield PER of riskless rate (1/a)	12.20 times	20.00 times
c Japanese riskless rate modified to include purchase of non-Japanese long government bonds		6.04%
d Japanese PER of riskless rate revised on the basis of c		16.56
e Japanese PER/U.S. PER of riskless rate (16.56/12.20)		1.36 times
f PER fully adjusted for MSCIP differences, accounting differences and crossholdings	13.50	19.09
g PER fully adjusted for above accounting differences and capitalization differences (19.09/1.36)	13.50	14.04
h Consensus estimate of 1989 GNP growth	2.7%	4.9%
i PER units per unit of growth	5.00 units	2.87 units

March 1990	U.S.	Japan
a Riskless rate-yield of 10 year central government bonds	8.4%	7.4%
b Earnings yield PER of riskless rate (1/a)	11.90 times	13.51 times
c Japanese riskless rate modified to include purchase of non-Japanese long government bonds		7.4%
d Japanese PER of riskless rate revised on the basis of c		13.51
e Japanese PER/U.S. PER of riskless rate (13.51/11.90)		1.14 times
f PER fully adjusted for MSCIP differences, accounting differences and crossholdings	13.50	19.09
g PER fully adjusted for above accounting differences and capitalization differences (19.09/1.14)	13.50	16.75
h Consensus estimate of 1989 GNP growth	2.7%	4.9%
i PER units per unit of growth	5.00 units	3.42 units

To close this section, we present an alternative calculation by Paul Aron that looks at earnings growth. The PER calculations, however adjusted, simply consider the PER at the same moment in time with the earnings forecast. The PER could also be related to GNP growth as a proxy of for earnings growth. When Aron did this in August 1989, Japan's projected 4.9% growth for 1989/90 versus 2.7% in the U.S. gave Japan the edge with 2.87 units of PER per unit growth versus 5.00 for the U.S. We recalculated this as of March 30, 1990, for the current interest rates, and not assuming any relative earnings changes in the U.S. or Japan since

August 1989, Japan still has the edge with 3.42 versus 5.00. Table 5.12 shows this calculation. One may argue with some of the assumptions but Japan's current prices were not excessively high as long as growth continues to be high. This calculation is, of course, related to the Miller-Modigliani infinite horizon model and suffers from the same criticisms.

PRICE EARNINGS RATIOS: THE NON-TRADING EFFECT

There are many reasons for the high PERs of Japanese stocks such as the deliberate understating of earnings, largely to minimize taxes, vast holdings of land and other assets listed on the books at values way below current market values, and the cross-holdings of shares in other companies most of which, to maintain proper business relations, is non-trading. Table 5.13, developed by Yoshihiro Nishimura, staff writer for *The Japan Times*, writing in the May 23, 1988 issue, shows what the PERs would be assuming that those investors whose holdings are never sold are in for the long haul and good business relations and they do not wish any of the current earnings but only a claim on the assets of the company.

This simplified "free market" PER analysis is not a correct way to account for this effect, but it does give some suggestive insights. Suddenly, shares in Bridgestone, Toyota, Sumitomo Bank and Tokyo Electric seem well-priced or even cheap. To more realistically estimate the current worth of various securities, one should try approaches that evaluate the true worth of companies and their future prospects. Measures that evaluate price to real book value and those that eliminate the land and other assets and gross up the earnings by standard account scale factors and adjust partially for the lack of trading will give you stocks with good value. This security analysis is very important and you can get good advice from analysts at the big four and other brokerage firms in addition to the emphasis on anomalies that we stress in this book. Some specific recommendations appear in Chapters 8 and 9.

The mochiai or non-trading effect is very strong in Japan as we can see from Table 5.13 which shows this for the largest stocks in each of the twenty-eight sectors in the first section of the TSE.

Table 5.13
Largest Companies in the TSE Sectors and Their Free Market PERs in 1988

TSE Sector	Largest Companies	Price ¥ 28/4/88	% Sector Mkt Cap end Apr. 1988	% Floating Shares	P/E Ratio (A)	Free Market P/E Ratio (B)	A/B
Fishery, agriculture	Nippon Suisan	675	30	20	79.4	15.9	5.0
Mining	Arabian Oil	5760	34	17	130.3	22.2	5.9
Construction	Kajima	1590	9	15	91.9	13.8	6.7
Food	Ajinomoto	3610	16	15	169.5	25.4	6.7
Textiles	Asahi Chemical	1150	20	25	104.5	26.1	4.0
Pulp & Paper	Oji Paper	1450	25	21	64.7	13.6	4.8
Chems & pharma.	Takeda Chemical	3050	8	17	117.3	19.9	5.9
Oil & coal products	Nippon Oil	1190	39	27	135.2	36.5	3.7
Rubber Products	Bridgestone	1460	49	12	32.5	3.9	8.3
Glass & ceramic	Asahi Glass	2100	34	14	73.2	10.2	7.1
Iron & steel	Nippon Steel	465	27	20	n/a	n/a	n/a
Non-ferrous metals	Sumitomo Electric	1660	19	24	90.2	21.7	4.2
Metal products	Toyo Seikan	3210	41	10	39.1	3.9	10.0
Machinery	Kubota	700	10	12	85.4	10.2	8.3
Electrical machinery	MEI	2790	12	17	52.5	8.9	5.9
Transportation equip.	Toyota Motor	2440	33	8	32.5	2.6	12.5
Precision instrument	Ricoh	1360	20	17	79.0	13.1	6.0
Other products	Dai Nippon	2750	30	10	66.7	6.7	10.0
Commerce	Mitsubishi Corp.	1330	8	12	93.0	11.2	8.3
Banking & insurance	Sumitomo Bank	3800	7	5	161.7	8.1	20.0
Real estate	Mitsubishi Estate	2410	45	16	122.3	19.6	6.2
Land transportation	Seibu Railway	4550	16	8	784.5	62.8	12.5
Marine transport	Nippon Yusen	646	33	20	2153.3	430.7	5.0
Air transportation	All Nippon Air	1880	51	24	458.5	109.9	4.2
Warehouse & transp.	Mitsubishi Ware.	1570	24	17	58.4	9.9	5.9
Communications	NTT	2490000	73	5	262.4	13.1	20.0
Electricity & gas	Tokyo Electric	6170	37	22	42.8	9.4	4.5
Services	Secom	7110	15	23	68.6	15.8	4.3

Kobayashi (1990) suggests adjusting for cross-holdings using the formula

$$\text{adjusted PER} = \frac{\text{Total value of marketed shares}}{\text{Reported net earnings - dividends received}}$$

$$= \frac{(\text{Total value of outstanding shares})(1\text{-holding ratio})}{(\text{Reported net earnings}) (1\text{- payout ratio x holding ratio})}$$

$$= \text{Reported PER} \left(\frac{1\text{-holding ratio}}{1\text{-payout ratio x holding ratio}} \right).$$

Estimates of the holding ratio and payout ratio by Nikko Securities and Sharpe-Tint, Inc., for 1990 are 0.33, and 0.30 or 0.35, respectively. These values give a correction factor of 0.74 or 0.76 for the two payout ratios.

McDonald's (1989) calculations on the cross-holding effect of a sample also yield a value of about 0.75 for this effect. Table 5.9 has additional calculations by French and Poterba (1990) who find values in the 0.67-0.69 range in the late 1980s. See also Ando and Auerbach (1990) and Ueda (1990).

DO LOW PER STOCKS HAVE AN EDGE?

In the United States and other countries, there is considerable evidence that securities with low PERs have outperformed high PER and other stocks. Basu (1977, 1983), Goodman and Peavy (1985,1986), Jacobs and Levy (1988abc) among others document this. Dreman (1982) suggests this as a fundamental approach for stock selection. A survey of this literature appears in Ziemba (1991e). In particular, the strategy of investing in stocks with PERs that are low, low compared to their industry and low compared to their historical norms, has consistently yielded portfolios with superior risk adjusted returns. To do a proper analysis, one must separate out the risk taken as well as the effect of other anomalies such as the January and small firm effects.

The PERs on the Tokyo stock exchange are very high, averaging about 70 at the end of December 1989, which is more than four times those in the U.S. On May 15, 1987 the PER of the NSA 225 index peaked at 80.15 based on estimated earnings as of May 1. Many observers believe these PERs do not tell much about the real valuation of securities prospects. Considerable effort can be expended to take apart the various companies to get at the *real* PERs by eliminating the land, buildings, and other hard asset holdings, the cross stock holdings, and the effects of non-trading of a high percentage of the outstanding stock, and the different accounting procedures used in Japan. With adjustments of this sort a more meaningful PER often results.

Thus, on the surface, one would not expect that the usual edges from low PER stocks would prevail. However, a look at the data of 574 firms on the TSE-I by Aggarwal, Hiraki and Rao (1988) shows that there actually was a low PER effect for the ten years from 1974 to 1983. Moreover, this effect was separate from monthly and size effects, and it was statistically significant and positive in all months except January. In January, the PER effect was reversed and that effect was also statistically significant. Still, with so much size and January effects going on, the simple model may fail to capture the effect correctly. In any event, there was a significant PER effect in the other eleven months.

Figure 5.5
The TOPIX Index Around the Period at the Aggarwal, Hiraki and Rao (1988) Low PER Study, 1970-88

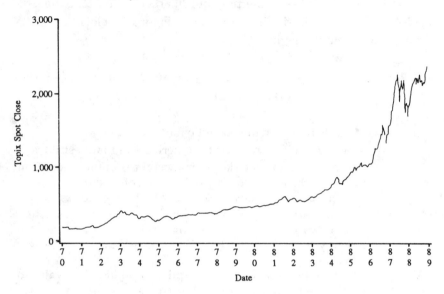

Source: Yamaichi Research Institute

Aggawal, Hiraki and Rao eliminated companies with negative earnings and found 574 firms that had complete data for the 1974-83 period. An earnings/price ratio is preferable to use because it avoids problems when earnings are zero and this ratio is computed as of December 31 of each year using the earnings per share of the most recent fiscal year end. They used 68,880 observations each for monthly returns and the two sets of risk-adjusted returns based on the value and equally weighted indices. The median of the size (market capitalization, number of shares outstanding times price), E/P ratio, and the beta of the firms studied was ¥30.11 billion, 0.046 and 0.87, respectively. Similar numbers for the size, E/P ratio, and beta for all firms on the Nikkei tape are ¥9.70 billion, and 0.045 and by construction 1.00, respectively. The E/P ratios as well as the inter-quartile ranges for their sample were virtually identical to those of companies on the Nikkei tape, while these values for the size of the sample are somewhat larger than for all companies on the Nikkei tape. However, the larger size of their sample means the observed size effect is likely to be less significant than if all firms on the Nikkei tape could have been used.

The 1974-83 period is in the post bull market period following the 1973-74 first OPEC oil price increase crash. Figure 5.5 plots the TOPIX during and around this period.

Aggarwal et al fit the following statistical model

$$R_{pt} - R_{ft} = a_0 + B_p (R_{mt} - R_{ft}) + a_1 JA + a_2 JU + a_3 JA \bullet LMV_{pt} + a_4 JU \bullet LMV_{pt} + a_5 NJJ \bullet$$
$$LMV_{pt} + a_6 JA \bullet LEP_{pt} + a_7 JU \bullet LEP_{pt} + a_8 NJJ \bullet LEP_{pt} + u_{pt}$$

where

R_{pt}	=	Monthly return on the portfolio for time period t.
R_{ft}	=	Monthly risk-free rate for time period t (all interest rates on unconditional loans to large financial institutions taken from Economic Statistics Monthly of the Bank of Japan).
R_{mt}	=	Monthly return on the market index for time period t.
JA	=	Dummy variable equal to 1 if month is January, 0 otherwise.
JU	=	Dummy variable equal to 1 if month is June, 0 otherwise.
NJJ	=	Dummy variable equal to 1 if month is January or June, 0 otherwise.
LMV_{pt}	=	Log of the average market equity capitalization value of portfolio p for time period t adjusted once a year.
LEP_{pt}	=	Log of the average E/P ratio of portfolio p for time period t adjusted once a year.
u_{pt}	=	Stochastic error term with zero mean and constant variance.

This model separates out the January and June, the January and June small firm, and the small firm effects in other months. Also, these effects are separated away from the CAPM model with its beta coefficient. This leaves the low PER effect which is further separated into its effect in January, June, and in the other ten months. The results that follow in Table 5.14 are based on the value weighted TOPIX index. The results using the equally weighted index indicate that while the seasonal (January and June) effect is weaker, the PER, size, and interaction effects are stronger than the results using the value weighted index.

Table 5.14 presents the estimates in six different ways. First estimation can proceed via ordinary least squares or by a more advanced statistical procedure called TSCSR (Time Series Cross Sectional Regression) that accounts for contemporaneous data correlations among the error terms, see Brown, Kleidon and Marsh (1983).

Table 5.14
Size, PER and Seasonal Effects of 574 Stocks on the First Section of the Tokyo Stock Exchange, 1974-83

$$R_{pt}-R_{ft} = a_0 + B_p (R_{mt} - R_{ft}) + a_1 JA + a_2 JU + a_3 JA \bullet LMV_{pt} + a_4 JU \bullet LMV_{pt} + a_5 NJJ \bullet LMV_{pt} + a_6 JA \bullet LEP_{pt} + a_7 JU*LEI_{pt} + a_8 NJJ \bullet LEP_{pt} + u_{pt}$$

Independent Groups

	a_0	B_p	a_1	a_2	a_3	a_4	a_5	a_6	a_7	a_8
OLS[a]	0.0010	0.9319	0.0266	0.0391	-0.0112	-.0043	0.0003	-.0080	0.0076	0.0022
	0.263	*67.369**	*2.202†*	*3.239**	*-6.474**	*-2.470†*	*0.551*	*-2.432†*	*2.313†*	*2.108†*
TSCSR[b]	0.0029	0.9333	0.0404	0.0392	-0.0116	-.0042	0.0003	-.0033	0.0084	0.0028
	0.617	*23.073**	*3.345**	*3.252**	*-7.977**	*-2.877**	*0.589*	*-1.176*	*2.946**	*3.063*

Within Groups MV/EP

	a_0	B_p	a_1	a_2	a_3	a_4	a_5	a_6	a_7	a_8
OLS	0.0008	0.9274	0.0260	0.0330	-0.0116	0.0040	0.0001	0.0086	0.0060	0.0020
	0.208	*67.885**	*2.170**	*2.749**	*-6.771**	*-2.352†*	*0.223*	*-2.664**	*1.848 +*	*1.946 +*
TSCSR	0.0029	0.9290	0.0400	0.0330	-0.0120	0.0039	0.0001	-.0039	0.0067	0.0026
	0.609	*22.815**	*3.333**	*2.757*	*-8.458**	*-2.768**	*0.168*	*-1.426*	*2.429†*	*2.952**

Within Groups EP/MV

	a_0	B_p	a_1	a_2	a_3	a_4	a_5	a_6	a_7	a_8
OLS	-.0001	0.9218	0.0293	0.0377	-0.0116	-.0040	0.0003	-.0080	0.0072	0.0019
	-0.037	*67.742**	*2.433†*	*3.134†*	*-6.755**	*-2.340†*	*0.519*	*-2.430*	*2.215†*	*1.797 +*
TSCSR	0.0020	0.9297	0.0432	0.0378	-0.0119	-.0039	0.0002	-.0031	0.0080	0.0025
	0.418	*22.877**	*3.589**	*3.144**	*-8.363**	*-2.740**	*0.542*	*-1.123*	*2.862**	*2.798**

t values in italics, * = .01, † = .05, + =.10
[a] estimates using ordinary least squares
[b] estimates using the TSCSR procedure

Source: Aggarwal, Hiraki and Rao (1988)

There were five size quintiles and five earnings price quintiles for a total of twenty-five categories in each monthly period. The size and earnings quintiles are updated yearly, but the returns are updated monthly.

Three portfolio formation methods were used. First, returns were examined for portfolios based on market value (MV) and earnings to price (EP) rankings independently. In the second and third methods, portfolios were formed taking into account both size and earnings/price ratios simultaneously. These different portfolio formation methods were used to avoid results that may be attributable to the formation process itself. The first of these is labeled as the independent groups method and the other two as the within groups methods.

In the independent groups method, stocks are initially ranked by size and assigned to five MV quintiles in ascending order. The stocks are then re-ranked by their EP ratio and assigned to five EP quintiles with the EP1 quintile containing the stocks with the lowest earnings/price ratios and the EP5 quintile those stocks with the highest earnings/price ratios. From the EP and MV quintiles, twenty-five portfolios are formed reflecting the twenty-five possible pairs of EP and MV quintiles.

In the within groups approach, stocks are first ranked by EP and formed into EP quintiles. Next, within each EP quintile, stocks are ranked by MV and assigned to five MV quintiles to give the twenty-five portfolios. This procedure is repeated, but with quintiles first formed on the basis of MV values, and then within each MV quintile stocks are assigned to EP quintiles to form the within groups MV/EP method. The within groups methods yield portfolio sizes that are generally equal while the independent groups method results in portfolios that vary in size since MV and EP are correlated.

The results show that beta was about 0.93 for this set of 574 firms over this ten year period. The January effect amounts to 3-4% and so does the June effect. In January, the small firm effect adds about another 1% per tenfold decrease in firm size. Logs are used and a minus coefficient suggests an edge for the smaller stocks. The June small firm effect is smaller, being about 0.4% per tenfold decrease, but it is still significant. In months other than January and June, there is no significant size effect.

The PER effects are then separated from these other effects. June has a positive effect of about 0.8% per tenfold increase in the earnings/price ratio (i.e., per tenfold decrease in the PER). Non January or June months gain about 0.2% per month per tenfold increase in the EP ratio. These effects are statistically significant. In January, the effect seems to reverse itself. The various estimation procedures give low PER losses of about 0.4 to 0.8% per tenfold decrease in PER, but only the OLS estimates are significant. It is not clear why this effect occurs, but with a 3-4% January effect plus a 1% per tenfold decrease low cap effect, it is not surprising that there is nothing left for the low PER stocks to add. In total, there is a small low PER effect of about 3% per year per tenfold decrease in the PER with January and June more or less offsetting themselves and the other months gaining about 0.30%. However, this effect is smaller than the January, June, and size effects.

Asaji Komatsu of the Yamaichi Research Institute in Tokyo and I looked into this. We computed the cumulative effect of the variable earnings over price, that is the reciprocal of PER. Values were normalized for all (some 1229 , autumn 1990 count) companies on the TSE-I by subtracting the mean and dividing by the standard deviation so one has a pure variable. The time period studied was the ten year period June 1979 to August 1989. Figures 5.17 and 5.18 at the end of this chapter have the cumulative effect graphs for both the univariate variable earnings over price and the seperate effect of this variable once the effects of twenty-nine other variables are eliminated. The results showed that the univariate effect of PER by itself is essentially zero relative to the TOPIX over the ten year period. However, once the other variables are accounted for, the low PER stocks had an edge of about 60% over the TOPIX. This is broadly consistent with the Aggawal et al. results.

PRICE TO SALES AS A PREDICTOR OF STOCK PRICES

Aggarwal, Rao and Hiraki (1989) did another study similar to their low PER analysis described above using price to sales ratios. The main idea is to simply use the PSR in place of the PER. Senchack and Martin (1987) and Jacobs and Levy (1988ab) found a significant PSR effect for the U.S. market. Low PSR stocks have higher returns, and portfolios of low PSR stocks outperform portfolios with high PSR stocks. The performance of smaller firms is even stronger if they have a low PSR. The idea is that earnings are influenced more by accounting procedures than are sales. Companies that are small, new, or have a history of low or negative earnings have meaningless PERs. Thus, given accounting problems and the temporal instability of reported earnings, the PSR is an alternative measure of relative valuation.

Aggarwal, Rao and Hiraki used monthly data from the first section of the TSE for the sixteen years 1968-83, a longer period than their PER study. Data from the Japan Securities Research Institute and the Nihon Keizai Shimbun Nikkei Financial Data tapes were merged to form the sample. The PSR is the year end market price divided by the annual sales per share. This is not the best measure to use for a monthly model, but that is all the data they had available. Year end total assets are used to evaluate firm size, again not the best measure for a monthly model. Size and PSR portfolios were formed in a matrix with five size and five PSR categories. They fit the following statistical model:

$$R_{pt} - R_{ft} = a_0 + B_p (R_{mt} - R_{ft}) + a_1 JA + a_2 JU + a_3 JA \cdot LTA_{pt} + a_4 JU \cdot LTA_{pt} + a_5 NJJ \cdot$$
$$LTA_{pt} + a_6 JA \cdot PSR_{pt} + a_7 JU \cdot PSR_{pt} + a_8 NJJ \cdot PSR_{pt} + u_{pt}$$

where

R_{pt}	=	Monthly return on the portfolio for time period t.
R_{ft}	=	Monthly risk-free rate in t.
R_{mt}	=	Monthly return on the market index in t.
JA	=	Dummy variable equal to 1 in January, 0 otherwise.
JU	=	Dummy variable equal to 1 in June, 0 otherwise.
NJJ	=	Dummy variable equal to 1 if month is not January or June, 0 otherwise.
LTA_{pt}	=	Log of the average total assets for portfolio p for time period t adjusted once a year.
PSR_{pt}	=	Average PSR ratio of portfolio p for time period t adjusted once a year.
u_{pt}	=	Stochastic error term with zero mean and constant variance.

Ranking by PSR they have the five quintiles:

PSR Quintile	Monthly Mean % Return	PSR	Total Assets, ¥ bil
1	0.01862	0.131	132.7
2	0.01716	0.253	128.4
3	0.01586	0.375	120.1
4	0.01448	0.549	97.6
5	0.01125	1.292	96.7

By size they have the quintiles:

PSR quintile	Monthly Mean, % Return	Total Assets	PSR
1	0.01757	0.1318	0.691
2	0.01611	0.2705	0.517
3	0.01535	0.4894	0.506
4	0.01448	0.9750	0.414
5	0.01388	3.7950	0.470

During the 1968-83 period, January and June had their usual high returns as did March and December. January and June also had excess returns relative to the CAPM.

	Monthly Returns			Monthly Returns above the Risk Free Rate		
	1968-83	1968-75	1975-83	1968-83	1968-75	1975-83
Jan	0.0523	0.0573	0.0487	0.0213	0.0208	0.0216
Feb	0.0104	0.0261	-0.0010	-0.0004	-0.0011	0.0001
Mar	0.0256	0.0454	0.0114	-0.0038	-0.0023	-0.0049
Apr	0.0066	-0.0022	0.0130	-0.0092	-0.0042	-0.0128
May	0.0065	0.0214	-0.0042	-0.0083	-0.0060	-0.0010
Jun	0.0278	0.0337	0.0235	0.0070	0.0098	0.0050
Jul	0.0120	0.0215	0.0053	0.0048	0.0072	0.0031
Aug	0.0024	-0.0227	0.0206	-0.0011	-0.0045	0.0012
Sep	0.0061	0.0056	0.0065	-0.0092	-0.0169	-0.0036
Oct	0.0033	0.0159	-0.0058	0.0014	0.0157	-0.0088
Nov	0.0093	0.0139	0.0060	-0.0089	-0.0141	-0.0052
Dec	0.0233	0.0236	0.0230	-0.0046	0.0024	-0.0096

Table 5.15 shows the absolute and excess returns by size and PSR quintiles, and Table 5.16 shows the regression results for their model.

Table 5.15
Size and PSR Absolute and Excess Returns by Quintile, TSE-I, 1968-83

Absolute Returns by Size Quintiles

	Jan	Feb	Mar	Apr	May	Jun	Jul	Aug	Scp	Oct	Nov	Dec
1	0.0634	0.0187	0.0214	0.0131	0.0072	0.0358	0.0142	0.0012	-0.0020	0.0106	0.0016	0.0256
2	0.0603	0.0163	0.0226	0.0077	0.0108	0.0309	0.0115	0.0054	0.0016	0.0018	0.0055	0.0189
3	0.0528	0.0099	0.0237	0.0091	0.0058	0.0277	0.0121	0.0032	0.0076	0.0047	0.0096	0.0178
4	0.0481	0.0053	0.0320	0.0033	0.0046	0.0267	0.0096	0.0020	0.0106	0.0001	0.0110	0.0206
5	0.0370	0.00015	0.0283	0.0000	0.0042	0.0177	0.0129	0.0007	0.0129	-0.0009	0.0188	0.0334

Excess Returns by Size Quintiles

	Jan	Feb	Mar	Apr	May	Jun	Jul	Aug	Scp	Oct	Nov	Dec
1	0.0311	0.0063	-0.0097	-0.0044	-0.0096	0.0133	0.0049	0.0050	-0.0196	0.0067	-0.0182	-0.0036
2	0.0286	0.0047	0.0079	-0.0089	-0.0051	0.0094	0.0031	0.0014	-0.0154	-0.0007	-0.0142	-0.0096
3	0.0224	-0.0003	-0.0055	-0.0056	-0.0085	0.0075	0.0053	0.0010	-0.0072	0.0043	-0.0080	-0.0093
4	0.0174	-0.0053	0.0030	-0.0124	-0.0097	0.0061	0.0026	-0.0016	-0.0042	-0.0019	-0.0069	-0.0072
5	0.0063	-0.0077	0.0010	-0.0146	-0.0088	-0.0013	0.0081	-0.0016	0.0004	-0.0013	0.0026	0.0069

Absolute Returns by PSR Quintiles

	Jan	Feb	Mar	Apr	May	Jun	Jul	Aug	Scp	Oct	Nov	Dec
1	0.0654	0.0075	0.0221	0.0057	0.0067	0.0378	0.0260	0.0007	0.0081	0.0086	0.0093	0.0257
2	0.0648	0.0113	0.0297	0.0013	0.0037	0.0320	0.0193	0.0016	0.0035	0.0025	0.0106	0.0258
3	0.0532	0.0114	0.0308	0.0068	0.0050	0.0255	0.0119	0.0033	0.0054	0.0041	0.0087	0.0242
4	0.0498	0.0128	0.0243	0.0090	0.0097	0.0270	0.0018	0.0022	0.0078	0.0004	0.0062	0.0228
5	0.0283	0.0088	0.0211	0.0104	0.0076	0.0166	0.0013	0.0047	0.0059	0.0008	0.0117	0.0178

Excess Returns by PSR Quintiles

	Jan	Feb	Mar	Apr	May	Jun	Jul	Aug	Scp	Oct	Nov	Dec
1	0.0306	-0.0079	-0.0096	-0.0153	-0.0124	0.0131	0.0141	-0.0167	-0.0110	0.0006	-0.0118	-0.0050
2	0.0329	0.0000	0.0003	-0.0157	-0.0122	0.0110	0.0120	-0.0041	-0.0126	0.0001	-0.0077	-0.0023
3	0.0230	0.0016	0.0019	-0.0077	-0.0093	0.0059	0.0059	0.0006	-0.0095	0.0036	-0.0084	-0.0026
4	0.0206	0.0044	-0.0041	-0.0044	-0.0033	0.0081	-0.0034	0.0022	-0.0057	0.0016	-0.0108	-0.0037
5	-0.0007	-0.0002	-0.0077	-0.0028	-0.0044	-0.0031	-0.0045	0.0063	-0.0072	0.0012	-0.0061	-0.0093

Source: Aggarwal, Rao and Hiraki (1989)

Table 5.16 Size, PSR and Seasonal Effects on the TSE-I, 1968-83

Regression Estimates Using Raw Returns
Regression Models

Independent Variable	(1)	(2)	(3)	(4)	(5)	(6)	(7)	(8)	(9)
Intercept	0.0118 (14.580)*	0.0221 (18.355)*	0.0153 (17.833)*	0.0171 (14.051)*	0.0103 (11.488)*	0.0150 (11.744)*	0.0112 (12.215)*	0.0157 (12.446)*	0.144 (10.851)*
JA	0.0425 (15.825)*			0.0425 (15.878)*	0.0425 (15.847)*	0.0600 (14.158)*	0.0136 (12.013)*	0.0425 (15.905)*	0.0543 (12.366)*
JU	0.0175 (6.510)*			0.0175 (6.532)*	0.0175 (6.519)*	0.0249 (5.885)*	0.0136 (4.499)*	0.0175 (6.543)*	0.0214 (4.880)*
PSR		-0.0104 (-5.634)*		-0.0104 (-6.532)*				0.0108 (-6.039)*	
JA*PSR						-0.0407 (-6.581)*			-0.427 (-6.920)*
JU*PSR						-0.0209 (-3.388)*			-0.0222 (-3.607)*
NJJ*PSR						-0.0063 (-3.214)*			-0.0065 (-3.325)*
LTA			-0.0024 (-3.707)**		-0.0024 (-3.812)			-0.0026 (4.174)*	
JA*LA							-0.0108 (-5.026)*		-0.0116 (-5.460)*
JU*LTA							-0.0072 (-3.347)*		-0.0076 (-3.577)*
NJJ*LTA							-0.0010 (-1.538)		-0.0012 (-1.741)***

Regression Estimates Using Risk-Adjusted Returns
Regression Models

Independent Variable	(1)	(2)	(3)	(4)	(5)	(6)	(7)	(8)	(9)
Intercept	-0.0035 (-5.567)*	0.0010 (1.116)	-0.0012 (-1.803)***	-0.0021 (-2.235)**	-0.0040 (-6.219)*	-0.0044 (-4.45)*	-0.0340 (-4.883)*	-0.0029 (-2.928)*	-0.0043 (-4.245)*
JA	0.0264 (12.669)*			0.0264 (12.673)*	0.0264 (12.678)*	0.0451 (13.731)*	0.0199 (8.501)*	0.0264 (12.683)*	0.0391 (11.505)*
JU	0.0114 (5.449)*			0.0114 (5.451)*	0.0114 (5.453)*	0.0202 (6.146)*	0.0072 (3.075)*	0.0114 (5.455)*	0.0164 (-4..28)*
PSR		-0.0027 (-1.926)**		-0.0027 (-1.961)**				-0.003 (-2.129)**	
JA*PSR						-0.0350 (-7.318)*			-0.0369 (-7.738)*
JU*PSR						-0.0156 (-3.259)*			-0.0168 (3.517)*
NJJ*PSR						0.0018 (1.183)			0.0013 (1.201)
LTA			-0.0013 (-2.717)*		-0.0013 (-2.767)*			-0.0014 (-2.888)*	
JA*LA							-0.0102 (-6.133)*		-0.0109 (-6.622)*
JU*LTA							-0.0065 (-3.917)*		-0.0068 (-4.146)*
NJJ*LTA							0.0001 (0.134)		0.0001 (0.205)**

*, **, *** significant at .01, .05, .10 level, respectively

Source: Aggarwal, Rao and Hiraki (1989)

The results show the January and June size and PSR effects by themselves in equations (1)-(3) of Table 5.16 The various other equations separate out the different effects. Finally equation (9) delineates all the effects studied. Not surprisingly, the PSR effect is strongest in January and June. However, it is significant in the other months as well and it is separate from small firm effects. The size effect is significant only in

January and June. Relative to the market index, the PSR and size effects are still significant but only in January and June.

The two studies by Aggarwal, Rao and Hiraki provide evidence that PER and PSR do provide significant fundamental valuation measures despite the inherent inaccuracy of their measurement.

The evidence and conclusion of Aggarwal, Rao and Hiraki is also consistent with the calculations Asaji Komatsu and I made of the cumulative effect of low PSR. This effect, as shown in Figures 5.17 and 5.18 is generally irrelevant from 1979 to 1985. However, from 1985 to 1989, the effect was a strong. The cumulative effect in its univariate form over the period June 1979 to August 1989 was a 70% gain for stocks relative to the Topix, with PSR ratios one standard deviation below the mean. Once the effects of other factors were eliminated, the low PSR effect was not as strong but still exceeded the TOPIX by about 10% over the ten years.

EFFECT OF PAR VALUES ON STOCK PRICES
Stocks with low par values seem to trade at higher prices once profits and assets at book value are accounted for. Most stocks have par values of ¥50 but some have values of ¥20, ¥500, and ¥5000. To investigate this, colleagues at YRI fit a cross section regression on 78 stocks from the Tokyo Stock Exchange's first section on May 16, 1989. They found that the following equation best captured the effect with all coefficients significant at the 5% level or better with t statistics in parentheses:

$$\ln(\text{price}) = \underset{(-3.15)}{4.821} \quad \underset{}{-0.384 \text{ par value of } ¥500} \quad \underset{(2.74)}{+0.771 \text{ par value of } ¥20}$$

$$\underset{(2.79)}{+0.257 \ln(\text{current yearly profit estimate})} \quad \underset{(2.84)}{+0.303 \ln(\text{book value per share})}$$

$$R^2_{df=73} = 0.676, s_{df=73} = 0.387.$$

The results indicate there is a significant price advantage to the low par values of ¥20 versus the ¥500 par value stocks. How much of this is subsumed in the small firm effect and how much can be explained by hidden assets remains to be explored.

However, Figures 5.17 and 5.18 show the cumulative effect diagrams for June 1979 to August 1989. The results indicate that relative to the

TOPIX stocks with low par values fared poorly in the 1982-87 bull market. However, this reversed itself in 1987, so the net effect from 1979 to 1989 is positive for the low par value securities and the revenue for high par value stocks that underperform.

DIVIDENDS AND YIELDS

Figure 5.6 shows the yield on the TSE-I from 1955 to 1990. Figures 5.7a and 5.7b show the weighted and arithmetic yields of all issues and all dividend paying stocks on the TSE-I and TSE-II from 1976 to 1988. Tables 5.17 and 5.18 supplement this for the TSE-I by showing the average yields by industry as of the end of 1989 and the dividends and yields going back to 1949. There is little difference across industries.

However, one sees fairly constant dividends yielding lower and lower percentage returns as the prices have increased since the 1960s. As capital gains are not taxed but dividends are, there is little incentive for having high yields; hence, the companies are not encouraged to increase these payouts. As of April 1989 capital gains have been taxed but at rates which are still well below those of dividend income. Capital gains of foreigners are still tax exempt, but foreigners must pay about 15% on dividends.

The average yields of all first and second section stocks have been dropping almost consistently since 1951. This is because businesses have mostly been utilizing a dividend policy that it is enough to pay a certain fixed percentage of the face value as a dividend steadily and continuously, while stock prices went up and remained high, thanks to the mutual stock holdings between businesses and the domestic funds surplus.

In the 1950s, yields were in the 5-10% range and in the 1960s, 3-5%. After falling below the 2% level in May 1976, the average yields fell below 1%, hitting 0.74% in 1986. At the end of December 1988, they averaged 0.52%. As of the end of December 1989, they averaged 0.38%. After the 1990 declines, the yield rose to about 0.7%

Figure 5.8 shows the distribution of dividend payments for the NSA by month for the year ending September 1987. The end of the fiscal year, March, has the highest dividend level followed by the end of the six month fiscal year in September.

Table 5.19a shows the ratio of dividends to total return for the TSE-I from 1952 to 1987. Table 5.19b the same for the second section from 1975 to 1987 and Table 5.20 shows the distribution of the number of stocks in various yield groups from 1978 to 1988. In 1988 versus 1978, the main difference is the majority of stocks paying 0.01 to 0.49% and 0.50 to 0.99% as shown in Figure 5.9. The actual number of stocks that pay no dividend at all has fallen from 281 to 216.

The percent of earnings paid out by the 1,810 companies on the TSE-I and TSE-II fell below 30% in 1988, and in 1989 was 28.13%. During 1989, 1619 or 89.4% of the companies paid dividends. Figure 5.10 shows the trend in the payout ratio from 1980-89. Since the dividend level is more or less fixed, the percent payout depends on the level of earnings in the given year. Table 5.21 details the payout ratios from 1980 to 1989. These ratios have been about a third of total earnings.

Roth (1989) points out that many companies give presents that are often worth a lot more than the dividends. The Japanese edition of the *Japan Company Handbook*, called the *Shikiho* lists these presents. One is eight Kabuki theater tickets each year for each 1000 shares of Kabukiza, a stock on the the TSE-II that sold for about ¥4500 per share in 1988.

Finally, Tables 5.22 and 5.23 show an international comparison of long term corporate and government bond yields versus stock yields for 1986 to 1988. The stock yields in Japan are far below those in other major countries, and the bond yields are 1-2% below those in West Germany and much lower than those in the U.S., the U.K., France and Italy.

Figure 5.6 Average Dividend Yield, TSE-I, 1955-90

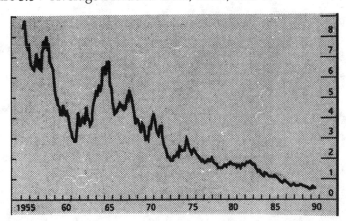

Source: TSE data from Jardine Fleming Securities

Figure 5.7a Stock Yields, First and Second Sections, 1976-88

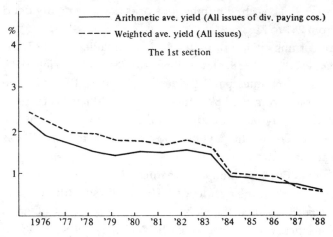

Figure 5.7b

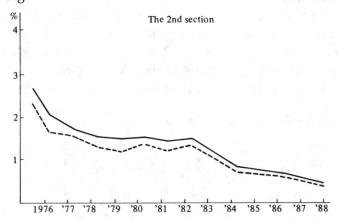

Source: Tokyo Stock Exchange

Table 5.17   Average Yields by Industry on the TSE-I end of 1989

1st Section					2nd Section					
#	with div	av yield	yield divid	wted yield	#	with div	av yield	yield divid	wted yield	industry
6	3	0.15	0.29	0.25	1	1	0.21	0.21	0.21	Fishery & Forestry
7	6	0.26	0.29	0.27	2	1	0.24	0.40	0.31	Mining
92	87	0.40	0.41	0.46	25	21	0.31	0.36	0.35	Construction
55	53	0.47	0.48	0.46	22	21	0.42	0.43	0 40	Foods
43	36	0.33	0.37	0.50	15	10	0.36	0.46	0.34	Textiles
20	17	0.45	0.50	0.50	6	4	0.35	0.49	0.39	Pulp & Paper
124	117	0.41	0.43	0.45	36	32	0.33	0.36	0.36	Chemicals
9	8	0.71	0.76	0.72	3	2	0.40	0.51	0.35	Oil & Coal Products
9	9	0.49	0.49	0.56	8	5	0.34	0.48	0.29	Rubber Products
31	29	0.37	0.39	0.41	14	13	0.39	0.41	0.43	Glass & Ceramics Prod
36	32	0.41	0.46	0.55	15	11	0.32	0.41	0.34	Iron & Steel
24	19	0.37	0.46	0.40	11	7	0.30	0.47	0.30	Nonferrous Metals
24	22	0.33	0.36	0.30	15	14	0.33	0.34	0.34	Metal Products
91	81	0.38	0.41	0.42	47	37	0.31	0.37	0.35	Machinery
109	101	0.42	0.44	0.53	60	51	0.33	0.36	0.36	Electric Appliances
51	47	9.44	0.47	0.57	23	19	0.40	0.47	0.44	Transportation Equip
20	19	0.49	0.51	0.61	14	10	0.29	0.37	0.31	Precision Instruments
29	27	0.37	0.38	0.41	11	11	0.31	0.31	0.30	Other Products
130	124	0.39	0.40	0.40	45	45	0.35	0.35	0.36	Commerce
137	137	0.36	0.36	0.32	11	11	0.32	0.32	0.32	Finance & Insurance
18	17	0.36	0.37	0.33	4	4	0.12	0.12	0.14	Real Estate
25	24	0.27	0.29	0.26	8	8	0.30	0.30	0.35	Land Transportation
13	2	0.04	0.21	0.10	10	3	0.12	0.28	0.07	Marine Transportation
4	4	0.28	0.28	0.23	1	1	0.22	0.22	0.22	Air Transportation
10	10	0.34	0.34	0.39	9	9	0.31	0.31	0.31	Warehousing & Harbor Transport
5	5	0.31	0.31	0.32	-	-	-	-	-	Communication
14	14	0.77	0.77	0.90	1	1	0.38	0.38	0.38	Electric Power & (;as
25	23	0.26	0.27	0.26	19	19	0.26	0.26	0.26	Services
1,161	1.073	0.38	040	0.43	436	371	0.32	0.35	0.33	Total

Source: TSE

Table 5.18   Dividends and Yields on the TSE-I, 1949-89

	All 1st Section Stocks		Dividend-Paying 1st Section Stocks	
	Weighted average yield, %	Av dividend per share ¥	Total amount of dividends (¥mils)	Simple average yield %
1949	...	6.09	1,869	6.77
1950	...	6.97	11,525	9.53
1951	...	10.69	28,264	11.91
1952	...	12.88	41,311	9.85
1953	...	11.17	52,414	7.44
1954	...	9.89	60,499	9.44
1955	...	8.70	69,734	7.96
1956	...	8.27	85,109	6.68
1957	...	7.71	113,006	7.14
1958	...	7.14	122,938	6.66
1959	4.68	6.76	138,102	4.54
1960	4.27	6.71	174,225	3.93
1961	4.47	6.63	230,781	3.24
1962	5.82	6.47	307,253	3.86
1963	5.08	6.26	348,900	4.24
1964	6.01	6.26	391,501	5.69
1965	6.01	6.08	409,041	5.92
1966	4.76	5.92	407,890	4.44
1967	4.96	5.97	456,892	4.74
1968	5.00	6.09	506,603	4.36
1969	4.19	6.28	569,413	3.34
1970	4.30	6.55	647,271	3.47
1971	4.01	6.65	710,819	3.41
1972	2.42	6.55	717,714	2.24
1973	2.02	6.75	849,748	2.09
1974	2.55	6.88	912,452	2.53
1975	2.54	6.51	881,019	2.31
1976	2.27	6.25	995,343	1.91
1977	2.16	6.34	1,040,454	1.82
1978	2.00	6.45	1,090,007	1.60
1979	1.87	6.49	1,191,842	1.57
1980	1.79	6.58	1,200,537	1.63
1981	1.65	6.69	1,498,879	1.55
1982	1.80	6.80	1,525,765	1.68
1983	1.55	6.88	1,594,659	1.39
1984	1.24	7.11	1,709,559	1.09
1985	1.05	7.25	1,829,277	0.99
1986	0.83	7.33	1,850,248	0.78
1987	0.56	7.36	2,042,359	0.63
1988	0.52	7.52	2,298,464	0.55
1989	0.46	7.78	2,495,041	0.47

Source: TSE

Figure 5.8
Distribution of Dividends on the NSA, by Month, Year Ending September
1987

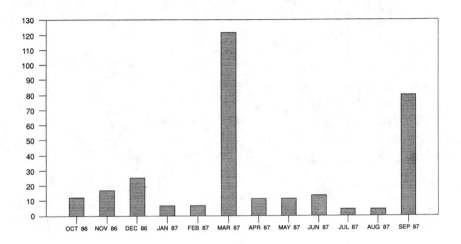

Source: Tokyo Stock Exchange and Brenner et al. (1989b)

Table 5.19a Ratio of Dividends to Total Return First Section, 1952-87

	1953	1954	1955	1956	1957	1958	1959	1960	1961	1962	1963	1964	1965	1966	1967	1968	1969	1970	1971	1972	1973	1974	1975	1976	1977	1978	1979	1980	1981	1982	1983	1984	1985	1986	1987
1952	17.4	40.1	43.0	29.7	32.4	34.5	24.2	20.5	18.8	20.2	20.7	33.8	37.9	33.6	36.5	35.8	29.5	29.9	28.6	18.5	16.0	20.5	21.6	20.7	20.4	19.6	19.5	19.7	17.8	19.2	17.1	14.4	12.3	9.6	7.1
1953		-111.7	101.8	30.0	32.9	39.0	25.2	20.8	20.0	26.8	27.0	34.9	39.1	34.3	37.3	36.6	29.8	30.2	28.8	18.5	16.0	20.5	21.7	20.7	20.4	19.6	19.5	19.7	17.8	19.2	17.1	14.4	12.3	9.5	7.1
1954			30.5	22.9	28.1	31.7	21.7	18.5	18.3	25.0	25.7	33.2	37.5	33.1	36.2	35.6	29.1	28.6	28.3	18.2	15.8	20.3	21.6	20.5	20.3	19.5	19.4	19.6	17.7	19.3	17.0	14.3	12.3	9.5	7.0
1955				17.3	25.8	30.7	20.0	17.5	17.5	24.4	25.3	33.1	37.6	33.1	38.2	35.6	29.0	29.5	28.2	18.2	15.7	20.2	21.4	20.4	20.2	19.4	19.3	19.5	17.7	19.1	17.0	14.3	12.2	9.5	7.0
1956					42.7	45.2	21.1	17.5	17.5	25.3	25.3	34.8	39.5	34.2	37.4	36.6	28.8	28.8	28.5	18.0	15.7	20.2	21.4	20.3	20.2	19.4	19.2	19.3	17.6	19.1	16.9	14.3	12.2	9.5	7.0
1957						43.7	12.5	15.2	13.8	24.1	24.1	34.3	39.4	33.8	37.3	38.4	29.2	28.7	28.1	17.8	15.5	20.1	21.3	20.4	20.2	19.4	19.2	19.1	17.5	19.0	16.8	14.2	11.3	9.4	7.0
1958							11.2	11.9	15.0	22.5	23.7	33.7	38.1	33.4	37.0	36.2	28.9	28.4	28.1	18.0	15.5	19.9	21.1	20.4	20.4	19.4	19.3	19.5	17.6	19.1	16.9	14.2	12.1	9.4	7.0
1959								12.8	17.7	28.6	28.6	47.7	49.1	30.5	42.4	40.3	30.8	31.1	30.8	18.3	15.4	20.2	21.4	20.7	20.4	19.4	19.3	19.6	17.7	19.2	16.9	14.2	12.1	9.4	6.9
1960										51.1	39.5	65.8	71.8	47.0	61.0	46.3	33.1	34.9	31.8	18.3	15.5	20.5	21.8	20.8	20.5	19.6	19.5	19.7	17.7	19.2	16.9	14.2	12.1	9.4	6.9
1961										-3.8	72.8	173.9	144.6	68.5	63.0	53.5	35.3	35.3	34.9	18.3	15.5	20.6	21.9	20.8	20.5	19.6	19.5	19.7	17.7	19.2	17.0	14.2	11.9	9.3	6.9
1962											29.2	81.4	87.8	45.7	60.8	45.4	31.3	31.9	31.6	17.2	14.7	19.8	21.0	20.0	19.8	18.8	19.0	19.2	17.3	18.8	16.7	14.0	11.8	9.2	6.8
1963												-133.7	78.2	54.4	69.9	49.7	31.6	31.9	29.4	16.7	14.3	19.3	20.7	19.8	19.8	18.8	18.8	19.0	17.2	18.7	16.5	13.8	11.6	9.1	6.8
1964													102.2	33.0	42.0	30.6	27.6	24.8	24.1	14.1	13.1	18.1	18.7	18.1	18.1	18.1	18.1	18.0	16.3	17.9	15.9	13.3	11.4	9.0	6.7
1965														19.8	33.0	32.7	24.8	26.0	23.9	13.7	12.0	17.2	18.7	18.0	18.1	17.6	17.8	18.0	16.3	17.8	15.8	13.3	11.3	8.8	6.8
1966															81.3	45.0	23.9	22.0	22.1	12.3	12.0	17.0	17.7	17.2	17.3	16.9	17.0	17.4	15.8	17.4	15.5	13.0	11.1	8.8	6.5
1967																32.2	18.4	20.4	20.4	11.0	11.0	15.9	17.0	17.0	16.8	16.7	16.8	17.1	15.5	17.4	15.3	12.8	11.0	8.6	6.4
1968																	13.2	13.7	18.1	10.5	11.0	15.3	17.5	17.2	17.2	15.0	16.4	17.4	15.7	17.4	15.3	12.5	10.9	8.5	6.3
1969																		13.2	16.0	8.2	10.5	13.8	15.5	17.0	15.9	15.0	18.9	18.9	15.2	16.8	14.7	12.2	10.7	8.4	6.2
1970																			22.1	8.2	9.6	12.5	15.5	15.4	15.9	15.0	17.0	16.3	14.9	16.8	17.0	13.2	10.4	8.0	6.1
1971																				5.0	8.2	12.5	15.5	15.4	15.9	15.0	18.9	16.3	15.2	18.9	15.3	12.5	11.0	8.5	6.0
1972																					5.0	3.2	15.3	25.6	23.8	20.9	15.9	15.2	14.9	16.8	14.7	12.2	10.9	8.4	5.9
1973																						-18.3	-9.3	71.5	40.3	20.5	25.7	20.9	16.4	16.8	17.0	13.2	10.7	8.0	5.6
1974																							40.8	21.5	20.3	18.2	23.8	24.9	18.1	18.9	16.3	13.1	10.4	8.0	5.5
1975																								14.8	16.4	15.6	16.3	17.2	19.6	22.2	17.8	17.8	11.2	8.3	5.3
1976																									15.4	16.0	16.0	17.8	14.6	17.5	17.4	18.2	11.2	7.3	5.1
1977																										14.4	16.1	17.7	14.0	17.3	14.5	11.6	9.7	7.1	4.9
1978																											18.2	13.9	14.0	17.8	14.5	11.3	9.4	6.8	4.7
1979																												21.8	12.6	18.5	14.1	10.9	9.0	6.4	4.4
1980																													9.2	18.5	13.4	10.6	8.7	6.0	4.0
1981																														85.8	14.2	9.9	8.2	5.5	3.8
1982																															7.8	9.0	7.2	5.2	3.2
1983																																8.2	5.8	4.3	2.9
1984																																	4.7	3.8	2.5
1985																																		2.7	2.1
1986																																			1.7

Table 5.19b Ratio of Dividends to Total Return, TSE-II, 1975 to 1987

	1976	1977	1978	1979	1980	1981	1982	1983	1984	1985	1986	1987
1975	8.3	7.9	6.0	6.2	6.0	7.6	9.9	6.6	6.0	6.3	6.0	4.7
1976		14.3	9.4	6.5	6.9	8.2	11.1	6.7	4.9	6.3	4.9	4.6
1977			4.2	6.2	6.1	7.8	10.7	6.3	4.6	6.0	6.0	4.5
1978				6.0	13.2	9.5	15.3	6.6	4.7	6.1	4.8	4.6
1979					90.9	11.6	23.5	6.9	4.6	6.0	4.6	4.4
1980							17.6	5.4	3.7	4.3	4.1	4.0
1981							-33.7	6.1	3.3	3.0	3.1	3.2
1982								2.3	2.2	3.0	3.1	3.2
1983									2.0	3.5	3.5	3.4
1984										6.6	6.0	4.2
1985											3.5	3.4

Source: JSRI (1988)

Table 5.20 Distribution of Number of Stocks by Yield Group, 1978-1988

	0%	0.01-0.49	0.50-0.99	1.00-1.49	1.50-1.99	2.00-2.49	2.50-2.99	3.00-3.99	4.00-4.99	5.00-5.99	≥6.00	Total
1978	281	15	133	291	310	225	81	39	10	3	-	1,388
1979	259	16	89	225	352	245	121	70	7	10	-	1,397
1980	218	25	90	244	326	273	128	93	5	-	-	1,402
1981	192	25	92	215	303	288	166	108	13	8	2	1,412
1982	214	24	104	172	275	278	174	158	18	9	-	1,426
1983	250	74	188	302	268	183	106	55	9	5	-	1,440
1984	252	102	277	332	246	126	67	37	5	-	-	1,444
1985	239	116	399	388	214	89	16	14	1	-	-	1,476
1986	232	217	498	366	147	31	5	3	-	-	-	1,449
1987	243	297	703	238	44	2	5	-	-	-	-	1,532
1988	216	697	544	113	1	-	-	-	-	-	-	1,571

Source: Tokyo Stock Exchange

Figure 5.9 Distribution of Number of Stocks by Yield Group, 1978 and 1988

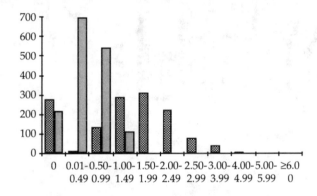

Source: Tokyo Stock Exchange

Figure 5.10
Profits on the TSE-I and II and Total and Percent of Profits Paid in
Dividends, 1980-89

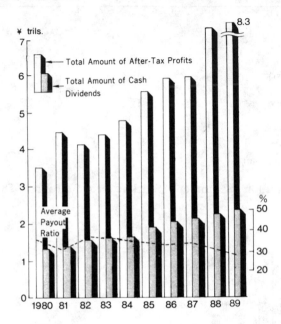

Source: Tokyo Stock Exchange

Table 5.21
Number of Companies on the TSE-I and II in Various Payout Percent
Categories, 1980-89

	1980	1981	1982	1983	1984	1985	1986	1987	1988	1989
Number Div.	305	262	296	346	358	320	304	320	258	191
Paying										
0.1 - 9.9	26	29	20	24	27	33	43	42	65	74
10.0-19.9	201	197	176	151	143	181	164	186	244	337
20.0-29.9	336	338	313	273	296	334	338	283	366	424
30.0-39.9	289	292	285	295	299	289	298	254	268	297
40.0-49.9	171	217	179	199	189	193	172	211	188	189
50.0-59.9	131	112	147	118	101	125	149	137	127	132
60.0-69.9	80	89	81	99	95	108	114	117	95	69
70.0-79.9	61	68	64	76	79	72	78	86	63	34
80.0-89.9	58	51	69	64	67	63	54	75	41	26
90.0-99.9	16	12	22	34	27	28	36	32	16	10
$\geq$100.0	37	58	86	83	100	53	64	66	46	27
Total	1,406	1,463	1,442	1,416	1,423	1,479	1,510	1,489	1,519	1,619
Average Payout Ratio (%)	35.86	31.84	37.69	37.54	36.68	33.51	32.96	34.76	29.24	28.13

Source: Tokyo Stock Exchange

Table 5.22
Yields of Long-Term Government Bonds and Stocks, Percent Per Annum

Year	Mon	Corporate Bonds						Stocks					
		Japan	U.S.	UK	FRG	Frarce	Italy	Japan	U.S	UK.	FRG	France	Italy
1986		6.14	9.71	10.82	6.6	9.94	10.56	0.78	3.49	4.01	1.75	2.55	1.58
19S7		5.40	9.91	10.62	6.6	10.94	9.87	0.63	3.08	3.50	2.83	-	2.01
1987	(0)	5.95	10.97	11.24	7.0	11.23	10.35	0.61	3.25	3.46	2.45	4.16	2.19
	(N)	5.59	10.54	10.63	6.8	10.96	10.69	0.62	3.66	4.46	2.77	4.33	2.67
	(D)	5.32	10.59	10.89	6.7	10.94	10.56	0.64	3.71	4.45	2.83	5.01	2.71
1988	(0)	5.06	10.37	10.92	6.7	10.38	10.28	0.58	3.66	4.17	2.95	5.03	2.81
	(F)	5.03	9.89	10.85	6.7	9.91	10.33	0.54	3.56	4.23	2.60	4.21	2.95
	(M)	4.99	9.86	10.65	6.6	10.02	10.31	0.54	3.48	4.18	2.59	4.62	2.64
	(A)	4.93	10.15	6.6	9.78	-	0.51	3.57	4.20	2.63	4.24	-	-
	(M)	4.95	10.37	10.68	6.8	-	-	0.52	3.80	4.25	-	-	-
	(0)	4.97	10.36	-	-	-	-	0.52	-	-	-	-	-

Source: National Data

Table 5.23   Yields of Corporate Bonds and Stocks Percent Per Annum

Year	Mon	Corporate Bonds						Stocks					
		Japan	U.S.	UK	FRG	Frarce	Italy	Japan	U.S	UK.	FRG	France	Italy
1986		6.14	9.71	10.82	6.6	9.94	10.56	0.78	3.49	4.01	1.75	2.55	1.38
19S7		5.40	9.91	10.62	6.6	10.94	9.87	0.63	3.08	3.50	2.83	-	2.01
1987	(0)	5.95	10.97	11.24	7.0	11.28	10.55	0.61	3.25	3.46	2.45	4.16	2.19
	(N)	5.79	10.54	10.63	6.8	10.96	10.69	0.62	3.66	4.46	2.77	4.33	2.67
	(D)	5.32	10.59	10.89	6.7	10.94	10.56	0.64	3.71	4.45	2.83	5.01	2.71
1988	(J)	5.06	10.37	10.92	6.7	10.38	10.28	0.58	3.66	4.17	2-95	5.03	2.81
	(F)	5.03	9.89	10.37	6.7	9.91	10.33	0.54	3.56	4.23	2.60	4.21	2.95
	(M)	4.99	9.86	10.65	6.6	10.02	10.31	0.54	3.48	4.18	2.59	4.62	2.64
	(A)	4.93	10.15	10.56	6.6	9.78	-	0.51	3.57	4.20	2.63	4.24	-
	(M)	4.95	10.37	10.68	6.8	-	-	0.52	3.80	4.25	-	-	-
	(0)	4.97	10.36	-	-	-	-	0.52	-	-	-	-	-

Source: National Data

THE Q RATIO

James Tobin of Yale University, Nobel laureate in economics, devised the
Q ratio in the 1960s.   Basically, Q is the ratio of the market value of a
firm's stock to the market value of its assets. He envisioned it as a broad
measure of overall tightness of a nation's financial markets rather than a
guide for buying and selling stocks. He is quoted as saying in an article
written by Marcus W. Branchli in the *Asian Wall Street Journal* that the idea
was to offer signals as to when companies should increase capital
investments. If their stock were worth more than the replacement value
of their assets, that is Q is more than one, then theoretically they could
afford to buy plant and equipment.

A report by the Japan Securities Research Institute in 1988, backed by
the securities industry, challenged the view that Japanese stock prices are
excessively high, defying the price-earnings ratio. The Tokyo stock
market's average PER has never been extremely high, due in part to tight
supply-demand conditions resulting from the mutual holding of shares by
different corporations, different depreciation, and Japanese accounting
methods. The average PER for Tokyo was then around 60 and has been
more than 70, compared with 12-22 for American and European stocks.
The Japan Securities report proposed the Q-ratio, the stock price to the
value of a company's net assets per share, for assessing stock price levels.

One may think of the PER as reflecting the corporation's future
earnings potential and the Q ratio as the current value of the corporation's
assets.

The Q ratio measures the market capitalization of the company's shares outstanding relative to the market value of its assets net of debt. Hence, the ratio is essentially the fraction of the worth of a company that it is selling for assuming that the assets could be sold at the current market prices. Ratios under 1.0 indicate undervaluation and those above 1.0 suggest overvaluation. Sanyo Securities Co., Fumiko Konyo and the Japan Securities Research Institute made the following estimates for a sample of 133 TSE first section stocks. See also Figure 5.11a.

Year End	Average PER	Average Yield	Q Ratio
1978	23.0	1.88%	0.364
1984	45.0	0.95	0.425
1985	49.6	0.88	0.425
1986	90.5	0.69	0.453
1987	68.3	0.60	0.630
1988	66.2	0.50	0.706

Figure 5.11a   A U.S.-Japan Comparison of Q-Ratios

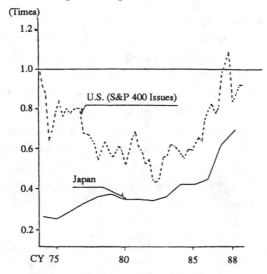

Source: Konya and Wakasugi (1987)

Additional calculations for the six month periods ending in March 1983 and September 1988 for major textile companies made by Konya and Wakasuji appear in Figure 5.12.

Hence, by this measure, the TSE even at its lofty levels is still undervalued and more so with individual stocks. For example, Roth (1989) refers to a list of the ten stocks with the lowest Q ratios as of October 1988 according to the daily newspaper the *Kabushiki Shimbun*. These are listed in Table 5.24.

Table 5.24
The Ten Stocks on the TSE-I with the Lowest Q Ratios, October 1988

Code	Name	Industry	PER Summer 89	Beta	Q Ratio	Price Oct 88	Dec 89	Jun 90	ROR Oct 88-Dec 89
5231	Nihon Cement	Cem & Con	38.0-74.7	0.89	0.22	970	1200	1040	41.60
8231	Mitsukoshi	Dept Stores	91.1-195.8	0.74	0.22	1940	2480	1800	43.89
8802	Mitsubishi Estate	Real Estate	45.5-94.5	1.74	0.17	2550	2610	1500	41.35
8804	Tokyo Tatemono	Real Estate	28.7-47.9	1.58	0.14	1620	2220	1510	48.00
9007	Odakyu Electric R'way	Railroads	76.1-131.7	0.86	0.25	1340	1840	1150	47.76
9042	Hankyu	Railroads	54.5-100.5	1.19	0.20	920	1550	961	36.33
9301	Mitsubishi W'house & Transport	Warehouse	23.2-49.7	1.11	0.25	1730	2250	1720	49.81
9302	Mitsui Warehouse	Warehouse	70.2-127.0	0.90	0.18	1020	1670	1240	37.96
9303	Sumitomo Warehouse	Warehouse	43.8-71.8	1.22	0.15	1040	1510	995	40.31
9671	Yomiuri Land	Leisure	60.8-119.9	0.56	0.14	1780	3150	2670	27.99

The problem with the use of Q ratios in Japan is that a very large part of the value of these TSE stocks is composed of land - which, as discussed in Chapter 2, has a value intimately tied to the stock levels themselves - and stock in other companies, most of which consists of high priced shares of stock on the TSE-I which, in turn, have stock and land and so on. Obviously, not many companies could dispose of their assets at the current market prices without precipitating a fall in these valuations. The above list of ten stocks with very low Q ratios are, not surprisingly, mostly major land holders. Hence, the Q ratios could stay about constant even if there was a steep fall in stock prices.[1] So the measure is suggestive rather than a definitive valuation measure.

---

[1]This assumes that the stock price correlates perfectly with overall land prices. We know that the level of the NSA correlates very close to 1 with the level of commercial land prices, but particular company's correlations may be much lower. Also, the value of a company's land holdings may move differently then those of the whole country or constitute a larger or smaller share than the average company. But for the sake of argument, suppose these relationships are approximately correct. Now let land prices fall by 50%. If A_i were zero then Q_i would not change at all. In fact, in this case Q is independent of the land and stock prices. So the change in Q_i when L_T changes depends upon the relative size of A_i versus $(\beta_i + \gamma_i)L_T$. If A_i is small relative to the other terms, then Q hardly changes at all when stock and land prices change.

$$Q_i = \frac{MV_i}{\text{Net Assets}_i} = \frac{\alpha_i L_T}{A_i + S_i + L_i} = \frac{\alpha_i L_T}{A_i + \beta_i L_T + \gamma_i L_T} = \frac{\text{Market Value of Company i}}{\text{Net Assets of Company i}}$$

In fact, there was a steep fall in stock prices in 1990, and the prices of large landholding companies fell even more, though land prices did not decline at all. In the first quarter of 1990, the NSA fell about 23%, but share prices of the twenty largest publicly traded land holders fell about 30%, as shown in Figure 5.11b. Thus, as low as the Q values were for these firms at the end of 1989, they were even lower at the end of the first quarter of 1990. Much or all of a huge real estate crash, which may or may not occur, has been already discounted in these shares.

Figure 5.11b
Decline in the First Quarter of 1990 of the Twenty Largest Publicly Traded Property Owners in Japan versus the NSA

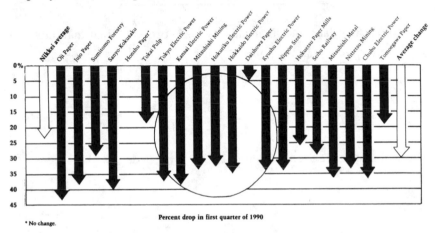

Percent drop in first quarter of 1990

* No change.

Source: *Japan Economic Journal*

A further problem with the Q ratio is that there are many alternative ways to measure it, and the estimates of the land assets are very subjective

$$= \frac{\text{conversion into land that fraction i holds of total land assets of Japan}}{\text{assets of i not in land or stocks + stocks i holds + land i holds}} =$$

$$\frac{\text{Conversion into land that fraction i holds of total land}}{\begin{array}{l}\text{assets of i} \\ \text{not land} \\ \text{or stocks}\end{array} + \begin{array}{l}\text{conversion of stocks i holds} \\ \text{into a fraction of total} \\ \text{land assests of Japan}\end{array} + \begin{array}{l}\text{conversion of land i holds} \\ \text{into a fraction of total} \\ \text{land assets of Japan}\end{array}} .$$

and subject to considerable error. Kobayashi (1990) summarized these approaches as follows: Let the assets and liabilites be broken down as

Capital Stock K	Liabilities B
Land L	Equity E
Financial Assets F	

Assume that land and financial assets are priced at their market value. Then

$$B+E \quad = \quad q_k(P_kK) + P_LL + F$$

or $\qquad q_k \quad = \quad \dfrac{B+E - P_LL - F}{P_kK}.$

This is the measure used by Hayashi (1982) and Ueda (1990).

Figure 5.12
Business Transformation and Hidden Assets - An Example of Three Major
Synthetic Textile Companies (Weighted Average)

Change in Sales and Profit (%)	Net Assets (Book Value)	Per-Share ( ) "Hidden" Assets Land Securities		Total	Stock Price ( )	Q-Ratio (Times)
(Term to Mar. 1983) Non-Textiles Textile	152.8	448.5	100.8	702.1	305.0	0.434
(Term to Sept. 1988)	214.6	895.6	441.2	1,551.4	882.4	0.569

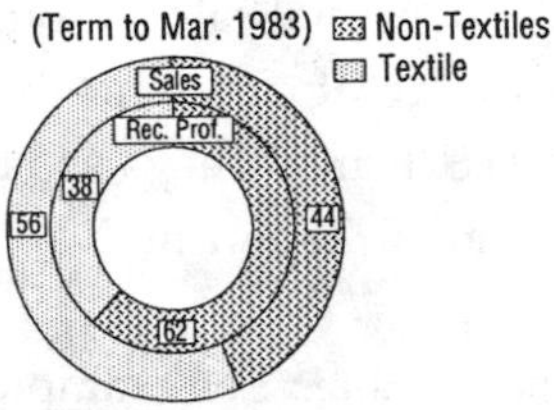

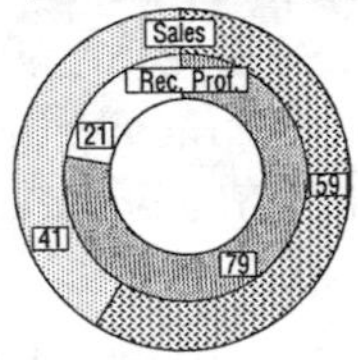

Source: Konya's calculations reported in Yamaichi Research Insititute's Outlook for the Japanese Stock Market, April 1989

Alternatively, assume that only financial assets are priced at their market value. Then

$$B+E = q_k(P_kK) + q_L(P_LL) + F.$$

Then there are two q's: one for land and one for capital goods. This approach was used by Asako, Kuninori, Inoue and Murase (1989). Konya and Wakasugi (1987) whose calculations were shown above used

$$q_k = \frac{B+E}{P_kK + P_LL + F}.$$

Finally, the *Japan Economic Journal* and the Japan Securities Research Institute utilize a **q** only on equity capital, namely

$$Q = \frac{E}{P_k K + P_L L + F - B}$$

which is the Q discussed above and the measure that seems to make the most sense.

Kobayashi (1990) summarized the results given in Table 5.25 for various q and Q ratios. There is a wide range of estimates. Table 5.26 shows details of the land calculations made by Konya and by Asako for all TSE-I companies, excluding financial companies that do not own much land relative to the other firms. Table 5.27 has additional calculations by French and Poterba (1990) which also shows the great difference in the percent of assets in land between Japanese and U.S. firms. They used data from the Japan Economic Planning Agency's Annual Report on National Accounts.

The difference in the land valuations is considerable. For example, in 1987, Konya's estimate is ¥270.37 trillion, while Asako et al. obtained only ¥114.11 trillion. French and Poterba's estimates include more stock companies than TSE-I; namely all the non-financials. Still, their estimate of ¥403.4 trillion is even higher than Konya's. Meanwhile, the book value was only ¥9.94 trillion. Other studies of the Q ratio in Japan include Ando and Auerbach (1988, 1990), Daiwa (1989), Hayashi and Inoue (1989), Hoshi and Kashyap (1990) and Ueda (1990).

Table 5.25: Various Estimates of q and Q in Japan, 1955-87

	Wakasuji & Konya 1980	Konya & Wakasugi 1987	Yonezawa 1982	Konya & Wakasugi 1987	Ueda 1989		Homma & Iwamuto 1985	Homma et al 1984	Homma et al 1984	Hayashi 1985	Hayashi & Inoue 1987	Hayashi & Inoue 1989	Homma et al 1989	Homma et al 1989
Universe	TSE-I	TSE-I	TSE-I	TSE-I	TSE-I,II Non-Financial	All listed	SNA	All	All	All	Listed	Listed	Private corps	Private corps
Companies Sectors	826 33	829 33	829 33	829 33			SNA	18	18	18	611 Manuf., panel data	656 Manuf., panel data	SNA	SNA
	q*	q	q	q	q	q	Q***	Q	Q***	Q	Q	q	Q	Q****
1955								-1.300	-1.880	-1.129				
1956								-1.190	-1.660	-0.980				
1957								-1.240	-1.610	-0.598				
1958								-0.880	-1.160	-0.460				
1959								-0.870	-1.070	1.110				
1960								-0.100	-0.060	1.061				
1961								-0.240	-0.380	0.437				
1962								-0.310	-0.780	-0.184				
1963								-0.540	-1.020	-0.501				
1964								-0.720	-1.000	-0.590				
1965	0.755	0.666	1.081					-0.640	-0.640	-0.228				
1966	0.763	0.671	1.136					-0.270	-0.720	0.037				
1967	0.733	0.642	1.048					-0.460	-0.560	1.445				
1968	0.759	0.643	1.107					-0.200	0.390	0.623				
1969	0.776	0.649	1.148					0.690	-0.270	0.060				
1970	0.737	0.629	1.041		-0.208		4.397	-0.060	-0.420	-0.204			4.973	2.600
1971	0.771	0.639	1.119		-0.143		3.729	-0.120	-0.590	-0.600			4.399	2.435
1972	0.857	0.672	1.372		0.494		2.745	-0.300	-0.930	-1.280			2.785	1.882
1973	0.752	0.625	1.139		0.120		2.268	-0.750	-1.360	-0.176			1.333	1.364
1974	0.747	0.623	0.957	0.572	-0.004		2.292	-1.310	-0.460	0.068			1.699	1.667
1975	0.778	0.654	1.016	0.585	-0.106		2.655	-0.010	-0.240	-0.101			1.895	1.964
1976	0.789	0.669	1.048	0.616	0.065		2.559	0.040	-0.370	0.084		1.019	1.455	1.548
1977	0.784	0.669	1.065	0.648	0.014		2.346	-0.080	-0.170	-0.188	1.590	1.012	1.679	1.673
1978	0.790	0.681	1.150	0.664	0.168		2.488	0.250	-0.450	-0.483	1.660	1.270	1.691	1.761
1979		0.664	1.149	0.658	0.058		1.806	-0.080	-0.720	0.108	3.350	1.007	0.886	1.139
1980				0.643	-0.094	0.668	1.746	-0.500	-0.190		1.990	1.151	0.979	1.217
1981				0.629	-0.092	0.873	1.734	0.160			2.590	0.967	0.970	1.212
1982				0.619	-0.177	0.819	1.606				2.080	1.036	0.886	1.076
1983				0.626	0.039	1.050	2.215				5.080	1.563	1.532	1.794
1984				0.653	0.248	1.350	2.306				5.740	1.580	1.646	1.902
1985				0.648	0.336	1.380	3.063					1.630	2.480	2.562
1986				0.641	0.788	2.030								
1987														

* Nontax adjusted marginal Q   ** Some small companies have negative book value   *** Tax adjusted marginal Q   **** Tax adjusted average Q

Source: Kobayachi (1990)

Table 5.26

Comparison of Market Values and Land Values for the TSE-I Excluding Financial Companies, in Trillions of Yen, Estimated by Konya and Asako et al, 1976-1989

Date	1976	1977	1978	1979	1980	1981	1982	1983	1984	1985	1986	1987	1988	1989
Konya and Asako et al in Kobayashi (1990)														
Operating income	4.96	6.52	6.2	6.96	8.93	11.01	10.67	10.05	10.55	12.06	11.13	9.4	11.56	13.86
Corporate tax	1.47	2.05	2.12	2.51	3.15	3.96	3.86	3.58	4.04	5.11	4.81	4.38	5.2	6.19
Depreciation	3.15	3.34	3.45	3.77	4.15	4.7	5.33	5.73	6.21	6.78	7.3	7.71	9.41	9.82
Operating cash flow	6.44	7.81	7.53	8.22	9.93	11.75	12.14	12.2	12.72	13.73	13.62	12.73	15.77	17.49
Grossinvestment	5.53	5.62	5.71	6.26	6.94	8.59	9.42	9.69	9.59	9.83	10.94	11.31	12.03	13.77
Net cash flow	1.11	2.19	1.82	1.96	2.99	3.16	2.72	2.51	3.13	3.9	2.68	1.42	3.74	3.72
Companies	976	983	987	1001	1004	1005	1010	1011	1015	1016	1016	1019	1021	1022
Equity	40.2	38.8	50.8	52.7	58.9	69.6	74.2	99	113.3	130.7	195.8	221	318	
Debt	58	61.81	64.07	64.85	69.06	73.72	79.2	83.77	86.05	88.43	90.86	94.22	103.98	
Interest	5.19	5.36	5.12	4.6	5.2	6.79	6.86	6.81	6.8	6.7	6.63	5.94	5.72	
Konya's calculations														
Cash & cash equity	13.1	13.79	14.02	14.54	15.51	16.67	18.24	18.35	19.6	20.86	21.84	25.13	32	
Securities (current)	3.5	4.59	5.29	6.39	6.63	7.28	7.53	7.86	9.03	9.54	9.7	11.73	12.55	
Securities (inv)	7.21	7.85	8.22	8.78	9.45	10.17	11.15	12.08	13	14.16	15.49	16.58	19.1	
Unrealized capital	15.26	17.79	18.78	22.77	20.82	23.44	24.69	24.91	43.13	54.32	67.03	111.82	145.27	
Financial assets	39.07	44.02	46.31	52.48	52.41	57.56	61.61	63.20	84.76	98.88	114.06	165.26	208.92	
Land (bv)	4.26	4.58	4.92	5.24	5.66	6.13	6.57	7.08	7.7	8.19	9.03	9.94	11.53	
Unrealized capital	71.14	73.28	77.24	85.41	100.18	118.92	134.03	150	158.62	169.53	218.53	260.43	372.42	
Land	75.4	77.86	82.16	90.65	105.84	125.05	140.6	157.08	166.32	177.72	227.56	270.37	383.95	
Asako et al's calculations														
Cash & cash equity	13.1	13.79	14.02	14.54	15.51	16.67	18.24	18.35	19.60	20.86	21.84	25.13		
Securities (current)	3.5	4.59	5.29	6.39	6.63	7.28	7.53	7.86	9.03	9.54	9.7	11.73		
Securities (inv)	7.21	7.85	8.22	8.78	9.45	10.17	11.15	12.08	13.00	14.16	15.49	16.58		
Unrealized capital	15.26	17.79	18.78	22.77	20.82	23.44	24.69	24.91	43.13	54.32	67.03	111.82		
Financial assets	39.07	44.02	46.31	52.48	52.41	57.56	61.61	63.20	84.76	98.88	114.06	165.26		
Land (bv)	4.26	4.58	4.92	5.24	5.66	6.13	6.57	7.08	7.7	8.19	9.03	9.94		
Unrealized capital	23.73	25.74	29.47	35.32	41.77	47.14	50.65	51.26	54.75	60.28	81.18	104.17		
Land	27.99	30.32	34.39	40.56	47.43	53.27	57.22	58.34	62.45	68.47	90.21	114.11		

Source: Kobayashi (1990)

Table 5.27
Asset Composition of U.S. and Japanese Firms in 1984 and 1987

| | U.S.($ billions) | | | | Japan(¥ trillions) | | | |
	1984		1987		1984		1987	
Land	464.0	(12%)	553.8	(13%)	221.7	(46%)	403.4	(55%)
Plant & Equip	2644.9	(69%)	3021.4	(69%)	206.4	(43%)	274.5	(38%)
Inventories	740.9	(19%)	809.7	(18%)	55.8	(12%)	53.5	(7%)
Totals	3849.8	(100%)	4384.9	(100%)	483.9	(100%)	731.4	(100%)

Source: French and Poterba (1990)

TAKING THE LAND OUT OF THE STOCK FOR SPECIFIC COMPANIES

Table 5.28 tries to take out the land from a number of companies on the TSE to see how much the PERs drop. Land carried on the books in earlier years was adjusted up to a current valuation, using indices for the six largest cities in Japan; see Table D1 in the appendix. Buildings on this land were valued at 50% of their land value. Table 5.28 further reduces the PERs by subtracting cross holdings of stocks owned by the various companies at current market prices. This stock is held in good faith and rarely, if ever, is sold. Obviously, other assets could also be accounted for but the separating out of land, buildings and cross-holdings does tend to lower the PERs by a large amount. In the case of NEC, the current PER of 82.3 becomes 80.7 without land, and 79.9 without land and buildings, which does not represent much of a drop. But it becomes 44.0, a drop of 46.5%, without the cross-holdings. Nippon Steel has a PER of 101.5, which drops to 83.3 without land, to 74.3 without buildings, and dramatically to 5.4 without cross holdings, a 94.7% drop, making its purchase at current levels seem cheap. Not all stocks show such dramatic declines in these adjusted PERs. Seibu Railway has one of the highest PERs on the first section at 777 as of early 1989. Without land it becomes 638 and

Table 5.28
Adjusting the PERs for Several Companies by Taking Out Land, Buildings and Cross-Holdings

Adjusting for Land

	(a) Market Value ¥ mil	(b) Profit ¥ mil	(d) PER	(c) Land ¥ mil	(e) Adjusted PER no land	(f) % Decrease in PER
Toray	1061480	16223	65.58	132532.78	57.26	12.69%
Nihon Sekiyu	1312784	16739	78.47	384088.71	5.48	93.02%
NEC	3079532	37477	82.29	57193.39	80.65	1.99%
Tokyo Marine	3010776	35980	83.72	349011.99	73.98	11.63%
Heiwa Fudousan	156642	1069	146.48	4521.00	142.30	2.85%
Nihon Yusen	678368	2434	279.74	75813.75	247.56	11.50%
Nippon Steel	3232076	31883	101.46	575963.32	83.31	17.89%
Seibu Railway	1945537	2504	776.8	347538.24	638.18	17.85%

Adjusting for Land and Buildings

	(g) Land and Buildings	(h) Value Net of Land and Bldgs	(i) Adj PER No Land & Bldgs	(j) % Decrease in PER
Toray	198799.17	862680.83	53.18	18.91%
Nihon Sekiyu	576133.07	736650.94	44.01	43.91%
NEC	85790.09	2993741.92	79.88	2.93%
Tokyo Marine	523517.99	2487258.02	69.13	17.43%
Heiwa Fudousan	6781.50	149860.50	140.19	4.29%
Nihon Yusen	113720.03	564647.98	231.98	17.07%
Nippon Steel	863944.98	2368131.02	74.28	26.79%
Seibu Railway	521307.36	1424229.64	568.78	26.78%

Adjusting for Land, Buildings and Crossholdings

	(k) Market - Book Value ¥ mil	(l) Book Value 3/31/88 ¥ mil	(m) B V increase Mar 87-88	(n) Value of Cross- holdings	(o) MV Net of Land, Bldgs & Crossh'gs	(p) Adj PER NoLand, Bldg or Crossh'gs	(q) % Decrease in PER
Toray							
Nihon Sekiyu							
NEC	950442	271324	1072098.58	1343422.58	1650319.34	44.04	46.49%
Tokyo Marine							
Heiwa Fudousan							
Nihon Yusen							
Nippon Steel	1605895	385406	1811449.56	2196855.56	171275.46	5.37	94.71%
Seibu Railway	50808	55141	57311.424	112452.42	1311777.22	523.87	32.56%

• Thanks are due to Hirokaza Yuihama of the Yamaichi Research Institute for his help on this calculation.

Table 5.29
Valuation of 1010 Non-Financial Companies in 34 groups on the TSE in 1989

Group	Firms	Tobin's Q*	Q Ratio	Equity*	Book Value*	Liabilities	β	Market Value of Land	Mkt Value of Securities
Fishing & forestry	6	0.94	0.88	719712	818206	687461	816332	461310	319540
Mining	7	0.60	0.50	916635	680738	437390	1822146	1340730	377012
Construction	91	0.74	0.57	15340006	20473344	16615540	26784317	20363550	4322336
Foods	55	0.79	0.75	12051576	6356297	3566755	16144275	12253530	2012872
Textiles	43	0.76	0.69	7749351	5332394	3611826	11260382	7919460	2512448
Pulp & paper	19	0.58	0.46	4463186	3615308	2775060	9693912	8272440	1142632
Chemicals	92	0.76	0.68	19758639	13270949	9114590	28990064	21186060	5605144
Medicine	30	1.39	1.49	11406594	4187858	1991922	7635930	4717680	1172764
Oil	9	0.46	0.32	4566618	4364470	3508474	14163820	12904620	1111144
Rubber products	9	0.91	0.87	2055022	1478920	955836	2353871	1444260	579560
Glass & ceramics	31	0.86	0.82	7198950	3899797	2427063	8827346	6509280	1416416
Iron & steel	36	0.79	0.71	20659561	14045925	11380684	29218422	25153470	2984220
Non-fer met	24	0.81	0.74	6423077	4650187	3595240	8700536	6424620	1913504
Fabricated metal	22	0.76	0.70	2422923	1563412	963353	3475203	2676180	384228
Machinery	85	0.77	0.71	11507433	8104210	4725316	16321935	11230530	2782488
Electrical Appliances	106	1.06	1.09	445575711	27529273	15744123	40989054	18747420	14775204
Shipbuilding	6	1.05	1.09	7150737	5492354	4613016	6561004	5166000	917156
Autos & parts	37	0.59	0.50	17891497	13999388	7626164	35799732	24182790	8066412
Other transport	12	0.79	0.72	966691	660601	444470	1338151	1044870	149304
Precision instr	18	0.77	0.71	4064273	28045115	1428614	5691356	3632700	1071792
Other products	28	0.79	0.75	6184026	3034525	1670720	8210528	6319650	963640
Trading company	80	0.81	0.57	14444015	35217055	31573120	25449160	13472880	11708604
Retail trade	43	0.63	0.56	13172017	6788865	4317051	23406680	20150490	1941416
Other finance	11	0.92	0.53	1950829	18377374	17675333	3670205	2150340	1186004
Real Estate	18	0.38	0.28	7675170	5451687	4232037	27086485	26150160	764464
Railroad & bus	16	0.66	0.58	12009018	5762145	4914655	20700347	19395990	1471200
Trucking	9	0.42	0.35	2776755	1393578	951398	7911197	7454460	350720
Ocean freight	14	1.11	1.18	3596649	2257211	1847183	3041085	1910700	1045396
Air cargo	4	1.87	2.52	4938795	1861880	1465415	1962917	1379430	310672
Warehousing & Harbor Transpt	10	0.67	0.61	1112846	547196	341460	1836714	1562910	160220
Communications	5	1.32	1.45	28084743	11848676	7689261	19380162	15490560	328720
Electric power	9	0.78	0.62	20918322	29101014	29101014	33807935	27715590	2593212
Gas	5	1.17	1.20	6018260	1843953	1109013	5004554	4192860	288688
Services	25	0.75	0.71	3620944	1477625	924466	5097489	4260270	568092
Totals	1010	0.80	0.71	328390581	269290930	198953734	463153248	347237790	77537224

*Notes:

Equity = equity at original book value plus hidden assets

Book value = book value at normal levels

$$\text{Tobin's Q} = \frac{\text{Assets}}{\text{Corporate value (owners equity net of liabilities)}}$$

$$Q = \frac{\text{Market capitalization}}{\text{Hidden assets (land and stocks) + owners equity at book value}} = \frac{\alpha}{\beta}$$

Source: Japan Securities Research Institute

without buildings it is 569 and without cross holdings 523. This is a 32.7% drop, but a PER of still over 500 indicates that our simple analysis is not considering much. Obviously, the firm has many other assets that we do not know about; and this firm is discussed in greater detail in Chapter 8.

HOW MUCH OF THE VALUE OF THE STOCKS IS LAND?
Much of the value of the stocks on the TSE is composed of land, albeit at very high prices. But how much is it? Does this explain the high PERs?

Table 5.29 provides some answers to these questions. It lists 34 groups of stocks totalling 1010 separate companies. The data consist of their Tobin Q ratio, which averages 0.80, assets divided by corporate value (liabilities plus owners equity at book value), their Q ratios (equity at original book value plus hidden assets) divided by hidden asssets (land and stocks) plus owners' equity (at book value), which averages 0.71, the book value of normal assets, liabilities, equity at original book value plus hidden assets at market value, the market value of land and the market value of the securities represented. The 1010 represent about 70% of the TSE. The financials, including insurance, banks, and security companies are excluded.

In total as of October 1988, the market value of the land was ¥347 trillion, the market value of land and stocks was about ¥425 trillion, but the market value of all the stocks that own these ¥425 trillion in stocks and land was only ¥300 trillion. Hence, the PER for the market at some 61.62 times in October 1988 was not high assuming that the land and stocks are worth something near their current market values. These data, from corporate research, provide an estimate as of October 1988 of this valuation. The market value of land is about thirty times its book value, and the market value of securities is about four times the value of these securities held on the books. The breakdown uses the following balance sheet schema:

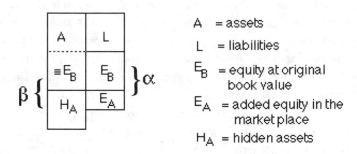

A = assets

L = liabilities

E_B = equity at original book value

E_A = added equity in the market place

H_A = hidden assets

SUMMING UP THE PER ADJUSTMENTS TO FAIRLY EVALUATE JAPANESE STOCKS

The PER adjustments provide handy ad hoc models to value stocks. Let's start with a stock with a PER of say 70. First, we can adjust this PER down 20-50% to account for the consolidated earnings, so the new PER is 35-56. Adjusting for the non-working aspect of the cross-holdings plus the land and other hidden assets drops the PER a further 25-80%, yielding an adjusted PER of 28 to 42. Comparing this with yields required to compete with money market instruments and bonds (about 4-8%) can result in a non overvalued stock in comparison to stocks elsewhere in the world.

Adding the confidence in the Japanese economy, the vast amount of money from savings and profits chasing few stocks, and the intense desire to invest at home, one can make the case for stocks in Japan not being over valued. Despite the critics, the evidence is that this ad hoc theory has been more correct than the Western view of impending disaster in the Japanese market. The road up to a gain in dollars of 500 times in the past forty years has been rocky with many pauses. In Chapter 7 we look more carefully at these twenty corrections, and the 21st and 22nd ones in 1990 and discuss current risks in the market. Among other things, we find that the simple ad hoc theory was a good predictor for the last four corrections, two in 1987 and two in 1990.

A BOND AND STOCK YIELD DIFFERENTIAL VALUATION MODEL FOR DETECTING OVERPRICED MARKETS

A measure of the *over-pricedness* of a stock market is the reciprocal of the PER, which is like a yield if all earnings were paid out, subtracted from the long term bond yield. This measures the bond minus stock earnings yield. Let us illustrate this in the context of the over valuation of the S&P 500 index prior to the October 1987 crash. Table 5.30 lists the S&P 500 index values and the corresponding price earnings ratios along with the interest rates on 30 year government bonds for 1986 to August 1988. From January 1962 to August 1988, this measure averaged -0.36% with a standard deviation of 2.00. From January 1973 to August 1988, it averaged -0.12% with a standard deviation of 2.46%. Finally during the 1980s it averaged 1.53% with a standard deviation of 1.62%. This premium was less than 2% from February 1986 to March 1987. It then leaped to high values above 2.5% from April to September, and it was 4.14% at the end of September.

After the October 1987 crash, the premium fell below 2% where it has since remained because of the drop in interest rates and the increase in stock price earnings yields due to lower stock prices and increasing earnings. Even the increase in interest yields to the 9.3% level in August 1988 did not move the premium above 2% because of the lower PE ratios. The historical values yield a premium of -0.36% with a 2.00% standard deviation. Then one can use a rule to *sell* when the premium gets above 1.65 standard deviations, which corresponds to 95% confidence of being out of whack with a one tail statistical test assuming that the premiums have a normal distribution. This gives the sell signal at 2.94% and you would have then cashed out at the end of April with a 289 S&P500 index. Or, at least, then one could have entered a trailing stop about 4% below the market as suggested by Zweig (1986). Specifically, Zweig suggests the rule: if the market rises by four percent or more in a week, buy; and if it falls by four percent or more, sell. The evidence in Zweig (1986) and later calculations show that this rule is far superior to a buy-and-hold stategy.

When would one get back in? According to Table 5.30, at the end of October 1987, when the premium was back down to 1.97% when the S&P 500 at 245.01. More conservative investors might not have gotten back in until the pendulum swung very much the other way with the premium close to its historical average of -0.36% and, certainly, below its 1980s bull market average of 1.53%. Such reasoning might have led an investor back in the market with a 0.59% premium at the end of January 1989 when the S&P 500 stood at 250.48. In any event, the 4.14% premium going into October certainly was excessive and indicative of the over valuation of stocks.

Table 5.30
S&P 500 Index Values, Yields, PE Ratios, Government Bond Yields, and
the Yield Premium over Stocks, January 1986 to August 1988

		S&P index	PER	(a) 30-day gov't bond yield	(b) 1/PE %	(a)-(b)
1986	Jan	208.19	14.63	9.32	6.84	2.48
	Feb	219.37	15.67	8.28	6.38	1.90
	Mar	232.33	16.50	7.59	6.06	1.53
	Apr	237.98	16.27	7.58	6.15	1.43
	May	238.46	17.03	7.76	5.87	1.89
	Jun	245.30	17.32	7.27	5.77	1.50
	Jul	240.18	16.31	7.42	6.13	1.29
	Aug	245.00	17.47	7.26	5.72	1.54
	Sep	238.27	15.98	7.64	6.26	1.38
	Oct	237.36	16.85	7.61	5.93	1.68
	Nov	245.09	16.99	7.40	5.89	1.51
	Dec	248.60	16.72	7.33	5.98	1.35
1987	Jan	264.51	15.42	7.47	6.49	0.98
	Feb	280.93	15.98	7.46	6.26	1.20
	Mar	292.47	16.41	7.65	6.09	1.56
	Apr	289.32	16.22	9.56	6.17	3.39
	May	289.12	16.32	8.63	6.13	2.50
	Jun	301.38	17.10	8.40	5.85	2.55
	Jul	310.09	17.92	8.89	5.58	3.31
	Aug	329.36	18.55	9.17	5.39	3.78
	Sep	318.66	18.10	9.66	5.52	4.14
	Oct	280.16	14.16	9.03	7.06	1.97
	Nov	245.01	13.78	8.90	7.26	1.64
	Dec	240.96	13.55	9.10	7.38	1.72
1988	Jan	250.48	12.81	8.40	7.81	0.59
	Feb	258.10	13.02	8.33	7.68	0.65
	Mar	265.74	13.42	8.74	7.45	1.29
	Apr	262.61	13.24	9.10	7.55	1.55
	May	256.20	12.92	9.24	7.74	1.50
	Jun	270.68	13.65	8.85	7.33	1.52
	Jul	269.44	13.59	9.18	7.36	1.82
	Aug	263.73	13.30	9.30	7.52	1.78

Source: Yamaichi Research Institute

Figure 5.13 Bond and Stock Yield Differential Model for Japan, 1980-90

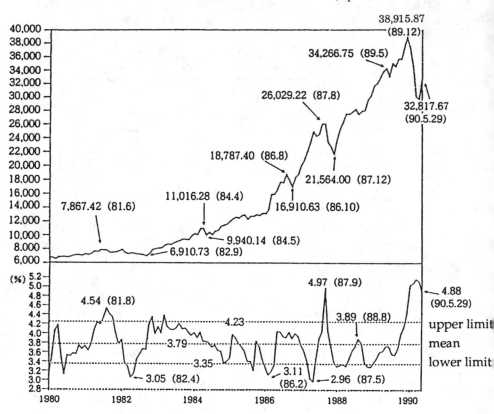

Source: Yamaichi Research Institute

Value of NSA for Various Spread Values[2]

Date/level	Spread	NSA
May 29, 1990	4.88%	32,818
Mean	3.79%	20,022
Upper Limit	4.23%	23,754
Lower Limit	3.35%	17,303

[2]Interestingly, at the bottom of the 22nd correction on October 1, 1990, the NSA was at 20222, which was almost exactly on the mean. See Chapter 7 for more discussion on the 1990 corrections.

Figure 5. 14
Bond and Stock Yield Differential Model for the S&P 500, 1980-1990

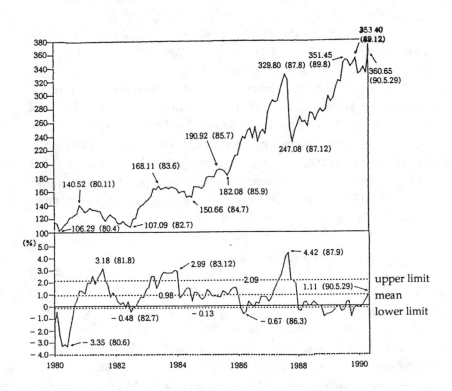

Source: Yamaichi Research Institute

Value of S&P 500 for Various Spread Values

Date/level	Spread	S&P 500
May 29, 1990	1.11%	360.65
Mean	0.98%	355
Upper limit	2.09%	415
Lower limit	-0.13%	309

This model also applies quite well in Japan. Calculations by Shigeru Ishii, a Yamaichi Research Institute colleague, show that the model has provided an excellent signal for many of the previous corrections in Japan.

We studied all twenty of the corrections in Japan from 1949 to 1989 listed in Table 2.7. We found that not all corrections began with this spread so far out of whack; but whenever the index was in the danger zone, there *always* was a correction.

Figure 5.13 shows the spread from 1980 to the end of May 1990. The data are for all of the 1980s; whereas Table 5.30 uses a longer sample, hence the numbers are slightly different. Each time the spread exceeded the 4.23 cutoff (which has higher than 95% confidence) there was a correction. The model also indicates that the valuation was still high as of May 29, 1990, at 4.88. Not much later, the 22nd correction began. Meanwhile, the same calculation for the S&P 500 shown in Figure 5.14 indicated the market then was not extremely overvalued. Indeed, it has been cheap, that is below the mean, since the September 1987 peak of 4.42. The May 29, 1990, value of 1.11 was, however, slightly above the mean level and the highest since the late fall of 1987.

JAPANESE ASSET PRICING MODELS

A variety of approaches can be used to help to understand, evaluate, and predict stock prices. In the modern financial literature, the main approaches are those based on the capital asset and arbitrage pricing models. The CAPM, which dates to the mid 1960s, was developed independently by Sharpe (1964), Lintner (1965) and Mossin (1966). The basic ideas are simple and so are the mathematics. Stock prices are subject to systematic, or market risk, and to unsystematic or diversification risk. The latter can be minimized with proper diversification.[3] The former, though, cannot, and this risk varies with how the stock price changes as the market moves. The mean return in a period of time from stock i equals the risk free rate of return plus the return the stock earns from bearing its market risk. Hence,

$$E(R_i) = R_f + \beta_i(R_m - R_f)$$

where $E(R_i)$ is stock i's mean return in the time period, R_f is the risk free return in the same time period, $E(R_m)$ is the market's mean return in the same period, and β_i is the stock's beta or risk measure which is the correlation of the stock's return with the market, divided by the market

---

[3]For example, with 100 independent securities all having the same variance, the resulting portfolio of equally weighted securities has a systematic risk that is only 1% of that of each component stock.

variance. The β_i measures how fast the stock goes up and down with the market variance. At $\beta_i = 1$ they move 1 to 1. When beta is more than one, the stock moves up and down faster than the market. For example, at $\beta_i = 1.5$, the stock moves 50% faster up and down. Stocks with betas less than one move slower than the market. Those with $\beta_i = 0$ do not move at all with the market (gold stocks often have a beta of about zero). This is not to say that they have no risk since one can have $\beta=0$ with high variance of returns. The few stocks that move contrary to the market have negative betas. The small stocks advocated in Chapter 4 have betas of about 0.5. The CAPM has been subject to numerous tests, variants and applications. A survey of this literature appears in Sharpe and Alexander (1990). The model is easy to use and interpret, and has become an important aspect of stock price evaluation. How well does it work?

We do not have space to fully answer this question. The papers by Roll(1988), Sharpe (1983), Ritter and Chopra (1989) and Cadsby (1991) provide much insight. Roll investigates how much of a stock's return variance the CAPM actually explains. He finds that over time it is about 20% for daily returns, and about 35% for monthly returns. Sharpe investigates how much of the monthly return variance the CAPM explained of U.S. stock returns for 1931-1979. His average of 33.9% is similar to Roll's results. Ritter and Chopra, using data from 1935 to 1986, argue that the risk factor is priced, that is you actually receive extra return for bearing additional risk only during January and then only for small stocks. In months other than January one simply is not paid for the risk borne. Cadsby shows that the CAPM prices risk only during the anomalous periods of the year, namely at the turn of the month, before holidays, etc.

Figures 5.17 and 5.18 provide a calculation of the cumulative effect of investing in high beta stocks from June 1979 to August 1989. The univariate effect of beta as a single predictor is slightly negative. Investing in stocks with betas one standard above the mean beta yields a total return over the period of about 16% less than the TOPIX. However, in a thirty factor model, once the other twenty-nine variables are separated out, the higher beta stocks outperformed the TOPIX by about 30% in the ten years. This reinforces our view that a high beta has not been an especially useful attribute to look for in Japanese stocks.

From a statistical point of view, it is not surprising that one has trouble predicting stock prices with only one variable, no matter how reasonable that effect might appear to be. A model that lends itself to many factors is the arbitrage pricing model of Ross (1976). This model is based on deeper mathematics and has many intricacies that require elaborate analysis and subtle interpretation. On the surface, though, the model suggests that mean stock returns are generated by a series of factors whose changes induce changes in the underlying stocks. A typical model is

$$E(R_i) = R_f + b_{1i}F_1 + b_{2i}F_2 + \ldots + b_{ni}F_n$$

where $E(R_i)$ is stock i's mean return in the time period, R_f is the risk free return in the same time period, F_1, F_2 to F_n are the level of the factors 1, 2, ..., n in this time period and they affect the mean return through the coefficients b_{1i}, b_{2i} to b_{ni}.

The theory does not specify the number of factors and what their factors are. Hence, one can either devise factors that are independent using multivariate factor analysis procedures or specify factors that seem to be reasonable. The former approach was tested in Roll and Ross (1980), Dhrymes, Friend and Gultekin (1984) and other authors using U.S. data. Sharpe's (1983) study of U.S. stock returns during 1931-79 indicated a set of five factors - yield, beta, size, bond beta and alpha - provides a model that explains 38.2% of the monthly variance of returns versus the 33.9% for beta. When one adds the sector factors - basic industries, capital goods, construction, consumer goods, energy, finance, transportation and utilities, the explanatory power increases slightly to 40.3%. Sharpe also investigated how much one could explain cross sectionally of the differences among stocks in a given month. This is a more difficult task than to explain a given stock's return over time. He found that beta explains only 3.7%, and common factors a further 7.7% for a total of only 10.4%.

Elton and Gruber (1988) have developed a model using a factor analysis approach for the Japanese stock market using a proprietary four factor model that has been used by Nomura Securities.

The four factors are able to explain 78% of the monthly variance of portfolios of about 20 stocks, formed by size of 393 of the 400 stocks in the Nomura Research Institute's stock index.[4] As of April 1987, this index, which is oriented toward large capitalized stocks, constituted 70.9% of the capitalization of the first section of the TSE and 62.9% of the entire TSE. Their study used data for the 180 months (15 years) from April 1971 to March 1986. The 78% adjusted R^2 compares with about 55% for a single

---

[4]The NRI 350 used by French and Poterba (1990) in their study discussed above consists of the 350 highest capitalized stocks in the NRI 400 index.

index CAPM type model for the same period. These R^2 are for portfolios of stocks, not individual stocks, and hence are much higher.

Table 5.31
Explanatory Power Measured in Adjusted R^2 of the Returns of 20 Size Ranked Portfolios with 393 Total Stocks of the NRI 400 Index, the Best Single Factor and the Best Four Factors along with the Portfolio Means Monthly Returns, Betas and Excess Returns

		Adjusted R^2			Mean monthly		Excess
		NRI 400	Best factor	Best 4 factor	return in%	Beta	Return, Alpha,%
Largest cap	1	0.9065	0.6447	0.8168	0.0117	1.1373	- 0.0018
	2	0.8790	0.6839	0.8201	0.0104	1.1289	- 0.0030
	3	0.8700	0.7502	0.8580	0.0122	1.0283	0.0000
	4	0.8180	0.7429	0.8239	0.0112	0.9610	- 0.0002
	5	0.7649	0.6995	0.7516	0.0144	0.9570	0.0030
	6	0.7525	0.7488	0.7689	0.0110	0.8697	0.0007
	7	0.6675	0.7190	0.7504	0.0115	0.7877	0.0022
	8	0.6693	0.7488	0.7767	0.0132	0.7942	0.0038
	9	0.6904	0.7996	0.8130	0.0096	0.8130	0.0000
	10	0.5650	0.7256	0.7266	0.0153	0.7067	0.0069
	11	0.5610	0.7376	0.7732	0.0121	0.7037	0.0037
	12	0.5081	0.7098	0.7642	0.0120	0.7097	0.0036
	13	0.4174	0.6564	0.7479	0.0172	0.6232	0.0098
	14	0.4022	0.6998	0.8112	0.0132	0.6203	0.0058
	15	0.3663	0.6363	0.7605	0.0147	0.6307	0.0073
	16	0.3365	0.6358	0.8086	0.0179	0.6137	0.0106
	17	0.2137	0.5033	0.7395	0.0181	0.4815	0.0124
	18	0.2916	0.5796	0.7371	0.0180	0.6001	0.0109
	19	0.2093	0.4900	0.6995	0.0199	0.5349	0 0135
Smallest cap	20	0.1419	0.4220	0.6626	0.0260	0.4841	0.0203
Average		0.5516	0.6667	0.7765			

*Alpha is defined as $\alpha_i = R_i - R_f - \beta_i (R_m - R_f)$, that is an actual return that exceeds that predicted by the CAPM.

Source: Elton and Gruber (1988)

Table 5.31 shows the explanatory power of the NRI 400 index, the best factor, and the best-four-factors, which average 55.16%, 66.67% and 77.65%, respectively. Each of the twenty portfolios ranked by size has about 20 stocks for the 393 sample. The NRI 400 predicts the largest capitalized portfolios the best with R^2s in the 80-90% range for portfolios one to four. This is not surprising since the NRI 400 is a large capitalized index. Nor is it that the NRI 400 does a much poorer job of explaining the small capitalized portfolios with the R^2s of portfolios 17-20 with R^2s in the range 14-21%. The mean monthly returns, beta and alpha excess return values are consistent with this. As we saw in Chapters 2 and 4, the small capitalized stocks have low betas, high returns and high alphas. This is also borne out by Elton and Gruber's sample from April 1971 to March 1986.

The best single factor found was better than the NRI 400 index even though the 393 stocks were chosen from this index. Factors 2 to 4 do add considerably to the predictive ability of the models. Tests done in different ways indicate that additional factors essentially add noise over the basic four. The four factors were also quite stable over time if one splits the 15 year sample into 5 year sub periods. Since the factors are not unique up to linear transformations, many sets of four factors and an infinite number of sets of four of them will do the same job. The four factors are highly correlated with linear combinations of continuously compounded changes of various macrovariables as detailed in Table 5.32. These correlations were 29.6% for the 15 year period, April 1971 to March 1986, and 63.9% in the final five year period ending in March 1986.

Table 5.32 Macrovariables Used in the Elton-Gruber Factor Analysis Study

(1) Inflation rate:
Consumer price index
Wholesale price index
Yen/dollar rate (US dollar central rate)
Export price index (yen based)
Import price index (yen base)
Nikkei commodity price index
Expected inflation rate

(2) Interest rate:
Call rate
10 yr. gov't bond yield
Difference in rates between short and long
    term interst rate
Difference in short term interests between
    Japan and US

(3) Foreign trade:
Export, quantum index
Imports quantum index
Crude oil import quantity

(4) Petroleum prices:
Crude oil import price

(5) Economic conditions:
Workers' households disposable income
Production index
Inventory index
Value of public contracts
Number of corporate bankruptcies
Index of business outlook about small enterprises
Retail trade index (seasonally adjusted)
Forecast industrial production rate

(6) U.S. interest rate and inflation:
Consumer price index of USA
3-month TB rate
Treasury securities yields (20 years avg.)

The factor approach used by Elton and Gruber has potentially much value, but it has many difficulties such as the inability to interpret the factors. These pros and cons are discussed in the context of the U.S. situation by Chen (1983), Cho (1984), Cho, Elton and Gruber (1984),

Brown and Weinstein (1983), Dhrymes, Friend and Gultekin (1984), Roll and Ross (1980), Burmeister, Wall and Hamilton (1986), Burmeister and Wall (1986), McElroy and Burmeister (1988), Burmeister and McElroy (1988), Shanken and Weinstein (1987), and others. If one uses portfolios of securities as Elton and Gruber did, rather than individual securities, then one has the following two disadvantages:[5]

- No matter how large the sample, one cannot determine if one has measured factors unique to that sample or general factors common to all securities.
- The results are sensitive to the portfolio formation technique used.

The factor approach is less satisfying because it is difficult to get much or any meaning at all from the factors. So we will henceforth concentrate on factor models that prespecify factors that seem to be reasonable. Such an approach originated with Chen (1983) and Brown and Weinstein (1983). Chen, Roll and Ross (1986) studied this approach using U.S. macroeconomic variables as proxies for the underlying risk factors that determined stock returns. They found that industrial production, inflation, risk premium, and the slope of the yield curve were significant factors. Moreover, the CAPM could not explain the returns better nor did adding the factors improve the explanatory power.

Hamao (1988) developed an APT model for the Japanese stock market using prespecified factors similar to the Chen, Roll and Ross (1986) study for the U.S. For the Japanese market, Hamao examined six factors - industrial production, inflation, investor confidence, interest rates, exchange rates and oil prices. He used monthly data from the TSE-1 from January 1975 to December 1984. The sample universe had 1066 stocks with some stocks excluded each month (53 to 188) because of missing or inaccurate data. The stocks were grouped, as Elton and Gruber had, into 20 equally weighted portfolios ranked by market capitalization. Portfolios were then reformed monthly. Since size is related to portfolio performance and size data are readily available, it is a good way to sort the portfolios.

---

[5]For individual securities, one has voluminous data problems plus the variability of individual stocks. Hence, even with a sample of stocks, the estimation will be difficult. This group or multi-sample approach first introduced by Roll and Ross (1980) has the added difficulty that the factors in each sample may be different and certainly will have different coefficients or even different signs.

Standard valuation in finance suggests that a firm's value equals its risk adjusted discounting of the future cash flows. Hence, variables that affect either the cash flows or the discount rates are good candidates for an asset pricing model. The variables, in addition to the equally and value weighted indices including dividends of all TSE-1 stock prices, were:

- *Industrial production:* The variable used was MPSA(t) which is the seasonally adjusted growth rate of industrial production. The growth rate of industrial production is MP(t) = lnIP(t)-lnIP(t-1) where lnIP(t) is the log of MITI's monthly production index. The variable is lagged forward by one month since MP(t) primarily reflects production in the previous month. To seasonally adjust, the average MP over the previous five years for each month is subtracted to yield the MPSA series.

- *Inflation:* The Gensaki rate, which is applied to bond transactions with repurchase or resale agreements, is used as the risk free interest rate. This rate for the 1975-84 period was for three months, so the one month compounded rate was used.

- *Investor confidence:* This is measured through changes in risk premiums measured by the difference between high and low quality bonds of similar duration. The risk premium variables were UPREL(T) =EL(t) - LGB(t) and UPRMF(T) =MF(t) - LGB(t) where EL(t), LGB(t), MF(t) are the monthly returns on the electricity bond (10 year maturity until March 1981, 12 year after), the long-term government bond (10 year maturity), and the managed fund, respectively

- *Interest rates:* To capture term structure effects, the return difference between long term bonds and the Gensaki rate was used via the variable UTS(t) = LGB(t)- GR(t-1). If UTS is positive, then long term bonds have risen so their yield has declined and the slope of the yield curve is lower.

- *Exchange rates[6]:* Due to the heavy reliance on imported energy and other natural resources, exchange rates have strong effects on various sectors of the economy. Hamao used the exchange rate variable UYEN(t) = ln $_{t-1}F_t$ - ln S_t, where $_{t-1}F_t$ is the forward exchange rate (yen/dollar) at the end of month t-1 applicable to the end of month t, and S_t is the spot rate at the end of month t. If forward rates are efficient, then $_{t-1}F_t$ is a forecast of S_t.

- *Oil prices:* The Japanese economy is very dependent on oil imports. As an example, one sees in Table 2.7a the extreme crash of 37.4% in

[6]Hamao also investigated a terms of trade variable DTT(t) = lnTT(t) - lnTT(t-1) where TT was the ratio of the prices of export to import goods. This variable was not significant

1973/74 during the first OPEC oil price crisis. Since then, the economy has become much more resilient to the dramatic increases in the price of oil; still, it is an important variable. The oil price growth variable OG is the monthly log difference of the Arabian Light spot price measure in yen using month-end spot exchange rates.[7]

Tables 5.33 and 5.34 show the correlation and autocorrelation matrices of Hamao's monthly economic variables over the ten years of the sample.

Table 5.33
Correlation Matrix of Economic Variables, January 1975- December 1984

	MP	MPSA	DEI	UI	UPRMF	UTS	UPREL	DTT	UYEN	OG	VW	EW
MP	1.000											
MPSA	0.315	1.000										
DEI	0.035	0.106	1.000									
UI	-0.079	0.020	0.043	1.000								
UPRMF	0.052	-0.002	--0.112	0.0044	1.000							
UTS	-0.101	-0.090	-0.196	-0.089	-0.630	1.000						
UPREL	0.134	-0.016	0.049	0.110	0.748	- 0.776	1.000					
DTT	-0.137	-0.059	-0.187	-0.041	-0.150	0.217	-0.203	1.000				
UYEN	-0.093	-0.001	-0.153	-0.059	-0.130	0.408	-0.329	0.234	1.000			
OG	0.169	0.006	0.127	0.045	0.154	-0.318	0.276	-0.340	-0.535	1.000		
VW	-0.104	-0.048	-0.108	-0.015	0.109	0.147	-0.016	0.038	0.224	-0.156	1.000	
EW	0.053	0.004	-0.179	-0.015	0.058	0.193	-0.071	0.174	0.291	-0.193	0.648	1.000

MP   - Monthly growth rate of industrial production (raw data).
MPSA   - Monthly growth rate of industrial production (filtered).
DEI   - Change in expected inflation.
UI   - Unanticipated inflation.
UPRMF   - Unanticipated change in risk premium using managed bond fund return.
UTS   - Unanticipated change in the term structure of interest rates.
UPREL   - Unanticipated change in risk premium using electricity company bond return.
DTT   - Change in tcrms of trade.
UYEN   - Unanticipated change in foreign exchange rates.
OG   - Growth rate of oil prices.
VW   - Retum on the value-weighted TSE-I index.
EW   - Return on the equally-weighted TSE-I index.

Source: Hamao (1988)

The relatively low correlation (0.648) in Table 5.33 between VW (the value weighted TSE-1 index) and EW (equally weighted TSE-1 index) suggests that several factors are needed to explain stock returns. High correlations between (1) oil price growth and the value of the yen, (2) unanticipated changes in risk premiums using managed bond fund

---

once other factors were considered; hence, its effect, if any, was subsumed by other pure variables.

[7]Since the OPEC oil crises, the *yen* value of oil has decreased dramatically, see Figure 7.9.

returns or electricity bond returns and unanticipated changes in the term structure of interest rates, and (3) unanticipated changes in risk premiums using managed bond fund returns and electricity bond returns are not surprising as these pairs have common variables: the spot exchange rate is used in both oil price growth and the value of the yen; long term government bond returns are used in both of the bond fund returns and in the term structure variables. These variables are not used together because of multicollinearity problems. The change in terms of trade (DTT) series is moderately autocorrelated, while the high autocorrelation of the monthly industrial production (MP) series at the 12th lag indicates an expected seasonality which is corrected using the MPSA.

Table 5.34
Autocorrelations of Economic Variables, Monthly Lags of Up to One Year
January 1975-December 1984

	ρ_1	ρ_2	ρ_3	ρ_4	ρ_5	ρ_6	ρ_7	ρ_8	ρ_9	ρ_{10}	ρ_{11}	ρ_{12}
MP	-0.333	-0.408	0.389	-0.123	-0.047	0.126	-0.074	-0.084	0.376	-0.432	-0.298	0.865
MPSA	-0.212	0.053	0.181	-0.151	0.132	-0.038	-0.109	0.045	0.203	-0.155	0.063	0.120
DEI	-0.144	0.070	0.132	0.043	0.052	0.086	-0.024	-0.105	0.198	-0.146	-0.077	0.144
UI	-0.038	0.303	-0.083	0.030	0.127	0.081	0.043	0.034	-0.064	-0.297	0.019	0.613
UPRMF	-0.063	0.039	0.034	0.067	-0.013	-0.055	-0.040	0.100	0.029	0.063	0.141	0.078
UTS	0.076	0.013	-0.087	0.080	0.064	-0.150	-0.048	0.161	0.134	0.182	0.047	0.035
UPREL	-0.256	0.119	-0.107	0.060	-0.054	-0.058	-0.075	-0.001	0.128	0.129	-0.033	0.016
DTT	0.689	0.473	0.378	0.295	0.292	0.319	0.271	0.169	0.048	-0.076	-0.055	-0.066
UYEN	0.094	-0.016	0.160	0.099	0.036	-0.044	-0.031	0.066	-0.053	-0.042	0.021	0.115
OG	0.079	-0.023	0.500	0.035	-0.069	0.287	-0.194	-0.018	0.138	-0.155	-0.111	0.042
VW	-0.017	-0.050	-0.035	-0.066	-0.110	-0.040	0.018	0.058	0.053	-0.021	0.014	0.013
EW	0.209	0.062	0.032	0.026	0.112	-0.111	0.050	-0.008	-0.122	-0.064	0.048	0.168

Source: Hamao (1988)

Hamao's estimates are of two basic kinds. The first are time series regressions to relate the various factors to the returns of the twenty size-ranked portfolios:

$$R_p = a_p + b_{1p} \bullet MPSA + b_{2p} \bullet DEI + b_{3p} \bullet UI + b_{4p} \bullet UPR + b_{5p} \bullet UTS + \varepsilon_p.$$

Then cross sectional regressions to estimate the risk premiums of each macrovariable were made using the time series estimates of the b's.

$$R_{pt} = \lambda_{0t} + \lambda_{1t} \bullet b_{1p} + \lambda_{2t} \bullet b_{2p} + \lambda_{3t} \bullet b_{3p} + \lambda_{4t} \bullet b_{4p} + \lambda_{5t} \bullet b_{5p} + \varepsilon_p.$$

Thus, a time series of estimates of risk premiums for each macrovariable is generated, and the mean of these estimates is tested for significance. Table 5.35 shows the risk premiums for three related models.

The time series regressions were run over a five year period to obtain the b's. Then a cross section regression was run for the month following the five year period. This procedure was repeated from each month for five years and a five year series of λs was obtained. The most recent estimate of the b's was then used for this rolling procedure. Eleven time series models were estimated as shown in Table 5.36 and three cross section APT models in Table 5.35. Very little is added with the six additional variables from the five factor APT model as most coefficients are not highly significant. The market variables VW and EW are not significant at the 5% level and EW has the *wrong* sign. Hence, the market factors do not contain missing priced factors.

Table 5.35
Pricing of Variables in Three APT Models, January 1975 - December 1984

	Constant	MPSA	DEI	UI	UPREL	UTS	DTT
1	0.02327	0.01690	0.00094	0.00597	0.01173	-0.01999	
	(4.366)	(3.064)	(2.964)	(2.616)	(2.678)	(-1.936)	
2	0.02239	0.01688	0.00103	0.00552	0.00744	-0.02002	
	(3.249)	(2.174)	(2.540)	(1.760)	(1.637)	(-1.465)	
3	0.02316	0.01730	0.00093	0.00606	0.01730	-0.01973	-0.01027
	(4.533)	(3.439)	(3.158)	(2.276)	(2.686)	(-1.997)	(-1.34)

The top rows give the time series means of λs with the t-statistics in ().

Source: Hamao (1988)

The third equation has the most significant variables with only the terms of trade variable, DTT, not significant.

Roll and Ross Asset Management use a confidential model that has some of its origins in the Chen, Roll and Ross (1986) and Hamao (1988) work, for asset management in the U.S., Japan and other localities. This model is used in connection with Daiwa International to jointly manage some $3 billion in Japanese equities. Their research suggests that five factors are key:

- Short term inflation measured by CPI changes.

- Long term inflation: measured by changes in real short term risk free interest rates.

- Business cycle: measured by changes in an industrial production index to reflect real output changes.

- Interest rates: measured by long term government bond yields to capture investor's expectations of future interest rates.

- Investor confidence: measured by the difference between high and low grade bonds.

Table 5.36
Time Series Regressions for Eleven Models, January 1975 - December 1984

	Const	MPSA	DEI	UI	UPREL	UTS	UPRMF	DTT	UYEN	OG	VW	EW
1	0.02013	0.0592	0.00039	0.00453	0.01369	-0.01500						
	(4.440)	(1.263)	(1.966)	(1.651)	(1.747)	(-1.452)						
2	0.01832	0.00619	0.00036	0.00419		-0.01340	0.00555					
	(3.952)	(1.385)	(1.954)	(1.520)		(1.247)	(1.478)					
3	0.01947	0.00725	0.00039	0.00436	0.01440	0.01345		- 0.0107				
	(4.500)	(1.532)	(1.985)	(1.504)	(1.892)	(-1.348)		(-1.425)				
4	0.01790	0.00442	0.00033	0.00394	0.01280	-0.01492			-0.00755			
	(4.417)	(0.965)	(1.717)	(1.543)	(1.830)	(-1.470)			(-0.712)			
5	0.02001	0.00470	0.00035	0.00043	0.01096	-0.01140				0.01253		
	(4.700)	(0.990)	(1.811)	(1.586)	(1.459)	(-1.149)				(0.477)		
6	0.02174	0.00877	0.00041		0.01920	-0.02572						
	(4.522)	(1.830)	(2.096)		(2.259)	(-2.286)						
7	0.02478	0.00966	0.00039		0.01893	-0.02199		- 0.1190				
	(4.476)	(1.963)	(1.972)		(2.331)	(-2.071)		(-1.551)				
8	0.01445	0.00640	0.00042		0.01280	-0.01849					0.00478	
	(2.167)	(1.581)	(2.233)		(1.806)	(-1.914)					(0.680)	
9	0.02357	0.00584	0.00032		0.01590	-0.01632						-0.01215
	(3.365)	(1.641)	(1.6658)		(2.277)	(-1.721)						(-1.716)
10	0.00266										0.02190	
	(0.408)										(2.817)	
11	0.01445	0.00642	0.00047		0.01309	-0.01954					0.01107	
	(2.167)	(1.605)	(2.579)		(1.846)	(- 2.018)					(1.757)	

Numbers in the top rows represent the time series means of λs with t-statistics in ().

Source: Hamao (1988)

The model has been back tested and used to manage real portfolios with the success shown in Figure 5.15. From January 1983 to December 1989, the month to month volatility of the TOPIX was 16.4% versus 14.9% for the APT portfolios. During the three year period September 1986 to September 1989, with actual investment results, the APT portfolios beat the TOPIX by an average of 3% per year. One yen on January 1, 1983, would have grown to 5.70 versus 4.55 if invested in the TOPIX.

CAPMD: A MODEL OF RISK AND RETURN IN THE JAPANESE EQUITY MARKET

All of the major Japanese brokerage firms as well as some foreign firms and consultants have various models to evaluate stock prices using factor models. The CAPMD (capital asset pricing, multiple dimensioned) model of Yamaichi Securities is typical of the best of these efforts. It utilized modern Western technology (supplied by consultant professors Steven Brown of New York University and Toshiyuki Otsuki of the International of Japan) along with a well funded team effort by members of the development branch of Yamaichi Securities who are familiar with Japanese security markets.

CAPMD attempts to bring together three separate models: the capital asset pricing model, the arbitrage pricing model, and the approach of Rosenberg and his co-workers[8] to relate betas and other factors to fundamental indicators that affect the financial environment of the firm.

Figure 5.15
Performance of Roll and Ross APT Portfolio versus the Topix, January 1983 to September 1989

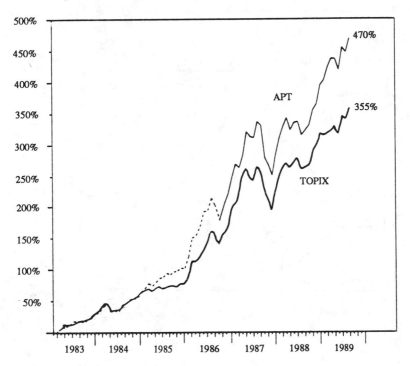

Source: Roll and Ross Asset Management (1990)

---

[8]See Rosenberg and McKibben (1973) and Rosenberg and Guy (1976ab).

Figure 5.16   Comparison of the CAPMD Portfolio and the Topix, 1983-87

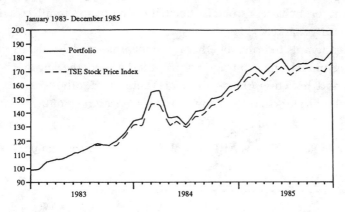

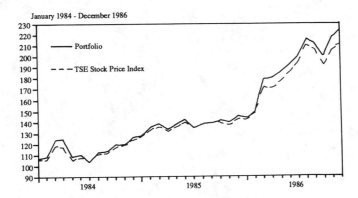

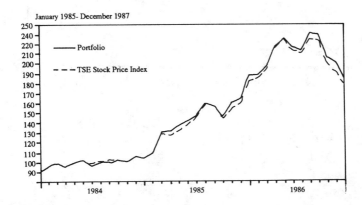

Source: Brown and Otsuki (1988)

The CAPMD model postulates that the security return equals the risk free rate, plus the risk premium and plus the excess return the model can provide. The risk premium is composed of macroeconomic, market and microeconomic factors. The excess return is composed of theme and idiosyncratic (security specific component) factors. The analysis of the CAPMD has several steps. First, the macroeconomic risk factors are defined and related to industry returns. By disaggregating the level of the individual firm, the model assesses the sensitivity of the returns to these sources of macroeconomic risk. The model then determines the impact of market risk and risk factors for individual firms. By measuring the relationship between returns and measures of risk in the cross section of all securities, it is possible to separate the returns into the three components: risk free rate, risk premium and excess return.

The macroeconomic factors are changes in interest rates and percentage changes in the money supply, production, price of oil, wholesale price index and the yen/dollar exchange rate.

The model explained about half the variance in these macroeconomic data. Unexpected changes in the variables are given by the implied innovations in these series and are uncorrelated. The six factors are essentially independent sources of risk that are priced in the Japanese capital markets.

Estimation of the relationship between the macroeconomic factors and industry returns begins with the development of a measure of industry returns. Firms are broken down into their component lines of business on the basis of sales data from their annual reports, yielding industry weights for each firm.[9] Industry returns are inferred by relating these weights to a cross section of individual security returns. These industry returns are analogous to, but more accurate than, those computed for the U.S. The industry returns diversify away the non-factor returns. These are then related to unexpected changes in the macroeconomic data to obtain the estimates of the relationship between industry returns and macroeconomic risk. In turn, these are disaggregated to the individual securities using the firm/industry weights. The sensitivity of the security to macroeconomic factors changes as the lines of business (reflected in the weights) change. These macroeconomic factor sensitivities are normalized

---

[9]One sees the Western influence of this model which tend to view the company as a portfolio of its component businesses rather than as an entity with synergies, as seen by Japanese management.

so that the value weighted average of each sensitivity is zero with unit variance in the cross section of securities.

Financial statements and investor expectations data form micro-economic factors that are priced.

The CAPMD model can be used for several purposes: as a valuation screen to identify potential buy and sell decisions, in portfolio management to allow the institution to offset the risk exposure generated by active management, and in portfolio management to attribute the performance to the investment decision process of an active manager.

Figure 5.16 shows the simulated performance of the model versus the TOPIX for three subperiods from 1983 to 1987. The model beats the index by 1-3% and can be thought of as an index plus alpha fund. The specific stocks in the simulated portfolio as of January 1986 and January 1987 appear in Table 5.37.

The model has a number of useful features. One can select the stocks with high alphas for buy signals, those with low alphas for sell signals. Alternatively, one can tilt the portfolio in a specific direction (say toward oil price exposure) while, if desired, keeping portfolio risk constant. One of the advantages of computerized systems such as CAPMD is that they provide a systematic basis for investment choice and risk measurement and control. The latter is especially important if several managers are selecting securities.

One important application of CAPMD is the measurement of investment performance of money managers. Just as CAPMD can attribute individual security returns to risk exposures or security specific factors, the same can be done for a portfolio of securities. Therefore, a particular money manager's portfolio return, R_p^τ, can be assessed by decomposing it into the level of risk, ρ_{pk}^τ, and price of that risk, λ_k^τ, in period τ for factor k.

Table 5.37   Stocks in the CAPMD Simulated Portfolios

Code	January 1986	Code	January 1987
1332	Nippon Suisan	1803	Shimizu Construction
1801	Taisei	1925	Daiwa House Industry
1925	Daiwa House Industry	1983	Toshiba Engineering & Corrstruction
2212	Yamazaki Banking	2002	Nisshin Flour Milling
2262	Snow Brand	2202	Meiji Seika
2503	Kirin Brewery	2262	Snow Brand
2897	Nisshin Food Products	2531	Takara Shuzo
3407	Asahi Chemical Ind.	3402	Toray Ind.
3702	Sanyo-Kokusai Pulp	3861	0ji Paper
4043	Tokuyama Soda	4010	Mitsubishi Chemical Industries
4452	Kao	4043	Tokuyama Soda
4471	Sanyo Chemical Ind.	4151	Kyowa Hakko Kogyo
4506	Dainippon Pharmaceutical	4522	Green Cross
4522	Green Cross	4711	Shiseido
4901	Fuji Photo Film	6005	Toa Nenryo Kogyo
5001	Nippon Oil	5238	Mitsubishi Mining & Cement
5108	Bridgestone	5332	Toto
5401	Nippon Steel	5451	Yodogawa Steel Works
5486	Hitachi Metals	5801	Furukawa Electric
5802	Sumitomo Electric Ind.	6326	Kubota
5901	Toyo Seikan	6444	Sanden
6583	Matsushita Refrigeration	6502	Toshiba
6107	Sonoike Mfg.	6762	TDK
6349	Komori Printing Machinery	6783	Matsushita-Kotobuki Electronics Ind
6407	CKD	6845	Yamatake Honeywell
6503	Mitsubishi Electric	6954	Fanuc
6756	Kokusai Electric	7203	Toyota Motor
6781	MatsLishita Communication Industrial	7267	Honda Motor
6782	Kyushu Matsushita Electric	7741	Hoya
6991	Matsushita Electric Works	7751	Cannon
7102	Nippon Sharyo Seizo	7712	Dai Nippon Printing
7259	Aisin Seiki	7974	Nintendo
7267	Honda Motor	7988	Nifco
7741	Hoya	8016	Kashiyama
7752	Ricoh	8058	Mitsubishi Corp.
7762	Citizen Watch	8183	Seven-Eleven Japan
7912	Dai Nippon Printing	8231	Mitstikoshi
8016	Kashiyama	8263	Daiei
8057	Uchida Yoko	8302	Industrial Bank of Japan
8183	Seven-Eleven Japan	8317	Fuji Bank
8231	Mitsukoshi	8332	Bank of Yokohama
8263	Daiei	8401	Mitsui Trust and Banking
8302	Industrial Bank of Japan	8604	Nomura Securities
8318	Sumitomo Bank	8752	Taisho Marine & Fire Insurance
8332	Bank of Yokohama	8801	Mitsui Real Estate Development
8402	Mitsubishi Trust and Banking	9001	Tobu Railway
8601	Daiwa Securities	9005	Tokyu
8761	Tokio Marine & Fire Insurance	9076	Seino Transpqration
8801	Mitsui Real Estate Development	9104	Mitsui O.S.K. Lines
8802	Mitsubishi Estate	9202	All Nippon Airways
9001	Tobu Railway	9401	Tokyo Broadcasting System
9101	Nippon Yusen	9431	Kokusai Denshin Denwa
9202	All Nippon Airways	9501	Tokyo Electric Power
9431	Kokusai Denshin Denwa	9531	Tokyo Gas
9503	Kansai Electric Power	9735	Secom
9531	Tokyo Gas	9738	Intec
9762	Daiwa Kosho Lease		

Source: Brown and Otsuki (1988)

Then the portfolio return is

$$R_p^\tau = c^\tau + \sum_k \lambda_k^\tau \rho_{p_k}^\tau + \varepsilon_k^\tau$$

where c^τ is the level of interest rates. The money manager's return can be attributed to the general market conditions, c^τ, the risk exposure (the summation), and the particular return from the manager's stock selection ability.

Market timing abilities can be measured by further decomposing the return:

$$R_p^\tau = c^\tau + \sum_k \lambda_k^\tau \bar{\rho}_{pk} + \sum_k \lambda_k^\tau (\rho_{p_k}^\tau - \bar{\rho}_{pk}) + .\varepsilon_p^\tau$$

The first term reflects the general market conditions; the second, the return attributed to the average factor risk exposure of the manager; the third, the return to market timing activities in the particular month, τ, and the final term, the stock selection ability of the manager. By averaging these measures over time, one can break down a favorable investment result into its component parts.

CUMULATIVE PAYOFF TO SINGLE FACTORS: JUNE 1979 TO SEPTEMBER 1989
Ziemba (1990b), assisted by Asaji Komatsu, did a study at the Yamaichi Research Institute of the factors that led to superior portfolio performance for the 123 months from June 1979 to August 1989. Thirty variables were investigated and in each case the variable was standardized by subtracting the mean and dividing by the standard deviation. Some variables are revised monthly, others yearly. The variables used are defined in Table 5.38.

Table 5.38

Definition of Fundamental and Technical Variables Used in the Factor Model Study

D=difference, A=acceleration, P=price, BV=book value, Div= dividend

Variable	Definition
1. PER	Most recent 1 year's earnings/price
2. PDER	(Most recent 1 year's earnings - previous year's earnings)/price
3. PAER	{(Most recent 1 year's earnings - previous year's earnings) - (previous year's earning - earnings of 2 year's ago)}/price
4. PSR	Most recent 1 year's sales/price
5. PDSR	(Most recent 1 year's sales - previous year's sales)/price
6. PADR	{(Most recent 1 year's sales - previous year's sales) - (previous year's sales - sales of 2 year's ago)}/price
7. PBR	Most recent BV/price
8. PDBR	(Most recent BV - BV of 2 year's ago)/price
9. PABR	{(Most recent BV- BV of 1 year ago) - BV of 1 year ago - BV of 2 years ago)}/price
10. YIELD	Most recent 1 year's Div/price
11. DYield	(Most recent 1 year's Div - previous year's Div)/price
12. AYield	{(Most recent 1 year's Div- previous year's Div) - (previous year's Div - Div of 2 years ago)}/price
13. Div-P	Most recent year's Div/most recent year's earnings
14. DDiv-P	(Most recent year's Div/most recent year's earnings) - (previous year's Div/previous year's earnings)
15. ADiv-P	{(Most recent year's Div/most recent year's earnings) - (previous year's Div/previous year's earnings)} - {(previous year's Div/most recent year's earnings) - (Div of 2 year's ago - earnings of 2 year's ago)}
16. D-Zero	$\begin{cases} 1 & \text{if no dividends were paid during the most recent year} \\ 0 & \text{otherwise} \end{cases}$
17. TMVLOG	Log(capitalization)
18. Shares	Outstanding shares
19. Price50	Price converted to par value of ¥50, measures low price effect
20. IND-R	Shares held by individual investors/outstanding shares
21. D-PAR	$\begin{cases} 1 & \text{if par value is at least ¥500} \\ 0 & \text{otherwise} \end{cases}$
22. EST-LACT (growth)	(Earnings estimate of the current fiscal year - most previous year's earning)/price

Variables 23-27 are based on the previous 60-month's regression

23. Beta	Slope of time series regression

24.	Alpha	Intercept of the time series regression
25.	Sigma	Mean squared error of the time series regression
26.	EPS	Most recent month's residual
27.	EPS-1	Previous month's residual
28.	RELSTR	Relative strength measured by $0.4\,Ret_t + 0.2\,Ret_{t-1} + 0.2\,Ret_{t-2} + 0.2\,Ret_{t-3}$
29.	D-RELSTR	$RELSTR_t - RELSTR_{t-1}$
30.	R-MAX24	Price/highest price during the last 2 years

Source: Yamaichi Research Institute reported in Ziemba (1990b)

The returns are computed relative to the TOPIX. For each variable x_i, the standardized variable is $\dfrac{x_i - Mkt\,x}{std\,x}$, where $Mkt\,x = \sum_{i=1}^{n} w_i x_i$, with the weights w_i = market value of i/total market value and

$$std\,x = \sqrt{\dfrac{\sum_{i=1}^{n}(x_i - Mkt\,x)^2}{n-1}},$$ and n = all TSE-I stocks, 1229 as of autumn 1990. Figure 5.18 shows these cumulative returns in a univariate one at a time sense. Jacobs and Levy (1988abc) who did a similar study for the U.S. call these the *naive* effects. Figure 5.19 has the pure or multivariate effects which are the effects when the other 29 variables are separated from each factor. Tables 5.39 and 5.40 present the results from the univariate and multivariate regressions. The means of the monthly returns from each of the thirty naive and pure effects, plus the t and p statistics for a two sided test of the hypothesis that there is an effect are shown.

The expected return of each stock i in the TSE-I universe was then estimated using the 30 variable regression model

$$E(R_{i,t+1}) = \sum_{j=1}^{30} b_{ij}\bar{A}_{jt}$$

where $E(R_{i,t+1})$ is the expected return of the ith security during month $t+1$ estimated at the end of month t, and $\bar{A}_{jt}$ is the average over the past sixty months of the jth attributes's pure anomaly return, namely

$$\bar{A}_{jt} = \frac{1}{60} \sum_{s=0}^{59} A_{jt-s}$$

where A_{jt} is the jth attribute's pure anomaly return in month t.

Table 5.39

Univariate (Naive) Effects of Thirty Factors on the TSE-I, June 1979 to August 1989

	Factor	Monthly Mean Return from Factor, %	t-Statistic	p-Significance, 2 sided test
1	ADiv-P	0.00013	0.12	0.904
2	Alpha	-0.00384	-3.99	0.000
3	AYield	0.00065	1.31	0.191
4	Beta	-0.00104	-0.45	0.066
5	D-PAR	-0.00370	-0.02	0.980
6	D-RELSTR	-0.00233	-1.92	0.058
7	D-Zero	0.60613	1.88	0.063
8	DDiv-P	0.00110	0.94	0.347
9	Div-P	0.00033	0.22	0.826
10	DYield	-0.00122	-0.18	0.067
11	EPS	-0.00350	-3.04	0.003
12	EPS-1	-0.00195	-1.46	0.146
13	EST-LACT	0.00820	8.74	0.000
14	INP-R	0.00240	2.50	0.014
15	PABR	0.00017	0.19	0.852
16	PAER	0.00263	3.25	0.002
17	PASR	0.00084	0.95	0.344
18	PBR	0.00398	3.31	0.001
19	PDBR	-0.00165	-1.39	0.167
20	PDER	0.00094	0.96	0.338
21	PDSR	-0.00117	-1.29	0.200
22	PER	-0.00038	-0.30	0.768
23	Price50	-0.00719	-3.04	0.003
24	PSR	0.00416	2.98	0.003
25	R-MAX24	-0.00279	-1.47	0.144
26	RELSTR	-0.00649	-3.85	0.000
27	Shares	-0.00017	-0.07	0.944
28	Sigma	-0.00434	-3.02	0.003
29	TMVLOG	-0.00396	-2.24	0.027
30	YIELD	0.00233	2.50	0.014

Source: Yamaichi Research Institute reported in Ziemba (1990b)

Some of the major conclusions are as follows:

- Low PER had no effect by itself but once the effects of other variables were eliminated the pure effect is quite strong.

- Earnings changes and acceleraton in earnings are very positive.

- Low price to sales and price to book value ratios are very positive by themselves but the pure effect gives only a 10% edge over the TOPIX over the ten years.

- As in the U.S., stocks with higher yields have higher returns and the highest returns are those with no dividends at all.

- As discussed in Chapter 4 there is a strong small stock effect. Low price stocks also do well as shown in Price 50.

- Stocks react positively to the number of outstanding shares.

- Stocks with higher percentages owned by individuals outperform those with lower.

- By far, the strongest positive variable with over a 250% edge on the TOPIX is earnings growth - EST-LACT.[10]

- Beta has a negative unvariate but a positive multivariate effect.

- There is mean reversion, negative alpha, in the univariate results but not in its pure effect according to the time series regression. But there is strong mean reversion of current and past residuals as well as relative return strength averaged over the past four months.

- Sigma, as expected, has a negative effect.

- Changes in relative strength and in price relative to its maximum price in the past two years are negative in univariate but strongly positive in their pure effects.

Figure 5.17 shows how one would have done with monthly revisions by choosing the best 50, 100, 200, 300, 400, 500 versus all the TSE-I equally weighted, the TOPIX (the TSE-I value weighted), and the NSA 225. This simulation re-estimated the model with new data from June 1979 to month t then the model selects the best stock for month t+1 and a revision is made to choose the best stocks, equally weighted in the portfolio. One yen invested in the best 50 stocks would have grown to ¥7.57 from January 1985 to December 1989. Meanwhile, the TOPIX and NSA were at ¥2.96 and ¥3.09, respectively. Table 5.41 details this.

---

[10]The detailed study of Darrough and Harris (1991) considers the effect of management forecasts of earnings on stock prices in Japan. Their empirical results demonstrate that: (1) management forecasts at both parent and consolidated earnings are generally more accurate than a random walk model using past earnings; (2) the analysts forecasts of parent-only earnings preceeding the announcement date is the most accurate measure of unexpected earnings and is most closely associated with unexpected returns; (3) it is difficult to distinguish between managment forecast, imputed (parent-earnings-based) and random walk measures of unexpected consolidated earnings relative to their associations with unexpected returns and (4) the sign of management forecasts - up or down - are associated with unexpected returns for both parent and consolidated earnings. This research suggests even more earnings variables to utilize in models. Whether or not they would improve on EST-LACT is not clear. What is clear is that these variables are strong predictors of future stock prices.

Table 5.40
Multivariate (Pure) Effects of Thirty Factors on the TSE-I, Ranked by t - Statistics, June 1979 to August 1989

	Factor	Monthly Mean Return from Factor, %	t-Statistic	p-Significance, 2 sided test
1	EST-LACT	0.00788	7.85	0.000
2	EPS	-0.00693	-3.65	0.000
3	RELSTR	-0.00645	-3.42	0.001
4	PDBR	-0.00397	-2.87	0.005
5	R-MAX24	0.00363	2.86	0.005
6	PER	0.00385	2.69	0.008
7	TMVLOG	-0.00429	-2.21	0.029
8	Shares	0.00382	1.87	0.065
9	Sigma	-0.00234	-1.72	0.088
10	PBR	0.00124	1.68	0.095
11	AYield	0.00105	1.49	0.139
12	DYield	-0.00136	-1.45	0.149
13	DDiv-P	0.00281	1.35	0.179
14	D-RELSTR	0.00250	1.22	0.224
15	PDSR	-0.01645	-1.20	0.233
16	Beta	0.00223	1.11	0.268
17	ADiv-P	-0.00147	-1.00	0.318
18	PDSR	0.00109	0.93	0.356
19	IND-R	0.00046	0.84	0.404
20	D-Zero	0.00184	0.83	0.407
21	PSR	0.00072	0.67	0.507
22	EPS=1	-0.00846	-0.63	0.528
23	PABR	0.00097	0.60	0.550
24	PDER	0.00092	0.53	0.596
25	YIELD	0.00033	0.38	0.706
26	Price50	-0.00068	-0.34	0.737
27	Alpha	0.00025	0.19	0.846
28	PAER	0.00020	0.18	0.854
29	D-PAR	-0.00042	-0.09	0.930
30	Div-P	-0.00012	-0.07	0.941

Source: Yamaichi Research Institute reported in Ziemba (1990b)

Figure 5.17
Cumulative Performance of ¥1 Invested in the Best 50, 100, 200, 300, 400,
500 and All Equally Weighted TSE-I Stocks versus the Topix and NSA225,
Monthly Revisions of Data and Model, January 1985 to September 1989

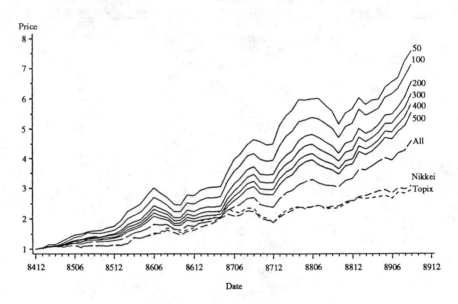

Source: Yamaichi Research Institute reported in Ziemba (1990b)

Table 5.41
Performance of the Best 50, 100, 200, 300, 400, 500 and All Equally Weighted TSE-I Stocks versus the Topix and NSA225 with Monthly Revisions, January 1985 to September 1989.

Portfolio		Value of ¥1 invested in Jan 85 at end of Sept 89	Annualized* Return in %	Monthly Mean Return, %	St Dev of Monthly Returns
Best	50	7.57	53.1	3.76	5.57
Best	100	7.12	51.2	3.64	5.36
Best	200	6.54	48.5	3.48	5.17
Best	300	6.16	46.6	3.37	5.13
Best	400	5.84	45.0	3.26	5.02
Best	500	5.54	43.4	3.16	4.88
Equally weighted	TSE-I	4.44	36.8	2.80	4.17
	Nikkei	3.09	26.8	2.09	4.42
	TOPIX	2.96	25.7	2.04	4.96

*Annualized return in percent equals $\left[\left(\frac{\text{total}}{\text{return}} \right)^{12/57} -1 \right] 100.$

Source: Yamaichi Research Institute reported in Ziemba (1990b)

SUMMARY OF CHAPTER - WHAT DO WE KNOW ABOUT VALUATION?

The adjusted PER and regression based models suggest strategies and methods to value stocks. Prices of stocks are, of course, dependent upon supply and demand. Hence, particular stocks or industries or the whole market can trade below, at, or above intrinsic values (based on historical means of summary statistics) for significant periods. However, over long periods, investing in undervalued stocks or at anomalous times of the year usually is a very succesful strategy. In Chapter 8 we compile sample portfolios that look promising and suggest in Chapter 9 good mutual funds. At the end of Chapter 4 we presented the results of a small stock portfolio run with real yen in 1988 to 1990.

Figure 5.18
Cumulative returns Relative to the Topix over the Period June 1979 to
August 1989 for Each of Thirty Univarate Variables: The *Naive* Effects

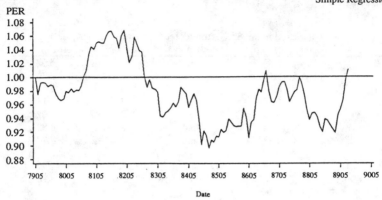

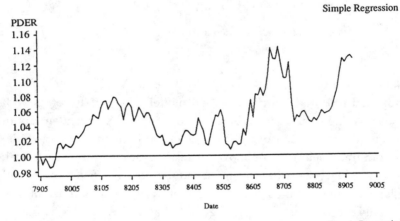

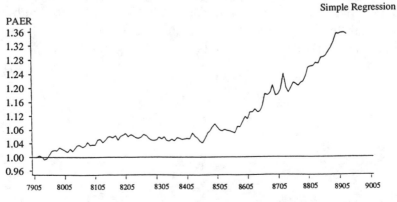

Source: Yamaichi Research Institute reported in Ziemba (1990b)

Figure 5.18 continued

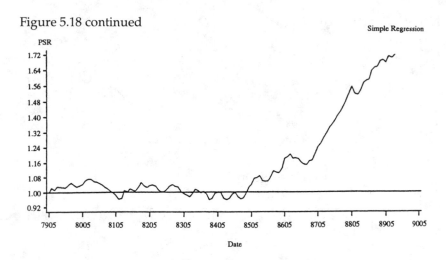

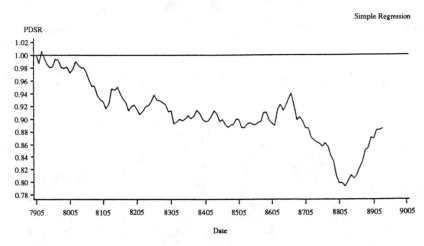

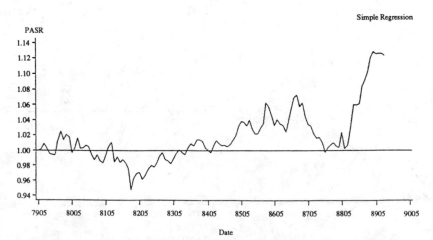

Figure 5.18 continued

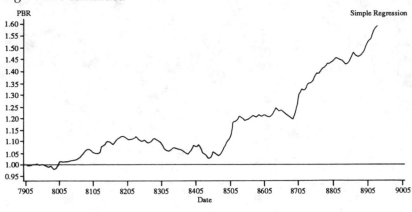

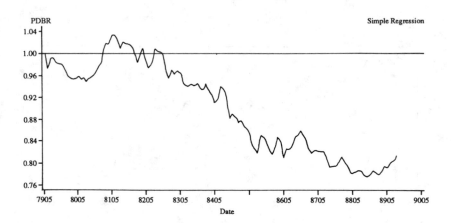

Figure 5.18 continued

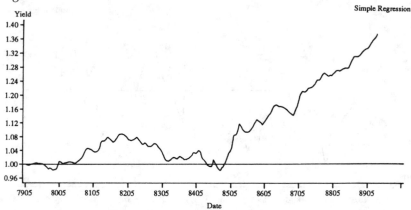

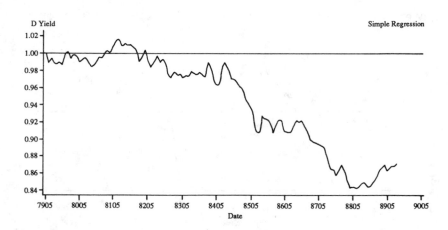

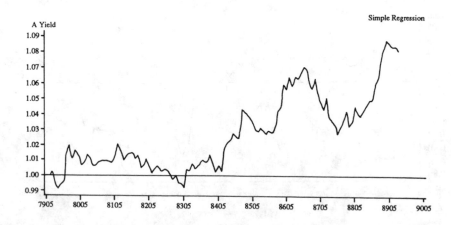

Figure 5.18 continued

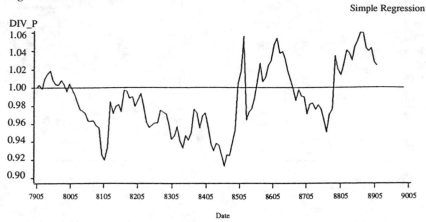

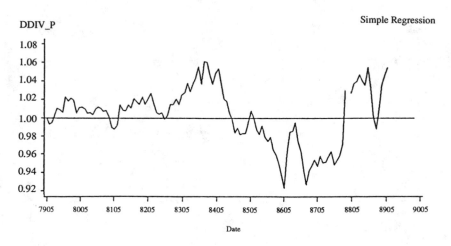

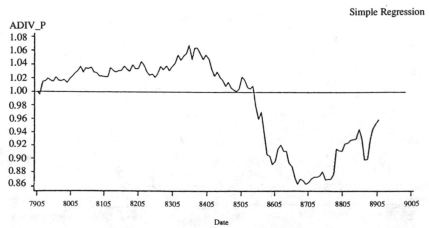

Figure 5.18 continued

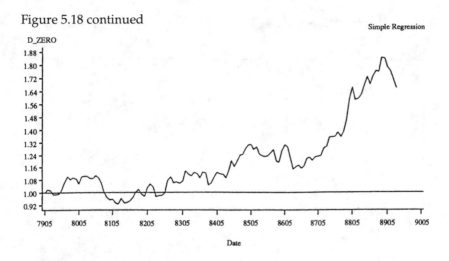

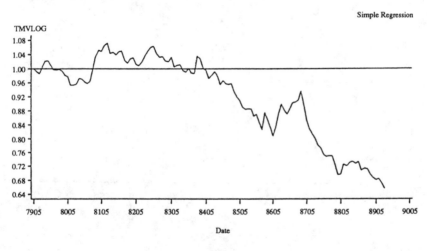

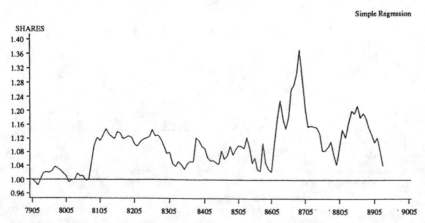

Figure 5.18 continued

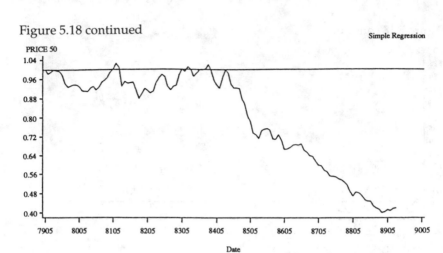

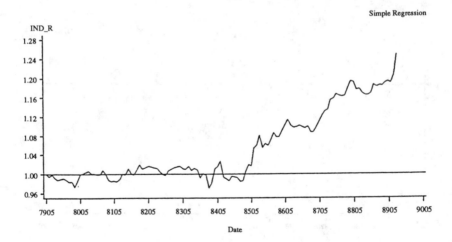

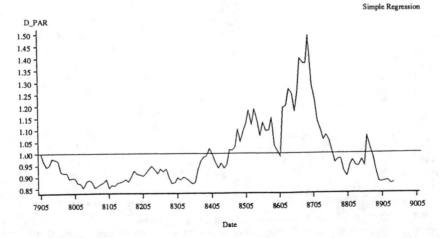

Figure 5.18 continued

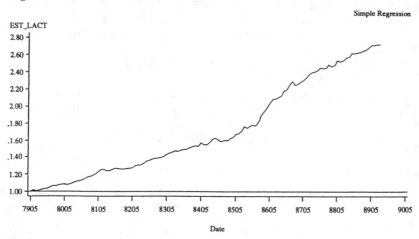

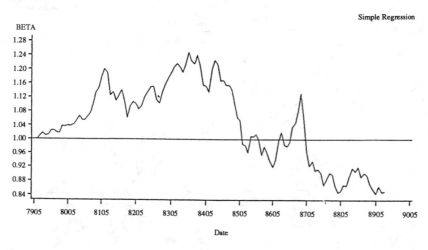

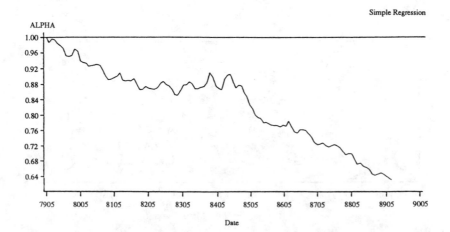

Figure 5.18 continued

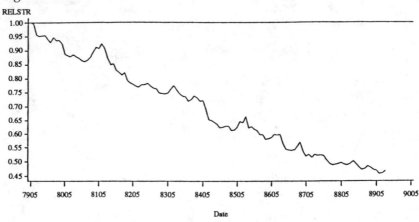

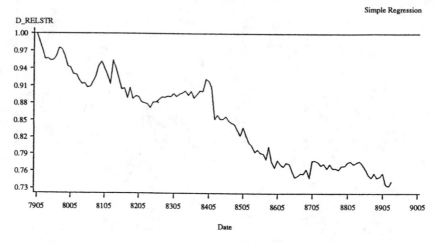

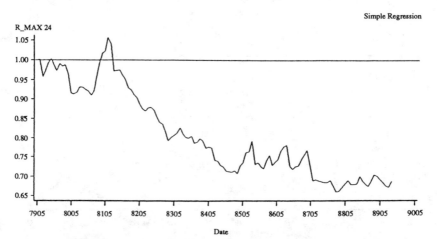

Figure 5.18 continued

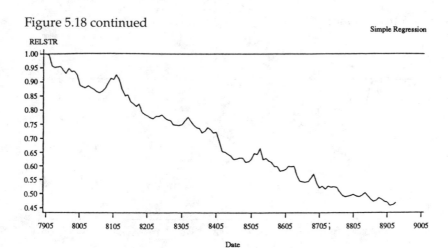

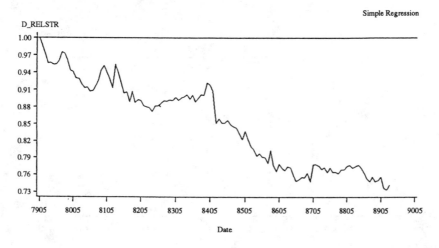

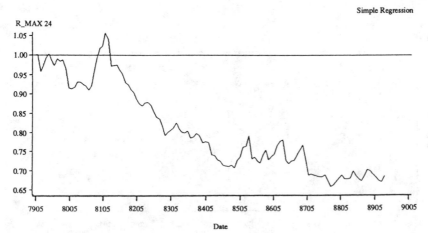

Figure 5.18 concluded

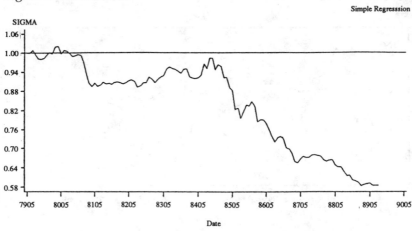

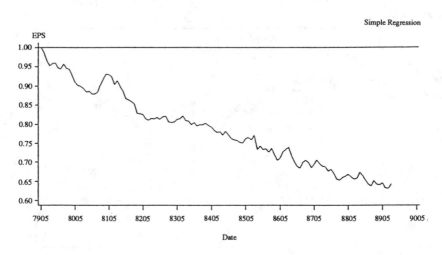

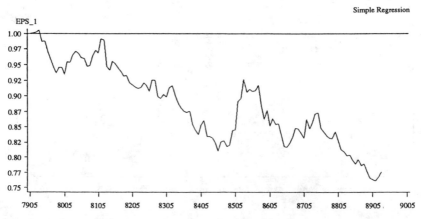

Figure 5.19
Cumulative Returns Relative to the Topix over the Period June 1979 to
August 1989 for Each of Thirty Multivariate Variables: The *Pure* Effects

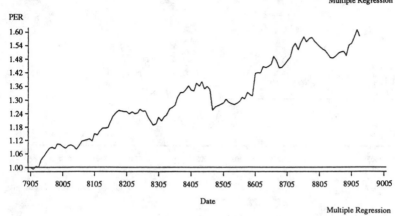

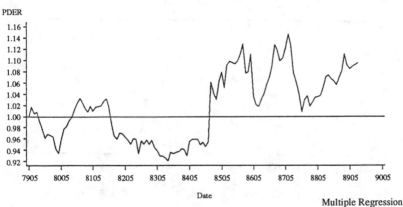

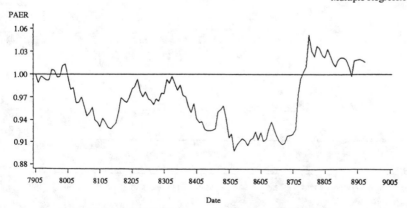

Source: Yamaichi Research Institute reported in Ziemba (1990b)

Figure 5.19 continued

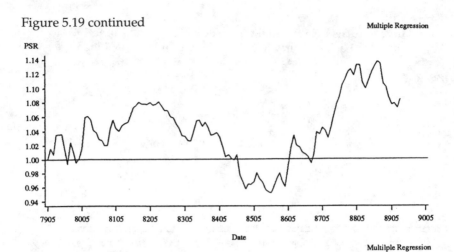

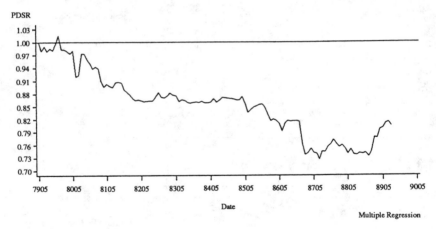

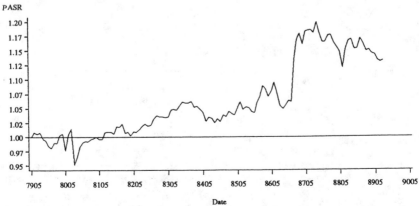

Figure 5.19 continued

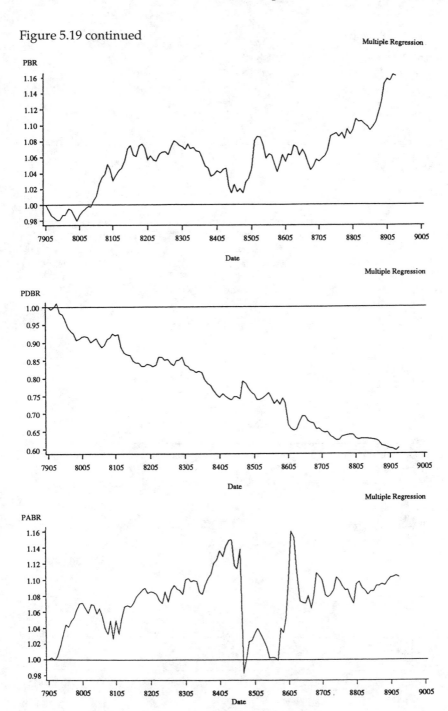

Figure 5.19 continued

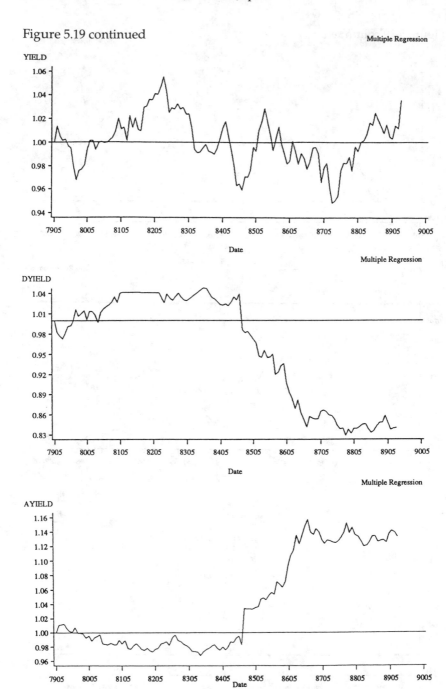

Figure 5.19 continued

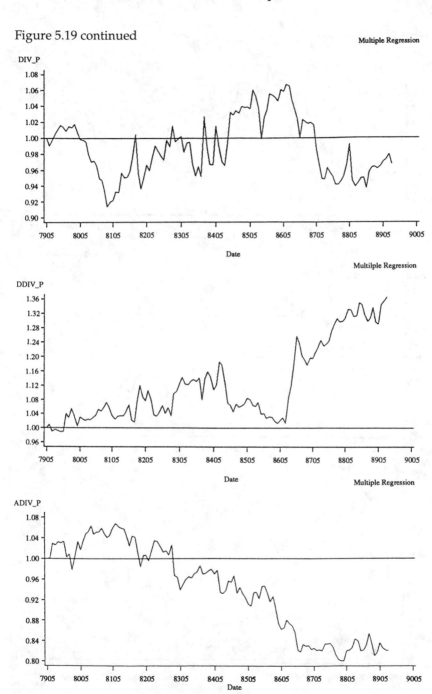

Figure 5.19 continued

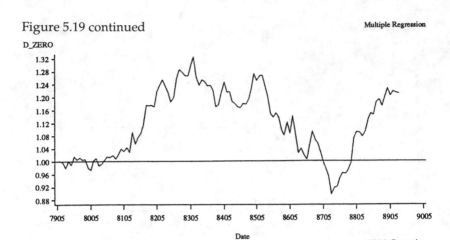

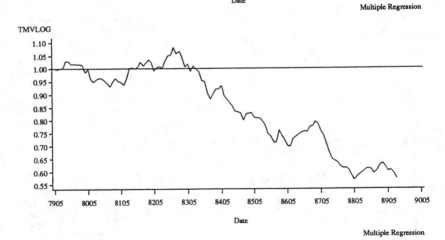

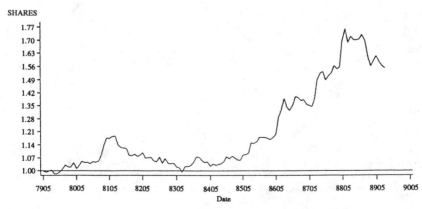

Figure 5.19 continued

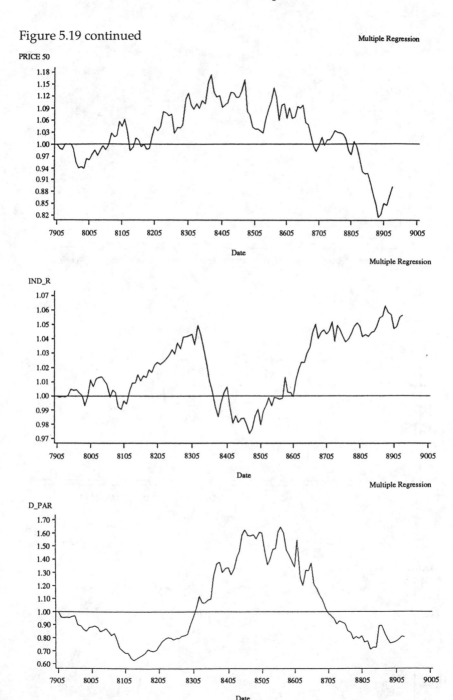

Figure 5.19 continued

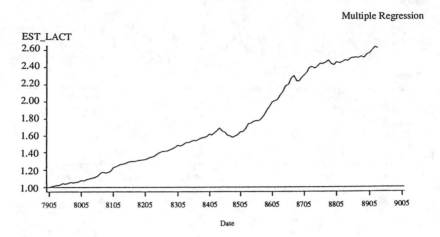

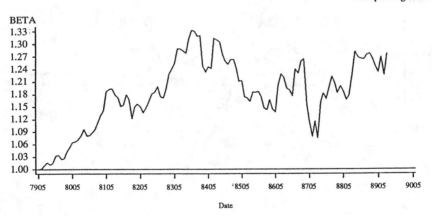

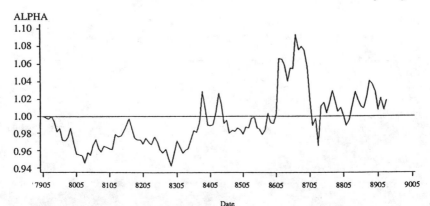

Figure 5.19 continued

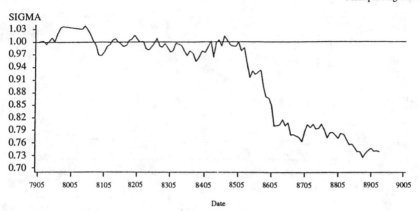

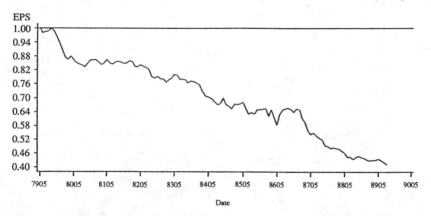

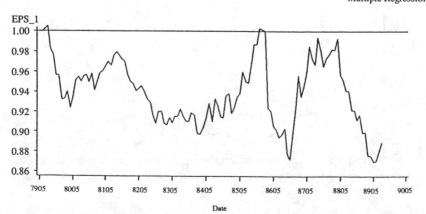

Figure 5.19 concluded

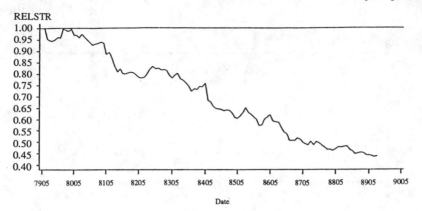

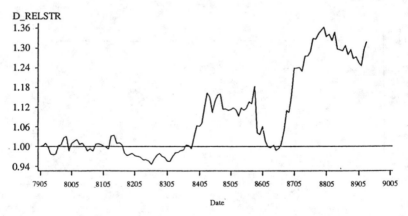

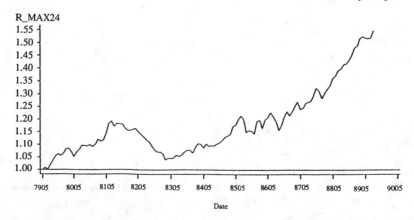

CHAPTER 6
HEDGING STRATEGIES FOR STOCKS
AND THE VALUE OF THE YEN

Futures and options can be used for hedging-risk reduction purposes as well as for speculation. For the yen, there are active options markets as well as futures markets around the world. Long term yen currency warrants are traded on the American Stock Exchange and yen futures markets in Japan began in June 1989. For the stock market, only index futures were available for use in Japan until the new NSA index options contracts began trading in Osaka in June 1989. Futures options contracts on the Topix, the TSE and the Nagoya 25 began trading in October 1989. However, long term puts and calls on the NSA and Topix have been trading for some time in markets outside Japan. Short and long term options on the Japan 210 index trade on the American Stock Exchange. The Chicago Mercantile Exchange trades futures and futures options on the NSA. There are no futures or options contracts in existence or planned regarding individual stocks or for small stocks. Hence, hedging strategies involving individual stock portfolios using the index derivative instruments will be subject to tracking error, which must be considered in the design of such strategies.[1]

When the yen strengthened from 260 in the fall of 1985 to its low near 120 in 1987 and 1988, the *seibo* (life insurance companies) lost some $50 billion from their U.S. Treasury bond investments by not hedging. During 1989 and 1990, the yen has fallen back to the 150-160 range and then to the 125-135 range. Hence, they have made back some of these losses. The strategy discussed here is a simple one that utilizes short-term puts and calls. Other instruments that could be used for currency hedging are put warrants as well as currency swaps, foreign exchange annuity swaps, foreign currency borrowing, interest rate caps and floors, investment or deposit in foreign currencies (such as dollar deposits with reverse floating

---

[1]This chapter is based on Ziemba (1991d). Thanks are due to Yuko Beppu of Seikei University, Tokyo, and an anonymous referee for some helpful comments on this work.

rates against option contracts), hybrid capital market instruments (such as index bonds), etc.

The *seiho* have generally neglected the currency risk for investing long-run in the higher interest rates in the U.S. and for international diversification of their portfolios. The main reason is that their capacity to take large risks has come from the soaring prices of their accumulated real estate, stocks, and bonds in the domestic markets since 1985. Altman and Minowa (1989) discuss risks and returns from Japanese investment in high yield corporate (junk) bonds using futures hedging strategies. Obviously with so much at stake, strategies to protect this investment against unfavorable currency movements is of considerable interest.

HEDGING A U.S. STOCK PORTFOLIO AGAINST A POSSIBLE INCREASE IN THE VALUE OF THE YEN FOR A JAPANESE INVESTOR

To begin our discussion, let's consider the case of a Japanese individual or institutional investor with a U.S. denominated portfolio that is either owned or contemplated. To make the case simplest, suppose the investor has $10 million in yen or about 1271.5 million yen at the spot rate of 127.15¥/$ in late October 1988. It does not matter if the money is in dollars from earnings in the U.S., or in yen because this sum can be immediately converted at very low cost from one currency to the other.

Strategies for Making and Keeping Excess Profits in the Stock Market (Ziemba, 1991e) provides strategies and suggestions for investment in the U.S., so we will not discuss how to wisely invest there. Assume that you are about to purchase the $10 million in U.S. denominated stocks, bonds, and treasuries. How can you protect against the chance that the yen will keep rising and possibly go to 100 against the dollar?[2]

A hedge involves the purchase of yen futures to match the sale of yen on day 0 - the conversion day - into dollars and the sale of these futures on day τ - the day you sell all or part of your stock in dollars and convert it back into yen. On Thursday, October 20, 1988 the futures displayed in

---

[2]Most of this chapter was written in the fall of 1988 and the winter of 1989 when the yen was in the 125-130 range and many predicted that it would increase further due to the U.S twin trade and budget deficits. The fear then was about a ¥100 per dollar rate. In May 1990 the yen stood at 150-160 to the dollar, and further falls seemed possible. Hence, in recent times, hedging may not have been the best strategy *ex post*. At these and higher levels, it may soon be very wise again. The yen was about 135 in February 1991.

Table 6.1 were available. The spot price was 0.7865 U.S. dollars per 100 yen, or 127.15 yen per dollar. The futures price of the yen is such that it is expected that the dollar will fall more than one yen in each three month period. Over a twelve month period, the dollar will fall in the futures market hedge by about 4.75 Yen or about 3.75%. This difference is the amount that it must fall in the futures market to account for the difference in interest rates in Japan and the United States. For example, the U.S. discount rate in late October 1988 was 6.5%, and the Japanese was 2.5% for a 4% difference.[3] If the futures were not priced this way then risk-free arbitrage would be possible by buying dollars with borrowed yen and investing them in U.S. dollars at the higher interest rates, meanwhile guaranteeing no loss by selling these dollars at high rates in the futures market.

Table 6.1   October 20, 1988 Futures for Japanese Yen

JAPANESE YEN (MM) 12.5 million yen; $ per yen (.00)

	Open	High	Low	Settle	Change	Lifetime High	Low	Open Interest	Yen/ US$
Dec 78	.7931	.7948	.7908	.7911	+ .0013	.8530	.7115	46,621	126.41
Mar 89	.8007	.8019	.7981	.7982	+ .0013	.8590	.7439	2,094	125.28
June 89	.8093	.8096	.8065	.8065	+ .0013	.8400	.7500	785	123.99
Sept 89	.8150	.8180	.8145	.8140	+ .0014	.8180	.7690	174	122.85

Est Vol 28,556; vol Wed 27,380; open into 49,674, -1,104.

The point is that an investor will lose about 3.75% per year by using this type of hedge. One buys

$$\frac{\$10 \text{ million U.S.} \times 127.15 \text{¥}/\$}{12.5 \text{ million ¥}/\text{contract}} = 101.7$$

or about 102 futures contracts and sells them when the stock is sold and the proceeds are converted back into yen. Since the 101.7 is not exactly 102 and one may not get exactly the same selling price for the futures contract as the spot price equivalent, except on an exact delivery date (because the futures price involves expectations, the so called basis risk, as well as interest rate differentials) there may be some additional small costs or benefits from this transaction.

The percentage gain on the portfolio in yen will be approximately

[3]In February 1991, the U.S. discount rate was 6.5% and that in Japan 6.0% for a 0.5% difference.

$$(100 + \quad \begin{array}{c} \text{Rate of increase} \\ \text{in the portfolio in} \\ \text{U.S. dollars in percent} \end{array} \quad) \quad (0.9625) - 100.$$

So if the portfolio gains 25% in dollars it will gain only about 20% in yen. Hence a full 5% of the gain is lost just to manage the hedge. Can one avoid this loss? Yes, to some extent, but not without bearing some currency risk.

A PARTIAL HEDGE: THE BASIC IDEA

One way is to partially hedge by selling put options on the yen. The short position in puts is equivalent to a long position in yen that pays a premium. This strategy eliminates the 3.75% annual loss because the yen is projected to strengthen in the futures markets and indeed provides a similar premium. So instead of losing 3.75% per year you gain about 7.60% per year (using the data below). The actual premium depends upon the usual factors that affect option prices: current volatility, time to expiry, the difference between the current yen price and the nearest strike price, the interest rates, and current market expectations regarding the yen-dollar exchange rate.

But this gain does not come for free, because one is only partially protected against falls in the dollar, to the tune of 7.60% or 11.35% per year in comparison to the futures approach. The spot price was 78.65 U.S. cents per 100 yen on October 20, 1988. The options were priced as listed in Table 6.2. With options, one has many choices of how to do the partial hedge but let us sell December puts.[4] They are the most liquid and have about two months to expiry. Since the yen is expected to strengthen and the spot price is already 78.65 we can sell the 79 puts for about 1.00¢.

---

[4]We could buy calls, such as the 79's for 1.11 cents but that would get us back into the interest rate loss situation as in the futures markets at roughly similar costs. At-the money calls would eliminate the currency risks as the futures hedge did, and out-of-the-money puts would partially protect against large losses with lower costs.

Table 6.2   October 20, 1988 Options on Japanese Yen

Strike Price	Calls - Settle			Puts-Settle		
	Nov-c	Dec-c	Jan-c	Nov-p	Dec-p	Jan-p
77	2.15	2.43	----	0.06	0.34	0.42
78	1.27	1.70	2.46	0.17	0.61	0.67
79	0.60	1.11	----	0.48	1.00	----
80	0.22	0.69	1.29	1.09	1.57	----
81	0.07	0.41	0.90	----	2.27	----
82	0.02	0.23	0.60	----	3.09	----

Let's see how this works out. Assume that in the ensuing two months the portfolio, including dividends, goes up 3% - a roughly 20% yearly rate of return which is similar to the historical returns from the Topix or NSA. The investor will leave some of this stock as collateral for the margin required and invest the premium proceeds in T-bills and interest-bearing accounts with the brokerage firm to cover losses on the short calls.

The investor will collect the premiums which, when rolled over every few months, amount to roughly 7.6% per year and does not lose the 3.75% interest premium decay in the futures markets. So if the time horizon is long, say three years, then the investor has more than 25% to play with in possible drops in the dollar against the yen, in comparison with the futures hedge. So, assuming one rolls up and dynamically updates this hedge one is better off with the partial hedge over the three year horizon as long as the dollar stays above 95 yen.

It's not so simple, though, because whipsawing volatility is hazardous to this strategy. For example, when the dollar falls the investor loses all the gains in the yen above about 2/3% per month in premiums and about 1/3% per month from the interest rate differential. Also, the investor, protecting against falls in the dollar, does not participate in the gains in the dollar. So, if there are sharp falls, such as the five yen fall in Table 6.3, it will take a while to recoup the losses. However, the five yen fall or 4% in only two months still results in a gain of 1.42% on the partially hedged yen, which is less than 1% worse than the straight hedge.

This strategy is appropriate for a market with a yen that is slightly on the increase against the dollar. After the fall to the lower end of the Group of Seven target area for the yen of 120 to 140, this may not be too risky a strategy. At some stage, the already grossly over-valued yen in price-parity terms will, once the U.S. twin deficits are held in check, start falling and then one will want to participate in its rise more fully than one can with the covered call strategy. One can then simply go long in the stocks or protect the other way by selling yen futures option puts.

As with all option positions, they must be carefully monitored because sudden movements in the spot price are magnified in the options markets. Still, with proper management, the short-put partial hedge strategy with dynamic adjustments can provide a useful way to hedge against possible future dollar drops again the yen.

Table 6.3
Results of the Short Put, Partial Hedging Strategy on the U.S. Portfolio for a Japanese Investor, Gains and Losses in U.S. $ on December 1988 Expiry (Second Friday in December)

Day 0	Hedge Comparison	Dollar Remains Constant @ 127.15¥/$ or $0.7865/100¥	Dollar Rises 1.75¥ to 129¥/$ or $0.7750/100¥	Dollar Rises 5¥ to 132.15¥/$ or 79.90¢/100¥	Dollar Falls 2¥ to 125.15¥/$ or 79.90¢/100¥	Dollar Falls 5¥ to 122.15¥/$ or 81.87¢/100¥
Convert 127,150,000¥ into $10 mil US @ $0.7865/100 ¥ or 127.15¥/$	$300,000 (gains on stock with dividends less 0.625% loss on hedge or $62,500	$300,000 (gains on stock with dividends)	$300,000 (gains on stock with dividends)	$300,000 (gains on stock with dividends)	$300,000 (gains on stock with dividends)	$300,000 (gains on stock with dividends)
Sell 102 Dec 79 puts @ 1.00¢/100¥ Collect $125,000 less commissions of about $2040 (assuming $20/contract)		$122,800 (in premiums $1228 (interest on premiums at 6%/year	$122,800 (in premiums $1228 (interest on premiums at 6%/year	$122,800 (in premiums $1228 (interest on premiums at 6%/year	$122,800 (in premiums $1228 (interest on premiums at 6%/year	$122,800 (in premiums $1228 (interest on premiums at 6%/year
		-0, since short puts expired worthless	a loss of $161,400, short puts 0.0125¢ in the money, with commission	a loss of $426,595, short puts 0.0333¢ in the money, with commission	-0, since short puts expired worthless	-0, since short puts expired worthless
Total Gain is in	$$1237,500	$424,028	$262,628	($2567)	$424,028	$424,028
% Gain in $	2.38%	4.24%	2.63%	(0.026%)	4.24%	4.24%
% Gain in ¥	2.38%	4.24%	4.12%	3.91%	2.60%	1.4%

TESTING OUT THE PARTIAL HEDGE IDEA: JAPANESE INVESTMENT IN U.S. TREASURY BONDS[5]

The short put strategy discussed above is useful for an investor especially if the dollar does not fall too much. But it does not participate in possible rises in the dollar. We discuss some related strategies that do participate in dollar advances and limit the loss for yen gains. These strategies are then compared by simulation to ascertain how good they really are.

---

[5]Mr. H. Maruyama of the Yamaichi Research Institute assisted in this test by preforming the simulation calculations that follow.

First, let's look at the various strategies. For the context and calculations, we move to Wednesday, November 23, 1988, when the yen was trading at 82.41¢ per 100¥ or 121.34¥/$ near its low for the year. At this time, the U.S. interest rates had risen to protect the dollar so the spread in the futures markets was about $4\frac{1}{2}\%$ per year. Figure 6.1 compares the various strategies. In these graphs, the profits or losses from the option trading are kept separate from the asset returns. One may think of the underlying asset as being in U.S. currency with zero mean return and no variance. This simplifies these diagrams. The most risky strategy, called N and shown in Figure 6.1a is simply to not hedge at all. This, of course, is what is done most frequently by investors. By not hedging, one does not lose the roughly $4\frac{1}{2}\%$ annual futures discount; but, there is no protection if the yen rises. All gains in the dollar against the yen are captured. But, all losses from gains in the yen are lost. If the yen rises less than $4\frac{1}{2}\%$ per year, this strategy beats the hedge.

Figure 6.1b shows the futures hedge, called H. This strategy is essentially riskless. One receives the same return, a loss of about $-4\frac{1}{2}\%/12$ per month or about -0.75% over two months, namely -0.91¥ or 0.618¢ per 100¥.

Strategy 0, shown in Figure 6.1c is the short put partial hedge described in the previous section. This strategy is the next most risky procedure. The investor sells yen puts near the money. The investor collects the premium of say 7% per year and does not pay for the $4\frac{1}{2}\%$ discount. So if the yen rises less than $11\frac{1}{2}\%$ per year, this strategy provides higher mean returns than the futures hedge. This strategy does not participate in dollar gains. It is only protected against yen gains by the roughly $11\frac{1}{2}\%$ per year.

The five new strategies limit the down-side risk of yen rises and participate in dollar rises in various ways. Figure 6.1d describes strategy A1: Sell put near the money, buy put 2¢ out of the money. The related strategy was also tested, A2: Sell put near the money, buy put 3¢ out of the money.

These strategies are less risky than strategy 0. They participate in the dollar rise once it moves 2¢ or 3¢, respectively, but the protection against the yen's rise is limited to the premium. This strategy is the opposite of strategy C described below and has similar risk, assuming one worries about yen falls as well as rises. It is more risky against yen rises than C.

The net premiums collected are less, say 4-5% per year, than with strategy 0 because the deep out put must be purchased.[6]

Figure 6.1
The Various Hedging Strategies Compared, N, H, O, A, B and C

a: Case N: No Hedge

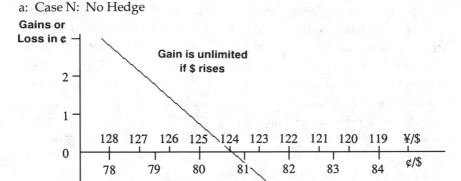

b: Case H: Futures Hedge

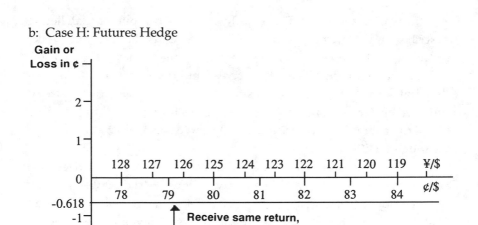

---

[6]Strategies like this would have worked well *ex post* during the dollar's rise in 1989 and 1990 while at the same time protecting against a sudden drop in the dollar.

c: Case O: The Partial Hedge with Put Sold Near Money, at 81¢/100¥

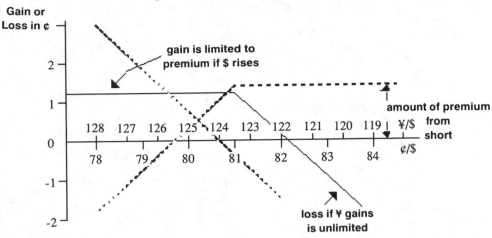

Gain or Loss in ¢

gain is limited to premium if $ rises

amount of premium from short

loss if ¥ gains is unlimited

d: Case A1: The Partial Hedge with Put Sold Near Money at 81¢/100¥ and Put Bought out of Money, at 79¢/100¥

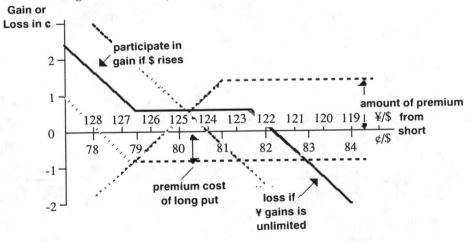

Gain or Loss in ¢

participate in gain if $ rises

amount of premium from short

premium cost of long put

loss if ¥ gains is unlimited

e: Case B1: The Partial Hedge with Put Sold Near Money, Put Bought 2¢
out of Money and Call Bought 2¢ Out of the Money

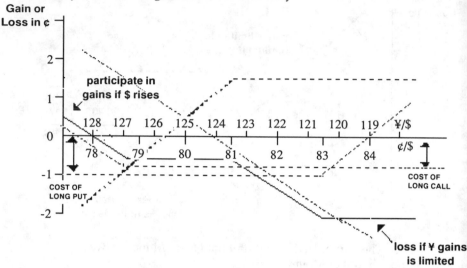

f: Case C: The Partial Hedge with Put Sold Near Money, at 81¢/100¥
and Call Bought Out of Money, at 83¢/100¥

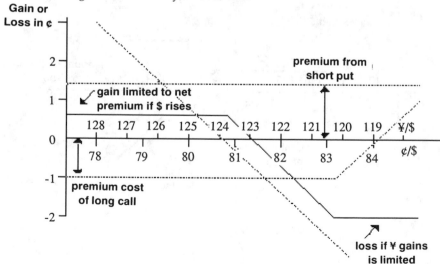

Figure 6.2   ¥/$ Exchange Rate, July 31, 1986 to January 19, 1989

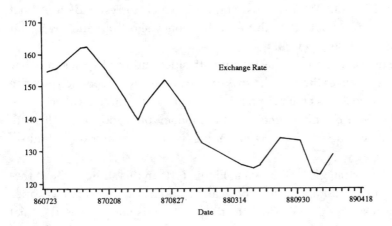

Figure 6.3
Results of Various Strategies, July 23, 1986 to January 19, 1989, U.S. T-Bonds Yielding 6.7% and a Reinvestment Rate of 6%

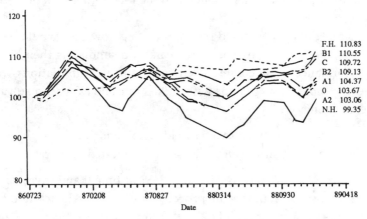

Strategies B1 and B2 are the least risky. B1, which is shown in Figure 6.1e, has the investor buy a call 2¢ out of the money in addition to strategy A1. So, the full position is to sell a put near the money, buy a put 2¢ out and a call 2¢ out. The related strategy B2, which corresponds to A2 but with the extra 2¢ out call with the at the money short put and the 3¢ out long put was tested as well.

The investor is now protected on both sides and participates in dollar rises once it moves through the strike price and the losses on the yen's rise are limited to 2¢ less the net premiums. The net premiums collected are from the short put minus the out of the money puts and calls. This will not be very much, maybe $\frac{1}{2}$% to 3% per year depending on volatility, execution, etc.

The final strategy, C is shown in Figure 6.1f. In this strategy the at-the-money put is sold and a deep out call is purchased. This is a cheaper strategy cost wise than B1 since the deep out put is not purchased. What one gains is to limit the maximum loss in any 2 month period if the yen rises sharply to a ¥2 change in the ¥/$ rate. So one has protection against the yen rising. But, one does not participate in dollar gains. The risk of this strategy is less than with A1. For this strategy, one collects less premium because a call is bought as well as the put sold. The options sold provide more money than those bought, so the total return is about 4-5% per year.

These strategies are compared by investigating how they would have performed in the previous two or more years, and simulating their likely future performance. The context used for the future simulations was investment in U.S. Treasury bonds with a fixed rate and a 3 year maturity. The specifics being:

Nov 1991 $8\frac{1}{2}$ Bid 98-02 Ask 98-06 yield 9.23%, and
coupons received on stream were assumed invested at 8% per year.

An amount ¥A=¥100 is converted into US$ at time 0 and invested in U.S. assets at time 0. At time τ the proceeds are converted back into ¥B. The data series used ran from July 23, 1986 to January 19, 1989. The test used a T-bond with a yield of 6.7% and it was assumed that the coupons were reinvested at 6%. This was a period of sharp increase for the yen, except during 1988. As shown in Figure 6.2, the yen started at about 154 and ended up about 128. The first year and a half the yen rose over 25% (154 → 120). Then it stayed in a volatile trading range of 120-135. With such a large gain in the yen, one would expect the futures hedge to work the best. It did, returning 110.83 without risk. Strategies B1, B2 and C were only about 1% behind, but they had more risk. The other strategies were 5-10% worse. Figure 6.3 shows the results.

The conclusion is: if the yen rises 15-20% in a year or so, the futures hedge will be the best strategy. One has to have the yen rise no more than say 10% per year for the other strategies to possibly be better. So, over three years, the rise in the yen must be less than, say, 30-35%. Given the dollar's sharp fall since 1985 a further 30% drop would take it under 90¥/$, an event that may or may not occur. Obviously, the yen cannot keep rising forever. Indeed, the dollar rose to the ¥150 level in 1989 and to ¥160 in April 1990 before it fell to the ¥125 to ¥135 range in late 1990 and early 1991. Hence, there may well be use for the partial hedge strategies that are now investigated with the simulation of possible futures for the ¥/$ exchange rate.

A Black-Scholes simulation shows how the strategies might do in various possible futures. The idea was to assume that the put and call prices were reasonably accurately estimated by their Black-Scholes options prices. Volatility was assumed to be 11.8%, which was that of 1988.[7] For interest rates we used 9% for the U.S. (the federal funds rate) and 3.9% for Japan (the call rate). The yen/dollar rate evolves day by day as[8]

$$(¥/\$)t+1 = (¥/\$)t \exp\left(-\frac{d}{252} + \sigma\delta\right)$$

d = the assumed yearly drift of the scenario over the 252 trading days

σ = the assumed volatility = 11.8% but double for the weeks with shocks

$\delta = \begin{cases} +1 \\ -1 \end{cases}$ for increases and decreases, the binominal model with drift.

The two month options are bought and sold at their Black Scholes prices and held to maturity when they either expire worthless or are covered at the then in-the-money price, assuming no bid-ask spread.

The following scenarios were tested:

---

[7]Constant volatility is a requirement of the Black-Scholes model inputs. Obviously, volatility is not constant, so this is simply a convenient simplification. There is much scope to consider alternative currency option pricing models here.

[8]This is a binomial currency change model. It was convenient to utilize when analyzing broad currency trends as we wished to do. There are alternative theories of currency movements, such as those based on the Fisher effect, purchasing power parity, and expectation theory, that could be utilized and compared as well.

1   The yen rises at 4% per year in each of the three years. This is roughly
    what the futures market expected (d=-0.04)

1' The same as 1, but every three months there is a shock and for one
    week the volatility doubles.

2   The yen has a zero (d=0) drift in the first year. In the second and third
    years the yen falls with a drift of 5% per year (d=0.05). This is a mildly
    stronger dollar scenario.

3   The yen drifts up 4% in year 1 (d=-0.04) but then the $ drifts up 15% in
    the second year (d=0.15) and 20% in the third year (d=0.20). This is the
    U.S. trade and budget improvement scenario moving close to price
    parity in 3 years.[9]

4   The yen drifts up 10% in the first year, 5% more in year 2 and 10%
    more in the third year. This is the hard landing scenario for the dollar
    with the $/¥ rate falling to less than 100.

These five scenarios seem to span the range of possibilities reasonably
well. There could be more violent moves in the market, but it seems
doubtful that the yen would fall much below 95-100 (scenario 4) or rise
much above about 165 (scenario 3). For some of the simulation outcomes,
the ¥/$ rate is outside these bands so we do have estimates of the strategic
performances of these cases are also available.

Observations
1   The mean yen/dollar rate was 120.4 with a minimum of 47.6 and a
    maximum of 254.1.

2   The future hedge returns 114.96 without risk.

3   The other strategies return more on average but they have more risk.
    Additional mean return is approximately linear in standard deviation
    risk with a slope of 0.334 units of mean return per unit of standard
    deviation. Figure 6.4 shows this tradeoff. B1 is slightly above the
    curve but more or less one gets what one pays for in a Markowitz
    mean-standard deviation sense. Another measure of risk is the lowest
    payoff. Figure 6.5 shows the minimum payoffs; the specific numbers
    appear in Table 6.4.

---

[9]This is the scenario that is closest to what has actually happened before the yen firmed
again in mid 1990.

Table 6.4
Summary of the 125 Simulation Runs, 25 per Scenarios Times 5 Scenarios for Each of the Eight Strategies, Both in Total and Individual

Variable Strategy	Sample Size	Mean Return	St Dev of Return	Min Return	Max Return	St Error of Mean Ret
Exchange Rate	125	120.42	37.46	47.60	254.08	3.35
N	125	128.29	39.91	50.71	270.67	3.57
H	125	114.96	0.00	114.96	114.96	0.00
O	125	120.24	22.13	60.01	170.47	1.92
A1	125	124.16	30.68	54.15	226.77	2.74
A2	125	122.48	27.35	55.21	205.31	2.45
B1	125	121.61	17.71	95.02	189.80	1.58
B2	125	120.12	14.31	97.66	171.69	1.28
C	125	118.53	8.06	102.24	148.48	0.72

Scenario	N	O	A1	A2	B1	B2	C
1	113.14	115.13	113.25	113.37	113.31	113.48	115.6
1'	114.05	111.69	113.29	112.50	117.44	116.68	116.7
2	140.96	129.18	135.11	132.46	126.46	124.05	121.1
3	173.92	138.57	157.25	151.22	143.36	137.88	126.3
4	99.37	106.61	101.88	102.88	107.44	108.53	113.0
Total	128.29	120.24	124.16	122.48	121.61	120.12	118.5

Scenario	STD N	STD O	STD A1	STD A2	STD B1	STD B2	STD C
1	25.69	18.79	22.07	20.48	10.10	8.31	6.12
1'	28.58	19.62	24.34	22.58	12.01	10.15	6.35
2	32.01	19.27	24.85	22.16	13.72	10.82	7.33
3	39.50	18.76	26.94	22.64	17.22	13.05	7.70
4	22.57	18.41	20.28	19.41	8.54	7.42	5.53
Total	39.91	22.13	30.68	27.35	17.71	14.31	8.06

The strategies N, O, A1 and A2 have very low minimum values. These are with very low dollar values. Assuming that the dollar cannot fall below ¥90 then the minimum values are (starting with 100 in year 0)

No Hedge	96
0	89
A1	99
A2	99

So, one could lose money with these strategies.

B1 and B1 and C have minimum payoffs of 95, 97 and 102, respectively, with all scenarios. With the yen no lower than 90, the minimum payoffs for these strategies are

B1	102	with ¥/$ at 93	¥/$ = 74 before loss of 5
B2	104	" at 94	¥/$ = 60 before loss of 2
C	105	" at 102	Never loses, its minimum is 102 when the exchange rate is 83¥/$

So C compares favorably with the hedge. Its mean is 3.5% higher. Its lowest return with yen at 92 is 105 versus the 115 with the futures hedge. Its standard deviation is low. Strategies B1 and B2 look promising as well. These strategies seem to promise a 2% minimum return per year and get more mean return 5.7% with B1 and 4.4% with B2 versus the futures hedge.

Table 6.5 gives the minimum returns for the various strategies given a variety of low final values for the dollar/yen exchange.

Figure 6.4
Mean-Standard Deviation Tradeoff of the Scenario Results for the Various Strategies

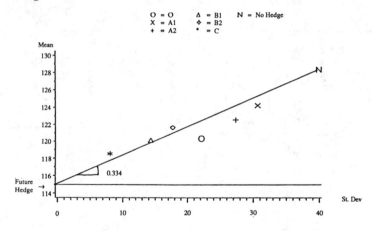

Figure 6.5
Mean-Standard Deviation Tradeoff plus Ranges of the Scenario Results for
the Various Strategies

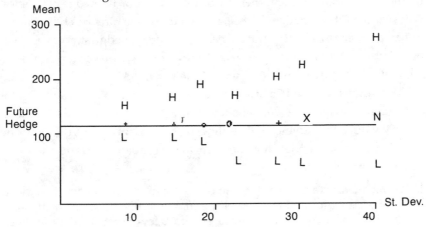

Table 6.5
Minimum Returns for the Various Strategies for Various Minimum
Final Values for the Dollar in Yen

Value of $ in ¥	NH	0	A1	A2	B1	B2	C	Futures Hedge
90+	96	89	99	99	102	104	105	115
95+	100	107	105	105	106	105	110	115
100+	106	108	109	110	108	112	112	115
105+	112	108	112	111	108	112	112	115
110+	117	101	115	113	108	110	111	115
115+	121	115	120	118	118	112	112	115
120+	127	126	126	124	119	117	118	115
125+	132	128	130	129	121	120	119	115
130+	138	132	139	137	126	126	119	115
135+	142	131	142	139	127	125	118	115
140+	147	130	138	138	130	130	121	115
145+	154	131	144	144	144	139	135	115
150+	159	148	145	144	125	123	127	115
160+	170	132	153	142	148	138	131	115
170+	176	150	168	159	140	132	123	115
Mean Returns	128	120	124	122	121	120	119	115

This study was oriented toward the concern that the yen would strengthen to provide poor returns on the investment. Should the dollar neither fall nor strengthen, then all of the partial or no hedge strategies will beat the futures hedge. Hence, at final exchange rates of ¥120+ for the dollar, one sees this effect. Not surprisingly, the no hedge strategy is then best, but the partial hedge strategies that were good protection against a fall in the dollar are pretty good should the yen fall.[10]

This simulation used 25 histories for each strategy. Each result is path dependent, the outcome depends upon how the yen/dollar rate reached its final value. For professional application one might do several things in addition to more model development and simulations to decide on a preferred strategy, such as:

1. Using a market maker, prices can be obtained that are better than those estimated from the Black-Scholes equations. One can sell at the ask and buy at the bid. This translates into a few percent over the three years.

2. These calculations use a 2 month rollover period with no dynamics. There is room for some improvement by altering slightly the strategy as the outcomes unfold. One also might be able to buy back shorts if prices are low and combine a little market timing on the margin.

3. The interest on the shorts is worth more than calculated here as are the coupons. The latter benefits the futures hedge as well. [11]

The analysis here and in most other literature assumes that stock prices and currency movements are uncorrelated. This is definitely not the case with the yen and Tokyo markets. Indeed, the Tokyo market generally reacts favorably to higher yen values and negatively to the reverse. This was especially true in the 1990 correction when the yen and the indices fell sharply, and then turned around together in late April and May. This relationship is not simple, however, during 1989, there was a sharp rise in the NSA coupled with a falling yen. It was higher interest

---

[10]The yen did in fact fall to the 150-160 range and the no hedge strategy did the best *ex post* returning 170 vs. 153 for strategy A1 and 176 versus 168 if the dollar rises past 170.

[11]More mathematical analyses emphasizing continuous time strategies using futures are discussed by Adler and Detemple (1988), Duffie and Jackson (1990), Duffie and Richardson (1989), Eaker and Grant (1987), Solnik (1989) Svensson (1988) and references therein. The goals of these authors differed from those here. We are searching for a way to minimize the effects of the deep futures discount on the yen, while they were more concerned with minimizing the variance of returns over time. See also Jorion (1989, 1990b), Stone and Hensel (1989), Pérold and Schulman (1988) and Thomas (1990).

rates that triggered the stock market fall in 1990. The point of this, for a complete analysis, is that one needs to consider the relationship between currency and stock price movements and their relationship with interest rates and other macro variables such as inflation.

HEDGING A JAPANESE PORTFOLIO AGAINST A POSSIBLE DROP IN THE VALUE OF THE YEN FOR A U.S. INVESTOR

This situation is the reverse of the previous case, except now the interest rate differential works in the investor's favor. Hence, the futures prices of the dollar are higher than the spot prices. In addition, because the dollar is expected to fall, the prices of the puts one would have to sell to produce the partial hedge are not as high as the calls. Hence, the futures hedge seems like the preferable way to protect against possible gains in the dollar. Let's look at it with some numbers.

Assume that U.S.$10 million has been invested in Japanese securities at the October 20, 1988 spot exchange rate of 78.65 cents per 100 yen or 127.15 ¥/$. The dollar can fall about 3.75% or about 4.75 yen to 122.40 ¥/$ before the advantage of the hedge ceases to give you an edge over the status quo considering a one year horizon.

The futures hedge allows one to change one's yen back into dollars at the currently favorable rate of 122.40 ¥/$. So one's U.S.$10 million is really worth $10,375,000 as long as the stock market performance in yen matches the performance in the U.S. stock market. This $375,000 edge provides a cushion for the yen tracking error risk as well as the market risk and transactions costs.

A short call partial hedge is illustrated in Table 6.6 and compared with the futures hedge. Assuming the stock portfolio plus dividends increases by 3% in the two month period from October 20, 1988, until the options expire on the third Friday in December, the hedge gains 3.63%; the 3% gain plus the two month bonus of 0.63% from the interest rate differential. If the exchange rate stays constant then the partial hedge returns 4.40% in yen as well as in dollars. One does not gain much extra with dollar falls because one has sold the calls short. The gains of 4.88% and 4.99% with dollar falls of 2 and 5 yen, respectively, differ slightly from the 4.40% of the constant exchange rate case because of transactions costs, the fact that the 102 short calls is not the exact cover for the partial hedge, and the basis difference beween the spot and strike prices of the options.

Table 6.6
Results of the Short Call, Partial Hedging Strategy on a Japanese Portfolio for a U.S. Investor, Gains and Losses in Yen on December 1988 Expiry (Second Friday in December)

Day 0	Hedge Comparison	Dollar Remains Constant at 127.15¥/$ or $0.7865/100¥	Dollar Rises 1.75¥ to 129¥/$ or $0.7750/100¥	Dollar Rises 5¥ to 132.15¥/$ or 79.90¢/100¥	Dollar Falls 2¥ to 125.15¥/$ or 79.90¢/100¥	Dollar Falls 5¥ to 122.15¥/$ or 81.87¢/100¥
Convert $10 million US into 127,150,000¥ @ $0.7865/100 ¥ or 127.15¥/$	3,814,500¥ (gains on stock with dividends) gain on hedge of 0.625% or 794,688¥	38,145,000¥	38,145,000¥	,145,000¥	38,145,000¥	38,145,000¥
Sell 102 Dec 79 calls @ 1.11¢/100¥ Collect $140,250 less commissions of $2040		$138,210 or 17,573,402¥	$138,210 or 17,573,402¥	$138,210 or 17,573,402¥	$138,210 or 17,573,402¥	$138,210 or 17,573,402¥
		-0, since short calls expired worthless	-0, since short calls expired worthless	-0, since short calls expired worthless	a loss of $116,790 or 14,849,849¥ short calls 0.009¢ in the money with commission	a loss of $367,965 or 44,946,625¥ short calls 0.0287¢ in the money with commission
Total Gain in $ % Gain in $ % Gain in ¥	46,091,880¥ 3.63% 3.63%	55,894,123¥ 4.40% 4.40%	55,894,123¥ 4.40% 2.90%	55,894,123¥ 4.40% 0.45%	41,041,274¥ 3.23% 4.88%	10,944,198¥ 0.86% 4.99%

The investor is pretty well fully protected on this side but does not participate in any further gains. When the dollar rises, the investor is only partially protected to the tune of the options premium; unlike the yen into dollars play, the investor does not gain the interest differential in comparison with the futures hedge. In addition, because the yen is projected to increase in value in the futures market, the calls are not as valuable to sell as the puts were. Still, our investor makes 2.90% when the dollar rises 1.75¥ ,and 0.45% when it rises 5¥ in this two month period. On balance the straight hedge seems preferable for this investor. The advantage of the essentially riskless 3.75% per year makes this strategy a hard one not to employ. The U.S. investor in Japan does not need to use the complicated strategies that the Japanese investor in the U.S. might wish to utilize.[12]

The Canadian investor, or those from England, France, Italy, Switzerland and other countries that have higher interest rates than in the

---

[12]In May 1990, this differential against the U.S. dollar was more on the order of 1% per year rather than the 3.75% it was in the fall of 1988 and in February 1991 it was slightly negative. Given this, one may wish to consider more risky strategies, such as those discussed above for Japanese investment in the U.S.

U.S., have even more advantages investing in Japan. Figure 6.6 shows this with four different approaches. In Figure 6.6a, the portfolio value in yen is displayed with a typical volatility pattern assuming an upward trend in prices. The portfolio value in Canadian dollars is much more volatile, as shown in Figure 6.6b. Huge jumps in value of the portfolio have occured often in these markets. For example, on Friday, May 11, 1990, the Canadian dollar fell 5 yen from 135 to 130. Since currency and stock price movements are highly correlated, one will have large moves in both directions from the trend line in yen. Figure 6.6c hedges the currency and the Canadian investor was able, as of October 1990, to eliminate the Canadian/yen risk and gain over 5% essentially risk free. Given this edge, the investor may well be wise to spend some of it on portfolio insurance protection through Nikkei put warrants or some other scheme. The situation is shown in Figure 6.6d where there is a floor on the minimum portfolio return that is above the nominal investment with a positive drift of 1-2% per year. Given the poor performance of Canadian portfolios and managers over the past twenty years, they would likely benefit from strategies like Figure 6.4d. The difference between hedged and unhedged returns is explored more fully after we discuss adjusting the amount of the hedge. The difference in interest rates closed up sharply from October 1990 to February 1991.

ADJUSTING THE AMOUNT OF THE HEDGE

The U.S. investor in Japan does need to adjust the number of contracts in the hedge as the portfolio of Japanese stocks varies in value. Since each yen currency contract is for ¥12.5 million, the number of contracts required to hedge the position when the currency is exchanged is

$$\text{int}\left[\frac{S_0 A}{\text{¥}12.5\text{M per contract}}\right] = c_0$$

where S_0 is the current spot exchange rate, say ¥140/\$, A is the investment, say \$10 milion, and int means that one takes the largest integer that is less than the quantity in the brackets. With these data, $c_0 = 112$ contracts exactly; but, usually one will have to round down so as not to over hedge. To update the hedge, one simply keeps the number of contracts sold on day t equal to

$$\text{int}\left[\frac{S_t A(1+r_t)}{\text{¥12.5M per contract}}\right] = c_0$$

where S_t is the yen/dollar spot exchange rate on day t and r_t is the gross rate of return on the portfolio from the start up to day t.

So if S_t is 150 and $r_t=16\%$ then

$$\text{int}\left[\frac{150(10 \text{ million})(1.16)}{\text{¥12.5 million}}\right] = \text{int}(139.2)=139.$$

Hence, one needs 27 more contracts. This day-by-day adjustment procedure works well in general. Problems can arise from basis risk when the futures gets out of whack with the spot rate or when there is a sharp move in stock or currency values. The former rarely amounts to more than one half yen so the tracking error is less than 0.5% which is small in comparison with the interest differential futures discount gain. The latter, a sharp move in the stock portfolio value or the yen/dollar rate, can cause hedging losses. Like portfolio insurance strategies used in the October 1987 stock market crash, one must dynamically adjust in a continuous fashion. Since one is not dealing with stock futures premiums that can get 5% or more out of whack with the cash indices but with currency futures, the risk from the potential basis change does not seem that great.

HEDGED AND UNHEDGED RETURNS[13]

The mean return from hedged and unhedged returns is the same for an investment from one country to another as long as the returns from investments and from currency changes are uncorrelated. The difference in actual returns is then equal to this mean return plus the return in the local currency plus the currency surprise. This is shown as follows. Let

r_u = the unhedged return

r_h = the hedged return

r_c = the currency return

r_e = the return in the local currency

S_t = the spot currency exchange rate to change local into foreign returns

F_t = the forward/futures rate local to foreign currencies

V_t = the asset values in the local currency

---

[13]Thanks to Andy Turner for his help on this section.

$$1 + r_u = \frac{S_t V_t}{S_{t-1} V_{t-1}} = \left(\frac{S_t}{S_{t-1}}\right)\left(\frac{V_t}{V_{t-1}}\right) = (1+r_c)(1+r_e)$$

$$1+r_h = \frac{F_t V_{t-1} + (V_t - V_{t-1}) S_t}{S_{t-1} \; V_{t-1}}$$

$$= \frac{(F_t - S_{t-1}) V_{t-1} - (S_t - S_{t-1}) V_{t-1} + S_t V_t}{S_{t-1} \; V_{t-1}}$$

$$= 1+r_e + \underbrace{\left(\frac{F_t - S_{t-1}}{S_{t-1}}\right)}_{p} - \underbrace{\left(\frac{S_t - S_{t-1}}{S_{t-1}}\right)}_{r_c} .$$

The actual return of the hedged portfolio equals that of the unhedged portfolio plus the futures hedge premium p minus the currency return. If we let $\varepsilon = r_c - p$, then the return of the hedged portfolio equals that of the unhedged portfolio plus the currency surprise ε. Taking expectations yields

$$E(r_h) = E(r_u) + E(\varepsilon) = E(r_u)$$

since currency surprise has mean zero.

In terms of local returns and currency returns, one has

$$1+ r_h \;\; = \;\; 1+ r_u - \varepsilon \;\; = \;\; (1 + r_c)(1+r_e) -\varepsilon \;\; = \;\; 1 + r_e + r_c + r_c r_e -\varepsilon$$

So. $\;\; r_h \;\; = \;\; r_e + p + r_c r_e$ and $E(r_h = E(r_e) + p + cov(r_c, r_e)$.
If $Cov(r_c, r_e) = \;\; 0$, then $E(r_h) = E(r_e) + p = E(r_u)$.

In practice, the currency returns and the local returns have low correlation,[14] so the expected hedged return equals the expected local return plus the futures hedge premium.

---

[14]This assumption, as discussed above, is not particularly valid for Japan.

Figure 6.6   Typical Portfolio Values in Yen and Dollars Over Time

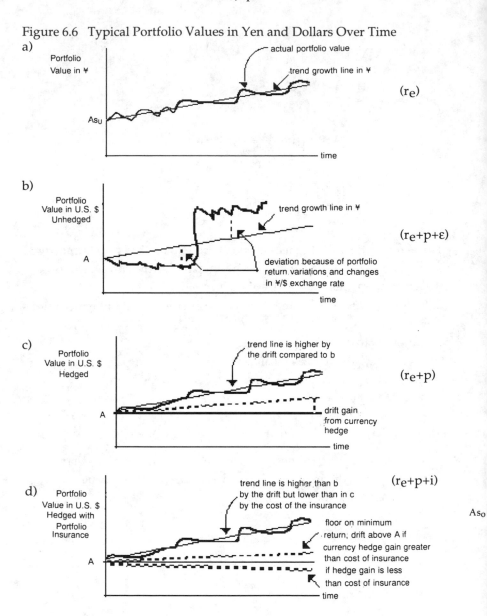

a)
Portfolio Value in ¥

actual portfolio value

trend growth line in ¥

(r_e)

As$_U$

time

b)
Portfolio Value in U.S. $ Unhedged

trend growth line in ¥

$(r_e+p+\varepsilon)$

A

deviation because of portfolio return variations and changes in ¥/$ exchange rate

time

c)
Portfolio Value in U.S. $ Hedged

trend line is higher by the drift compared to b

(r_e+p)

A

drift gain from currency hedge

time

d)
Portfolio Value in U.S. $ Hedged with Portfolio Insurance

(r_e+p+i)

trend line is higher than b by the drift but lower than in c by the cost of the insurance

As$_0$

floor on minimum return; drift above A if currency hedge gain greater than cost of insurance

A

if hedge gain is less than cost of insurance

time

Figure 6.6 shows the typical behavior of the various portfolios for a Canadian investor. For a U.S. investor, the situation is similar except that the drift in Figure 6.6 is about 1% and the floor in Figure 6.6d has a slight negative drift of 1-2% per year.[15] The return in local currency r_e shown in (a) has the same volatility as the hedged portfolio (b), namely $\sigma(r_e)$. The hedged portfolio has return r_e+p with volatility $\sigma(r_e)$. The unhedged portfolio has return $r_e+p+\varepsilon$ which has the same mean return as the hedged portfolio but higher volatility assuming $\sigma^2(\varepsilon)$ is positive but $\text{cov}(r_e,\varepsilon) = \text{cov}(r_e,r_c) = 0$.

---

[15]In December 1990, the Cdn$/yen futures was at a discount of about 4.5% per year. Hence, an the investor could hedge currency and stock price level risks and still have a floor well above zero since long term NSA put warrants had costs that were much less than this per year. By February 1991, this discount was only about 2.5%. For U.S. investors, the currency difference was actually slightly negative. Hence, the floor is slightly below A.

CHAPTER 7
RISKS FOR THE STOCK MARKET

I have been hearing warnings of impending disaster for the last twenty years. Although almost consistently wrong, the spokesmen argue that their contention is correct, but their timing is premature. Paul Aron[1]

The volume of funds flowing around the world for speculative transactions is more than 10 times the volume of international trade.

The Japanese have taken a large risk by allowing their land prices to reach totally astronomical levels. Hence most of their wealth is in land and corporations whose main assets are land and stock in corporations owning more land. Despite their recent diversification into stock, bonds and property abroad, the vast majority of their wealth is indeed the land that they started with. Should these land values ever collapse, the Japanese stock market and many other markets in the world would be profoundly affected.

THE TWENTY-TWO CORRECTIONS, 1949-1990

Where is the Japanese market headed? Will it crash again as countless North American observers believe?

Most North American investment analysts and casual observers of the stock market argue that the Japanese stock market is overvalued. They cite the extraordinarily high PERs and see a crash as inevitable.[2] It's not whether or not the market will crash, but when. As we were leaving Vancouver to go to Japan in July 1988, Ziemba remarked to a colleague, a senior finance researcher, that he would be studying the market in Japan to investigate when it would peak out and when and if it might crash. He remarked, "I'm sure we have already seen the peak." But in mid-November 1988, the NSA had six consecutive days of gains and was at a record high in excess of 29,000. Many analysts saw 30,000 as a virtual

---

[1] Aron (1988a).

[2] Indeed in 1986 alone they doubled from about 30 to about 60 versus 12-18 for the U.S. market. NTT, the most highly capitalized stock in the world, joined the first section in 1987 with a PER of an astounding 285. Other stocks have even higher PERs.

certainty and 32,000 as plausible soon. With low interest rates, low oil prices, a strong yen, high confidence in the economy, and rather bleak prospects in the United States, Japanese investors would rather invested in themselves. Hence, there was strong upward pressure on the market. Also with January right around the corner, it would not have been surprising if the NSA had risen to this range. This turned out to be what happened and the market rose well above 32,000 in 1989. At the end of December 1989, the NSA was 38,915.87. This was its peak for the year, and was the second year in a row that the peak for the year occurred on the final trading day of that year.

So will there be another crash, and when? The NSA rose from 176.21 on May 16, 1949 to 29,180.20 at the close on Friday, November 18, 1988, a gain of an amazing 165.6 times. This is the gain in yen without dividends or taxes. The yen was at 360 to the U.S. dollar in 1949, and on November 18, 1988 it was 122.4 per dollar; the gain in U.S. dollars was a staggering 487.06 times! At the end of 1989, the gain was 220.84 times in yen and 553.04 times in dollars when the NSA closed at its record 38,916. In 1949, a \$10,000 bet that Japan would come back from its wartime devastation would then have been worth well over \$5 million. You could not buy much land in Tokyo with this because, as we saw earlier, those prices have been in a lock step movement with the NSA. But it sure would have been a handsome sum if you live elsewhere or you are happy as a renter.

Despite this phenomenal growth, the rise has not been straight up. At dinner at the Q group meetings in Tokyo in November 1988, Ziemba asked one of America's most distinguished finance experts, who was doing research on the Japanese market the following question: How many market corrections do you think Japan has had over 20% and over 10% since 1949? He replied, three and seven, respectively. What's your answer?

Surprisingly, there have been ten times when the market fell by 20% or more, and twenty times when a correction of 10% or more occurred up to the end of 1989. These are listed in Table 2.7 along with a discussion of some plausible causes of and details about the various declines. The 21st and 22nd corrections in 1990 are discussed after we look at the relevance of some U.S. market research.[3]

MARKET TIMING: THE U.S. LESSONS[4]

Market timing is very difficult. The majority of successful investment advisors simply do not try to time the market. They buy, hold, and switch stocks that have better value, such as those with low PERs, or concentrate on anomalous prospects, such as small stocks in January. This is the style Peter Lynch used to run Fidelity Magellan, the largest U.S. mutual fund, and one of the most successful. As described in his book, which we heartily recommend, Lynch (1989) suggests that a concentration on companies making good products that people want to buy, will reap gains over the long haul well above market index gains. Lynch argues, as we do, that with a sound approach through either fundamentals, under-valuation or anomalies, the small investor can do just as well or better than the average professional and need not be intimidated by the ups and downs of the market caused by temporary aberrations. Once transactions costs are considered, most market timers simply cannot do better than chance. Only about 25% to 40% of professional portfolio managers in the U.S. and Japan beat the S&P 500, NSA or Topix indices. This is the same across the world. An example of this is the record of 148 fund managers in Hong Kong in 1988 who were investing in various parts of the world. Less than 30% of those managers actually beat their benchmark indices, see Table 2.43.

One very successful market timer in the U.S. is Martin Zweig, and we strongly endorse and recommend his useful book, Zweig (1986), and his advisory services and newsletters. Among other things, a $20 investment in his book would have kept investors out of the October 1987 crash. Zweig observed that three conditions seem to signal impending crashes in the U.S. stock market: extreme deflation, very high PERs, and an inverted yield curve, see Table 7.1. Table 7.2 indicates that each of the fourteen bear markets in the U.S. from 1919 to 1990 had at least one of these

---

[3]The October 1987 world wide crash is discussed in Roll (1988) and Ziemba (1991e).

[4]See also the section in Chapter 5 on a bond and stock yield differential valuation model for detecting overpriced markets.

conditions. We added the 1987 crash to Zweig's table as the fifteenth crash because it qualifies via its high PERs.

Table 7.1   Zweig's Three Bear Market Signals

Signal	Usual Range	Bear Market Signal	Synopsis
Extreme deflation; Producer (wholesale) price index declines; annualized drop averaged over six months is high.	Usually PPI is rising	Six month annualized average is -10% or less.	Economy in bad trouble. Prices have to be cut to stimulate demand.
High PERs	10 to 14	S&P PER 18 or higher; or DJIA at 20 or higher.	Overvaluation of stocks is caused by excessive speculation.
Inverted yield curve	Long-term interest rates exceed short-term rates by 2 to 4%.	Moody's six month Commercial papers exceed Moody's Corporate Bond Rate.	Short-term interest rates are rising rapidly as the Federal Reserve is tightening. Bonds are less risky because rates are peaking. They are now cheap.

The declines are more severe when two of the signals are present, as in 1966, 1969-70, and 1973-74. All three signals have been present only once. That was during the great crash of 1929-32 when the market fell an amazing 89.2%! Zweig concludes:

> There is no guarantee that a bear market will begin when one of the three extremely bearish market conditions is first present. But the longer such a condition persists, or the more severe it becomes, or when a second or third negative condition joins the first, the odds of a bear market become overwhelming. On the other hand, should the major averages experience a decline of, say, 10% or more with none of these three negative conditions present, the odds of that decline's becoming a major bear market are quite small.

So if the background environment is reasonably sound, that is, there is no extreme deflation, PERs are normal, and there is a positive yield curve, then a decline of 10% sets in motion a buying opportunity with overwhelming odds that you will not lose more than 5% before the market begins to rally once more.

Table 7.2   Fifteen Bear Markets in the U.S. during 1919-1990

Bear Markets	Extreme Deflation	Very High PER	Inverted Yield Curve	% Decline in DJIA
1919-21	Yes	No	Yes	-47.6
1923	No	No	Yes	-18.6
1929-32	Yes	Yes	Yes	-89.2
1933	Yes	No	No	-37.2
1937-38	Yes	No	No	-49.1
1938-42	No	Yes	No	-41.3
1946-49	No	Yes	No	-24.0
1056-57	No	No	Yes	-19.4
1962	No	Yes	No	-27.1
1966	No	Yes	Yes	-25.2
1969-70	No	Yes	Yes	-36.1
1973-74	No	Yes	Yes	-45.1
1978-80	No	No	Yes	-16.4
1981-82	No	No	Yes	-24.1
1987	No	Yes	No	-30.5
Average				-35.3%

Source: Updated from Zweig (1986)

THE DECLINE OF 1990

The Japanese stock market as measured by the NSA peaked at ¥38,915.87 at the end of December 1989. This was an all time high, up 29.0% in 1989 and 220.84 times since 1949. Late in 1989, there were three increases in the discount rate from 2.5% to 3.25 and then to 3.75 and 4.25%. Interest rates were increased in an attempt to dampen inflation and to protect the weak yen. Japanese interest rates had remained artificially low out of deference to the U.S. to strengthen the dollar and improve the bilateral trade balance. As Japanese inflation began to increase, initially largely because of the April 1989 3% consumption tax, various interest rates rose as well. Deregulaton also had a considerable impacts. Rates on postal savings and other accounts rose, which increased the cost of money to the government for public works. The postal savings accounts were no longer tax exempt. Up to that time nearly 70% of all the savings in Japan were in tax exempt accounts, according to the Japan Securities Research Institute. These increases led to the eventual hikes of the central bank rate by the Bank of Japan. The weakness in the yen was caused by a number of factors coming together at the same time:

1. A continual badgering of Japan by U.S. politicians and press regarding so called unfair trade practices. While it is certainly more difficult to export to Japan than to the U.S., the real culprit was the insatiable U.S. appetite to consume more than they produced as well as the desire for superior goods from Japan and West Germany.

2. A dramatic rise in investment abroad by Japanese financial institutions in the U.S., Canada, Australia, Europe and especially Germany and Eastern Europe. These purchases meant there was a huge demand in Japan for foreign currency, especially dollars and marks, at the expense of the high priced yen. These financial institutions were investing abroad because they could not find as good investments in Japan, and they also wished to diversify their holdings both in terms of locality and currency risk.

3. Continual infighting in the LDP, where the party could not agree to support Prime Minister Kaifu , and infighting between the Ministry of Finance, which wanted lower interest rates to protect the economy and stock markets, and the Bank of Japan, which wanted higher interest rates to control inflation which had already risen from the 1% range to nearly 3% and was threatening to go higher.

4. A mounting set of troubles in the world leading people to believe that dollars were the safest haven for their investments.

In early January 1990, in a very strong seasonal period, the stock market began to weaken. The fall in January was 4.5%. This is not large by absolute standards, but relative to historical norms it represented a substantial weakness in the market. That the market failed to rally at the start of the year with huge bonus sums available, was a strong negative signal to market watchers. The crisis deepened, and the declines in February and March, 6.2% and 14.1%, respectively, were even larger. Table 7.3 shows the decline in these three months.

Table 7.3   Declines on the NSA in early 1990

Month	Start	End	Decline	Cumulative
Jan	38916	37189	-4.5%	-4.5%
Feb	37189	34189	-6.2%	-10.6%
Mar	34891	29980	-14.1%	-23.0%

The decline in Japan in the first quarter was about 25.5%, the largest drop in local currency of the twenty stock markets listed in Table 7.4.

Table 7.4
First Quarter of 1990 Performance of Twenty Stock Markets in Local Currency

Country	% Increase	Country	% Decrease
Austria	46.0	France	-3.0
Norway	18.9	Italy	-3.1
W. Germany	10.7	Netherlands	-3.1
Hong Kong	6.0	U.S.	-3.7
Denmark	5.8	Finland	-5.0
Singapore	1.4	Switzerland	-6.3
		Australia	-6.5
		Belgium	-6.8
		Britain	-7.4
		Canada	-7.8
		Sweden	-10.0
		New Zealand	-13.8
		Spain	-17.4
		Japan	-25.5

Source: Morgan Stanley Capital International Perspective

The LDP was reelected February 18, 1990, with a reasonably strong mandate given the fractionalism in the LDP and their recruit and other troubles. Still the market and yen continued to slide. Interest rates were raised again after unprecedented fighting between the Bank of Japan and the Ministry of Finance. The discount rate rose a full 1% to 5.25% on March 20, 1990 its highest level since 1986.

There are several explanations one can give for the January to April 1990 correction, which is the 21st decline of at least 10% since 1949. Let us loosely list them:

1. The market was simply overvalued in PER terms and it needed to return to more typical historical levels in Japan.

2. When one properly readjusts Japanese PERs to make them comparable to U.S. PERs, and capitalizes both of these to reflect current interest rates and required rates of return from alternative investments, the resulting PERs were extremely high in December 1989 and prices simply had to fall back in line.

3. Reasons (1) and (2) started the decline, and then sellers of NSA put warrants in the U.S., Canada and Europe and other traders used various forms of programmed trading to exacerbate the decline. The sheer size of this market and the low trading volumes in Tokyo made the warrant portfolio hedge adjustments the *portfolio insurance* of 1990. The resulting cheap futures then led to arbitrage trading and lowered the stock prices even more. Meanwhile, the large Japanese firms showed themselves quite naive in letting a handful of not that highly

capitalized foreign firms make devastating moves in the Japanese stock market. All the while, the foreign firms were making large sums, and Japanese financial institutions were piling up enormous paper and real losses.[5]

This latter point is one of the major new activities that resulted from the financial deregulation and globalization of the Japanese economy. This changing structure of the Japanese markets took control away from the big four and other major players inside Japan and provided easy access and influence on the markets via derivative instruments, many of which were not traded in Japan and the Japanese were barred from trading them.

Before we go into these effects more carefully let us record and recall some useful data. Figures 7.1 and 7.4ab shows the day-by-day movements in the NSA for all of 1990 and January and February 1991. The day-by-day data appear in Table F-1 in the appendix. The 21st correction had a high close of 38,916 on December 29, 1989, and a low close of 28,002 on April 2, 1990, for a fall of 28.04%. The market moved lower during April 3 and 5, touching a low of 27,251 on April 5, down 29.97% and then the market turned around. It then rose to 15.9% to 33,293 on July 17, 1990. The market then began a second decline in 1990, the 22nd correction, which bottomed out on October 1, 1990, at 20,222, a decline of 39.3. This decline began prior to the August 2 Iraqi invasion of Kuwait and ended prior to the resolution of this crisis on January 16, 1991. This decline ended with panic selling in October 1 followed by credit easing and a thaw in the oil crisis which led to a dramatic 2675 or 13.2% increase in the NSA on October 2nd.

---

[5]The extent of the losses by major brokerage firms will not be known for some time. As of mid April, 1990, the Japanese securities firms were believed to have lost about $250 million U.S. from customers who placed large orders to buy stocks and were unable to pay for them. The largest reported loss from a single customer was by Yamaichi. The customer, a speculator, placed an order for several million shares of Nippon Seisen, Japan's largest maker of stainless steel rods. When he failed to pay for the shares, Yamaichi's loss was a staggering ¥7 billion about $45 million U.S.

To support the market, the big Japanese firms often took to bidding up the futures to premiums above fair value. This was easier to do than to buy stocks or to try to convince customers to buy. The market was then set up for profitable index arbitrage trading by the foreign brokerage firms. This raised stock prices but the main profits went to foreign firms.

Table 7.5 shows the number of large (±500 and ±350) moves by month in 1990 and 1991. One sees how the correction's character changed as the number of big moves shifted from more declines to more and more increases in April, signaling the decline was close to being over. We had a similar effect in the 22nd correction with eleven declines of at least 500 points on the NSA in August. Figure 7.2a shows the interest rate movements in 1989, 1990 to February 1991 in Japan, and Figure 7.2b compares interest rates in Japan, the U.S. and West Germany from 1988 to 1990. Figure 7.2c has the Japanese short and long term prime rates in 1989 and 1990. Figure 7.2d has government bond yield curves for the U.S., Japan, Britain, Germany and France by term to maturity for July 1990 and January 1991. Figure 7.3 has the yen dollar exchange rate for U.S. and Canadian funds.

Table 7.5   Number of Large (±500) Moves by Month in 1990 and 1991

Month	Number of Large Moves			
	≥500	≤-500	≥350	≤-350
January	0	3	2	5
February	2	3	3	4
March	2	7	2	9
April	5	3	5	4
May	3	0	7	1
June	1	1	2	4
July	4	4	4	6
August	5	11	7	11
September	2	5	2	9
October	6	3	8	4
November	1	3	2	7
December	2	2	4	3
January	1	2	2	3
February	3	0	3	0

In February of 1991, the U.S. discount rate was lowered 0.5% to 6.5%. Table 2.7 gives data on the previous twenty corrections which have averaged a fall of (22.6%) over 6.5 months. The last decline of the magnitude of the 21st correction was the 1973/74 oil crisis, when the price of oil quickly quintupled. The level of this correction and its length pointed dramatically to a need to restructure the Japanese economy to confront high inflation and high interest rates. The 22nd correction had an even steeper fall; the largest since the 51.8% decline in 1949/50. The total decline in 1990 was 14,864.17 NSA points or 38.4%. Let's now look at the reasons for the declines in turn.

Figure 7.1   The NSA in 1989 and the First Quarter of 1990

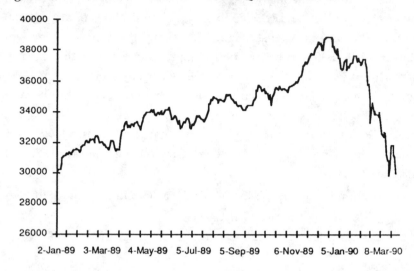

Figure 7.2a   Interest Rates in Japan in 1989, and 1990 to February 1991

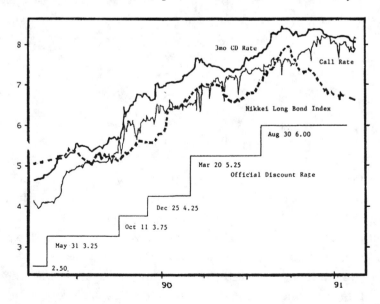

Source: Yamaichi Securities

Figure 7.2b Official Discount Rates, U.S., Germany and Japan , 1988-1990

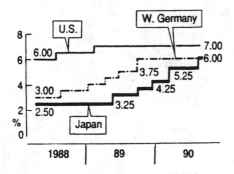

Source: Gordon Capital Corporation

Figure 7.2c   Long and Short Term Prime Rates in Japan, 1989-1990

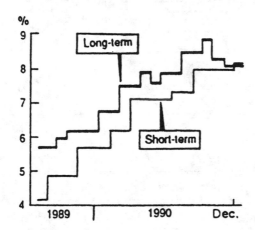

Source: *Japan Economic Journal*

Figure 7.2d
Government Bond Yields for the U.S., Japan, Britain, Germany and France
by Term to Maturity for July 1990 and January 1991

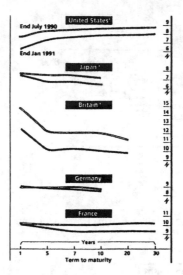

Source: *The Economist*

Figure 7.3   Yen versus U.S. and Canadian Dollars, 1989 to 1991 (February)

Source: Gordon Capital

Figure 7.4a
NSA Day-by-Day from December 1, 1989 to February 28, 1991

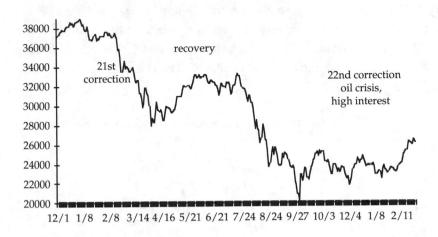

Source: Reuters Historical Information

Figure 7.4b
Changes in the NSA from December 1, 1989 to February 28, 1991

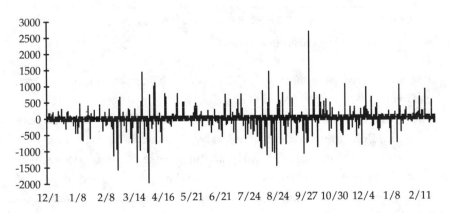

Source: Reuters Historical Information

Reason 1: the PERs were too high and had to correct to more historical norms.
Figure 7.4c shows the PERs of Japan over time. There had been a gradual increase in these PERs and then a dramatic increase in 1986. The line

drawn in Figure 7.4c projects the 1974-85 growth rate onto the 1986-1990 values. Despite the positive trend of PERs, 14.7 in 1974 to 26.6 in 1985, the 1986-89 values were way above this trend. For the end of 1989 PER to drop to the historical norm as measured by this increasing trend, the PER would need to fall from 57.1 to 30.6, or a drop of 46.4%. The NSA's 38,916 at the end of 1989 would then fall to 20,858. The low close on October 1, 1990, was 20,222.

Figure 7.4c   PERs of Japan, United States, Canada and United Kingdom

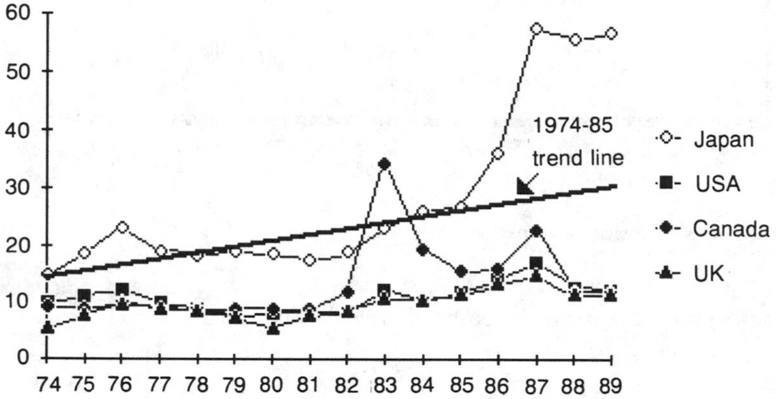

Source: Morgan Stanley Capital International

Reason 2: the properly adjusted PERs were too high given the new interest rates and had to correct to more historical norms.

Paul Aron, chairman emeritus of Daiwa Securities in New York, has been adjusting PERs to make them comparable to those in the U.S. since 1981. Although controversial and fairly ad hoc, these methods do seem to provide numbers that make sense and have been good inputs to investment decision making. In Chapter 5 we discussed technique, criticisms and alternative approaches. Table 7.6 shows some of Aron's calculations plus additional ones we made for the end of December 1989, March, June, September, October 1 and 2, the end of December 1990 and the end of February 1991.[6] The boxed values point to overvalued markets. As of early October 1990, the market moved out of the danger zone and it

---

[6]See Aron (1990) for his latest calculations as of August 1990.

was not overvalued. The close on October 1, with an adjusted PER of 13.5, was a strong buy signal.

Table 7.6
Paul Aron's Adjusted PERs for Japan Compared with those in the U.S., April 26, 1981, to August 31, 1989 with Adjustments for End of December 1989 and March, June, September, October 2 and December 1990

Date	U.S. PER	Japan, adj PER	NSA
Apr 26, 1981	9.1	4.0	7548
Oct 19, 1984	10.0	11.5	10929
Apr 17, 1986	13.7	13.5	15827
May 26, 1987	17.4	17.4	24533
Sept 11, 1987	20.3	18.1	24829
Dec 31, 1987	14.4	14.5	21533
May 31, 1988	13.1	15.4	26963
Aug 30, 1988	11.3	15.5	27679
Aug 31, 1989	13.5	17.5	34808
Dec 31, 1989	13.5	23.9	38915
Mar 30, 1990	15.5	19.7	29980
Jun 29, 1990	17.0	19.8	31940
Sept 30, 1990	13.6	15.2	20983
Oct 1, 1990	14.3	13.5	20022
Oct 2, 1990	14.3	15.4	22896
Dec 31, 1990	13.6	14.8	23849
Feb 28, 1991	16.2	15.2	26409

The □s indicate very overvalued periods and the Os undervalued periods. October 1, 1990, is signalled as a major low and was a strong buy signal.

The values since August 31, 1989, use the following assumptions.

	Interest		Earnings Gain
	U.S	Japan	over August 89
Dec 1989	8.2	6.4	5%
Mar 1990	8.4	7.4	10%
June 1990	8.2	7.0	12%
Sept 1990	8.2	7.75	8%
Oct 1, 1990	8.1	7.5	7.5%
Oct 2, 1990	8.1	7.5	8%
Dec 30, 1990	7.6	6.5	8%
Feb 28, 1991	7.6	6.0	8%

Hence, the adjusted PER at the end of December 1989 was in the 23.9 range when the NSA was 38,916. Even after the fall to 29,980 at the end of March 1990 assuming an earnings increase of 5% in 1990, the adjusted

PER was still about 19.7. Then, with a slight decrease in interest rates and small increase in earnings, the rise from 29,980 at the end of March 1990 to 31,940 at the end of June 1990 resulted in an increase in the market's adjusted PER to 19.9. Thus the market in June 1990 was still pricey and vulnerable should interest rates rise again or business conditions falter. If these interest rates remain at these high levels and earnings are flat, the market would have to fall a further 24% to the 23,000 level for the PER to be about 15, the recent historical range for a healthy market.

Reason 3: NSA put hedging and arbitrage trading exacerbated the decline.
The decline has also been compounded by the widespread purchase of Nikkei put warrants in the U.S., Canada and Europe. We have seen many days when the Tokyo market behaved like the U.S. market in 1986 and 1987 when portfolio insurance and widespread use of arbitrage trading were prevalent.

There are now six Nikkei put warrants trading in Toronto, four more on the American stock exchange, and many others in London. Many private puts are also in this market across the world. These puts are discussed in Ziemba and Schwartz (1992). The delta neutral hedging required to keep positions in balance for the backers of these instruments during a falling market has led to much downward pressure on the Tokyo stock market. Given that about 71% of shares are held by non-traders, the volume is low in any event. The big four and other major brokers have been largely on the sidelines, while foreign firms have exacerbated the decline with two forms of programmed trading. The scenario starts with an initial fall in the spot or futures market, followed hedging of the Nikkei puts, which drives the futures lower. Then the arbitrage traders buy the cheaper futures and sell the stocks. So one has a double whammy. The magnitudes of the declines are much larger because of the low volumes. Hence, we have a virtual repeat of the October 1987 activities in the U.S. except that it is occurring over a longer time.

There was about $90 billion of index futures portfolio insurance in place in October 1987 in the U.S. On a typical trading day, 200 million shares might trade hands at an average price of $40 per share or $8 billion total. On some days, 10-40% of the volume in the futures markets was related to portfolio insurance, and their trades were virtually all sales.

These were often very violent down and up days (if the market was rising). The key is that volatility increased dramatically, and a small decline could end up in a big rout.

There was little programmed trading in Japan until recently. But the widespread selling of Nikkei put warrants changed this. The total size of the Nikkei put warrant market is approximately $600 million, but each of these puts is equivalent to 5-10+ times in futures. So the total impact is $5-10+ billion. Adding up the value of the four U.S. put warrants alone gives about $2 billion of NSA equivalents. Combining this with the Canadian, London, over the counter, and private arrangements gives a total of at least $5 billion. On a typical day, with its light volume, the TSE might trade 500 million shares at an average price of about ¥1800 or about $6 billion. Hence, the exposure is much less than was in the U.S. in 1987 but it is still considerable. For example on the ¥1161 fall on February 21, 1990, the volume was only 430 million shares, a third of the normal day's trading. On some strong upward days, volume reaches 3 billion. So the hedging for the put warrants can easily be over 10% of the total futures volume on a given day.

During most of January to March 1990, we saw this trading magnify the downside but it affected the upside as well. The ¥1468.33 rise, some 4.8% in the NSA on Monday, March 26, shows this. The previous Friday's ¥528.82 rise led to sharply higher futures prices that were well above arbitrage buy program levels. Hedge adjustment by the Nikkei put backers was a major cause of the high price futures. This then set the stage for sell futures - buy stocks arbitrage and a nearly 5% gain.

Throughout 1990 one could obtain a pretty good forecast of the next day's trading direction in Tokyo based on the day's trading in the Nikkei put warrants in Toronto and New York, see Ziemba and Schwartz (1992). Table 7.7 shows the effect using implied NSA values on day t based on deep in the money NSA put warrants and the actual NSA close in Tokyo. It is assumed that there is no time value to the warrants which during this period were trading near their intrinsic values with periodic discounts and premiums. The real effect is, of course, the early in the day hedging but more often than not, the forecast was correct as of the close.

The result checks whether or not the implied NSA previous close signal is correct, that is, has the same sign as the next day's NSA close to close change. Table 7.7 shows that 23 out of 25 were predicted correctly.

Table 7.7
The Salomon Nikkei January 1993 Put Warrants Record at Predicting the Following Day's Change in the NSA in Tokyo

Date	SXAWSj93	(Implied Nikkei)	Nikkei Close	Prediction	
9/6/90	17.75	(23,906)	23,812	fall	√
9/5	17.00	(24,442)	24,078	fall	√
9/4	16.25	(24,997)	24,907	fall	√
8/31	15.625	(25,452)	25,978	rise	√
8/30	16.00	(25,179)	24,895	rise	× (even)
8/29	16.00	(25,179)	24,895	fall	√
8/28	15.50	(25,543)	25,710	rise	√
8/27	14.625	(26,180)	25,142	rise	√
8/24	16.625	(24,725)	24,166	rise	√
8/23	18.125	(23,633)	23,738	fall	√
8/22	16.00	(25,179)	25,211	fall	√
8/21	14.75	(26,089)	26,298	fall	√
8/20	13.50	(26,998)	26,490	rise	×
8/17	14.125	(26,544)	26,787	fall	√
8/16	13.875	(26,726)	27,549	fall	√
8/15	12.375	(27,817)	28,112	rise	√
8/14	12.875	(27,453)	26,673	rise	√
8/13	13.75	(26,817)	26,176	fall	√
8/10	12.875	(27,453)	27,329	fall	√
8/9	11.75	(28,272)	27,615	fall	√
8/8	11.125	(28,726)	28,509	rise	√
8/7	12.00	(28,090)	27,653	fall	√
8/6	12.625	(27,635)	28,600	fall	√
8/3	10.875	(28,908)	29,516	fall	√
8/2	10.50	(29,181)	30,245	fall	√
8/1	9.375	(30,000)	30,838		

Source: Modified from The Wall Street Journal.

Implied NSA = $36,821.14 - 5P_{SXA}(145.52)$. Each put is worth 0.2 of a NSA with a fixed exchange rate of 145.52.

Conclusion

Upon reflection, Reason 2 is the most convincing. The market was simply overvalued when properly measured and evaluated with current interest rates. It seems quite likely that the NSA put warrant hedging increased the volatility and exacerbated the decline. Some additional valuation measures also pointed to a decline in December 1989.

A. Nomura's Regression Model

The rise in the NSA from ¥6849 in October 1982 to ¥27,849 in October 1988 can be attributed to increases in industrial production and real money supply and decreases in long term interest rates. The model was

Factor	% Change	% Rise in NSA	Amount of Oct 82-Oct 88 Gain Explained
industrial production index	+1%	0.6%	3000
real money supply	+1%	1.0%	10000
long term interest rate	-0.5%	8.8%	8000
			¥21,000

During 1989 the Bank of Japan increased the discount rate from 2.5 to 4.25% with final 0.5% rise occuring on December 15, 1989. The rate then rose a further 1% on March 20, 1990, to 5.25%. A rough approximation of the fall - assuming constant industrial production and real money supply and that the December 1989 and March 1990 interest rate hikes are those that count is

$$2(1.5)8.8 = 26.4\%.$$

This is close to the actual fall in the 21st correction. If all of the interest rate rise is factored in this model, the calculation yields a fall of

$$2(2.75)8.8 = 48.4\%.$$

Such a fall would move the NSA from 38,916 to 20,000. The market did fall to this level at the beginning of October, but there was an additional rise of 0.75% to 6% in the discount rate on August 25, 1990.

B. Excess Volatility

Gennotte and Leland (1990), Ziemba (1991e), and others have utilized excess volatility models to *explain* stock market falls such as the October 1987 crash. In a standard, continuous time, investment model, the optimal fraction to hold in risky assets is

$$x = \text{Constant (risk tolerance)} \left(\frac{\mu\text{-r}}{\sigma^2} \right),$$

where μ is the mean return on stock (the risky asset), r is the risk free rate, and σ is the standard deviation volatility. Using data from Chapter 2 for mid 1989, we have $\mu \cong 0.145$ (1949-89), r = 0.04 (the mid 1989 Gensaki rate), and $\sigma = 0.125$ (1949-89). One then has

$$\frac{\mu\text{-r}}{\sigma^2} = \frac{0.145 - 0.04}{0.125^2} = 6.72.$$

Increasing the risk free interest rate by 1.5% as in A, and increasing the volatility to the level of the implied volatilities of the put options sold by Salomon Brothers in London, namely, 18% yields $\mu = r + 6.72\ \sigma^2 = 0.055 + 6.72(0.18)^2 = 0.285$. This implies a decline of $\frac{0.273 - 0.145}{0.273} = 46.9\%$. Pricing at 20%, which was the implied volatility of the NSA puts on the American Stock Exchange in early 1990 and the one month puts and calls sold by the major Japanese brokerage firms in 1989, gives $\mu = 0.324$ and a decline of 56.8%.

One sees how sensitive and hair triggered these related models (some of which were discussed in Chapter 5) are to small changes in the input parameters. Since it is current and expected volatility that is crucial, these short term implied volatilities may be somewhat high and over estimate the expected decline. However, it is clear that the increase in interest rates and volatility is consistent with a substantial fall in equilibrium asset prices.

JAPAN'S DEPENDENCE ON OIL

Figures 7.5 to 7.9 show schematically many aspects of Japan's dependence on foreign oil. Some observations, in light of the Iraq induced oil crisis that began on August 2, 1990, include:

- Oil reserves amount to 54 days (31.36 million kiloliters) for the government run Japan National Oil Company and 88 days (51.27 million kiloliters) in the private oil industry for a total of 142 days as of the end of September 1990. In 1973 at the first oil shock, the reserve was only 49 days. While the private stock has been used on several occasions such as in 1979, the government has never released its holdings.

- The minimum reserves industry needs to avoid regional shortages is 45 days according to the Petroleum Association of Japan. In a crisis, the government might release its national reserves when private stocks fall to the 45 day level.

- Gasoline prices are very high in Japan, about ¥120 per liter (about $1 Canadian versus 50-65¢ in Canada). On September 7, MITI obtained cabinet approval for a price rise of about ¥10 per liter.

- Japan owes Iraq and Kuwait more than ¥50 billion for past exports. With economic sanctions it is not clear when they will pay or if there will be late penalties.

- Japanese trading and oil companies will more than double their imports from Iran. The increase of 410,000 barrels a day is almost equivalent to the 440,000 barrels a day that Japan imported from Iraq and Kuwait in the first half of 1990. This brings imports from Iran to a total of some 690,000 barrels a day.

Figure 7.5
Japan's Crude Reserves
Source: MITI

Figure 7.6
Japan's Crude Oil Suppliers
Source: MITI

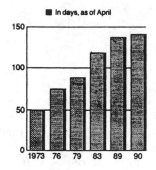

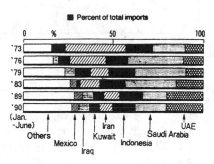

Figure 7.7
Oil Import Cost and CPI Increase
Source: MITI

Figure 7.8
Economic Impact of Costlier Crude
Source: Nippon Credit Bank

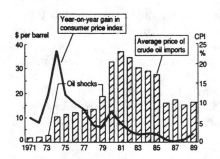

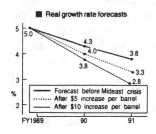

Figure 7.9
Crude Oil in Local Currency (U.S. Refiners Acquisition Price per Barrel)

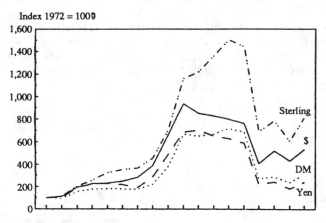

Source: Brinson Partners

- Japan in 1990 was much less vulnerable to oil price increases than in the 1973/74 and 1979 oil crises. Between 1973 and 1989 the ratio of oil to total energy sources fell from 75.5% to 56.6%, according to the OECD. The rate of energy consumption per unit of GNP fell by an average of 2.8% per year since 1973 versus 1.8% for the 24 OECD nations. Energy requirements as a whole have declined nearly 40% from 1973 to 1989. Also, with the strong yen, oil prices in yen have not risen that much as shown in Figure 7.9.

- The short term price elasticity of demand for petroleum over a 1-2 year period is about -0.2, according to Japan's Economic Planning Agency. If prices rise 50% from $18 to $27 then purchases might fall about 10%.

- The economy is much less vulnerable to oil shocks than in the 1970s. First, the rate of consumption is down. For example, steel makers now use 20% less energy per unit of steel output. Second, the core of the industrial structure has shifted from heavy industries to high value-added microelectronics. Finally Japan has replaced petroleum with nuclear power, liquefied petroleum gas, imported coal and other energy sources. These measures have left Japan's ratio of crude oil imports to GNP at 0.8% in 1989. Adding gasoline and other petroleum products, the ratio is still only 1.1%.

- Japan continued to pursue energy conservation when oil prices dropped while the U.S., more sensitive to market signals, began to increase consumption. MITI encouraged the appointment of energy conservation engineers and allowed energy suppliers to keep prices and profits high provided the funds went into energy research. This energy tax both contributed to price sensitive conservation and new methods of using energy efficiently.

The extent of the 1990 Iraq oil shock was about one-eighth that of the 1973/74 and 1979 crises.

- At the time of the first and second oil crises, the income transfers per 50% increase in oil prices were 4.3% and 3.8% of the GNP, respectively. In 1990 a 50% permanent increase in oil prices from $18 to $27 would bring a transfer of about 0.5% of Japan's GNP to the oil producing countries. Thus the 1990 oil price shock was only about one eighth of that of the previous two oil crises. Moreover, the price increases in 1973/74 and 1979 were four fold and 2.5 fold, respectively. Hence, even if there was $60 oil for a short period and $27 oil later, the effects would not have been that great.

- Simulations show that the CPI would rise about 0.2% and real GNP would fall about 0.1% in 1990. In 1991 the changes would be about 0.5% for the CPI and 0.3% for the GNP and a 0.4% rise in long term interest rates. Before the Kuwait invasion, the forecasts for Japan in 1991 projected inflation at 2.5% and real GNP growth at 4.5%. Adding the expected impact of a 50% increase in oil prices would result in inflation of about 3% and real GNP growth of 4%.

- Another difference between the 1990 and the earlier crises is the yen. In late 1990, it was strong while it was battered the last two times as inflation was high because of low interest rates. *The CPI increased 24% in 1974 and 11% in 1979.*

In conclusion, there are effects in Japan of higher oil prices. But it hardly merited a correction of the magnitude that the NSA had in August and September of 1990.

EARTHQUAKE[7]

In the search for risk factors for a crash of the TSE, the possibility of a devastating earthquake has been gaining notoriety. *The Economist* discussed the results of a study by the Tokai Bank of Nagoya on the economic impact of an earthquake. The next great quake is due about 1993 based on a 70 year cycle. The Japanese archipelago is very earthquake prone. Tokyo lies over the intersection of four of the earth's twelve biggest plates and is more likely than California to experience a

---

[7]Special thanks go to Hajime Eto for his help on this section.

devastating quake. Japan and its surrounding waters experience 10% of the quake activity in the world.

On September 1, 1923, a major earthquake measuring about 8.3 on the Richter scale, leveled the then downtown Tokyo. The city was not prepared, and some 100,000 people died, largely of fire and smoke inhalation. The damage cost fully 40% of Japan's GNP. Now the gas systems are designed to cut off automatically with major shaking. The quake's epicenter was at Sagamü, see Figure 7.10. This was not an isolated occurrence, there has been a major earthquake in a roughly 80 year cycle - plus or minus about 20 years - for the past 2000 years. Earthquakes off the coasts tend to be large, while those inland are always small but are very damaging if near large cities. Frequent minor quakes are a part of daily life in Japan; houses and buildings rattle every month or so.

The first such experience was a nervous one for us, but one quickly gets used to them as we witnessed our Japanese friends carry on with their business. Although there have been serious quakes of 4 to 5 on the Richter scale, they so far have caused little damage. Most of the buildings in Tokyo and other major cities and nearly all the new ones are built to withstand all but the most severe earthquakes. Newer buildings are designed to endure 8 on the Richter scale. In particular, despite the incredible land prices one sees few skyscrapers, most buildings are not over ten to fifteen floors. The tallest building in Tokyo, with about 40 stories and standing 146 meters, is the Sunshine Building in Ikeburkuro. Research has shown that hillside buildings have less quake risk, so they tend to be taller. Areas near the sea tend to be muddy underneath and they are much riskier, so the buildings are shorter; this includes the Ginza, which is on land reclaimed from Tokyo Bay about 200 years ago. Other risky reclaimed areas are Tokyo station, Haneda airport, and Ueno station, which was reclaimed about 300 years ago. At that time, Tokyo had a population of one million putting it above London as the biggest city in the world. These areas also face the risk from the *Tsunami*, the big waves that follow an earthquake.

Another less known but large quake occurred in two waves; first on December 7, 1944, with a major after-shock January 13, 1945. The first quake was at Enshu and the second nearby at Mikawa. Details about this destruction were hushed up in the war, but it is known to have been a major double quake with much destruction and loss of some 3000 lives; see Figure 7.13. Another major quake measuring 8.9 occurred on March 2, 1933, and killed 2990 people. A quake measuring 7.3 on June 28, 1948, killed 5131 at Fukui. Tables 7.8 and 7.9 list some details of known large quakes in the twentieth century in Japan and the rest of the world, respectively.

Another noteworthy earthquake occurred in the 1930s at Hoku-Izu, which is south of Mt. Fuij. The Tokaido Super Express passes through Hoku-Izu with the Kodama stopping. Only a few hundred people were killed in this quake. Fujitsu and several other high technology companies such as Toray and Kyowa Fermentation (the biotechnology and cancer cure giant) are located there. There was a volcanic eruption at Mihara Mountain on Oshima Island in November 1987 and again on July 13, 1989, at Teishi in Ito Bay. Each of these towns is on a direct volcanic belt emanating through Mt. Fuji. There is some risk of a volcanic eruption at Mt. Fuji itself.

Figure 7.10 Quakes near Tokyo

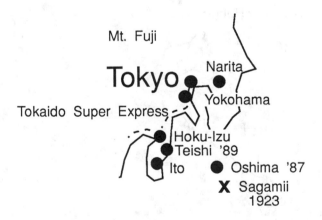

Many quakes have also occurred in the vicinity of Tokachi off the island of Hokkaido in the north of Japan, as shown in Figure 7.11.

Although frequent and large, these quakes have caused little damage and loss of life because this area is remote from major population centers.

Table 7.8   Major Earthquakes in Japan in the Twentieth Century

Date	Level	Epicenter	Damage
1. Sept 1, 1923	8.3	Sagamii, near Tokyo	100,000 killed
2. Mar 2, 1933	8.9	in the north, Sanriku	2990 killed including 1535 by *Tsunami*
3. Mid 1930s		in Hoku-izu, north of Nagoya	Inland quake; many casualties
4. Dec 7, 1944 & Jan 13, 1945		Enshu Mikawa	998 killed, 26,130 houses destroyed 1961 killed, Nagoya not damaged. There were two waves. This quake is not well known as information about it was hushed up in the war.
5. Dec 21, 1946	8.4	Nankai	Osaka, slightly to the north of Nankai, was not damaged
6. Jun 28, 1948	7.3	Fukui	3769 killed, 36,000 homes destroyed
7. Jun 16, 1964		Sanriku	26 killed, 2250 homes destroyed
8. 1960s-80s		Tokachi	Many quakes have occurred in this undeveloped area in Hokkaido in the north

Figure 7.11   Quake Area near Hokkaido

There is a very serious possibility that a major earthquake would destroy or damage a significant part of Tokyo, Osaka or other major cities. The Japanese are as prepared as possible for this. They simply will rebuild virtually immediately. Loss of data and computer files could

cause serious disruption for a considerable period. Even in light of the high probability of a major quake, there is no backup computer system at the TSE, where computers account for more than 25% of the world's stock transactions. One can easily imagine that the markets would close for a while!

After the California quake in 1989, Japanese experts visited to study why some buildings collapsed and others didn't. Essentially, Japan and California have different codes: Japan follows rigid construction while California has margins of deformability.

The next center is likely to be Odawara, 65 kilometers south of Tokyo, and then the next great quake is likely to be in the heavily populated Tokai region further south. These are predicted to begin a period of frequent quakes in Tokyo Bay. It has been estimated that if a quake of the 1923 intensity hit in the winter, there would be 37,000 dead and 78,000 injured with one third the homes and offices destroyed and disruption in communication and power. Others have higher estimates with up to 3 million casualties!

So what does the Tokai Bank's computer model expect to be the economic and stock market effects of a major quake? Reconstruction would cost ¥119 trillion, so Japanese institutions would sell investments in the U.S. Capital flows to the U.S. would be cut, causing high interest rates and a significant debt crisis.[8] Japan's GNP would fall 4.8% and the world economy would fall 0.3 points with effects continuing over the years. Increased demand to rebuild would quickly boost Japan's growth to 12% while in Canada and the U.S., the growth rate would fall about 2.5%. The Tokai Bank estimated that in order to undertake the rebuilding, Japanese institutions would have to sell many of their foreign investments of some $1.5 trillion, in turn depressing stock and bond markets in the U.S. and elsewhere and further causing a world wide stagflation with world wide production and income shrinking 0.3%.

Many foreign investors would immediately sell their shares on the TSE unless trading was halted. But there probably will not be a panic on the Tokyo and Osaka stock exchanges, both of which are in not very tall

---

[8]To keep this in perspective, the ¥119 trillion is less than the paper loss *in either of the two 1990 corrections* from top to bottom.

buildings that are essentially earthquake proof. A drop of 10-20% or more
in the immediate confusion particularly with the magnification in the
futures markets, is the likely near term effect. If the October 1987 crash is
any example to follow, there was panic among foreign investors and
much selling among large institutional investors, so the TOPIX and NSA
averages fell sharply. The average investor holding small stocks did do
some selling, but then stocks, which had more than doubled in 1987, did
not crash as similar stocks did in the U.S. and other countries. Moreover
they came back in value to reach new highs and finished the year up 50-
200% ahead; see Figure 7.12. The prices of large construction stocks like
Kajima could rise sharply and possibly double in three months with the
acute demand for their services. Small construction companies will
prosper even more with the flexibility and availability of their work and
ability to expand their operations.

Figure 7.12
The Performance of the 10, 25, 50, 100, 150 and 200 Smallest Capitalized
Stocks on the TSE-I and the NSA and TOPIX Indices in 1987

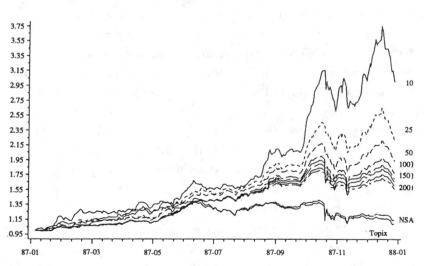

Index Scale 1.00 = beginning of 1987

Source: Yamaichi Research Institute

Japan will be aggrieved and focused inward for a period. Large sums of foreign investments would be sold to provide ready cash to pay for the reconstruction[9] There would be an avoidance of sales in Japan out of respect and so as not to depress stock prices at home. Depending on the speed of this withdrawal, the extent of the quake and the reaction of parties involved, we could see a sharp increase in U.S. interest rates, a flight from the dollar into the yen by the Japanese, and hence a sizeable fall in U.S. stock and bond prices.

Figure 7.13
Epicenters for the 1923, 1944-45 Quakes and the Most Dangerous Current Locale Suruga

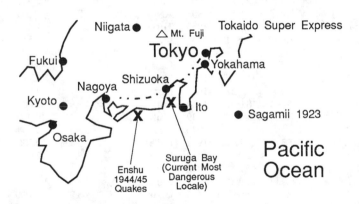

The stock market crash in New York following a quake in Tokyo could exceed that in Tokyo itself, particularly given the fears of Western investors who would perceive this as the end of prosperity and the onset of world wide depression. Foreign currencies might drop sharply, and

---

[9]Japan would likely be importing supplies and other needed goods. We must be careful not to confuse cash with the basic materials needed to rebuild. Consider that rebuilding itself is expansionary and would put pressure on materials prices and cause a realignment in production.

there would be many margin calls, credit failures, and bankruptcies. In the panic, volatility would increase sharply along with option premiums, and in the midst of it there would be substantial bargains to be had. We expect the Japanese to handle the crisis well. They expect it and they are continually reminded of it. Such a crisis is just part of the continuation of life on the Japanese archipelago. Growth rates in Japan within a year or two would, according to the Tokai Bank study, increase by at least 12%.

Table 7.9   Major Earthquakes in the 20th Century

Year	Place	Richter scale	Deaths	Year	Place	Richter scale	Deaths
1990	Iran	na	48,000	1963	Yugoslavia	6.0	1,100
1989	California	6.9	67	1962	Iran	7.1	12,230
1988	Armenia	6.9	25,000	1960	Chile	8.3	5,000
1985	Mexico	8.1	9,500	1960	Morocco	5.8	12,000
1983	Turkey	7.1	1,300	1957	Iran	7.1	2,000
1982	Yemen	6.0	2,800	1957	Iran	7.4	2,500
1980	Italy	7.2	4,800	1956	Afghanistan	7.7	2,000
1980	Algeria	7.3	4,500	1953	Turkey	7.2	1,200
1979	Columbia, Ecuador	7.9	800	1950	India	8.7	1,530
1978	Iran	7.7	25,000	1949	Ecuador	6.8	6,000
1977	Romania	7.5	1,541	1948	Japan	7.3	5,131
1976	Turkey	7.9	4,000	1946	Japan	8.4	2,000
1976	Philippines	7.8	8,000	1939	Turkey	7.9	30,000
1976	China	7.8	200,000*	1939	Chile	8.3	28,000
1976	Italy	6.5	946	1935	India	7.5	30,000
1676	Guatemala	7.5	22,778	1934	India	8.4	10,700
1975	Turkey	6.8	2,312	1933	Japan	8.9	2,990
1974	Pakistan	6.3	5,200	1932	China	7.6	70,000
1972	Nicaragua	6.2	5,000	1927	China	8.3	200,000
1972	Iran	6.9	5,057	1923	Japan	8.3	100,000
1970	Peru	7.7	66,794	1920	China	8.6	100,000
1970	Turkey	7.4	1,086	1915	Italy	7.5	29,980
1968	Iran	7.4	12,000	1908	Italy	7.5	83,000
1966	Turkey	6.9	2,520	1906	Chile	8.6	20,000
1964	Alaska	8.4	131	1906	California	8.3	700

*Official estimate, may be as many as 800,000.

Source: Associated Press

It is extremely difficult to predict the size of an earthquake, how much damage it would do, when it would occur and with how much warning. However, current seismographic research suggests the chance of a major quake that would destroy Tokyo before the year 2000 is small. The highest risk area is Suruga, and the nearest large city is Shizuoka, see

Figure 7.13. Should a quake occur there it would affect but not destroy Tokyo, which is about 200 kilometers away.

Although a giant earthquake will slow the Japanese exports for a year or two, it will not cause a depression in Japan, and its spillover effects on the U.S. and elsewhere depend largely on the extent of cooperation versus panic.[10]

PRICE LIMITS AND CRASHES: TAIWAN'S 3% LIMIT

The Taiwan stock market is one of the world's most exciting and dangerous. It goes up and down frequently in violent moves. Figure 7.14 plots its price movements and volume from 1985 to 1991. The daily trading value is about U.S.$3 billion, which is more than half that in New York. It has also been one of the world's best performers. With huge foreign reserves in the $75 billion U.S. range, a trade surplus of $13.8 billion in 1988, private savings in excess of $40 billion; a high savings rate of over 30% far exceeding even that of Japan; low rates on cash-like instruments in the 3.5% per year range; a small number (some 144) of stocks; limited land, and virtually no bonds, the excess liquidity goes as in Japan into stocks and land. As measured by the Gini coefficient, Taiwan has an even more equal income distribution than Japan and everyone owns stock.

Property prices in Taipei, as we have noted in Chapter 2, exceed those in New York and London and rival those in Paris and Osaka. Similarly, the stock market with its huge run up has been a favorite playground for taxi drivers and homemakers as well as the new rich business and land owner. The economy is run very differently than in Japan. The wealth is not in the giant corporations, as in Japan where the population has a tight income distribution. Rather, the wealth is in the export businesses run by small family groups. Each business concentrates on a small set of products and then makes huge profits on low costs and huge volume. The growth in exports has been extremely fast, and the profits have poured in. With exchange controls, the money finds its way into the land

---

[10]In any major quake trading would likely be halted. The real problem would be dealing with grief and then reactivating the workers to rebuild, and this requires not so much money - which can, after all, be printed but the materials to rebuild and the means to clear the rubble. One could probably build a new island with the tons of rubble.

and stock markets. There is much speculation and borrowing of money for speculation in land or stocks using one or the other as collateral in a pyramiding fashion.

Figure 7.14   The Taiwan Stock Market Index, 1986 to 1991

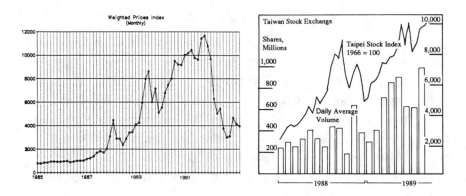

Source: *The Economist*

As in Japan, the Taiwanese financial system has a tightly regulated banking system. The money of the nouveau riche of the 80s found its way into the stock market. Seemingly minor rules changes, particularly those involving taxes, can cause big moves in the stock market given the very high PERs and inherent risks in the market. While a case can be made for the safety of the Japanese stock market despite the high PERs it is more difficult to do the same thing in Taiwan. Hidden assets are important there, but one does not have the strong stability and openness of the Japanese markets.[11] There is limited foreign financial investment. The

---

[11]A very major problem is the limited stock offerings. Because the firms developed as small businesses with limited financial needs, the stock market did not evolve in the normal way to fund new enterprise and expansion. Many of the important Taiwanese businesses are not even on the exchange. The other real problem was the increase in local currency due to hoarding of U.S. dollars and increased trade balance which recently have been reduced to satisfactory level.

only exceptions being four local-foreign joint ventures traded in London and New York that each manages one open and one closed end fund. Locals use these funds to avoid individual stock selection and for diversification and not for investment in the general market because, as we have seen in most parts of the world, the funds have underperformed the market indices.

In 1988, the Taiwan stock market rose 276% in the first nine months. Its capitalization was then larger than that in Osaka and London and some 135% of the country's GNP. The market rose in a steady fashion given its 3% daily market move limit. The rise was halted because of the announcement in September of a capital gains tax on stock market gains to take effect the following January. The proposed tax was intended to cool the overheated market and it did.

Not surprisingly, the market fell its 3% limit on the first day of the *crisis* and with many sellers and few if any buyers, the volume dropped to 1% of its average turnover; see Figure 7.15.

Local mutual funds suspended valuation of their holdings in the wake of redemption requests from 50% of shareholders. The market place was complicated by the over 200 illegal investment houses with some NT$100 billion in unsecured deposits and their need to make their promised return of 4-10% per month. Margin calls abounded. Half the small players had about two thirds of their net worth in the market, with 10-15% more leveraged up with margin to more than 100% of their net worth. (Then U.S. $1 was worth about NT$29.) The market fell the 3% limit for an amazing 19 straight days.

To improve volume, the government adjusted the law before trading on October 3. This improved the volume but did not alter the slide. Specifically, the government announced it would raise the NT$3 million annual ceiling for non-taxable share trading to NT$10 million and lower the existing transaction tax from 0.3% to 0.15%. Since the rise was not based on fundamentals but on a speculative emotional binge, one could not really predict where the bottom would be and if the market might just come back in a new rise. The market did bottom out in mid October 1988. Since then, it has gone on its traditional path - up - with violent moves reacting to the perceived consequences of new government policies.

One of the policies that did not cool off the economy was the relaxation of exchange controls allowing virtually unlimited foreign investment with a limit being U.S.$5 million per person per year. This was subsequently reduced to $3 million. The government is also hoping to soak up a lot of excess liquidity by selling shares in ten state industries over the next six years, notably the three big state-run banks. The government is also trying to curb and legalize the activities of the underground investment companies. Eventually, Taiwan will also open the market to foreign financial investment through convertible bonds. Will the market, now capitalized in the $250 billion range versus a GDP of about $120 billion, crash again and when?[12]

Figure 7.15
Trading Volume and the Taipei Weighted Index Values at the Time of the September 1988 Crash

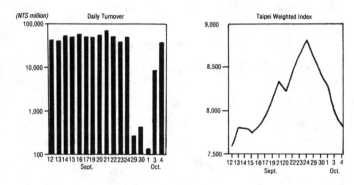

Source: Review Data

What do we learn from the Taiwan experience that might be instructive for the Japanese markets? First, while the markets have some

---

[12]In 1990, the Taiwan market had another steep fall, see Figure 7.14. Lower industrial output and exports coupled with a weakening of the usually strong New Taiwan dollar against the U.S. dollar, as well as the world wide weakness, are part of the reason for the decline as well as its usual over-valuedness. The index rose from 1,063.13 in January 1987 to a peak of 12,495.34 February 10, 1990. On June 28, it fell below 5,000 to 4,995.38, down already 60.02% from its peak. But, even with this gigantic fall in 1990, the market closed up more than four times since the beginning of 1987.

similarities, such as high PERs and land prices; the differences are many, particularly much greater economic stability and inward directedness, sounder economic fundamentals and a less emotional, secure personal nature. The price limits of 3% on the futures and options contracts based on the underlying index and 15% on stocks have so far tended to moderate and not accelerate market moves. On Black Tuesday in October 1987, it was the SIMEX, which had no limit on moves, that fell over 25% prompting the authorities to institute a 15% limit.

CHAPTER 8
SUGGESTIONS FOR STOCK INVESTMENT IN JAPAN
BY JAPANESE AND BY FOREIGNERS

It is difficult to make specific portfolio recommendations far into the future because conditions can change quickly. It is even more difficult with individual securities. However, we will try to provide some guidance in both of these areas based on information available at the end of 1990. The individual stocks are analyzed in terms of valuation measures, anomalous aspects, and likely future trends for the Japanese economy. The portfolios are put together with particular goals in mind. We begin with four sample portfolios and then discuss the prospects for a number of individual securities and for particular strategies such as the purchase of new issues. Mutual funds are discussed in Chapter 9.[1]

SAMPLE PORTFOLIOS
Portfolio 1
Portfolio 1 is a small stock portfolio - the type that should be purchased in late December. This portfolio, listed in Table 8.1 consists of a diversified portfolio of 50 securities from the 100 smallest capitalized stocks on the TSE-I. The idea is to invest in the smallest capitalized securities but to sufficiently diversify the portfolio. Since the trading volume of these

---

[1]We are not generally in favor of firms diversifying. U.S. companies diversify into non-related products in a portfolio approach to spread risk but really increase it by going into products that they do not understand and cannot manage. They neglect their main lines of business and treat them as cash cows. This has been at the heart of the deterioration of U.S. management, innovation and productivity (see Schwartz, 1989). Noritake is a good example of the Japanese approach to diversification: They can encompass mass production table ware, custom tableware, museum quality custom pieces and the new industrial ceramics and pay attention to all of them. U.S. firms would begin to treat the mass produced ware as a mature segment and neglect it. The Japanese have a knack of diversifying and maintaining a company mission that encompasses the new business and thus often makes diversification work. Perhaps as well, they let separate products maintain their separateness and are non-interfering, so again, it works. This follows perhaps from the Japanese tradition of forming loose associations among different firms in networked groupings.

413

Table 8.1 Sample Portfolio 1 - Small Capitalized Stocks

	Code	Company	Industry	Cap (¥100 mil)	Daily Vol*	Beta	Yrly ROR	Price 28 Dec 90
1	1865	Komatsu Const	Construction	339	88	0.08	58.20	1000
2	1867	Uekigumi	Construction	233	44	0.30	27.38	755
3	1975	Asahi Kogyosha	Construction	254	52	0.04	24.90	970
4	2003	Nitto Flour Milling	Foods	254	93	0.62	24.24	710
5	2604	Yoshihara Oil Mill	Foods	171	46	0.67	26.23	615
6	3004	Shinyei	Textiles	281	157	0.14	31.57	540
7	3524	Nitto Seimo	Textiles	125	86	0.19	23.69	1190
8	3553	Kyowa Leather Cloth	Textiles	424	26	-0.15	38.60	1250
9	3577	Tokai Senko	Textiles	205	141	0.11	16.58	1190
10	3887	Chuo Paperboard	Paper&Pulp	383	137	1.15	29.26	610
11	4210	Toyo Chemical	Chemicals	169	69	0.43	28.34	538
12	4614	Toa Paint	Chemicals	160	26	0.84	27.43	733
13	4992	Hokko Chem Ind	Misc Chems	218	20	0.76	18.33	1100
14	5011	Nichireki Chem Ind	Petro Prod	269	64	0.21	25.04	1190
15	5234	Daiichi Cement	Cement&Con	315	57	0.46	51.78	900
16	5262	Nippon Hume Pipe	Cem & Con	204	33	0.22	39.70	761
17	5263	Daido Concrete	Cem & Con	178	159	0.39	35.23	725
18	5457	Nippon Pipe Mfg	Iron & Steel	199	138	0.17	40.34	448
19	5544	Yahagi Iron	Iron & Steel	185	168	0.33	37.01	480
20	5913	Matsuo Bridge	Metal Prod	119	54	0.43	35.08	1130
21	5915	Komai Tekko	Met Prod	205	30	0.18	32.69	1850
22	5957	Nitto Seiko	Met Prod	286	75	0.17	11.48	751
23	6138	Dijet Industrial	Mach Tools	332	8	0.36	33.82	760
24	6363	Torishima Pump Mfg	Ind Mach	350	2	0.16	21.92	1280
25	6373	Daido Kogyo	Ind Mach	233	73	0.04	4.36	555
26	6375	Nippon Conveyor	Ind Mach	206	72	0.18	19.22	930
27	6378	Kimura Chemical	Machinery	127	69	0.48	21.19	500
28	6590	Shibaura Eng Works	Elec Mach	196	94	0.36	26.14	750
29	6644	Osaki Electric	Heavy El Mach	276	68	0.25	27.59	1120
30	6851	Ohkura Electric	Electric Appl	336	50	0.71	31.24	980
31	6901	Sawafuji Elec	Elec Mach	154	52	0.23	27.99	566
32	6921	Toko Elect	Misc Elec Mach	290	46	0.70	32.63	706
33	6937	Furukawa Battery	Electric Appl	207	58	0.19	19.35	530
34	6999	KOA	Misc Elec Mach	254	107	0.30	-2.33	678
35	7104	Fuji Car Mfg	Trans Equip	190	103	0.42	38.55	789
36	7105	Nippon Yusoki	Rollingstock	252	89	0.20	26.08	1210
37	7961	Nissan Nihrin Kogyo	Misc Manu	171	140	0.28	13.02	493
38	8005	Mutow	Commerce	322	17	0.86	13.38	1230
39	8038	Tohto Suisan	Commerce	362	94	0.26	39.94	562
40	8042	Nihon Matai	Commerce	183	14	0.20	28.66	781
41	8052	Tsubakimoto M& Eng	Commerce	202	72	0.47	28.87	870
42	8064	Kinsho-Mataichi	Commerce	239	99	0.44	38.03	501
43	8103	Meiwa Trading	Commerce	299	160	0.79	42.16	480
44	8122	OSG Corp	Commerce	200	4	-0.09	9.88	110
45	8181	Totenko	Commerce	229	36	0.24	9.03	999
46	8211	Sotetsu Rosen	Commerce	208	31	0.27	20.42	966
47	8239	Yokohama Matsu	Dept & Ch St	230	31	-0.05	43.35	700
48	9113	Inui Steamship	Marine trans	211	102	0.48	53.21	470
49	9632	Subaru Enterprise	Leisure&Hot	208	40	0.42	28.71	849
50	9727	Tokyu Tourist	Leisure&Hot	387	32	0.43	30.90	800
		Average				1.07	34.97	

*Since the trading volume of these stocks is low, limit prices and a little patience should be used to enter and exit these positions.

Capitalization in ¥100 mil, Yearly ROR average from 1 Oct 1983 to 1 Oct 1988.

stocks is quite low, limit prices and a little patience should be used to enter and exit these positions.

This portfolio should have strong gains in January and February and in April to July, and reasonable returns during the rest of the year. At the end of the next year, it is advisable to rebalance new diversified securities from the then 100 lowest capitalized stocks on the TSE-I. Studies have shown that the end of July may be a good exit point for small capitalized stocks, so the investor may sell the portfolio, invest the money elsewhere in the meantime and then start again for the next January with a new small stock portfolio. This strategy will lower the portfolio risk. See the discussion in Chapter 4 on this and the December 1988 to December 1990 results from an actual portfolio of 15 selected small stocks. These low beta portfolios have had excellent returns in the past. The beta of this portfolio is low. The portfolio standard deviation risk is higher than the Topix and NSA indices. But, risk adjusted, this type of stock portfolio has historically bettered the NSA or Topix by about 10% per year.

Portfolio 2

The second sample portfolio is meant to mirror and move with the market indices, specifically the Topix. As discussed in Chapter 2, only about 25% to 35% of all portfolio managers actually beat the market indices in any given year. The percentage is even lower over a long period. This portfolio, as listed in Table 8.2, is for a buy-and-hold strategy. Since there are only forty stocks, it will have some tracking error with the Topix index of some 1,225 stocks and the NSA. With equal weighting, it has a beta of 1.09 versus 1.00 for the Topix and 0.86 for the NSA. However, despite its tracking ability and high correlation with the Topix and NSA indices, this portfolio consists of stocks that may well beat these indices. The higher beta suggests it will on average outperform the Topix and the NSA in up markets and underperform these indices in down markets. This portfolio is for a long buy-and-hold investor with or without any portfolio insurance or other protection strategy.

Table 8.2   Sample Portfolio 2 - Index Tracking Stocks

	Code	Company	Industry	Cap (¥100M)	Daily Mean Trading (1000)	Beta	Yrly ROR Oct 83 Oct 88	Price 28 Dec 1990
1	1301	Kyokuko	Fish & Forest	697	519	0.93	32.88	777
2	1515	Nittetsu Mining	Mining	997	329	1.42	29.52	1490
3	1812	Kajima	Const	14583	1128	1.13	43.43	1580
4	2107	Toyo Sugar Refin'g	Food	359	556	0.48	41.98	500
5	2503	Kirin Brewery	Food	15566	900	1.27	31.61	1440
6	3201	Japan Wool Textile	Textiles	1670	66	0.90	36.05	1580
7	3863	Jujo Paper	Pulp & Paper	4931	1774	0.94	35.78	645
8	4001	Mitsui Toatsu Chem	Chemicals	5472	4044	1.45	43.30	490
9	4452	Kao	Chemicals	7815	607	0.84	30.85	1200
10	5002	Showa Shell Sekiyu	Oil & Coal	4314	699	0.71	30.70	1090
11	5004	Mitsubishi Oil	Oil & Coal	4466	3464	0.51	30.65	900
12	5108	Bridgestone	Rubber Prods	8818	1310	0.67	23.71	990
13	5261	Misawa Resort	Cem & Con	332	58	1.02	59.42	2250
14	5407	Nisshin Steel	Iron & Steel	10727	11750	1.19	55.71	540
15	5801	Furukawa Electric	Wires & cable	5596	1914	1.27	28.46	656
16	5938	Toyo Sash	Metal Products	3830	189	0.53	33.71	3230
17	6013	Takuma	Machinery	682	219	1.35	30.42	770
18	6302	Sumitomo Heavy Ind	Machinery	5134	11134	0.68	35.13	531
19	6502	Toshiba	Electric Appl	30804	24100	1.26	23.67	706
20	6752	Matsushita Elect Ind	Electric App	43608	5297	0.60	7.81	1590
21	6851	Ohkura Electric	Electric Appl	336	50	0.71	31.24	980
22	7012	Kawasaki Heavy Ind	Trans Equip	11047	20217	1.27	41.22	516
23	7201	Nissan Motor	Trans Equip	31706	7936	0.70	17.21	700
24	7724	Kimmon Mfg	Prec Inst	393	19	1.00	38.19	1020
25	7976	Mitsubishi Pencil	Other Products	808	42	0.98	37.36	2050
26	8001	C. Itoh	Commerce	10439	2739	1.24	29.06	645
27	8231	Mitsukoshi	Commerce	9003	936	0.74	43.89	1160
28	8263	Daiei	Commerce	7037	576	1.15	30.31	1220
29	8317	Fuji Bank	Fin & Ins.	78417	336	1.68	46.76	2440
30	8318	Sumitomo Bank	Fin & Ins.	84492	668	2.01	49.24	1990
31	8602	Yamaichi Securities	Fin & Ins.	19870	550	2.04	35.139	45
32	8801	Mitsui Real Estate	Real Estate	19278	2091	1.70	37.28	1250
33	8804	Tokyo Tatemono	Real Estate	2623	755	1.58	48.08	775
34	9001	Tobu Railway	Land trans	11287	3246	1.18	52.57	753
35	9101	Nippon Yusen	Marine trans	9297	6828	1.32	31.06	555
36	9202	All Nippon Airways	Air transport	22523	846	0.66	43.441	280
37	9310	Yokkaichi Warehse	Warehousing	405	96	1.07	37.95	1040
38	9401	Tokyo Broadcasting	Communic	3902	417	0.94	29.55	2020
39	9532	Osaka Gas	Elec & Gas	20514	3906	1.20	48.59	498
40	9710	Dai-ichi Hotel	Services	616	22	0.35	33.76	1320
		Average				1.07	36.17	

Portfolio 3

The third portfolio, listed in Table 8.3, looks to the future. What are the areas that should perform the best over the next five years in the Japanese economy? Areas that seem very likely to do well are services, banks and

Table 8.3 Sample Portfolio 3 - Strong Future Growth Portfolio

	Code	Company	Industry	Cap (¥100 mil)	Daily Vol*	Beta	Yrly ROR	Price 28 Dec 90
1	1803	Shimizu Corp	Const	9969	1216	0.97	43.36	1570
2	1812	Kajima	Const	14583	1128	1.13	43.43	1580
3	1886	Aoki	Const	3247	964	0.46	8.46	785
4	1925	Daiwa House	Const	8591	1444	0.77	32.24	1820
5	2502	Asahi Breweries	Foods	5104	516	0.99	43.47	1210
6	5001	Nippon Oil	Oil & Coal	15919	1947	0.49	8.06	915
7	5407	Nisshin Steel	Iron & Steel	10727	11750	1.19	55.71	540
8	6501	Hitachi	Electric Appl	44874	10698	0.71	12.58	1130
9	6502	Toshiba	Electric Appl	30804	24100	1.26	23.67	706
10	6702	Fujitsu	Electric Appl	25594	7712	0.55	8.91	980
11	6752	Matsushita Elect Ind	Electric App	43608	5297	0.60	7.81	1590
12	6758	Sony	Electric Appl	16401	1677	0.23	12.33	5840
13	7011	Mitsubishi Heavy Ind	Trans Equip	33110	30799	1.32	34.60	668
14	7203	Toyota Motor	Trans Equip	67575	15777	0.37	17.10	1750
15	7731	Nikon	Prec Inst	3919	1321	0.55	16.75	1030
16	8001	C. Itoh	Commerce	10439	2739	1.24	29.06	645
17	8231	Mitsukoshi	Commerce	9003	936	0.74	43.89	1160
18	8263	Daiei	Commerce	7037	576	1.15	30.31	1220
19	8264	Ito-Yokado	Commerce	14460	269	0.59	26.84	3550
20	8318	Sumitomo Bank	Fin & Ins.	84492	668	2.01	49.24	1990
21	8603	Nikko Securities	Fin & Ins.	23413	499	2.22	35.30	929
22	8604	Normura Securities	Fin & Ins.	66261	1685	2.32	41.93	1770
23	8801	Mitsui Real Estate	Real Estate	19278	2091	1.70	37.28	1250
24	9001	Tobu Railway	Land trans	11287	3246	1.18	52.57	753
25	9002	Seibu Railway	Land trans	20365	19	0.73	48.97	3600
26	9101	Nippon Yusen	Marine trans	9297	6828	1.32	31.06	555
27	9107	Kawasaki Kisen	Marine trans	2898	3279	0.58	29.13	435
28	9113	Inui Steamship	Marine trans	211	102	0.48	53.21	470
29	9201	Japan Air Lines	Air Transport	20029	161	-0.03	42.81	1080
30	9202	All Nippon Airways	Air transport	22523	846	0.66	43.44	1280
31	9401	Tokyo Broadcasting	Communic	3902	417	0.94	29.55	2020
32	9531	Tokyo Gas	Elec & Gas	38978	9232	1.19	64.80	565
33	9725	Tokyo Hotel Chain	Services	1458	334	0.23	33.94	1570
		Average				0.93	33.09	

brokerage firms (that did not get into trouble in the 1990 corrections and whose stocks were depressed in the general market declines) those involved in vacation and related travel, marina and golf course construction and management (again those whose stock prices fell in 1990 more than their net asset values); hotel, food and beverage distributors; those investing in foreign farms and food processing, and real estate companies encompassing land management including golf course development outside central Tokyo. Included here also are stocks in automobiles, electronics and food distribution that should benefit from the December 1988 tax reform. This portfolio is somewhat similar in spirit to the Nagoya 25 index, but it is intended to be even more tilted toward the future. For investors with limited capital, the purchase of call options on the Nogoya 25 - when its implied volatility is low - may be a good substitute for such a portfolio. This and other indices along with derivative securities based on them are discussed in Ziemba and Schwartz (1992).

Portfolio 4

The final portfolio is based on value. The portfolio, as listed in Table 8.4, emphasizes securities that are cheap relative to their current valuation - that is, securities whose current prices are below estimated equilibrium prices based on improperly capitalized and hidden assets, poor image, etc. Many of these stocks have vast holdings of land in Japan valued on the books at far less than its current market value. The idea is that these securities' values will rise to their equilibrium values eventually, and, hence investors will then make the market gain plus the undervalued premium.

Table 8.4 Sample Portfolio 4 - Undervalued Securities

	Code	Company	Industry	Cap (¥100 mil)	Daily Vol*	Beta	Yrly ROR	Price 28 Dec 90
1	1812	Kajima	Construction	14583	1128	1.13	43.43	1580
2	5401	Nippon Steel	Iron & Steel	56411	69392	1.37	40.83	448
3	5451	Yodogawa Steel	Iron & Steel	2234	1332	0.91	32.57	830
4	7007	Sasebo Heavy Ind	Trans Equip	817	556	0.37	19.22	720
5	8001	C. Itoh	Commerce	10439	2739	1.24	29.06	645
6	8751	Tokio Marine & Fire	Fin & Ins.	31123	2092	1.88	36.30	1320
7	8753	Sumitomo Mar&Fire	Fin & Ins.	7596	700	2.37	43.52	945
8	8755	Yasuda Fir & Mar	Fin & Ins.	9863	1106	1.84	40.64	890
9	8759	Dowa Fire & Mar	Fin & Ins.	2584	129	1.17	35.47	780
10	9001	Tobu Railway	Land trans	11287	3246	1.18	52.57	753
11	9009	Keisei Elect RR	Land trans	8150	5870	0.86	55.61	1300
12	9107	Kawasaki Kisen	Marine trans	2898	3279	0.58	29.13	435
13	9303	Sumitomo Warehouse	Warehousing	1343	283	1.22	40.31	709
14	9531	Tokyo Gas	Elec & Gas	38978	9232	1.19	64.80	565
15	9532	Osaka Gas	Elec & Gas	20514	3906	1.20	48.59	498
		Average				1.23	40.80	

Table 8.3 has additional stocks that can be considered similar to those in sample Portfolio 4. These ten stocks have enormous hidden assets relative to their stock price. The Q-ratio which estimates the market value of the stock divided by the market value of the firm's tangible assets - land, buildings, stock, inventory, net accounts receivable etc. is 0.25 or less. This means that at current market values these companies could, if they wish, cash in their assets for four to ten times the current market price of

its shares. This is unlikely because most of the companies utilize their assets in an integral way in their business. To sell the assets would necessitate scaling down or moving out of business. This points to large undervaluation of the company's assets by the market. A small hint of sales of some of the hidden assets would be very positive for the stock price. Each of them has a strong underlying business. All of them look good for long term investments with relatively low risk. Only a gigantic crash in land prices, which is extremely unlikely, would put them in financial trouble, and the market fall in 1990 has discounted most or all of this.

As with all recommendations in this book, the sample portfolios are for informational purposes. They do not imply any offer or inducement to buy or sell any security. We may hold positions in some of these securities. Before acting on any information, investors may wish to seek professional help from one or more brokerage firms or securities advisors and current information such as the *Japan Company Handbook*, the Tokyo Stock Exchange, and other sources. Currently, all commissions on the TSE are regulated, so one would pay the same transactions costs regardless of with whom one trades, so preference should be given to organizations that provide good service and efficient executions.

A somewhat similar portfolio to sample Portfolio 2 is the stocks in the Kabusaki 50 index traded on the Osaka stock exchange. This basket of stocks is meant to track the NSA, however, not the Topix, so it will usually under (over) perform the Topix in rising (falling) markets. Of course one can also simply go long the SIMEX- or OSE-NSA or TSE-Topix futures contract directly as discussed in Ziemba and Schwartz (1992). The best time to do this, on average is when they are trading at a discount, preferably just before the turn of the month.

THE EXPERTS' SELECTIONS FOR 1991

Table 8.5 gives the top three recommended stocks by fifty market experts along with their projections for the high and low for the NSA. The average high was 30,548 and the average low 21,910. The projections ranged from a high of 35,600 and a low of 17,000. Most of the experts see a low before the end of the 1990 fiscal year in March and then a rise to a high late in the year.

Table 8.5 The Experts' Choices in 1991

Survey summary: 1991 Nikkei average range		
HIGH	Highest projection	35,600
	Average	30,548
	Lowest projection	26,000
LOW	Highest projection	25,000
	Average	21,910
	Lowest projection	17,000

Name/title, company	Nikkei (high, low)	Issues with brightest prospects
Kimitoshi Hasegawa Manager Dai-ichi Mutual Life Insurance	33,000 (Dec.) 23,000 (May)	1. Tokyo Electric Power 2. Kajima 3. Nomura Securities
Yasushi Yamada General manager Sumitomo Life Insurance	30,000 (Dec.) 22,000 (Jan.)	1. Okumura 2. Daicel Chemical Industries 3. Nintendo
Takeshi Inui Senior fund manager Daido Mutual Life Insurance	30,000 (Nov.) 20,000 (Feb.)	1. Shimizu 2. JGC 3. Nintendo
Hiroyasu Mizuno General manager Asahi Mutual Life Insurance	33,000 (Aug.) 23,000 (Jan.)	1. All Nippon Airways 2. Okumura 3. C. Itoh
Tadao Nishioka General manager Nippon Life Insurance	33,000 (Dec.) 23,000 (Mar.)	1. Kato Works 2. Citizen Watch 3. Raito Kogyo
Yasuhisa Sato Vice president Meiji Mutual Life Insurance	30,000 (Dec.) 22,000 (Jan.)	1. Tokio Marine & Fire Insurance 2. Tokyo Electric Power 3. Mitsubishi Corp.
Isao Ushikubo General manager Toyo Trust & Banking	33,000 (July) 23,500 (Nov.)	1. Canon 2. Kirin Brewery 3. Fujisawa Pharmaceutical
Hiroshi Momoi General manager Mitsubishi Trust & Banking	27,000 (Aug.) 21,000 (Mar.)	1. Kajima 2. Tokyo Electric Power 3. Mitsubishi Heavy Industries
Teruo Watanabe Manager Mitsui Trust & Banking	27,000 (Dec.) 18,000 (Mar.)	1. Hitachi 2. Mitsubishi Heavy Industries 3. Kyocera
Kunio Ueki General manager Yasuda Trust & Banking	32,500 (Dec.) 21,000 (Mar.)	1. Secom 2. Komori Printing Machinery 3. Takaoka Electric Mfg.
Tetsuro Arita Director Fuji Bank	28,000 (July) 22,000 (Feb.)	1. Nishimatsu Construction 2. Marubeni 3. Tokyo Electric Power
Akio Yamamoto General manager Sanwa Bank	28,500 (Dec.) 20,300 (Feb.)	1. Sekisui Jushi 2. Eisai 3. Mutoh Industries
Toshihiro Tanaka Deputy general manager Daiwa Bank	32,000 (Dec.) 20,000 (Feb.)	1. Fuji Bank 2. Nomura Securities 3. Mitsui Real Estate Development
Fumio Mizuno General manager Nomura Securities	33,000 (Dec.) 23,000 (Mar.)	1. Kajima 2. Tokyo Electric Power 3. Taisho Pharmaceutical
Masuo Nishizawa Director Daiwa Securities	31,500 (Dec.) 23,500 (Mar.)	1. Kajima 2. Tokyo Electric Power 3. Takeda Chemical Industries
Misao Maehara Director Nikko Securities	33,000 (Dec.) 23,000 (Feb.)	1. Matsushita Communication Ind. 2. Taisei 3. Toyo Communication Equipment
Takeshi Kanasaki General manager Yamaichi Securities	33,000 (Dec.) 23,500 (Feb.)	1. Shimizu 2. Marubeni 3. Mitsubishi Heavy Industries
Toyoharu Tsutsui Managing director CS First Boston (Japan)	30,000 (Dec.) 23,000 (Mar.)	1. Shimizu 2. Mitsubishi Corp. 3. Matsushita Communication Ind.
Minoru Itoh Tokyo Branch manager Smith Barney, Harris Upham International	32,000 (Nov.) 23,000 (Jan.)	1. Japan Airlines 2. Matsushita Communication Ind. 3. Sankyo
Hideo Ueno Vice president Goldman Sachs Japan	31,800 (Dec.) 21,200 (Feb.)	1. Hitachi 2. Kajima 3. Tokyo Electron
Yoshiaki Saito Vice president Morgan Stanley Japan	30,000 (June) 22,000 (Feb.)	1. Hitachi 2. Mitsubishi Petrochemical 3. Sankyo
Eiichi Akioka Managing director Cosmo Securities	32,000 (Dec.) 22,000 (Apr.)	1. Sony 2. Kajima 3. Ebara
Akihiro Ieda Director Kankaku Securities	31,000 (Dec.) 23,000 (Apr.)	1. Nishimatsu Construction 2. Sankyo 3. Matsushita Communication Ind.

Source: The Japan Economic Journal

Table 8.5 continued

Name/title, company	Nikkei (high, low)	Issues with brightest prospects
Akio Yamamoto Vice president Nomura Securities Investment Trust Management	35,600 (Oct.) 23,500 (Feb.)	1. Kajima 2. Sumitomo Electric Industries 3. Kirin Brewery
Hiroyuki Wada Managing director Japan Investment Trust Management	32,000 (Dec.) 22,000 (Mar.)	1. Matsushita Communication Ind. 2. Mitsubishi Heavy Industries 3. Sanki Engineering
Norikazu Nakamura President Hyogin Investment Management	30,000 (May) 23,000 (Feb.)	1. Hazama-gumi 2. Hitachi 3. C. Itoh
Takashi Ohtsubo Director Daiwa Investment Trust Management	33,000 (Dec.) 21,000 (Mar.)	1. Kajima 2. Fuji Photo Film 3. Ebara
Masahiko Tokutake Manager Warburg Investment Trust Management	27,000 (Dec.) 21,000 (Aug.)	1. Sankyo 2. Seven-Eleven Japan 3. Santen Pharmaceutical
Yukio Itagaki Managing director Kokusai Investment Trust Management	33,000 (Dec.) 22,000 (Feb.)	1. Nintendo 2. Tokio Marine & Fire Insurance 3. Sumitomo Electric Industries
Sakio Maeda Director Shin-Wako Sec. Investment Trust Management	32,000 (Dec.) 23,000 (Feb.)	1. Kajima 2. Sankyo 3. Sony
Tsuyoshi Matsumoto Senior managing director Taiyo Investment Trust & Management	30,000 (Oct.) 23,000 (Jan.)	1. Okumura 2. Matsushita Electric Industrial 3. Marubeni
Takashi Murakami Managing director Nikko International Capital Investment	33,000 (Dec.) 21,000 (Feb.)	1. Mitsubishi Heavy Industries 2. Amada 3. Godo Steel
Toru Ohara Senior portfolio manager Tokio Marine MC Asset Management	28,000 (Dec.) 20,500 (Apr.)	1. Hitachi 2. Yamanouchi Pharmaceutical 3. Seven-Eleven Japan
Atsushi Deguchi President Sumitomo Marine Investment Management	28,000 (Dec.) 21,000 (Feb.)	1. Tokyo Electric Power 2. Ebara 3. Sumitomo Marine & Fire Insurance
Yoshiyuki Ataigawa Managing director Nissay Asset Management	30,000 (Dec.) 22,000 (Mar.)	1. Matsushita Electric Industrial 2. Ito-Yokado 3. Komatsu Construction
Sohichiro Ishii General manager IBJ Capital Management	30,000 (Nov.) 22,000 (Mar.)	1. Tokyo Gas 2. Kajima 3. Matsushita Communication Ind.
Toshitaka Okada General manager LTCB Investment Management	32,000 (Dec.) 23,500 (Jan.)	1. Kajima 2. Kokusai Electric 3. Sony
Masahiko Moriyama Director NCB Investment Management	30,000 (Dec.) 21,000 (Mar.)	1. Kajima 2. Sankyo 3. Sony
Mamoru Uehara General manager Dai-Ichi Kangyo Investment Management	29,000 (Oct.) 21,000 (Feb.)	1. Mitsubishi Corp. 2. Kajima 3. Taisho Marine & Fire Insurance
Shinji Okumura President SB Investment Management	30,000 (Dec.) 22,000 (Feb.)	1. Nintendo 2. Nippon Hodo 3. Matsushita Electric Industrial
Kunio Wada Managing director Sanyo Investment Management	29,000 (Aug.) 22,000 (Feb.)	1. NTT 2. Sega Enterprises 3. Tokyo Steel Mfg.
Junpei Kimoto Director Yamatane Investment Management	28,000 (Dec.) 18,000 (Mar.)	1. Fanuc 2. Ono Pharmaceutical 3. Sumitomo Metal Mining
Yasuhiro Ishii President Rothchild Asset Management (Japan)	26,000 (Nov.) 21,000 (Apr.)	1. Komatsu 2. Matsushita Electric Industrial 3. Kandenko
Masayoshi Hiromatsu President Merrill Lynch International Capital Management	29,500 (Oct.) 21,000 (Feb.)	1. Kajima 2. Mitsubishi Heavy Industries 3. Sony
Yuji Kudo Managing director Schroder Investment Management (Japan)	28,000 (Dec.) 21,000 (Apr.)	1. Ines 2. Shimachu 3. Skylark
Atsuto Sawakami President Pictet (Japan)	27,000 (Oct.) 17,000 (Apr.)	1. Takuma 2. Hoxan 3. Osaka Titanium

Figure 8.1
Performance of Sectors on the TSE-I Relative to the NSA 500, 1984 to April
1989

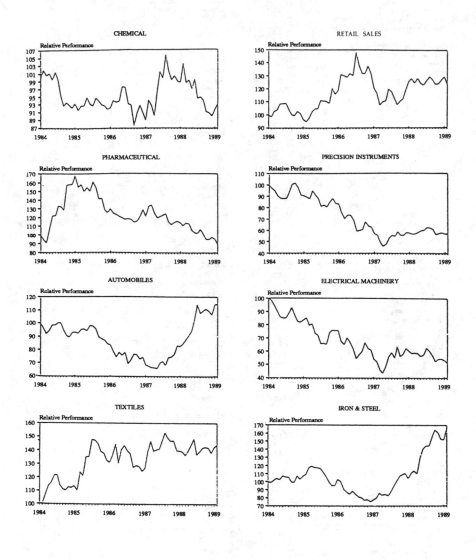

Source: Goldman Sachs and TSE

Figure 8.1 concluded

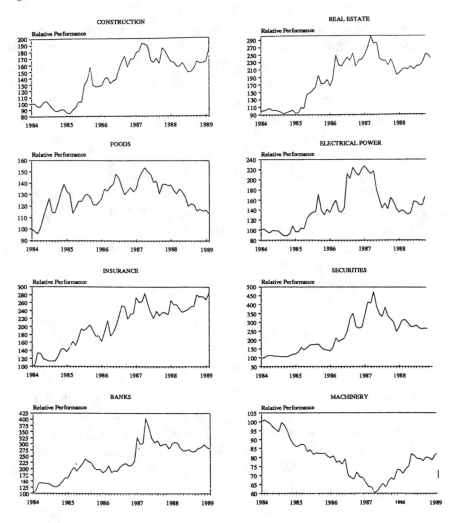

SECTOR PERFORMANCE: 1984 TO APRIL 1989

Performance in particular sectors depends on general market effects, fads, trends, and how economic conditions affect the companies in the grouping. The data in Figure 8.1, courtesy of Goldman Sachs and computed from the TSE valuations, show how a number of sectors performed relative to the NSA 500 index from 1984 to April 1989. Risk through beta or standard deviation measures is not considered. Machinery, general or electrical, chemicals, and precision instruments lagged the index. The big gainers were construction, real estate, electric power, insurance, securities and banks. The graphs indicate that few of these moves were straight up and some, notably the banks and security houses, peaked just prior to the October 1987 crash. Since the TSE maintains separate sub indices for all twenty-eight industry sectors, it is easy to keep track of these trends should you wish to use this approach as part of your stock selection analysis.

NEW ISSUES

For a variety of reasons, new issues are generally priced below market values. The price that they bring on offering and shortly after is usually higher than their offering price.[2]

The new stock issues in Japan are made following the 1973 Guideline for Raising Capital via Public Offering Method, which limits the size and frequency of new issues. A study by Kunimura and Severn (1989) concluded that the guideline limited the size of new issues especially by large capitalized companies. The guideline's main points in 1973 were:

1. The dividend must be at least 10% of par value.
2. Net profit must be at least 10 yen per 50 yen of par value.
3. The number of new shares is restricted to specified portions of outstanding equity, especially for large firms.
4. Public offerings of any firm must be at least a year apart.

There have been minor changes since then with points 3 and 4 being made more flexible, but it is still a constraint for many companies.

---

[2]For the U.S. literature, see Ritter (1991). From 1975 to 1984, initial public offerings underperformed similar stocks already listed by 17% over a three year horizon. However, the short run performance of these issues is often positive, particularly when they go public near the peak of industry-specific fads.

New issues are sold at a discount of about 5% from the pre-announced market prices. How much extra returns are obtainable by investment in these new issues? Kunimura and Severn, using a sample of 551 from 1969 to 1980, estimated there is an abnormal return over the Topix of 1.4% in the month after the date of issue and normal returns in the following two months. The large issues did somewhat better than the small issues, as shown in Figure 8.2. The guidelines made large issues more profitable than small issues according to Kunimura and Severn's data. After two years, large issues are about 7% above the Topix, and small issues have an edge of about 4%.

Figure 8.2
Cumulative Excess Returns for 551 Small and Large Issues, 1973-80

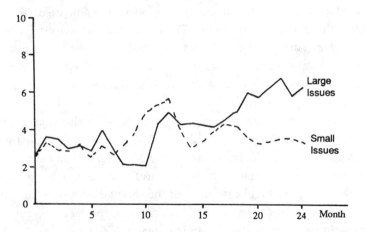

Source: Kunimura and Severn (1989)

A sampling of the usual effect on the TSE is shown in Table 8.6 for nine new issues from 1988.

Table 8.6 Effect of a Public Offering on Market Price

	Public Offering	Initial Market	Dec 1988
Fuji Denki Reiki	2230	5100	4000
Nippon Avionics	1760	5050	2670
Mitsuba Electric Mfg	1580	2040	1700
Fujitsu Kiden	1750	6200	3300
Taio Paper Mfg	1612	2350	2000
Namu Co.	1950	3800	2150
Iwaki Glass	1880	2070	1800
Shinkawa	7860	8350	6990
Mitsubishi Motor Corp.	850	1380	1440

The pattern here was fairly consistent. A low public offering price, followed by a sharp rise in the initial public offering, and then a downward drift toward the public offering price. In some cases, the price falls below the public offering price. The maximum profits relative to risk are to sell very soon after the stock is listed if you are able to purchase such stock and are confident that the stock will actually be listed on the TSE. The latter is crucial because it is very hard to sell unissued stock in the period before it is listed.

The recent Recruit scandal is a painful reminder of this phenomenon. For a small amount of profits, the country lost the services of the finance minister, the head of NTT, and the Prime Minister. Many others also suffered more embarrassment than their profits were worth. Only time will tell the full impact and casualties of the shady dealings of this public offering. More on the Recruit scandal and its impact on the future of insider trading appears in Ziemba and Schwartz (1991).

As of the end of 1990, there were very few new issues coming to the market becasue of the steep decline in 1990. New issues will appear when the market regains its strength again.

ANALYSIS OF PARTICULAR SECURITIES

In this section we discuss briefly the current situation and probable future prospects for a number of leading Japanese companies. Since conditions can change rapidly, the reader should get up to date information before making any transactions concerning these securities. We do not recommend all the securities that follow nor do we have a comprehensive list. The idea here is to discuss briefly some interesting and influential companies.[3]

The amount of new stock issues, of course, affects the total supply of the stock and the general level of the entire market. Mergers and acquisitions tend to lower this available stock, while the new issues expand it. Obviously, more stock enters the market when it is strong. Not surprisingly, there was a considerable increase in the 1984-89 estimated new public offerings of stock and convertible warrant bonds. The following data were provided by Goldman Sachs, the 1989 yearly estimates were based on an annualization of the first quarter. These new issues, in billions of yen, were:

Total New Stock Issues

1984	¥3,603.6
1985	4,286.6
1986	5,530.3
1987	16,587.1
1988	18,775.1
1989	20,000.0 (estimate)

In 1990, there were very few new stock or equity warrants being issued because of the market correction. As the market has strengthened from October 1990 to February 1991, when we went to press, the activity has accelerated considerably.

---

[3]Without implicating them in any way, we wish to thank the Nomura Securities Co. Ltd through its daily columns in the *Japan Times*, the *Japan Times* itself; the *Asian Wall Street Journal*, the *Wall Street Journal*, the *Far Eastern Economic Review*, the *Japan Company Handbook*, the Tokyo Stock Exchange, and colleagues at the Yamaichi Research Institute for some helpful background information on some of the companies that follow.

Seibu Railway/Saison Group

Code[4]	Price	CAP	Beta	Vol	PER	ROR	Div	Recommendation
9002	4750	20581	0.75	19	703.5-	48.97	5	Buy, in moderation on
	5020				1117.5			price dips and sell on
								substantial rises

Seibu Railway had an astonishingly high PER of 777 as of December 1988. The stock is closely held and lightly traded. A casual calculation to subtract known land holdings, estimates of the value of the buildings on them and their known stock holdings lowers the PER to 567. As shown above the PER has been even higher. Obviously this is not the story.

The story is of Yasajiro Tsutsumi, who founded the Seibu Railway Group with its vast real estate, railway, and distribution empire, and his two sons Yoshiaki and Seiji. The sons are half brothers; Yoshiaki is the son of a mistress and Seiji the son of a wife. Yoshiaki Tsutsumi heads the Seibu Railway Group and by some accounts is the world's richest businessman with a personal wealth of more than $25 billion. Yoshiaki was the heir to the largest part of his father's fortune. Seiji Tsutsumi controls the Seibu/Saison Group, which recently became more widely known with its purchase of the Inter-Continental Hotel chain for $2.15 billion. The two half brothers may well be the two most influential businessmen in Japan in the 1990s.

Yasujiro began building his fortune in the 1920s, and he cleaned up in the devastation of post-war Japan, buying huge tracts of land from people impoverished by the war. He used his land holdings as collateral to borrow money and as sites for resorts and railways. He had at least two wives, three mistresses and seven children. The only children born to wives were Seiji and his younger sister. Misao Aoyama, his eventual

---

[4]For the stocks described in this section we provide some fundamental data. Additional information appears in the *Japan Company Handbook*. Code is the stock's code number. Two prices are given. The top is the closing market price in yen on the TSE on October 31, 1988, and the bottom is the price at the end of December 1990. CAP is the capitalization in ¥100 million and is the stock price times the number of shares outstanding. Beta is the covariance of the stock with the TOPIX index divided by the variance of the TOPIX as estimated by the TSE as of October 31, 1988. Trading volume is the mean trading volume on the TSE per day. PER is the stock price divided by the per share net profit after taxes. The two values shown - from the *Japan Company Handbook* - are the averages of the highest and lowest PER in each of the five previous account settlement periods ending in the fall of 1990. ROR is the yearly geometric rate of return for the period October 1983 to October 1988. Dividend is the yearly dividend payment in yen. The price charts are from the Japan Company Handbook.

widow and once his mistress, was the mother of Yoshiaki and two other sons. While Yoshiaki was devoted to his father, Seiji became a radical and Communist Party activist during his student days at Tokyo University. This did not sit well with his father. When he died, Yasujiro gave Yoshiaki the bulk of the empire and Seiji only one department store.

Despite considerable ideological differences between Yoshiaki's traditional conservative Japanese business approach and Seiji's idealism, they both have thrived in their businesses. Seibu Railway Group has an estimated $400 billion network of hotels, resorts and amusement parks that have been a careful expansion of the businesses started by Yasujiro. This includes a major resort in Maui. There are 50 to 100 separate companies involved, with operations opening and closing regularly. Some 48.4% of Seibu Railway is held by the family through Kokudo Keikaku and a further 5.3% by Seibu Construction. Minor, but stable, shareholders include major trust, bank and life insurance companies such as Yasuda, Mitsui, IBJ, Mitsubishi and Nippon. Revenues in the fiscal year ended in March 1989 were split as follows: railway activities, 48%, real estate, 14%, and tourism, 38%.

Yoshiaki is the only link between the various companies, and the whole empire is run to preserve his father's image and his conservative establishment ideas. The Seibu companies are mostly held by family members, but they operate in a highly competitive fashion. Between them, they own entire regions in northern Japan, control much of Tokyo's suburban railway service, dominate Japanese retailing, operate hotels and resorts across the country, and promote the Seibu Lions, the baseball team that usually wins the professional championship in Japan.

Seiji is more of an aggressive entrepreneur. He has built the single department store into a conglomerate of about 100 companies with sales of about $30 billion per year. Seiji's prize is the fashionable Seibu/Saison retail store group. Companies he controls are Seibu Credit, code number 8253 and Seibu Department Stores, which is a private holding company. According to Paul Maidment (1988), *The Economist*'s Tokyo correspondent, the key to Seiji's success was a correct judgment about how Japan would grow richer. He believed the young, highly paid workers would become yuppies and spend rather than save their income, and flaunt their wealth by buying. He then envisioned stores that would be one-store lifestyle upscale markets where travel, tourism and consumer finance would be bought as readily as fashions, foods and faxes. The Seibu/Saison credit card, which is now linked with VISA and Mastercard, has over six million holders and fully 60% are in the hands of those in their twenties, a large and growing consumer group. Loans for cars, durables and even land are available, and instant credit up to ¥300,000 can be obtained on the road. Seibu/Saison also has some joint ventures with Sears to expand activities in the U.S.

Until the mid 1980s, the brothers' businesses did not conflict, but now they are often head to head in the leisure hotel business. Their mothers both died days apart in November 1984. This, in Seiji's mind, ended the connection and started the direct competition, particularly in hotel and resort development. For example, Seiji's Inter-Continental hotel chain competes directly with Yoshaiki's Prince hotels in Japan and in foreign locales. The sibling hostility reveals itself in policies such as not accepting Seibu/Saison credit cards in the Prince Hotels. The younger brothers play an active but less forceful role in the businesses. These two businesses are hard to evaluate but their success and influence cannot be denied. They are in businesses that seem to have strong features. Most likely both will do very well and we recommend their purchase in moderate amounts on price declines. Expanding real estate sales have generated increased revenue but interest charges are large. Their Makuhari Prince Hotel will open in 1993 and they are building several new railway stations. Given the low trading volume, the price should be carefully watched, and price limit orders may be warranted. A January purchase is recommended because the stock usually is at a low for the year then.

Prices	high	low	Yearly G/L (%)
To 1985	2180 (1984)	48 (1949)	
1986	7200 (Dec)	1850 (Jan	110.4
1987	5800 (Apr)	3400 (Dec)	-20.2
1988	5300 (May)	3140 (Jan)	45.3
1989	8000 (Sep)	4600 (Jan)	63.9
1990	7850 (Feb)	3250 (Oct)	-56.6

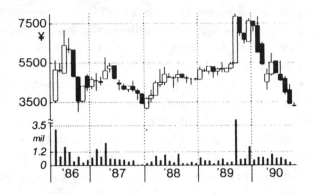

JAPAN AIR LINES

Code	Price¥	CAP	Beta	Vol	PER	ROR	Div	Recommendation
9201	1280	20029	-0.03	161	119.1-	42.81	40	Hold for long term
	1080				174.8			

Japan Air Lnes is well poised to capture a substantial fraction of the revenues from Japan's overseas travel boom. Travel by Japanese abroad is increasing at about 25% per year, and business travel in and out of Japan is increasing as well. JAL is a high-status airline and its tickets command premium prices. It is the favored airline for most Japanese. JAL also owns part of Hawaiian Airlines.

JAL is pushing ahead with a number of innovative upscale schemes to attract customers. It has its own passage card that enables passengers to reserve seats on about 220 domestic and international airlines with no ceiling on ticket purchase amounts. Later the card will likely be useable for meal and retail purchases at outlets affiliated with member carriers. JAL also offers in-flight personal video screens in January 1990 for first class and business class passengers on 747 - 400 international flights. The 12 centimeter liquid crystal screens developed by Matsuhista Electric Industrial are located in seat arms and fold out for viewing. The video service will expand to six channels featuring movies, music, travel and tourist information along with a channel devoted to business news and information in English and Japanese.

JAL reported record profits for 1988 and 1989. Sales are about ¥1 trillion and pre-tax earnings were about ¥50 billion for the first five

months of fiscal 1988. Earnings per share of about ¥160 were predicted for
the 1990 fiscal year. JAL was privatized in 1987 and has been undergoing
a reorganization, including diversification. Shares are widely held with
no one holding more than 2.9%. All the major owners are banks and
insurance companies.

On the negative side for JAL's outlook, Narita Airport is already
overcrowded, so adding flights there is becoming more difficult.
Moreover, there is pressure to decrease airfares, particularly the
exorbitant fares to leave Japan. These fares are based on old values of the
yen (¥296 per dollar) and lead to fares about double those of the reverse
trip into Japan from overseas. The fares are likely to be decreased in the
next few years. Finally, even with the Iraq oil crisis in 1990, the world oil
price is fairly low in yen now and, since it is priced in dollars, the risks are
definitely high. Forward hedging and long term contracts cushion this.
As of March 1990 revenues were divided as follows:

Domestic line passengers	22
International line passengers	53
Cargoes	15
Postal service	2
Other air transport	1
Related businesses	7

In general, the future looks rosy for JAL. Efficiency of flight operation
is improving with high load factors and an overdemand for the available
seats. The overseas travel boom is also helping JAL's subsidiaries such as
Japan Asia Airways, which flies between Japan and Taiwan, Japan Air
Lines Development, which manages hotel businesses, Japan Creative
Tours, which sells package tours, and JAL's development of hotel chains
and resort complexes outside of Japan. Moreover, JAL Trading, the
commercial division of JAL, may be spun off into a separate company on
the TSE. JAL Trading develops resort hotels in Guam and Hawaii and has
an equity participation in Hawaii Airlines.

Prices	high	low	Yearly G/L (%)
To 1986	1374 (1986)	43 (Apr)	
1987	2010 (Oct)	1180 (Jan)	-3.8
1988	1620 (Mar)	1230 (Jan)	27.4
1989	1960 (Dec)	1500 (Mar)	20.5
1990	1940 (Jul)	921 (Oct)	-43.0

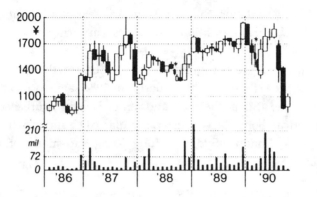

SONY

Code	Price¥	CAP	Beta	Vol	PER	ROR	Div	Recommendation
6758	5990 5840	16401	0.23	1677	30.3- 49.8	12.33	50.0	Buy for long term, hold

Sony is one of the world's leading consumer electronics manufacturers and one of the early and leading Japanese global companies. Sales in the U.S. surpass those in Japan. Its stock is listed on stock exchanges worldwide. Its par value is ¥50,000, so it can be purchased in Japan in units of 100 shares. The earnings estimates by Nomura Securities, listed in Table 8.7, show greatly increased earnings in total and per share that are returning the company to the peak levels of ¥73 billion earned in the period that ended in October 1985.

The firm has completely caught up with the high yen problem in profit terms; although, it tends to make even more profit if the yen is weak. Several factors are behind this performance. The household electrical appliance division, including the highly successful 8mm videotape recorders, had growth of about 30% in 1988 after falling in 1987. The non-household electrical appliance areas, including video tape recorders and semi-conductors for commercial use, have also had growth in the 30%

range. U.S.-based CBS Records, which was acquired in January 1988 has been very profitable and is growing at a double digit pace.

Sony is marketing, in a joint venture with the U.S. firm Geostar Corp, a new line of mobile communication equipment that uses a satellite link. These devices are expected to be used by trucking companies to radio instructions to drivers caught in traffic jams or involved in accidents. In June 1988, Sony sold more than 2,000 one-way telecommunication systems to about 50 U.S. transportation companies, capturing about 70% of the total U.S. market.

Sales in Japan are rising sharply, and the growth is even faster in Europe and the U.S. In the third quarter of 1988 sales rose 27% in Japan, 36% in Europe, 46% in the U.S., and about 50% in Southeast Asia and South America. Sony stock is also a popular ADR and is actively traded in New York, London, Sydney, Hong Kong and many other foreign exchanges.

Table 8.7   Sales and Earnings Estimates for Sony, Millions of Yen

| Period Ending | Sales | Profit | | After-Tax | EPS |
		Dividend	Current		
Year Mar 1987	396,095	13,195	7,515	32.5	18.50
Year Mar 1988	1,029,891	43,405	30,661	128.5	44.60
9 mos Dec 1988	1,606,000	128,650	58,090	194.5	33.45
Year Mar 1989	2,201,472	165,516	72,469	241.7	44.60
Year Mar 1990	2,945,242	227,429	102,808	306.9	50.00
Year Mar 1991 est	3,670,000	310,000	115,000	340.7	50.00

Source: Nomura Securities, *Asian Wall Street Journal* and *Japan Company Handbook*

Foreign holders account for 15% of the shares outstanding. R&D is high at about 9% of sales. Sony is moving into the software business and is promoting sales of hardware. Nonconsumer product sales are expanding. The company recently purchased Columbia Pictures for a then record Japanese acquisition in the U.S. for $3.4 billion. Sony also purchased the Gubers Peters production company for $400 million. They were responsible for many of Columbia's recent successes.

Prices	high	low	Yearly G/L (%)
To 1985	5860 (1981)	251 (1965)	
1986	4190 (Jan)	2800 (Jul)	-15.2
1987	5710 (Oct)	2560 (Apr)	41.8
1988	7290 (Dec)	4600 (Feb)	55.2
1989	9500 (Oct)	6550 (Apr)	10.6
1990	9150 (Jul)	5360 (Oct)	-22.9

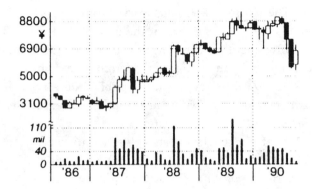

NIPPON TELEGRAPH AND TELEPHONE (NTT)

Code	Price¥	CAP	Beta	Vol	PER	ROR	Div	Recommendation
9432	1850000	99900	1.04	6	99.3-	-19.78	5000	Sell or short
	980,000				159.6			

NTT is a giant firm with nearly 300,000 employees and dominates the domestic telephone business in Japan. KDD dominates the international call business. NTT's market capitalization of about U.S.$164 billion as of October 1988 was by far the largest of any company in the world exceeding that of IBM, Ford Motor Co., Exxon and General Motors combined. It amounts to nearly 4% of the capitalization of the TSE-I. At the height of its valuation in 1987, its shares amounted to about 7% of all the stock value in Japan. At a price of about seven times sales with earnings lower than much smaller firms such as Toyoda, with less than a fourth the employees, or Nomura, with about 3% as many employees, it certainly is expensive. Even with the notoriously highly capitalized business of telephones, this is very, very high.

In 1987 it had the fourth highest earnings of all Japanese corporations, some ¥413.2 billion. But it does seem over-priced. In 1989 the stock fell to the ¥1.5 million range and in 1990 to about ¥1 million. It is currently only the second largest capitalized stock in Japan behind the Industrial Bank of Japan. There was great difficulty in selling the stock to the public in the later stages of its offering. This held down the whole market and gave a strong signal of the general market weakness. Until September 1987, NTT monopolized the country's telecommunications service. At that time, three new firms entered the market mostly for long-distance calls between the big cities. These firms use circuits leased from NTT. The firm faces challenges similar to those of AT&T at the time of its breakup, and, like AT&T, it is highly capital intensive in comparison with its competitors in related fields. The company will face a dilemma if earnings keep rising, because its users regard its service in the public interest and likely will demand telephone rate cuts. NTT is also expected to encounter political pressure to break itself up sooner or later.

The Ministry of Finance has been selling off its shares of NTT in a massive public offering (privatization). It still owns 66.2% of the shares. Mitsubishi Trust, Nippon Life, Dai Ichi Insurance and employees each with 0.5% are the next largest owners. Each year a block of shares have been offered for sale. The major brokerage firms are expected to sell their share of the offering. They sold 1.95 million shares in 1986 and 1987 and 1.5 million in 1988. A further 1.95 million shares were to be offered in 1989 at an estimated average price per share of ¥1.81 million, which was the average price between December 14, 1988, and January 13, 1989. This would have raised about ¥3.53 trillion, or some U.S.$28.2 billion. Even the transactions costs (commissions) at ¥36.2 billion, some $290 million, are staggering. Due to the stock's weakness, the sale was postponed in 1989 and in 1990. The stock's price peaked at ¥3.18 million in 1987. This company is simply too big to operate in an efficient, profitable fashion. The problem is with the privatization and not the company, as the government is trying to get a lot of money out of it. We recommend selling these shares. But if you purchase the shares you can do so one share at a time because NTT's par value is ¥50,000.[5]

---

[5]The Ministry of Posts and Telecommunications recommends splitting NTT's monopoly. Now there are 50 firms that compete with NTT in long distance and local telephone markets, leased circuit market, radio pager and satelitte communications market. The ministry proposes dividing it into one long distance firm and 11 local service firms at a cost of ¥300 billion.

Prices	high	low	Yearly G/L (%)
1987	3,180,000 (Apr)	1,600,000 (Feb)	35.0
1988	2,530,000 (May)	1,700,000 (Nov)	-14.6
1989	1,930,000 (Jan)	1,350,000 (Apr)	-21.8
1990	1,470,000 (Jun)	720,000 (Oct)	-46.9

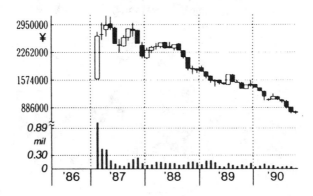

KAJIMA

Code	Price¥	CAP	Beta	Vol	PER	ROR	Div	Recommendation
1812	1730	14583	1.13	1128	55.0-	43.43	11	Hold for long term
	1580				94.3			

This large construction firm seems poised to benefit from the increased consumption orientation of the Japanese economy. Despite the stock market decline in 1990, Kajima's profits are at an all time high. Current and future projects include a highway across Tokyo Bay, development of 38 hectares of land in Kemigawa for housing, construction of the World Business Garden in Makuhari and the Shigi New Town, and one of the world's largest indoor skiing grounds. Profits in 1989 were up 49% to reach record levels of ¥41.2 billion for the six months ended in March 1989. The firm suffered losses on foreign projects and has re-emphasized the market it knows best back in Japan. This has led to high profit levels of about 10% of sales.

The future looks good for Kajima with plenty of work in the domestic economy, its backlog alone is about 17 months and over ¥2 trillion. The company looks poised to capture much of it. It is progressing with a large redevelopment project centering on new hotel construction on its own land in Tokyo. It is accumulating intelligent building technologies and would be a prime beneficiary of rebuilding after a major earthquake.

Prices	high	low	Yearly G/L (%)
To 1986	1540 (1986)	123 (1965)	
1987	2160 (Apr)	1240 (Dec)	-9.0
1988	1860 (Dec)	1230 (Jul)	29.1
1989	2670 (Mar)	1820 (Jan)	8.6
1990	2200 (Jan)	1190 (Sep)	-37.5

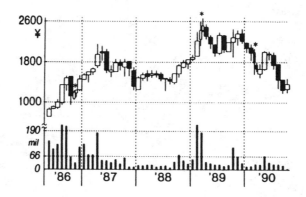

FUJITSU, LTD.

Code	Price¥	CAP	Beta	Vol	PER	ROR	Div	Recommendation
6702	1460 980	25594	0.55	7712	38.7-66.5	8.91	9	Aggressively accumulate to hold for long run unless earnings growth falters, then sell

This electronic manufacturer, Japan's largest domestic computer maker, has had earnings per share grow from ¥10.2 in fiscal 1987, to ¥18.8 in fiscal 1988, to an estimated ¥33.4 in fiscal 1989. This latter gain of nearly 80% is the result of huge sales gains in optical communications, semi-conductors, computers and industrial electronics. Total sales in fiscal 1991 are estimated to be about ¥2.3 trillion, and net after-tax profit about ¥85 billion. The firm is one of the leaders in information and communication, and its mid to long term prospects look bright. It controls Amdahl, has DRAM production plants in California, produces printer heads in Thailand, has an IC plant in Malaysia, and is a major producer of semiconductors and communications equipment. Fujitsu has supercomputers that equal or surpass those of Cray and all purpose computers that rival IBMs Summit.

Based on recent sharp earnings and future growth of earnings in very competitive areas, one must be a little cautious about the industry competition. Hence, if sales and earnings are surprisingly low in the future, the stock should be sold immediately. However, the future looks attractive for investors at the currently depressed price.

Prices	high	low	Yearly G/L (%)
To 1986	1560 (1984)	35 (1950)	
1987	1610 (Oct)	700 (Apr)	4.7
1988	1950 (Aug)	1160 (Jan)	29.1
1989	1710 (Aug)	1390 (Mar)	0.0
1990	1640 (Jan)	995 (Oct)	-26.6

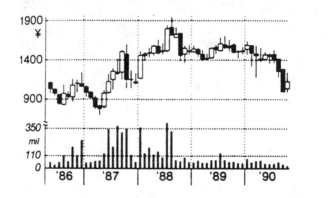

KEISEI ELECTRIC RAILWAY

Code	Price¥	CAP	Beta	Vol	PER	ROR	Div	Recommendation
9009	3000	8150	0.86	5870	na	55.61	4	Hold for long term up-
	1300							ward valuation of its land
								holdings in stock price.
								Buy its subsidiary
								Oriental Land when it is
								listed on the TSE in 1991
								for a 1-3 year play

Keisei has very valuable land holdings, and its book value is about ¥7500 per share compared to a share price of about ¥1300. Its land is centered in Chiba prefecture, which likely will be developed into a major housing and resort area. With the addition of the JR Kieyo line and the probable construction of a second Disneyland, the value of its land holdings are poised to increase further. Keisei's subsidiary, Oriental Land, which operates and owns 45% of Tokyo Disneyland, will be spun off to form a new TSE company in 1991. Shares of both look attractive. If the Chiba prefectural government invests in Oriental Land, this would also benefit the company. Keisei's railway line to Narita is very successful. Additional benefits will accrue when the direct access line to Narita opens in the spring of 1991. The company also operates a bus line from Narita to the domestic Hanada airport. Current profits are depressed because of the termination of interest reduction and exemption measures and high interest rates. But the stock looks promising as a long term hold based on its land value.

Prices	high	low	Yearly G/L (%)
To 1985	504 (85)	47 (49)	
1986	750 (Sep)	360 (Jan)	46.2
1987	900 (Oct)	545 (Jan)	14.5
1988	3260 (Nov)	590 (Jan)	345.8
1989	3150 (Nov)	2200 (Mar)	12.9
1990	2950 (Jun)	1010 (Oct)	-57.3

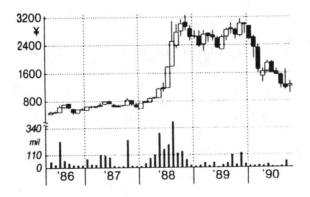

TOKYO GAS

Code	Price¥	CAP	Beta	Vol	PER	ROR	Div	Recommendation
9531	1430	38978	1.19	9232	66.0-	64.80	5	Buy at depressed price.
	565				120.0			Sell when the market
								discounts its assets less.

Just behind Tokyo Electric Power in market size, Tokyo Gas looks even more attractive for mid and long term investment at its currently depressed market value. Household and industrial gas sales are increasing sharply, so its main business is sound. The firm also has considerable valuable land, much of which will be developed soon and increase in price. This includes its Toyosu Works on Tokyo Bay and 660,000 square meters in the Tokyo suburbs near the proposed Tokyo Bay highway. The company supplies city gas to the Kanto area, including Tokyo and eight other prefectures. It leads other gas companies in converting petroleum products into LNG.

With a solid business, diversification into technologies such as fuel, batteries, and home security services, and large undervalued land holdings, Tokyo Gas is safer than most TSE stocks, yet its potential for gain in value above the market averages is substantial. However, revenues are sensitive both to the price of oil and the yen/dollar exchange rate. It loses ¥4.6 billion for each $1 increase in the price of crude and ¥800 million for each ¥1 decline per dollar.

Tokyo Gas is also constructing a 52 storey building on its own land scheduled for completion in October 1993. The top six shareholders are life insurance companies which collectively hold 28.2% of the outstanding shares.

The stock in the ¥565 range seems very reasonable. The pull back from the ¥1500 range because of the discounting of the value of its land holdings and higher material costs provides a good entry point.

Prices	High	Low	Yearly G/L (%)
To 1985	370 (85)	48 (50)	
1986	1250 (Dec)	277 (Jan)	264.8
1987	1590 (Apr)	796 (Dec)	-24.8
1988	1560 (Nov)	780 (Jan)	61.4
1989	1440 (Jan)	1010 (Oct)	-14.0
1990	1170 (Jan)	430 (Sep)	-60.7

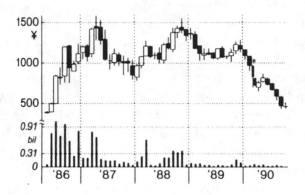

TOBU RAILWAY

Code	Price¥	CAP	Beta	Vol	PER	ROR	Div	Recommendation
9001	1470	11287	1.18	3246	167.7-	52.57	5	Hold for long term
	753				286.5			

Tobu is the third largest railway company behind Seibu and Tokyu, but it has the longest track. Like many of the railway companies, it has vast land holdings valued on the books at far less than current market prices. It is also moving into the rental, real estate and hotel business to provide more current income. The company has plans to build hotels in Urawa and Tokyo, to expand resort operations in Aizu and Nikko and to build a large sale sports club in Tokyo. It has just opened a world architecture museum in Kinugawa Its main business is about 470 kilometers of tracks in the Kanto area.

Prices	High	Low	Yearly G/L (%)
To 1985	498 (85)	48 (49)	
1986	984 (Sept)	385 (Jan)	84.4
1987	1280 (Apr)	781 (Jan)	3.6
1988	1610 (Nov)	770 (Jan)	87.7
1989	1840 (Nov)	1300 (Jun)	15.6
1990	1700 (Jan)	608 (Oct)	-60.2

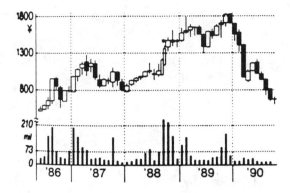

YODOGAWA STEEL WORKS

Code	Price¥	CAP	Beta	Vol	PER	ROR	Div	Recommendation
5451	1090	223	0.91	1332	21.3-	32.57	7	Buy for long term, hold
	830				35.9			

Yodogawa is the largest independent manufacturer of surface steel sheets. Its earnings and profits have been increasing steadily. Strong sales growth, increased prices, greater efficiency, and an expanding real estate business have led to this growth. Profit is expected to increase sharply due to a higher operating rate and reduced depreciation. Sales and earnings were:

Year ending in March	Sales Billions of ¥	After Tax π Billions of ¥	Earnings (¥) per Share	Dividends (¥)
1987	130.6	3.89	23.5	5.0
1988	147.1	7.40	39.1	5.5
1989	176.9	8.51	41.4	6.5
1990	187.6	10.12	49.2	7.0

Its land holdings also make the stock attractive. These include office buildings, golf courses, driving ranges, and motor pools in Osaka with revenues in excess of ¥2 billion, and plants under construction in Osaka near the Kansai International Airport near Osaka. Yodogawa also owns part of a Taiwanese rolled sheet maker. At current market prices of the land, the stock is estimated to be worth about ¥1800.

Prices	High	Low	Yearly G/L (%)
to 1985	521 (85)	33 (54)	
1986	540 (Jul)	390 (Oct)	13.8
1987	1430 (Sep)	445 (Jan)	124.2
1988	1390 (Jun)	980 (Jan)	14.3
1989	1660 (Apr)	1100 (Jan)	33.9
1990	1510 (Feb)	900 (Oct)	-29.3

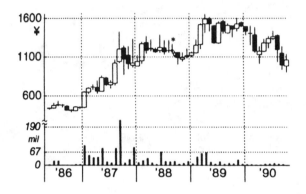

TOYOTA

Code	Price¥	CAP	Beta	Vol	PER	ROR	Div	Recommendation
7203	2510 1750	67575	0.37	15777	19.3- 28.5	17.10	19	Hold for medium term

Toyota has 43% of Japan's domestic market and has the widest array of expensive cars including its new Lexus. Its aim is 10% of the world wide car market. They are Japan's largest and the third largest auto maker in the world. Sales in Japan are expected to be about 2.53 million cars in 1990 with exports up 7.6% at 1.73 million cars. The tax reform should boost sales significantly because of the lower prices from the elimination of the large car tax. The total excise, purchase, and ownership taxes often amounted to 30% or more of the auto's value. With the tax reform, this drops to the 20% range, and further drops are planned. As well as increased sales because of lower prices, Toyota and the other large car manufacturers can slightly raise their price to make money both ways: more sales and more profit per sale.

Toyota will likely get more and more of the market, particularly the high end, with its higher profit margins. Worldwide sales had dropped slightly because of the high yen, but customer acceptance and loyalty is high (the writers of this book included). With the lower yen, sales should increase and foreign currency profit will also increase. The Camry plant in Kentucky has been very successful, and its sales do not count in any import quotas. It is currently building a second 200,000 capacity plant in Kentucky and is also developing production facilities in Europe.

Toyota's net income in the period July-December 1988 rose 64% to ¥120.6 billion, or ¥22.14 per share. Sales rose 8.8% to a record ¥3.508 trillion. Sales for the fiscal year ending in June 1989 were expected to exceed ¥7 trillion, a company record. In the last few years, it has been quite active in financial engineering and has made considerable profit. The company also has some $20 billion in cash and has one of the lowest PERs in Japan.

Prices	high	low	Yearly G/L (%)
To 1985	1650 (1981)	21 (1950	
1986	2350 (Dec)	1130 (Mar)	80.3
1987	2450 (Oct)	1360 (Apr)	-13.2
1988	3030 (Jul)	1780 (Jan)	41.9
1989	2940 (Oct)	2410 (Apr)	-1.2
1990	2620 (Jun)	1750 (Sept)	-24.8

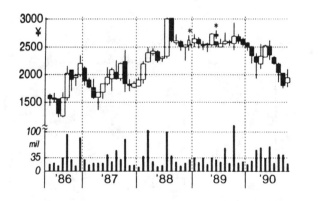

ASAHI BREWERIES

Code	Price¥	CAP	Beta	Vol	PER	ROR	Div	Recommendation
2502	1680	5104	0.99	516	106.6-	43.47	8	Hold for the long run
	1210				174.6			

Asahi Breweries has had the fastest growth and is the most profitable of
Japan's breweries. It is the third largest beer brewer with a 13% market
share. It also owns Nikka Whiskey. The entire industry is strong, with
good sales and profitability. The future, with the Japanese enjoying more
leisure time, patronizing hotels, restaurants and resorts, looks bright for
Asahi. Its profits should strengthen even further because of previous
absorptions of expenses for new bottles and boxes, advertising and
promotion costs. It has also expanded into foods and pharmaceuticals,
the latter through the addition of Torii and Co. Asahi is licensed to
produce Coors beer. Its new Ibaraki plant, which cost ¥88 billion, has just
begun production. Investment of ¥150 billion was made in the December
1989 half year to expand production capacity by 50% at seven existing
plants. It is probably best to buy the stock in January as the following
chart from the *Japan Company Handbook* suggests.

Prices	High	Low	Yearly G/L (%)
To 1985	810 (61)	95 (71)	
1986	1110 (Dec)	392 (Jan)	180.6
1987	2010 (Jun)	1040 (Jan)	45.8
1988	2440 (May	1470 (Jan)	32.0
1989	2500 (Sep)	1890 (Jan)	11.5
1990	2110 (Jan)	1000 (Oct)	-47.6

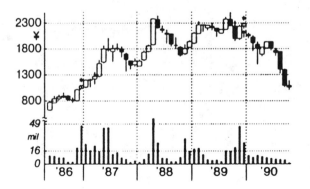

ITO-YOKADA

Code	Price¥	CAP	Beta	Vol	PER	ROR	Div	Recommendation
8264	3950	14460	0.59	269	26.7-	26.84	22	Aggressively accumulate
	3550				43.7			for mid-term holding; sell
								if recession hits

Japan's second largest but by far the most profitable supermarket chain seems poised for continued growth in sales and earnings. The company has the most advanced retailing technology in the industry. Japan's increasing emphasis on consumption plus the effective tax cut from the new tax law for most of Ito-Yokada's customers will add to sales over time. The big retailers will take more and more of the business from the *mom-and-pop* operations which dominate the current marketing structure.

Ito-Yokada opened a second department store (Robinson's) and a store in Utsunomiya in 1990. It also opened new stores in Koriyama in Fukushima prefecture, Shinkawa on the island of Hokkaido. and in Abiko in Chiba prefecture during 1989. It has several profitable and growing subsidiaries such as 7-Eleven Japan and the CVS chain.

Prices	High	Low	Yearly G/L (%)
To 1985	3280 (73)	760 (82)	
1986	4690 (Jul)	2910 (Jan)	33.4
1987	4320 (Aug)	3100 (Oct)	-7.7
1988	4850 (Apr)	3570 (Jan)	24.4
1989	5050 (Sep)	3350 (Apr)	3.8
1990	4680 (Jan)	3080 (Sep)	-26.9

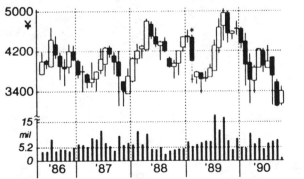

Nomura Securities

Code	Price¥	CAP	Beta	Vol	PER	ROR	Div	Recommendation
8604	3460	66261	2.32	1685	23.8-	41.93	15	Buy for long run, hold
	1770				39.2			

Nomura is the world's largest and most profitable securities firm. Traditionally, it has been the innovative leader in Japanese finance, with the other big four firms -Daiwa, Nikko and Yamaichi - following suit. Today, the other firms and the top foreign firms, have begun to be more innovative and competitive in some areas, particularly in high tech finance. Still, Nomura is the established leader. It is the world's sole investment bank with an AAA credit rating. Its 1987 earnings of ¥478.4 billion (up 28.6% from 1986) were the second highest of all companies in Japan, only behind Toyota.

Nomura, like the other major brokerage firms, makes the bulk of its income, some 80% from brokerage fees on stock, bond and warrant trading. The 1990 decline has seriously cut into this profit. However, a stock market recovery will enhance these profits. Its overseas operations are large and expanding and beginning to become profit centers. Once presence is established and market share expanded, particularly in the U.S. and Europe, these foreign operations may eventually be profitable. Nomura is also active in the very profitable underwriting business.

Prices	High	Low	Yearly G/L (%)
1985	1420 (85)	55 (65)	
1986	3720 (Oct)	1010 (Jan)	171.6
1987	5990 (Apr)	2500 (Dec)	-10.4
1988	4470 (Apr)	2500 (Jan)	46.3
1989	4120 (Jan)	3050 (Oct)	-8.0
1990	3500 (Jan)	1320 (Sep)	-55.8

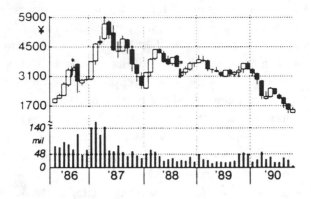

NIKON

Code	Price¥	CAP	Beta	Vol	PER	ROR	Div	Recommendation
7731	1080	3919	0.55	1321	61.0-	16.75	9	Hold for long term
	1030				122.0			

The Japanese camera makers have dominated the world wide market. Leica still has a small part of the ultra luxury market, and there is some small production in U.S. and other countries but Olympus, Minolta, Yashica and the other Japanese cameras have taken over. At the top of the heap is Nikon. Originally used by professionals and serious amateurs, Nikon cameras are known for quality of lenses and durability. The outfits we bought in Hong Kong in 1978 to do the photography work for the book *Turkish Flat Weaves*, Ziemba, Akatay, and Schwartz (1979) are still in top shape. The vast majority of professional photographers at the Seoul Olympics used Nikon equipment. Nikon's equipment is well priced and competitive with other manufactures for the general good quality camera market.

The firm is doing very well. The *Japan Company Handbook's* sales and profits given below show increases in sales and growth of earnings per share:

Year ended in March	Sales Millions of ¥	Current Profit	After Tax π Millions of ¥	Earnings (¥) per Share	Dividends (¥)
1988	170.3	5,693	2,313	6.4	5.0
1989	218.9	18,661	6,855	18.9	7.5
1990	241.1	20,201	10,869	29.6	8.75
1991 (forecast)	260.0	20,500	11,000	29.8	9.0

The camera business is doing fine, sales of single-lens reflex cameras are expected to contribute to the higher profitability. The F4 model series is Nikon's basic top-of-the-line model. But the big profit item is steppers for semi-conductors, which now amounts to over half of Nikon's total sales. It has about half of the world stepper market, and this market is expanding rapidly. Many semi-conductor manufacturers are intensively investment oriented, causing demand for steppers to increase sharply. A new machine developed as an alternative to the 4-megabit DRAMs has been faring well and is expected to develop overwhelming strength even when the age of the 4-megabit DRAM has emerged. Nikon has plans to invest more in preparation for the mass production of the next generation 4-megabit DRAMs. Nikon also produces eye glasses, microscopes and measuring instruments.

Nikon seems well poised to continue to improve its profitable operations. It has adjusted well to the increased value of the yen and is operating well at current levels. At higher dollar levels, profits will escalate further.

Nikon is an example of a company that has diversified on strength, not to balance portfolio risk. From cameras to video recorders to telescopes to computer stations for surveying, from lithographer for semi-conductors to data storage with magneto-optical disks to coating for lenses and glass tooth roots, "...our integration of highly advanced optics, electronics and precision engineering is pushing the frontiers of technology to create products that set new higher standards of quality."

Prices	High	Low	Yearly G/L (%)
to 1985	1650 (84)	43 (71)	
1986	1210 (Apr)	790 (Oct)	-17.9
1987	1380 (Oct)	576 (Apr)	3.5
1988	2440 (May)	860 (Jan)	48.8
1989	1640 (Oct)	1150 (Feb)	19.0
1990	1780 (Jul)	949 (Sep)	-29.1

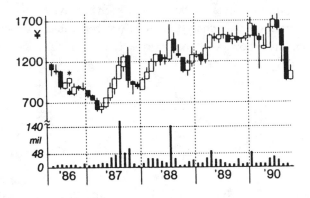

MITSUKOSHI

Code	Price¥	CAP	Beta	Vol	PER	ROR	Div	Recommendation
8231	1940	9003	0.74	936	127.6-	43.89	6	Hold for steady growth
	1160				199.1			over the long term

Mitsukoshi Ltd. is Japan's largest department-store operator and is part of the Mitsui group. Mitsukoshi operates the largest and busiest store in Japan. The main store in Nihonbashi is noted for its deluxe merchandise and high profitability. It accounts for 44% of total sales. This fashionable store has 990,425 square feet of floor space. Total sales in fiscal 1989 were $2.589 billion or $2614 per square feet up 11.4% on the year.

Robust personal consumption, which forms a major part of Japan's continuing economic growth, led to increased sales, revenue and net profits, which were up 49% to ¥4.769 billion, or ¥10.29 per share in the fiscal year that ended March 31, 1989. Clothing sales represent 36.5% of overall sales, food, 22%, and household utensils, 13%. The company is expanding into housing and mail order sales and operates foreign stores in the U.S., Madrid, Vienna, and elsewhere. It also owns 13% of Tiffany and Co., the New York retail jewelry institution. They are opening a second store in Shinjuku in the spring of 1991 and have just expanded the Mataiyama store.

The main stores in the center of Tokyo, Osaka and elsewhere sit on very valuable land, and this and other assets provide for a very low Q ratio of 0.22, as of October 1988. With the current price at 1160 versus 1940 in October 1988, the current Q ratio is well below 0.15. It is, of course, almost inconceivable that Mitsukoshi would sell this land, but this does point to the stock price not being very high relative to the company's assets. The price growth chart that follows, reprinted from the *Japan Company Handbook*, shows the steady growth in stock prices. Earnings are also increasing:

Feb 1988	¥9.6
Feb 1989	12.6
Feb 1990	14.2
Feb 1991 forecast	15.6
Feb 1992 forecast	16.6

With a low Q ratio , the company is also quite undervalued, so it can be considered as a land play also. It's a good bet for the future. With most stocks in Japan, January is a good entry point, and we see that its low for the year in three of the past five years was in January, and in another, an entry in January would still have produced considerable profits.

Prices	High	Low	Yearly G/L (%)
to 1985	1710 (51)	168 (56)	
1986	1410 (Aug)	580 (Jan)	87.2
1987	1980 (Jun)	1060 (Feb)	30.4
1988	2170 (Dec)	1410 Jan)	49.7
1989	2740 (Dec)	2140 (Jan)	25.8
1990	2730 (Jan)	1000 (Oct)	-57.5

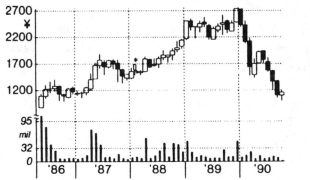

KOITO

Code	Price¥	CAP	Beta	Vol	PER	ROR	Div	Recommendation
7276	2804	4552	0.04	1081	83.7	44.84	8	Watch the action from the
	3080				209.1			sidelines

Koito is a major manufacturer of automotive lighting equipment and is closely linked to Toyota Motor. This business is growing in volume and value due to consumer preferences for luxury cars. It has a subsidiary that produces traffic signals and sanitary equipment. It also produces circuit boards and aircraft parts. Koito has a number of joint ventures in the U.S., Thailand, and elsewhere.

The stock has made the news because of the acquisition of 20.2% and then a further 6% of the shares by legendary corporate greenmailer T. Boone Pickens. Pickens bought these shares at a discount from Kitaro Watanabe, the president of Azabu Motors, who purchased them beginning in 1987 for ¥550 per share. Watanabe, also known as a corporate raider, was unable to sell the shares back to Koito or Toyota and sold them to Pickens. By Japanese law, Koito could claim back the profits of this sale and it did. This ¥1.17 billion is still being held by Koito. Pickens claimed to be a long term investor but he had a difficult time convincing the Japanese of this. They refused to give him board seats. However, his pressure to increase the dividend may have worked as an increase to ¥10 is expected. Since this activity and its political aspects for Pickens and U.S.-Japanese relations are detracting from the main business of Koito we recommend not being involved. Pickens finally gave up and sold his stock to Watanabe.

The stock's price rose sharply from the ¥500 range where it was from 1984 to mid 1987, to the ¥4500-5000 range, an increase of about ten times. Profits have increased hardly at all. The current price of ¥3080 is reflecting more the hidden assets and the 1990 decline. Koito was one of the few large capitalized Japanese stocks to rise in 1990. Boone Co. is the largest owner, followed by Toyota, which owns 19%, Nissan, 5.9%, and Matsushita, 5.3%.

Prices	High	Low	Yearly G/L (%)
To 1985	685 (1985)	10 (1950)	
1986	722 (Jul)	505 (Oct)	-9.0
1987	1660 (Dec)	510 (Apr)	182.6
1988	3820 (Aug)	1520 (Jan)	123.7
1989	5470 (Mar)	3300 (Aug)	3.2
1990	3890 (Jul)	2800 (Mar)	4.3

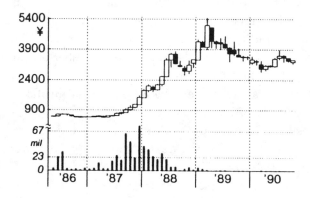

MITSUBISHI ESTATE CO. LTD

Code	Price¥	CAP	Beta	Vol	PER	ROR	Div	Recommendation
8802	2550	32,335	1.74	2859	61.9-	41.35	7.5	Buy for long term,
	1400				112.7			hold and land play

Mitsubishi Estate is the largest owner of office buildings in downtown Tokyo. It has at least 24 major buildings. Each new building in downtown Tokyo costs about ¥50-100 billion to develop, so it has emphasized development in other areas. These include housing developments in Forest Park Town on the outskirts of Sapporo (102 hectares), Kanazawabunko Park Town in Yokahama (31 hectares), Inagawa Park Town in Hyuogo Prefecture (122 hectares) and Iguchidai Park Town in Hiroshima (61 hectares). It has constructed 738 large condominiums at Park Town Tamagawa in Tokyo and 1000 more at Suma Park Hills in Hyogo prefecture. It also has many joint activities and has diversified into other areas of business including resort development, and is expanding investments in large scale development projects such as MM21 on the coast, mainly in Yokahama.

Recently Mitsubishi Estate purchased 51% of the 19 building complex known as Rockefeller Center in New York for $846 million, or some ¥120 billion. While the price and boldness raised eyebrows in the U.S., the price is not expensive in comparison with many of the company's single buildings in Tokyo. This purchase puts its overseas assets at 15% of total consolidated assets. Later they bought another $400 million stake to increase their ownership to over 70%.

Sales and profits are growing rapidly and they are expected to continue to improve with the aggressive tactics of Mitsubishi Jisho, as it is called in Japan. But interest charges are high. With a Q ratio of about 0.17 at the end of 1990, the land holdings are only valued at a tenth of their market values so the stock can also be considered to be a land play. The *Japan Company Handbook's* estimates of sales, profits and earnings for the fiscal years 1988 to 1992 in millions of yen are:

		Profit			
Year Ending	Sales	Current	After-Tax	EPS	Dividend
Mar 1988	236,354	64,187	29,891	23.6	7.20
Mar 1989	274,409	76,262	35,542	26.0	7.50
Mar 1990	314,925	85,400	43,853	34.4	8.50
Mar 1991,est.	330,000	88,000	44,000	34.4	7.5-8.5
Mar 1992,est.	350,000	90,000	46,000	36.0	7.5-8.5

Prices	High	Low	Yearly G/L (%)
To 1985	1550 (1953)	121 (1964)	
1986	2850 (Sep)	1070 (Jan)	104.1
1987	3520 (Apr)	1580 (Dec)	-34.9
1988	3000 (Nov)	1510 (Jan)	66.7
1989	2950 (Feb)	2220 (Jan)	-7.1
1990	2500 (Jul)	995 (Sep)	-54.0

CHAPTER 9
MUTUAL FUNDS FOR INVESTMENT IN JAPAN
BY JAPANESE AND BY FOREIGNERS

FUNDS MANAGED IN THE U.S. WITH JAPANESE EQUITIES

Table 9.1 lists thirteen mutual funds that invest at least a part of their assets in Japanese securities.[1] All of them had outstanding performances during the bull market from 1983 to 1987. These thirteen were all in the top fourteen of the 555 funds in the universe of the rating agency Lipper Analytic Services, Inc. As the Japanese market has gone higher and higher some of these funds have lowered their holdings in Japan. It may be hard for the Japanese investments to keep pace with the four tigers (Taiwan, Singapore, Hong Kong and Korea) and other countries in Asia. A fund that invests in several of these areas may be preferable. Good funds in this category are the Asia Pacific Fund and the Scudder New Asia Fund, both of which are discussed below. All these funds will send you free prospectuses. Check them carefully for current holdings, load, charges and management fees. Do not forget that your return can be affected by currency movements as well as share price gains if the fund does not hedge. The yen may not appreciate much more against the U.S. dollar, but it is not unlikely that the other currencies will because their economies are strong and growing and these currencies have been held in check to maximize exports. Slowly the exchange rates are creeping up.

The Japan Fund Inc. was the first major U.S. fund to invest in Japan. Figure 9.1 and Table 9.2 show how a $10,000 investment in April 1962 when the fund began would have fared. Reinvesting all capital gains and dividends provides a tidy sum of some $1.53 million or a growth of 153 times the original investment as of the end of 1989. The fund does not hedge, so these results reflect the favorable move in the currency from 360 yen per dollar to 143.76 at the end of 1989. This appears to be more than

---

[1]Like all the suggestions in this book, the authors have no stake in the management of these companies; although, we may invest in some of these suggestions in personal or managed accounts.

the NSA or Topix indices gained, as we discussed in Chapter 2, which is the mark of good management based on fundamentals or anomalies or other sound investment strategy.

Table 9.1
How Mutual Funds with Japanese Securities Fared, December 31, 1982 to December 31, 1987

International & Global Funds	5-Year Lipper-Rank (of 555)	Portfolio % in Japanese securities	Total Assets (mil. $)	Total Return Performance			$10,000 Invested 12/31/82 worth on 12/31/87
				1986	% 1/1/87 through 9/30/87	1987	
Merrill Lynch Pacific Fund	1	44	490.2	78.05	53.47	13.77	$40,504
Japan Fund*	2	100	538.0	69.50	32.16	31.62	39,337
Vanguard World-Int'l Growth	3	34	645.5	56.71	29.22	12.48	39,138
BBK International	4	39	113.4	61.97	17.60	3.30	36,458
Putnam Int'l Equities	5	7	718.3	37.66	32.28	8.45	31,747
T. Rowe Price Int'l Fund	6	20	1,091.0	61.29	30.48	7.99	30,636
Transatlantic Growth Fund	7	28	95.7	52.62	33.92	9.28	29,259
Scudder International Fund	8	22	900.8	50.70	31.35	0.85	29,105
Kemper International Fund	9	39	249.3	44.17	26.65	6.46	27,853
Alliance International Fund	10	19	106.4	43.90	24.82	-5.37	27,848
Templeton Foreign Fund	11	0	327.9	28.78	49.90	24.72	27,487
United Int'l Growth Fund	13	21	324.4	30.31	36.82	17.10	26,461
GT Pacific Growth Fund	14	22	58.2	70.04	33.59	2.89	25,485

*This closed end fund was open ended in 1987 and it now so trades through its management by Scudder, Stevens and Clark.

Source: *Investor's Monthly*, February 1988

Such calculations typically appear in fund prospectuses and greatly *overstate* the fund's performance because one would have had to pay considerable *taxes* on the dividends and capital gains reinvested along the way. Table 9.2 indicates that the $10,000 grew to $34,248 with $993,110 in capital gains and $559,731 in income paid along the way. Hence the total investment to net the $1.53 million was well over $100,000. To properly compare the growth with the NSA and Topix, one must discount all the investment costs back to 1949, and to evaluate it for a given person one must consider the after tax returns. Still the results are impressive.

Ziemba invested in the Japan Fund for a client in 1986 and 1987. At that time, the fund was a closed-end mutual fund whose price was determined on the NYSE via a bid-ask process because, for such funds, the number of shares is fixed. Many closed-end mutual funds trade at a substantial discount, others at premiums. The net asset values in Table 9.2 do not give the market prices for which one could have sold the shares.

Researchers, such as Thompson (1978), have shown that investments in a diversified portfolio of deep discount, closed-end mutual funds have returns that exceeds the market averages by about 4% per year when risk adjusted. For surveys of recent results, see Lee, Shleifer and Thaler (1990) and Ziemba (1991e). At the time of our purchase, the Japan Fund was at a large discount. One could buy the fund at a price much below the net asset value of the Japanese and other shares and assets the fund owned. The reasons why some closed-end funds sell at such heavy discounts and others at hefty premiums is not well understood. Investor sentiment, liquidity, riskiness of the assets held, investment restrictions, future prospects and currency risk are part of the story. However, for an investor, buying deep discounted closed-end mutual funds can be an effective strategy, especially if they are investing in stocks one would like to own. With a 20% discount one could then buy stocks in Japan at 80¢ on the dollar.

Figure 9.1
Results of $10,000 Investment in the Japan Fund, Dividends and Capital Gains Reinvested, Before Taxes, April 1962 to the End of 1989

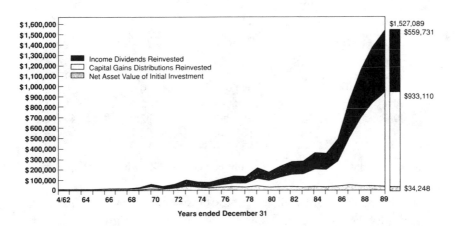

Source: The Japan Fund

Table 9.2
Results from a $10,000 Investment in the Japan Fund, April 1962 to the
End of 1989, Dividends and Capital Gains Reinvested, Before Taxes*

End of Year	Net Asset Value Initial Investment	Capital Gains Reinvested	Income Dividends Reinvested	Total Net Asset Value
April 1962	$10,000			$10,000
1962	9,240	0	0	9,240
1963	8,016	376	279	8,671
1964	8,328	377	663	9,368
1965	11,328	532	1,605	13,465
1966	12,120	569	2,290	14,979
1967	11,633	1,098	2,707	15,438
1968	16,327	4,339	5,023	25,689
1969	33,912	11,406	11,764	57,082
1970	19,176	9,500	7,754	36,430
1971	24,168	19,769	12,488	56,425
1972	39,744	35,741	22,008	97,493
1973	28,032	31,357	17,749	77,138
1974	22,056	33,149	18,536	73,741
1975	27,048	49,813	27,282	104,143
1976	31,440	65,599	36,419	133,458
1977	27,720	66,110	36,942	130,772
1978	38,976	109,337	62,808	211,121
1979	27,192	90,296	52,187	169,675
1980	30,840	112,689	71,720	215,249
1981	33,024	148,419	89,112	270,555
1982	28,800	153,181	93,661	275,642
1983	33,360	198,646	123,655	355,661
1984	30,240	195,911	123,184	349,335
1985	37,272	274,986	172,921	485,179
1986	48,672	504,968	307,771	861,411
1987	40,728	689,290	415,714	1,145,732
1988	38,976	831,796	497,276	1,368,048
1989	34,248	933,110	559,731	1,527,089

* The fund operated as a closed end fund until August 14, 1987 when it was open ended

The Japan Fund did well as the stocks rose and the yen strengthened.
Ziemba also believed that at some time somebody might take over the
fund and make it open ended. This they could do by buying the shares at
80%, 81%, 82%, 83% etc until they had enough shares to attempt to force
the present management, via a shareholder vote, to open up the fund so it
would become a regular, open ended, mutual fund and trade at its net
asset value. If such a takeover is successful, then the fund is open-ended

Table 9.3

Closed End Equity and Convertible Mutual Funds September 4, 1989

Fund Name	Exch	NAV	Price	% Diff	Fund Name	Exch	NAV	Price	% Diff
1st Australian	AMEX	10.83	10.25	-6.51	Hampton Utils Tr Cap	AMEX	11.60	9.94	-14.26
1st Iberian	AMEX	10.19	10	-1.86	Hampton Utils Tr Pref	AMEX	49.17	49.94	-2.51
ASA Ltd,	NYSE	55.93	42.5	-23.79	Helvetia Fund	NYSE	12.59	11.25	-10.64
American Capital Conv	NYSE	24.52	21.88	-10.79	India	NYSE	14.08	16.75	16.3
Asia Pacific	NYSE	13.74	13	-5.39	Italy Fund	NYSE	11.91	9.75	-18.14
BGR Prec Metals	TOR	11.60	10	-13.79	Korea Fund	NYSE	19.28	39.5	104.88
Bancrott Convertible	AMEX	21.76	18	-13.26	MG Small Cap	NYSE	z	z	z
Bergstrom Capital	AMEX	63.42	59	-6.58	Malaysia Fund	NYSE	11.43	11.75	1.71
Brazil	NYSE	18.37	10	-41.48	Meeschaert G&C	MWST	8.1	7.88	-2.78
CNV Holdings Capital	NYSE	10.73	5.75	-49.91	Mexico Fund	NYSE	12.18	11.63	-4.56
CNV Holdings Income	NYSE	9.55	11.75	23.04	Patriot Premium Div Fd	NYS.E	9.9	10.5	6.06
Castle Convertible	AMEX	22.65	19.5	-13.91	Petrol & Resources	NYSE	30.45	26.13	-14.2
Central Fund Canada	AMEX	4.93	4.94	0.15	Pilgrim Reg Bk Shms	NYSE	11.47	10.13	-11.73
Central Securities	AMEX	13.09	10.25	-21.7	Real Estate Sm Inc Fd	AMEX	8.7	8.75	0.57
Counselers Tandem Secs	AMEX	12.87	10.75	-16.47	ROCTwn	NYSE	15.36	15	-2.34
Cypress Fund	NYSE	11.05	10.75	-6.11	Regional Fin Shrs Inv	NYSE	9.93	8.88	-10.62
Duff & Phelps Sel Utils	AMEX	8.52	8.25	-3.17	Scudder New Asia	NYSE	15.31	11.75	-23.25
Ellsworth Conv Gr&Inc	NYSE	9.03	7.88	-12.79	Spain Fund	NYSE	14.01	17.25	23.13
Engex Inc	AMEX	14.289	9.94	-30.41	TCW Convertible Secs	NYSE	9.16	8.38	-8.57
Financial News Composite	AMEX	21.40	20	-2.45	Taiwan Fund	NYSE	z	z	z
First Financial Fund	NYSE	11.88	10.88	-8.46	ThaiFund	NYSE	16.59	19	14.53
France Fund	NYSE	12.59	11	-5.68	Temp Energy Mkts	AMEX	12.44	12.13	-2.53
Gabelli Equity Trust	NYSE	14.70	14	-4.76	Templeton Value Fd	NYSE	10.98	9.63	-12.34
Germany Fund	NYSE	9.70	8.88	-8.51	UK Fund	NYSE	12.14	10.25	-15.57
H&Q Healthcare Inv	NYSE	10.22	8.25	-19.28	Z-Seven	OTC	14.59	14.75	1.1

z= not avilable

Source: *Barron's*

and new investors are simply given new shares and shares are cancelled for sales. A group did in fact do this and the Japan Fund was open-ended on August 14, 1987. Those holding the fund at the time made a huge gain. Table 9.2 shows the gain from the beginning of 1986 to the end of 1987, which includes the stockmarket crash, to be 1,145,732/485,179, or 188%. Overall for sample periods ending December 31, 1989, the Japan Fund was in the top 1% of all funds in Lipper's universe which consisted of 710 and 427 funds, for five and ten year periods, respectively.

Is the Japan Fund a good investment now? We think so. It is run by strong management in the Scudder group as a no load fund. The only costs for investors are the advisory fee of about 0.63% and trading and other expenses of about 0.38% or about 1.01% per year. One must bear yen/dollar risk though. Investors could hedge this separately by themselves.

All the Japanese funds listed in Table 9.1 are to be recommended. One should check current holdings in the prospectus and fees. With very strong management available at 0.30% to 1% per year in fees, we see no reason to recommend funds with loads unless the loads are small and the management is truely exceptional. There is considerable evidence that, on average, you will do better with no load funds.

Some funds try to beat the market and others try to match an attractive index. Index funds have lower fees in the 0.30% per year range plus transactions costs. An example is the Vanguard International Equity Index Fund. Its Pacific Portfolio attempts to match the 400 stock Morgan Stanley Capital International Pacific Index with stocks from Japan, Australia, New Zealand, Hong Kong and Singapore. From 1970 to 1989, this index returned an average of 18.7% per year versus 11.8% for the S&P 500. Most stocks were Japanese which accounted for 91% of the index as of March 30, 1990.

Many of the funds listed in Table 9.1, being Asia-Pacific funds, are only partially invested in Japan. Very good closed-end funds in 1989 were the Asia Pacific Fund Inc and the Scudder New Asia Fund, Inc. both of which trade on the NYSE. Again, with sizeable discounts, one can, at times, buy these funds at 80¢ or so on the dollar and benefit from possible open ending at some stage as well as strong gains on the securities held. Table 9.3 lists closed-end funds and their discounts as of September 4. Current information can be found in *Barron's*, *The Wall Street Journal* or *Investors Daily*. *Barron's*, which comes out on the weekend, has the most thorough treatment.

We have listed all the equity and convertible funds. Asia Pacific was trading at $13 per share, a 5.39% discount from its net asset value of $13.74. Hence, one is essentially buying the fund's assets and there is not much of an open-ending play. Scudder New Asia was more appealing on these latter grounds with a sizeable 23.25% discount while trading at 11.75

with a 15.31 net asset value. At 11.75 the fund made substantial gains during 1989 from its low of 8.125. However it has traded as high as 12.625, and it was a new issue of 7 million shares at $12 per share with an underwriting fee of 7% for an initial net asset value of $11.16. We would not want to buy at the initial $12 because the 7% is immediately lost, plus the fund did, as did many others, trade at a discount. See Lee, Shleifer and Thaler (1990) for evidence on this point. But later when the fund is at a 20% discount, it is a good investment risk. Also, at a total size of about $90 million, its chances of being opened up are not small. On June 30, 1989, the fund was 90.2% invested in Asian equity and bonds, with 9.8% held in short-term money market instruments. The largest holding was in Japan with other sizeable investments in Thailand, Hong Kong, the Philippines, and other Asian countries as detailed in the following list:

	% of Portfolio
Japan	43.3%
Thailand	13.3
Hong Kong	9.2
The Philippines	5.9
Korea	4.6
India	3.7
Singapore	3.6
Malaysia	1.7
Indonesia	1.0
Other	3.9
Total invested	90.2%

One sees no exposure to the profitable but violently explosive and risky Taiwan market. The fund can hedge foreign currency risks, as discussed in Chapter 6 using forward contracts. This presumably lowers the fund's risk and adds to its expected return in U.S. dollars.

ASIAN EQUITY FUNDS IN HONG KONG

Table 9.4 shows the ten best and worst performing Asian equity funds available in Hong Kong for the past three months, the past year and the past five years during the period ended August 31, 1988. The performance is measured in U.S. dollars, so the gains or losses reflect equity returns compounded with currency fluctuations. During the past three months the U.S. dollar increased in value against the yen by about 8.4%, see Figure 9.2, and not surprisingly Japanese funds predominate the

Table 9.4
How Asian Equity Funds Available in Hong Kong Fared in % Gained:
Past Three Months, Past Year, Five Years ending August 31, 1988

June-Aug Top 10		One Year Top 10		Five Years Top 10	
Thornton Philip. Redevelopment	21.93	NM Australian	24.28	Jardine Fleming P.C.	482.87
Baring Australia	14.98	Scimitar Japanese	20.36	Jardine Fleming Japan	411.85
Connaught World Gwth	12.05	NM Schroder J.S.C.	15.34	GT Honshu Pathfinder	390.10
NM Australian	10.75	G.T. Berry Japan	12.11	Wardley Japan	369.79
Connaught Pacific Ent.	10.16	Japan Technology	9.99	MIM Japan Growth	353.93
Citicorp CI Hong Kong	9.41	NM Schroder Tokyo	8.73	Schroders Japan	352.41
Citicorp CI U.K.	9.35	Jardine Fleming J.T.	8.60	Hambro-Pacific Jpn	345.54
Jardine Fleming Philip.	8.50	Fidelity Japan Sit.	8.32	Jardine Fleming P.S.	333.83
Thornton Little Dragons	8.40	Hambro-Pacific J.E.	7.91	NM Schroder Tokyo	321.83
MIM Brit. Amer. S.C.	8.36	GT Honshu Pathfinder	6.51	Fidelity Sp. Sit. Jpn.	298.71
Bottom 10		**Bottom 10**		**Bottom 10**	
Jardine Fleming J.S.C.	-17.69	Thornton Kangaroo	-60.00	Foreign Inv. Fund. Am.	-37.17
Hambro-Pacific Jpn. E.	-16.76	Gartmore Orient. V.	-58.00	Gartmore Australia	-19.48
Jardine Fleming Jpn.	-14.94	Thornton HK/China	-56.74	C.T. Technology	-13.20
Hambro-Pacific Japan	-14.62	SHK Hong Kong	-56.05	Jardine Fleming Am. G.	-13.10
Fedelity Japan Sit.	-14.45	Gartmore Australia	-55.59	MIM Britannia A.S.C.	-11.50
NM Port Sel. Jpn. S.C.	-14.37	Gartmore Hong Kong	-52.24	Jardine Fleming Aust.	-11.38
GT Honshu Pathfinder	-14.23	Hambro-Pacific Aust.	-49.78	G.T. Australia	-11.15
Federated Japan	-14.17	Gartmore Sing/Mal.	-47.89	Singapore/Malaysia	-10.82
G.T. Japan Sm. Co.	-13.95	Jardine Fleming Aust.	-47.59	G.T. Dollar	-0.74
Baring Japan	-13.38	GAM Australia	46.70	Gartmore N. Amer.	-0.33

Source: *The Asian Wall Street Journal*, September 23-24, 1988

bottom ten in this period. The best performing Japanese mutual fund lost 3.8% in this three-month period. However, over longer periods, the Japanese funds have done very well. All ten of the top funds over the five year period are invested in Japanese securities. They had the compound gains of high market returns coupled with strong currency gains. Of course, with currency hedging even these funds would have had gains in the past three months. With the benefits of hedging, that we discussed in

Chapter 6, it is surprising that none of these funds hedges. As mentioned above, one can always hedge separately from the fund.

According to Todd (1988), among the 26 fund categories monitored by Wyatt Co., which tracks fund returns for the Hong Kong Unit Trust Association, only nine bond funds have a five-year track record. The $16.3 million Schroders Currency & Bond Fund was the best performer with a 128.5% return. Todd writes,

> ...so-called ASEAN trusts registered a median gain of 3.3%. Currency funds denominated in Australian dollars and Canadian dollars also gained 2% to 4%. Trusts invested in Asia's smaller markets and in U.S.-dollar bond and currency funds eked out median gains of less than 2%.
>
> Over the year ended in August, non-dollar currency and bond funds dominate in terms of fund categories, reflecting the weakness of the dollar early in the period. Canadian-dollar and Australian-dollar funds gained more than 10%, as did British currency and bond funds. Equity funds generally registered median losses for the year.
>
> In terms of individual funds, however, managers of some Japanese equity trusts maintained their leadership for the year. The exception and top performer was the $35.2 million National Mutual Australian Fund, with a 24.3% gain. The fund was largely in cash before last October's global crash and has been able to profit from the Australian market's subsequent rebound. Other Australian funds weren't so fortunate and continued to occupy prominent places among the one year losers.
>
> Over the five years ended in August, Jardine Fleming Pacific Income Trust, Jardine Fleming Japan Trust and G.T. Honshu Pathfinder retained their long-standing positions as the top three equity performers. All three are large trusts that manage well over $100 million. The losers list also was little-changed over the long term. U.S. equity funds remained prominent in the list, along with a sprinkling of Asian funds.
>
> Among bond funds, the top performer for the quarter was the $1.4 million National Mutual Portfolio Selection. The Dollar Fixed Interest Fund, had a 4% gain. Other U.S.-dollar bond funds also did almost as well. The biggest loser for the quarter was the $1.5 million Wardley Global Select Sterling Bond Fund, with a 13.2% loss. Non-dollar bond funds generally performed poorly during the quarter.
>
> But because the dollar didn't strengthen until recently, bond funds denominated in pounds, yen and the European currencies turned in the best one-year performances. U.S.-dollar bond funds generally registered losses for the year despite their recent strength.

TRUST FUNDS AVAILABLE IN JAPAN

Table 9.5 lists foreign investment trust shares sold in Japan.

Table 9.5
Foreign Investment Trust Shares Sold in Japan as of December 31, 1986

Issue	Type	Domicile	Marketing Securities Companies	Date Launched Period	Balance (Net Asset Value) Japan	Balance (Net Asset Value) Total
Fidelity Discovery Fund	Corporate	Luxembourg	Marusan	1985 Jan. 22-29	¥m 17,577	¥m 20,236
Dreyfus American Fund	—	—	Daiwa	April 18-26	22,176	22,321
Save-and-Prosper Balance Fund	—	—	Nomura	June 25-28	38,703	39,514
U.S. Filadel Securities Fund S.A.	—	—	Toyko Branch of Merrill Lynch	July 27-31	8,491	87,537
World Bond Fund	—	—	Nikko	Aug. 30 - Sept. 4	27,333	28,208
U.S. Pacific Stock Fund, S.A.	—	—	Yamaichi	Sept. 2-6	10,824	11,061
Industria Fund	Contractual	West Germany	Daiwa	Oct. 23-26	4,635	9,889
Target International Growth Fund	—	Luxembourg	New Japan	Nov. 8-13	15,562	18,561
Pacific Growth Fund	—	—	Pacific	Dec. 2-6	8,855	9,073
NM Income Fund	—	—	Nomura	1986 Jan. 13-17	83,615	84,033
Top-Brand Fund International S.A.	—	—	Yamaichi	Feb. 17-21	16,127	18,348
World Stock Fund	—	—	Nikko	Mar. 17-20	14,605	15,958
Okasan Britania Global Strategy Fund	—	—	Okasan	Mar. 24-27	2,619	3,267
International Bond Index Fund	—	—	Kokusai	Apr. 1-4	6,971	7,138
Alliance Global Bond Fund	—	—	Nomura	Apr. 28-30	8,946	9,097
Australia Fund	—	—	Daiwa	May 20-23	8,554	8,829
Henderson International Select Fund	—	—	Nippon Kangyo Kakumaru	July 21-24	8,701	10,479
First Convertible Securities Fund	—	—	Tokyo Branch of Merrill Lynch	Aug. 20-26	12,758	26,479
Nomura-Prudential Global Portfolio Fund	—	—	Nomura	Aug. 25-27	6,098	11,356
Fidelity International Fund	—	—	Yamatane	Aug. 26-28	3,569	21,266
International Specialty Fund S.A.	—	—	Yamaichi	Sept. 2-4	10,452	11,264
Prudential Special Equity Fund	—	—	Nikko	Sept. 8-12	17,939	21,243
Transworld Bond Trust Fund	Contractual	—	Pacific	Sept. 29 - Oct. 3	5,682	6,420
Nomura Capital International Equity Fund	Corporate	—	Nomura	Oct. 6-8	15,059	18,301
World Capital Growth Fund	—	—	New Japan	Nov. 13-19	8,220	9,903
World Balance Fund	—	—	Daiwa	Nov. 26-27	29,715	30,845
Inter-Stock Fund Nomura-Robeco	—	—	Nomura	Dec. 8-10	15,976	18,280
GT International Bond Fund	—	—	Tokyo	Dec. 10-16	4,928	6,365
Fidelity Global Industries Fund	—	—	Universal	Dec. 11-17	4,890	5,892

Figure 9.2
The Currency Factor, The Dollar's Rise Against Four Major Units, Percent
Change May 31 to August 31, 1988

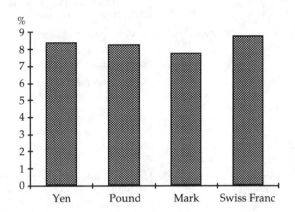

JAPANESE VERSUS AMERICAN STYLES OF RUNNING MUTUAL FUNDS

There are many criteria one can employ in the selection of a mutual fund. Fees, current and past performance, goals, transactions costs, and security are among them. Presumably long-run risk adjusted performance net of all costs should be the primary criteria. Even that is hard to measure, and the academic world has not settled into a set of procedures that most agree are the correct way to performance evaluate a fund.

According to Viner (1988), there are the old and new rules for running mutual funds in Japan which are as follows:

Old Rules	New Rules
The management of money shadows the management of relationships.	A new pragmatism will shift corporate vision to promises of improved portfolio performance, pushing some old relationships into disuse.
At trust banks and insurance companies, Portfolio performance = Gross yield.	Portfolio performance = Yield ... but not forever.
Low return and low risk.	Higher return and higher risk.
Just as performance is not the goal of management institutions in Japan, it is also not the goal of individual fund managers.	New performance: the be-all and the end-all of the investment management business.
At investment trusts, portfolio performance = Brokerage commissions.	At investment trusts, portfolio performance will rise while brokerage commissions decline.
Japanese capital management firms, like the investment trusts, provide the parent securities company with a vital source of brokerage commissions.	Japanese capital management firms, gradually forced to compete with foreign managers in the domestic market, will be obliged to improve portfolio performance at the expense of brokerage commissions for their parents.

Not surprisingly, given this modus operandi, foreign mutual funds specializing in Japanese securities have outperformed Japanese fund managers. But this is changing, and all the big four and other major brokerage houses now have state of the art models that attempt to beat the market or to stay up with it using index funds. The weak market in 1990 has put further focus on actual performance. More and more, the ability of the major Japanese firms to retain their accounts will depend on good performance.

CHAPTER 10
FAVORABLE SEASONALITY CALENDARS FOR 1988-92

Many factors – interest, inflation, exchange rate changes, industrial productivity and earnings, growth in real money, commodity prices, particularly oil, debt, and trade numbers – affect the Japanese stock market. During the steep rise in 1988, it was often said that low oil prices, low inflation, low interest rates and a strong yen propelled the market to new highs. A strong yen decreases the profits of many exporters. This effect was considered to be negative until recently.[1] However, there are many favorable consequences of the strong yen, particularly low interest rates. In fact, econometric studies, such as those discussed in Chapter 5, have shown that a strong yen, which allows interest rates to fall (with high savings), has been a plus for the stock market over long periods. In 1990 a weaker yen plus higher inflation, much of which was caused by the consumption tax, led to a substantial increase in interest rates and sharply lower stock prices. The yen finally strengthened when the discount rate became 6% but by then the damage to the stock market was done.

PREDICTING VERSUS TIMING THE MARKET

A Nomura study for the six year bull market from October 1982 to October 1988 cites steady growth in industrial production, real money supply and a downturn in interest rates as the forces behind this rise. Starting at ¥6,849, the rise was about ¥21,000 from October 1982 to October 1988. Over this period, industrial production expanded about 30% while the real money supply doubled, causing real interest rates to fall about 37% from 8.3% to 5.2%. The regression model indicates that the ¥21,000 gain can be attributed to a ¥3,000 gain from the growth in industrial production, an ¥8,000 gain from a decline in long term interest rates, and a

---

[1]The worry is that a strong yen would hurt exports. This is referred to as the *endaka* crisis which we discussed in Ziemba and Schwartz (1991). This happened for a number of companies. In total, the volume of trade did decrease, but not the value in dollars of this export, because of the J-curve effect. Other pluses perceived by the general market are the ability to purchase foreign assets and imported goods, such as oil, cheaply.

¥10,000 gain from the growth in real money supply. This model provides the following handy model for predicting changes in the NSA 225:

Factor	% Change	% Rise in NSA
Industrial production index	+1	0.6
Real money supply	+1	1.0
Long term interest rate	-0.5	8.8

This and the other models discussed in Chapter 5 give us some ways to predict with some success the general level of the market, particularly if we can evaluate longer periods such as six months or a year. The shorter the prediction interval is, the more difficult an accurate prediction becomes.

Timing the market is extraordinarily difficult. When we get down to weekly or daily periods, the prediction models have more and more trouble. We know that particular months are more favorable to the general market and to specific groups of stocks. In this book, we have tried to present information on good strategies for investing in Japan. Some of this research concerns security market regularities or anomalies that lead to strategies that usually beat the market. Several of the strategies involve seasonal regularities, and these have been combined to form the calendars for 1991 and 1992 that follow. These calendars reflect the elimination of Saturday trading at the end of January 1989. These are preceded by the calendars for 1988 and January 1989 with Saturday trading for the NSA and the Topix, and the calendars without Saturday trading for the rest of 1989 and for 1990. The tests that follow are supportive of the hypothesis that the seasonality calendars do help performance. Obviously, if the market is crashing or bursting to the upside based on other considerations that have captivated the market of the moment, the market may rise or fall when it is unlikely based on the seasonality. But more often than not, these seasonality effects should work to your advantage.

SEASONALITY CALENDARS FOR 1988 TO 1992: RATING RULES
The seasonality calendars for 1989 (February and later) to 1992 were formed on the following basis. Modified ratings for 1988 to February 1989 with Saturday trading and their results appear below. The days are graded on a scale of -4 (the worst) to +4 (the best).[2]

---

[2]The ratings for 1989 (February) to 1992 were developed using a 52 variable computer model developed by Asaji Komatsu and William Ziemba at the Yamaichi Research

1. **Days of the Week Effects.** Since Saturday trading stopped at the end of January 1989, day of the week effects now proceed via the results in Table 3.4 for the third week of the month, which ended with Friday trading following a week that also ended with Friday trading. The estimated mean returns are

Monday	Tuesday	Wednesday	Thursday	Friday
-0.3489	0.1931	0.2479	0.2609	0.2193.

All days are strongly positive, except Mondays, which are strongly negative. The strongly positive Tuesday is somewhat of a speculation but that's what the data indicate. However, given the evidence in the U.S. of only mildly positive Tuesdays and the tradition of negative Tuesdays in Japan, its positive rating is lower than for Wednesday to Friday.

2. **Holiday Effect.** Days before a holiday are rated +4, except Mondays, which are at +2, Tuesdays +3, and holidays in September and October are 0's.

3. **January, Turn of the Year Effect.**

   Trading Days   -4, -3, -1, +3, +4, +5, +7, +9, +10, +11, and +14 are rated +4
   Trading Days   -8, -7, -6, -5, -2, +1, +2, +6, +8, +12, and +13 are rated +2

   with adjustments to account for days of the week effects.

4. **Turn of the Month Effect.**

   Days   -5 to +2 at the turn of the month are the best
   Days   +3 to +7 in the *second* week of the month are good
   Days   +8 to -6 in the second half of the month are bad

   Then with the days of week effects with no Saturday trading:

Trading Days -5 to +2		Trading Days +3 to +7		Trading Days +8 to -6	
T	+2	T	+1	T	-3
W	+4	W	+2	W	-2
Th	+4	Th	+2	Th	-2
F	+4	F	+2	F	-2
M	0	M	-2	M	-4

The -1 day of month gets one or two points higher rating except for May, depending upon where it falls.

Institute that formalizes these simple rules. That model yields fewer +3 or +4 or -3 or -4 ratings than this ad hoc approach because it is based on standard deviations above or below the predicted mean TOPIX return. Special thanks go to Asaji Komatsu for her help on this material.

5. **Monthly Effect.** Lower one grade on all effects during September and October.

6. **Golden Week Effect.** The pre-holiday trading days of April 28, May 2, and May 4 and the in-between trading day, May 1, all receive +4. The post-holiday and -1 day of the month, April 30, has poor returns, on average, and is rated a -2. Trading on May 4 has been eliminated, making a three day holiday, May 3 to 5. We would expect then that the -1 day would improve to a rating of at least 0. The birthday of previous Emperor Showa, April 29, was retained as a holiday but renamed Greenery Day while December 23, Emperor Akihito's birthday, has become a new holiday.

7. **Small Firm Effect.** Small stocks have high returns in January and June, and the ratings of all days for these stocks should be increased. Because of portfolio adjustments, large stocks beat small stocks in March handily and in December by a small margin, and the ratings for these stocks should be slightly upgraded during this period.

The 1988 to February 1989 ratings with Saturday trading use the following ratings with some judgment:

1. **Days of the Week Effects.** We use the following rate of return data from Table 3.4 to influence the ratings:

Month		Trading Ends: This Week	Last Week	Mon	Tues	Wed	Thurs	Fri	Sat
1st,5th		A1	Sat	Sat	0.0198	-0.1072	0.1790	0.0581	0.0605	0.1678
4th	A2	Sat	Fri	-0.1008	-0.1102	0.1074	0.0306	0.1582	0.0793
2nd	B1	Fri	Sat	0.1135	-0.0649	0.0980	0.0933	0.1341	
3rd	B2	Fri	Fri	-0.3489	0.1931	0.2479	0.2609	0.2193	

Mondays are negative following weeks without Saturday trading, and positive or neutral otherwise. Tuesdays are negative except in the third week, when they are quite positive. Wednesdays are strongly positive. Thursdays are mildly positive except the third week, when they are strongly positive. Fridays and Saturdays are strongly positive except for Fridays in A1 and Saturdays in A2.

2. **Holiday Effect.** Days before a holiday are rated +4 except Mondays which are -2 in weeks 3 and 4, 0 in weeks 1 and 5 ,and Tuesdays, which are -2 in weeks 1, 2, 4 and 5 and +4 in week 3 and pre-holidays

in September and October are given 0's. Days after holidays are downgraded one point.

3. **January, Turn of the Year Effect.** The historical record indicates that days -8 to +14 are all strong. The data suggest the following ratings:

   Trading Days   -4, -3, -1, +3, +4, +5, +7, +9, +10, +11, and +14 are rated +4
   Trading Days   -8, -7, -6, -5, -2, +1, +2, +6, +8, +12, and +13 are rated +2

with adjustment to account for days of the week effects.

4. **Turn of the Month Effect.**

   Days   -5 to +2 at the turn of the month are the best
   Days   +3 to +7 in the second week of the month are good
   Days   +8 to -6 in the second half of the month are bad

The day of the week effect with Saturday trading, formerly on the 1st, 4th and 5th weeks of the month is illustrated below. The three columns indicate the effect of the time of the month and the four rows indicate the effect of Saturday trading. The missing blocks do not occur.

	Trading Days -5 to +2		Trading Days +3 to +7		Trading Days +8 to -6	
1st & 5th	W,S	+4	W,S	+3		
Weeks	Th,F	+3	Th,F	+2		
(A1)	M	+2	M	+1		
	T	+1	T	-3		
4th	W,S	+4			W,S	+1
Week	Th,F	+2			Th,F	0
(A2)	T	+1			T	0
	M	-2			M	-3
2nd			W,S	+3	W,S	+2
Week			Th,F	+2	Th,F	+1
(B1)			T	-3	T	-4
3rd					T,W	+2
Week					Th,F	+1
(B2)					M	-4

The -1 day of month gets a one or two point higher rating except for May depending upon its day of the week effect.

5. **Monthly Effect.** Lower one grade on all effects during September and October.

6. **Golden Week Effect.** The pre-holiday trading days of April 28, May 2 and May 4 and the in between trading day May 1 all receive +4. The post holiday and -1 day of the month, April 30, has poor returns, on average, and is rated a -2. Trading on May 4 has stopped. We would

expect then that the -1 day would improve to a rating of at least 0. The birthday of previous Emperor Showa, April 29, was retained as a holiday but renamed Greenery Day while Emperor Akihto's birthday, December 23, became a new holiday.

7. **Small Firm Effect.** Small stocks have high returns in January and June, and the ratings of all days for these stocks should be increased. Because of portfolio adjustments, large stocks beat small stocks in March handily and in December by a small margin, and the ratings for these stocks should be slightly upgraded during this period.

THE RESULTS FOR 1988 AND JANUARY 1989

The results are summarized in Table 10.1 and visually in Figure 10.1. In general, the calendar worked quite well. Days +3 and +4 returned 0.339% per trading day versus only 0.016% for days -3 and -4, and this difference is significant at the 10% level. Also, days +3 and +4 have returns that are significantly higher at the 5% level than those on days +1 and +2, which returned 0.102% on average. Similarly, days -2 and -1 returned 0.186% per day versus the 0.016% on days -3 and -4, and days +4, +3, +2 and +1 returned 0.177% versus 0.064% on days -1, -2, -3 and -4. However, even though these mean returns are much higher, the daily variation is so large the differences are not statistically significant. Days +1 and +2 did not have higher returns than on days -1 and -2 as expected; although, with the sample variation, one cannot reject the hypothesis that these returns are equal. Table 10.2 presents statistical tests concerning various hypotheses that the higher rated days have higher returns.

Table 10.1
Summary of the Seasonality Calendar Results, January 1988 to end of January 1989

Rank	Sample Size	MeanDaily ReturnNSA225	Mean Daily Return Topix	Stand Dev on NSA	Stand Dev on Topix
-4	14	0.213	0.166	0.455	0.409
-3	19	-0.129	-0.080	0.517	0.538
-2	6	0.281	0.240	0.668	0.732
-1	7	0.104	0.002	0.781	0.834
0	27	-0.111	-0.117	0.675	0.687
1	79	0.132	0.081	0.627	0.659
2	71	0.067	0.085	0.650	0.676
3	30	0.154	0.149	0.610	0.595
4	40	0.478	0.512	1.060	1.224

Categories to be Compared

Rank				Sample Size	MeanDaily ReturnNSA225	Mean Daily Return Topix	Stand Dev on NSA	Stand Dev on Topix
4	3			70	0.339	0.356	0.904	1.014
-4	-3			33	0.016	0.025	0.514	0.496
2	1			150	0.102	0.083	0.637	0.665
-2	-1			13	0.186	0.112	0.706	0.765
4	3			70	0.339	0.356	0.904	1.014
2	1			150	0.102	0.083	0.637	0.665
-2	-1			13	0.186	0.112	0.706	0.765
-4	-3			33	0.016	0.025	0.514	0.496
4	3	2	1	220	0.177	0.170	0.738	0.801
-4	-3	-2	-1	46	0.064	0.049	0.572	0.577

Table 10.2
Statistical Tests Concerning the Seasonality Calendars, January 1988 to End of January 1989

Statistical Hypothesis	NSA 225	Topix
(+4,+3) > (-3,-4)	Yes, with 94% confidence.	Yes, with 92% confidence.
(+2,+1) > (-2,-1)	No, this ranking did not work with this sample.	No, this ranking did not work with this sample.
(+4,+3) > (+2,+1)	Yes, with 97% confidence.	Yes, with 98% confidence.
(-2,-1) > (-3,-4)	The mean return is much higher but the variation is so high that the difference is not significant.	The mean return is much higher but the variation is so high that the difference is not significant.
(+4,+3,+2,+1) > (-1,-2,-3,-4)	The mean return is much higher but the variation is so high that the difference is not significant.	The mean return is much higher but the variation is so high that the difference is not significant.

Figure 10.1
Mean Daily Returns on the NSA 225 for Days Ranked -4 to +4 by the
Seasonality Calendars, January 1988 to End January 1989

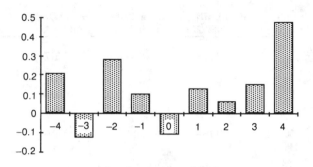

Mean Daily Return ND225

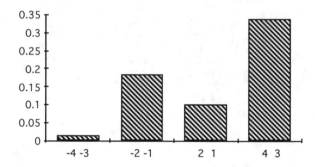

THE RESULTS FOR FEBRUARY TO SEPTEMBER 1989

The ratings for February to September 1989 used our model that forecasts
an expected daily rate of return for the market as measured by the Topix.
For example, February 1's forecast is 0.15% and February 7's forecast is -
0.04%. Consequently, these days are rated +1 and -1, respectively. The
projected returns differ from the mean, which is rated 0, by one standard
deviation. The ratings are rounded to the nearest integer, so 0.75 becomes
+1 and -1.10 becomes -1. Because -2 or +2 involves a two standard
deviation difference, such days are, according to the seasonality calendar
model, very poor or very good. Rarely will a day be rated + or -3 or + or -
4. December 27, 1989, at the turn of the year with an estimated mean

return of 0.53%, is a +4. Some other days in December and January also have +3 or +4 ratings. But, in general, this rating system and the future projections for 1990 use this more compact distribution as compared to our ad hoc approach for 1988. Table 10.3 shows the spread for 1989-92. If you wish to recalculate the 1990-92 ratings with a wider range, simply modify the *script* given above.

Table 10.3 Distribution of Seasonality Model Ratings, 1989-1992

Ratings	Feb-Dec 1989	1990	1991	1992
-2	14	13	11	12
-1	67	70	68	65
0	83	90	97	103
1	55	53	51	50
2	7	16	12	11
3	2	3	5	4
4	1	2	2	2

In general, the ratings for February to September 1989 worked reasonably well. For example, the days ranked +1 or higher did have higher returns than those ranked -1 or lower, particularly for the Topix.

Rank	Sample Size	Mean Daily Return on NSA	on Topix	Standard Deviation on NSA	on Topix
+1 or higher	44	0.0787	0.0801	0.503	0.444
-1 or lower	58	0.0677	0.0406	0.475	0.492

Rank	Sample Size	Mean Daily Return on NSA	on Topix	Standard Deviation on NSA	on Topix
3	1	0.479	0.5680	--	--
2	6	-0.0286	0.1070	0.515	0.566
1	37	0.0853	0.0624	0.508	0.429
0	65	0.0761	0.0548	0.646	0.639
-1	50	0.0876	0.0594	0.474	0.502
-2	8	-0.5670	-0.7680	0.491	0.429

The sample size is too small to have any statistically significant conclusions. Table 10.4 which lists the -2 and +2 days, shows this and explains the poor -0.0286 return on the NSA on the +2 days. June 2, 1989, a +2 day was the Friday before the Beijing massacres and a big down day, particularly for the big stocks in the NSA as the institutional portfolio managers moved out of the market.

Table 10.4
Comparison of Days Rated + or - 2, February to September 1989

Ratings	Date	Model Mean Return Estimate	NSA Return	Topix Return
-2	May 9	-0.133	-0.303	-0.250
-2	May 15	-0.187	-0.443	-0.514
-2	May 16	-0.153	0.653	0.576
-2	May 22	-0.187	0.194	0.052
-2	May 23	-0.153	-0.738	-0.462
-2	July 17	-0.144	-0.353	-0.384
-2	July 24	-0.144	0.572	0.535
-2	Sept 11	-0.141	-0.0063	-0.169
2	Mar 31	0.260	0.0382	0.526
2	Apr 28	0.268	0.634	0.689
2	May 1	0.315	0.237	0.592
2	Jun 2	0.280	-0.924	-0.661
2	Jun 30	0.280	-0.0231	-0.188
2	Aug 25	0.291	-0.134	-0.314

THE RESULTS FOR 1990[3]

Nineteen ninety was a terrible year for the Japanese stock market. As discussed in Chapters 2, 5 and 7 the market fell sharply in the face of greatly increased interest rates. The market began January 1990 by falling 4.5% in the supposedly strongest month of the year. It was then weak all year and suffered two strong declines, finishing the year down 38.7% from its record close at the end of 1989. The seasonality calendars did not work well as the market was dominated by these inflation and interest rate worries. As a parallel, Ziemba (1991e) found that anomalies did not work in the precrash portion of 1987, which was driven by takeovers and mergers.

It remains to be seen how the seasonality calendars will do in 1991 and 1992. The experience has been that such calendars work well if the market is regular and not dominated by some major outside force. As we entered 1991, with the prospect of war in the Middle East, we had that situation again. The early evidence in December and the first half of January was looking more like 1990 than earlier years. But the prospect of lower world wide interest rates due to recession, assuming that the war with Iraq was

---

[3]Thanks are due to Mr. Bruno Vander Cruyssen for help with these calculations.

not too costly, bode well for the future once the 1990 fiscal year ends in March 1991. The short war was very positive for world wide stock markets. There are many problems in the world and the Japanese economies. However, interest rates and inflation in Japan are at or near their peaks. In fiscal year 1991, the market seems likely to be reasonably positive and hence the script is likely to be a useful guide again once the Japanese security scandals of 1991 are settled.

Table 10.5a Summary of the Seasonality Calendar Results for 1991

Rank	Sample Size	Mean Daily Return	Std Dev on NSA
-2	13	0.7513	1.9418
-1	70	-0.3816	1.9429
0	90	0.0335	2.5226
1	51	-0.3821	1.6726
2	16	-0.8660	1.1269
3	3	-0.7358	0.5656
4	2	1.0676	0.5626
+1 or higher	72	-0.4641	1.5475
0	90	0.0335	2.5226
-1 or lower	83	-0.2041	1.9858

THE CALENDARS FOR 1990-92 AND DETAILED RESULTS FOR 1988 AND 1989
The calendars for 1988 to 1992 follow. For 1988 and January 1989 the ratings and actual NSA and Topix daily percentage changes are given. For February 1989 to December 1992, the ratings and the model's forecast of the Topix's daily percentage change are given.

The code is as follows:

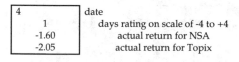

Saturday trading ended in January 1989. The ratings beginning February 1989 are given along with the expected return for the Topix estimated by our model.

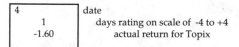

Table 10.5b 1990 NSA Data

Date	Rank	%on Day	Date	Rank	%on Day	Date	Rank	%on Day	Date	Rank	%on Day	Date	Rank	%on Day	Date	Rank	%on Day
May 8	-2	0.0452	Jun 11	-1	-1.3730	Oct 2	0	13.2260	Feb 15	0	0.8605	Jan 30	0	0.1130	Dec 27	1	0.2219
Dec 10	-2	1.1180	Sep 12	-1	2.4832	Apr 3	0	2.7034	Mar 15	0	0.9860	Oct 30	0	-0.3438	Apr 27	1	-0.5404
Sep 10	-2	4.6699	Dec 12	-1	0.1753	Oct 3	0	-0.2071	Nov 15	0	-1.5935	May 30	0	0.3321	Dec 28	1	-0.3843
May 14	-2	1.6819	Jul 12	-1	-0.6699	Jul 3	0	1.8521	Jan 16	0	-1.7752	May 31	0	0.6196	Mar 29	1	-1.7659
Oct 15	-2	3.2113	Mar 12	-1	-1.8386	Oct 4	0	-2.4990	Aug 16	0	-2.0027	Jul 31	0	1.9479	Feb 28	1	2.0474
May 15	-2	-0.1342	Dec 13	-1	2.6834	Jul 4	0	0.0966	Oct 17	0	1.0718	Feb 1	1	0.0484	Sep 28	1	-3.6239
Jul 16	-2	2.3740	Aug 13	-1	-4.2190	Jun 4	0	0.1338	May 18	0	-0.1497	Aug 1	1	-0.6380	Nov 28	1	-2.4113
Dec 17	-2	-1.0719	Nov 13	-1	4.5433	Jan 4	0	-0.5216	Oct 18	0	2.1292	Nov 1	1	-3.5681	Jun 28	1	-0.6375
Sep 17	-2	-2.1328	Feb 13	-1	-0.4854	Apr 4	0	-1.1023	Apr 18	0	2.7665	Aug 3	1	-1.9230	Nov 29	1	-1.4900
May 21	-2	-0.2310	Mar 13	-1	-2.2417	Jul 5	0	-0.6010	Jul 18	0	-0.7599	Oct 5	1	-2.4103	Aug 29	2	-3.1737
May 22	-2	-0.5479	Sep 13	-1	-0.5592	Sep 5	0	-3.3323	Apr 19	0	2.3810	Jul 6	1	2.4688	Mar 29	2	-0.7581
Oct 22	-2	2.4100	Aug 14	-1	1.8987	Apr 5	0	-0.6796	Jul 19	0	0.0484	Apr 6	1	0.6047	Aug 30	2	3.1131
Jul 23	-2	-1.6254	Oct 16	-1	2.1507	Jul 6	0	0.0972	Jul 20	0	-1.9180	Jun 6	1	3.6426	Jan 31	2	-0.0726
Oct 1	-1	-3.6274	Apr 16	-1	-2.5701	Sep 6	0	-1.1089	Mar 20	0	-1.4586	Mar 9	1	-0.5995	Oct 31	2	-0.1898
Mar 2	-1	0.6740	May 16	-1	-0.0969	Jun 7	0	0.7253	Jun 20	0	0.1479	Jan 9	1	0.8964	Mar 1	2	-2.2029
Jul 2	-1	-0.2661	May 17	-1	0.2940	Dec 7	0	4.2965	Nov 21	0	0.8403	Nov 9	1	-1.1538	May 1	2	-0.3549
Dec 3	-1	1.2085	Jul 17	-1	0.9338	Mar 7	0	-1.2696	Nov 21	0	0.1467	Aug 10	1	-0.1655	Jun 1	2	-0.7214
Sep 3	-1	-2.1477	Dec 18	-1	1.3949	Sep 7	0	0.6342	Sep 21	0	0.7414	Oct 12	1	-1.0357	Nov 2	2	1.1934
Dec 4	-1	-3.7974	Sep 18	-1	-0.4979	Nov 7	0	-1.9424	Feb 21	0	-3.1468	Apr 13	1	-0.8678	Feb 2	2	-1.1314
Sep 4	-1	-2.0142	Jun 19	-1	-1.9742	Feb 7	0	-0.9690	Mar 21	0	-3.1292	Jun 15	1	-1.3807	Jan 5	2	0.3135
Jun 5	-1	-0.0425	Jun 19	-1	-1.0378	Mar 8	0	9.9862	Nov 22	0	2.5564	Mar 16	1	-0.3979	Jun 8	2	-1.7134
Mar 5	-1	-0.6225	Sep 19	-1	-0.6657	Aug 8	0	3.0955	Aug 22	0	-4.1334	Apr 16	1	-0.1683	Jan 12	2	-0.2499
Dec 5	-1	1.5140	Feb 19	-1	-0.6346	Nov 8	0	-2.2572	Jan 23	0	0.3248	Nov 16	1	-1.6317	Jan 18	2	0.2913
Feb 5	-1	-0.0505	Nov 19	-1	1.4948	Feb 8	0	0.5764	Aug23g	0	-0.5229	Feb 16	1	-0.6645	Jan 19	2	2.6126
Nov 5	-1	0.7967	Mar 19	-1	-4.1483	Aug 9	0	-3.1359	Apr 23	0	-5.8427	Oct 19	1	-2.7691	Feb 23	2	-0.2570
Nov 6	-1	-1.7206	Nov 20	-1	-1.3309	Feb 9	0	-8.6077	Oct 24	0	-1.6642	Dec 13	1	0.4678	Jan 26	2	-0.5170
Mar 6	-1	-0.1596	Feb 20	-1	-0.8785	Oct 9	0	-0.5713	Apr 24	0	-0.5998	Apr 20	1	1.8547	Jun 29	2	-3.3714
Feb 6	-1	0.0930	Aug 20	-1	-3.8441	Jan 11	0	1.2547	Jul 25	0	-1.8142	Dec 21	1	-0.3687	Mar 30	2	-1.1362
Dec 6	-1	1.6176	Sep 20	-1	-0.5184	Jul 11	0	0.9225	Jun 26	0	-0.0032	Feb 22	1	-3.0430	Aug 31	2	-0.9739
Aug 6	-1	-3.1034	Apr 21	-1	-0.7248	May 11	0	1.7172	Sep 26	0	1.4525	Jun 22	1	0.2575	Nov 30	2	-0.6693
May 7	-1	2.5950	Jan 22	-1	1.1429	Apr 11	0	-0.6234	Jul 26	0	-4.7434	Mar 23	1	-1.2249	Jan 10	3	-0.0787
Aug 7	-1	-3.3112	Oct 23	-1	0.9054	Jul 12	0	1.8122	Nov 26	0	-1.0441	Aug 24	1	1.8061	Jan 17	3	-1.4594
Oct 8	-1	3.5132	May 23	-1	0.5446	Apr 12	0	0.6216	Feb 26	0	1.5507	Jan 24	1	1.8030	Dec 25	3	1.6392
Apr 9	-1	3.8220	Jul 24	-1	-0.6051	Jun 13	0	0.1516	Mar 26	0	-4.4970	May 25	1	-1.6052	May 2	4	0.5049
May 9	-1	-0.0807	May 24	-1	1.7100	Jul 13	0	0.4364	Nov 27	0	4.7989	Jan 25	1	1.4917			
Jul 9	-1	-1.3592	Sep 25	-1	-1.7621	Nov 14	0	-0.1511	Nov 27	0	1.7286	Oct 25	1	0.5193			
Jul 10	-1	-2.4466	May 28	-1	1.2136	Feb 14	0	0.1294	Aug27	0	-0.5864	Apr 25	1	1.9134			
Apr 10	-1	-2.5408	Oct 29	-1	0.1297	Mar 14	0	-0.8216	Sep 27	0	4.0387	Oct 26	1	-0.8034			
May 10	-1	0.1131	May 29	-1	-1.1298	Sep 14	0	0.7099	Mar 27	0	-2.1527	Apr 26	1	-1.3687			
Dec 11	-1	0.7231	Jul 30	-1	-1.3609	Dec 14	0	-1.1930	Aug 28	0	-0.0471	Jul 27	1	-0.5502			
Oct 11	-1	-3.8689	Apr 2	0	-6.5977	Jun 14	0	0.9175	Jan 29	0	2.2631	Jun 27	1	-1.6162			
Sep 11	-1	-1.8979				Aug 15	0	5.3950		0	0.8109		1	2.3471			

1988 Jan-Mar

January 1988

Sunday	Monday	Tuesday	Wednesday	Thursday	Friday	Saturday
					1	2
3	4 1 -1.60 -2.05	5 3 1.68 1.03	6 4 5.63 6.56	7 4 0.00 0.00	8 4 0.35 -0.09	9
10	11 0 -1.28 -1.28	12 4 0.20 0.23	13 2 -1.32 -1.31	14 4 1.24 1.38	15	16
17	18 -2 1.35 1.54	19 3 -0.05 -0.41	20 2 -0.24 -0.28	21 2 -0.58 -0.44	22 4 0.73 0.79	23 4 1.08 1.86
24 31	25 2 0.83 1.40	26 1 0.77 0.88	27 4 -0.69 -0.74	28 3 1.07 1.56	29 4 0.14 0.23	30 4 0.40 0.66

February 1988

Sunday	Monday	Tuesday	Wednesday	Thursday	Friday	Saturday
	1 2 0.05 -0.19	2 -2 -0.25 -0.51	3 3 -0.32 -0.26	4 2 0.48 0.67	5 2 -0.24 -0.21	6 3 0.59 0.42
7	8 2 -0.08 -0.04	9 -3 -0.45 -0.10	10 4 0.46 0.46	11	12 0 0.88 0.79	13 3 0.59 0.42
14	15 -4 0.94 0.68	16 1 0.57 0.97	17 1 0.34 0.73	18 1 1.00 0.93	19 1 0.39 0.84	20
21	22 -3 0.29 0.32	23 1 0.41 0.36	24 4 0.07 0.21	25 2 0.52 1.05	26 2 0.25 0.00	27 4 0.47 0.27
28	29 3 -0.16 0.01					

March 1988

Sunday	Monday	Tuesday	Wednesday	Thursday	Friday	Saturday
		1 -2 0.76 0.53	2 4 0.97 1.11	3 2 -0.33 -0.29	4 2 0.07 0.15	5 3 0.04 -0.01
6	7 2 -0.04 -0.05	8 -3 -0.58 -0.66	9 1 0.54 0.49	10 1 0.04 -0.08	11 1 -0.28 -0.52	12
13	14 -4 -0.43 -0.80	15 1 0.16 0.49	16 1 0.89 1.02	17 1 0.65 0.71	18 4 0.36 0.64	19
20	21	22 -3 -0.47 -0.35	23 1 0.20 0.26	24 0 -0.44 -0.53	25 0 -0.59 -0.90	26 4 -1.19 -1.50
27	28 2 1.19 1.27	29 1 1.28 1.15	30 4 1.41 1.52	31 4 -0.22 -0.26		

1988 Apr-Jun

April 1988

Sunday	Monday	Tuesday	Wednesday	Thursday	Friday	Saturday
					1 3 -0.59 -0.82	2 4 0.68 0.51
3	4 2 0.20 0.07	5 -3 -0.07 -0.32	6 2 0.74 0.66	7 2 0.97 0.84	8 2 -0.07 0.23	9
10	11 -4 0.65 0.46	12 1 0.02 -0.07	13 1 0.20 0.26	14 1 0.46 0.28	15 1 -0.80 -0.91	16
17	18 -3 -0.82 -0.85	19 0 -0.05 -0.20	20 1 0.77 0.53	21 0 -0.13 -0.44	22 0 0.03 -0.01	23 1 0.82 0.67
24	25 2 0.57 0.40	26 1 0.12 0.02	27 3 -0.20 -0.26	28 4 0.89 0.87	29	30 0 0.27 0.27

May 1988

Sunday	Monday	Tuesday	Wednesday	Thursday	Friday	Saturday
1	2 3 0.58 0.80	3	4	5	6 2 -0.48 -0.50	7 3 -0.16 -0.21
8	9 2 -0.81 -0.76	10 -3 0.54 0.24	11 2 -0.91 -0.70	12 2 0.18 -0.27	13 2 0.93 0.82	14
15	16 -4 1.06 0.69	17 1 0.21 0.24	18 1 -0.18 -0.12	19 1 -1.42 −1.35	20 1 0.07 -0.20	21
22	23 -3 -0.52 -0.58	24 0 0.23 -0.03	25 1 0.47 0.27	26 2 -0.05 -0.31	27 2 -0.50 -0.89	28 4 -1.20 -1.30
29	30 2 0.96 0.32	31 2 0.71 0.81				

June 1988

Sunday	Monday	Tuesday	Wednesday	Thursday	Friday	Saturday
			1 4 1.04 1.06	2 3 0.59 0.57	3 2 -0.17 0.12	4 3 0.30 0.51
5	6 2 0.32 0.28	7 -3 -0.10 0.06	8 2 -0.19 -0.12	9 2 0.57 1.17	10 2 -0.54 -0.37	11
12	13 -4 0.41 0.41	14 1 0.09 0.20	15 1 0.11 0.28	16 1 0.19 -0.12	17 1 0.69 -0.09	18
19	20 -3 -0.71 -0.68	21 0 -0.75 -0.64	22 1 -0.23 -0.19	23 0 -0.45 -0.31	24 0 0.06 -0.26	25 4 -0.69 -0.46
26	27 2 -0.43 -0.32	28 1 -0.13 0.12	29 4 0.76 0.39	30 4 0.58 0.74		

1988 Jul-Sep

July 1988

Sunday	Monday	Tuesday	Wednesday	Thursday	Friday	Saturday
					1 3 -0.95 -0.89	2 4 -0.51 -0.67
3	4 1 0.00 -0.03	5 -3 0.79 0.73	6 3 0.68 0.57	7 2 -0.13 0.19	8 2 0.68 0.78	9
10	11 -4 0.24 0.12	12 1 0.40 0.33	13 1 -0.28 -0.45	14 1 0.22 0.04	15 1 -0.60 -0.56	16
17	18 -3 -0.90 -0.90	19 0 -1.85 -1.66	20 1 1.49 1.52	21 0 0.44 0.59	22 0 -1.41 -1.31	23 1 0.05 0.24
24 31	25 -2 -0.43 -0.25	26 1 0.44 0.36	27 4 1.59 1.55	28 2 0.20 0.33	29 2 0.41 1.30	30 4 1.03 1.00

August 1988

Sunday	Monday	Tuesday	Wednesday	Thursday	Friday	Saturday
	1 2 0.44 0.09	2 -2 0.14 0.17	3 3 -0.06 -0.33	4 2 -0.19 -0.55	5 2 0.46 -0.17	6 3 -0.21 0.07
7	8 2 -0.38 -0.35	9 -3 -0.29 -0.12	10 1 -2.18 -2.13	11 1 0.83 0.76	12 1 0.17 -0.10	13
14	15 -4 0.24 0.12	16 1 -0.01 -0.10	17 1 1.01 0.87	18 1 -0.17 -0.12	19 1 0.28 0.08	20
21	22 -3 -0.46 -0.38	23 0 -0.56 -0.62	24 1 -0.43 -0.56	25 2 0.25 0.19	26 2 -1.09 -0.93	27 4 0.41 0.20
28	29 2 -1.08 -1.04	30 1 0.48 0.20	31 4 -0.52 -0.62			

September 1988

Sunday	Monday	Tuesday	Wednesday	Thursday	Friday	Saturday
				1 2 -1.57 -1.63	2 2 0.67 0.14	3 2 1.37 1.31
4	5 1 -0.53 -0.51	6 -4 -0.07 -0.11	7 1 0.67 0.69	8 1 0.85 0.45	9 1 -0.33 -0.24	10
11	12 -4 0.39 0.44	13 0 0.13 0.38	14 1 0.04 -0.03	15	16 -1 0.21 0.19	17
18	19 -4 0.12 0.04	20 -1 -1.26 -1.31	21 0 0.59 -0.07	22 3 -1.02 -0.63	23	24 2 -0.13 -0.44
25	26 1 -0.20 -0.16	27 0 0.60 1.00	28 3 0.91 0.78	29 2 -0.18 -0.07	30 4 0.80 0.90	

1988 Oct-Dec

October 1988

Sunday	Monday	Tuesday	Wednesday	Thursday	Friday	Saturday
						1 3 -0.80 -0.73
2	3 1 -0.55 -0.46	4 -4 -0.16 0.18	5 1 -0.34 -0.61	6 1 -0.85 -0.96	7 3 0.31 0.26	8
9	10	11 -1 0.77 0.57	12 0 -0.21 0.11	13 0 -0.49 -0.33	14 0 0.12 0.73	15
16	17 -4 -0.13 0.15	18 -1 -0.46 -0.91	19 0 0.55 0.45	20 -1 0.35 0.27	21 -1 0.03 0.12	22 0 -0.22 -0.35
23	24 1 -0.20 -0.36	25 0 0.51 0.45	26 3 0.72 0.47	27 2 0.37 0.47	28 2 0.06 -0.31	29 4 0.79 0.57
30	31 2 0.07 0.46					

November 1988

Sunday	Monday	Tuesday	Wednesday	Thursday	Friday	Saturday
		1 -2 0.11 -0.03	2 4 -0.10 -0.24	3	4 1 -0.11 -0.28	5 3 0.33 0.04
6	7 2 -0.64 -0.72	8 -3 0.50 0.76	9 2 0.73 1.15	10 1 -0.16 0.27	11 1 1.14 1.67	12
13 0.65	14 -4 0.10 0.30	15 1 1.08 0.65	16 1 0.57 0.03	17 1 0.27 0.22	18 1 0.35 0.53	19
20	21 -3 0.35 0.62	22 4 0.49 0.56	23	24 1 -0.30 -0.23	25 2 0.22 0.08	26 4 -0.14 -0.07
27	28 2 -1.29 -1.24	29 1 1.15 1.05	30 4 0.88 0.73			

December 1988

Sunday	Monday	Tuesday	Wednesday	Thursday	Friday	Saturday
				1 3 -0.12 -0.14	2 3 -0.03 0.03	3 3 0.45 0.52
4	5 2 -0.17 -0.24	6 -3 0.18 0.24	7 2 1.28 0.82	8 2 -0.97 -0.50	9 1 0.11 0.12	10
11	12 -4 -0.40 -0.40	13 1 -0.25 -0.17	14 1 0.53 0.39	15 1 -0.16 -0.17	16 1 -0.56 -0.78	17
18	19 -3 -0.22 -0.14	20 0 0.33 0.21	21 2 0.44 0.38	22 2 0.25 0.60	23 2 -0.29 0.22	24 3 0.00 0.28
25	26	27	28 4 1.59 0.28	29	30	31

1989 Jan-Mar

January 1989

Sunday	Monday	Tuesday	Wednesday	Thursday	Friday	Saturday
1	2	3	4 4 0.28 0.77	5 3 -0.19 -0.30	6 4 0.08 -0.04	7
8	9 2 1.55 1.47	10 -1 1.06 1.08	11 2 0.44 0.59	12 2 0.00 0.15	13 2 0.49 0.48	14
15	16	17 1 -0.22 -0.35	18 1 0.40 0.12	19 1 -0.13 -0.66	20 1 -0.45 -0.40	21
22	23 -3 0.52 0.60	24 0 0.71 0.84	25 1 0.03 0.08	26 2 -0.17 -0.19	27 2 0.42 0.46	28 4 0.10 0.35
29	30 2 -0.35 -0.42	31 2 0.04 -0.11				

February 1989

Sunday	Monday	Tuesday	Wednesday	Thursday	Friday	Saturday
			1 1 0.15	2 1 0.15	3 1 0.17	4
5	6 -1 -0.08	7 -1 -0.04	8 0 0.07	9 0 0.06	10 1 0.15	11
12	13 -1 -0.10	14 -1 -0.06	15 0 0.04	16 0 0.04	17 1 0.15	18
19	20 -1 -0.10	21 0 0.04	22 1 0.15	23 1 0.15	24	25
26	27 0 0.05	28 0 0.04				

March 1989

Sunday	Monday	Tuesday	Wednesday	Thursday	Friday	Saturday
			1 1 0.15	2 1 0.15	3 1 0.17	4
5	6 -1 -0.08	7 -1 -0.05	8 0 0.06	9 0 0.06	10 1 0.15	11
12	13 -1 -0.10	14 -1 -0.07	15 0 0.04	16 0 0.04	17 1 0.15	18
19	20 -1 -0.01	21	22 0 0.01	23 0 0.04	24 1 0.15	25
26	27 0 0.00	28 0 0.03	29 1 0.15	30 1 0.05	31 2 0.26	

1989 Apr-Jun

April 1989

Sunday	Monday	Tuesday	Wednesday	Thursday	Friday	Saturday
						1
2	3 0 0.02	4 0 0.05	5 0 0.08	6 0 0.08	7 1 0.19	8
9	10 -1 -0.06	11 -1 -0.03	12 0 0.06	13 0 0.06	14 1 0.17	15
16	17 -1 -0.08	18 -1 -0.05	19 0 0.06	20 0 0.06	21 1 0.17	22
23 30	24 0 0.02	25 0 0.05	26 1 0.17	27 1 0.17	28 2 0.26	29

May 1989

Sunday	Monday	Tuesday	Wednesday	Thursday	Friday	Saturday
	1 2 0.31	2 3 0.39 SELL	3	4	5	6
7	8 -1 -0.11	9 -2 -0.13	10 -1 -0.01	11 -1 -0.01	12 0 0.09	13
14	15 -2 -0.18	16 -2 -0.15	17 -1 -0.03	18 -1 -0.03	19 0 0.07	20
21	22 -2 -0.18	23 -2 -0.15	24 -1 -0.03 BUY	25 0 0.07	26 1 0.18	27
28	29 -1 -0.07	30 -1 -0.04	31 0 0.07			

June 1989

Sunday	Monday	Tuesday	Wednesday	Thursday	Friday	Saturday
				1 1 0.17	2 2 0.28	3
4	5 -1 -0.06	6 -1 -0.03	7 0 0.08	8 0 0.08	9 1 0.19	10
11	12 -1 -0.08	13 -1 -0.05	14 0 0.06	15 0 0.06	16 1 0.17	17
18	19 -1 -0.08	20 -1 -0.05	21 0 0.06	22 0 0.06	23 1 0.17	24
25	26 0 0.02	27 0 0.05	28 1 0.17	29 1 0.17	30 2 0.28	

1989 Jul-Sep

July 1989

Sunday	Monday	Tuesday	Wednesday	Thursday	Friday	Saturday
						1
2	3 -1 -0.03	4 0 0.00	5 0 0.02	6 0 0.02	7 1 0.13 SELL	8
9	10 -1 -0.12	11 -1 -0.08	12 0 0.00	13 0 0.00	14 0 0.11	15
16	17 -2 -0.14	18 -1 -0.11	19 0 0.00	20 0 0.00	21 0 0.11	22
23	24 -2 -0.14	25 0 0.00 BUY	26 0 0.11	27 0 0.11	28 1 0.22	29
30	31 -1 -0.03					

August 1989

Sunday	Monday	Tuesday	Wednesday	Thursday	Friday	Saturday
		1 0 0.06	2 1 0.18	3 0 0.09	4 1 0.20	5
6	7 -1 -0.05	8 -1 -0.02	9 0 0.09	10 0 0.07	11 1 0.18	12
13	14 -1 -0.07	15 -1 -0.04	16 0 0.07	17 0 0.07	18 1 0.18	19
20	21 -1 -0.07	22 -1 -0.04	23 0 0.07	24 0 0.07	25 2 0.29	26
27	28 0 0.03	29 0 0.06	30 1 0.18	31 1 0.18		

September 1989

Sunday	Monday	Tuesday	Wednesday	Thursday	Friday	Saturday
					1 1 0.20 SELL	2
3	4 -1 -0.05	5 -1 -0.10	6 0 0.01	7 0 0.01	8 0 0.11	9
10	11 -2 -0.14	12 -1 -0.12	13 -1 0.00	14 -1 0.00	15	16
17	18 -1 -0.11	19 -1 -0.12	20 -1 0.00	21 -1 0.00 BUY	22 0 0.09	23
24	25 -1 -0.05	26 -1 -0.01	27 0 0.09	28 0 0.09	29 1 0.20	30

1989 Oct-Dec

October 1989

Sunday	Monday	Tuesday	Wednesday	Thursday	Friday	Saturday
1	2 -1 -0.02	3 0 0.00	4 0 0.03	5 0 0.03	6 1 0.14	7
8	9 -1 -0.02	10	11 0 0.00	12 0 0.01	13 1 0.12 SELL	14
15	16 -2 -0.13	17 -1 -0.10	18 0 0.01	19 0 0.01	20 1 0.12	21
22	23 -2 -0.13	24 -1 -0.10 BUY	25 1 0.12	26 1 0.12	27 1 0.23	28
29	30 -1 -0.02	31 0 0.00				

November 1989

Sunday	Monday	Tuesday	Wednesday	Thursday	Friday	Saturday
			1 1 0.14	2 1 0.14	3	4
5	6 -1 -0.04	7 -1 -0.05	8 0 0.05	9 0 0.05	10 1 0.16	11
12	13 -1 -0.11	14 -1 -0.08	15 0 0.03	16 0 0.03	17 1 0.14	18
19	20 -1 -0.11	21 -1 -0.08	22 1 0.12	23	24 1 0.22	25
26	27 0 0.00	28 0 0.02	29 1 0.14	30 1 0.14		

December 1989

Sunday	Monday	Tuesday	Wednesday	Thursday	Friday	Saturday
					1 1 0.19 SELL	2
3	4 -1 -0.06	5 -1 -0.12	6 -1 0.00	7 -1 0.00	8 0 0.10	9
10	11 -2 -0.15	12 -2 -0.14	13 -1 -0.02	14 -1 -0.02	15 0 0.08	16
17	18 -2 -0.17	19 -2 -0.14 BUY	20 0 0.08	21 1 0.14	22 2 0.35	23
24	25 0 0.02	26 3 0.38	27 4 0.53	28 1 0.17	29 1 0.24 SELL	30
31						

1990 Jan-Mar

January 1990

Sunday	Monday	Tuesday	Wednesday	Thursday	Friday	Saturday
	1	2	3	4 0 0.07 BUY	5 2 0.30	6
7	8 2 0.25	9 1 0.15	10 3 0.43	11 0 0.10	12 2 0.26	13
14	15	16 0 0.02	17 3 0.38	18 2 0.28	19 2 0.37	20
21	22 -1 -0.06	23 0 0.02	24 1 0.24	25 1 0.21	26 2 0.31	27
28	29 0 0.05	30 0 0.09	31 1 0.21			

February 1990

Sunday	Monday	Tuesday	Wednesday	Thursday	Friday	Saturday
				1 1 0.15	2 2 0.26	3
4	5 -1 -0.08	6 -1 -0.04	7 0 0.07	8 0 0.06	9 0 0.02	10
11	12	13 -1 -0.06	14 0 0.04	15 0 0.04	16 1 0.15	17
18	19 -1 0.10	20 -1 -0.06	21 0 0.04	22 1 0.15	23 2 0.26	24
25	26 0 0.00	27 0 0.04	28 1 0.15			

March 1990

Sunday	Monday	Tuesday	Wednesday	Thursday	Friday	Saturday
				1 1 0.05	2 2 0.26	3
45	5 -1 -0.08	6 -1 -0.05	7 0 0.06	8 0 0.06	9 1 0.17	10
11	12 -1 -0.10	13 -1 -0.07	14 0 0.04	15 0 0.04	16 1 0.15	17
18	19 -1 -0.10	20 0 0.01	21	22 0 0.00	23 1 0.15	24
25	26 0 0.00	27 0 0.03	28 1 0.15	29 1 0.15	30 2 0.26	31

1990 Apr-Jun

April 1990

Sunday	Monday	Tuesday	Wednesday	Thursday	Friday	Saturday
1	2 0 0.02	3 0 0.05	4 0 0.08	5 0 0.08	6 1 0.19	7
8	9 -1 -0.06	10 -1 -0.03	11 0 0.06	12 0 0.06	13 1 0.17	14
15	16 -1 -0.08	17 -1 -0.05	18 0 0.06	19 0 0.06	20 1 0.17	21
22	23 0 0.02	24 0 0.05	25 1 0.17	26 1 0.17	27 1 0.12	28
29	30					

May 1990

Sunday	Monday	Tuesday	Wednesday	Thursday	Friday	Saturday
		1 2 0.34	2 4 0.51 SELL	3	4	5
6	7 -1 -0.11	8 -2 -0.13	9 -1 -0.01	10 -1 -0.01	11 0 0.09	12
13	14 -2 -0.18	15 -2 -0.15	16 -1 -0.03	17 -1 -0.03	18 0 0.07	19
20	21 -2 -0.18	22 -2 -0.15	23 -1 -0.03 BUY	24 -1 -0.03	25 1 0.18	26
27	28 -1 -0.07	29 -1 -0.04	30 0 0.07	31 0 0.07		

June 1990

Sunday	Monday	Tuesday	Wednesday	Thursday	Friday	Saturday
					1 2 0.28	2
3	4 0 0.02	5 -1 -0.03	6 0 0.08	7 0 0.08	8 1 0.19	9
10	11 -1 -0.06	12 -1 -0.05	13 0 0.06	14 0 0.06	15 1 0.17	16
17	18 -1 -0.08	19 -1 -0.05	20 0 0.06	21 0 0.06	22 1 0.17	23
24	25 0 0.02	26 0 0.05	27 1 0.17	28 1 0.17	29 2 0.28	30

1990 Jul-Sep

July 1990

Sunday	Monday	Tuesday	Wednesday	Thursday	Friday	Saturday
1	2 -1 -0.03	3 0 0.00	4 0 0.02	5 0 0.02	6 1 0.13 SELL	7
8	9 -1 -0.12	10 -1 -0.08	11 0 0.00	12 0 0.00	13 0 0.11	14
15	16 -2 -0.14	17 -1 -0.11	18 0 0.00	19 0 0.00	20 0 0.11	21
22	23 -2 -0.14	24 -1 -0.11 BUY	25 0 0.11	26 0 0.11	27 1 0.22	28
29	30 -1 -0.03	31 0 0.00				

August 1990

Sunday	Monday	Tuesday	Wednesday	Thursday	Friday	Saturday
			1 1 0.18	2 1 0.18	3 1 0.20	4
5	6 -1 -0.05	7 -1 -0.02	8 0 0.09	9 0 0.09	10 1 0.18	11
12	13 -1 -0.07	14 -1 -0.04	15 0 0.07	16 0 0.07	17 1 0.18	18
19	20 -1 -0.07	21 -1 -0.04	22 0 0.07	23 0 0.07	24 1 0.18	25
26	27 0 0.03	28 0 0.06	29 1 0.18	30 1 0.18	31 2 0.29	

September 1990

Sunday	Monday	Tuesday	Wednesday	Thursday	Friday	Saturday
						1
2	3 -1 -0.05	4 -1 -0.01	5 0 0.01	6 0 0.01	7 0 0.11 SELL	8
9	10 -2 -0.14	11 -1 -0.10	12 -1 0.00	13 -1 0.00	14 0 0.09	15
16	17 -2 -0.16	18 -1 -0.12	19 -1 0.00	20 -1 0.00	21 0 0.05	22
23	24 30	25 -1 -0.01	26 0 0.09	27 0 0.09	28 1 0.20	29

1990 Oct-Dec

October 1990

Sunday	Monday	Tuesday	Wednesday	Thursday	Friday	Saturday
	1 -1 -0.02	2 0 0.00	3 0 0.03	4 0 0.03	5 1 0.14	6
7	8 -1 -0.11	9 0 0.00	10	11 -1 -0.01	12 1 0.12	13
14	15 -2 -0.13	16 -1 -0.10	17 0 0.01	18 0 0.01	19 1 0.12	20
21	22 -2 -0.13	23 -1 -0.10 BUY	24 0 0.01	25 1 0.12	26 1 0.23	27
28	29 -1 -0.02	30 0 0.00	31 1 0.12			

November 1990

Sunday	Monday	Tuesday	Wednesday	Thursday	Friday	Saturday
				1 1 0.14	2 2 0.25	3
4	5 -1 -0.09	6 -1 -0.05	7 0 0.05	8 0 0.05	9 1 0.16	10
11	12 -1 -0.11	13 -1 -0.08	14 0 0.03	15 0 0.03	16 1 0.14 SELL	17
18	19 -1 -0.11	20 -1 -0.08 BUY	21 0 0.03	22 0 0.03	23	24
25	26 0 0.04	27 0 0.02	28 1 0.14	29 1 0.14	30 2 0.25 SELL	

December 1990

Sunday	Monday	Tuesday	Wednesday	Thursday	Friday	Saturday
						1
2	3 -1 -0.06	4 -1 -0.03	5 -1 0.00	6 -1 0.00	7 0 0.10	8
9	10 -2 -0.15	11 -1 -0.12	12 -1 -0.02	13 -1 -0.02	14 0 0.08	15
16	17 -2 -0.17	18 -1 -0.03 BUY	19 1 0.14	20 1 0.25	21 1 0.13	22
23	24	25 3 0.38	26 4 0.53	27 1 0.17	28 1 0.24 SELL	29
30	31					

1991 Jan-Mar

January 1991

Sunday	Monday	Tuesday	Wednesday	Thursday	Friday	Saturday
		1	2	3	4 1 0.18 BUY	5
7	8 0 0.04	9 2 0.28	10 2 0.27	11 3 0.43	12 1 0.21	13
14	15 1 0.24	16	17 0 0.10	18 3 0.38	19 3 0.39	20
21	22 0 0.11	23 -1 -0.02	24 1 0.13	25 1 0.24	26 2 0.31	27
28	29 0 0.05	30 0 0.09	31 1 0.21	1 0.21		

February 1991

Sunday	Monday	Tuesday	Wednesday	Thursday	Friday	Saturday
					1 2 0.26	2
3	4 0 0.00	5 -1 -0.04	6 0 0.07	7 0 0.06	8 0 0.02	9
10	11	12 -1 -0.04	13 0 0.04	14 0 0.04	15 1 0.15	16
17	18 -1 -0.10	19 -1 -0.06	20 0 0.04	21 0 0.04	22 2 0.26	23
24	25 0 0.00	26 0 0.04	27 1 0.15	28 1 0.15		

March 1991

Sunday	Monday	Tuesday	Wednesday	Thursday	Friday	Saturday
					1 2 0.26	2
3	4 0 0.00	5 -1 -0.05	6 0 0.06	7 0 0.06	8 1 0.17	9
10	11 -1 -0.08	12 -1 -0.07	13 0 0.04	14 0 0.04	15 1 0.15	16
17	18 -1 -0.10	19 -1 -0.07	20 1 0.13	21	22 0 0.11	23
24	25 0 0.00	26 0 0.03	27 1 0.15	28 1 0.15	29 2 0.26	30
31						

1991 Apr-Jun

April 1991

Sunday	Monday	Tuesday	Wednesday	Thursday	Friday	Saturday
	1 0 0.02	2 0 0.05	3 0 0.08	4 0 0.08	5 1 0.19	6
7	8 -1 -0.06	9 -1 -0.03	10 0 0.06	11 0 0.06	12 1 0.17	13
14	15 -1 -0.08	16 -1 -0.05	17 0 0.06	18 0 0.06	19 1 0.17	20
21	22 -1 -0.18	23 0 0.05	24 1 0.17	25 1 0.17	26 1 0.12	27
28	29	30 -2 -0.21				

May 1991

Sunday	Monday	Tuesday	Wednesday	Thursday	Friday	Saturday
			1 3 0.46	2 4 0.51 SELL	3	4
5	6	7 -1 -0.13	8 -1 -0.01	9 -1 -0.01	10 0 0.09	11
12	13 -2 -0.16	14 -2 -0.15	15 -1 -0.03	16 -1 -0.03	17 0 0.07	18
19	20 -2 -0.18	21 -2 -0.15	22 -1 -0.03	23 -1 -0.03	24 0 0.07	25
26	27 -1 -0.07	28 -1 -0.04 BUY	29 0 0.07	30 0 0.07	31 1 0.18	

June 1991

Sunday	Monday	Tuesday	Wednesday	Thursday	Friday	Saturday
						1
2	3 0 0.02	4 0 0.05	5 0 0.08	6 0 0.08	7 1 0.19	8
9	10 -1 -0.06	11 -1 -0.03	12 0 0.06	13 0 0.06	14 1 0.17	15
16	17 -1 -0.08	18 -1 -0.05	19 0 0.06	20 0 0.06	21 1 0.17	22
23 30	24 0 0.02	25 0 0.05	26 1 0.17	27 1 0.17	28 2 0.28	29

1991 Jul-Sep

July 1991

Sunday	Monday	Tuesday	Wednesday	Thursday	Friday	Saturday
	1 -1 -0.03	2 0 0.00	3 0 0.02	4 0 0.02	5 1 0.13 SELL	6
7	9 -1 -0.12	9 -1 -0.08	10 0 0.00	11 0 0.00	12 0 0.11	13
14	15 -2 -0.14	16 -1 -0.11	17 0 0.00	18 0 0.00	19 0 0.11	20
21	22 -2 -0.14	23 -1 -0.11 BUY	24 0 0.00	25 0 0.11	26 1 0.22	27
28	29 -1 -0.03	30 0 0.00	31 0 0.11			

August 1991

Sunday	Monday	Tuesday	Wednesday	Thursday	Friday	Saturday
				1 1 0.18	2 2 0.29	3
4	5 -1 -0.05	6 -1 -0.02	7 0 0.09	8 0 0.09	9 1 0.20	10
11	12 -1 -0.07	13 -1 -0.04	14 0 0.07	15 0 0.07	16 1 0.18	17
18	19 -1 -0.07	20 -1 -0.04	21 0 0.07	22 0 0.07	23 1 0.18	24
25	26 0 0.03	27 0 0.06	28 1 0.18	29 1 0.18	30 2 0.29	31

September 1991

Sunday	Monday	Tuesday	Wednesday	Thursday	Friday	Saturday
1	2 -1 -0.05	3 -1 -0.01	4 0 0.01	5 0 0.01	6 0 0.11 SELL	7
8	9 -2 -0.14	10 -1 -0.10	11 -1 0.00	12 -1 0.00	13 -1 -0.05	14
15	16	17 -1 -0.12	18 -1 0.00	19 -1 0.00	20 -1 -0.05	21
22	23	24 -1 -0.01 BUY	25 0 0.09	26 0 0.09	27 1 0.20	28
29	30 -1 -0.05					

1991 Oct-Dec

October 1991

Sunday	Monday	Tuesday	Wednesday	Thursday	Friday	Saturday
		1 0 0.00	2 1 0.12	3 0 0.03	4 1 0.14	5
6	7 -1 -0.11	8 -1 -0.08	9 1 0.12	10	11 0 0.09	12
13	14 -1 -0.13	15 -1 -0.10	16 0 0.01	17 0 0.01	18 1 0.12	19
20	21 -1 -0.13	22 -1 -0.10	23 0 0.01	24 0 0.01	25 1 0.23	26
27	28 -1 -0.02	29 0 0.00	30 1 0.12	31 1 0.12		

November 1991

Sunday	Monday	Tuesday	Wednesday	Thursday	Friday	Saturday
					1 0 0.10	2
3	4	5 0 0.02	6 0 0.05	7 0 0.05	8 1 0.16	9
10	11 -1 -0.09	12 -1 -0.05	13 0 0.03	14 0 0.03	15 1 0.14	16
17	18 -1 -0.11	19 -1 -0.08	20 0 0.03	21 0 0.03	22 1 0.14	23
24	25 0 -0.00	26 0 0.02	27 1 0.14	28 1 0.14	29 2 0.25 SELL	30

December 1991

Sunday	Monday	Tuesday	Wednesday	Thursday	Friday	Saturday
1	2 -1 -0.06	3 -1 -0.03	4 0 -0.00	5 0 -0.00	6 0 0.10	7
8	9 -2 -0.15	10 -1 -0.12	11 -1 -0.02	12 -1 -0.02	13 0 0.08	14
15	16 -2 -0.17	17 -2 -0.14	18 0 0.08	19 1 0.14	20 1 0.20	21
22	23	24 0 0.06	25 3 0.50	26 4 0.53	27 2 0.28	28
29	30 1 0.14 SELL	31				

1992 Jan-Mar

January 1992

Sunday	Monday	Tuesday	Wednesday	Thursday	Friday	Saturday
			1	2	3	4
5	6 -1 -0.02	7 0 0.08	8 3 0.40	9 2 0.27	10 4 0.54	11
12	13 -1 -0.04	14 2 0.28	15	16 0 0.10	17 3 0.49	18
19	20 1 0.13	21 1 0.15	22 0 0.09	23 1 0.13	24 2 0.35	25
26	27 0 0.05	28 0 0.09	29 1 0.21	30 1 0.21	31 2 0.31	

February 1992

Sunday	Monday	Tuesday	Wednesday	Thursday	Friday	Saturday
						1
2	3 0 0.00	4 0 0.04	5 0 0.07	6 0 0.06	7 1 0.17	8
9	10 0 0.00	11	12 0 0.03	13 0 0.04	14 1 0.15	15
16	17 -1 -0.10	18 -1 -0.06	19 0 0.04	20 0 0.04	21 1 0.15	22
23	24 0 0.00	25 0 0.04	26 1 0.15	27 1 0.15	28 2 0.26	29

March 1992

Sunday	Monday	Tuesday	Wednesday	Thursday	Friday	Saturday
1	2 0 0.00	3 0 0.03	4 0 0.06	5 0 0.06	6 1 0.17	7
8	9 -1 -0.08	10 -1 -0.05 BUY	11 0 0.04	12 0 0.04	13 1 0.15 SELL	14
15	16 -1 -0.10	17 -1 -0.07	18 0 0.04	19 0 0.04	20	21
22	23 -1 -0.06	24 -1 -0.07	25 1 0.15	26 1 0.15	27 2 0.26	28
29	30 0 0.00	31 0 0.03				

1992 Apr-Jun

April 1992

Sunday	Monday	Tuesday	Wednesday	Thursday	Friday	Saturday
			1 1 0.17	2 1 0.17	3 1 0.19	4
5	6 -1 -0.06	7 -1 -0.03	8 0 0.08	9 0 0.08	10 1 0.17	11
12	13 -1 -0.08	14 -1 -0.05	15 0 0.06	16 0 0.06	17 1 0.17	18
19	20 -1 -0.08	21 -1 -0.05	22 0 0.06	23 1 0.17	24 2 0.28	25
26	27 0 0.02	28 1 0.13	29	30 -1 -0.12		

May 1992

Sunday	Monday	Tuesday	Wednesday	Thursday	Friday	Saturday
					1 3 0.41	2
3	4	5	6 0 0.04	7 -1 -0.01	8 0 0.09 SELL	9
10	11 -2 -0.16	12 -1 -0.13	13 -1 -0.01	14 -1 -0.03	15 0 0.07	16
17	18 -2 -0.18	19 -2 -0.15	20 -1 -0.03	21 -1 -0.03	22 0 0.07	23
24	25 -1 -0.07	26 -1 -0.04 BUY	27 0 0.07	28 0 0.07	29 1 0.18	30

June 1992

Sunday	Monday	Tuesday	Wednesday	Thursday	Friday	Saturday
	1 0 0.02	2 0 0.05	3 0 0.08	4 0 0.08	5 1 0.19	6
7	8 -1 -0.06	9 -1 -0.03	10 0 0.06	11 0 0.06	12 1 0.17	13
14	15 -1 -0.08	16 -1 -0.05	17 0 0.06	18 0 0.06	19 1 0.17	20
21	22 -1 -0.08	23 -1 -0.05	24 1 0.17	25 1 0.17	26 2 0.28	27
28	29 0 0.02	30 0 0.05				

1992 Jul-Sep

July 1992

Sunday	Monday	Tuesday	Wednesday	Thursday	Friday	Saturday
			1 0 0.11	2 0 0.11	3 1 0.13 SELL	4
5	6 -1 -0.12	7 -1 -0.08	8 0 0.02	9 0 0.02	10 0 0.11	11
12	13 -2 -0.14	14 -1 -0.11	15 0 0.00	16 0 0.00	17 0 0.11	18
19	20 -2 -0.14	21 -1 -0.11 BUY	22 0 0.00	23 0 0.00	24 0 0.11	25
26	27 -1 -0.03	28 0 0.00	29 0 0.11	30 0 0.11	31 1 0.22	
30	31					

August 1992

Sunday	Monday	Tuesday	Wednesday	Thursday	Friday	Saturday
2	3 0 0.03	4 0 0.06	5 0 0.09	6 0 0.09	7 1 0.20	1 8
9	10 -1 -0.05	11 -1 -0.02	12 0 0.07	13 0 0.07	14 1 0.18	15
16	17 -1 -0.07	18 -1 -0.04	19 0 0.07	20 0 0.07	21 1 0.18	22
23	24 -1 -0.07	25 0 0.06	26 1 0.18	27 1 0.18	28 2 0.29	29
30	31 0 0.03					

September 1992

Sunday	Monday	Tuesday	Wednesday	Thursday	Friday	Saturday
		1 -1 -0.01	2 0 0.09	3 0 0.01	4 0 0.11 SELL	5
6	7 -2 -0.14	8 -1 -0.10	9 0 0.01	10 -1 0.00	11 0 0.09	12
13	14 -1 -0.07	15	16 -1 -0.04	17 -1 0.00	18 0 0.09	19
20	21 -2 -0.16	22 -1 -0.03 BUY	23	24 0 0.06	25 1 0.20	26
27	28 -1 -0.05	29 -1 -0.01	30 0 0.09			

1992 Oct-Dec

October 1992

Sunday	Monday	Tuesday	Wednesday	Thursday	Friday	Saturday
				1 1 0.12	2 1 0.23	3
4	5 -1 -0.11	6 -1 -0.08	7 0 0.03	8 0 0.03	9 1 0.14 SELL	10
11	12 -2 -0.13	13 -1 -0.10	14 0 0.01	15 0 0.01	16 1 0.12	17
18	19 -2 -0.13	20 -1 -0.10 BUY	21 0 0.01	22 0 0.01	23 1 0.12	24
25	26 -1 -0.02	27 0 0.00	28 1 0.12	29 1 0.12	30 1 0.23	31

November 1992

Sunday	Monday	Tuesday	Wednesday	Thursday	Friday	Saturday
1	2 0 0.08	3	4 0 0.11	5 0 0.05	6 1 0.16	7
8	9 -1 -0.09	10 -1 -0.05	11 0 0.05	12 0 0.03	13 1 0.14	14
15	16 -1 -0.11	17 -1 -0.08	18 0 0.03	19 0 0.03	20 -1 0.00	21
22	23	24 0 0.02	25 1 0.14	26 1 0.14	27 2 0.25	28
29	30 0 0.00	31				

December 1992

Sunday	Monday	Tuesday	Wednesday	Thursday	Friday	Saturday
		1 -1 -0.03	2 0 0.08	3 0 -0.00	4 0 0.10 SELL	5
6	7 -2 -0.15	8 -1 -0.12	9 0 0.00	10 -1 -0.02	11 0 0.08	12
13	14 -2 -0.17	15 -2 -0.14	16 -1 -0.02	17 -1 -0.02 BUY	18 1 0.19	19
20	21 0 0.00	22 1 0.22	23	24 1 0.14	25 4 0.61	26
27 31	28 3 0.38	29 0 0.06	30 2 0.29 SELL			

APPENDICES

APPENDIX A SOURCES OF DATA IN ENGLISH FOR JAPANESE SECURITIES

Data in English pertinent to Japanese securities is available from five basic sources:

- The Tokyo, Osaka and Nagoya stock exchanges as well as the other five stock exchanges in Japan.

- The big four and other domestic security companies as well as foreign securities companies.

- Government agencies such as the Bank of Japan and the National Land Agency.

- Independent data sources providing hard copy or on-line information.

- Other sources such as books and research reports from academic researchers.

The Japan Company Handbook provides considerable up to date information (with quarterly revisions) on all the stocks on the first and second sections of the TSE. It is available from Toyo Keizai Inc., 1-2-1, Hongokucho, Nihonbashi, Chuo-ku, Tokyo 103, Japan or Toyo Keizai America Inc., 65 East 55th St, 28th floor, New York, NY 10022, tel: 212-418-7610. Toyo Keizai Inc. also publishes an *Asian Company Handbook* covering over 800 companies listed in Hong Kong, the Republic of Korea, Taiwan, Thailand, Malaysia and Singapore.

Hamao and Ibbotson (1989) provide much data on past returns for research purposes. Much data and economic news analysis comes from the Nihon Keizai Shimbun, Inc., 9-5, Otemachi 1-chome, Chiyoda-ku, Tokyo 100, tel: 03-270-0251. Among other excellent publications, it produces the weekly *Japan Economic Journal*.

Japan Periodicals: A Guide to Business and Economic Studies in English,, published in Japan (1990) by the Keizai Koho Center, describes the major English language publications emanating from Japan. The address is Keizai Koho Center, Otemachi Bldg, 6-1 Otemachi 1-chome, Chiyoda-ku, Tokyo 100, tel: 03-201-1415, fax: 03-201-1418.

Examples of publications available from the Tokyo Stock Exchange include:

- *TSE Fact Book*, updated yearly

- Tokyo Stock Exchange
- Constitution of the TSE
- Business Regulations of the TSE
- Listing Regulations of the TSE
- Brokerage Agreement Standards of the TSE
- TOPIX - Tokyo Stock Price Index
- TOPIX Data Book
- TOPIX Futures - Outline of the TSE Price Index Futures
- TOPIX Options
- Japanese Government Bond Futures
- TSE U.S. T-Bond Futures
- Options on Japanese Government Bond Futures
- Tokyo Stock Exchange's Computer-assisted Order Routing and Execution System (CORES)
- TSE Monthly Statistics Report

For further information contact the Tokyo Stock Exchange, International Affairs Dept. 2-1, Nihombashi-Kabuto-cho, Chuo-ku, Tokyo 103, tel: Tokyo 666-0141 or fax: 663-0625 or Tokyo Stock Exchange, NY Research Office, 100 Wall St, NY, NY 10005, tel: (212)-363-2350.

Information from the other stock exchanges can be obtained by contacting them. The OSE has many useful data publications: Osaka Securities Exchange, 8-16 Kitahama 1-chome, Chuo-Ku, Osaka 541, Japan.

Information from the securities companies are for institutional and other clients.

From Yamaichi Securities and Yamaichi Research Institute:

- Yamaichi Research: Monthly Commentary and Investment Outlook for Japan by the Yamaichi Research Institute
- Yamaichi Research Institute Monthly Digest of Statistics
- Monthly Stock Market Outlook
- Yamaichi Investment Briefs on Individual Stocks

The addresses are Yamaichi Securities Co, Ltd, 4-1, Yaesu 2-chome, Chuo-ku, Tokyo 104, Japan, tel: 03-276-3181, and Yamaichi Research Institute of Securities and Economics, Inc (YRI), 14-8 Ningyo-cho, Nihonbashi 1-chome, Chuo-ku, Tokyo 103, Japan, tel: 03-660-5511, fax: 03-

663-0906. For the New York office: Yamaichi Research Institute of Securities and Economics, Inc (YRI), Two World Trade Center, Suite 9846, NY, NY 10048, tel: (212) 524-0836, fax: (212) 466-6849.

From Gordon Capital Corporation, Box 67, Suite 5300, Toronto Dominion Centre, Toronto, Ontario, Canada M5K 1E7, tel: (416)-364-9393, fax: (416)-868-0445. Ziemba writes an occasional *Japan Guide* as well as a *Quantitative Studies Guide* for Gordon's institutional investors.

Examples of government information sources include:

Organization	Sample Publications
The Bank of Japan, 2-1, Nihonbashi Hongoku-cho 2-chome, Chuo-ku, Tokyo 103, tel: 03-279-1111	Balance of Payments Monthly Economic Statistics Annual Economic Statistics Monthly Price Indexes Annual Price Indexes Monthly
Japan Economic Research Center, Nikkei Kayabacho Bldg. Bekkan, 6-1, Nihonbashi Kayabacho 2-chome, Chuo-ku, Tokyo 103 tel: 03-639-2801	A Five-year Economic Forecast Long-term Economic Forecast Series Quarterly Forecast of Japan's Economy
Japan Securities Research Institute, 5-8, Nihonbashi Kayabacho 1-chome, Chuo-ku, Tokyo 103 tel: 03-669-0737	Securities Market in Japan
Ministry of Finance, Printing Bureau, 2-4, Toranomon 2-chome, Minato-ku, Tokyo 105, tel: 03-582-4411	Economic Survey of Japan Japanese Economic Indicators An Outline of Japanese Taxes
The Japan Times Ltd, 5-4, Shibaura 4-chome, Minato-ku, Tokyo 108, tel: 03-4543-2013	Defense of Japan The Japan Times The Japan Times Weekly Overseas Edition

Examples of independent data sources include:

Information Service	Publisher	Information Type	Language	Update Frequency	Number	Format
Analysts Guide	Daiwa Securities Co. Ltd.	Full B/S & US Acts	English/ Japanese	Annual	900	Hard copy
Japan's Business Directory	Diamond Lead Co., Ltd	Selected B/S & US Acts	English	Annual	1500	Hard copy
Financial Leaders of Japan	Japan Export Magazine Pub. Co.	Selected B/S & US Acts	English	Annual	N.P.	Hard copy
IBJ Data	Industrial Bank of Japan	B/S & US Acts, Ratios stock analysis	English	Quarterly	100	On line
Japan Co. Handbook	First Securities Co., Second Securities Co.	Selected B/S & US Acts	English	Semi- annual	1104 671	On line/ hard copy
Jiji Press Ticker Service	Jiji Press	Share price data	English	Daily	N.P.	On line
Needs -Company	Nihon Keizai Shimbun	B/S & US data	English	Monthly	15,000	On line
Needs - Stock & Bond Price File	Nihon Keizai Shimbun	Stock & bond quotes	English	Twice a day	N.P.	On line
Survey of Japance & Ind	Ref & Statistics Center	Selected B/S & US Acts	Japanese/ English	Annual	N.P.	Hard copy
Japan Information Exchange	Contex Scientific Corp/Kyodo News	Stock market data	English	Continuous	N.P.	On line
The President Directory	President Inc.	Selected B/S & US Acts	English	Annual	N.P.	Hard copy
Toyokeizai Corp. Financial Data	The Oriental Economist	Complete B/S & US Acts	Japanese/ English	Daily	1811	On line
TSR-BIGS	Tokyo Shoko Research Corp	Selected financial data	Japanese	Monthly	360,000	On line
TSR-FINES	Tokyo Shoko Research Corp	Selected B/S & US Acts	Japanese	Monthly	35,000	On line

Source: Choi (1988)

Examples of reports and books from academic researchers include the references listed in this book as well as the material in the text and appendix.

APPENDIX B SOME BASIC DATA ON FISCAL 1989 FINANCIAL PERFORMANCE
OF MAJOR FIRMS

1. Life Insurance Companies' Premiums and Assets in FY (fiscal
    year) 1989

Table B1 provides the seven major life insurance companies' premium
revenue, total assets and profits (losses) from stock portfolios in fy 1989.
Premiums continued to rise, as did total assets, but the stock market fall in
the first quarter of 1990 led to considerable stock portfolio losses.

Table B1
Financial Performance of the Major Life Insurance Companies in FY 1989
in Billions of Yen with Yearly Percentage Changes in ()

	Premium Revenue	Total Asset	Latent Profits of Stock Portfolio
Nippon	5051.3 (+4.6)	24881.4 (+16.4)	8841.7 (-21.5)
Dai-Ichi	3638.9 (+3.9)	17380.8 (+18.4)	5640.4 (-23.7)
Sumitomo	3357.6 (+4.6)	14861.6 (+17.2)	3251.3 (-27.0)
Meji	2558.0 (+16.9)	10085.6 (+22.4)	4338.5 (-22.2)
Asahi	1796.2 (+9.0)	7954.4 (+16.0)	2594.1 (-26.6)
Mitsui	1597.2 (+16.3)	6302.8 (+20.7)	1422.5 (-29.3)
Yasuda	1474.9 (+12.5)	5420.9 (+21.5)	1659.7 (-20.2)

Source: *Japan Economic Journal*

The share of assets as of the end of 1989 is shown in Figure B1. So far the
life insurers have been conservative investors and stable stockholders.
They have typically had the same policy payout return and have held
onto their huge profits using book values. There is increasing pressure to
open up these companies through the general deregulation of the
Japanese economy. The deregulation of interest rates is hitting the life
insurers hard. Sales of policies, which are primarily investment vehicles,
were down 60% in 1990. Yields on variable-insurance funds of major
insurers have been dropping steadily as shown in Figure B2, and were in
the red in 1990.

Table B9 shows the profits of trust banks. Profits were down 45% in
the six months ending September 1990 from 1989 profits which are shown
in ( ). Forecasts for all of fy 1990 to March 1991 for a decline of 55.4% in
net profits from fiscal 1989 to ¥241.5 billion.

Figure B1   Life Insurers' Assets (¥111,266.6 billion) at the End of 1989

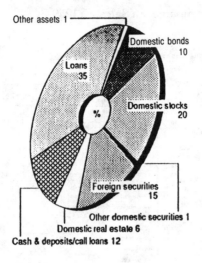

Source: Life Insurance Association of Japan

Figure B2
Yields on Variable Life Insurance Funds of Major Insurers, 1987-1990

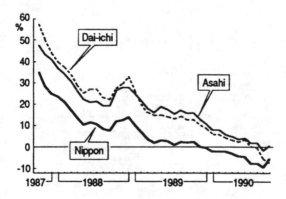

Source: Life Insurance Association of Japan

2. Fiscal 1989 Performance of Various Companies, 1990

Table B2   Top 100 Listed Companies in Sales, FY1989

	Billions of Yen	% Change from Previous Year		Billions of Yen	% Change from Previous Year
1 Sumitomo Corp.	21,403.6	(46.9)	51 Sharp	1,057.2	(6.5)
2 C.Itoh & Co.	20,532.7	(31.9)	52 Sanyo Electric	1,040.1	(5.3)
3 Mitsui & Co.	20,300.0	(36.9)	53 Seiyu	1,004.0	(3.5)
4 Marubeni	18,248.2	(28.6)	54 Dainippon Ink & Chemicals	956.7	(5.5)
5 Mitsubishi Corp.	16,614.0	(20.1)	55 Asahi Glass	925.9	(10.9)
6 Nissho Iwai	15,047.5	(36.5)	56 Jusco	922.8	(7.0)
7 Toyota Motor	7,190.5	(7.4)	57 Asahi Chemical Industry	879.3	(7.5)
8 Toyo Menka Kaisha	6,324.3	(20.8)	58 Matsushita Electric Works	865.1	(12.2)
9 Nichimen	5,893.7	(24.6)	59 Suzuki Motor	843.6	(3.3)
10 NTT	5,769.2	(2.0)	60 Sekisui House	841.6	(15.6)
11 Kanematsu Gosho	5,501.7	(25.5)	61 Nippon Mining	822.3	(14.5)
12 Matsushita Electric Industrial	4,248.7	(4.2)	62 Canon	814.2	(21.1)
13 Tokyo Electric Power	4,086.8	(3.7)	63 Kawasaki Heavy Industries	812.8	(5.9)
14 Nissan Motor	4,005.5	(11.8)	64 Chugoku Electric Power	810.7	(1.2)
15 Hitachi	3,525.2	(9.0)	65 Mitsukoshi	787.8	(10.5)
16 Toshiba	3,060.8	(4.7)	66 Toppan Printing	781.5	(6.4)
17 NEC	2,760.6	(8.6)	67 Fuji Photo Film	777.5	(5.0)
18 Honda Motor	2,748.8	(4.2)	68 Hanwa	771.9	(16.3)
19 Nippon Steel	2,573.1	(7.8)	69 Mitsubishi Oil	764.5	(15.8)
20 Mitsubishi Electric	2,387.8	(7.0)	70 Mitsubishi Kasei	731.8	(·)
21 Fujitsu	2,125.6	(6.0)	71 Tokyo Gas	707.1	(1.8)
22 Mitsubishi Heavy Industries	2,094.2	(22.3)	72 Chori	700.6	(5.8)
23 Kansai Electric Power	2,075.2	(2.7)	73 Sumitomo Electric Industries	700.3	(15.7)
24 Mazda Motor	2,045.5	(·)	74 Bridgestone	698.8	(12.4)
25 Mitsubishi Motors	2,025.7	(6.6)	75 Daihatsu Motor	694.6	(1.5)
26 Toyota Tsusho	1,957.3	(10.6)	76 All Nippon Airways	672.0	(16.3)
27 Nippon Oil	1,853.7	(11.2)	77 Fujita	664.3	(23.3)
28 Daiei	1,777.3	(6.0)	78 Toshoku	664.3	(1.9)
29 Chubu Electric Power	1,706.7	(2.8)	79 House Food Industrial	664.2	(19.1)
30 Kawasho	1,611.6	(13.4)	80 Kubota	662.8	(5.8)
31 Sony	1,536.4	(22.1)	81 Fuji Heavy Industries	658.0	(−0.8)
32 Shimizu	1,476.6	(17.6)	82 Ricoh	656.3	(8.9)
33 Cosmo Oil	1,465.3	(21.1)	83 Asahi Breweries	655.0	(20.2)
34 Kajima	1,419.8	(14.3)	84 Takashimaya	653.6	(8.6)
35 Taisei	1,406.0	(10.4)	85 Nichii	647.3	(6.7)
36 Showa Shell Sekiyu	1,366.2	(10.9)	86 Mitsubishi Metal	642.7	(−10.5)
37 NKK	1,277.5	(1.3)	87 Itoman & Co.	638.3	(22.3)
38 Ito-Yokado	1,258.1	(7.5)	88 Ishikawajima-Harima Heavy Industries	632.8	(2.8)
39 Nippondenso	1,230.6	(10.3)	89 Komatsu	628.4	(10.9)
40 Kobe Steel	1,221.7	(3.8)	90 Victor Co. of Japan	618.4	(·)
41 Kirin Brewery	1,199.8	(·)	91 Mitsui Real Estate Development	604.2	(28.5)
42 Ohbayashi	1,151.9	(21.9)	92 Sumitomo Chemical	601.8	(8.1)
43 Sumitomo Metal Industries	1,119.6	(6.1)	93 Hino Motors	599.9	(12.1)
44 Kawasaki Steel	1,112.2	(5.6)	94 Hitachi Sales	591.4	(−10.1)
45 Kumagai Gumi	1,100.2	(·)	95 Takeda Chemical Industries	587.7	(0.4)
46 Isuzu Motors	1,092.1	(6.7)	96 Toda Construction	587.7	(·)
47 Nippon Express	1,086.1	(8.2)	97 Taiyo Fishery	581.4	(·)
48 Tohoku Electric Power	1,067.9	(3.3)	98 Furukawa Electric	577.7	(9.9)
49 Kyushu Electric Power	1,065.8	(2.6)	99 Daimaru	568.9	(7.3)
50 Japan Airlines	1,060.3	(13.3)	100 Osaka Gas	559.3	(−0.6)

Note: (·) companies with irregular settlement terms in previous year

Source: *Japan Economic Journal*

Table B3   Top 100 Listed Companies in Pretax Recurring Profits, FY1989

Name	Year-to-Year Growth (%)	Pretax Profits Projections (¥ Billion)	Name	Year-to-Year Growth (%)	Pretax Profits Projections (¥ Billion)
1 General Sekiyu	191.7	10.0	51 Keyence	21.4	10.5
2 Cosmo Oil	105.7	15.0	52 Dowa Mining	21.2	5.0
3 Ishikawajima-Harima Heavy Industries	95.5	30.0	53 Cleanup	21.2	7.1
4 Kawasaki Kisen Kaisha	83.3	9.5	54 Kyokuto Kaihatsu Kogyo	21.2	4.5
5 Janome Sewing Machine	68.9	6.0	55 Shimizu Construction	20.7	98.5
6 Nagoya Railroad	56.6	5.7	56 Yamaha Motor	20.5	8.5
7 Daifuku	47.0	11.0	57 Tateyama Aluminium Industry	20.5	8.3
8 Daito Trust Construction	45.7	22.0	58 KYC Machine Industry	20.4	3.7
9 Toyo Information Systems	45.6	4.5	59 Senko	20.3	5.2
10 Itoman & Co.	45.3	20.0	60 Komatsu Forklift	20.2	5.7
11 Aoyama Trading	43.4	18.0	61 Osaka Building	19.9	6.5
12 Nippon Oil	41.4	30.0	62 Makino Milling Machine	19.7	8.8
13 Mitsubishi Oil	38.8	16.0	63 Hankyu Department Stores	19.5	11.0
14 Stanley Electric	38.7	6.0	64 Takara Shuzo	19.4	5.5
15 Japan Airlines	38.4	73.0	65 Nisshin Oil	18.7	6.5
16 Shokusan Jutaku Sogo	36.3	6.0	66 Fujikura	18.7	9.5
17 Kurimoto	36.2	7.5	67 Kato Works	18.3	3.6
18 Ines	33.2	4.3	68 Nissan Construction	17.8	3.9
19 Nihon Cement	32.9	16.5	69 Nippon Hodo	17.7	14.0
20 Okumura	31.6	20.0	70 Mitsui Real Estate Development	17.6	62.0
21 Autobacs	31.1	5.8	71 Nichiei	17.6	10.0
22 Roland	30.2	4.0	72 Pioneer	17.6	41.0
23 Mitsui Construction	29.5	10.5	73 Toei	17.5	4.9
24 Crown	29.5	6.5	74 Mitsubishi Heavy Industries	17.4	165.0
25 Niigata Engineering	29.2	4.2	75 Itoham Foods	17.2	13.5
26 Sony	28.7	120.0	76 Bunka Shutter	17.2	7.2
27 Ohbayashi	28.6	65.0	77 Shinko Electric	17.0	4.7
28 Tosoh	27.6	13.0	78 Tochigi Fuji Industrial	16.8	4.0
29 Sumitomo Heavy Industries	27.5	4.5	79 Yamato Transport	16.7	10.0
30 JDC	27.3	8.2	80 Sun Wave Industrial	16.6	6.0
31 Hitachi Seiki	27.3	6.0	81 Furukawa	16.6	13.0
32 Sanwa Shutter	27.1	21.0	82 Kawasaki Heavy Industries	16.5	20.0
33 Mitsubishi Metal	26.8	33.0	83 Chubu-Nippon Broadcasting	16.4	5.8
34 Daiwa House Industry	26.5	60.0	84 Teac	16.4	5.4
35 Suzuki Motor	26.1	20.0	85 Seiren	16.3	3.6
36 Nakanogumi	26.1	4.1	86 Kyocera	15.8	62.3
37 Kurita Water Industries	25.6	8.3	87 Sumitomo Forestry	15.8	17.5
38 Royal Hotel	25.0	5.2	88 Sumitomo Densetsu	15.6	3.8
39 Kajima	24.6	90.0	89 Sangetsu	15.5	11.0
40 Toda Construction	24.5	34.2	90 Toshiba Chemical	15.1	4.0
41 Dia Kensetsu	24.2	12.0	91 Nisshin Steel	15.0	5.0
42 Kuraray	24.1	19.0	92 Ando Construction	14.9	7.5
43 Japan Vilene	24.1	5.3	93 Mitsubishi Warehouse & Transportation	14.8	9.3
44 Meitec	23.7	3.6	94 Ebara	14.6	10.5
45 Taisei Construction	23.4	70.0	95 Settsu	14.4	11.7
46 Toyo Construction	22.9	4.7	96 Fujita	14.4	35.0
47 Daihatsu Motor	22.3	13.5	97 Nippon Densan	14.3	3.5
48 Toyota Motor	21.9	7.0	98 Sumitomo Corp.	14.2	80.0
49 Mitsui Real Estate Sales	21.7	12.6	99 Mazda Motor	14.1	55.0
50 Mitsubishi Corp.	21.3	100.0	100 Daikyo	14.1	39.0

Source: *Japan Economic Journal*

Table B4 Top 100 Listed Companies in Pretax Profits Growth, FY1989

		Billions of Yen	% Change from Previous Year				Billions of Yen	No Change from Previous Year
1	Toyota Motor	569.8	(9.2)		51	Tohoku Electric Power	73.4	(– 17.4)
2	Nomura Securities	488.8	(•)		52	Sharp	72.4	(31.0)
3	NTT	484.7	(13.8)		53	Kajima	72.2	(45.8)
4	Sumitomo Bank	352.6	(– 15.3)		54	Dainippon Ink & Chemicals	71.0	(11.6)
5	Sanwa Bank	319.6	(– 2.6)		55	Sekisui House	70.7	(28.9)
6	Daiwa Securities	313.1	(•)		56	Sumitomo Corp.	70.0	(26.6)
7	Fuji Bank	296.8	(– 24.5)		57	Nippon Credit Bank	69.1	(– 10.3)
8	Dai-Ichi Kangyo Bank	295.4	(– 23.7)		58	Kyushu Electric Power	67.5	(– 20.8)
9	Mitsubishi Bank	270.9	(– 23.8)		59	Fanuc	66.0	(38.8)
10	Matsushita Electric Industrial	265.2	(6.3)		60	Mitsui & Co.	65.0	(18.4)
11	Nikko Securities	260.4	(•)		61	Kirin Brewery	64.6	(•)
12	Yamaichi Securities	233.6	(•)		62	House Food Industrial	63.2	(43.6)
13	Hitachi	220.8	(15.5)		63	Kyowa Bank	62.8	(– 20.0)
14	Nippon Steel	202.3	(26.1)		64	Arabian Oil	62.5	(165.4)
15	Toshiba	201.8	(35.4)		65	Daiwa Bank	61.9	(– 30.1)
16	Tokyo Electric Power	184.9	(– 32.8)		66	Matsushita Electric Works	61.5	(19.4)
17	Nissan Motor	184.2	(19.0)		67	Nisshin Seiko	58.5	(3.5)
18	Industrial Bank of Japan	158.6	(– 18.6)		68	Yamanouchi Pharmaceutical	58.0	(•)
19	Fuji Photo Film	151.2	(14.5)		69	Toppan Printing	57.6	(11.2)
20	Mitsubishi Heavy Industries	140.4	(61.2)		70	Marui	56.7	(19.0)
21	Mitsubishi Electric	135.3	(45.3)		71	Taisei	56.7	(33.8)
22	NEC	133.2	(30.4)		72	Kobe Steel	56.0	(18.7)
23	Sumitomo Trust & Banking	133.0	(– 15.5)		73	Toray Industries	55.3	(5.9)
24	Mitsubishi Trust & Banking	133.0	(– 22.5)		74	Mitsubishi Petrochemical	54.1	(•)
25	Kansai Electric Power	127.9	(– 14.8)		75	C. Itoh & Co.	54.0	(6.5)
26	Fujitsu	127.0	(19.4)		76	Kyocera	53.7	(6.7)
27	Mitsui Taiyo Kobe Bank	125.9	(– 26.9)		77	Seven-Eleven Japan	53.0	(17.4)
28	Mitsui Trust & Banking	118.4	(– 12.3)		78	Japan Airlines	52.7	(20.7)
29	Long-Term Credit Bank of Japan	114.8	(– 10.3)		79	Mitsui Real Estate Development	52.7	(15.5)
30	Yasuda Trust & Banking	105.1	(– 19.2)		80	Canon	52.6	(20.9)
31	Tokio Marine & Fire Insurance	103.7	(– 7.6)		81	Tokyo Gas	50.5	(– 32.6)
32	Tokai Bank	103.6	(– 26.9)		82	Marubeni	50.5	(11.8)
33	Kawasaki Steel	103.5	(9.6)		83	Saitama Bank	50.5	(– 33.0)
34	Nippondenso	98.3	(10.2)		84	Ohbayashi	50.5	(53.6)
35	Chubu Electric Power	96.2	(– 36.7)		85	Yasuda Fire & Marine Insurance	50.5	(8.6)
36	Sumitomo Metal Industries	95.6	(9.4)		86	New Japan Securities	50.0	(•)
37	Sony	93.2	(20.7)		87	Toyo Seikan	48.8	(17.5)
38	Honda Motor	90.5	(1.3)		88	Mazda Motor	48.1	(•)
39	Bank of Tokyo	89.6	(– 12.3)		89	Wako Securities	47.7	(•)
40	Bridgestone	87.0	(24.0)		90	Sanyo Securities	47.0	(•)
41	Mitsubishi Estate	85.4	(11.9)		91	Tokyo Steel Mfg.	46.0	(26.1)
42	Asahi Glass	84.7	(11.4)		92	Taisho Pharmaceutical	45.6	(4.1)
43	Mitsubishi Corp.	82.4	(13.0)		93	Chugoku Electric Power	45.4	(– 27.1)
44	NKK	82.0	(– 18.7)		94	Hokkaido Takushoku Bank	44.8	(1.4)
45	Shimizu	81.5	(104.9)		95	TDK	44.2	(•)
46	Ito-Yokado	79.7	(9.1)		96	Nippon Kangyo Kakumaru Sec.	44.1	(•)
47	Toyo Trust & Banking	76.7	(– 17.2)		97	Daiichi Pharmaceutical	43.8	(1.9)
48	Kokusai Securities	76.5	(•)		98	Sekisui Chemical	43.5	(18.2)
49	Asahi Chemical Industry	75.3	(4.8)		99	Sumitomo Chemical	43.3	(18.2)
50	Takeda Chemical Industries	74.9	(1.1)		100	Toyo Sash	43.3	(•)

Note: (•) companies with irregular settlement terms in previous year

Source: *Japan Economic Journal* [1]

Table B5   Top 30 Retailers, FY 1989

'89	'88	Company (Category)	Sales (¥ million)	Year-to-Year Increase (%)
1	1	Daiei (s)	1,777,335	(+6.1)
2	2	Ito-Yokado (s)	1,258,190	(+7.5)
3	3	Seiyu (s)	1,004,094	(+3.6)
4	5	Seibu Department Store (s)	994,620	(+34.3)
5	4	Jusco (s)	922,866	(+7.1)
6	6	Mitsukoshi (d)	787,857	(+10.6)
7	8	Takashimaya (d)	653,603	(+8.7)
8	7	Nichii (s)	647,332	(+6.7)
9	9	Daimaru (d)	569,935	(+7.3)
10	10	Marui (d)	543,312	(+9.4)
11	11	Uny (s)	469,712	(+3.5)
12	12	Matsuzakaya (d)	438,565	(+6.0)
13	13	Nagasakiya (s)	406,449	(+20.8)
14	—	Isetan (d)	371,156	(—)
15	16	Tokyu Department Store (d)	346,523	(+10.5)
16	14	Izumiya (s)	340,677	(+3.1)
17	15	Hankyu Department Store (d)	327,045	(+4.2)
18	17	Chujitsuya (s)	302,873	(+5.5)
19	19	Nadakobe Consumers' Co-op (cp)	297,574	(+6.6)
20	20	Sogo (d)	292,610	(+11.7)
21	18	Kotobukiya (s)	285,167	(+1.4)
22	21	Maruetsu (s)	272,179	(+4.4)
23	22	Uneed (s)	271,613	(+4.4)
24	25	Kintetsu Department Store (d)	264,773	(+15.4)
25	23	Yokohama Takashimaya (d)	258,686	(+6.3)
26	34	Daiei Convenience Systems (cn)	256,936	(+97.7)
27	24	Tokyu Store Chain (s)	242,303	(+4.1)
28	26	Higashi Nippon Kiosk (—)	199,494	(+3.2)
29	27	Best Denki (sp)	194,361	(+13.8)
30	28	Heiwado (s)	174,722	(+7.2)

Note: Parentheses after name of company indicates; (d) department store, (s) supermarket, (sp) specialty shop, (cp) consumers' co-operative, (cn) convenience store, (—) others.

Source: *Nikkei Marketing Journal* Survey

Table B6   Zaitek Profits from Trading in FY 1989 in Billions of Yen

1	(1)	Toyota Motor	139.0	17	(22)	Sekisui Chemical	15.6
2	(2)	Mataushita Elec. Ind.	115.0	18	(1,326)	Mitsubishi Electric	15.3
3	(3)	Hitachi	61.9	19	(14)	Komatsu	15.0
4	(-)	Kirin Brewery	28.4	20	(17)	Kyocera	14.6
5	(4)	Sharp	26.6	21	(47)	Asahi Breweries	14.2
6	(6)	Fuji Photo Film	25.8	22	(62)	Honda Motor	12.9
7	(15)	Sumitomo Corp.	25.0	23	(23)	Sekisui House	12.8
8	(12)	Sony	23.7	24	(11)	Ajinomoto	12.4
9	(8)	Mitsubishi Heavy lnd.	23.6	25	(16)	Dai Nippon Printing	12.3
10	(5)	Nissan Motor	22.7	26	(19)	Takeda Chemical lnd.	12.2
11	(7)	Hanwa	21.4	27	(20)	Ricoh	11.6
12	(9)	Nippon Oil	19.2	28	(426)	Toshiba	10.6
13	(13)	Nippondenso	19.1	29	(18)	Tonen	10.2
14	(32)	Mitsubishi Corp.	18.4	30	(24)	Tejiin	10.0
15	(I 0)	Sanyo Electric	17.9	31	(-)	Yamanouchi Pharm.	10.0
16	(21)	Asahi Glass	16.4	32	(43)	Fanuc	10.0

Note: Ranking in previous year in parentheses. - Indicates irregular accounting period in previous year. Survey covers 1,799 firms listed on Japan's stock exchanges, excluding banks, securities firms, insurers and firms whose fy 1989 was an irregular accounting period.

Source: *Japan Economic Journal*

Table B7
Consolidated Pretax Profits of the Big Four Securities Companies, FY 1989 in Millions of Yen

	Consolidated		U.S. units		UK units	
Nomura	538.010	(+0.1)	2,845	(-523)	25,653	(1 2,329)
Daiwa	339,195	(+0.9)	1,496	(498)	13,902	(7,015)
Nikko	274,665	(+0.1)	- 873	(54)	11,252	(6,128)
Yamaichi	247,607	(+8.3)	90	(- 496)	4.450	(3,044)

Note: Figures in parentheses for consolidated profits are adjusted percentage changes from the irregular 6-month period ending March 1989, when the month of book-closing was changed. Figures in parentheses for U.S. and UK operations are pre-tax profits in the six-month ending March 1989.

Source: *Japan Economic Journal*

Table B8

The 100 Lowest Consolidated PER Stocks in Japan among Nonfinancials
Based on fy1990 Net Earnings Forecasts

	Consol PERs	Unconsol PERs			Consol PERs	Unconsol PERs
1 Orix	13.03	57.34	51 Daiichi		30.71	31.17
2 Mitsubishi Metal	14.33	15.61	52 Omron		30.76	44.09
3 Matsushita Electric Industrial	17.78	28.60	53 Daiichi Pharmaceutical		30.95	31.38
4 Honda Motor	19.05	31.75	54 Toyo Kohan		31.08	31.97
5 Toyota Motor	20.02	21.14	55 Hitachi Credit		31.11	31.63
6 Mitsubishi Petrochemical	20.33	21.04	56 Mitsui & Co.		31.14	56.05
7 Yamato Kogyo	21.23	31.99	57 House Food Industrial		31.25	31.65
8 Hitachi	21.67	37.51	58 Mori Seiki		31.32	32.53
9 Fuji Photo Film	21.82	23.36	59 Toyota Tsusho		31.33	36.49
10 Shin-Etsu Chemical	21.87	48.99	60 Nissho Iwai		31.35	62.71
11 Kanematsu	21.96	77.27	61 Dainippon Ink & Chemicals		31.45	36.75
12 Nissan Motor	22.58	30.11	62 Nippon Steel		31.57	37.89
13 Mitsui Petrochemical Industries	23.18	23.64	63 Rengo		31.66	46.53
14 Toshiba	23.33	32.21	64 Nichimo Corp.		31.78	32.13
15 Toyo Seikan Kaisha	23.48	34.15	65 Rinnai		31.80	38.79
16 Sumitomo Corp.	24.12	33.16	66 Nichimen Corp.		31.88	57.14
17 Fujitsu	24.14	31.24	67 Ezaki Glico		31.91	35.62
18 Nichicon	24.98	36.56	68 Toagosei Chemical Industry		31.94	38.72
19 YamanouchiPharmaceutical	25.19	29.53	69 Aisin Seiki		32.44	22.61
20 Mitsubishi Electric	25.20	30.47	70 Sumitomo Chemical		32.53	52.05
21 Sony	25.40	41.74	71 Canon		32.54	34.98
22 Sekisui Chemical	25.53	32.40	72 Hitachi Cable		32.55	39.94
23 Yamatake-Honeywell	26.02	41.84	73 Nisshinbo Industries		32.65	51.69
24 Yodogawa Steel Works	26.06	26.98	74 Mitsui Real Estate Development		32.69	43.93
25 Nisshin Steel	26.17	29.78	75 Nippon Light Metal		32.72	61.08
26 Ito-Yokado	26.58	36.70	76 Pioneer Electronic		32.73	50.92
27 Toray Industries	26.70	38.14	77 Matsushita Refrigeration		32.75	38.11
28 Nihon Cement	27.00	40.50	78 Toyo Suisan		32.76	39.48
29 Kanegafuchi Chemical Industry	27.10	33.87	79 Yokogawa Bridge Works		32.81	34.45
30 Amada	27.17	31.78	80 Jujo Paper		32.83	45.14
31 Asahi Chemical Industry	27.29	33.19	81 JVC		32.85	44.58
32 Sekisui House	27.58	28.60	82 Citizen Watch		32.87	43.05
33 Sumitomo Realty & Development	27.64	27.91	83 Amadasonoike		32.94	37.48
34 Teijin	27.70	32.52	84 Teac		33.05	49.57
35 Nagase & Co.	27.73	31.70	85 Mazda Motor		33.11	33.11
36 Japan Synthetic Rubber	29.02	31.92	86 Oji Paper		33.11	40.14
37 Joshin Denki	29.27	30.79	87 Tokuyama Soda		33.14	38.23
38 Itoman & Co.	29.61	32.90	88 Hitachi Express		33.20	46.11
39 Daiwa House Industry	29.71	29.71	89 TDK		33.24	38.77
40 Nippon Konpo Unyu Soko	29.73	37.16	90 Gunze		33.29	32.37
41 Kawasaki Steel	29.81	35.77	91 Oki Electric Industry		33.44	42.09
42 Mitsui Toatsu Chemicals	29.89	40.65	92 Nippon Meat Packers		33.53	33.53
43 Hitachi Koki	29.90	34.58	93 Kobori Juken		33.56	32.68
44 Sintokogio	29.97	42.81	94 Wacoal		33.63	36.99
45 C.Itoh & Co.	30.17	57.32	95 NEC		33.67	37.88
46 Sumitomo Metal Industries	30.18	36.89	96 Haseko		33.69	38.50
47 Murata Mfg.	30.27	51.71	97 Misawa Homes		33.75	34.85
48 Makita Electric Works	30.31	35.52	98 Tokyo Leasing		33.77	49.92
49 Marubeni	30.61	63.03	99 Toppan Printing		33.77	36.50
50 Seino Transportation	30.64	38.31	100 Yokogawa Electric		33.78	46.91

Note: PERs are based on closing share prices on July 10. Survey covers companies listed on nationwide exchanges with projected consolidated net profits of Y3 billion or more, excluding banks, insurers, brokerages and companies whose net profits exceed pretax recurring profits. Irregular accounting periods have been adjusted to annualized figures.

Source: Japan Economic Journal, July 28, 1990

Table B9
Business Results of Trust Banks for the Six Months Ending September 1990 in Billions of Yen

	Operating revenue	Net profits	Balance of deposits	Balance of money trust	Balance of pension trust	Balance of loan trust	Latent profits in securities portfolio	Latent profits in stock portfolio	Margin on operated funds (%)	Profits or losses from bond transactions	Profits from stock transactions	Profits from bond transactions in bond trading accounts	% of funds raised through money truments	Balance of real estate loans	BIS capital adequacy ratio, %
Sumitomo	827.3 (688.3)	29.5 (40.1)	9443.6	5,673.7	3,227.7	9,332.1	866.1 (1,614.3)	897.3 (1,638.2)	-0.07 (0.41)	-18.4 (1.80)	39.1 (30.00)	2.8 (2.10)	31.8 (32.60)	1497 (0)	8.6 (11.10)
Mitsubishi	822.8 (662.5)	29.8 (42.0)	10760.7	5,934.9	3,264.0	9,652.5	772.7 (1,680.2)	935.9 (1,766.6)	-0.28 (0.27)	0.1 (3.80)	50.1 (37.90)	2.8 (1.20)	29.2 (35.70)	1596.7 (12.40)	8.5 (11.10)
Yasuda	634.3 (470.6)	22.6 (32.0)	6064.4	5,176.4	2,839.8	7,005.6	647.4 (1,375.5)	693.5 (1,409.1)	-0.42 (0.08)	0.4 (-0.07)	43.5 (36.30)	1.7 (-2.6)	35.7 (45.70)	1094.2 (-8.2)	8.52 (10.29)
Mitsui	663.0 (528.7)	19.2 (32.6)	6830.6	6,595.0	2,827.0	9,371.4	962.6 (1,814.3)	1,162.3 (1,920.0)	-0.23 (0.19)	-9.5 (1.10)	13.6 (39.80)	3.20 (1.70)	25.7 (32.50)	1684.9 (-57.5)	9.14 (10.23)
Toyo	456.9 (362.9)	12.1 (22.3)	4564.7	3,596.9	2,803.4	5,847.8	514.2 (960.4)	561.1 (991.9)	-0.31 (0.40)	-4.1 (1.00)	7.2 (8.90)	2 (2.80)	35.6 (33.10)	966.6 (-5.9)	9.1 (12.10)
Chuo	285.8 (191.9)	6.3 (7.5)	2623.6	3,201.3	1,319.8	3,242.6	219.4 (478.4)	249.6 (502.7)	-0.61 (0.05)	-0.9 (-0.3)	19.1 (3.2)	1.1 (0.4)	42 (31.5)	720 (10.3)	7.4 (9.2)
Nippon	91.2 (70.6)	2.2 (3.2)	591.9	1,000.2	396.6	1,451.8	95.9 (201.4)	107.7 (213.3)	-0.1	-5.9 (0.80)	12.6 (3.5)	0.2 (0.20)	41.6 (29.30)	416.2 (5.80)	11.7 (13.30)
Total	3,781.3 (2,975.5)	121.9 (179.7)	40,879.5	31,178.4	16,678.3	45,904.3	4,098.3 (8,124.5)	4,607.4 (8,441.8)	0.20	-36.50 (7.5)	185.2 (156.9)	14.2 (6.0)		7,975.6 (-67.9)	

Note: - shows losses or negative interest rate spreads. Net business, profits are pretax recurring profits excluding profits management in tokkin funds.

Source: *Japan Economic Journal*

Table B10   Top 100 Corporate Landowners in Japan
in thousands of sq meters, % change from previous year in parentheses

#	Company	Area	(%)	#	Company	Area	(%)
1	Oji Paper	960,979	(1.0)	51	Kobe Steel	12,301	(0.9)
2	Jujo Paper	551,352	(0.0)	52	Chichibu Cement	11,738	(0.3)
3	Sumitomo Forestry	406,190	(0.0)	53	Nitchitsu	11,487	(0.0)
4	Sanyo-Kokusaku Pulp	275,643	(2.3)	54	Fujita Tourist Enterprises	10,940	(0.2)
5	Honshu Paper	271,758	(1.2)	55	Tokyu	10,339	(20.9)
6	Tokai Pulp	255,292	(0.0)	56	Sumitomo Chemical	9,494	(13.1)
7	Tokyo Electric Power	166,332	(0.2)	57	Komatsu	9,423	(– 4.5)
8	Kansai Electric Power	127,470	(– 0.7)	58	Denki Kagaku Kogyo	9,243	(0.3)
9	Hokuriku Electric Power	117,809	(0.0)	59	Chuetsu Pulp Industry	8,957	(0.2)
10	Mitsubishi Mining & Cement	116,369	(– 2.1)	60	Mitsubishi Kasei	8,641	(– 5.5)
11	Hokkaido Electric Power	99,276	(2.4)	61	Meiji Milk Products	8,522	(– 1.4)
12	Kyushu Electric Power	85,150	(1.1)	62	Tokyu Land	8,281	(*)
13	Nippon Steel	74,012	(– 0.2)	63	Isuzu Motors	7,872	(– 2.3)
14	Hokuetsu Paper Mfg.	69,182	(0.0)	64	Aisin Seiki	7,797	(187.3)
15	Daishowa Paper Mfg.	68,869	(– 28.0)	65	IHI	7,506	(0.4)
16	Seibu Railway	57,050	(– 0.5)	66	Mitsui Toatsu Chemicals	7,234	(1.1)
17	Mitsubishi Metal	51,111	(0.0)	67	Kumiai Chemical Industry	7,169	(0.2)
18	Nittetsu Mining	49,893	(0.9)	68	Nippon Oil	7,106	(0.8)
19	Chubu Electric Power	49,063	(2.0)	69	Mazda Motor	6,960	(6.6)
20	Tomoegawa Paper	43,338	(0.0)	70	Toshiba	6,744	(0.4)
21	Chugoku Electric Power	43,222	(0.6)	71	KDD	6,702	(0.4)
22	Nihon Cement	43,108	(0.0)	72	Cosmo Oil	6,660	(59.4)
23	Tohoku Electric Power	37,548	(– 3.1)	73	Daiwa House Industry	6,450	(– 10.9)
24	NTT	33,210	(– 0.3)	74	Odakyu Electric Railway	6,159	(13.4)
25	Toyota Motor	31,254	(0.8)	75	Osaka Cement	6,050	(– 0.2)
26	Onoda Cement	30,818	(0.0)	76	Daido Steel	5,980	(2.1)
27	Ube Industries	29,194	(2.7)	77	Nippondenso	5,901	(6.5)
28	NKK	26,676	(– 1.5)	78	Mitsubishi Motors	5,720	(3.2)
29	Kinki Nippon Railway	25,882	(– 0.9)	79	Asahi Glass	5,659	(– 0.8)
30	Sumitomo Metal Mining	24,817	(1.3)	80	Kajima	5,607	(0.0)
31	Furukawa	23,976	(0.0)	81	Fuji Heavy Industries	5,568	(0.5)
32	Kawasaki Steel	22,667	(0.6)	82	Izuhakone Railway	5,545	(1.9)
33	Mitsubishi Paper Mills	21,893	(8.6)	83	Showa Denko	5,495	(0.0)
34	Nissan Motor	21,529	(0.0)	84	Toray Industries	5,378	(– 0.6)
35	Nippon Mining	20,578	(– 0.8)	85	Nippon Light Metal	5,328	(33.4)
36	Sumitomo Metal Industries	19,797	(11.5)	86	Kawasaki Heavy Industries	5,235	(– 0.5)
37	Asahi Breweries	19,229	(3.2)	87	Yamaha Motor	5,233	(18.8)
38	Dowa Mining	17,973	(4.3)	88	Mitsubishi Electric	5,222	(0.3)
39	Hitachi	17,215	(– 0.3)	89	Japan Steel Works	5,130	(– 0.2)
40	Nagoya Railroad	17,123	(3.7)	90	Suzuki Motor	5,052	(0.6)
41	Mitsui Mining	16,650	(0.4)	91	Kubota	4,951	(0.1)
42	Honda Motor	16,035	(67.8)	92	Ohbayashi	4,871	(1.6)
43	Shikoku Electric Power	15,988	(1.7)	93	Mitsubishi Corp.	4,814	(9.8)
44	Daio Paper	15,604	(0.8)	94	Kirin Brewery	4,747	(– 1.2)
45	Sumitomo Cement	15,448	(– 2.5)	95	Tonen	4,624	(0.0)
46	Yamaha	15,150	(1.4)	96	Nippon Beet Sugar Mfg.	4,598	(– 0.2)
47	Mitsubishi Heavy Industries	14,358	(0.3)	97	Yomiuri Land	4,568	(2.9)
48	Asahi Chemical Industry	14,300	(– 1.7)	98	Mitsui Engineering & Shipbuilding	4,545	(– 0.2)
49	Tobu Railway	13,420	(0.0)	99	Teijin	4,490	(– 1.9)
50	Nippon Express	12,717	(0.7)	100	Showa Shell Sekiyu	4,488	(– 1.9)

Note: Survey covers April 1989 through March 1990. (*)Tokyu Land changed its accounting periods.

Source: *Japan Economic Journal*

APPENDIX C JAPANESE ECONOMIC INDICATORS, FEBRUARY 1991

Top band

Items (Unit or base)	(11) Gross national product — Nominal (seas adj annual rates) ¥ billion (*1)	(12) Money supply — M1 outstanding (end of month of year) ¥ billion (*2)	Yr-to-yr change %	M2+CD outstanding (end of month or year) ¥ billion (*3)	Yr-to-yr change %	(12) Account of Bank of Japan — Bank notes issued (end of month or year) ¥ billion	Yr-to-yr change %	Loans & discounts (end of month or year)	Gov't securities (end of month or year)	(12) Account of all banks — Deposits (end of month or year) ¥ billion	Loans & discounts (end of month or year)	Securities (end of month or year)	(13) Balance of treasury Accounts with the public [(-)pay'm't excess] ¥ billion (*1)	(12) Average contracted interest rates on loans and discounts of all banks (end of month or year) %	(13) Customs clearances — Exports (fob) $ million	Yr-to-yr %	Imports (cif) $ million	Yr-to-yr %	(16) Department store sales — National Value ¥ billion	Yr-to-yr %
1987	356,263.6	102,927.7	4.8	360,867.3	10.8	29,186.8	8.6	6,566.8	19,640.2	328,877.1	336,556.0	83,878.6	-2,555.7	5.208	229,221	9.6	149,515	18.3	8,879.3	5.5
1988	378,963.0	111,844.0	8.6	419,732.3	10.2	32,318.3	10.7	8,473.9	22,520.8	358,337.8	370,802.0	96,743.0	-731.2	5.034	264,917	15.6	187,354	25.3	9,551.8	7.6
1989	406,744.9	114,473.6	2.4	470,020.3	12.0	37,420.0	15.8	6,945.1	25,348.1	405,502.3	410,572.3	112,586.1	-2,095.8	5.287	275,175	3.9	210,847	12.4	10,516.6	10.1
1989 Dec				470,020.3	12.0	37,420.0	15.8	6,945.1	25,348.1	405,502.3	410,572.3	112,586.1	1,979.7	5,782	24,655	-5.8	18,446	12.1	1,517.8	10.2
1990 Jan		106,661.2	-0.4	460,417.1	11.8	31,316.8	11.0	5,523.3	20,959.8	396,917.9	411,394.7	114,253.8	3,398.7	5,993	18,673	-3.5	18,336	13.8	828.1	12.4
Feb		106,889.5	1.4	464,418.0	11.7	31,760.0	7.3	6,115.3	22,047.5	403,178.3	414,679.3	116,129.8	-2,034.2	6.212	22,006	-1.7	16,993	12.2	715.5	10.8
Mar	418,266.6	109,985.9	5.8	472,477.8	11.7	33,529.6	12.1	5,341.1	26,878.0	419,580.5	424,343.0	121,113.3	-2,873.9	6.431	26,039	-1.7	18,973	4.6	1,008.6	-4.6
Apr		122,020.4	3.2	485,764.4	13.7	34,640.8	14.6	4,546.5	29,059.4	419,100.1	420,781.8	121,174.6	-5,567.7	6.625	21,916		19,673	15.3	878.6	22.6
May		120,203.4	-1.8	472,564.8	12.4	31,172.7	8.4	3,585.2	26,243.4	421,715.6	418,805.8	121,546	831.7	6.761	23,782	-4.8	18,438	2.7	868.2	17.9
June	426,860.5	107,458.8		480,654.2	12.6	31,615.6	12.4	3,615.6	25,410.4	425,882.5	425,882.5	122,514.9	2,466.9	6.815	23,949	2.1	17,088	4.8	872.2	14.6
July		108,164.5		485,115.7	11.7	32,731.4	7.6	4,350.0	26,409.2	427,228.5	427,228.5	122,156.6	3,359.4	6.844	22,442	2.8	18,562	6.3	734.4	10.6
Aug		108,620.4	3.0	484,552.1	11.7	31,985.4	7.9	4,437.2	28,148.5	429,770.6	429,770.6	121,902.7	-230.8	6.929	25,854	6.3	18,977	2.8	817.7	8.7
Sept	431,003.9	106,160.0	2.9	495,901.3	13.1	32,246.4	8.6	3,633.6	27,266.3	424,553.1	434,172.6	123,000.8	491.3	7.161	25,725	16.1	18,935	10.5	912	9.7
Oct		114,856.8	3.5	486,418.2	10.7	31,637.3	6.8	4,001.9	29,017.8	441,499.6	433,951.4	124,820.3	-1,112.5	7.427	25,743	16.6	23,191	27.9	959.8	5.3
Nov		105,239.0	3.3	487,840.0	9.3	31,986.7	5.8	6,303.3	27,619.6	424,279.0	438,138.2	—	-2,592.8	7.477	25,743	—	23,496	26.7	948.9	6.7
Dec		107,067.8	4.7	—	—	39,797.8	6.4	—	31,542.1	436,241.6	441,172.2	—	1,885.6	—	28,291	14.7	22,903	24.2		

Bottom band

Items (Unit or base)	(12)(13) Balance of payments $ million (*4) — Overall	Current	Trade	Long term capital	(12) Gold & foreign exchange reserves (end of year or month) $ million (*5)	(12) Wholesale prices — Overall index 1985=100 (*6)	Yr-to-yr %	Domestic price index 1985=100 (*7)	Yr-to-yr %	Export price index (fob) (yen base) 1985=100 (*8)	Yr-to-yr %	Import price index (yen base) 1985=100 (*9)	Yr-to-yr %	(14) Consumer price index — General (Tokyo) 1985=100 (*10)	Yr-to-yr %	(15) Bankruptcies (*11) Cases	Yr-to-yr %	(16) Department store sales — National Value ¥ billion	Yr-to-yr %
1987	-29,545	87,015	96,386	-136,532	81,479	87.5	-3.8	92.3	-3.1	80.6	-5.1	58.9	-8.2	101.3	0.4	12,655	-27.6	2,122.4	5.5
1988	-28,982	79,631	95,012	-130,930	97,662	86.6	-1.0	91.8	-0.5	78.8	-2.3	56.2	-4.6	102.3	1.0	10,122	-20.0	2,001.0	7.6
1989	-33,286	57,157	76,917	-89,246	84,895	88.8	2.6	93.6	1.9	82.3	4.4	60.5	7.6	105.1	2.7	7,234	-28.5	1,232.3	10.1
1989 Dec	7,348	4,013	6,424	3,224	84,895	89.6	3.9	94.1	2.5	83.8	7.2	61.9	15.3	106.1	3.0	493	-40.0	1,517.8	10.2
1990 Jan	-4,525	-559	1,069	-2,698	82,717	89.7	3.7	94.1	2.6	84.2	6.3	62.6	13.0	106.3	3.4	455	-24.7	828.1	12.4
Feb	5,216	4,817	5,352	-7,905	80,443	89.8	3.5	94.2	2.5	84.2	6.0	63.4	11.8	106.7	3.8	448	-25.0	715.5	10.8
Mar	-757	8,047	7,972	-5,483	73,496	90.4	3.9	94.3	2.5	86.1	7.4	65.9	14.0	107.1	3.5	502	-36.1	1,008.6	-4.6
Apr	-19,836	1,960	3,976	-5,377	73,024	90.9	2.7	94.4	0.7	87.9	9.1	67.3	13.3	107.9	2.8	526	-22.4	878.6	22.6
May	8,891	1,399	2,618	-5,607	73,557	90.6	1.7	94.4	0.6	86.5	5.4	65.8	7.0	108.5	2.7	501	-24.1	868.2	17.9
June	3,008	4,533	7,020	-8,001	73,649	90.5	0.9	94.5	0.5	86.1	2.3	64.8	3.0	107.9	2.3	516	-18.7	872.2	14.6
July	-12,732	1,925	5,323	-8,062	74,585	90.4	0.8	94.9	0.6	85.2	2.3	64.6	1.9	107.9	2.0	482	-12.5	1,043.4	10.6
Aug	150	850	4,061	-4,886	75,315	90.7	1.0	95.1	1.8	85.1	2.5	64.0	3.6	108.0	2.8	514	-6.2	877.4	8.7
Sept	10,245	1,925	5,701	5,001	75,723	90.9	1.5	95.6	1.5	85.6	1.8	66.4	2.8	109.0	3.6	531	9.7	734.4	10.6
Oct	471	2,733	5,986	7,092	76,190	90.9	1.9	95.8	—	80.3	—	67.7	9.7	109.0	2.8	646	23.2	817.7	8.7
Nov	5,901	1,749	4,515	-2,850	76,672	91.3	2.0	96.2	2.2	79.8	2.2	68.4	10.5	110.0	3.8	633	44.8	912	9.7
Dec	—	—	—	—	77,053	91.6	2.2	96.3	2.3	81.1	3.2	69.0	11.5	109.9	3.6	714	—	959.8	6.7

Source: NEEDS (Nikkei Economic Electronic Databank System)

(16), (11), (17), (18) — Indexes, orders, construction, employment and wages

Unit or base	Production index (sea adj.) Mfg 1985=100	Prod. Mining mfg Yearly or monthly change %	Shipment index (sea adj.) Mfg 1985=100	Ship. Mfg change %	Inventory index of finished goods (sea adj.) Mfg 1985=100	Inv. Mfg change %	Operating rate index (sea adj.) Mfg 1985=100	Orders for machinery Private (excl ships, sea adj.) ¥ billion	Orders change %	Housing starts New construction 1,000 no	Housing Yr-to-yr change %	Building construction starts Non dwelling use ¥ billion	Building Yr-to-yr change %	Employment index of regular workers (mfg) 1985=100	Employment Yr-to-yr change %	Wage index (mfg) Nominal 1985=100	Wage Real 1985=100	Wage Yr-to-yr change %
1987	103.2	3.4	104.5	3.9	110.6	0.5	95.5	9,394.0	21.0	1,674.3	22.7	11,708.3	11.4	99.7	-1.5	103.9	103.6	2.2
1988	113.0	9.5	113.5	8.6	110.2	-0.4	101.1	10,265.3	9.3	1,684.6	0.6	14,436.5	23.3	100.1	0.6	108.3	107.5	3.8
1989	120.1	6.1	120.6	6.1	110.6	0.4	103.3	12,482.5	21.6	1,662.6	-1.3	17,800.3	23.3	101.7	1.8	113.0	109.7	3.0
1989 Dec	120.8	0.0	122.3	0.7	110.0	0.5	102.6	1,052.2	-6.4	143.8	0.6	1,917.2	46.5	102.5	2.0	115.3	111.1	1.6
1990 Jan	120.7	0.1	122.5	0.3	110.5	-0.4	102.8	1,073.1	2.0	108.6	6.3	1,345.1	25.0	102.2	2.0	111.7	107.3	0.7
Feb	121.1	0.3	124.0	1.3	108.5	-1.8	102.3	1,149.8	7.1	122.1	5.6	1,558.7	30.9	102.1	2.0	114.5	109.7	-0.3
Mar	123.1	1.7	126.1	1.7	107.4	-1.0	104.3	1,028.3	-10.6	134.1	-2.0	1,869.7	4.5	102.4	2.1	114.5	109.3	1.3
Apr	121.9	-1.0	121.4	-3.7	107.0	-0.5	104.2	1,162.5	13.0	147.8	-0.5	1,651.4	12.6	105.4	2.1	117.5	112.2	2.1
May	125.0	2.5	127.5	4.9	106.8	-1.8	107.1	1,115.3	-4.1	146.6	8.4	1,945.4	50.1	105.1	2.1	117.7	112.1	2.5
June	124.8	-0.2	127.5	0.1	108.1	0.2	105.3	944.2	-15.3	162.0	7.8	2,181.7	37.8	105.0	2.1	120.4	110.6	2.4
July	127.0	1.8	128.4	0.4	108.4	0.7	106.8	1,206.8	27.8	158.4	6.3	2,199.1	34.0	105.0	2.0	120.0	113.9	1.7
Aug	126.1	-1.0	127.7	-0.5	108.9	0.5	104.4	1,277.7	5.9	143.1	-0.2	1,962.2	15.0	104.4	2.9	117.7	113.6	1.7
Sept	130.0	-1.2	128.0	0.4	110.0	1.0	107.9	1,062.2	-0.2	158.1	15.0	1,977.2	16.0	104.4	1.9	119.7	113.6	1.6
Oct	130.8	3.1	127.7	-0.2			108.6	1,147.5	-1.5	151.9	0.7	2,113.4	23.9	104.5		120.4	110.8	
Nov	129.3	-0.8	131.0				109.7	1,292.0	12.6	138.4	-3.7	2,018.7	32.9			120.8	111.6	0.6
Dec																		

(16) Output of principal products

Items / Unit	Electric power million kWh	Fuel oil C 1,000 kl	Crude steel m t	Machine tools m t	Color TV sets 1,000 sets	Electronic switching systems ¥ million	VCRs (*14) 1,000 units	ICs million units	Passenger cars no. of vehicles	35mm still cameras (*15) 1,000 units	Ethylene	Caustic soda	Poly-ethylene	Poly-styrene	Synthetic fiber	Poly-propylene	Paint	Ink	Paper, paperboard
1987	584,885	38,077	98,513	263,000	13,081	344,165	27,489	11,557	7,891,087	16,399	4,585	3,227	2,181	1,735	1,388	1,405	1,894	320	22,537
1988	619,326	39,354	105,681	340,215	13,220	406,681	28,154	13,758	8,198,400	15,560	5,057	3,508	2,381	1,891	1,403	1,559	2,032	341	24,624
1989	660,640	41,243	107,907	417,733	12,577	388,360	28,242	14,490	9,052,406	16,746	5,603	3,674	2,712	1,997	1,436	1,719	2,127	364	26,809
1989 Dec	58,750	4,202	9,247	37,568	1,155	29,903	2,158	1,183	769,072	1,453	515	338	254	173	121	161	175	32	2,298
1990 Jan	59,074	3,900	9,172	33,323	874	26,435	1,811	1,085	678,533	1,199	525	343	265	173	120	166	155	27	2,700
Feb	54,414	3,806	8,274	36,733	949	32,328	2,092	1,136	837,830	1,410	447	312	220	167	111	144	163	28	2,131
Mar	57,511	3,786	9,170	45,213	1,021	53,747	2,276	1,195	910,687	1,557	456	336	245	153	121	162	192	33	2,357
Apr	52,624	3,167	9,126	35,042	1,071	37,208	2,171	1,238	814,203	1,377	446	316	231	159	122	163	182	33	2,257
May	53,282	2,986	9,335	35,253	1,027	27,873	2,147	1,203	799,933	1,221	491	318	252	181	127	160	175	31	2,332
June	59,022	2,844	8,980	38,893	1,150	29,929	2,480	1,308	869,104	1,364	457	304	253	165	125	146	186	33	2,369
July	68,144	3,645	9,189	38,384	1,207	39,352	2,574	1,364	894,463	1,395	485	328	239	174	128	154	187	34	2,351
Aug	70,072	3,871	9,157	42,558	1,015	37,179	2,294	1,294	709,785	1,264	490	311	244	179	125	164	179	31	2,331
Sept	61,600	3,946	9,077	35,746	1,140	43,395	2,463	1,371	834,572	1,439	475	324	223	183	123	158	196	32	2,270
Oct	57,116	4,107	9,822		1,203	34,449	2,623	1,423	932,309	1,481	489	330	249		127	172	209	36	2,402
Nov	55,612	4,336	9,394		1,292	34,259	2,557	1,405	856,700	1,517	497	341	241		126	172	198	35	
Dec	61,049																		

Notes

(*1)...Fiscal year for yearly figures; In constant 1980 prices;(*2)...Total of cash currency in circulation and demand deposit; (*3)...Issuance of certificates of deposit (CD) began in May 1979 in Japan;(*4)...IMF basis; (*5)...Total of gold, foreign exchange, SDRs and IMF Reserve Position; (*6)...320 items; (*7)...1,076 items; (*8)...312 items; (*9)...265 items; (*10)...540 items; (*11)...Business failures involving liabilities of ¥10 million or more; (*12)...Figures of 178 companies (before adjustment of overlapped orders); (*13)...Regular monthly pay, excluding bonuses; (*14)...Excluding kits and those for use by broadcasters; (*15)...Excluding half-sized cameras.

Sources

(*11)...Economic Planning Agency; (*12)...Bank of Japan;(*13)...Ministry of Finance; (*14)...Management and Coordination Agency; (*15)...Tokyo Shoko Reserch; (*16)...Ministry of International Trade & Industry; (*17)...Ministry of Construction; (*18)...Ministry of Labor.

Appendix D Land Prices

In *Land Prices in Japan: No Cause for Alarm*, May 1990, Hugh Canaway of Baring Securities made a number of points consistent with our information and views. His main points are listed Below. Figure D1 shows the land value by region in Japan and Figure D2 shows year by year land price changes in various major cities and prefectures from 1980 to 1989.

Main Land Points

- Inherent in the tax structure of Japan are huge disincentives to land sales; capital gains tax is high, while the cost of holding land is very low. In particular, agricultural land is taxed at a low level, but across the board, taxation has not kept pace with land price increases.

- Limiting supply further is the regulatory framework, which both discourages land sales, and decreases the level of efficiency at which it is used. Plot ratios, height restrictiors and zoning all exacerbate the poor supply of land.

- Attempts to increase the supply of land are half hearted and do not address the root of the problem, though will go some way to limiting speculative demand. There are a number of proposals, in particular by the Ministry of Construction, but these are either not enough, or unlikely to be carried out.

- Much of what has to be done is at the expense of the farmers, major corporations and rich individuals. How can the LDP realistically undertake tax reforms that are directed at these groups, which represent so much of its electoral support?

- The theoretical value of land: how far from the truth are we in Tokyo? If the plot ratio were to double in Central Tokyo - an eventual likelihood - yields might not look so bad.

- Land prices themselves: Tokyo commercial and residential land will remain stable, while Osaka should see a correction. Smaller regional investment is seeing a decline in yields, as construction costs rise, so a slowdown in growth rates can be expected here too.

- While supply is low, there will still be some land coming onto the market. This will meet with adequate demand from real estate companies and individuals. Though some bankruptcies will occur, these will not bring a flood of real estate onto the market nor drive prices down.

- Only if the economy goes into recession are land prices likely to collapse. At that point, the stock market would go first, then the economy, and finally the property market.

- Evaluation of share prices under higher interest rates and slower growth in land prices must be rethought, and we are led to the conclusion that the only way to include landholdings into share price evaluation is on the basis of the earnings that are to be received from land, discounted to present values at current interest rate levels.

Source: Canaway (1990)

Table D1
Land Price Indices: Six Largest Japanese Cities and Nationwide
Average for the First and Last Six Months of Each Year, 1955-90

	Nationwide				Six Largest Cities				CPI
	All	Comm	Housing	Indus	All	Comm	Housing	Indus	
1955:1	3.1	3.7	2.5	3.2	2.4	4.9	1.7	2.2	
1955:2	3.3	4.0	2.7	3.4	2.6	5.1	1.9	2.3	
1956:1	3.5	4.3	2.9	3.7	2.8	5.6	1.9	2.6	
1956:2	3.9	4.8	3.2	4.1	3.2	6.1	2.2	3.0	
1957:1	4.5	5.5	3.6	4.8	3.6	6.7	2.6	3.5	
1957:2	5.0	6.1	4.0	5.4	4.2	7.4	2.9	4.1	
1958:1	5.5	6.6	4.5	5.9	4.6	7.8	3.3	4.7	
1958:2	6.1	7.2	5.0	6.5	5.0	7.9	3.6	5.3	
1959:1	6.8	8.1	5.5	7.3	5.5	8.4	4.0	5.9	
1959:2	7.7	9.1	6.2	8.3	6.3	9.6	4.6	6.8	
1960:1	8.7	10.5	6.8	9.5	7.2	11.2	5.2	7.9	
1960:2	10.2	12.4	7.8	11.4	9.3	14.1	6.0	10.6	
1961:1	12.3	14.4	9.3	14.6	12.1	18.0	7.5	14.8	
1961:2	14.5	16.7	10.8	17.4	15.7	22.9	9.5	20.0	
1962:1	15.7	17.9	11.8	19.1	17.3	24.3	10.5	22.2	
1962:2	17.1	19.2	12.8	21.0	19.0	25.4	11.9	24.2	
1963:1	18.4	21.0	13.6	22.7	20.5	27.1	13.1	26.1	
1963.2	19.6	22.1	14.5	24.5	22.3	29.0	14.5	28.4	
1964:1	21.0	23.5	15.5	26.3	24.1	31.1	15.9	30.4	
1964:2	22.5	25.4	16.6	28.0	25.6	32.9	17.1	32.0	
1965:1	23.8	26.6	17.8	29.6	26.4	33.8	17.8	33.1	
1965:2	24.4	27.5	18.2	30.1	26.6	34.1	18.0	33.2	
1966:1	25.0	28.4	18.9	30.5	26.9	34.5	18.4	33.2	
1966:2	25.8	29.5	19.6	30.8	27.2	34.8	18.9	33.2	
1967:1	27.1	31.4	20.8	31.9	28.1	36.3	19.6	34.0	
1967:2	28.8	33.3	22.4	33.2	29.2	37.6	20.7	35.0	
1968:1	30.8	35.7	24.2	35.1	30.5	38.8	22.0	36.3	
1968:2	33.2	38.6	26.3	37.4	32.4	41.1	23.9	38.1	
1969:1	36.1	41.8	29.0	40.2	35.1	44.4	26.1	40.9	
1969:2	39.6	46.1	32.2	43.2	38.1	48.0	28.7	44.1	
1970:1	43.2	49.9	35.5	47.0	41.3	51.4	31.3	47.8	
1970:2	46.8	53.8	38.7	50.7	44.8	54.1	34.4	52.0	
1971:1	50.0	57.0	41.8	54.1	48.0	56.5	37.2	55.8	
1971:2	53.2	59.8	44.9	57.8	51.0	58.8	40.0	59.4	
1972:1	56.5	63.2	47.8	61.8	54.1	61.7	42.8	62.7	
1972:2	61.2	67.8	52.1	66.7	59.6	66.7	48.1	68.6	
1973:1	70.8	76.6	61.6	77.0	71.2	77.0	59.2	80.8	
1973:2	81.1	85.9	71.8	88.5	81.1	85.8	68.5	91.7	
1974:1	87.0	91.4	77.8	94.8	84.1	88.7	71.0	95.3	
1974:2	88.2	92.4	79.1	95.7	84.5	89.1	71.5	95.4	
1975:1	83.3	87.8	74.6	89.7	77.3	82.1	65.6	86.7	100.0
1975:2	83.5	88.0	75.0	89.7	77.5	82.1	66.2	86.8	
1976:1	83.9	88.3	75.7	89.9	78.0	82.4	66.9	86.8	108.3
1976:2	84.7	88.7	77.0	90.2	78.8	82.8	68.3	87.1	
1977:1	85.7	89.3	78.7	90.7	79.9	83.9	69.9	87.4	118.1
1977:2	86.9	90.0	80.5	91.1	80.9	84.5	71.6	87.8	
1978:1	88.1	91.0	82.5	91.8	82.2	85.7	73.6	88.4	112.6

Table D1 continued

	Nationwide				Six Largest Cities				
	All	Comm	Housing	Indus	All	Comm	Housing	Indus	CPI
1978:2	89.8	92.2	85.1	92.9	84.5	87.4	77.2	89.7	
1979:1	92.1	93.9	88.7	94.4	88.3	90.3	82.9	92.0	127.0
1979:2	95.5	96.5	93.7	96.8	94.2	95.3	91.6	96.0	
1980:1	100.0	100.0	100.0	100.0	100.0	100.0	100.0	100.0	137.2
1980:2	104.6	103.7	106.5	103.5	104.6	104.3	106.2	103.4	
1981:1	108.7	106.9	112.2	106.7	108.5	108.1	110.6	106.7	143.7
1981:2	112.8	110.3	117.6	109.9	112.4	112.5	114.8	109.9	
1982:1	116.4	113.4	122.4	112.6	115.7	116.7	117.9	112.6	147.6
1982:2	119.4	116.0	126.4	115.0	118.5	120.6	120.2	114.8	
1983:1	121.9	118.3	129.5	117.0	121.3	124.6	122.5	116.7	150.5
1983:2	124.0	120.2	131.9	118.9	123.9	128.5	124.6	118.6	
1984:1	125.8	122.0	134.1	120.3	127.6	135.7	126.8	120.6	153.8
1984:2	127.6	123.8	136.0	121.8	132.2	144.4	129.6	123.1	
1985:1	129.3	125.7	137.7	123.2	137.1	153.6	133.8	125.0	157.0
1985:2	131.0	127.8	139.2	124.5	143.3	167.1	138.1	127.1	
1986:1	133.0	130.9	140.7	125.8	156.6	197.9	146.7	131.2	158.1
1986:2	135.6	134.9	142.7	127.3	173.8	229.3	165.3	137.0	
1987:1	140.2	141.1	147.0	130.1	197.2	264.7	186.3	153.6	158.3
1987:2	149.9	153.3	156.1	137.0	234.8	336.7	216.1	175.4	
1988:1	154.2	159.9	159.3	140.1	252.2	375.2	229.4	183.2	159.3
1988:2	159.2	166.9	162.7	144.7	279.9	420.0	240.0	213.1	
1989:1	165.9	175.9	168.1	150.1	318.8	467.5	264.5	243.7	163.4
1989:2	174.8	186.8	176.0	157.8	356.6	528.8	300.7	279.4	
1990:1	189.3	203.9	189.6	170.2	408.2	599.2	352.0	315.7	
1990:2	203.1	220.5	202.9	181.4	429.1	625.9	372.4	331.7	

Source: JREI

Indices of agricultural and forest land appear in Figures D1 and D2 and Table D2. The agricultural land indices are the averages of the prices of the medium-grade paddy fields and upland fields as valued by local government agricultural experts in about 1600 cities, towns and villages across Japan. The forest land indices are averages of the prices of medium grade forest lands (excluding the prices of standing timber) for sawlogs and fuelwood, valued by local government forestry experts in about 1600 cities, towns and villages. Agricultural and forest lands that are expected to soon be classified as building sites have relatively high prices and are excluded from the data.

Quarterly golf course membership index data for various locales for the period 1981(4) to 1991(1) appear in Table D3.

Figure D1   Price Indices of Agricultural Land and Forest Land (Semi Log)

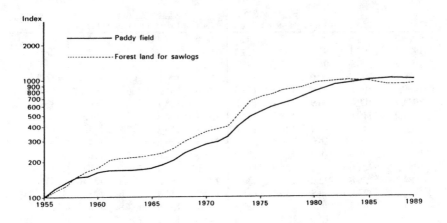

Source: JREI

Figure D2
Annual Rates of Change of Agricultural Land and Forest Land Prices

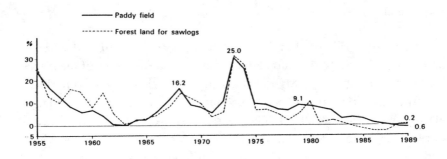

Source: JREI

Table D2
Agricultural Land and Forest Land Prices, Yen per Hectare, end of March
1943 to 1990

	Paddy Field	Upland Field	Forest Land for Sawlogs	Forest Land for Fuelwood
1943	7,150	4,080	1,570	1,350
1944	7,890	4,710	-	-
1945	8,970	5,640	-	-
1946	13,930	9,430	3,820	2,860
1947	41,890	27,310	5,120	4,000
1948	94,200	61,630	9,660	8,380
1949	159,450	103,880	17,690	13,830
1950	208,210	130,320	17,290	14,540
1951	291,100	186,450	22,130	18,950
1952	447,110	285,460	28,670	24,760
1953	633,150	391,450	49,250	40,880
1954	935,460	557,530	70,720	56,580
1955	1,160,180	676,940	89,270	69,670
1956	1,357,240	797,280	101,040	78,740
1957	1,524,800	914,800	110,920	84,520
1958	1,654,950	981,130	128,840	96,910
1959	1,724,180	1,074,810	148,510	110,540
1960	1,866,110	1,120,130	160,050	121,880
1961	1,943,010	1,147,700	183,160	135,940
1962	1,945,440	1,157,850	192,360	144,270
1963	1,938,600	1,175,850	194,750	144,670
1964	1,984,760	1,201,200	199,320	150,080
1965	2,039,020	1,232,020	205,860	152,640
1966	2,162,170	1,295,690	216,870	158,780
1967	2,396,010	1,433,320	234,710	170,100
1968	2,783,490	1,630,770	267,930	189,710
1969	3,030,740	1,711,820	301,070	211,470
1970	3,277,060	1,844,220	327,050	227,530
1971	3,444,160	1,966,240	340,820	234,370
1972	3,797,510	2,203,480	362,790	253,090
1973	4,746,960	2,893,540	476,170	324,740
1974	5,712,500	3,527,710	604,600	413,240
1975	6,266,850	3,872,010	647,970	435,290
1976	6,849,070	4,190,950	694,870	461,760
1977	7,350,460	4,482,320	730,120	483,800
1978	7,835,200	4,787,930	748,120	494,780
1979	8,546,270	5,162,220	782,790	514,580
1980	9,284,740	5,559,060	859,900	559,590
1981	10,000,230	5,956,390	871,900	569,720
1982	10,660,390	6,309,450	887,310	573,820
1983	10,945,760	6,507,940	893,830	573,470
1984	11,301,190	6,653,330	883,460	564,120
1985	11,622,080	6,741,920	868,200	560,610
1986	11,685,090	6,823,730	840,770	545,830
1987	11,710,700	6,824,660	820,370	534,280
1988	11,692,620	6,771,110	820,650	532,440
1989	11,628,180	6,660,290	822,520	535,470
1990	11,729,120	6,725,950	830,380	542,380

Source: JREI

Table D3
Nikkei Golf Course Membership Indices for Various Areas of Japan and
the NSA , 1982-91:1 Quarterly, End of 1981 = 100

Date	All	East	West	Tokyo	Osaka	Kyoto	Nara	Waka-yama	NSA
81:4	100	100	100	100	100	100	100	100	100
82:1	108	109	106	104	108	103	103	101	94
82:2	116	117	113	109	111	105	110	101	94
82:3	122	122	116	113	112	110	114	100	92
82:4	126	127	122	119	116	113	116	100	105
83:1	135	136	130	120	127	119	120	117	105
83:2	138	134	142	117	146	130	133	128	109
83:3	144	135	161	115	166	147	155	133	122
83:4	151	139	173	119	176	160	176	132	130
84:1	158	145	183	123	181	192	189	135	144
84:2	163	149	189	126	181	202	200	138	137
84:3	164	149	192	126	176	200	197	139	139
84:4	166	152	193	129	174	196	190	145	151
85:1	175	163	196	137	178	200	186	154	165
85:2	180	169	201	142	181	206	187	176	169
85:3	187	175	206	148	185	219	190	185	166
85:4	197	188	212	156	191	234	192	191	172
86:1	234	236	221	195	203	270	207	210	208
86:2	261	262	248	214	251	341	250	255	231
86:3	284	284	271	241	265	409	301	290	234
86:4	359	382	286	330	276	429	326	293	245
87:1	479	511	381	470	411	547	469	431	282
87:2	483	506	408	474	414	583	489	493	317
87:3	466	473	428	418	434	559	475	567	341
87:4	441	431	445	376	442	579	477	631	282
88:1	446	433	459	381	459	582	480	717	344
88:2	454	432	484	382	505	634	519	904	364
88:3	472	438	531	405	604	713	595	1182	366
88:4	487	447	560	407	668	754	633	1365	395
89:1	528	472	635	419	840	1008	758	1599	430
89:2	570	504	698	432	977	1169	891	1757	431
89:3	714	616	911	505	1329	1616	1382	2756	467
89:4	846	703	1133	588	1646	2134	1742	3967	510
90:1	901	739	1230	592	1657	2299	1701	4147	398
90:2	844	727	1079	593	1374	1762	1410	3375	418
90:3	767	667	967	565	1120	1477	1163	2540	274
90:4	696	616	854	506	948	1181	1012	2100	311
91:1	663	595	816	487	940	1177	999	2083	374

APPENDIX E BACKGROUND DATA ON SMALL STOCK PORTFOLIO

Table E1
Day by Day Results of the 15 Stock Small Capitalized Portfolio Versus the NSA, December 1988 to July 1989

Date	¥ profit or loss	% gain or loss		NSA	change in NSA	% gain or loss on NSA
88/12/13				29,597.81		
88/12/14				29,754.73	156.92	
88/12/15				29,705.75	-48.98	
88/12/16				29,536.71	-169.04	
88/12/19				29,470.08	-66.63	
88/12/20	-80,000		-0.27%	29,567.94	97.86	0.35%
88/12/21	-121,000		-0.40%	29,698.19	130.25	0.79%
88/12/22	-267,000		-0.89%	29,774.61	76.42	1.05%
88/12/23	-242,000		-0.81%	29,686.26	-88.35	0.75%
88/12/24	-415,000		-1.38%	29,686.36	0.10	0.75%
88/12/25						
88/12/26	-412,000		-1.37%	29,868.01	181.65	1.37%
88/12/27	-353,000	-1.21%	-1.18%	30,050.93	182.92	0.00%	1.09%
88/12/28	-337,000	-1.15%	-1.12%	30,159.00	108.07	0.36%	2.36%
88/12/29						
88/12/30						
88/12/31						
89/01/01						
89/01/02						
89/01/03						
89/01/04	46,000	0.16%	0.15%	30,243.66	84.66	0.64%	2.65%
89/01/05	-140,000	-0.48%	-0.47%	30,183.79	-59.87	0.44%	2.44%
89/01/06	-73,000	-0.25%	-0.24%	30,209.54	25.75	0.53%	2.53%
89/01/07						
89/01/08						
89/01/09	160,000	0.55%	0.53%	30,678.39	468.85	2.09%	4.12%
89/01/10	370,000	1.27%	1.23%	31,006.51	328.12	3.18%	5.23%
89/01/11	792,000	2.71%	2.64%	31,143.45	136.94	3.64%	5.70%
89/01/12	986,000	3.37%	3.29%	31,143.45	0.00	3.64%	5.70%
89/01/13	1,192,000	4.08%	3.97%	31,298.38	154.93	4.15%	6.23%
89/01/14						
89/01/15						
89/01/16						
89/01/17	1,722,000	5.89%	5.74%	31,227.52	-70.86	3.92%	5.98%
89/01/18	1,734,000	5.93%	5.78%	31,354.55	127.03	4.34%	6.42%
89/01/19	1,674,000	5.73%	5.58%	31,311.40	-43.15	4.19%	6.27%
89/01/20	1,860,000	6.36%	6.20%	31,170.38	-141.02	3.73%	5.79%
89/01/21						
89/01/22						
89/01/23	2,257,000	7.72%	7.52%	31,332.88	162.50	4.27%	6.34%
89/01/24	2,722,000	9.31%	9.07%	31,557.68	224.80	5.01%	7.11%
89/01/25	2,750,000	9.41%	9.17%	31,567.79	10.11	5.05%	7.14%
89/01/26	3,016,000	10.32%	10.05%	31,511.81	-55.98	4.86%	6.95%
89/01/27	3,078,000	10.53%	10.26%	31,646.13	134.32	5.31%	7.41%
89/01/28	3,147,000	10.77%	10.49%	31,679.07	32.94	5.42%	7.52%
89/01/29						
89/01/30	3,397,000	11.62%	11.32%	31,567.50	-111.57	5.05%	7.14%
89/01/31	3,833,000	13.12%	12.78%	31,581.30	13.80	5.09%	7.19%
89/02/01	3,986,000	13.64%	13.29%	31,360.68	-220.62	4.36%	6.44%
89/02/02	4,337,000	14.84%	14.46%	31,498.30	137.62	4.82%	6.90%
89/02/03	4,148,000	14.19%	13.83%	31,685.78	187.48	5.44%	7.54%
89/02/04						
89/02/05						
89/02/06	4,164,000	14.25%	13.88%	31,828.75	142.97	5.92%	8.03%
89/02/07	3,713,000	12.71%	12.38%	31,880.65	51.90	6.09%	8.20%
89/02/08	4,029,000	13.79%	13.43%	32,065.12	184.47	6.70%	8.83%
89/02/09	4,063,000	13.90%	13.54%	32,078.43	13.31	6.75%	8.87%
89/02/10	4,092,000	14.00%	13.64%	32,131.99	53.56	6.93%	9.05%
89/02/11						
89/02/12						
89/02/13	3,682,000	12.60%	12.27%	31,985.32	-146.67	6.44%	8.56%
89/02/14	3,551,000	12.15%	11.84%	31,982.89	-2.43	6.43%	8.55%
89/02/15	3,683,000	12.60%	12.28%	32,149.48	166.59	6.98%	9.11%
89/02/16						

Table E1 continued

89/03/01	3,476,000	11.89%	11.50%	31,964.30	-21.30	6.37%	8.40%
89/03/02	3,385,000	11.58%	11.28%	32,073.73	109.43	6.73%	8.86%
89/03/03	3,400,000	11.63%	11.33%	32,000.10	-73.63	6.40%	8.61%
89/03/04							
89/03/05							
89/03/06	3,302,000	11.30%	11.01%	31,876.86	-123.24	6.08%	8.19%
89/03/07	3,562,900	12.19%	11.88%	31,937.94	61.08	6.28%	8.40%
89/03/08	3,164,000	10.83%	10.55%	31,837.66	-100.28	5.95%	8.06%
89/03/09	3,279,000	11.22%	10.93%	31,656.45	-181.21	5.34%	7.44%
89/03/10	3,625,000	12.40%	12.08%	31,701.78	45.33	5.49%	7.59%
89/03/11							
89/03/12							
89/03/13	3,514,000	12.02%	11.71%	31,552.96	-148.82	5.00%	7.09%
89/03/14	3,405,000	11.65%	11.35%	31,724.35	171.39	5.57%	7.67%
89/03/15	3,293,000	11.27%	10.98%	32,100.48	376.13	6.82%	8.95%
89/03/16	3,336,000	11.42%	11.12%	32,098.24	-2.24	6.81%	8.94%
89/03/17	3,080,000	10.54%	10.27%	32,021.01	-77.23	6.56%	8.68%
89/03/18							
89/03/19							
89/03/20	2,986,000	10.22%	9.95%	31,654.80	-366.21	5.34%	7.43%
89/03/21	2,728,000	9.33%	9.09%	31,443.24	-211.56	4.63%	6.72%
89/03/22	2,811,000	9.62%	9.37%	31,588.66	145.42	5.12%	7.21%
89/03/23	2,591,000	8.87%	8.64%	31,568.52	-20.14	5.05%	7.14%
89/03/24							
89/03/25							
89/03/26							
89/03/27	1,841,000	6.30%	6.14%	31,512.40	-56.12	4.86%	6.95%
89/03/28	1,980,000	6.78%	6.60%	32,306.36	793.96	7.51%	9.65%
89/03/29	2,844,000	9.73%	9.48%	32,737.28	430.92	8.94%	11.11%
89/03/30	3,017,000	10.32%	10.06%	32,826.13	88.85	9.23%	11.41%
89/03/31	2,958,000	10.12%	9.86%	32,838.68	12.55	9.28%	11.45%
89/04/01							
89/04/02							
89/04/03	3,229,000	11.05%	10.76%	33,042.07	203.39	11.75%	12.14%
89/04/04	3,593,000	12.29%	11.98%	33,312.25	270.18	12.66%	13.06%
89/04/05	3,374,000	11.55%	11.25%	33,360.79	48.54	12.83%	13.22%
89/04/06	3,434,000	11.75%	11.45%	32,995.78	-365.01	11.59%	11.99%
89/04/07	3,588,000	12.28%	11.96%	33,185.05	189.27	12.23%	12.63%
89/04/08							
89/04/09							
89/04/10	4,244,000	14.52%	14.15%	32,999.02	-186.03	11.60%	12.00%
89/04/11	4,028,000	13.78%	13.43%	33,249.58	250.56	12.45%	12.85%
89/04/12	4,102,000	14.04%	13.67%	33,256.45	6.87	12.47%	12.87%
89/04/13	3,866,000	13.23%	12.89%	33,063.94	-192.51	11.82%	12.22%
89/04/14	3,857,000	13.20%	12.86%	33,150.44	86.50	12.12%	12.51%
89/04/15							
89/04/16							
89/04/17	3,898,000	13.34%	12.99%	33,308.33	157.89	12.65%	13.05%
89/04/18	4,120,000	14.10%	13.73%	33,321.66	13.33	12.70%	13.09%
89/04/19	4,242,000	11.52%	14.14%	33,363.83	42.17	12.84%	13.24%
89/04/20	4,162,000	14.24%	13.87%	33,185.15	-178.68	12.23%	12.63%
89/04/21	4,414,000	15.10%	14.71%	33,029.81	-155.34	11.71%	12.10%
89/04/22							
89/04/23							
89/04/24	4,547,000	15.56%	15.16%	32,805.92	-223.89	10.95%	11.34%
89/04/25	4,645,000	15.89%	15.48%	33,244.78	438.86	12.44%	12.83%
89/04/26	4,696,000	16.07%	15.65%	33,434.93	190.15	13.08%	13.48%
89/04/27	5,029,000	17.21%	16.76%	33,500.83	65.90	13.30%	13.70%
89/04/28	5,654,000	19.35%	18.85%	33,713.35	212.52	14.02%	14.42%
89/04/29							
89/04/30							
89/05/01	5,995,000	20.52%	19.99%	33,793.17	79.82	14.29%	14.69%
89/05/02	6,163,000	21.09%	20.54%	33,954.99	161.82	14.84%	15.24%
89/05/03							
89/05/04							
89/05/05							
89/05/06							
89/05/07							
89/05/08	6,450,000	22.07%	21.50%	33,954.99	0.00	14.84%	15.24%
89/05/09	5,938,000	20.32%	19.79%	34,135.24	180.25	15.45%	15.85%
89/05/10	5,615,000	19.21%	18.72%	34,031.87	-103.37	15.10%	15.50%
89/05/11	5,785,000	19.80%	19.28%	34,081.49	49.62	15.27%	15.67%
89/05/12	5,929,000	20.29%	19.76%	33,866.33	-215.16	14.54%	14.94%
89/05/13							
89/05/14							
89/05/15	5,789,000	19.81%	19.30%	33,716.29	-150.04	14.03%	14.43%
89/05/16	5,521,000	18.89%	18.40%	33,926.45	210.16	14.74%	15.14%
89/05/17	5,686,000	19.46%	18.95%	33,992.45	66.00	14.96%	15.37%
89/05/18	5,602,000	19.17%	18.67%	33,856.33	-136.12	14.50%	14.91%
89/05/19	5,258,000	17.99%	17.53%	34,001.96	145.63	15.00%	15.40%

Table E1 concluded

89/05/20							
89/05/21							
89/05/22	5,096,000	17.44%	16.99%	34,067.86	65.90	15.22%	15.62%
89/05/23	4,670,000	15.98%	15.57%	33,816.61	-251.25	14.37%	14.77%
89/05/24	4,899,000	16.76%	16.33%	33,851.82	35.21	14.49%	14.89%
89/05/25	5,175,000	17.71%	17.25%	34,005.39	153.57	15.01%	15.41%
89/05/26	5,261,000	18.00%	17.54%	34,191.62	186.23	15.64%	16.04%
89/05/27							
89/05/28							
89/05/29	5,148,000	17.62%	17.16%	34,160.83	-30.79	15.53%	15.94%
89/05/30	5,149,000	17.62%	17.16%	34,076.89	-83.94	15.25%	15.66%
89/05/31	5,739,000	19.64%	19.13%	34,266.75	189.86	15.89%	16.30%
89/06/01	5,457,000	18.78%	18.29%	33,951.35	285.40	14.93%	15.33%
89/06/02	5,311,000	18.28%	17.80%	33,667.42	-313.93	13.86%	14.27%
89/06/03							
89/06/04							
89/06/05	4,832,000	16.53%	16.11%	33,457.08	-210.34	13.15%	13.55%
89/06/06	4,722,000	16.16%	15.74%	33,452.01	-5.07	13.11%	13.53%
89/06/07	4,827,000	16.52%	16.09%	33,626.89	174.88	13.73%	14.13%
89/06/08	5,061,000	17.33%	16.88%	33,718.29	91.40	14.04%	14.44%
89/06/09	5,681,000	19.44%	18.94%	33,639.98	-78.31	13.77%	14.17%
89/06/10							
89/06/11							
89/06/12	5,361,000	18.34%	17.87%	33,398.01	-241.97	12.95%	13.35%
89/06/13	5,543,000	18.97%	18.48%	33,213.55	-184.46	12.33%	12.73%
89/06/14	5,202,000	17.80%	17.34%	33,402.99	189.44	12.97%	13.37%
89/06/15	5,543,000	18.98%	18.49%	32,913.09	-489.90	11.31%	11.71%
89/06/16	5,240,000	17.96%	17.50%	33,055.17	142.08	11.79%	12.19x
89/06/17							
89/06/18							
89/06/19	5,145,000	17.61%	17.15%	33,013.18	-41.99	11.65%	12.05%
89/06/20	5,285,000	18.08%	17.62%	33,233.47	220.29	12.40%	12.79%
89/06/21	5,790,000	19.81%	19.30%	33,345.28	111.81	12.78%	13.17%
89/06/22	5,840,000	19.98%	19.47%	33,324.97	-20.31	12.71%	13.10%
89/06/23	5,740,000	19.64%	19.13%	33,530.71	205.74	13.40%	13.80%
89/06/24							
89/06/25							
89/06/26	5,669,000	19.40%	18.00%	33,625.82	95.11	13.72%	14.12%
89/06/27	5,523,000	18.90%	18.41%	33,469.21	-156.61	13.19%	13.59%
89/06/28	5,325,000	18.22%	17.75%	33,245.60	-223.61	12.44%	12.83%
89/06/29	5,225,000	17.88%	17.42%	32,956.31	-289.28	11.46%	11.85%
89/06/30	5,042,000	17.25%	16.81%	32,948.69	-7.62	11.43%	11.83%
89/07/01							
89/07/02							
89/07/03	5,162,000	17.66%	17.21%	33,236.42	287.73	12.41%	12.80%
89/07/04	5,417,000	18.54%	18.06%	33,190.38	-46.04	12.25%	12.65%
89/07/05	5,568,000	19.05%	18.56%	33,309.71	110.33	12.66%	13.05%
89/07/06	5,596,000	19.15%	18.65%	33,423.48	113.77	13.04%	13.44%
89/07/07	5,803,000	19.86%	19.34%	33,703.97	280.49	13.90%	14.39%
89/07/08							
89/07/09							
89/07/10	6,111,000	20.91%	20.37%	33,676.02	-27.95	13.89%	14.29%
89/07/11	5,954,000	20.37%	19.85%	33,746.77	70.75	14.13%	14.53%
89/07/12	5,982,000	20.47%	19.94%	33,701.52	-45.25	13.98%	14.38%
89/07/13	5,921,000	20.26%	19.74%	33,631.16	-70.36	13.74%	14.14%
89/07/14	5,860,000	20.05%	19.53%	33,574.77	-56.39	13.55%	13.95%
89/07/15							
89/07/16							
89/07/17	5,849,000	20.01%	19.50%	33,456.22	-118.55	13.15%	13.55%
89/07/18	5,437,000	18.60%	18.12%	33,343.73	-112.49	12.77%	13.17%
89/07/19	5,481,000	18.76%	18.27%	33,557.17	213.44	13.49%	13.89%
89/07/20	5,707,000	19.53%	19.02%	33,664.87	107.70	13.80%	14.20%
89/07/21	5,752,000	19.68%	19.17%	33,899.43	234.56	14.65%	15.05%
89/07/22							
89/07/23							
89/07/24	5,304,000	18.15%	17.68%	34,093.33	193.90	15.31%	15.71%
89/07/25	5,409,000	18.51%	18.03%	34,538.90	445.57	16.41%	17.22%
89/07/26	6,052,000	20.71%	20.17%	34,515.83	-23.07	16.73%	17.16%
89/07/27	5,976,000	20.46%	19.93%	34,785.28	269.45	17.66%	18.09%
89/07/28	6,437,000	22.03%	21.46%	34,705.63	-79.65	17.38%	17.79%

APPENDIX F NSA AND TOPIX DATA

Table F1   The NSA Day by Day, December 1, 1989 - February 28, 1991

Date	Close	Change	if ≤500 % decline	if ≥500 % increase	Date	Close	Change	if ≤500 % decline	if ≥500 % increase
1989					Feb 13	37107	-181		
Dec 1,	37133								
Dec 4	37304	171			Feb 14	37155	48		
Dec 5	37494	190			Feb 15	37471	316		
Dec 6	37654	160			Feb 16	37222	-249		
Dec 7	37858	204			Feb 20	36895	-327		
Dec 8	37724	-134			Feb 21	35734	-1161	-3.1%	
Dec 11	37753	29			Feb 22	35826	92		
Dec 12	37804	51			Feb 23	34890	-936	-2.6%	
Dec 13	38063	259			Feb 26	33321	-1569	-4.5%	
Dec 14	38181	118			Feb 27	33897	576		1.7%
Dec 15	38271	90			Feb 28	34591	694		2.0%
Dec 18	38586	315			Mar 1	33829	-762	-2.2%	
Dec 19	38439	-147			Mar 2	34057	228		
Dec 20	38512	73			Mar 5	33845	-212		
Dec 21	38215	-297			Mar 6	33791	-54		
Dec 22	38423	208			Mar 7	33362	-429		
Dec 26	38681	258			Mar 8	33691	329		
Dec 27	38801	120			Mar 9	33993	302		
Dec 28	38876	75			Mar 12	33368	-625	-1.8%	
Dec 29	38915	39			Mar 13	32620	-748	-2.2%	
1990					Mar 14	32352	-268		
Jan 4,	38712	-204							
Jan 5	38274	-438			Mar 15	32671	319		
Jan 8	38394	120			Mar 16	32616	-55		
Jan 9	37951	-443			Mar 19	31263	-1353	-4.1%	
Jan 10	37697	-254			Mar 20	30807	-456		
Jan 11	38170	473			Mar 22	29843	-964	-3.1%	
Jan 12	37516	-654	-1.7%		Mar 23	30382	539		1.8%
Jan 16	36850	-666	-1.8%		Mar 26	31840	1458		4.8%
Jan 17	36821	-29			Mar 27	31825	-15		
Jan 18	36729	-92			Mar 28	31263	-562	-1.8%	
Jan 19	36836	107			Mar 29	31026	-237		
Jan 22	37257	421			Mar 30	29980	-1046	-3.4%	
Jan 23	37378	121			Apr 2	28002	-1978	-6.6%	
Jan 24	36778	-600	-1.6%		Apr 3	28759	757		2.7%
Jan 25	36969	191			Apr 4	28442	-317		
Jan 26	36874	-95			Apr 5	28249	-193		
Jan 29	37173	299			Apr 6	29278	1029		3.6%
Jan 30	37215	42			Apr 9	30397	1119		3.8%
Jan 31	37188	-27			Apr 10	29625	-772	-2.5%	
Feb 1	37206	18			Apr 11	29440	-185		
Feb 2	37650	444			Apr 12	29623	183		
Feb 5	37631	-19			Apr 13	29214	-409		
Feb 6	37666	35			Apr 16	28463	-751	-2.6%	
Feb 7	37301	-365			Apr 17	28462	-1		
Feb 8	37516	215			Apr 18	29249	787		2.8%
Feb 9	37288	-228			Apr 19	29945	696		2.4%

Table F1 continued

Date	Close	Change	if ≤500 % decline	if ≥500 % increase	Date	Close	Change	if ≤500 % decline	if ≥500 % increase
Apr 20	29835	-110			Jun 29	31940	-166		
Apr 23	29679	-256			Jul 2	31855	-85		
Apr 24	29501	-178			Jul 3	32445	590		1.9%
Apr 25	29264	-237			Jul 5	32250	-195		
Apr 26	29425	161			Jul 6	32445	195		
Apr 27	29584	159			Jul 9	32004	-441		
May 1	29689	-264			Jul 10	31221	-783	-2.4%	
May 2	30173	484			Jul 11	31509	288		
May 7	30956	783		2.6%	Jul 12	32080	571		1.8%
May 8	30970	14			Jul 13	32220	140		
May 9	30945	-25			Jul 16	32985	765		2.4%
May 10	30980	35			Jul 17	33293	308		
May 11	31512	532		1.7%	Jul 18	33040	-253		
May 14	32042	530		1.7%	Jul 19	33056	16		
May 15	31999	-43			Jul 20	32422	-634	-1.9%	
May 16	31968	-31			Jul 23	31895	-527	-1.6%	
May 17	32062	94			Jul 24	31702	-193		
May 18	32014	-48			Jul 25	31701	-1		
May 21	31940	-74			Jul 26	31370	-331		
May 22	31765	-175			Jul 27	30863	-507	-1.6%	
May 23	31938	173			Jul 30	30443	-420		
May 24	32312	374			Jul 31	31036	593		1.9%
May 25	32794	482			Aug 1	30838	-198		
May 28	33192	398			Aug 2	30245	-593	-1.9%	
May 29	32817	-375			Aug 3	29516	-729	-2.4%	
May 30	32926	109			Aug 6	28600	-916	-3.1%	
May 31	33130	204			Aug 7	27653	-947	-3.3%	
Jun 1	32891	-239			Aug 8	28509	856		3.1%
Jun 4	32935	44			Aug 9	27615	-894	-3.1%	
Jun 5	32921	-14			Aug 10	27329	-286		
Jun 6	32953	32			Aug 13	26176	-1153	-4.2%	
Jun 7	33192	239			Aug 14	26673	497		
Jun 8	32993	-199			Aug 15	28112	1439		5.4%
Jun 11	32540	-453			Aug 16	27549	-563	-2.0%	
Jun 12	32322	-218			Aug 20	26490	-1059	-3.8%	
Jun 13	32371	49			Aug 21	26298	-192		
Jun 14	32668	297			Aug 22	25211	-1087	-4.1%	
Jun 15	32538	-130			Aug 23	23738	-1473	-5.8%	
Jun 18	32376	-162			Aug 24	24166	428		
Jun 19	32040	-336			Aug 27	25142	976		4.0%
Jun 21	32087	47			Aug 28	25711	569		2.3%
Jun 22	31694	-393			Aug 29	24895	-816	-3.2%	
Jun 25	31119	-575	-1.8%		Aug 30	25670	775		3.1%
Jun 26	31571	452			Aug 31	25420	-250		
Jun 27	32312	741		2.3%	Sep 4	24908	-512	-2.0%	
Jun 28	32106	-206			Sep 5	24078	-830	-3.3%	

Table F1 continued

Date	Close	Change	if ≤500 % decline	if ≥500 % increase	Date	Close	Change	if ≤500 % decline	if ≥500 % increase
Sep 6	23811	-267			Nov 1	24295	-899	-3.6%	
Sep 7	23962	151			Nov 2	24195	-100		
Sep 10	25081	1119		4.7%	Nov 5	24385	190		
Sep 11	24605	-476			Nov 6	23966	-420		
Sep 12	25216	611		2.5%	Nov 7	23500	-466		
Sep 13	25075	-141			Nov 8	22970	-530	-2.3%	
Sep 14	24897	-178			Nov 9	22932	-38		
Sep 17	24366	-531	-2.1%		Nov 13	23974	1042		
Sep 18	23885	-481			Nov 14	23937	-36		
Sep 19	23726	-159			Nov 15	23556	-381		
Sep 20	23603	-123			Nov 16	23172	-384		
Sep 21	23778	175			Nov 19	23518	346		
Sep 25	23359	-419			Nov 20	23205	-313		
Sep 26	22251	-1108	-4.7%		Nov 21	23400	195		
Sep 27	21772	-479			Nov 26	23763	363		
Sep 28	20983	-789	-3.6%		Nov 27	23624	-139		
Oct 1	20222	-761	-3.6%		Nov 28	23054	-570		
Oct 2	22896	2675			Nov 29	22713	-341		
Oct 3	22849	-47			Nov 30	22455	-258		
Oct 4	22278	-571	-2.5%		Dec 3	22726	271		
Oct 5	22828	550			Dec 4	21863	-863	-3.8%	
Oct 8	23630	802			Dec 5	22194	331		
Oct 9	23495	-135			Dec 6	22553	359		
Oct 11	22586	-909	-3.9%		Dec 7	23522	969		
Oct 12	22390	-196			Dec 10	23785	263		
Oct 15	23109	719			Dec 11	23957	172		
Oct 16	23606	497			Dec 12	23999	42		
Oct 17	23859	253			Dec 13	24643	644		
Oct 18	24367	508			Dec 14	24349	-294		
Oct 19	24481	114			Dec 17	24088	-261		
Oct 22	25071	590			Dec 18	24424	336		
Oct 23	25298	227			Dec 19	24877	453		
Oct 24	24877	-421			Dec 20	24526	-351		
Oct 25	25353	476			Dec 21	24120	-406		
Oct 26	25006	-347			Dec 25	23767	-353		
Oct 29	25329	323			Dec 26	23887	120		
Oct 30	25242	-87			Dec 27	23940	53		
Oct 31	25194	-48			Dec 28	23848	-92		

High close	38915	Dec 29	
Low close	20222	Oct 1	-48.04%
Final close	23849	Dec 26	-38.72%

Table F1 continued

Date 1991	Close	Change	if ≤500 % decline	if ≥500 % increase	Date	Close	Change	if ≤500 % decline	if ≥500 % increase
Jan 2	23941	53			Feb 1	23410	-50		
Jan 5	23849	-92			Feb 2	23293	-117		
Jan 6	24069	220			Feb 3	23157	-136		
Jan 7	23737	-332			Feb 4	23287	130		
Jan 8	22898	-839	-3.5%		Feb 5	23822	535		2.3%
Jan 9	22969	71			Feb 6	23952	130		
Jan 12	23047	78			Feb 10	24104	152		
Jan 14	23241	194			Feb 11	24296	192		
Jan 15	23213	-28			Feb 12	24935	639		2.6%
Jan 16	22443	-770	-3.3%		Feb 13	25139	204		
Jan 19	23447	1004		4.5%	Feb 16	25356	217		
Jan 20	23808	361			Feb 17	25344	-12		
Jan 21	23352	-456			Feb 18	26230	886		3.5%
Jan 22	23254	-98			Feb 19	26170	-60		
Jan 23	23050	-204			Feb 20	26199	29		
Jan 26	23269	219			Feb 21	26024	-175		
Jan 27	23573	304			Feb 22	25902	-122		
Jan 28	23569	-4			Feb 25	26463	561		2.2%
Jan 29	23460	-109			Feb 26	26283	-180		
					Feb 27	26094	-189		
					Feb 28	26409	315		

Invest Japan

Table F2   TOPIX Values Day by Day in 1988 and 1989

Source: TSE

1988

January 4, 1968 = 100

	Jan	Feb	Mar	Apr	May	June	July	Aug	Sept	Oct	Nov	Dec
1	—	1,925.83	2,089.11	○2,130.20	—	○2,151.17	2,163.66	2,249.10	○2,093.20	2,135.62	2,155.62	2,282.50
2	—	1,915.84	2,112.39	2,141.26	●2,213.08	2,163.55	2,148.97	●2,253.10	2,096.22	—	2,150.29	2,283.22
3	—	○1,910.81	2,106.20	—	—	2,166.28	—	2,245.47	2,123.73	2,125.78	—	2,295.16
4	○1,690.44	1,923.65	2,109.48	2,142.93	—	2,177.51	2,148.25	2,232.95	—	2,129.78	2,144.08	—
5	1,707.89	1,919.56	2,109.17	2,136.02	—	—	2,164.11	2,229.06	2,112.82	2,116.76	2,145.05	2,289.57
6	1,820.03	1,927.73	—	2,150.17	2,201.93	2,183.79	2,176.55	2,230.79	2,110.40	○2,096.31	—	2,295.24
7	1,820.17	—	2,107.98	2,168.35	2,197.20	2,185.18	2,180.86	—	2,125.14	2,101.95	○2,129.44	2,314.20
8	1,818.43	1,926.94	2,094.00	2,173.46	—	2,182.53	2,197.91	2,222.96	2,134.81	—	2,145.73	2,302.60
9	—	1,924.87	2,104.33	—	2,180.47	2,208.13	—	2,220.29	2,129.64	—	2,170.51	2,305.48
10	—	1,933.88	2,102.55	—	2,185.77	2,199.92	—	2,172.80	—	—	2,176.57	—
11	1,795.15	—	2,091.42	2,183.58	2,170.33	—	2,220.56	2,189.43	—	2,113.97	2,212.97	—
12	1,799.42	1,949.31	—	2,182.02	2,164.43	—	2,207.97	2,187.04	2,139.20	2,116.40	—	2,296.15
13	1,775.80	—	—	2,187.78	2,182.22	2,209.03	2,197.97	—	2,147.38	2,109.30	—	2,292.24
14	1,800.36	—	2,074.52	2,193.95	—	2,213.63	2,198.88	—	2,146.73	2,124.74	2,219.69	2,301.34
15	—	1,962.60	2,084.80	2,173.80	—	●2,219.98	2,186.42	2,189.85	—	—	2,234.15	2,297.36
16	—	1,981.70	2,106.18	—	2,197.49	2,217.18	—	2,187.49	2,150.82	—	2,234.98	2,279.36
17	—	1,996.24	2,121.20	—	2,202.83	2,219.33	—	2,206.55	—	2,128.05	2,240.10	—
18	1,828.09	2,014.82	2,134.89	2,155.29	2,200.06	—	2,166.56	2,203.87	—	2,108.66	2,252.11	—
19	1,820.46	2,031.90	—	2,150.89	2,170.31	—	○2,130.57	2,205.80	●2,151.86	2,118.17	—	○2,276.02
20	1,815.23	—	—	2,162.46	2,165.87	2,204.19	2,163.14	—	2,123.64	2,123.90	—	2,280.89
21	1,807.13	—	—	2,152.93	—	2,189.87	2,176.08	—	2,122.03	2,126.56	2,266.10	2,289.56
22	1,821.51	2,038.56	2,127.40	2,152.50	—	2,185.54	2,147.46	2,197.37	2,108.55	2,118.91	2,278.83	2,303.43
23	1,855.56	2,045.92	2,133.05	2,166.99	2,153.12	2,178.64	2,152.63	2,183.54	—	—	—	2,308.55
24	—	2,050.29	2,121.64	—	2,152.39	2,172.88	—	2,171.31	2,099.24	2,111.24	2,273.51	2,315.17
25	1,881.71	2,071.93	2,102.38	2,175.77	2,158.22	2,162.67	2,147.16	2,175.49	—	2,120.78	2,275.41	—
26	1,896.95	2,072.08	2,070.81	2,176.38	2,151.38	—	2,155.08	2,155.09	2,095.84	2,130.80	2,273.70	2,340.28
27	1,882.75	2,077.84	—	2,170.51	2,132.23	2,155.70	2,188.56	2,159.58	2,116.81	2,140.96	—	2,350.44
28	1,912.28	—	2,097.29	2,189.42	2,104.41	2,158.48	2,195.84	—	2,133.46	2,134.32	2,245.50	●2,357.03
29	1,916.75	●2,078.07	2,121.41	—	—	2,166.90	2,224.58	2,137.08	2,131.96	2,146.56	2,269.15	—
30	●1,929.50	—	●2,153.66	●2,195.39	2,111.31	2,183.10	●2,247.03	2,141.49	2,151.36	—	●2,285.75	—
31	—	—	2,147.90	—	2,128.58	—	—	○2,128.02	—	●2,156.44	—	—
High	1,929.50	2,078.07	2,153.66	2,195.39	2,213.08	2,219.98	2,247.03	2,253.10	2,151.86	2,156.44	2,285.75	2,357.03
Low	○1,690.44	1,910.81	2,070.81	2,130.20	2,104.41	2,151.17	2,130.57	2,128.02	2,093.20	2,096.31	2,129.44	2,276.02
Ave	1,828.36	1,985.47	2,109.32	2,165.74	2,167.79	2,185.63	2,177.78	2,195.02	2,124.77	2,123.30	2,217.24	2,302.54

Note: ● Highest in month (year) ○ Lowest in month (year)

Table F2   continued
1989

	Jan	Feb	Mar	Apr	May	June	July	Aug	Sept	Oct	Nov	Dec
1	—	2,445.05	2,443.76	—	2,503.26	2,518.21	—	2,627.62	2,602.51	—	2,691.19	2,819.63
2	—	2,456.35	2,442.68	—	2,517.49	2,501.56	—	2,633.24	—	2,703.58	2,685.03	—
3	—	2,465.62	2,439.90	2,467.52	—	—	2,467.15	2,616.69	—	2,688.80	—	—
4	2,375.30	—	—	2,483.01	—	—	2,469.55	2,613.27	2,614.59	2,679.40	—	2,837.73
5	2,368.09	—	—	2,494.74	—	2,486.57	2,478.02	—	2,613.34	2,676.99	—	2,850.82
6	2,366.91	2,473.59	2,426.34	2,469.78	—	2,482.58	2,489.31	—	2,602.70	2,659.38	2,681.48	2,867.32
7	—	2,472.30	2,427.10	2,474.35	—	2,487.29	2,507.29	2,615.48	2,593.39	—	2,663.39	2,879.02
8	—	2,490.07	2,421.78	—	2,544.60	2,504.73	—	2,624.70	2,583.12	—	2,674.31	2,871.93
9	2,401.81	2,489.07	2,403.61	—	2,538.23	2,503.41	—	2,643.91	—	2,673.56	2,684.12	—
10	2,427.75	2,485.71	2,408.24	2,458.80	2,535.08	—	2,504.15	2,640.13	—	—	2,692.77	—
11	2,442.10	—	—	2,470.23	2,537.99	—	2,518.33	2,638.20	2,578.76	2,660.49	—	2,873.66
12	2,445.82	—	—	2,466.39	2,518.64	2,483.76	2,516.10	—	2,595.85	2,623.60	—	2,868.02
13	2,457.58	2,478.82	2,392.89	2,455.21	—	2,464.14	2,513.97	—	2,599.16	2,646.54	2,700.95	2,878.46
14	—	2,473.46	2,407.52	2,457.42	—	2,472.82	2,509.38	2,632.97	2,618.43	—	2,709.98	2,871.90
15	—	2,475.71	2,432.77	—	2,505.69	2,440.16	—	2,633.33	—	—	2,717.87	2,874.56
16	—	2,468.19	2,432.69	—	2,520.13	2,440.17	—	2,650.61	—	2,600.88	2,721.03	—
17	2,448.93	2,473.33	2,419.59	2,468.99	2,523.45	—	2,499.74	2,652.96	—	2,642.64	2,717.90	—
18	2,451.90	—	—	2,464.62	2,509.72	—	2,487.93	2,652.50	2,622.23	2,642.88	—	2,884.80
19	2,435.55	—	—	2,460.53	2,518.15	2,443.71	2,499.71	—	2,619.07	2,665.66	—	2,852.59
20	2,425.72	2,470.37	2,393.04	2,447.42	—	2,456.63	2,509.41	—	2,615.58	2,679.72	2,717.63	2,849.17
21	—	2,452.91	—	2,438.19	—	2,469.40	2,533.06	2,659.08	2,633.52	—	2,717.65	2,826.76
22	—	2,472.04	2,370.06	—	2,519.46	2,473.54	—	2,653.45	2,629.40	—	2,737.20	2,810.74
23	2,440.35	2,487.24	2,380.17	—	2,507.85	2,486.23	—	2,644.02	—	2,687.53	—	—
24	2,460.92	—	2,373.00	2,422.98	2,509.73	—	2,546.61	2,630.97	—	2,681.22	2,759.60	—
25	2,462.99	—	—	2,448.73	2,519.50	—	2,584.07	2,622.70	2,643.20	2,672.57	—	2,847.30
26	2,458.09	—	—	2,461.02	2,531.16	2,489.80	2,586.13	—	2,675.22	2,697.58	—	2,866.95
27	2,469.45	2,468.97	2,364.33	2,471.50	—	2,481.74	2,605.48	—	2,681.66	2,681.76	2,795.38	2,867.97
28	2,478.12	2,447.23	2,422.46	2,488.52	—	2,466.23	2,606.61	2,610.29	2,696.18	—	2,799.94	2,870.32
29	—	—	2,447.59	—	2,531.27	2,453.99	—	2,615.63	2,702.22	—	2,815.98	2,881.37
30	2,467.60	—	2,456.23	—	2,522.59	2,449.38	—	2,607.07	—	2,676.60	2,829.54	—
31	2,464.83	—	2,469.15	—	2,537.14	—	2,628.90	2,603.38	—	2,692.65	—	—
High	2,478.12	2,490.07	2,469.15	2,494.74	2,544.60	2,518.21	2,628.90	2,659.08	2,702.22	2,703.58	2,829.54	2,884.80
Low	2,366.91	2,445.05	2,364.33	2,422.98	2,503.26	2,440.16	2,467.15	2,603.38	2,578.76	2,600.88	2,663.39	2,810.74
Ave.	2,437.49	2,470.84	2,417.04	2,463.50	2,522.56	2,475.28	2,526.71	2,631.40	2,626.01	2,668.29	2,725.65	2,859.57

Note: ●Highest in month (year) ○Lowest in month (year)

Table F3   Monthly Closes of the NSA, May 1949 to February 1991

Month	1949	1950	1951	1952	1953	1954	1955	1956	1957	1958	1959	1960	1961	1962	1963	1964	1965	1966	1967	1968	1969
Jan		92.54	115.43	188.96	456.43	352.66	369.45	423.46	567.78	522.70	692.12	957.13	1,493.58	1,511.14	1,458.47	1,326.96	1,240.86	1,470.38	1,463.11	1,312.20	1,830.26
Feb		113.40	121.84	181.40	392.10	352.51	366.99	439.39	571.64	528.16	721.06	1,015.16	1,524.53	1,502.88	1,500.51	1,257.26	1,212.88	1,507.41	1,494.82	1,349.77	1,758.54
Mar		97.61	124.53	175.51	307.05	322.99	351.50	458.58	587.00	529.98	764.85	1,059.49	1,587.10	1,449.78	1,614.13	1,222.17	1,132.77	1,584.28	1,455.58	1,377.58	1,841.02
Apr		99.31	120.82	202.72	339.37	345.63	351.39	473.34	589.69	556.57	745.68	1,091.21	1,645.55	1,378.42	1,592.57	1,232.24	1,176.64	1,557.97	1,437.24	1,456.07	1,904.94
May	176.52	94.22	127.23	225.38	331.13	325.82	349.93	488.43	520.44	563.46	803.08	988.47	1,679.33	1,367.08	1,554.75	1,318.81	1,096.60	1,514.15	1,505.94	1,462.34	2,002.46
Jun	146.92	86.17	130.49	246.15	346.27	348.09	352.47	499.17	524.70	584.42	810.07	1,089.63	1,737.05	1,450.25	1,570.58	1,359.31	1,060.11	1,494.93	1,494.18	1,544.70	1,984.58
Jul	144.86	97.59	135.89	253.21	386.13	331.93	366.90	500.34	586.16	571.60	854.91	1,097.09	1,745.26	1,410.40	1,386.98	1,309.21	1,105.54	1,502.13	1,476.33	1,602.97	1,865.59
Aug	175.18	114.55	145.30	254.72	409.47	345.02	387.12	493.69	530.37	592.57	881.53	1,175.75	1,602.37	1,416.97	1,349.22	1,276.11	1,255.58	1,463.04	1,342.68	1,703.91	1,915.68
Sep	163.29	104.98	154.27	268.90	450.87	351.33	388.42	491.71	529.35	586.20	902.48	1,226.47	1,526.03	1,289.61	1,301.68	1,217.23	1,223.74	1,465.43	1,318.77	1,839.81	2,016.15
Oct	141.54	106.16	165.09	313.23	434.79	328.19	409.17	568.16	510.81	607.72	955.64	1,250.06	1,329.51	1,259.52	1,358.60	1,212.56	1,257.31	1,441.02	1,376.05	1,745.29	2,130.30
Nov	122.84	109.75	157.35	351.10	423.06	326.85	393.28	556.58	492.00	629.04	976.93	1,287.17	1,325.78	1,441.82	1,278.23	1,209.31	1,373.16	1,390.21	1,277.27	1,726.09	2,211.90
Dec	109.91	101.91	166.06	362.64	377.85	356.09	425.69	549.14	474.55	666.54	874.88	1,356.71	1,432.60	1,420.43	1,225.10	1,216.55	1,417.83	1,452.10	1,283.47	1,714.89	2,359.96

Month	1970	1971	1972	1973	1974	1975	1976	1977	1978	1979	1980	1981	1982	1983	1984	1985	1986	1987	1988
Jan	2,316.98	2,099.37	2,856.50	5,165.24	4,449.90	3,957.53	4,684.25	4,962.47	5,111.67	6,212.78	6,768.16	7,284.15	7,938.83	8,103.47	10,196.10	11,992.31	13,024.30	20,023.55	23,719.13
Feb	2,374.45	2,246.36	3,021.98	5,121.32	4,486.58	4,273.39	4,624.63	5,079.11	5,222.66	6,072.88	6,764.89	7,149.57	7,440.46	8,085.57	10,030.70	12,321.92	13,640.83	20,766.66	25,242.81
Mar	2,523.75	2,403.30	3,187.62	5,226.02	4,473.58	4,484.97	4,596.48	5,011.75	5,447.76	6,141.31	6,556.19	7,334.31	7,260.48	8,478.70	10,986.41	12,590.20	15,859.75	21,566.66	26,260.26
Apr	2,114.32	2,468.18	3,339.08	4,598.47	4,622.35	4,484.84	4,656.96	5,102.39	5,534.18	6,216.76	6,865.19	7,674.19	7,390.71	8,682.36	10,016.28	12,426.29	15,825.50	23,274.83	27,509.54
May	2,072.46	2,456.33	3,636.79	4,557.36	4,772.66	4,402.52	4,622.28	5,026.14	5,469.77	6,252.59	6,865.56	7,558.65	7,325.65	8,617.57	10,940.14	12,758.46	16,629.09	24,901.59	27,416.70
Jun	2,138.11	2,637.35	3,710.70	4,675.21	4,614.22	4,532.54	4,852.13	4,975.93	5,542.13	6,273.12	6,865.66	7,867.42	7,213.87	8,870.95	10,428.43	12,923.05	17,654.19	24,176.40	27,769.40
Jul	2,159.16	2,655.20	3,938.40	5,041.18	4,492.42	4,333.04	4,655.78	4,923.71	5,601.34	6,313.34	6,870.70	7,828.26	7,189.94	9,042.24	10,998.50	12,232.27	17,509.71	24,488.11	28,199.94
Aug	2,150.29	2,297.60	4,066.78	4,882.09	4,168.15	4,089.98	4,738.41	5,243.46	5,585.41	6,436.13	6,819.63	7,815.78	7,123.38	9,189.43	10,584.20	12,716.52	18,787.40	26,029.22	27,365.95
Sep	2,065.44	2,428.25	4,352.95	4,607.18	3,950.00	3,886.39	4,830.40	5,264.38	5,783.16	6,590.69	6,910.87	7,455.50	6,910.73	9,402.58	10,637.16	12,700.11	17,852.86	26,010.88	27,923.67
Oct	2,114.41	2,275.84	4,537.99	4,699.73	3,594.55	4,352.05	4,658.61	5,079.61	5,902.93	6,444.13	7,150.75	7,499.42	7,295.92	9,356.79	10,252.98	12,936.47	16,910.63	23,328.91	27,982.54
Nov	1,990.47	2,442.71	4,868.96	4,461.84	3,954.21	4,331.14	4,506.60	4,936.89	5,967.43	6,450.19	7,165.45	7,549.33	7,895.62	9,320.24	10,428.90	12,779.53	18,325.50	22,686.78	29,578.90
Dec	1,987.14	2,713.74	5,207.94	4,306.80	3,817.22	4,358.60	4,990.85	4,865.60	6,001.85	6,569.47	7,116.38	7,681.84	8,016.67	9,893.82	10,542.60	13,113.32	18,701.30	21,564.00	30,159.00

Month	1989	1990	1991
Jan	31,581	37,189	23,460
Feb	31,986	34,891	26,409
Mar	32,839	29,980	
Apr	33,713	29,689	
May	34,267	33,131	
Jun	32,949	32,042	
Jul	34,954	31,036	
Aug	34,431	25,420	
Sept	35,637	20,983	
Oct	35,544	25,194	
Nov	37,269	22,455	
Dec	38,916	23,848	

Table F4 Details on the 225 Stocks in the NSA

		(A)	(B)	(C)	(D)	(E)	(F)	(G)	(H)	(I)	(J)	(K)	(L)
Foods													
1	NIPPON FLOUR MILLS	865	0.2849%	1577	433	2.40	41.90	2.41	0.69	3.00	1.10	1.94	8.54
2	NISSHIN FLOUR MILLS	1490	0.4908%	3039	130	-3.90	26.43	3.78	0.47	-3.50	0.99	-5.81	14.71
3	TAITO	1470	0.4842%	729	81	26.70	155.08	0.64	0.34	27.10	0.31	30.02	14.52
4	NIPPON BEET SUGAR	1290	0.4249%	1977	1062	63.90	94.14	1.06	0.39	64.50	0.97	48.72	12.74
5	MORINAGA	838	0.2760%	2222	661	0.40	111.10	0.90	0.60	1.00	0.82	0.38	8.28
6	MEIJI DEIKA	906	0.2984%	3528	722	-7.60	50.40	1.98	0.66	-7.00	0.91	-7.17	8.95
7	MEIJI MILK PRODUCTS	836	0.2754%	2346	412	-10.10	80.89	1.24	0.72	-9.60	1.09	-9.10	8.26
8	SAPPORO BREWERIES	1500	0.4941%	5005	532	-11.80	111.22	0.90	0.33	-11.50	1.05	-19.37	14.81
9	ASAHI BREWERIES	1810	0.5962%	7201	705	-11.50	120.01	0.83	0.44	-11.20	1.29	-25.08	17.87
10	KIRIN BREWERY	1550	0.5105%	15535	1081	-14.40	53.20	1.88	0.48	-14.00	1.46	-25.18	15.31
11	TAKARA SHUZO	930	0.3063%	1964	500	3.30	78.55	1.27	0.65	4.00	0.91	2.91	9.18
12	GODO SHUSEI	1880	0.6192%	890	145	16.00	329.45	0.30	0.27	16.30	0.59	25.18	18.57
13	SANRAKU	1130	0.3722%	1615	258	-11.00	89.74	1.11	0.44	-10.60	0.62	-13.56	11.16
14	HONEN	935	0.3080%	777	223	7.50	776.54	0.13	0.55	8.00	0.70	6.30	9.23
15	NISSHIN OIL MILLS	1170	0.3854%	1621	456	13.60	54.05	1.85	0.60	14.20	0.75	13.56	11.55
16	KIKKOMAN	1320	0.4348%	2237	301	14.80	111.86	0.89	0.53	15.40	1.09	16.46	13.04
17	AJINOMOTO	1900	0.6258%	12295	597	-32.90	76.84	1.30	0.53	-32.60	1.09	-90.07	18.76
18	NICHIREI	1010	0.3327%	3110	989	-11.40	81.84	1.22	0.59	-11.00	1.15	-12.59	9.97
Textile Products													
1	KATAKURA INDUSTRIES	5000	1.6469%	1754	45	85.90	167.00	0.60	0.16	86.20	0.99	223.73	49.38
2	TOYOBO	630	0.2075%	4351	1697	-30.80	58.01	1.72	0.79	-30.20	1.46	-27.12	6.22
3	KANEBO	685	0.2256%	3402	861	-18.90	100.05	1.00	0.73	-18.30	0.84	-15.50	6.76
4	UNITIKA	610	0.2009%	2903	1120	-23.40	87.98	1.14	0.82	-22.70	1.19	-18.01	6.02
5	FUJI SPINNING	736	0.2424%	795	275	-4.30	83.67	1.20	0.68	-3.70	0.50	-3.20	7.27
6	NISSHINBO INDUSTRIES	1200	0.3953%	2811	580	-13.70	46.85	2.13	0.58	-13.20	1.46	-18.40	11.85
7	NITTO BOSEKI	675	0.2223%	1672	596	-14.70	79.61	1.26	0.96	-13.90	0.93	-11.60	6.67
8	JAPAN WOOL TEXTILE	2160	0.7115%	2067	121	24.90	76.54	1.31	0.27	25.20	1.51	41.65	21.33
9	DAITO WOOL SPINNING	1430	0.4710%	429	86	58.90	NA	NA	0.00	58.90	0.93	51.33	14.12
10	TEIKOKU SEN-I	2130	0.7016%	574	59	145.40	NA	NA	0.00	145.40	0.11	122.23	21.03
11	TEIJIN	700	0.2306%	6747	2760	-19.10	32.13	3.11	1.00	-18.40	1.15	-15.98	6.91
12	TORAY INDUSTRIES	715	0.2355%	9909	3098	-27.00	33.03	3.03	1.05	-26.40	1.28	-25.67	7.06
13	TOHO RAYON	900	0.2964%	818	457	-3.20	109.07	0.92	0.56	-2.80	0.92	-2.91	8.89
14	MITSUBISHI RAYON	610	0.2009%	3807	1753	-26.90	66.79	1.50	0.82	-26.30	1.05	-21.69	6.02
15	KURARAY	1470	0.4842%	3947	858	16.70	56.38	1.77	0.41	17.10	0.75	20.34	14.52
16	ASAHI CHEMICAL IND.	805	0.2651%	10928	2206	-39.90	33.12	3.02	1.12	-39.30	1.14	-51.82	7.95
Paper and Pulp													
1	SANYO-KOKUSAKU PULP	650	0.2141%	2918	1200	-46.30	32.42	3.08	1.15	-45.70	1.21	-54.52	6.42
2	OJI PAPER	1000	0.3294%	6072	1447	-49.50	26.40	3.79	0.85	-49.10	1.35	-94.92	9.88
3	HONSHU PAPER	1710	0.5632%	5708	2006	67.60	190.26	0.53	0.35	68.40	0.80	66.83	16.89
4	JUJO PAPER	730	0.2404%	3483	826	-44.30	30.29	3.30	0.96	-43.80	1.13	-56.17	7.21
5	MITSUNISHI PAPER	849	0.2796%	2734	648	-39.80	32.55	3.07	0.94	-39.30	0.86	-54.33	8.38
6	HOKUETSU PAPER MILLS	980	0.3228%	1217	232	-16.20	33.82	2.96	0.71	-15.70	0.86	-18.40	9.68
Chemicals													
1	MITSUI TOATSU CHEMICAL	661	0.2177%	5009	2730	-43.70	41.74	2.40	0.91	-43.20	1.59	-51.25	6.53
2	SHOWA DENKO	659	0.2171%	6835	2536	-44.20	42.72	2.34	0.91	-43.70	1.31	-50.46	6.51
3	SUMITOMO CHEMICAL	630	0.2075%	10214	1955	-41.70	46.43	2.15	0.95	-41.20	1.59	-43.58	6.22
4	MITSUNISHI KASEI	700	0.2306%	9047	1576	-42.10	54.70	1.83	0.86	-41.70	1.47	-49.39	6.91
5	NISSAN CHEMICAL IND.	1030	0.3393%	1426	1143	21.50	95.06	1.05	0.49	22.10	0.71	17.63	10.17
6	RASA INDUSTRIES	931	0.3066%	519	405	21.40	97.98	1.02	0.53	22.00	0.86	15.88	9.19
7	NIPPON SODA	900	0.2964%	756	476	1.10	88.94	1.12	0.56	1.70	1.07	0.97	8.89
8	TOSOH	605	0.1993%	2749	1313	-39.20	54.98	1.82	0.83	-38.80	1.35	-37.77	5.97
9	TOAGOSEI CHEMICAL	841	0.2770%	1758	506	-25.70	35.51	2.82	0.71	-25.30	1.33	-29.88	8.30
10	DENKI KAGAKU KOGYO	646	0.2128%	3070	1142	-40.20	51.16	1.95	0.93	-39.70	1.42	-42.03	6.38
11	SHIN-ETSU CHEMICAL	1490	0.4908%	4780	881	-24.70	40.86	2.45	0.49	-24.40	1.08	-47.46	14.71
12	NIPPON CARBIDE IND.	899	0.2961%	595	194	5.50	77.46	1.29	0.68	6.50	0.74	4.55	8.88
13	NIPPON CHEMICAL IND.	2340	0.7707%	1755	701	141.20	168.75	0.59	0.13	141.50	0.75	132.69	23.11
14	KYOWA HAKKO KOGYO	1300	0.4282%	5801	609	-16.10	52.47	1.91	0.46	-15.70	1.54	-24.21	12.84
15	NIPPON SYNTHETIC	1100	0.3623%	799	194	11.40	57.07	1.75	0.45	11.90	0.62	10.94	10.86
16	UBE INDUSTRIES	618	0.2036%	5141	1215	-33.50	64.27	1.56	0.81	-33.00	1.37	-30.22	6.10
17	NIPPON KAYAKU	1060	0.3491%	1028	1119	-15.20	38.56	2.59	0.71	-14.70	1.15	-18.40	10.47
18	ASAHI DENKA KOGYO	1200	0.3953%	877	309	22.40	67.44	1.48	0.42	22.90	0.54	21.31	11.85
19	NIPPON OIL AND FATS	980	0.3228%	2132	449	-16.90	62.71	1.59	0.61	-16.50	1.14	-19.37	9.68
20	FUJI PHOTO FILM	3910	1.2879%	16556	2500	23.20	20.19	4.95	0.38	23.60	0.50	78.55	38.61
21	KONICA	1400	0.4611%	4991	1082	30.80	55.46	1.80	0.71	31.80	0.69	31.96	13.83
Drugs													
1	SANKYO	2150	0.7082%	7683	1108	-10.40	65.67	1.52	0.35	-10.10	1.31	-24.21	21.23
2	TAKEDA CHEMICAL IND.	1750	0.5764%	15268	830	-28.60	41.26	2.42	0.57	-28.20	1.29	-67.80	17.28
3	YAMANOUCHI PHARMACEUTICAL	2620	0.8630%	7455	519	-27.00	31.90	3.14	0.30	-26.80	0.62	-93.95	25.87
4	DAINIPPON PHARMACEUTICAL	2530	0.8333%	3797	193	14.00	63.28	1.50	0.30	14.20	0.58	30.02	24.98

(A) Closing price as of 3/30/90
(B) Weight in Index
(C) Market Value as of 3/30/90
(D) Average Daily Volume 4/89 to 3/90 (1000 shares)

(E) Annual Return from 4/89 to 3/90
(F) Price to Earnings Ratio (3/30/90)
(G) 1/PER
(H) Dividend Yield as of 3/30/90

(I) N/A
(J) Beta as of 3/30/90
(K) N/A
(L) N/A

Source: TSE and Chicago Mercantile Exchange

Table F4 continued

Petroleum

1 NIPPON OIL	1050	0.3458%	12814	3112	-34.80	116.49	0.86	0.57	-34.50	0.92	-54.24	10.37
2 SHOWA SHELL SEKIYU	1180	0.3887%	3222	344	-15.70	53.71	1.86	0.51	-15.30	1.01	-21.31	11.65
3 MITSUBISHI OIL	955	0.3146%	3299	1965	-25.40	54.99	1.82	0.63	-24.80	0.97	-31.48	9.43
4 TONEN	1580	0.5204%	10215	377	-11.20	56.75	1.76	1.58	-1.00	0.61	-19.37	15.60

Rubber

1 YOKOHAMA RUBBER	1200	0.3953%	2925	731	12.10	37.50	2.67	0.50	12.80	0.69	12.59	11.85
2 BRIDGESTONE	1420	0.4677%	10898	2297	-4.70	23.19	4.31	0.85	-3.80	0.92	-6.78	14.02

Clay and Glass

1 ASAHI GLASS	1730	0.5698%	20150	1236	-24.50	42.87	2.33	0.52	-24.10	0.87	-54.24	17.08
2 NIPPON SHEET GLASS	851	0.2803%	3713	1607	-17.40	33.75	2.96	0.71	-16.90	0.98	-17.34	8.40
3 NIHON CEMENT	920	0.3030%	2992	675	-31.30	49.87	2.01	0.65	-30.90	1.17	-40.68	9.09
4 SUMITOMO CEMENT	680	0.2240%	2081	718	-31.30	39.27	2.55	0.88	-30.80	1.12	-30.02	6.72
5 ONODA CEMENT	705	0.2322%	3266	982	-37.10	48.03	2.08	0.78	-36.60	1.56	-40.19	6.96
6 MITSUBISHI MINING	650	0.2141%	2937	928	-35.60	36.71	2.72	0.92	-35.10	1.21	-34.87	6.42
7 TOKAI CARBON	850	0.2800%	1335	650	-13.10	111.28	0.90	0.59	-12.60	0.82	-12.40	8.39
8 NIPPON CARBON	831	0.2737%	983	1135	7.90	409.70	0.24	0.24	7.90	0.97	5.91	8.21
9 NORITAKE	1480	0.4875%	2084	288	22.30	69.46	1.44	0.54	22.90	0.73	26.15	14.62
10 TOTO	1980	0.6522%	6647	858	-0.05	39.10	2.56	0.45	0.03	1.05	-0.10	19.55
11 NGK INSULATORS	1310	0.4315%	4624	1119	-22.00	51.38	1.95	0.61	-21.60	0.70	-35.84	12.94
12 SHINAGAWA REFRACTORY	1690	0.5566%	1115	256	20.70	202.80	0.49	0.30	21.10	0.77	28.09	16.69

Iron and Steel

1 NIPPON STEEL	520	0.1713%	35812	15969	-44.40	35.81	2.79	1.15	-43.80	1.40	-40.19	5.14
2 KAWASAKI STEEL	519	0.1709%	16874	8747	-43.70	42.19	2.37	1.16	-43.10	1.29	-40.15	5.13
3 NKK	500	0.1647%	17614	7694	-44.40	58.71	1.70	1.20	-43.90	1.41	-40.19	4.94
4 SUMITOMO METAL IND.	539	0.1775%	16621	14765	-36.00	46.46	2.15	1.11	-35.40	1.34	-29.35	5.32
5 KOBE STEEL	555	0.1828%	15637	7736	-38.00	62.55	1.60	1.08	-37.50	1.10	-32.93	5.48
6 NIPPON STAINLESS	930	0.3063%	885	347	-36.70	32.19	3.11	0.54	-36.40	0.56	-52.30	9.18
7 NIPPON METAL IND.	879	0.2895%	1400	594	+24.90	51.87	1.93	0.58	-24.50	0.50	-28.18	8.68
8 NIPPON YAKIN KOGYO	750	0.2470%	1245	687	-49.70	49.78	2.01	0.67	-49.40	0.93	-71.67	7.41
9 NIPPON DENKO	915	0.3014%	1040	456	-21.10	104.00	0.96	0.55	-20.60	0.44	-23.73	9.04
10 JAPAN STEEL WORKS	753	0.2480%	2797	1705	-35.10	17.48	5.72	0.53	-34.70	1.09	-39.42	7.44
11 MITSUBISHI STEEL MFG	1450	0.4776%	2088	417	-40.30	696.01	0.14	0.00	-40.30	0.74	-94.92	14.32

Metal products

1 NIPPONLIGHT METAL	780	0.2569%	3436	1094	-12.00	49.08	2.04	0.64	-11.50	1.07	-10.96	7.70
2 MITSUI MINING & SMELTING	668	0.2200%	3246	2790	-28.00	43.29	2.31	0.60	-28.50	0.80	-26.34	6.60
3 TOHO ZINC	985	0.3244%	985	382	23.10	42.64	2.35	0.51	23.80	0.60	17.92	9.73
4 MITSUBISHI METAL	770	0.2536%	5274	3748	-31.30	47.95	2.09	0.78	-30.70	1.12	-33.90	7.60
5 NIPPON MINING	799	0.2632%	7054	4002	-20.00	70.54	1.42	0.63	-19.40	1.15	-19.37	7.89
6 SUMITOMO METALMINING	1290	0.4249%	6447	3870	-9.20	67.87	1.47	0.54	-8.70	1.04	-12.59	12.74
7 DOWA MINING	910	0.2997%	2209	1628	-3.10	81.82	1.22	0.55	-2.60	0.88	-2.81	8.99
8 FURUKAWA	872	0.2872%	2143	1175	-9.80	47.62	2.10	0.69	-9.20	0.92	-9.20	8.61
9 SHIMURA KAKO	1580	0.5204%	646	336	122.80	248.29	0.40	0.00	122.80	0.32	84.36	15.60
10 SHIMITOMO ELECTRIC	725	0.2388%	4731	3057	-38.60	63.08	1.59	0.83	-38.20	1.48	-44.07	7.16
11 SUMITOMO ELECTRIC	1400	0.4611%	9847	1368	-10.80	61.54	1.62	0.54	-10.40	1.02	-16.46	13.83
12 FUJIKURA	850	0.2800%	2835	883	-36.10	65.93	1.52	0.76	-35.70	1.01	-46.49	8.39
13 SHOWA ELECTRIC WIRE	929	0.3060%	1971	1008	-28.00	65.71	1.52	0.65	-27.60	1.03	-34.96	9.17
14 TOYO SEIKAN	3400	1.1199%	5715	213	42.30	32.66	3.06	0.22	42.60	0.68	97.82	33.58
15 TOKYO ROPE MFG.	1440	0.4743%	2037	331	-38.70	185.19	0.54	0.35	-38.50	0.58	-88.14	14.22

Machinery

1 NIIGATA ENGINEERING	746	0.2457%	2488	820	-16.00	138.20	0.72	0.54	-15.60	1.07	-13.75	7.37
2 OKUMA MACHINERY WORK	1546	0.5092%	2042	426	13.20	40.03	2.50	0.42	13.60	0.45	17.43	15.21
3 KOMATSU	1030	0.3393%	10183	1990	-27.00	59.90	1.67	0.78	-26.40	0.83	-36.80	10.17
4 KUBOTA	920	0.3030%	12954	1318	-27.60	66.43	1.51	0.71	-27.10	1.23	-33.90	9.09
5 EBARA	1670	0.5501%	4742	2641	-8.20	105.38	0.95	0.51	-7.90	0.91	-14.53	16.49
6 CHIYODA	2470	0.8136%	4822	1595	83.00	241.10	0.41	0.16	83.00	0.33	108.47	24.39
7 NIPPON PISTON RING	1260	0.4150%	807	111	17.80	120.45	0.83	0.40	18.20	0.38	18.40	12.44
8 NIPPONSEIKO	1120	0.3689%	6205	2578	6.70	53.95	1.85	0.71	7.30	0.54	6.78	11.06
9 NTV	948	0.3122%	4357	1014	-2.50	44.48	2.25	0.95	-1.70	0.48	-2.63	9.36
10 KOYO SEIKO	1250	0.4117%	2442	390	7.80	42.11	2.37	0.56	8.30	0.11	8.72	12.34
11 NACHI-FUJIKOSHI	1020	0.3360%	2317	622	-4.70	68.16	1.47	0.59	-4.20	0.30	-4.84	10.07

Table F4 continued

Electric Equipment

1	HITACHI	1590	0.5237%	51188	6076	10.60	44.51	2.25	0.69	11.30	0.51	15.45	15.70
2	TOSHIBA	1060	0.3491%	33592	10549	-10.20	37.32	2.68	0.94	-9.40	1.07	-11.62	10.47
3	MITSUBISHI ELECTRIC	970	0.3195%	20708	4987	-8.50	37.65	2.66	1.03	-7.70	0.82	-8.72	9.58
4	FUJI ELECTRIC	900	0.2964%	6382	2262	-25.00	60.78	1.65	0.78	-24.50	1.04	-29.06	8.89
5	MEIDENSHA	1170	0.3854%	2361	615	0.90	73.32	1.36	0.51	1.30	0.89	0.97	11.55
6	NEC	2120	0.6983%	32170	3062	22.50	46.62	2.14	0.47	23.10	0.43	37.77	20.94
7	FUJITSU	1480	0.4875%	26649	3364	5.00	36.51	2.74	0.61	5.60	0.63	6.78	14.62
8	OKI ELECTRIC IND.	1050	0.3458%	6239	2303	10.50	38.99	2.56	0.67	11.20	0.75	6.69	10.37
9	MATSUSHITA ELECT. IND.	2150	0.7082%	44636	2549	-10.80	31.21	3.20	0.47	-10.40	0.69	-25.18	21.23
10	SHARP	1770	0.5830%	18548	4502	36.20	40.81	2.05	0.62	37.00	0.40	45.52	17.48
11	SONY	8000	2.6350%	26446	2182	19.20	40.69	2.46	0.63	19.90	0.33	124.94	79.00
12	SANYO ELECTRIC	825	0.2717%	15720	4154	-11.20	68.35	1.46	0.97	-10.40	0.90	-10.07	8.15
13	YOKOGAWA ELECTRIC	1630	0.5369%	4213	890	-3.60	46.82	2.14	0.46	-3.20	0.46	-5.81	16.10
14	NIPPONDENSO	2020	0.6653%	16539	822	8.90	35.19	2.84	0.64	9.60	0.36	17.63	19.95
15	YUASA BATTERY	1070	0.3524%	1909	823	-18.30	119.34	0.84	0.46	-18.00	0.62	-23.24	10.57

Shipbuilding

1	MITSUI ENGIN & SHIP	780	0.2569%	5952	4715	-14.70	297.61	0.34	0.51	-14.20	1.07	-12.98	7.70
2	HITACHI ZOSEN	745	0.2454%	7466	4085	2.50	746.64	0.13	0.00	2.50	1.01	1.74	7.36
3	MITSUBISHI HEAVY IND.	870	0.2866%	29090	10281	-23.70	37.79	2.58	0.80	-23.20	1.22	-26.15	8.59
4	KAWASAKI HEAVY IND.	720	0.2372%	9584	8468	-26.90	95.84	1.04	0.69	-26.40	1.54	-25.67	7.11
5	IHI	991	0.3264%	12868	6460	-20.10	116.98	0.85	0.50	-19.80	1.42	-24.12	9.79

Motor Vehicles

1	NISSAN MOTORS	1070	0.3524%	26815	2952	-29.60	33.52	2.98	1.31	-28.80	0.84	-43.58	10.57
2	ISUZU MOTORS	675	0.2223%	6824	1119	-20.80	45.50	2.20	0.74	-20.40	0.86	-18.93	6.67
3	TOYOTA MOTORS	2220	0.7312%	67438	1858	-7.50	18.73	5.34	0.90	-6.80	0.45	-18.31	21.92
4	HINO MOTORS	1020	0.3360%	3644	715	-1.90	36.44	2.74	0.74	-1.30	0.85	-1.94	10.07
5	MAZDA MOTOR	845	0.2783%	9039	1386	-7.40	36.16	2.77	0.89	-6.70	0.56	-6.59	8.34
6	HONDA MOTOR	1760	0.5797%	16996	1262	-7.40	33.46	2.99	0.80	-6.60	0.43	-13.56	17.38
7	SUZUKI MOTOR	740	0.2437%	3021	1070	-10.30	35.54	2.81	0.88	-9.60	0.83	-8.23	7.31

Transportation Equipment

1	NIPPON SHARYO	1450	0.4776%	2116	429	-7.10	72.98	1.37	0.41	-6.70	0.35	-10.65	14.32

Precision Instrument

1	NIKON	1450	0.4776%	5315	1136	6.60	53.15	1.88	0.59	7.20	0.58	8.72	14.32
2	CANON	1680	0.5534%	12328	3739	12.00	41.09	2.43	0.74	12.80	0.49	19.18	16.59
3	RICOH	1120	0.3689%	7179	1296	1.40	39.88	2.51	0.89	2.20	0.25	1.55	11.06
4	CITIZEN WATCH	960	0.3162%	2962	1255	-5.90	37.98	2.63	0.86	-5.10	0.22	-5.81	9.48

Other Manufacturing

1	TOPPAN PRINTING	1840	0.6061%	11807	1023	-4.70	39.75	2.52	0.54	-4.20	0.76	-8.72	18.17
2	DAI NIPPON PRINTING	1870	0.6159%	13954	642	-18.30	40.45	2.47	0.53	-18.00	0.86	-40.68	18.47
3	YAMAHA	1740	0.5731%	3410	417	4.20	79.30	1.26	0.56	4.70	0.85	6.78	17.18

Marine Products

1	KYOKUYO	1310	0.4315%	1484	1211	78.20	247.33	0.40	0.23	78.50	1.24	55.69	12.94
2	NICHIRO	691	0.2276%	1137	779	-10.10	378.90	0.26	0.00	-10.10	1.45	-7.55	6.82
3	NIPPON SUISAN	669	0.2204%	1983	678	-20.30	132.22	0.76	0.75	-19.80	0.99	-16.46	6.61

Mining

1	MITSUI MINING	1060	0.3491%	1613	727	-1.90	268.80	0.37	0.00	-1.90	0.90	-1.94	10.47
2	SUMITOMO COAL MINING	1100	0.3623%	840	305	37.50	101.24	0.99	0.45	38.00	1.14	29.06	10.86
3	TEIKOKU OIL	1100	0.3623%	2928	2098	-0.90	94.46	1.06	0.50	-0.40	0.87	-0.97	10.86

Construction

1	TAISEI	1180	0.3887%	12014	3132	-39.20	53.40	1.87	0.76	-38.70	1.18	-73.61	11.65
2	OHBAYASHI	1430	0.4710%	10619	4105	-24.30	45.19	2.21	0.49	-24.00	1.26	-44.55	14.12
3	SHIMIZU	1740	0.5731%	13652	2363	-25.30	53.54	1.87	0.63	-24.90	1.14	-57.14	17.18
4	SATO KOGYO	2300	0.7576%	5678	2265	-7.30	157.72	0.63	0.26	-6.90	0.11	-17.43	22.71
5	TOBISHIMA	1550	0.5105%	3567	507	-0.60	118.91	0.84	0.40	-0.10	-0.19	-0.97	15.31
6	FUJITA	1650	0.5435%	7386	2338	-24.70	73.86	1.35	0.55	-24.20	1.20	-52.30	16.29
7	KAJIMA	1660	0.5468%	15859	1812	-30.80	61.00	1.64	0.66	-30.40	1.36	-75.25	16.39
8	TEKKEN CONSTRUCTION	1710	0.5632%	2662	1278	9.60	146.56	0.60	0.44	10.10	0.21	14.53	16.89
9	TOA	1060	0.3491%	1878	366	-23.70	117.40	0.85	0.47	-23.30	1.17	-31.96	10.47
10	DAIWA HOUSE INDUSTRY	1980	0.6522%	9256	2803	-1.00	28.92	3.46	0.85	-0.20	1.29	-1.94	19.55

Trade

1	C. ITOH	728	0.2398%	10324	3953	-34.70	57.35	1.74	0.69	-34.30	1.60	-39.28	7.19
2	MARUBENI	700	0.2306%	10346	5862	-27.60	60.86	1.64	0.71	-27.10	1.36	-25.86	6.91
3	MITSUI	850	0.2800%	12987	3520	-29.80	61.04	1.62	0.71	-29.30	1.67	-34.87	8.39
4	SUMITOMO	1120	0.3689%	11844	3243	-13.20	34.84	2.87	0.71	-12.70	1.39	-18.21	11.06
5	MITSUBISHI	1240	0.4084%	19344	2367	-22.50	48.36	2.07	0.73	-22.00	1.74	-34.87	12.25
6	IWATANI	1090	0.3590%	2576	78?	7.90	95.41	1.05	0.46	8.40	1.18	7.75	10.76

Table F4 concluded

	(A)	(B)	(C)	(D)	(E)	(F)	(G)	(H)		(J)		
Retail Stores												
1 MITSUKOSHI	1630	0.5369%	7858	842	-31.88	116.86	0.86	0.37	-31.60	1.54	-73.61	16.10
2 TOKYU DEPARTMENT	1400	0.4611%	3845	1884	3.00	67.45	1.48	0.57	3.40	1.00	4.07	13.83
3 TAKASHIMAYA	2950	0.9717%	6537	194	2.80	78.76	1.27	0.36	3.10	1.12	7.75	29.13
4 MATSUZAKAYA	6870	2.2628%	10686	46	19.50	159.50	0.63	0.14	19.70	0.51	108.47	67.84
5 MARUZEN	1430	0.4710%	1443	431	40.20	131.21	0.76	0.52	40.90	0.96	39.71	14.12
Banks												
1 DAI-ICHI KANGYO BANK	2370	0.7806%	73946	490	-24.30	47.71	2.10	0.36	-24.10	1.05	-78.85	23.40
2 BANK OF TOKYO	1350	0.4447%	26918	520	-20.60	48.94	2.04	0.59	-20.20	1.09	-33.90	13.33
3 MITSUI TAIYO KOBE	2150	0.7082%	40564	399	-5.70	62.41	1.60	0.40	-5.40	1.16	-12.59	21.23
4 MITSUBISHI BANK	2500	0.8234%	71830	569	-15.30	51.31	1.95	0.34	-15.10	1.07	-46.00	24.69
5 FUJI BANK	2940	0.9684%	85027	549	-10.80	53.14	1.88	0.29	-10.50	0.97	-36.13	29.03
6 SUMITOMO BANK	2620	0.8630%	82498	833	-22.20	45.83	2.18	0.32	-22.10	1.40	-78.73	25.87
7 MITSUI TRUST & BANK	1580	0.5204%	18926	322	-24.80	33.20	3.01	0.54	-24.40	1.61	-50.36	15.60
8 MITSUBISHI TRUST & BANK	1800	0.5929%	23427	311	-34.50	30.03	3.33	0.47	-34.30	2.22	-92.01	17.78
Other Financial Services												
1 NIPPON SHINPAN	1120	0.3689%	3479	1029	-14.50	31.62	3.16	0.94	-13.90	1.48	-18.40	11.06
Securities												
1 JAPAN SECURITIES FINANCE	2100	0.6917%	2599	354	39.10	28.88	3.46	0.29	39.30	1.64	57.14	20.74
2 NIKKO SECURITIES	1250	0.4117%	18299	590	-33.50	14.64	6.83	1.12	-32.80	2.14	-61.02	12.34
3 NOMURA SECURITIES	2170	0.7147%	42505	1552	-36.90	20.24	4.94	0.71	-36.50	2.11	-123.00	21.43
Insurance												
1 TOKIO MARINE & FIRE	1400	0.4611%	21615	1723	-29.00	51.47	1.94	0.57	-28.60	1.72	-58.11	13.83
2 TAISHO MARINE & FIRE	980	0.3228%	6754	1119	-25.20	42.21	2.37	0.71	-24.70	1.65	-31.96	9.68
3 YASUDA FIRE & MARINE	980	0.3228%	8693	2703	-27.40	52.68	1.90	0.71	-26.90	1.63	-35.84	9.68
Real Estate												
1 MITSUI REAL ESTATE	1650	0.5435%	13125	3601	-35.80	47.73	2.10	0.61	-35.50	2.07	-89.10	16.20
2 MITSUBISHI ESTATE	1530	0.5039%	19526	1456	-41.60	45.94	2.18	0.56	-41.30	1.89	-105.57	15.11
3 HEIWA REAL ESTATE	1460	0.4809%	1563	416	-20.50	77.35	1.29	0.41	-20.20	1.48	-40.10	14.42
Railroad Transport												
1 TOBU RAILWAY	970	0.3195%	7790	2452	-41.20	165.76	0.60	0.52	-41.00	1.66	-65.86	9.58
2 TOKYU	1580	0.5204%	17203	6541	-7.60	256.76	0.39	0.32	-7.40	1.46	-12.59	15.60
3 KEIHIN ELECTRIC RAILWAY	1030	0.3393%	5060	688	-44.00	167.54	0.60	0.49	-43.80	1.52	-78.45	10.17
4 ODAKYU ELECTRIC RAILWAY	1080	0.3557%	7087	1386	-32.50	181.71	0.55	0.46	-32.20	1.29	-50.36	10.67
5 KEIO TEITO RAILWAY	1000	0.3294%	5875	818	-28.60	172.81	0.58	0.50	-28.30	1.51	-40.68	9.88
6 KEISEI ELECTRIC RAILWAY	1690	0.5566%	4591	1963	-37.40	167.38	0.60	0.24	-37.30	1.18	-97.82	16.69
Trucking												
1 NIPPON EXPRESS	1000	0.3294%	10690	3264	-35.90	80.38	1.24	0.60	-35.60	1.45	-54.24	9.88
Sea Transport												
1 NIPPON YUSEN	820	0.2701%	9396	4554	-15.00	156.61	0.64	0.49	-14.60	1.61	-14.04	8.10
2 MITSUI O.S.K. LINES	785	0.2586%	8228	3489	-14.70	182.83	0.55	0.51	-14.20	1.37	-13.08	7.75
3 NAVIX LINE	921	0.3034%	3610	1482	12.90	164.10	0.61	0.00	12.90	0.91	5.08	9.09
4 KAWASAKI	780	0.2569%	4567	3336	-2.50	130.48	0.77	0.00	-2.50	1.01	-1.94	7.70
5 SHOWA	1210	0.3985%	3309	1441	39.10	66.18	1.51	0.00	39.10	0.62	32.93	11.95
Air Transport												
1 ALL NIPPON AIRWAYS	1600	0.5270%	21977	1031	-10.10	137.36	0.73	0.31	-9.80	0.92	-17.43	15.80
Warehousing												
1 MITSUBISHI WAREHOUSE	1620	0.5336%	2705	365	-3.60	60.79	1.65	0.37	-3.30	1.13	-5.81	16.00
2 MITSUI WAREHOUSE	1300	0.4282%	1799	253	-0.80	138.41	0.72	0.46	-0.30	1.26	-0.97	12.84
Communications												
1 NTT	1160000	0.3821%	180960	4492	-25.20	76.68	1.30	0.52	-24.80	0.87	-37.77	11.46
Electric Power												
1 TOKYO ELECTRIC POWER	3920	0.1291%	52501	8867	-33.90	58.33	1.71	1.28	-33.20	0.95	-19.87	3.87
2 KANSAI ELECTRIC POWER	3120	0.1028%	30210	7819	-29.30	50.35	1.99	1.60	-28.40	1.02	-12.76	3.08
Gas Services												
1 TOKYO GAS	720	0.2372%	20221	3208	-33.90	80.88	1.24	0.69	-33.40	0.92	-36.65	7.11
2 OSAKA GAS	580	0.1910%	14632	2189	-30.00	73.16	1.37	0.86	-29.50	0.97	-25.28	5.73
Services												
1 SHOCIKU	4380	1.4427%	2671	67	34.80	667.78	0.15	0.11	34.90	0.65	109.44	43.25
2 TOHO	38500	1.2681%	5407	138	72.20	117.54	0.85	0.26	72.60	0.88	171.91	38.02
3 TOEI	1200	0.3953%	1768	723	10.10	73.66	1.36	0.50	10.50	1.35	10.65	11.85
4 NIKKATSU	521	0.1716%	1260	1459	17.80	NA	NA	0.00	17.80	0.97	7.79	5.14
5 KORAKUEN	3700	1.2187%	5373	183	-7.30	103.32	0.97	0.32	-7.00	0.83	-28.09	36.54

(A) Closing price as of 3/30/90
(B) Weight in Index
(C) Market Value as of 3/30/90
(D) Average Daily Volume 4/89 to 3/90 (1000 shares)

(E) Annual Return from 4/89 to 3/90
(F) Price to Earnings Ratio (3/30/90)
(G) 1/PER
(H) Dividend Yield as of 3/30/90

(I) N/A
(J) Beta as of 3/30/90
(K) N/A
(L) N/A

APPENDIX G CLOSING PRICES ON JANUARY 4, 1991 OF THE STOCKS ON THE FIRST, SECOND AND FOREIGN SECTIONS OF THE TSE

Table G1
Closing Prices of the Stocks on the TSE-I on January 4, 1991, in Yen

■ Jan. 4

Stock	Close	Chg. in yen

1st section

Stock	Close	Chg.
FISHERY & FARM		
Hohsui	720	+30
Hoko Fishing	435	+5
Kyokuyo	799	+22
Nichiro	525	+30
Nippon Suisan	558	-24
Sakata Seed	3640	-50
Taiyo Fishery	440	-11
MINING		
Arabian Oil	7450	+220
Kanto Natural Gas	1400	-100
Mitsui Matsushima	595	+10
Mitsui Mining	735	+6
Nittetsu Mining	1520	+30
Sumitomo Coal	914	+23
Teikoku Oil	957	-3
CONSTRUCTION		
Ando Const.	1230	+50
Aoki Corp	781	-4
Arai-Gumi	3270	
Asahi Kogyosha	990	+20
Asanuma Gumi	1050	
Chudenko	3310	-60
Chugai Ro	1030	-60
Dai Nippon Const.	1480	-120
Daiho Const.	996	+11
Daimei Telecom	1220	
Daisue Const.	707	+2
Daito Kogyo	700	
Daiwa House Ind.	1800	-20
Fudo Const.	850	+30
Fujiko	587	+2
Fujita	1180	+30
Fukuda Const	1470	-30
Haseko	801	+1
Hazama-Gumi	1080	+30
Hitachi Plant E&C	1020	-20
Ichiken	1030	-60
JDC	903	
JGC	1900	+100
Kajima	1630	+50
Kandenko	2720	-10
Katsumura Const.	1000	+19
Kinden	2700	
Kitano Const	1320	+20
Komatsu Const.	1000	-20
Kumagai Gumi	737	-8
Kyowa Densetsu	1000	+8
Kyudenko	1750	-40
Maeda Corp	1700	+20
Maeda Road Const.	2110	-30
Magara Const.	1080	+50
Maisui Const.	1600	
Misawa Homes	1600	
Mitsui Const.	855	-10
Nakanogumi	1300	
National House Ind.	1020	+10
Nichiei Const	1700	-100
Nippon Comsys	1120	-10
Nippon Densetsu	1380	-10
Nippon Hodo	2510	-30
Nippon Koei	1030	+20
Nippon Road	1420	-10
Morinaga & Co.	630	-5
Morinaga Milk	541	-24
Morozoff	990	+10
Nagatanien-Honpo	1110	-40
Nakamuraya	905	+4
Nichirei	805	+14
Nihon Nosan	503	-7
Nippon Beet Sugar	735	+35
Nippon Flour Mills	635	+21
Nippon Formula F.	445	-5
Nippon Meat Pack.	1350	
Nisshin Flour Mill	1480	-30
Nisshin Oil Mills	1040	+40
Nissin Food	2060	-20
Nitto Flour Milling	687	-23
Pokka	1270	-10
Prima Meat Pack	608	-5
Q.P.	940	-10
Sapporo Breweries	1340	-50
Showa Sangyo	551	-19
Snow Brand Milk	759	-1
Taito	1130	+70
Takara Shuzo	659	-1
Toyo Sugar Refining	495	-35
Toyo Suisan	1220	-30
Toyojozo	970	-10
Yakult Honsha	1860	-60
Yamazaki Baking	1350	-10
Yomeishu Seizo	1180	-30
Yoshihara Oil Mill	608	-2
TEXTILES		
Asahi Chem. Ind.	740	-4
Ashimori Ind.	920	-15
Atsugi Nylon Ind.	840	-12
Daidoh	1090	-10
Daito Wool. Spin.	1280	-20
Daiwabo	910	-30
Dynic	599	+24
Fuji Spinning	2740	+160
Fukusuke	715	-20
Gunze	715	-20
Ichikawa Woolen	647	-14
Japan Vilene	1000	-10
Japan Wool Tex.	1630	+50
Kanebo	550	-7
Katakura Ind.	3260	+40
Kawashima Textile	820	-30
Kobe Kiito	415	-35
Komatsu Seiren		
Kurabo Industries	940	-9
Kuraray	1260	-20
Kyowa Leather	1250	
Mitsubishi Rayon	455	-5
Miyuki Keori		
Nippon Felt	1350	+50
Nippon Lace	1140	-40
Nisshinbo Ind.	1040	+30
Nitto Boseki	559	-11
Nitto Seimo	1120	-70
Omikenshi		
Sakai Textile Mfg.	653	+2
Seiren		
Shikibo		
Shinyei	512	-28
Suminoe Textile	717	
Teijin	525	
Teikoku Sen-i	2900	-180
Tesac		
Toa Wool Spin.		
Toho Rayon	730	+6
Tokai Senko	1210	+20
Toray Industries	604	+24
Toyobo	530	-20
Unitika	473	-2
Wacoal	970	-25
PULP & PAPER		
Chuetsu Pulp Ind.	481	-7
Chuo Paperboard	590	-20
Daio Paper	1030	
Daishowa Paper	3130	-60
Nichiban	664	+11
Nihon Nohyaku	900	+12
Nihon Parkerizing	959	-11
Nikken Chemicals	708	-7
Nippon Carbide	690	+40
Nippon Chem. Ind.	1150	+30
Nippon Chemiphar	1680	+10
Nippon Kasei	453	+3
Nippon Kayaku	770	
Nippon Oil & Fats	716	+1
Nippon Paint	665	-5
Nippon Sanso	609	
Nippon Shinyaku		
Nippon Shokubai	1300	
Nippon Soda	720	+15
Nippon Steel Chem	602	+20
Nippon Syn. Chem.	959	+24
Nippon Zeon	540	+1
Nissan Chem. Ind.	665	-10
Nitto Chem. Ind.	901	-24
Okura Industrial	765	+5
Ono Pharm.	—	
Osaka Sanso	560	-10
Osaka Soda	—	
Rasa Industries	809	+38
Rhoto Pharm.	—	
Riken Vinyl	672	-28
Sakai Chem. Ind.	980	
Sakata Inx	662	-18
Sankyo	2430	+10
Santen Pharm.	—	
Sanyo Chem. Ind.	1100	-20
Seitetsu Kagaku	610	
Sekisui Chem.	1050	-20
Sekisui Jushi	1460	
Sekisui Plastics	830	-3
Shikoku Chemicals	650	-19
Shin-Etsu Chem.	1200	-10
Shionogi & Co.	1060	+20
Shiseido	2020	
Showa Denko	515	+25
Showa Hpolymer	710	
SS Pharm	1010	-40
Sumitomo Bakelite	550	-13
Sumitomo Chem.	469	+14
Taisho Pharm.	2060	-50
Taiyo Sanso	750	-8
Takasago Intl	680	-30
Takeda Chem. Ind.	1620	+20
Takiron	660	-4
Tanabe Seiyaku	878	-52
Tayca	580	+18
Teisan	635	+2
Terumo	992	-18
Titan Kogyo	1000	-30
Toa Paint	803	
Toagosei Chem.	622	-5
Toda Kogyo	782	+1
Tokuyama Soda	521	-5
Tokyo Ohka	3680	
Tokyo Tanabe	780	-20
Tosoh	550	
Toyama Chem.	640	+4
Toyo Chemical	537	-1
Toyo Ink Mfg.	527	-13
Toyo Sanso	1100	-10
Tsumura & Co.	1600	
Tsutsunaka Plastic	1190	-80
Ube Industries	555	+15
Wakamoto Pharm.	960	-6
Yamanouchi Pharm.	2730	+30
Yoshitomi Pharm.	1400	+20
OIL PRODUCTS		
Cosmo Oil	650	+10
Fuji Kosan	480	
General Sekiyu	979	+6
Koa Oil	625	-23
Mitsubishi Oil	913	+13
Nichireki Chem Ind	1210	+20
Nippon Oil	911	-4
Sanyo Spec Steel	495	+5
Sumitomo Metal Ind	471	+13
Toa Steel	1180	
Tokyo Steel	3030	-40
Tokyo Tekko	2740	+20
Toyo Kohan	660	-1
Yahagi Iron	475	-5
Yamato Kogyo	1420	
Yodogawa Steel W.	808	-22
NON-FERROUS METALS		
Dowa Mining	629	-1
Fujikura	820	+25
Furukawa Co.	820	
Furukawa Elec.	670	+14
Hitachi Cable	930	-10
Mitsubishi Cable	730	
Mitsubishi Materials	574	-1
Mitsubishi Shindoh	500	+1
Mitsui M. & S.	455	-7
Nippon Light Metal	841	+3
Nippon Mining	484	+14
Oki Elec Cable	681	-30
Optec Dai-Ichi Denko	596	-8
Osaka Titanium	—	
Ryobi	595	-6
Shimura Kako	850	+2
Showa Aluminum	718	-17
Showa El. W & C	712	+6
Sumitomo Elec.	1430	+40
Sumitomo L. Metal	550	-1
Sumitomo Metal M.	1100	-30
Tatsuta El. W & C	994	-36
Toho Zinc	706	+1
Totoku Electric	975	-4
Toyo Aluminum	870	+5
METAL PRODUCTS		
Bunka Shutter	2340	+40
Chugokukogyo	426	-5
Chuo Spring	760	
Hokkai Can	1780	
Kawada Industries	1280	-20
Komai Tekko	1840	-10
Matsuo Bridge	1130	
Miyaji Iron	580	
Neturen	1210	-40
NHK Spring	545	+10
Nihon Kentetsu	2000	
Nitto Seiko	710	-41
Noritz	1520	
Rinnai	760	
Sakurada	1190	
Sankyo Aluminum	1220	-20
Sanwa Shutter	1240	-40
Sanyo Industries	1380	+10
Tokyo Rope Mfg.	1020	+28
Topre	1550	
Toyo Exterior	3040	+20
Toyo Sash	3090	-140
Toyo Seikan	4600	+80
Toyo Shutter	3090	
Yokogawa Bridge	3260	-10
GENERAL MACHINERY		
Aichi Sharyo	2650	
Aida Engineering	851	-24
Amada	1040	-10
Amada Wasino	605	+3
Amadasonoke	743	+7
Amano	1790	-30
Asahi Diamond	1800	-30
Brother Ind.	577	-3
Chiyoda	1730	+100
CKD	785	-45
Daido Kogyo	530	-5
Daifuku	2220	+10
Daikin Industries	1460	-10
Djiet Industrial	801	+41
Ebara	1300	
Enshu	485	
Fujitec		
Hisaka Works	2260	+10

Source: TSE

Table G1 continued

Company	Price	Chg
Nishimatsu Const.	1250	+20
Nissan Const.	1460	+50
Nittoc Construction	1410	+20
Odakyu Const.	—	
Ohbayashi Corp	1170	+40
Ohbayashi Road	1650	
Okumura	1480	+30
Penta-Ocean Const.	815	+6
Raito Kogyo	2340	-40
S x L	1150	-40
Saeki Kensetsu	631	-4
Sanki Engineering	1810	-110
Sanko Metal Ind.	1360	+50
Sata Const.	1040	
Sato Kogyo	1390	+10
Seikitokyu Kogyo	875	
Sekisui House	1390	-10
Shimizu Corp	1580	+10
Sho-Bond Const.	—	
Shokusan Jutaku	670	-19
Sumitomo Const.	710	-15
Sumitomo Forestry	1370	-40
Tada Const	1210	
Taihei Dengyo	1400	+20
Taihei Kogyo	1200	+40
Taikisha	2600	+10
Taisei	1000	+6
Taisei Road Const.	1020	
Takasago Thermal	2820	-70
Tekken Const.	1160	+30
Toa Doro Kogyo	1050	
Toa Harbor Works	862	+2
Tobishima	878	-9
Toda Const.	1570	
Toenec	1640	
Tohoku Elec. Const.	3270	+90
Tokai Kogyo	1100	
Tokyo Denki K.	1710	
Tokyu Const.	1150	
Tomoegumi Iron W.	—	
Toshiba Eng & C.	1400	-20
Totetsu Kogyo	913	+18
Toyo Const.	669	-12
Toyo Telecom.	910	
Uekigumi	755	
Wakachiku Const.	1100	-20
Yondenko	1400	-100
FOOD PRODUCTS		
Ajinomoto	1550	-20
Asahi Breweries	1180	-30
Calpis Food Ind.	863	-10
Chukyo Coca-Cola	1450	-10
Ezaki Glico	970	-20
First Baking	650	-10
Fuji Oil	860	-50
Fujiya	700	-5
Godo Shusei	1300	
Hayashikane	472	
Honen	760	+11
House Food Ind.	1550	+20
Itoham Foods	810	-10
Kagome	1350	
Katokichi	2440	
Kikkoman	1050	
Kirin Brewery	1450	+10
Kyodo Shiryo	640	-20
Maruha Food	960	-16
Meiji Milk	708	-7
Meiji Seika	689	-1
Meito Sangyo	1890	
Mercian	1020	+39
Mikuni Coca-Cola	2510	
Mitsui Sugar	541	+5
Hokuetsu Paper	781	+26
Honshu Paper	1850	+90
Japan Paper Ind.	535	+20
Jujo Paper	645	...
Kanzaki Paper	665	
Mitsubishi Paper	675	+20
Nippon Kakoh	672	+2
Oji Paper	840	+30
Rengo	700	+13
Sanyo-Kokusaku	514	+5
Settsu Corp	730	-15
Takasaki Paper	400	+15
Tokai Pulp	758	+10
Tokushu Paper	964	...
Tomoegawa Paper	540	...
Tomoku	822	-18
CHEMICALS		
Aica Kogyo	722	-19
Asahi Denka Kogyo	847	+7
Asahi Organic Chem.	920	-2
Banyu Pharm.	1020	-20
Central Glass	528	-7
Chugai Pharm.	1050	...
Chugoku Marine P	520	-10
Co-Op Chemical	471	+6
Dai Nippon Toryo	474	-5
Dai-ichi Kogyo	875	+23
Daicel Chem. Ind.	720	+10
Daido Sanso	560	...
Daiichi Seiyaku	2200	-30
Dainichiseika	731	-19
Dainippon Ink	472	-1
Dainippon Pharm.	1870	+20
Denki Kagaku	455	-10
Eisai	1800	-30
Fuji Photo Film	3160	-30
Fujirebio	1210	-10
Fujisawa Pharm.	1520	+50
Fuso Pharm.		...
Green Cross	1050	+20
Gun-ei Chem. Ind.	1090	+40
Harima Chemicals	1180	+30
Hisamitsu Pharm.	895	+5
Hitachi Chem.	1280	...
Hodogaya Chem.	494	+4
Hokko Chem Ind	1100	...
Hokuriku Seiyaku	2300	...
Hoxan	850	...
Ibiden	790	-16
Ihara Chemical Ind.	650	+20
Ishihara Sangyo	488	+3
Japan Carlit	—	
Japan Syn. Rubber	572	...
Kaken Pharm.	1250	+20
Kanegafuchi Chem.	660	-1
Kansai Paint	636	-14
Kanto Denka Kogyo	535	-5
Kao	1210	+10
Koatsu Gas Kogyo	715	-50
Konica	830	-20
Kumiai Chem. Ind.	551	+1
Kureha Chem. Ind.	590	-19
Kyowa Hakko Kogyo	1010	-10
Lion	633	-7
Mitsubishi Gas C	520	+3
Mitsubishi Kasei	555	...
Mitsubishi Petro.	763	-13
Mitsubishi Plastics	635	-35
Mitsui Petrochem.	737	-1
Mitsui Toatsu	500	+10
Miyoshi Oil & Fat	536	+16
Mochida Pharm.	2380	+20
Showa Shell Sekiyu	1020	-70
Tonen	1450	+120
RUBBER PRODUCTS		
Achilles	519	-1
Bando Chem. Ind.	571	...
Bridgestone	989	-1
Kinugawa Rubber	560	+10
Mitsuboshi Belting	772	-9
Okamoto Ind.	720	-38
Sumitomo Rubber	730	-20
Toyo Tire & Rubber	625	-5
Yokohama Rubber	784	-16
GLASS & CERAMICS		
Asahi Glass	1260	+30
Ask	560	...
Chichibu Cement	1430	...
Daido Concrete	720	-5
Daichi Cement	895	-5
Danto	1380	+50
Inax	1090	-30
Ishizuka Glass	915	...
Kurosaki Refract.	609	-11
Misawa Resort	—	
NGK Insulators	1080	...
NGK Spark Plug	776	-17
Nichias	705	-5
Nihon Cement	1050	...
Nippon Carbon	551	-21
Nippon Concrete	890	+5
Nippon Elec. Glass	1300	-40
Nippon Hume	771	+10
Nippon Sheet G.	588	-3
Noritake	1510	-30
Onoda Cement	619	-6
Osaka Cement	565	+15
Sasaki Glass	616	+4
Shinagawa Refract.	1090	+60
Sumitomo Cement	610	-5
Tokai Carbon	646	+7
Tokyo Yogyo	820	+15
Toshiba Ceramics	691	-20
Toto	1590	...
Yamamura Glass	652	+22
IRON & STEEL		
Aichi Steel Works	630	-15
Asahi Tec	585	-10
Daido S. Sheet	850	-10
Daido Steel	555	-15
Godo Steel	1760	-10
Hitachi Metals	1260	+20
Japan Metals & C.	690	-9
Japan Steel Works	515	+10
Kanto Spec Steel	552	+2
Kawasaki Steel	415	+5
Kobe Steel	485	+15
Kurimoto	1210	-40
Maruichi S. Tube	1420	-10
Mitsubishi Steel	1270	+60
Mory Industries	1000	-20
Nakayama Steel	1010	+14
Nichia Steel	1000	...
Nippon Denko	654	+9
Nippon Kinzoku	511	-11
Nippon Koshuha	516	-14
Nippon Metal	551	-29
Nippon Pipe	1060	+50
Nippon Stainless	805	+3
Nippon Steel	459	+11
Nippon Yakin	591	+12
Nisshin Steel	549	+9
NKK	404	+2
Pacific Metals	530	+8
Hitachi Const.	1390	-10
Hitachi Seiki	810	-27
Howa Machinery	808	-17
Ikegai	443	-17
Iseki & Co.	539	i 4
Ishii Iron Works	720	...
Ishikawa Seisaku	628	+3
Iwata Air Compr	760	...
Janome Sewing	—	
Japan Organo	1190	
Juki	802	-61
Kato Works	980	-10
Kimura Chem. Plants	490	-10
Kioritz	471	+1
Kitagawa Iron	925	-15
Kitz	1000	-30
Komatsu	988	+19
Komori	4040	-10
Koyo Seiko	900	...
Kubota	641	-9
Kurita Water Ind.	2260	-10
Makino Milling	1070	-10
Maruyama Mfg.	470	+10
Max	2140	-40
Minebea	834	1
Mitsubishi Kakoki	635	...
Miura	1300	-40
Mori Seiki	2310	l 10
Morita Fire Pump	—	
Nachi-Fujikoshi	695	...
Nihon Spindle	669	-11
Niigata Eng.	624	+21
Nikkiso	900	-11
Nikko	945	...
Nippon Conveyor	929	-1
Nippon Piston	717	+17
Nippon Seiko	695	-10
Nippon Thompson	945	+5
NTN Toyo Bearing	715	...
O-M Ltd	548	...
Okuma & Howa Mach	840	-10
Okuma Machinery	1240	-10
Osaka Kiko	700	...
OSG Mfg.	1170	+20
Rheon A Mach	2010	...
Riken	545	-5
Sakai Heavy Ind.	1530	-20
Sanden	715	-10
Shibuya Kogyo	2480	-110
Silver Seiko	480	+20
Sintokogio	1580	-60
SMC	4880	-10
Sumitomo Heavy	551	+20
Sumitomo Precision	1210	-20
Takuma	1870	+20
Takara	755	-15
Teijin Seiki	—	
Tokyo Kikai Seisaku	925	-5
Torishima Pump	1270	-30
Toshiba Machine	854	-11
Toshiba Tungaloy	715	+5
Toyo Engineering	1270	+80
Toyo Kanetsu	710	-15
Toyo Umpanki	660	-35
Toyoda Machine	1020	-50
Toyota Auto Loom	2320	-30
Tsubakimoto Chain	730	...
Tsubakimoto Pre	2290	+10
Tsudakoma	1150	...
Tsugami	630	+15
Tsukishima Kikai	1070	-30
Tsurumi Mfg	1200	...

Table G1 continued

Company	Price	Chg
Yuken Kogyo	620	-10
Zexel	602	-13
ELECTRIC MACHINERY		
Advantest	3450	
Aiwa	1140	-40
Akai Electric	575	+17
Alps Electric	1290	+10
Amada Metrecs	2580	+30
Anritsu	1650	-50
Casio Computer	970	+7
Chino	636	+10
Claron	618	-3
CMK	2340	
Crown	3060	-120
Daihen	807	-18
Denki Kogyo	780	
Fanuc	4350	-100
Fuji Electric	775	+5
Fuji Electrochem	609	-1
Fujitsu	988	+8
Fujitsu General	551	+21
Furukawa Battery	550	+20
Futaba Corp.	3730	+10
Graphtec	1840	-30
Hirose Electric	4950	-80
Hitachi	1100	-30
Hitachi Koki	1180	-70
Hitachi Maxell	1840	+30
Hochiki	1420	-40
Hokuriku Elec Ind	602	-37
Horiba	—	
Idec Izumi	1040	+20
Ikegami Tsushinki	1200	
Iwasaki Electric	891	
Iwatsu Electric	705	+10
Japan Aviation Elec.	1050	-40
Japan Radio	2230	-30
Japan Storage	655	-10
Jeol	900	-4
JVC	1480	+20
Kenwood	676	-18
Keyence	10900	+400
Kinseki	2420	+20
Koa	685	+7
Kokusai Electric	3300	-80
Kyocera	5970	+100
Kyosan Electric	920	+5
Kyushu Matsushita	2350	-50
Mabuchi Motor	5200	
Makita Electric	1410	-10
Matsushita Com.	3260	+30
Matsushita E I	1560	-30
Matsushita Refri.	999	-31
Matsushita Seiko	861	-19
Meidensha	1140	+40
Mitsubishi Elec.	619	-18
Mitsumi Electric	1200	-20
Mshita Elec W	1550	+20
Mshita-Kotobuki	1510	-70
Murata Mfg.	2300	-40
NCR Japan	1300	-20
NEC	1290	
Nichicon	1090	
Nihon Kohden	1120	+50
Nippon Chemi-Con	775	-9
Nippon Columbia	900	+21
Nippon Elec. Ind.	547	-5
Nippon Signal	971	-11
Nippondenso	1590	-10
Nissin Electric	1040	-20
Nitsuko	877	-23
Nitto Denko	1070	
Ohkura Electric	980	—
Oki Electric	708	+13
Omron	1650	
Ono Sokki	1150	-10
Origin Electric	835	+4
Osaki Electric	1160	+40
Pioneer Electronic	3990	+80
Rohm	2060	+40
Sanken Elec.	714	-36
Sansui Electric	399	+9
Sanyo Electric	567	-31

Company	Price	Chg
Nissan Shatai	570	...
NOK	740	-10
Pacific Ind	505	+4
Press Kogyo	481	-14
Sasebo Heavy Ind.	756	+36
Shimano Ind.	4250	...
Shin Meiwa Ind.	1340	...
Shiroki	633	-7
Showa Mfg	591	+9
Suzuki Motor	620	+15
Tokico	565	+10
Tokyu Car	1090	-10
Topy Industries	501	-11
Toyo Radiator	931	-9
Toyota Auto Body	1040	+10
Toyota Motor	1750	...
Yamaha Motor	710	-11
PRECISION MACHINERY		
Aichi Tokei Denki	620	+18
Asahi Optical	552	-12
Canon	1270	-10
Citizen Watch	841	-5
Copal	630	+10
Dainippon Screen	1250	+20
Hoya	1830	-70
Japan Medical Supply	872	-11
Kimmon Mfg.	1040	+20
Minolta Camera	601	-7
Nikon	1050	+20
Olympus Optical	998	...
Rhythm Watch	549	-2
Ricoh	710	-5
Sankyo Seiki	800	...
Shimadzu	690	-6
Sokkisha	2060	...
Star Micronics	2850	-50
Tokimec	669	-3
Tokyo Seimitsu	1030	...
Topcon	1180	-10
OTHER PRODUCTS		
Asics	482	+1
Bandai	5910	+10
Dai Nippon Print.	1470	+20
Daiken Trade & Ind	695	-5
Daiwa Seiko	582	-3
Dantani Plywood	633	-5
France Bed	800	+10
Itoki Kosakusho	2400	-90
Juken Sangyo	665	+15
Kawai Musical	637	+7
Kokuyo	3150	-30
Kyodo Printing	2270	...
Lintec	—	
Mitsubishi Pencil	—	
Mutoh Industries	—	
Nakabayashi	749	+9
Nifco	1390	+20
Nintendo	18700	-200
Nippon Valqua	570	-11
Nissan Notvin	499	+6
Nissha Printing	1550	+30
Okamura	1470	-30
Pilot Pen	1100	+50
Sega Enterprises	11400	-100
Shin-Etsu Polymer	603	+13
Takara Standard	896	...
Toppan Printing	1370	+30
Tosho Printing	780	...
Toyo Linoleum	712	-8
Yamaha Corp	1720	+30
COMMERCE		
Best Denki	1320	-70
C. Itoh & Co.	697	+52
C. Itoh Fuel	851	-4
Cabin	1180	+60
Canon Sales	3410	...
Chori	900	+10
Chujitsuya	3250	...
D'urban	708	-4
Dai-Ichi Katei	—	
Daiei	1190	-30
Daiei Finance	—	
Daiichi Corp.¹	2300	+20

Company	Price	Chg
Renown	717	-20
Renown Look	—	
Restaurant Seibu	1440	+20
Royal	1810	+10
Ryosan	2060	+90
San-ai Oil	841	...
Sankyo Seiko	1180	-10
Sanrio	3500	-120
Sanyo Shokai	880	...
Sato Shoji	—	
Seibu Credit	1920	+20
Seika Sangyo	580	-5
Seiyu	1560	-10
Senshukai	2700	+10
Seven-Eleven	6590	+110
Shinko Shoji	1030	+10
Shinsho	620	+11
Shoko	497	+4
Sinanen	1000	-10
Skylark	2230	...
Sogo	1000	...
Sotetsu Rosen	—	
Sumitomo Corp.	1010	-10
Suntelephone	1360	+10
Suzutan	1910	+60
Taka-Q	1190	+40
Takashima & Co.	660	+3
Takashimaya	2170	-30
TEC Electronics	996	+6
Tobu Store	1020	-40
Tohto Suisan	555	+3
Tokai	704	-13
Tokyo Electron	2780	-40
Tokyo Nissan	1100	...
Tokyo Style	1450	-50
Tokyu Depart.	1450	+10
Tokyu Store	1000	-10
Tomen	540	+25
Toshoku	1340	+30
Totenko	975	-24
Toyo Corp	1040	-10
Toyota Tsusho	810	-20
Tsubakimoto Mach.	850	-20
Tsukamoto Shoji	1130	+60
Uchida Yoko	1070	-20
Uni-Charm	1300	...
Uny	1450	+30
Viva Home	3050	-150
Yamazen	1000	-50
Yaohan Depart.	1300	-40
Yhama Mzakaya	—	
York-Benimaru	3440	+40
Yuasa Shoji	879	-17
Yuasa Trading	498	-5
Zenchiku	487	-13
BANKING & INSURANCE		
Akita Bank	666	-19
Aomori Bank	670	...
Ashikaga Bank	1040	-10
Awa Bank	665	-10
Bank of Fukuoka	940	-1
Bank of Hiroshima	920	-40
Bank of Ikeda	—	
Bank of Iwate	5210	...
Bank of Kinki	—	
Bank of Kyoto	2080	...
Bank of Nagoya	1160	-20
Bank of Okinawa	—	
Bank of Osaka	—	
Bank of Ryukyus	6440	-50
Bank of Saga	670	-10
Bank of Tokyo	1070	-10
Bank of Yokohama	1020	-40
Central Finance	540	-20
Chiba Bank	930	+5
Chiba Kogyo Bank	7280	...
Chiyoda F. & M.	763	+2
Chugoku Bank	—	
Chukyo Bank	850	...
Chuo T. & B.	2560	...

Company	Price	Chg
Nishi-Nippon Bk	749	-16
Nissan F. & M.	4090	...
Nisshin F. & M.	692	+10
Nomura Securities	1820	+50
Ogaki Kyoritsu Bk	692	+2
Oita Bank	980	+10
Okasan Securities	870	+20
Orient Finance	944	-30
Orix	2720	+10
Saitama Bank	1000	+4
San-in Godo Bank	900	...
Sanwa Bank	1930	...
Sanyo Securities	862	-3
Shiga Bank	1000	...
Shikoku Bank	765	...
Shimizu Bank	—	
Shinwa Bank	—	
Shizuoka Bank	1000	...
Sumitomo Bank	2000	+10
Sumitomo Leasing	1220	+20
Sumitomo M. & F.	975	+30
Sumitomo T. & B.	1590	+10
Suruga Bank	970	...
Taiheiyo Sec	915	...
Taisei F&M	909	-1
Taisho M. & F.	976	+40
Tochigi Bank	1710	...
Toho Bank	850	+20
Tokai Bank	1410	-20
Tokio M. & F.	1350	+30
Tokuyo City Bank	530	+25
Tokyo Securities	821	...
Tokyo Sowa Bank	1360	...
Tokyo Tomin Bank	8700	+100
Toyo Securities	946	+2
Toyo T. & B.	1760	+40
Wako Securities	875	-2
Yamagata Bank	711	...
Yamaguchi Bank	1100	...
Yamaichi Sec.	959	+14
Yamanashi Chuo Bk	840	-31
Yamatane Sec.	1350	...
Yasuda F. & M.	910	+20
Yasuda T. & B.	1590	+10
77 Bank	758	+1
REAL ESTATE		
Daikyo	1570	+20
Daiwa Danchi	1000	-70
Heiwa R. Estate	1060	+50
L Kakuei	410	...
Mitsubishi Estate	1400	...
Mitsui R. Estate	1250	...
Nichimo	980	-30
Odakyu Real Estate	600	+1
Osaka Building	1100	...
Sankei Building	1180	...
Sumitomo Realty	955	+5
Taiheyo Kouhatsu	440	-14
TOC	—	
Toho Real Estate	1100	...
Tokyo Rakutenchi	714	-16
Tokyo Tatemono	760	-15
Tokyu Land	586	+1
Towa Real Estate	529	-1
LAND TRANSPORTATION		
Fuji Kyuko	—	
Fukuyama Trans.	1220	+20
Hakone Tozan	880	...
Hankyu Corp.	670	+25
Hanshin Elec. Ry.	535	+10
Hitachi Transport	1270	+60
Japan Oil Transp.	700	...
Kanagawa Chuo	1350	...
Keihin Elec Exp	841	+10
Keio Teito	825	...
Keisei Elec. Ry.	1300	...
Kinki Nippon Ry.	765	+3
Maruun	900	...
Maruzen Showa	667	...
Nagoya Railroad	673	-12
Nippon Express	755	...
Nishi-Nippon	610	-10
Nissin Corp	700	...
Odakyu Elec. Ry.	834	-30
Sanami Railway	663	-7

Table G1 concluded

Company	Price	Chg
Sawafuji Elec.t.	570	+4
Sharp	1160	...
Shibaura Engi.	730	-40
Shin-Kobe Electric	—	...
Shindengen Elec.	705	-20
Shinko Electric	830	-5
Shintom	661	-8
SMK	661	-8
Sony	5990	+150
Stanley Electric	745	+5
Sumitomo S. Metals	1320	...
Tabai Espec	1480	...
Taiyo Yuden	795	-20
Takaoka Elec.	953	...
Tamura Electric	2040	...
Tamura Seisakusho	745	-20
TDK	4190	-10
TEAC	893	-7
Teikoku Tsushin	939	-11
Tokai Rika	1290	-10
Tokin	1220	-20
Toko	666	...
Toko Electric	706	...
Tokyo Elec Co	621	-19
Toshiba	700	-6
Toyo Comm	2380	-70
Toyo Denki Seizo	—	...
Uniden	2000	...
Ushio	815	-5
Yamatake-H'ywell	1530	+10
Yaskawa Elec.	652	-13
Yokogawa Elec	1150	+10
Yuasa Battery	990	-9
TRANSPORT EQUIPMENT		
Aichi Machine	585	...
Aisin Seiki	1120	-50
Akebono Brake	722	-23
Araya Industrial	—	...
Atsugi Unisia	735	...
Calsonic	565	...
Daihatsu Motor	550	-16
Fuji Car Mfg.	790	+1
Fuji Heavy Ind	442	-4
Futaba Ind	1580	-40
Hino Motors	923	...
Hitachi Zosen	478	+13
Honda Motor	1250	-40
Ichikoh Ind	492	-39
IHI	675	+5
Isuzu Motors	505	-1
Japan Aircraft	865	+15
Kanto Auto Works	889	-11
Kanto Seiki	768	+8
Kawasaki Heavy	530	+14
Kayaba Industry	581	-4
Kiriki Sharyo	605	...
Koito Mfg.	3030	...
Komatsu Forklift	1460	...
Komatsu Zenoah	675	+10
Mazda Motor	568	...
Mitsuba Electric	959	+11
Mitsubishi Heavy	685	+17
Mitsubishi Motors	710	...
Mitsui E & Shipbldg	548	+23
Nippon Air Brake	1200	...
Nippon Sharyo	1200	+10
Nippon Yusoki	1190	-20
Nissan Diesel	552	-23
Nissan Motor	696	-4

Company	Price	Chg
Daiichi Jitsugyo	819	+29
Daimaru	900	+9
Denny's Japan	3590	+90
Descente	585	...
FamilyMart	9370	-210
Fuji Denki Reiki	1620	-80
Fuji & Co.	—	...
Gastec Service	1000	...
Gunze Sangyo	920	-9
Hankyu Depart.	1340	-40
Hanwa	2090	-60
Hattori Seiko	4250	-40
Heiwado	1560	+60
Hitachi Sales	696	...
Ichida & Co.	805	-11
Inabata & Co.	648	...
Inageya	2820	-40
Isetan	2220	+10
Ito-Yokado	3650	+100
Itoman & Co.	447	+12
Iwatani Intl	860	+3
Izumi	1640	+80
Izumiya	—	...
Izutsuya	598	-2
Japan Pulp & P	628	-12
Joshin Denki	2260	...
Jujiya	570	-5
Jusco	1390	-70
Kamei	1090	+10
Kanaden	1440	-40
Kanematsu	635	+22
Kasho	—	...
Kasumi	—	...
Kawasho	525	-5
Keiyo Co	2700	-50
Kinsho-Mataichi	485	-16
Kyotaru	—	...
Life Stores	1000	-20
Marubeni	691	+31
Maruei Depart.	970	...
Maruetu	1510	-50
Maru	2100	-20
Maruzen	1060	+30
Matsuya	950	-31
Matsuzakaya	4600	-160
Meiwa Trading	480	...
Mitsubishi Corp.	1380	+10
Mitsui & Co	792	+24
Mitsukoshi	1150	-10
Mitsuuroko	850	+9
Mizuno	1460	-20
Mutow Co.	1210	-20
Nagasakiya	2300	...
Nagase & Co.	962	-38
Naigai	920	...
Nichiei	867	-21
Nichii	1490	+50
Nichimen	530	+15
Nichimo	—	...
Nihon Matai	785	+4
Nihon Unisys	2760	+60
Nippon Gas	—	...
Nissei Sangyo	1600	...
Nissho Iwai	557	+6
Nozaki & Co.	590	...
Okura & Co.	850	...
Onward Kashiyama	1700	+10
OSG Corp.	1130	+30
Parco	—	...

Company	Price	Chg
Cosmo Securities	820	-10
Dai-ichi Kangyo Bk	1990	+40
Dai-ishi Sei	800	...
Dai-Tokyo F. & M.	790	...
Daichi Sogo Bk	—	...
Daisan Bank	814	+4
Daishi Bank	930	-15
Daiwa Bank	1260	...
Daiwa Securities	1170	+30
Diamond Lease	1440	...
Dowa F. & M.	770	-10
Ehime Bank	1040	...
Eighteenth Bank	665	-5
Fuji Bank	2440	...
Fuji F. & M.	940	-60
Fukui Bank	750	...
Fukuoka City Bank	1750	...
Fukutoku Bank	—	...
Gunma Bank	920	+1
Hachijuni Bank	1150	...
Hanshin Bank	—	...
Higashi-Nippon Bank	—	...
Higo Bank	697	-8
Hiroshima-Sogo Bk	1030	+20
Hitachi Credit	1300	-30
Hokkaido Bank	585	-5
Hokkaido Takushoku	770	-16
Hokkoku Bank	940	...
Hokuetsu Bank	770	...
Hokuriku Bank	1040	+20
Hyakugo Bank	780	...
Hyakujushi Bank	795	...
Hyogo Bank	1640	...
Industrial Bank	3270	-30
Iyo Bank	930	...
Jaccs	491	+1
Japan Sec. Finance	1400	+120
Joyo Bank	887	+7
Juroku Bank	795	+20
Kagoshima Bank	637	-10
Kankaku Securities	842	+3
Kanto Bank	5350	+50
Keiyo Bank	919	...
Kita-Nippon Bank	—	...
Kiyo Bank	675	+5
Koa F. & M.	830	+1
Kokusai Securities	1390	+10
Kyowa Bank	1050	+20
Kyushu Bank	1000	+20
Long-T Credit Bk	1390	-20
Maruman Sec	1290	...
Marusan Sec	1440	...
Michinoku Bank	—	...
Mitsubishi Bank	2150	+70
Mitsubishi T. & B.	1820	+20
Mitsui T. & B.	1490	+30
Mitsui Taiyo Kobe Bank	1950	+50
Miyazaki Bank	—	...
Musashino Bank	6270	-90
Nanto Bank	—	...
National Sec.	950	...
New Japan Sec.	762	-8
Nichiboshin	1480	+30
Nichido F. & M.	800	...
Niigata Chuo Bank	620	-10
Nikko Securities	960	+3
Nippon Credit Bk	8710	-190
Nippon F. & M.	761	-19
Nippon H Loan	982	...
Nippon Shinpan	839	-1
Nippon Trust Bank	869	-11

Company	Price	Chg
Sankyu	483	...
Seibu Railway	3400	-300
Seino Transport	1980	-30
Senko	754	-11
Tobu Railway	753	...
Tokyu Corp.	1110	-20
Tonami Transport	770	-7
Yamato Transport	1150	-30
MARINE & AIR TRANSPORT		
All Nip. Airways	1340	+60
Daichi Chuo K	492	-9
Iino Kaiun	1020	-30
Inui Steamship	481	+11
JAL	1090	+10
Kansai Kisen	375	-5
Kawasaki Kisen	445	+10
Kokusai Kogyo	1480	...
Kyoei Tanker	495	+5
Meiji Shipping	1000	...
Mitsui O.S.K.	486	+5
Navix Line	515	+30
Nippon Yusen	578	+23
Pasco	980	+20
Shinwa Kaiun	443	+6
Showa Line	490	+20
Taiheiyo Kaiun	385	-5
WAREHOUSING & COMM.		
Gakken	1290	-50
Kamigumi	930	-6
KDD	11000	...
Keihin	830	...
Mitsubishi Whs.	1500	+50
Mitsui Whs.	980	...
Nippon TV	20200	+290
NTT*	9990	+190
Shibusawa Whs.	799	-19
Sumitomo Whs.	695	-14
TBS	2030	+10
Toyo Wharf & Whs	543	-7
Utoku Express	869	-17
Yamatane Corp.	968	+18
Yokkaichi Whs.	1010	-30
ELECTRIC POWER & GAS		
Chubu Elec Power	2850	+80
Chugoku E Power	2460	+60
Hokkaido E Power	2430	+30
Hokkaido Gas	549	+19
Hokuriku E Power	2570	+80
Kansai E Power	3050	+90
Kyushu E Power	2500	+110
Osaka Gas	499	+1
Saibu Gas	485	...
Shikoku E Power	2530	+50
Toho Gas	454	-10
Tohoku E Power	2600	+80
Tokyo Elec Power	3800	+150
Tokyo Gas	579	+14
SERVICES		
Asatsu	5500	...
Chisan-Tokan	920	-15
CSK Corp.	4040	...
Dai-ichi Hotel	1300	-20
Daiwa Kosho Lease	1400	+20
Fujita Tourist	—	...
Gajoen Kanko	1290	-10
Hakuyosha	1280	...
Ines	2940	+30
Intec	2810	-40
Joban Kosan	810	+5
Kinki N Tourist	1160	-60
Konami Industry	5570	-10
Nikkatsu	367	+19
Secom	4140	...
Shochiku	3880	+50
Subaru Enterprise	849	...
Toei	930	-10
Toho	27700	...
Tokai Kanko	423	+53
Tokyo Dome	3190	+90
Tokyo Theatres	801	-9
Tokyotokeiba	755	-15
Tokyu Hotel Chain	1510	-60
Tokyu Tourist	800	...
Yomiuri Land	1520	-40
Yoshimoto Kogyo	—	...

Table G2

Closing Prices of the Stocks on the Second Section of the TSE on January 4, 1991, in Yen

FARM, MINING & CONST.

Stock	Price	Change
Chitose El Const	—	—
Chugai Mining	850	+50
Chuo Build Ind	981	+1
Daiwa Const	1340	...
Hibiya Engineer	15300	...
Hoan Kogyo	—	—
Hokuriku Elec. Const.	764	+4
Inoue Kogyo	763	+3
Ishihara Const	560	+28
Kodensha	2540	...
Kokune Const	908	-61
Miyaji Const	—	—
NEC System	—	—
Nippon Tetrapod	820	-16
Nisseki House	615	-3
Ohki Const	992	...
P.S. Concrete	9700	...
Sanwa-Daiei Elec	520	-10
Sanyo Engineer	946	+5
Shin Nippon Air	2980	-10
Showa Mining	415	...
Sumitomo Densetsu	1750	...
Suzunui Ind	—	—
Taisei Prefab	—	—
Tatsumura Gumi	—	—
Tohoku Telecom	6000	...
Toyoko Riken	1200	...
Yamato Setsubi	1400	+10
FOOD PRODUCTS		
Boso Oil & Fat	480	-5
Bull-Dog Sauce	—	—
Chubu Shiryo	675	-15
Ensuiko Sugar	570	-15
Fuji Seito	—	—
Hkaido Coca-Cola	—	—
Ishii Food	—	—
Kanro	—	—
Mihiro Shokuhin	720	...
Myojo Foods	949	-21
Nihon Shokuhin	571	...
Nihon Sugar	—	—
Nikka Whisky	1550	+10
Nissin Sugar	—	—
Oriental Yeast	—	—
S&B Shokuhin	—	—
Snow Brand Food	685	+10
Sonton Food	1200	...
Surugaya	—	...
Tofuku Flour	600	...
Torigoe Flour	480	-1
Yokohama Reito	1310	+10
TEXTILES		
AuBex	939	...
Carolina	660	+5
Chuo Woolen Mills	440	...
Hirabo	475	+15
Hotta Textile	—	—
Jomo Twisting	376	+4
Kitanihon Spin	565	...
Nankai Worsted	865	-64
Nihon Seima	352	-5
Saibo.	—	—

Stock	Price	Change
Ube Chemical	—	—
METALS		
Ahresty	—	—
Automobile Found	—	—
Chuo Denki Kogyo	780	-35
Daiwa Heavy Ind	—	—
Hitachi Powdered	675	...
Hitachi Tool Eng	1060	...
J Steel Tower	—	—
Japan Casting	949	-1
Kato Spring	521	+1
Kawagishi Bridge	2200	-60
Kawaguchi Metal	820	...
KDK	—	—
Kokoku Steel	529	...
Kyosan El Wire	3480	+30
Kyoto Die-Casting	—	—
Nasu Denki	—	—
New Tachikawa	3350	...
Nihon Mining	450	...
Nihon Seikan	—	—
Nippon Chutetsu	—	...
Nippon Filcon	1450	+20
Nippon Foil	430	...
Nippon Seisen	990	...
Nippon Shindo	371	...
Okabe	—	—
Riken Elec Wire	480	...
Shin Nikkei	2350	-50
Suzuki Metal	625	...
Takasago Tekko	—	—
Takigami Steel	—	...
TDF	882	...
Toho Titanium	1100	-30
Tokyo Knife	646	+5
Tokyo Rika Mfg	—	—
Tokyo Shearing	511	-20
Tokyo Sintered	—	—
Tokyo Tungsten	1170	...
Toshiba Steel	411	-33
Toyo Steel Mfg	1460	-20
GENERAL MACHINERY		
Akasaka Diesels	611	...
Amatsuji Steel	—	—
Copyer	690	-30
Daito Seiki	—	—
DMW	—	—
Eagle Industry	1190	-10
Fuji Ribon Ind	443	...
Fuso Ind Works	—	—
Hamai	587	+5
Hitachi Tomioka	500	...
Ishii Precision	830	...
Kiriu Machine	—	—
Koike Sanso	855	-1
Kojima Iron	707	+7
Koyo Iron Works	—	—
Meiji Machine	463	+1
Misawa-Van	799	...
Miyairi Valve	385	-10
Nip Carbureter	—	—
Nip Typewriter	1320	...
Nippei Toyama	850	...
Nippon Gear	—	—
Nittan Valve	741	+6
Okamoto Machine	580	-10
Okano Valve	—	—
Oye Kogyo	—	—
Sanjo Machine	732	+8
Sanko Engineer	735	-5
Seirei Industry	730	...
Shin Nippon Mach	—	—
Shinkawa	3240	+40
Shoun Machine	754	...
SNT	1530	+20
Sodick	1520	+30
Sumikura Ind	—	—
Takakita	—	—
Takisawa Machine	920	+20
Tanifuji Machine	490	...
Teikoku Piston	560	+5
Toa Valve	468	+9
Tokyo Automatic	—	—

Stock	Price	Change
Keihin Seiki Mfg	551	...
Maruishi Cycle	—	—
Meiwa Industry	620	-30
Mikuni Corp	468	...
Miyata Industry	1170	-20
Nichibei Fuji	—	—
Nippon Seiki	1870	-30
Nitchitsu Ind	1390	...
Showa Aircraft	1580	...
Tachi-S	—	—
Tochigi Fuji Ind	1460	-40
Tokyo Buhin	610	...
Tokyo Radiator	—	—
PRECISION MACHINES		
Canon Elec	940	...
Chinon Ind	650	...
Jeco	1010	-20
Kawasumi Lab	1400	...
Kuroda Precision	785	...
Orient Watch	—	—
Oval Engineering	584	+9
Ricoh Elemex	2050	+40
Riken Keiki	636	+6
Sekonic	—	—
Sony Magne	—	—
Tokyo Sokuhan	1600	...
Tokyokoki	500	...
Union Optical	—	—
OTHER PRODUCTS		
Cleanup	2800	+40
JSP	1710	...
Melx	—	—
Mitsumura Print	1290	-10
Miura Printing	—	—
Nippon	—	—
Nozaki Insatsu	699	-10
Olympic	580	...
Sailor Pen	1300	-20
Sun Wave	—	—
Tachikawa Corp	—	—
Takara	3120	...
Tenma	2850	...
COMMERCE		
Aderans	1450	...
Aoki Intl	7900	-50
Aoyama Trading	11700	...
Chiyoda	5930	...
Chuo Gyorui	—	—
Chuo Subaru	—	—
Daito Gyorui	1060	...
Fujitsu B System	7700	...
Iwaki & Co	565	-10
Kaga Electronics	1550	-50
Kanematsu Elec	1180	+10
Kosugi Sangyo	600	...
Kyokuto Boeki	—	—
Lapine	690	...
LEC	—	—
Marufuji Sheet	1830	-90
Marusho	1010	...
MOS Food	4550	-180
Nagahori	1240	...
Narasaki Sangyo	620	-15
Oak & Co	1440	...
Rikei	949	...
Ryoden Trading	1050	...
Ryoyo Electro	2400	-90
Sagami	1300	+20
Saikaya	—	—
Sanshin Elec	2680	+40
Sapporo Lion	1970	...
Shimachu	3100	...
Shimamura	—	—
Shinko Sangyo	410	...
Shoei Foods	941	...
Soda Nikka	910	-10
Somar	—	—
Tachikawa Co	—	—
Tokyo Isuzu	800	...
Tokyo Sangyo	520	-10
Tokyo Soir	970	...
Tokyo Toyota	—	—
Tsukiji Uoichiba	—	—

Source: TSE

Table G2 concluded

Company	Price	Chg	Company	Price	Chg	Company	Price	Chg
Saitama Seni	445	...	Toyo Eng Works	—	...	Tsuzuki	1180	60
Shoei	—	...	Trinity Ind	—	...	Xebio	5260	...
Soto Kogyo	1100	+20	Uchida Oil	655	+6	Yuasa Funashoku	505	-10
Tokyo Ramie	440	...	Unozawa-gumi Iron	661	...	**FINANCE & REAL ESTATE**		
Tosco	—	...	Yamada	1020	-40	Cesar	1200	...
PULP & PAPER			**ELECTRIC MACHINERY**			Daiichi Housing Loan	1740	...
Chiyoda Shigyo	689	+10	Alpine Elec	—	...	Dia Construction	3000	-150
Chuetsu	445	-4	Ando Electric	1470	-20	Ichiyoshi Sec	—	...
Mishima Paper	—	...	Daido Signal	—	...	Kagawa Bank	—	...
Superbag	—	...	Denyo	—	...	Meiko Securities	—	...
Taihei Paper	1900	...	Elna	610	...	Mito Securities	—	...
Tokyo Serofan	570	...	Enplas	2250	...	Mitsui R. Estate Sales	2780	+30
CHEMICALS			Foster Electric	700	+5	North Pacific Bank	—	...
Cemedine	—	...	Fujitsu Denso	1550	...	Tachihi Enterprise	5870	...
Daiki Engineering	—	...	Fujitsu Kiden	2560	+10	Takagi Sec	—	...
Eiken Chemical	—	...	Hitachi AIC	675	...	Tokyo Leasing	1780	-30
Fudow	550	-10	Hitachi Electron	1130	...	Towa Bank	—	...
Fuji Titanium	749	...	Japan Resistor	444	-1	Universal Sec	1200	...
Fujikura Kasei	550	...	Japan Servo	449	-2	Yuraku Real	620	-11
Fujikura Rubber	701	+10	Kanda Tsushin	591	+5	**TRANSPORTATION**		
Fumakilla	470	-7	Kasuga Electric	1340	...	Asia Air Survey	—	...
Heisei Polymer	559	-2	Kawasaki Elec	—	...	Daiwa Motor	—	...
Honshu Chem Ind	615	...	Koito Industries	—	...	Fuji Kisen	—	...
Ise Chemicals	1520	...	Kokusan Denki	559	...	Hinode Kisen	411	+16
Katakura Chikkarin	630	-20	Kyoei Sangyo	811	...	Izuhakone Rail	—	...
Kawaguchi Chem	485	-30	Kyowa El Inst	750	...	Izukyu	6300	...
Kawasaki Kasei	700	...	Lead	990	-50	Kuribayashi Steam	—	...
Kibun Food Chem	—	...	Marantz Japan	1060	+10	Nihonkai Steam	340	+15
Kissei Pharm	4450	-50	Meisei Electric	640	-10	Nippon Konpo	800	...
Kodama Chemical	505	-15	Mitsui High-tec	2400	...	Sea-Com	2150	-50
Lonseal	374	-1	Mori Denki Mfg	—	...	Shin Yei Steam	—	...
Misawa Ceramic	—	...	Morio Denki	—	...	Shin-Keisei Elec	—	...
Morishita Jintan	—	...	Nakamichi	701	+1	Sotetsu Trans	1500	...
Nihon Kagaku	—	...	Nakayo Telecom	—	...	Taiyo Kaiun	—	...
Nihon Tokushu	1230	+20	Nihon Dempa Kogyo	3550	...	Tokai Kisen	950	...
Nippon Pigment	—	...	Nihon Inter	590	-10	Tokyo Kisen	955	...
Nippon Seiro	435	...	Nikko Electric	—	...	Tokyo Senpaku	353	-24
Nissui Pharm.	—	...	Nippon Avionics	985	+4	**WAREHOUSING & GAS**		
Nitto Kako	365	-1	Nippon Conlux	1250	+30	Asagami	—	...
Oriental Photo	710	+10	Nippon Tungsten	—	...	Fushiki Kairiku	—	...
Plas-Tech	—	...	Nishishiba Elec	569	-1	Inui Tatemono	—	...
Riken Vitamin	—	...	Nitto Elec Works	3020	-60	Keiyo Gas	—	...
S.T. Chemical	1520	+30	Nohmi Bosai	—	...	Maruhachi Whs	751	...
Sagami Rubber	—	...	Okaya Elec Ind	—	...	Mitsui Wharf	951	-4
Sakura Rubber	760	...	Sanoh Ind	780	...	Nihonbashi Whs	750	...
Showa Chemical	680	...	Sanyo Denki	921	+20	Niigata Rinko	930	...
Showa Rubber	—	...	Shinko Elec Ind	1700	+80	Sanwa Soko	630	...
Showa Tansan	600	-11	Shizuki Elec	611	-19	3S Shinwa	1120	...
Teikoku Hormone	3250	-10	Sony Chemical	—	...	**SERVICES**		
Teraoka Seisaku	1120	-20	SPC Electronics	—	...	CEC	—	...
Toa Oil	400	+15	Taiko Elec Works	486	...	Central Security	—	...
Toho Acetylen	367	+2	Takamisawa Elec	522	-18	Giken Kogyo	1150	...
Toho Chemical	750	...	Tensho Elec	—	...	Hitachi Software	4350	-110
Tokyo Printing	—	...	Toa Electronics	819	...	Imperial Hotel	—	...
Toshiba Chemical	1440	-10	Togami Elec Mfg	610	...	Japan Airport Terminal	2190	-10
Toyo Bosuifu	—	...	Tokyo Cosmos	555	...	Kabukiza	—	...
Tsurumi Soda	760	+10	Towa Electron	510	+10	Kagetsuenkanko	1750	...
Wakodo	9000	...	Towa Espo	550	+10	KFC Japan	5360	...
Yuki Gosei	825	...	Toyo Takasago	—	...	Marubeni Const	1110	+10
Yushiro Chemical	—	...	U-shin	1510	...	Musashino Kogyo	—	...
GLASS & CERAMICS			uniden 21	770	...	Namco	2650	-40
Arisawa Mfg	—	...	Y E Data	1040	...	Nikken Kogaku	730	-20
Asahi Concrete	1610	+10	**TRANSPORT EQUIPMENT**			Nippon B Consult	2740	-10
Asano Slate	512	-2	Fuji Kiko	827	-23	Nissho Electronics	2260	-20
Haneda Hume Pipe	750	+7	Fuji Tekko	960	-20	Nittetsu Shoji	869	+9
Ishikawajima Const.	1220	...	Hashimoto Form	560	...	Ohba	—	...
Iwaki Glass	680	...	Hino Auto Body	696	...	SRL	3250	...
Nippon Crucible	1000	...	Ikeda Bussan	—	...	Sumisho Computer	2810	-40
Nippon Muki	720	...	Jidosha Buhin	449	...	Sunseisha	5040	-260
Riken Corundum	599	...	Jidosha Denki	—	...	TKC	2960	...
Teihyu	—	...	Jidosha Kiki	844	-10	Toei Chemical	607	...
Tokai Konetsu	—	...	Kansai Kogyo	—	...	Tokai Lease	2540	+40
Toyo Carbon	456	...				Tokyo Kaikan	—	...
Toyo Pile Hume	5910	...				Tokyu Recreation	1210	...
						Toyo Information	3300	—

The TSE foreign stock market opened in December 1973. Keeping pace with the recent expansion of the foreign stock market shown in Table G3, the trading hours for foreign stocks were extended from 10:30-11:00 and 14:30-15:00 to 9:00-11:00 and 13:00-15:00, respectively, on January 4, 1986.

Foreign firms find that being listed on the TSE-FS is a symbol of a long term commitment and makes recruiting easier. There are 120 firms listed and some expect to see 20 to 30 new listings a year. On the TSE-FS, the opening price is based on the previous day's closing price in the main exchange abroad so it is not a real independent market but a facilitator of trade. Japan's Big Four have recently been pushing the TSE-FS stocks as a bargain. Since January 1990, Motorola's yen-based stock has risen 50%. Institutional investors, on the other hand, buy the shares on foreign markets.

Foreign stocks did well on the TSE in 1990. From January to June 1990, the foreign section outperformed the NSA 225, see Figure G1. They were up 15% versus the NSA, which was down 10%. Volume was also at a record. In 1989, 480 million shares valued at ¥2.8 trillion were traded on the TSE-FS, more than on five of the eight exchanges in Japan. Ownership has increased with more than 210,000 Japanese owning foreign section stocks, a four-fold increase since 1985.

Figure G1   Foreign Section versus NSA225

Source: *JEJ*, July 21, 1990

The daily average trading value continues to increase, reflecting the increase in the number of listed corporations and the growing interest in foreign stocks among Japanese investors. Table G3 lists the foreign corporations trading as of the end of 1989, and Table G4 gives the volume and value of these stocks listed on the TSE from 1982 to 1989.

Table G5 gives the current listing of foreign stocks on the TSE and their closing values on December 28, 1990.

Table G3   Volume and Value of Foreign Stocks Listed on the TSE, 1982-90

	Trading Days	Listing	Delisting	Number, year end	Volume Total	Daily Average	Value ¥ mil Total	Share-holders
1982	285			12	1271	4.5	64.1	na
1983	286			11	4974	17.4	113.6	na
1984	287			11	4522	15.8	324.5	na
1985	285	10	-	21	131424	461.1	2994.2	55598
1986	279	31	-	52	309701	1110	4128.5	128714
1987	274	36	-	88	755203	2756	12661	192234
1988	273	26	2	112	216332	792	2913	203755
1989	249	10	3	119	480193	1928	11235	212935
1990 *		1	-	120	120842	1206	13812	na

*January to May

Table G4   Foreign Securities Listed on the TSE, End of 1989

	Date of Listing	Industrial Classification	Unit of Trading (Shares)
Australia			
Broken Hill Proprietary	Apr. 12, 1988	Mining	1,000
Elders IXL	June 28, 1988	Commerce	1,000
National Australia Bank	Sept. 6, 1985	Finance and Insurance	1,000
News Corp.	Apr. 27, 1989	Communication	1,000
Pacific Dunlop	Feb. 25, 1987	Rubber Products	1.000
Westpac Banking Corp.	May 9, 1986	Finance and Insurance	1,000
Canada			
Alcan Aluminum	June 20, 1989	Nonferrous Metals	1,000
BCE Inc.	Nov. 19, 1985	Communication	50
Canadian Imperial Bank of Commerce	Sept. 9, 1986	Finance and Insurance	1,000
Northern Telecom	Nov. 12, 1986	Electric Appliances	100
Royal Bank of Canada	Oct. 17, 1986	Finance and Insurance	100
Royal Trustco	Dec. 19,1986	Finance and Insurance	100
Toronto-Dominion Bank	May 13, 1986	Finance and Insurance	100
France			
Compagnie Financière de Paribas	Dec. 23, 1988	Finance and Insurance	50
Compagnie Générale d'Electricitè	Dec. 20, 1988	Electric Appliances	100
Germany			
Bayer AG	Oct. 26, 1988	Chemicals	50
Commerzbank AG	Oct. 1, 1986	Finance and Insurance	10
Deutsche Bank AG	Nov. 9, 1989	Finance and Insurance	10
Dresdner Bank AG	Oct. 24, 1985	Finance and Insurance	50
Volkswagen AG	Dec. 2, 1988	Transportation Equipment	50
Netherlands			
Aegon N.V.	Oct. 4, 1988	Finance and Insurance	100
N.V. Gemeenschappelijk Bezit van Aandeelen Philips' Gloeilampenfabrieken	Sept. 30, 1988	Electric Appliances	1,000
ROBECO N.V.	Dec. 8, 1976	Finance and Insurance	50
Spain			
Telefónica Nacional de España S.A.	Oct. 4, 1985	Communication	1,000
Sweden			
AGA AB	Dec. 10, 1986	Chemicals	100
AB VOLVO	Dec. 12, 1986	Transportation Equipment	50
Pharmacia AB	Feb. 26, 1987	Chemicals	100
Switzerland			
CS Holding	Feb. 18, 1988	Finance and Insurance	1
Swiss Bank Corporation	Dec. 15, 1987	Finance and Insurance	10
Union Bank of Switzerland	Dec. 24, 1985	Finance and Insurance	1
United Kingdom			
Barclays PLC	Aug. 1, 1986	Finance and Insurance	1,000
BOC Group PLC	July 25, 1989	Chemcials	1,000
British Gas PLC	Sept. 29, 1988	Electric Power and Gas	1,000
British Petroleum Company PLC	Aug. 28, 1987	Oil and Coal Products	1,000
British Telecommunications PLC	May 30, 1986	Communication	1,000
BTR PLC	Nov. 5, 1986	Conglomerate	1,000
Cable & Wireless PLC	Apr. 2, 1986	Communication	1,000
Dixons Group PLC	May 31, 1988	Commerce	1,000
Fisons PLC	Dec. 22, 1988	Chemicals	1,000
Foreign and Colonial Investment Trust PLC	Dec. 18, 1987	Finance and Insurance	1,000
GKN PLC	Dec. 23, 1988	Transportation Equipment	1,000
Glaxo Holdings PLC	June 17, 1987	Chemicals	1,000

Table G4   continued

	Date of Listing	Industrial Classification	Unit of Trading (Shares)
Globe Investment Trust PLC	Feb. 4, 1988	Finance and Insurance	1,000
Imperial Chemical Industries PLC	Dec. 8, 1988	Chemicals	1,000
Lonrho PLC	July 23, 1987	Conglomerate	1,000
National Westminster Bank PLC	Oct. 18, 1988	Finance and Insurance	1,000
Peninsular & Oriental Steam Navigation	Dec. 22, 1987	Marine Transportation	1,000
Saatchi & Saatchi Company PLC	Oct. 13, 1988	Services	1.000
Standard Chartered PLC	Dec. 22, 1986	Finance and Insurance	1,000
United States			
Abbott Laboratories	Oct. 30, 1987	Chemicals	50
Allied-Signal Inc.	Dec. 21, 1987	Transportation Equipment	50
American Brands, Inc.	Aug. 15, 1989	Foods	50
American Express	Nov. 14, 1985	Finance and Insurance	50
American Family Corp.	Dec. 17, 1987	Finance and Insurance	1,000
American Information Technology	Dec. 18,1986	Communication	50
American International Group, Inc.	Sept. 18, 198	Finance and Insurance	50
American Telephone and Telegraph	Nov. 17, 1987	Communication	100
Anheuser-Busch Companies, Inc.	Oct. 6, 1987	Foods	100
Archer-Daniels-Midland	Jan. 19, 1988	Foods	100
Avon Products, Inc.	Dec. 17, 1987	Chemicals	100
BankAmerica Corp.	Dec. 22, 1975	Finance and Insurance	100
Bell Atlantic Corp.	Dec. 18, 1986	Communication	50
BellSouth Corp.	Nov. 26, 1987	Communication	100
Borden, Inc.	Aug. 25, 1987	Foods	50
Brunswick Corp.	Feb. 4, 1987	Transportation Equipment	100
Chase Manhattan Corp.	Sept. 20, 1974	Finance and Insurance	50
Chrysler Corp.	Sept. 19, 1986	Transportation Equipment	50
Citicorp	Dec. 18, 1973	Finance and Insurance	50
Dow Chemical	Dec. 18, 1973	Chemicals	50
Dun & Bradstreet Corp.	Feb. 5, 1988	Services	50
Du Pont	Oct. 2, 1986	Chemicals	50
Eastman Kodak	Aug. 26, 1986	Chemicals	50
Eli Lilly	Nov. 20, 1986	Chemicals	50
Exxon Corp.	Dec. 16, 1986	Oil and Coal Products	50
First Chicago Corp.	Dec. 18, 1973	Finance and Insurance	50
Ford Motor	Sept. 20, 1988	Transportation Equipment	100
FPL Group, Inc.	Dec. 9, 1986	Electric Power and Gas	100
General Electric	Nov. 10, 1987	Electric Appliances	50
General Motors Corp.	Dec. 20, 1974	Transportation Equipment	50
Georgia-Pacific Corp.	July 9, 1987	Fishery, Agriculture and Forestry	50
Goodyear Tire & Rubber	Jan. 7, 1988	Rubber Products	50
Greyhound	Nov. 10, 1989	Services	100
Grumman Corp.	Dec. 4, 1987	Transportation Equipment	100
GTE Corp.	Sept. 29, 1989	Communication	50
Hewlett-Packard	May 24, 1988	Electric Appliances	50
IBM Corp.	Nov. 27, 1974	Electric Appliances	10
ITT Corp.	Dec. 16, 1974	Conglomerate	50
J.P. Morgan	Sept. 30, 1987	Finance and Insurance	50
K mart Corp.	Dec. 8, 1987	Commerce	50
Knight-Ridder, Inc.	Sept. 13, 1988	Communication	100
The Limited, Inc.	July 16, 1987	Commerce	100
Lincoln National Corp.	Dec. 15, 1987	Finance and Insurance	50
Marriott Corp.	Sept. 17, 1987	Services	100
McDonald's Corp.	July 3, 1986	Commerce	50
Merrill Lynch	Nov. 18, 1986	Finance and Insurance	100
3M	Oct. 17, 1985	Chemicals	50
Mobil Corp.	Oct. 19, 1988	Oil and Coal Products	100
Monsanto	Oct. 4, 1989	Chemicals	50
Motorola, Inc.	Nov. 10, 1988	Electric Appliances	50

Table G4 concluded

	Date of Listing	Industrial Classification	Unit of Trading (Shares)
NCNB Corp.	July 1, 1987	Finance and Insurance	100
NYNEX Corp.	Oct. 29, 1987	Communication	50
Occidental Petroluem Corp.	Dec. 18, 1987	Mining	100
PepsiCo, Inc.	Nov. 13, 1986	Foods	100
Philip Morris	Oct. 16, 1985	Foods	10
Potomac Electric Power	Sept. 29, 1987	Electric Power and Gas	100
PPG Industries	Sept. 4, 1987	Glass and Ceramics Products	100
Proctor and Gamble	May 28, 1986	Chemicals	50
Rockwell International Corp.	Nov. 30, 1987	Transportation Equipment	100
Scott Paper	July 15, 1988	Pulp and Paper	100
Sears, Roebuck	June 29, 1984	Commerce	50
Security Pacific Corp.	Sept. 4, 1985	Finance and Insurance	50
SCE Corp.	Dec. 11, 1987	Electric Power and Gas	100
Texas Instruments Inc.	Nov. 15, 1989	Electric Appliances	1,0
Transamerica Corp.	Dec. 22, 1987	Finance and Insurance	100
US WEST, Inc.	Dec. 19, 1986	Communication	50
Walt Disney	June 27, 1985	Services	50
Warner-Lambert	Sept. 6, 1989	Chemicals	50
Waste Management, Inc.	July 22, 1986	Services	50
Weyerhaeuser	Dec. 17, 1986	Fishery, Agriculture and Forestry	100

Total 119 (United States : 70, United Kingdom : 19, Canada : 7, Australia : 6, Germany : 5, Netherlands : 3, Sweden : 3, Switzerland : 3, France : 2, Spain : 1)

Table G5
Closing Prices of the Stocks on the Foreign Section of the TSE on January 4, 1991, in Yen

Abbott Lab	—	—
ADM(c)	—	—
Aegon N.V. (c)	—	—
AGA(c)	—	—
AIG	—	—
Alcan Aluminium (d)	—	—
Allied-Signal	—	—
American Brands	—	—
American Family(c)	2360	– 250
Ameritech	—	—
Amex	2750	– 100
Anheuser-Busch(c)	—	—
Apple Computer	5700	– 140
AT&T(c)	3910	– 250
Avon Products(c)	—	—
B Petroleum(d)	—	—
B Telecom(d)	—	—
Banco Bilbao (c)	3350	....
Banco Santander	—	
BankAmerica (c)	3430	– 180
Barclays(d)	—	—
BASF (b)	17700	– 500
Bayer	19100	– 200
BCE	4530	+ 80
Bell Atlantic	—	—
BellSouth(c)	—	—
BHP	1030	—
BOC Group (d)	—	—
Boeing	5950	– 320
Borden	3790	—
British Gas (d)	—	—
Brunswick(c)	—	—
BTR(d)	—	—
C S Holding (a)*	—	—
C&W(d)	—	—
CGE (c)	—	—
Chase Manhattan	1490	+ 70
Chrysler	1620	– 140
CIBC(d)	—	—
Citicorp	1760	– 40
Commerzbank(b)	—	—
Daimler-Benz (b)	47500	– 2000
Deutsche Bank (b)	51800	– 2000
Dixons (d)	337	– 11
DNB	—	—
Dow Chemical	—	—
Dresdner	30100	– 1500
Du Pont	4690	– 280
Eastman Kodak	—	—
Eli Lilly	9410	– 590
Exxon	—	—
F Colonial(d)	—	—
First Chicago	2170	...
Fisons (d)	946	—
Ford Motor	—	—
Foster's Brewing (d)	140	– 5
FPL(c)	—	—
General Electric	—	—
Georgia-Pacific	—	—
GKN (d)	—	—
Glaxo(c)	2130	– 60
Globe(d)	—	—
GM	4470	– 230
Goodyear	2370	– 150
Greyhound Dial (c)	—	—
Grumman	—	—
GTE	—	—
Hewlett-Packard	—	—
IBM(b)	14900	– 400
ICI	—	—
ITT	—	—

J. P. Morgan	—	—
K mart	—	—
Knight-Ridder (c)	—	—
Limited(c)	—	—
Lincoln National	—	—
Lonrho(d)	—	—
Marriott(c)	1420	– 70
McDonald's	3750	– 70
Merrill Lynch(c)	2640	– 260
Mobil (c)	—	—
Monsanto	—	—
Motorola	—	—
N Telecom(c)	—	—
N.V. Philips' (d)	—	—
NAB(d)	—	—
NatWest (d)	—	—
NCNB(c)	3010	– 200
News Corp (d)	—	—
Nynex	—	—
Occi Petroleum(c)	2540	– 100
P Dunlop(d)	—	—
P&G	11200	– 400
P&O(d)	—	—
Paribas	—	—
PepsiCo(c)	—	—
Ph Morris(b)	6580	– 310
Potomac Elec(c)	—	—
PPG(c)	—	—
R Trustco(c)	1120	...
RBC (c)	—	—
Robeco	—	—
Rockwell(c)	—	—
S Chartered(d)	—	—
Saatchi & Saatchi	102	+ 6
SCE(c)	—	—
Schlumberger	7300	– 320
Scott Paper (c)	—	—
Sears	3360	– 40
SePac	2670	– 250
Swiss Bank(b)	—	—
T Dominion(c)	—	—
Telefonica(d)	1200	+ 30
Texas Instruments (c)	—	—
Transamerica(c)	—	—
UBS(a)*	2780	– 40
US West	4920	– 260
Volkswagen	—	—
Volvo	4970	...
Walt Disney	13500	– 300
Warner-Lambert	—	—
Waste Manage	4610	– 90
Westpac (d)	350	– 30
Weyerhaeuser(c)	—	—
3M	—	—

Notes: Standard trading unit for foreign stocks is 50 shares. (a) One share. (b) 10 shares. (c) 100 shares. (d) 1,000 shares.
R...ex-rights.
*Figures in 100s.
'Close': closing price of the week.
'Week's chg.': change from preceding week's 'close.'
... for unchanged.
—for no comparison.

Source: Tokyo Stock Exchange

APPENDIX H SECURITIES TAXATION

The information in tables H1-H5 on securities taxation is provided by the TSE effective April 1989.

Table H1 Corporation Tax

Income	Corporation	
	General	Paid-in capital ≤¥100 million and annual income ≤¥8 million
Paid out in dividends	33.3%	25%
Retained	43.2%	31%

Table H2 Securities Transfer Tax (Payable by Sellers)

Securities	Seller (% of trading value)	
	Other than securities company	Securities Company
Shares and stock investment trust certificates	0.30%	0.12%
Straight bonds and bond investment trust certificates	0.03%	0.01%
Convertible bonds and bonds with warrants	0.16%	0.06%

Table H3 Exchange Transfer Tax

Securities	% of trading value	
	Buyer	Seller
Japanese government bond futures and U.S. T-bond futures	0.001%	0.001%

Notes: 1. Exchange transfer tax is not imposed on stock index futures and options.
2. The tax rates for stock index futures and all options will be 0.001% and 0.01%, respectively from October 1, 1990.
3. The tax rate for Stock Futures 50 is 0.01% and will be 0.001% from October 1, 1990.

Table H4   Tax on Dividends

Income	Taxation (as of April, 1990)	Remarks
Individual		
Dividend on shares	1. If annual dividend per issue of stock is ≤¥100,000, choice from the following: a. Aggregate taxation (20% tax withheld at source); or b. No statement of dividend in tax return - hence, separate taxation (20% withheld at source)	In case of aggregate taxation, 10% of dividend income can be credited to tax liabilities. If the aggregate taxable income is >¥10 million, the tax credit rate on dividend is reduced to 5% for the amount of dividend up to the balance derived by subtracting ¥10 million from the aggregate taxable income.
	2. If annual dividend per issue of stock is >¥100 thousand but <¥500 thousand, and if the number of shares held are <5%, choice from the following: a. Aggregate taxation (20% withheld at source); or b. Separate taxation (35% withheld at source).	Dividend payment record filed by dividend-paying company with tax authorities for identification of recipient is not required for those recipients who receive ≤¥100,000 of dividends in a year
	3. If annual dividend per issue of stock is ≥¥500,000 or the number of shares held is ≥5% of the total outstanding shares, aggregate taxation is applicable (20% withheld at source)	
Dividend on stock investment trusts and bond investment trusts	Separate taxation (20% withheld at source)	
Corporation		
Dividend on shares	80% of the total amount of dividend received is not taxable	In case a corporation owns ≥25% shares of another corporation, the amount of dividend received on the said shares is not taxable.

Table H5 Tax on Interest

Income	Taxation (as of April, 1990)	Remarks
Individual		
Interest on bonds	Separate taxation (20% tax withheld at source)	
Redemption profit of no-coupon bonds	Separate taxation (18% tax withheld at source)	Tax is collected at time of issuance of such bonds
Corporation		
Interest income	Taxable	Interest paid deductible from taxable income.

Table H6 Tax on Capital Gains

Taxpayer	Taxation (as of April, 1990)
Individual	Capital gains from sales of shares, subscription rights, warrants, convertible bonds, and bonds with stock subscription warrants are taxable. Choice of the following: 1. Effective 1% withholding tax on the value of the sale 2. 20% of the profits from the sale.
Corporation	Capital gains are taxable. Capital losses are deductible from taxable income.

APPENDIX I MEMBERS OF THE TOKYO STOCK EXCHANGE

Table I1
Domestic and Foreign Members of the Tokyo Stock Exchange (124 members) as of April 1990

Member	Address	Telephone
Domestic		
ACE*	2-12, Nihombashi-Kayaba-cho, Chuo-ku, Tokyo 103	5695-5153
Aizawa*	20-3, Nihombashi 1-chome, Chuo-ku, Tokyo 103	272-3111
Akagiya	7-1, Nihombashi 2-chome, Chuo-ku, Tokyo 103	271-0011
Ando	10-3, Nihombashi-Kabuto-cho, Chuo-ku, Tokyo 103	666-1471
ARK	Shuwa Daini-Sakurabashi Bldg., 8-2, Hachiobori 4-chome, Chuo-ku Tokyo 104	297-5811
Century*	Itopia Nihombashi-Honcho Bldg. 7-1, Nihombashi-Honcho 2-chome, Chuo-ku, Tokyo 103	667-0371
Chiyoda*	2-15, Nihombashi-Muromachi 3-chome, Chuo-ku, Tokyo 103	271-2311
Chuo*	7-8, Nihombashi-Kabuto-cho, Chuo-ku, Tokyo 103	660-4700
Cosmo*	16-10, Nihombashi 1-chome, Chuo-ku, Tokyo 103	272-4611
Daiichi*	6-2, Nihombashi-Muromachi 1-chome, Chuo-ku, Tokyo 103	244-2600
Dainana	10-9, Ginza 3-chome, Chuo-ku, Tokyo 104	545-9111
Daisei	1-10, Nihombashi-Kabuto-cho, Chuo-ku, Tokyo 103	661-6006
Daito*	4-3, Nihombashi-Kabuto-cho, Chuo-ku, Tokyo 103	660-4311
Daiwa*	6-4, Ohtemachi 2-chome, Chiyoda-ku, Tokyo 100	243-2111
Fukuyama	9-4, Hachiobori 4-chome, Chuo-ku, Tokyo 104	297-2980
Hinode*	Shuwa Higashi Yaesu Bldg. 9-1, Hachiobori 2-chome, Chuo-ku, Tokyo 104	297-5111
Hiraoka	6-6, Nihombashi-Kobuna-cho, Chuo-ku, Tokyo 103	667-7676
Hirota	7-3, Nihombashi-Kayaba-cho 1-chome, Chuo-ku, Tokyo 103	667-1181
Ichiyoshi*	14-1, Hacchobori 2-chome, Chuo-ku, Tokyo 104	555-6200
Imagawa	10-1, Nihombashi 2-chome, Chuo-ku, Tokyo 103	273-7788
Issei	Dainichi Yaesu Bldg., 8-5, Yaesu 2-chome, Chuo-ku, Tokyo 104	273-9111
Iwai	Yaesu Kato Bldg., 15-12, Nihombashi-Kabuto-cho Chuo-ku, Tokyo 103	662-7151
Izumi*	17-24, Shinkawa 1-chome, Chuo-ku, Tokyo 104	555-4811
Jujiya	6-17, Nihombashi-Kayaba-cho 1-chome, Chuo-ku, Tokyo 103	666-0101
Kaisei*	13-2, Nihombashi-Kabuto-cho, Chuo-ku, Tokyo 103	666-1431
Kaneju	7-15, Nihombashi-Kabuto-cho, Chuo-ku, Tokyo 103	666-0191
Kaneman	3-8, Nihombashi-Kabuto-cho, Chuo-ku, Tokyo 103	666-1191
Kaneyama	11-8, Nihombashi-Koami-cho, Chuo-ku, Tokyo 103	668-3111
Kanto	8-1, Kanda-Ogawa-cho 1-chome, Chiyoda-ku, Tokyo 101	253-6721
Kokusai*	27-1, Shinkawa 2-chome, Chuo-ku, Tokyo 104	297-2111
Kosei*	Nihon Bldg., 6-2, Ohtemachi 2-chome, Chiyoda-ku, Tokyo 100	246-0811
Kurokawa Kitoku	16-3, Nihombashi 1-chome, Chuo-ku, Tokyo 103	278-7800
Kyokuto*	4-7, Nihombashi-Kayaba-cho, 1-chome, Chuo-ku, Tokyo 103	667-9171
Kyoritsu	7-3, Nihombashi 2-chome, Chuo-ku, Tokyo 103	272-3361
Kyowa	8-3, Nihombashi-Kabuto-cho, Chuo-ku, Tokyo 103	666-1381
Marutiachi	15-12, Nihombashi-Kabuto-cho, Chuo-ku, Tokyo 103	639-0808
Maruichi	13-1, Nihombashi-Koami-cho, Chuo-ku, Tokyo 103	666-0411
Marukin	7-9, Nihombashi-Kakigara-cho 1-chome, Chuo-ku, Tokyo 103	668-8381
Marukuni	10-2, Nihombashi-Koami-cho, Chuo-ku, Tokyo 103	666-2291
Maruko	3-3, Nihombashi-Kabuto-cho, Chuo-ku, Tokyo 103	666-2431
Maruman*	1-10, Nihombashi 2-chome, Chuo-ku, Tokyo 103	272-6011
Maiusan*	5-2, Nihombashi 2-chome, Chuo-ku, Tokyo 103	272-5211
Maruso	9-14, Nihombashi-Kabuto-cho, Chuo-ku, Tokyo 103	666-7901
Maruwa	8-2, Nihombashi 3-chome, Chuo-ku, Tokyo 103	274-5341

Matsui	20-7, Nihombashi 1-chome, Chuo-ku, Tokyo 103	281-3111
Meiko*	14-1, Nihombashi-Koami-cho, Chuo-ku, Tokyo 103	666-5211
Meiwa	7-15, Nihombashi-Kabuto-cho, Chuo-ku, Tokyo 103	666-2541
Miki	20-9, Nihombashi 1-chome, Chuo-ku, Tokyo 103	278-1111
Misaways	5-4, Nihombashi-Hakozaki-cho, Chuo-ku, Tokyo 103	667-4411
Milo*	13-5, Nihombashi 3-chome, Chuo-ku, Tokyo 103	274-6111
Murosei	1-10, Nihombashi-Kabuto-cho, Chuo-ku, Tokyo 103	666-1451
Naigai*	7-3, Nihombashi-Kabuto-cho, Chuo-ku, Tokyo 103	665-4321
Naito	10-1, Nihombashi-Ningyo-cho 3-chome, Chuo-ku, Tokyo 103	668-2090
Nakahara	1-10, Nihombashi-Kabuto-cho, Chuo-ku, Tokyo 103	666-0241
Natuse	4-2, Nihombashi-Kabuto-cho, Chuo-ku, Tokyo 103	666-2101
National*	6-7, Nihombashi-Kabuto-cho, Chuo-ku, Tokyo 103	666-0321
New Japan*	1 1, Kanda-Surugadai 3-chome, Chiyoda-ku, Tokyo 101	219-1111
Nichiei	10-7, Nihombashi-Koami-cho, Chuo-ku, Tokyo 103	667-3181
Nihon Kyoei	2-18, Nihombashi-Kayaba-cho 1-chome, Chuo-ku, Tokyo 103	668-2211
Nikko*	3-1, Marunouchi 3-chome, Chiyoda-ku, Tokyo 100	283-2211
Nippon Kangyo Kakumaru*	6-1, Marunouchi 1-chome, Chiyoda-ku, Tokyo 100	286-7111
Nippon*	9-10, Nihombashi-Horidome-cho 1-chome, Chuo-ku, Tokyo 103	668-0311
Nissan	7-6, Nihombashi-Kabuto-cho, Chuo-ku, Tokyo 103	666-3151
Nomura*	9-1, Nihombashi 1-chome, Chuo-ku, Tokyo 103	211-1811, 3811
Okachi	3-12, Nihombashi-Kayaba-cho 1-chome, Chuo-ku, Tokyo 103	668-3661
Okasan*	17-6, Nihombashi 1-chome, Chuo-ku, Tokyo 103	272-2211
Osawa	2-13, Nihombashi-Kayaba-cho 1-chome, Chuo-ku, Tokyo 103	666-0311
Ryoko*	17-12, Nihombashi 1-chome, Chuo-ku, Tokyo 103	246-5711
Sanei	12-7, Kyobashi 3-chome, Chuo-ku, Tokyo 104	562-3321
Sanyo*	8-1, Nihombashi-Kayaba-cho 1-chome, Chuo-ku, Tokyo 103	666-1233
Shinei-Ishino	15-1, Nihombashi 1-chome, Chuo-ku, Tokyo 103	271-5661
Tachibana	13-14, Nihombashi-Kayaba-cho 1-chome, Chuo-ku, Tokyo 103	669-3111
Taiheiyo*	17-10, Kyobashi 1-chome, Chuo-ku, Tokyo 104	566-4511
Takagi*	12-1 1, Nihombashi 1-chome, Chuo-ku, Tokyo 103	281-3231
Tokai	8-8, Yaesu 2-chome, Chuo-ku, Tokyo 104	274-3441
Tokyo*	7-3, Marunouchi 2-chome, Chiyoda-ku, Tokyo 100	214-3211
Tokyo Rengo	7-6, Nihombashi-Kayaba-cho 3-chome, Chuo-ku, Tokyo 103	667-2085
Tows*	16-7, Nihombashi 1-chome, Chuo-ku, Tokyo 103	278-1511
Toys*	20-5, Nihombashi 1-chome, Chuo-ku, Tokyo 103	274-0211
Universal*	4-2, Marunouchi 3-chome, Chiyoda-ku, Tokyo 100	284-3511
Utsumiya	12-4, Nihombashi-Kayaba-cho 1-chome, Chuo-ku, Tokyo 103	661-8855
Wako*	6-1, Nihombashi-Koami-cho, Chuo-ku, Tokyo 103	667-8111
World*	Sumitomo Real Estate Hakozaki Bldg. 16-9, Nihombashi-Hakozaki-cho, Chuo-ku, Tokyo 103	661-0241
Yamabun	18-3, Nihombashi-Koami-cho, Chuo-ku, Tokyo 103	666-1121
Yamaichi*	4-1, Yaesu 2-chome, Chuo-ku, Tokyo 104	276-3181
Yamaka	13-10, Nihombashi 2-chome, Chuo-ku, Tokyo 103	273-8681
Yamakichi	1-7, Nihombashi-Kabuto-cho, Chuo-ku, Tokyo 103	666-2281
Yamamaru	3-1 1, Nihombashi-Kabuto-cho, Chuo-ku, Tokyo 103	668-0211
Yamani	4-1, Nihombashi-Kabuto-cho, Chuo-ku, Tokyo 103	666-1151
Yamatane*	7-12, Nihombashi-Kabuto-cho, Chuo-ku,Tokyo 103	669-3211
Yamawa	1-3, Nihombashi-Kabuto-cho, Chuo-ku, Tokyo 103	668-5411
Yutaka	10-14, Nihombashi-Horidome-cho 1-chome, Chuo-ku, Tokyo 103	668-3621

Admitted as regular members in or after November, 1990

Daika	11-5, Nihombashi-Koami-cho, Chuo-ku, Tokyo 103	668-5531
Kimura	22-1 1, Hacchobori 3-chome, Chuo-ku, Tokyo 104	5566-0881
Kokyo	14-9, Nihombashi-Kabuto-cho, Chuo-ku, Tokyo 103	669-0121
Maeda	Futabakaikan Bldg. 1F, 16-5, Nihombashi-Kabuto-cho, Chuo-ku, Tokyo 103	662-2667
Marufuku	Yokokawa Bldg. 7F, 17-27, Shinkawa 1-chome, Chuo-ku, Tokyo 104	297-9111

Yahata Yamagen	Koura Bldg. 4F, Nihombashi-Kayaba-cho, Chuo-ku, Tokyo 103	669-2429
	1-17, Nihombashi-Ningyo-cho 3-chome, Chuo-ku, Tokyo 103	662-4451

Foreign

Baring*	Shin-Kasumigaseki Bldg. IOF, 3-2, Kasumigasek* 3-chome, Chiyoda-ku, Tokyo 100	595-8811
Citicorp Scrimg-eour Vickers*	Ark Mori Bldg. 24F. 12-32, Akasaka 1-chome, Minato-ku, Tokyo 107	589-7400
County Natwest*	AIU Bldg., 1-3, Marunouchi 1-chome, Chiyoda-ku, Tokyo 100	285-1300
DB Capital Markets*	Ark Mori Bldg. 22F, 12-32, Akasaka 1-chome, Minato-ku, Tokyo 107	589-1986
Dresdner-ABD*	Shionogi Honcho Kyodo Bldg. 5F, 7-2, Nihombashi-Honcho, 3-chome, Chuo-ku, Tokyo 103	662-3450
First Boston*	Asahi Seimei Hibiya Bldg., 5-1, Yurakucho 1-chome, Chiyoda-Ku, Tokyo 100	508-0261
Goldman Sachs*	Ark Mori Bldg. 1 OF, 12-32, Akasaka 1 -chome, Minato-ku, Tokyo 107	589-7000
Jardine Fleming*	Yamato Seimei Bldg., 1-7, Uchisaiwai-cho 1-chome, Chiyoda-ku, Tokyo 100	508-0261
Kidder Peabody*	Tokyo Kaijo Bldg. Shinkan, 2-1, Marunouchi 1-chome, Chiyoda-ku, Tokyo 100	213-6111
Kleinwort Benson*	Kokusai Bldg. 810, 1-1, Marunouchi 3-chome, Chiyoda-ku, Tokyo 100	284-0647
Merrill Lynch*	Ote Center Bldg. II F, 1-3, Otemachi 1-chome, Chiyoda-ku, Tokyo 100	213-7000
Morgan Stanley*	Ote Center Bldg. 8F, 1-3, Otemachi 1-chome, Chiyoda-ku, Tokyo 100	286-9000
Prudential-Bache*	Sumitomo Shibadainion Bldg., 5-5, Shibadaimon 2-chome, Minato-ku, Tokyo 105	578-0505
Salomon Brothers*	Ark Mori Bldg. 9F, 12-32, Akasaka 1-chome, Minato-ku, Tokyo 107	589-9111
SBCI*	Shin-Kasumigaseki Bldg. 19F, 3-2, Kasumigaseki 3-chome, Chiyoda-ku, Tokyo 100	595-4300
Schroder*	Ark Mori Bldg. 17F, 12-32, Akasaka 1-chome, Minato-ku, Tokyo 107	587-6800
S. G. Warburg*	New Edobashi Bldg., 7-2, Nihombashi-Honcho 1-chome, Chuo-ku, Tokyo 103	246-4111
Shearson Lehman Hutton*	Ark Mori Bldg. 36F, 12-32, Akasaka 1-chome, Minato-ku, Tokyo 107	505-9000
Smith Barney*	Mitsubishi Bldg., 5-2 Marunouchi 2-chome, Chiyoda-ku, Tokyo 100	201-3101
Société Générale*	Sumitomo Shibadaimon Bldg. 12F, 5-5, Shibadaimon 2-chome, Minato-ku, Tokyo 105	459-6841
UBS Phillips &Drew*	Yamato Seimei Bldg., 1-7, Uchisaiwaicho 1-chome, Chiyoda-ku, Tokyo 100	595-0211
W. I. Carr*	Yaesu Dai-Bldg. 4F, 1-1, Kyobashi 1-chome, Chuo-ku, Tokyo 104	278-4600

Admitted as regular members in or after November, 1990

Barclays de Zoete*	Sin-Kasumigaseki Bldg. 18F, 3-2, Kasumigaseki 3-chome, Chiyoda-ku, Tokyo 100	591-0890
Crédit Lyonnais*	Sumitomo-Fudosan-Hibiya Bldg, 5F, 8-6, Nishi-Shimbashi 2-chome, Minato-ku, Tokyo 105	504-3932
James Capel Pacific*	Kokusai Bldg. 7F, 1-1, Marunouchi 3-chome, Chiyoda-ku, Tokyo 100	282-0111

Note: * *Integrated* securities companies.

Source: Tokyo Stock Exchange

REFERENCES

Adler, Michael and J. Detemple (1988) Hedging with futures in an intertemporal portfolio context. *Journal of Futures Markets 8::* 249-269.

Adler, Michael and Bernard Dumas (1983) International portfolio choices and corporate finance: a synthesis. *Journal of Finance 38:* 925-984.

Adler, Michael, and Bruce Lehmann (1983) Deviations from purchasing power parity in the long run. *Journal of Finance 38:* 1471-87.

Adler, Michael and S. Simon (1986) Exchange rate surprises in international portfolios. *Journal of Portfolio Management 12 (Winter):* 44-53.

Admati, Anat R. and Paul Pfleidler (1988) A theory of intraday patterns: volume and price variability. *Review of Financial Studies 1:* 3-40.

Admati, Anat R. and Paul Pfleidler (1989) Divide and conquer: a theory of intraday and day of the week mean effects. *Review of Financial Studies 2:* 189-223.

Aggarwal, Raj, Ramesh P. Rao and Takato Hiraki (1988) Japanese equity returns: empirical evidence of skewness and kurtosis. Working Paper, John Carroll University, University Heights, Ohio, April.

Aggarwal, Raj, Ramesh P. Rao and Takato Hiraki (1989) Price/sales ratios and equity returns on the Tokyo Stock Exchange: an empirical study. Working Paper, John Carroll University, University Heights, Ohio, February.

Aggarwal, Raj, Takato Hiraki and Ramesh P. Rao (1988) Price/earnings ratios and equity returns on the Tokyo Stock Exchange: a note. Working Paper, John Carroll University, University Heights, Ohio, September.

Akgiray, V. and C. G. Lamoureux (1989) Estimation of stable-law parameters: a comparative study. *Journal of Business and Economic Statistics 7:* 8-93.

Altman, Edward J. (1988) Measuring corporate bond mortality and performance. Salomon Brothers Center for the Study of Financial Institutions Working Paper 468 (June), Graduate School of Business Administration, New York University, New York.

Altman, Edward J. and Scott A. Nammacher (1987) *Investing in Junk Bonds.* John Wiley & Sons, NY (translated into Japanese by Toyo Keizai Shinposha, Tokyo, 1988).

Altman, Edward J. and Yoshiki Minowa (1989) Analyzing risks and returns and potential interest in the U.S. high yield corporate debt market for Japanese investors. *Japan and the World Economy 13:* 163-86.

Amaya, Nashiro (1988) The Japanese economy in transition: optimistic about the short term; pessimistic about the long term, *Japan and the World Economy 1:* 101-111.

Amihud, Yakov and Haim Mendelson (1989) Market microstructure and price discovery on the Tokyo Stock Exchange. *Japan and the World Economy 1:* 341-370.

Ando, Albert and Alan J. Auerbach (1988) The cost of capital in the U.S. and Japan: a comparision. *Journal of the Japanese and International Economies 2:* 134-158.

Ando, Albert and Alan J. Auerbach (1990) The cost of capital in Japan: recent evidence and further results. Mimeo, University of Pennsylvania, Philadelphia.

Ariel, Robert A. (1987) A monthly effect in stock returns. *Journal of Financial Economics, 18:* 1-14.

Ariel, Robert A. (1991) High stock returns before holidays. *Journal of Finance,* forthcoming.

Aron, Paul H. (1981) Are Japanese P/E multiples too high? Daiwa Securities of America, NY.

Aron, Paul H. (1988a) Japanese P/E ratios and accountancy: rhetoric and reality. Daiwa Securities America Paul Aron Report 32, August 29.

Aron, Paul H. (1988b) Japanese P/E multiples: the shaping of a tradition. Daiwa Securities America Paul Aron Report 33, August 31.

Aron, Paul H. (1989a) Japanese P/E multiples: the tradition continues. Daiwa Securities America Paul Aron Report 35, October 23.

Aron, Paul H. (1989b) Japanese non-life insurance companies final analysis & report. Daiwa Securities America Paul Aron Report 37, December 29.

Aron, Paul H. (1990) Japanese P/E multiples in an era of increasing uncertainty. Daiwa Securities America, Paul Aron Report 41, August 31.

Asako, Kuninori, Inoue and Murase (1989) Q ratios in Japan, mimeo.

Asian Society of Security Analysts (1988) *Securities Markets in Asia.*

Bailey, Warren and Rene Stulz (1990) Measuring the benefits from international diversification: the case of Pacific-Basin stock markets. *Journal of Portfolio Management (Summer):* 57-61.

Bailey, Warren, Rene Stulz and Simon Yen (1989) Properties of daily stock returns from the Pacific Basin stock markets: evidence and implications, in S. Ghon Rhee and Rosita P. Chang, eds (1989).

Bailey, Warren and William T. Ziemba (1991) An introduction to Japanese stock index options in Ziemba, Bailey and Hamao (1991).

Balassa, Bela and Marcus Noland (1988) *Japan in the World Economy.* Washington, D.C.: Institute for International Economics.

Bank of Japan (1987) *Comparative Economics Statistics.*

Barclay, Michael J., Robert H. Litzenberger and Jerold B. Warner (1990) Private information, trading volume and stock return variances. *Review of Financial Studies 3:*233-253.

Basu, Sanjoy (1977) Investment performance of common stocks in relation to their price-earnings ratios: a test of the efficient market hypothesis. *Journal of Finance 32:* 663-682.

Basu, Sanjoy (1983) The relationship between earnings' yield, market value and return for NYSE common stocks: further evidence, *Journal of Financial Economics 12:* 129-156.

Bauer, R. and R. Wirick (1986) Investment strategies to exploit the small-firm and January anomalies. Working Paper, School of Business Administration, Univesity of Western Ontario, London, Ontario, October.

Bergsten, C. Fred and William R. Cline (1985) *The United States-Japan Economic Problem.* Institute for International Economics, Washington, D.C.

Blume, Marchall E. and Donald B. Keim (1987) Risk and return characteristics of lower grade bonds. *Financial Analysts Journal 43:* 26-33.

Boone, P. (1989) High land values in Japan: is the archipelago worth eleven trillion dollars? Mimeo, Department of Economics, Harvard University, Cambridge, Mass.

Bose, Mihir (1988) *Crash.* Bloomsbury, London.

Brenner, Menachem, Marti G. Subrahmanyam, and Jun Uno (1989a) Behavior of prices in Nikkei spot and futures markets. *Journal of Financial Economics 23:* 363-383 .

Brenner, Menachem, Marti G. Subrahmanyam, and Jun Uno (1990b) The volatility of the Japanese stock indices: evidence from the cash and futures markets, mimeo, New York University.

Brown, Christie (1988) How to short Japan. *Forbes*, June 27, 288-289.

Brown, Philip, Alan Kleidon and Terry Marsh (1983) New evidence on the nature of size-related anomalies in stock prices. *Journal of Financial Economics 12:* 33-56.

Brown, Stephen J. and Toshiyuki Otsuki (1988) CAPMD: a model of risk and return in the Japanese equity market. Mimeo, New York University.

Brown, Stephen J. and Toshiyuki Otsuki (1989) Macroeconomic factors and the Japanese equity markets: the CAPMD project in Elton and Gruber (1989).

Brown, Stephen J. and Mark Weinstein (1983) A new approach to testing asset pricing models: the bilinear paradigm. *Journal of Finance 38:* 711-743.

Brown, Stephen J. and Mark Weinstein (1985) Derived factors in event studies. *Journal of Financial Economics 14:* 491-495.

Burmeister, Edwin and Marjorie McElroy (1988) Joint estimation of factor sensitivities and risk premia for the arbitrage pricing theory. *Journal of Finance 43:* 721-735.

Burmeister, Edwin, and Kent Wall (1986) The arbitrage pricing theory and macroeconomic factor measures. *The Financial Review 21:* 1-20.

Burmeister, Edwin, Kent Wall and James Hamilton (1986) Estimation of unobserved expected monthly inflation using Kalman filtering. *Journal of Business and Economic Statistics 4:* 147-160.

Burnstein, Daniel (1988) *Yen!* Simon & Schuster, NY.

Cadsby, Charles B. (1991) The CAPM and the calendar: empirical anomalies and the risk-return relationship. *Management Science* (forthcoming).

Campbell, John Y. and Yasushi Hamao (1988) Predictable bond and stock returns in the U.S. and Japan: a study of long-term capital market integration. Mimeo, University of California, San Diego.

Canaway, Hugh (1990) Land prices in Japan: no cause for alarm. Baring Securities, May.

Chan, K.C. and G. Andrew Karolyi (1991) The volatility of the Japanese stock market: evidence from 1977 to 1990 in Ziemba, Bailey and Hamao (1991).

Chan, Louis, Yasushi Hamao and Josef Lakonishok (1990) Fundamentals and stock returns in Japan. Working Paper.

Chen, Nai-fu (1983) Some empirical tests of theory of arbitrage pricing. *Journal of Finance 38:* 1393-1414.

Chen, Nai-fu and Jonathan E. Ingersoll, Jr. (1983) Exact pricing in linear factor models with finitely many assets: a note. *Journal of Finance 38:* 985-988.

Chen, Nai-fu, Richard Roll and Stephen Ross (1986) Economic forces and the stock market. *Journal of Business 59:* 383-403.

Cho, D. Chinhyung (1984) On testing the arbitrage pricing theory: inter-battery factor analysis. *Journal of Finance 19:* 1-10.

Cho, D. Chinhyung, Edwin Elton, and Martin Gruber (1984) On the robustness of the Roll and Ross arbitrage pricing theory. *Journal of Financial and Qualitative Analysis 19:* 1-10.

Choi (1988) Sources of Data for Japanese securities in English. *Financial Management 17:* 80-98.

Christopher, Robert C. (1983) *The Japanese Mind: The Goliath Explained.* Simon & Schuster, NY.

Clark, Ross and William T. Ziemba (1987) Playing the turn of the year effect in the futures markets. *Operations Research 35:* 799-813.

Condoyanni, L., J. O'Hanlon and C.W.R. Ward (1987) Day of the week effect on stock returns: international evidence. *Journal of Business Finance and Accounting 144 :* 159-174.

Connolly, Robert A (1989) An examination of the robustness of the weekend effect. *Journal of Financial and Quantitative Analysis 24:* 133-169.

Connolly, Robert A (1988) A posterior odds analysis of the weekend effect. Working Paper, University of California, Irvine.

Conrad, Jennifer (1989) The price effect of option introduction. *Journal of Finance 44:* 487-498.

Conrad, Jennifer and Gautam Kaul (1989) Mean reversion in short-horizon expected returns. *Review of Financial Studies 2:* 225-240.

Corhay, A., G. Hawawini and P. Michel (1987) Seasonality in the risk-return relationship: some international evidence. *Journal of Finance 42:* 49-68.

Cornell, Bradford (1985) The weekly pattern in stock returns: cash versus futures: a note. *Journal of Finance XL:* 583-589.

Coulson, D. Robert (1987) *The Intelligent Investor's Guide to Profiting from Stock Market Inefficiencies.* Probus Publishing Co., Chicago.

Credit Suisse First Boston (1988) *The SCFB Guide to the Yen Bond Markets,* Probus Publishing.

Cults, R.L. (1990) Power from the ground up: Japan's land bubble, *Harvard Business Review* (May-June) 164-172.

Cutler, David M., James M. Poterba and Lawrence H. Summers (1989) What moves stock prices? *Journal of Portfolio Management 15 :* 4-12.

Cutler, David M., James M. Poterba and Lawrence H. Summers (1990) Speculative dynamics and the role of feedback traders. *American Economic Review 80 (May):* 63-68.

Daiwa Secruities Company Ltd (1989) Net asset value special report: new asset value of 450 companies and Q-ratio rankings. *Investment Monthly* (November) 17-69.

Damodaran, A. and J. Lim (1988) The effects of option listing on the underlying stocks' return processes: a study. Working Paper, Salomon Brothers Center for the Study of Financial Institutions, New York University, NY.

Darrough, Masako and Trevor Harris (1991) Do management forecasts of earnings affect stock prices in Japan? in Ziemba, Bailey and Hamao (1991).

Detemple, J. and P. Jorion (1988) Option listing and stock returns. Working Paper, Columbia University, NY.

Dhrymes, Phoebus I., Irwin Friend, and N. Bulent Gultekin (1984) A critical reexamination of the empirical evidence on the arbitrage pricing theory. *Journal of Finance 39:* 323-346.

Dhrymes, Phoebus I., Irwin Friend, and N. Bulent Gultekin (1985) New tests of the APT and their implications. *Journal of Finance 40:* 659-675.

Dimson, Elroy, ed. (1988) *Stock Market Regularities.* Cambridge University Press, Cambridge, Mass.

Dornbusch, Rudiger (1987) *Dollars, Debts and Deficits.* MIT Press, Cambridge, Mass.

Dornbusch, Rudiger (1988) *Exchange Rates and Inflation.* MIT Press, Cambridge, Mass.

Dreman, David (1982) *The New Contrarian Investment Strategy.* Random House, NY.

Drexel Burnham Lambert (1989) Financing America's future, High Yield Market Report.

Duffie, Darrell and Henry R. Richardson (1989) Mean-variance hedging in continuous-time. Working Paper, Stanford University, Stanford, CA.

Duffie, Darrell and Mathew O. Jackson (1989) Optimal innovation of futures contracts. *Review of Financial Studies 2:* 275-296.

Duffie, Darrell and Mathew O. Jackson (1990) Optimal hedging and equilibrium in a dynamic futures market. *Journal of Economic Dynamics and Control 14:* 21-33.

Eaker, M. and D. Grant (1987) Cross-hedging foreign currency risks. *Journal of International Money and Finance 6:* 85-105.

Economist (1990) Japanese finance (December 8).

Elton, Edwin J. and Martin J. Gruber (1988) A multi-index risk model of the Japanese stock market. *Japan and the World Economy 1:* 21-44.

Elton, Edwin J. and Martin J. Gruber, eds (1989) *Japanese Financial Markets.* Harper and Row, NY.

Eun, C.S. and B.G. Resnick (1988) Exchange rate uncertainty, forward contracts and international portfolio selection. *Journal of Finance, 43:* 197-216.

Fallows, James (1989) Containing Japan. *Atlantic Monthly* (May)

Fama, Eugene F. (1965) The behavior of stock-market prices. *Journal of Business 38:* 34-105.

Fama, Eugene F. and G. William Schwert (1977) Asset returns and inflation. *Journal of Financial Economics 8:* 115-146.

Feldman, Robert A. (1986) *Japanese Financial Markets: Deficits, Dilemmas and Deregulation.* MIT Press, Cambridge, Mass.

Figlewski, Stephen, John Kose and John Merrick (1986) *Hedging with Financial Futures for Institutional Investors: From Theory to Practice.* Ballinger, Cambridge, Mass.

Fingleton, E. (1990) Japan's other capital market hits a bunker, *Institutional Investor* April.

Flack, S. (1990) The land of the setting property values. *Forbes,* April 30.

Flannery, Mark and Aris Protopapadakis (1988) From T-Bills to common stocks: investigating the generality of intra-week return seasonality. *Journal of Finance 43*: 431-450.

Frankel, Jeffrey A. (1989) Japanese finance: a survey. National Bureau of Economic Research Working Paper No. 3156, New York.

French, Kenneth R. (1980) Stock returns and the weekend effect. *Journal of Financial Economics 8*: 55-69.

French, Kenneth R. and Bradford Cornell (1983) The pricing of stock index futures. *Journal of Futures Markets 3:* 1-14.

French, Kenneth R. and James M. Poterba (1990a) Were Japanese stock prices too high? *Journal of Financial Economics,* forthcoming.

French, Kenneth R. and James M. Poterba (1990b) Japanese and U.S. cross-border common stock investments. *Journal of the Japanese and International Economies 4:* 476-493.

French, Kenneth R. and James M. Poterba (1991) Investor diversification and international equity markets. Working Paper 3609, National Bureau of Economic Research, Inc.

French, Kenneth R., G. Wiliam Schwert and Robert F. Stambaugh (1987) Expected stock returns and volatility. *Journal of Financial Economics 19:* 3-29.

French, Kenneth R. and Richard Roll (1986) Stock return variances: the arrival of information and the reaction of traders. *Journal of Financial Economics 17*: 5-26.

Fridson, Martin S., Steven B. Jones and Fritz Wahl (1989) The anatomy of the high yield debt market: 1988 update. Morgan Stanley Credit Research Report (February), New York.

Friedland, Jonathan (1988) Controlled collapse. *Far Eastern Economic Review,* October 13.

Garman, Mark B. and Steven W. Kohlhagen (1983) Foreign currency options values. *Journal of International Money and Finance 2 (3):* 231-238.

Gennotte, Gerard and Hayne E. Leland (1990) Market liquidity, hedging and crashes. *American Economic Review 80:* 909-1021.

Gibbons, Michael R. and Patrick Hess (1981) Day of the week effects and asset returns. *Journal of Business 54:* 579-596.

Giovannini, A. and P. Jorion (1989) The time-variation of risk and return in the foreign exchange and stock markets. *Journal of Finance, 44:* 307-325.

Glen, Jack (1989) Exchange rate uncertainty, forward contracts and the performance of global equity portfolios. Working Paper, Wharton School, University of Pennsylvania, Philadelphia, PA.

Goldsmith, Raymond W. (1983) *The Financial Development of Japan, 1868-1977.* Yale University Press, New Haven.

Goodman, David A. and John W. Peavy III (1985) The risk universal nature of the P/E effect. *Journal of Portfolio Management 11:* 14-16.

Goodman, David A. and John W. Peavy III (1986a) The interaction of Firm size and price-aarnings ratio on portfolio performance. *Financial Analysts Journal 42:* 9-12.

Goodman, David A. and John W. Peavy III (1986b) The low price effect: relationship with other stock market anomalies. *Review of Business and Economic Research 22 (Fall):* 18-37.

Grossman, Stanford J. (1988) An analysis of the implications for stock and futures price volatility of program trading and dynamic hedging strategies. *Journal of Business 61:* 278-298.

Gultekin, Mustafa N. and N. Buletin Gultekin (1983) Stock market seasonality: international evidence. *Journal of Financial Economics 12:* 469-481.

Gyourko, J. and Donald B. Keim (1990) The risk and return characteristics of stock market-based real estate indices. Mimeo, Wharton School, University of Pennsylvania, Philadelphia, Pa.

Hakansson, Nils H. (1990) Asset allocation via supershares, presentation at Berkeley Program in Finance in Asia Seminar, Tokyo, June.

Hamada, Koichi, Kazumasa Iwata, Giorgio Basevi and Paul Krugman (1989) On the international capital ownership pattern at the turn of the Twenty-First Century. *European Economic Review 33:* 1055-1085.

Hamao, Yasushi (1986) A standard database for the analysis of Japanese security markets. Working Paper, Yale School of Management, New Haven, Conn.

Hamao, Yasushi (1988) An empirical examination of the arbitrage pricing theory using Japanese data. *Japan and the World Economy 1:* 45-61.

Hamao, Yasushi (1989) Japanese stocks, bonds and inflation (SBI) 1973-1987. *Journal of Portfolio Management 15 :* 20-26.

Hamao, Yasushi and Roger F. Ibbotson (1989) *The Stocks, Bonds and Inflation (SBI) Japan Yearbook.* Ibbotson Associates, Chicago.

Hamao, Yasushi, Ronald W. Masulis and Victor Ng (1990) Correlations in price changes and volatility across international stock markets. *Review of Financial Studies 3:* 281-307.

Hamao, Yasushi, Ronald W. Masulis and Victor Ng (1991) The effect of the 1987 stock crash on international financial integration in Ziemba, Bailey and Hamao (1991).

Hardouvelis, Gikas and Steve Peristani (1989) Do margin requirements matter? Evidence from U.S. and Japanese stock markets. *FRBNY Quarterly Review:* 16-35.

Harris, Lawrence (1986) A transaction data study of weekly and intra-daily patterns in stock returns. *Journal of Financial Economics 16:* 99-117.

Harris, Lawrence (1989) S&P 500 cash price volatilities *Journal of Finance , 44:* 1155-1175.

Haugen, Robert and Josef Lakinshok (1988) *The Incredible January Effect,.* Dow Jones-Irwin, Homewood, Ill.

Hawawini, Gabriel (1988) Market efficiency and equity pricing: international evidence and implications for global industry. Working paper, INSEAD, Fontainbleu, March.

Hawawini, Gabriel (1991) Stock market anomalies and the pricing of equity on the Tokyo Stock Exchange, in Ziemba, Bailey and Hamao (1991).

Hayashi, Fumio and Tohru Inoue (1989) The relation between firm growth and Q with multiple capital inputs: theory and evidence. Mimeo, University of Pennsylvania, Philadelphia, Pa.

Higgins, R. C. (1985) Introduction to Japanese finance: markets, institutions and firms. *Journal of Financial and Quantitative Analysis 20:* 169-172.

Hiraki, Takato, Raj Aggaarwal and Ramesh P. Rao (1988) Stock market anomalies and investors behavior in Japan. Working Paper, International University of Japan.

Hirsch, Yale (1986) *Don't Sell Stocks on Monday.* Facts on File Publications.

Hodder, James E. (1986) Evaluation of manufacturing investments: a comparison of U.S. and Japanese practices. *Financial Management 15:* 17-24.

Hodder, James E. (1991) The cost of capital for industrial firms in the U.S. and Japan, in Ziemba, Bailey and Hamao (1991).

Hodder, James E. and A. E. Tschoegl (1985) Some aspect of Japanese corporate finance. *Journal of Financial and Quantitative Analysis 20:* 173-191.

Horimoto, Saburo (1988) private correspondence.

Hoshi, Takeo (1987) Stock market rationality and price volatility: tests using Japanese data. *Journal of the Japanese and International Economies 1:* 441-462.

Hoshi, Takeo and Anil Kashyap (1990) Evidence on Q and investment for Japanese firms. *Journal of Japanese and International Economies,* forthcoming.

Hoshi, Takeo, Anil Kashyap and David Scharfstein (1990) Corporate structure, liquidity, and investment: evidence from Japanese industrial groups. *Quarterly Journal of Economics,* forthcoming.

Ibbotson and Associates (1989) *Stocks, Bonds, Bills and Inflation: 1926-88.* Chicago, Illinois.

Ibbotson, Roger G. and Gary P. Brinson (1989) *Investment Markets: Gaining the Performance Advantage.* McGraw Hill, NY.

Ibbotson, Roger G., Jody L. Sindelar and Jay R. Ritter (1988) Initial public offerings. *Journal of Applied Corporate Finance 1:* 37-45.

Ikeda, M. (1985) The day of the week effects and monthly effects in the Tokyo Stock Exchange (in Japanese). Working Paper, University of Tokyo, October.

Ikeda, M. (1988) Day of the week effects and the mixture of normal distributions hypothesis (in Japanese). *Japan Financial Review 8:* 27-53.

Ikeda, M. and Y. Kanazaki (1991) Diffusion-jump model to measure information release and its effects on captial markets. Mimeo, University of Tsukuba.

Ishizumi, H. (1988) On Japanese Q ratios. Mimeo.

Ito, Takatoshi and V.V. Roley (1987) News from the U.S. and Japan: which moves the yen/dollar exchange rate? *Journal of Monetary Economics 19:* 255-77.

Ito, Takatoshi (1988) Japan's structural adjustment: the land/housing problem and external balances. Mimeo, Hitsosubashi University.

Ito, Takatoshi (1990) *The Japanese Economy.* MIT Press, Cambridge, Mass, forthcoming.

Jacobs, Bruce I. and Kenneth N. Levy (1988a) Disentangling equity return regularities: new insights and investment opportunities. *Financial Analysts Journal 44:* 18-43.

Jacobs, Bruce I. and Kenneth N. Levy (1988b) On the value of value. *Financial Analysts Journal 44:* 47-62.

Jacobs, Bruce I. and Kenneth N. Levy (1988c) Calendar anomalies: abnormal returns at calendar turning points. *Financial Analysts Journal* 44:: 28-39.

Jacobs, Bruce I. and Kenneth N. Levy (1989) Forecasting the size effect. *Financial Analysts Journal 45:* 38-54.

Jaffe, J. and R. Westerfield (1985a) The weekend effect in common stock returns: the international evidence. *Journal of Finance 40*: 433-454.

Jaffe, J. and R. Westerfield (1985b) Patterns in Japanese common stock returns: day of the week and turn of the year effects. *Journal of Financial and Quantitative Analysis 20*: 243-260.

Japan Securities Research Institute (1988a) *Rates of Return on Common Stocks.* Tokyo.

Japan Securities Research Institute (1988b) *Report of Japan's Stock Price Level.* Tokyo.

Japan Securities Research Institute (1990) *Securities Market in Japan. 1990.* Tokyo.

Japanese Ministry of Finance and the United State Department of the Treasury, Working Group on Yen/Dollar Exchange Rate Issues (1984) *Report by the Working Group on Yen/Dollar Exchange Rate, Financial and*

Capital Market Issues to Japanese Minister of Finance Noboru Takeshita (and) U.S. Secretary of the Treasury Donald T. Regan. Tokyo, May.

Jardine Flemming (1989) *Japanese Indices.* April.

JETRO (1989) *Nippon Business, Facts and Figures.* Tokyo.

Jorion, Philippe (1985) International portfolio diversification with estimation risk *Journal of Business 58:* 259-278.

Jorion, Philippe (1989) Asset allocation with hedged and unhedged foreign stocks and bonds. *Journal of Portfolio Management 15:* 49-54.

Jorion, Philippe (1990a) Portfolio optimization in practice: an application to international diversification, mimeo, Columbia University.

Jorion, Philippe (1990b) Currency hedging for international portfolios, mimeo, Columbia University.

Kahn, Herman (1973) *The Emerging Japanese Superstate.* Penguin Books, Harmondsworth, England.

Kahn, Herman and Thomas Petter (1973) *The Japanese Challenge.* Penguin Books, Harmondsworth, England.

Kallberg, Jarl G. and William T. Ziemba (1983) Comparisons of alternative utility functions in portfolio selection problems. *Management Science 29:* 1257-1276.

Kanter, Rosabeth Moss (1989) *When Giants Learn to Dance.* Simon and Schuster, NY.

Kariya, T. Y. Tsukuda, and J. Mru (1989) The stock price changes in Japan (in Japanese). Toyo Keizai Inc, Tokyo.

Karpoff, J. M. (1987) The relation between price changes and trading volume: a survey. *Journal of Financial and Quantitative Analysis 22:* 109-126.

Kato, Kiyoshi (1990a) Weekly patterns in Japanese stock returns. *Management Science 36:* 1031-1043.

Kato, Kiyoshi (1990b) Being a winner in the Tokyo stock market: the case for an anomaly fund. *Journal of Portfolio Management* (in press).

Kato, Kiyoshi and James S. Schallheim (1985) Seasonal and size anomalies in the Japanese stock market, *Journal of Financial and Quantitative Analysis 20:* 243-272.

Kato, Kiyoshi, Sandra L. Schwartz and William T. Ziemba (1989) Day of the week effects in Japanese securities markets in Elton and Gruber (1989).

Kato, Kiyoshi, Scott Linn and James Schallheim (1987) A test of stock price parity using American Depository Receipts. Mimeo, Nanzan University.

Keim, Donald B. (1983) Size related anomalies and stock return seasonality. *Journal of Financial Economics 12*: 13-22.

Keim, Donald B. (1986a) Dividend yield and the January effect. *Journal of Portfolio Management, 13*: 54-60.

Keim, Donald B. (1986b) The CAPM and equity return regularities. *Financial Analysts Journal 42:* 19-34.

Keim, Donald B. (1987) Daily returns and size-related premiums: one more time, *Journal of Portfolio Management. 13:* 41-47.

Keim, Donald B. (1989) Trading patterns, bid-ask spreads and estimated security returns: the case of common stocks at calendar turning points. *Journal of Financial Economics 25:* 75-97.

Keim, Donald B. and Michael Smirlock (1987) The behavior of intraday stock index futures prices. *Advances in Futures and Options Research 2:* 143-166.

Keim, Donald B. and Robert F. Stambaugh (1984) A further investigation of the weekend effect in stock returns. *Journal of Finance 39*: 819-840.

Keizai Koho Center (1988) *Japan 1988: An International Comparison.* Japan Times.

Keizai Koho Center (1989) *Japan Periodicals.* Japan Institute of Social and Economic Affairs.

Kennedy, Paul (1989) *The Rise and Fall of the Great Powers,.* Vintage Books, NY.

Kim, Myung Jig, Charles R. Nelson, and Richard Startz (1988) Mean reversion in stock prices: a reappraisal of the empirical evidence. Mimeo, University of Washington, Nov 21.

Kishimoto, Kazuo (1990) A new approach for testing the randomness of heteroscadastic time series data. Mimeo, University of Tsukuba.

Kobayashi, Kaoru (1988) Japanese corporations expanding abroad, in *Top 1500 Japanese Corporations,* Japan Times.

Kobayashi, Takao (1990) The fundamental value of Japanese stocks. Mimeo, University of Tokyo.

Konya and Asako et al (1990) Japanese Q ratios. Mimeo.

Konya and Wakasugi (1987) Tobin's Q and stock price. *Securities Research* 80: 221-233.

Krugman, Paul (1988) Exchange rates and international adjustment. *Japan and the World Economy 1*: 63-87.

Krugman, Paul (1989) Persistent trade effects of large exchange rate shocks. *Quarterly Journal of Economics 104*: 635-654.

Krugman, Paul and Richard Baldwin (1987) The persistence of the U.S. trade deficit. *Brookings Papers on Economic Activity 1*: 1-43.

Kuboi, Takashi (1989) *Business Practices and Taxation in Japan*, The Japan Times.

Kunimura, Michio (1984) The information content of forecasts by corporate officials and by financial analysts in the Japanese capital karket. Working Paper No. 84-3 U.S.-Japan Management Studies Center, University of Pennsylvania, Philadelphia, Pa.

Kunimura, Michio and Alan K. Severn (1989) The market performance of new issues of Japanese stocks. Nagoya City University Working Paper, Nagoga.

Kurokawa (1988) On the stock market collapse: a view from Tokyo. Speech to the Brookings Institution, March 8.

Lakonishok, Josef and Maurice Levi (1982) Weekend effects on stock returns: a note. *Journal of Finance 37*: 883-889.

Lakonishok, Josef and Seymour Smidt (1989) Are seasonal anomalies real? A ninety-year perspective. *Review of Financial Studies 1*: 403-425.

Lau, S., S. Quay and C. Ramsey (1974) The Tokyo Stock Exchange and the Capital Asset Pricing Model, *Journal of Finance 28*: 507-514.

Lee, Charles M.C., Andrei Shleifer and Richard H. Thaler (1990) Anomalies: closed-end mutual funds. *Journal of Economic Perspectives 4*: 153-164.

Levy, Haim and M. Sarnat (1970) International diversification of investment portfolios. *American Economic Reveiw 60*: 668-675.

Lincoln, Edward J. (1988) *Japan, Facing Economic Maturity* . Brookings Institution, Washington, D.C.

Lintner, John (1965) The valuation of risky assets and the selection of risky investments in stock portfolios and capital budgets. *Review of Economics and Statistics 47:* 13-37.

Lothian, James R. (1991) A history of yen exchange rates in Ziemba, Bailey and Hamao (1991).

Lynch, Peter (1989) *One Up On Wall Street.* Simon and Schuster, NY.

McDonald, Jack (1989) The *Mochiai* Effect: Japanese corporate cross-holdings. *Journal of Portfolio Management 16:* 90-94.

McElroy, Marjorie and Edwin Burmeister (1988) Arbitrage pricing theory as a restricted nonlinear multivariate regression model. *Journal of Business and Economic Statistics 6:* 29-42.

McInish, Thomas H. and Robert A. Wood (1985) Intraday and overnight returns and day-of-the-week effects. *Journal of Financial Research 8:* 119-126.

MacKinlay, A. C. and K. Ramaswamy (1988) Index futures arbitrage and the behavior of stock index futures prices. *Review of Financial Studies 1:* 137-158.

McKinnon, Ronald and Kenichi Ohno (1986) Getting the exchange rate right: insular versus open economies. Mimeo, Stanford University, Stanford, CA.

Maidment, Paul (1988) Japanese finance: The end of an era. *The Economist:* December 10.

Mandelbrot, B. B. (1963) The variation of certain speculative prices. *Journal of Business 36:* 394-419.

Mandelbrot, B. B. (1973) Comments on: "A subordinated stochastic process model with finite variance for speculative prices" by Peter K. Clark. *Econometrica 41:* 157-159.

Mankiw, N.G. and D.N. Weil (1988) The baby boom, the baby bust and the housing market, W.P. No 2794 (December), National Bureau of Economic Research, Cambridge, MA.

Mansfield, M. (1989) The century of the Pacific, *Speaking of Japan*, KKC, March.

Marris, S. (1985) *Deficits and the Dollar: The World Economy at Risk.* Policy Analyses in International Economics #14. Institute for International Economics. Washington, D.C.

Marris, S. (1987) *Deficits and the Dollar: The World Economy at Risk. Revised Edition* Policy Analyses in International Economics #14. Institute for International Economics. Washingtcn, D.C.

Masato, Numako and Adisak Taveerojkumsri (1989) Mergers and acquisitions: Japanese style. Term paper in Finance III, University of Tsukuba.

Matsumoto, Toru (1989) *Japanese Stocks: A Basic Guide for the Intelligent Investor.* Kodansha International, Tokyo

Merville, Larry J. and Dan R. Pieptea (1989) Stock-price volatility, mean-reverting diffusion and noise. *Journal of Financial Economics 24:* 193-214.

Metz, Tim (1988) *Black Monday.* William Morrow, NY.

Miller, Edward, M. (1988) Why a weekend effect? *Journal of Portfolio Management 15:* 42-48.

Miller, Merton and Franco Modigliani (1961) Dividend policy, growth and the valuation of shares. *Journal of Business 34:* 411-33.

Mills, Edwin S. (1988) Social returns to housing and other fixed capital. Mimeo, Kellogg Graduate School of Management, Northwestern University, Evanston, Ill., October.

Modest, D. M. and M. Sundaresan (1983) The relationship between spot and futures prices in stock index futures markets: some preliminary evidence. *Journal of Futures Markets 3:* 15-41.

Mossin, Jan (1966) Equilibrium in a capital asset market. *Econometrica 34:* 768-783.

Mulvey, John M. (1988) Reducing portfolio risks: a surplus optimization perspective. Mimeo, Princeton University, Princeton, NJ.

Mulvey, John M. (1989) Incorporating transactions costs in models for asset allocation. Mimeo, Princeton University, Princeton, NJ.

Mulvey, John M. and Herculus Vladimirou (1988) Stochastic network optimization models for investment planning. Mimeo, Princeton University, Princeton, NJ.

Murphy, R. Taggart (1989) Power without purpose: the crisis of Japan's global financial dominance. *Harvard Business Review Mar-Apr:* 71-83.

Myers, David H. and Sachiko Ujiie (1988) Performance measurement in Japan: the coming of age. *Benefits and Compensation International,* June 27-33.

Nakamura, T. and N. Terada (1984) The size effect and seasonality in Japanese Stock Returns. Unpublished manuscript, Institute for Quantitative Research in Finance.

Ng, N. (1987) Detecting Spot price forecasts in futures prices using causality tests. *Review of Futures Markets 6:* 250-267.

Nihon Keizai Shimbun, Inc. (1988) *The Nikkei Stock Average Data Book, 1988.*

Noland, Marcus (1988) Japanese household portfolio allocation behavior. *Review of Economics and Statistics 70:* 135-139.

Nomura Research Institute (1988) *Nomura Fact Book,* Tokyo.

Norris, Floyd (1990) Investors relish bet against Japan. *New York Times,* January 15, page D4.

Ohno, Kenichi (1986) Estimating purchasing power parities in the 1970s and 80s: the price pressure approach,. Mimeo, Stanford University, Stanford, CA.

Okuda, H. (1975) Estimation of the efficiency of stock market (2) (in Japanese). *Zaikaikansoku 40:* 20-29.

Patrick, Hugh and Henry Rosovsky, eds. (1976) *Asia's New Giant: How the Japanese Economy Works,* Brookings Institution, Washington, D.C.

Patrick, Hugh and Ryuichiro Tachi, eds. (1986) *Japan and the United States Today: Exchange Rates, Macroeconomic Policies, and Financial Market Innovations.* Center for Japanese Economy and Business, Columbia University, NY.

Peavy, John W., III (1990) Returns on initial public offerings of closed end funds. *Review of Financial Studies 3:* 695-708.

Peavy, John W., III and D. A. Goodman (1983) Industry-relative price-earnings ratios as indicators of investment returns. *Financial Analysts Journal 39:* 60-66.

Pérold, Andre and Evan Schulman (1988) The free lunch in currency hedging: implications for investment policy and performance standards. *Financial Analysts Journal 44:* 45-50.

Pettway, Richard and T. Tapley (1984) The Tokyo Stock Exchange: an analysis of stock market prices. *Keio Business Review*, 75-93.

Pettway, Richard S. and Takeshi Yamada (1986) Mergers in Japan and their impacts upon stockholders wealth.*Financial Management 15:* 43-52.

Pettway, Richard S., Neil W. Sicherman and Takeshi Yamada (1989) Japanese mergers: relative size, corporate collectivism, and shareholders' wealth, in Rhee and Chang (1989).

Pettway, Richard S., Neil W. Sicherman and Takeshi Yamada (1989) The market for corporate control, the level of agency costs and corporate collectivism in Japanese mergers in Elton and Gruber (1989).

Pieptea, Dan R. and Eliezer Prisman (1988) The Monday effect and speculative opportunities in the stock index futures markets. Mimeo, University of Texas, Dallas.

Poterba, James M. and Lawrence H. Summers (1986) The persistence of volatility and stock market fluctuations. *American Economic Review 76:* 1142-1151.

Poterba, James M. and Lawrence H. Summers (1988) Mean reversion in stock prices: evidence and implications. *Journal of Financial Economics 22:* 27-59.

Prestowitz, Clyde V., Jr. (1988) *Trading Places: How We Allowed Japan to Take the Lead.* Basic Books, NY.

Rao, Ramesh P., Raj Aggarwal and Takato Hiraki (1988) Dividend yields and stock returns: evidence in the Tokyo Stock Exchange. Mimeo International University of Japan, Nigata, Japan.

Reischauer, Edwin O. (1977) *The Japanese.* Harvard University Press, Cambridge, Mass.

Rhee, S. Ghon and Rosita P. Chang, eds (1989) *Research on Pacific Basin Capital Markets,* North Holland, Amsterdam.

Ritter, Jay (1988) The buying and selling behavior of individual investors at the turn of the year. *Journal of Finance 43:* 701-717.

Ritter, Jay and Nisan Chopra (1989) Portfolio rebalancing and the turn of the year effect. *Journal of Finance 44:* 149-166.

Roberts, Gerald (1985) *Guide to World Commodity Markets.* Kogan Page, Ltd, London.

Rock, Kevin (1988) The specialist's order book: a possible explanation for the year-end anomaly. Working Paper, Harvard Business School, Cambridge, Massachusetts.

Roehl, Tom (1985) Data sources for research in Japanese finance. *Journal of Financial and Quantitative Analysis 20*: 273-276.

Roglaski, Richard J. (1984) New findings regarding day-of-the-week returns over trading and non-trading periods: a note. *Journal of Finance 39*: 1603-1614.

Roley, V. Vance (1987) U.S. money announcements and covered interest parity: the case of Japan. *Journal of International Money and Finance 6*: 577-70.

Roll, Richard (1977) A critique of the asset pricing theory's tests; Part I: On past and potential testability of the theory. *Journal of Financial Economics 4*: 129-176.

Roll, Richard (1984) A simple measure of the effective bid-ask spread in an efficient market. *Journal of Finance 39*: 1127-1139.

Roll, Richard (1988a) The international crash of 1987, in *Black Monday and the Future of Financial Markets* R. W. Kamphuis, R. C. Kormendi and J. W. H. Watson, eds, Dow-Jones Irwin, Homewood, Ill.

Roll, Richard (1988b) R^2. *Journal of Finance 63*: 541-566.

Roll, Richard and Stephen Ross (1980) An empirical investigation of the arbitrage pricing theory. *Journal of Finance 35*: 1073-1103.

Rosenberg, Barr and James Guy (1976a) Prediction of Beta from Investment Fundamentals. *Financial Analysts Journal 32*: 62-70.

Rosenberg, Barr and James Guy (1976b) Prediction of beta from investment fundamentals; Part II. *Financial Analysts Journal 32*: 71-79.

Rosenberg, Barr and Walt McKibben (1973) The prediction of systematic and specific risk in common stocks. *Journal of Financial and Quantitative Analysis 8*: 317-333.

Ross, Stephen (1976) The arbitrage theory of capital asset pricing. *Journal of Economic Theory 13*: 341-360.

Roth, Martin (1989) *Making Money in Japanese Stocks.* Rutland, Vermont and Tokyo: Charles E. Tuttle Co.,

Rubinstein, Mark (1987) Derivative assets analysis, *Journal of Economic Perspectives, 1*: 73-93.

Sakakibara, Shigeki, Hidetoshi Yamaji, Hisakatsu Sakurai, Kengo Shiroshita, and Shimon Fukuda (1988) *The Japanese Stock Market: Pricing Systems and Accounting Information,* New York: Praeger.

Sato, Ryuzo (1988) The U.S.-Japan trade imbalance from the Japanese perspective, Working Paper No. 2379, National Bureau of Economic Research, Cambridge, Massachusetts.

Schieneman, Gary S (1986) *Understanding Japanese Financial Statements: A Guide for the U.S. Investor.* Arthur Young, New York.

Schieneman, Gary S. (1988) *Japanese P/E Ratios: Are they Overstated by Conservative Accounting Practices?* Prudential Bache Securities, June 20.

Schwert, G.W. (1983) Seasonal regularities in securities markets. *Journal of Financial Economics* 12: 3-12.

Schwert, G.W. (1989) Why does Stock Market Volatility Change over Time? *Journal of Finance 44:* 1115-1154.

Senchak, A. J. and J. D. Martin (1987) The relative performance of the PSR and the PER investment strategies. *Financial Analysts Journal 43:* 46-56.

Shanken, Jay and Mark Weinstein (1987) Macroeconomic variables and asset pricing: estimation and tests. Mimeo, University of Rochester, Rochester, NY.

Sharpe, William F. (1964) Capital asset prices: a theory of market equilibrium under conditions of risk. *Journal of Finance 19:* 425-442.

Sharpe, William F. (1977) The capital asset pricing model: a multi-beta interpretation in *Financial Decision Making Under Uncertainty,* Haim Levy and Marchall Sarnat, N.Y: Academic Press.

Sharpe, William F. (1978) Major investment styles. *Journal of Portfolio Management 5:* 68-74.

Sharpe, William F. (1983) Factors in New York stock exchange returns: 1931-1979. *Journal of Portfolio Management (Winter):* 5-19.

Sharpe, William F. (1987) *Asset Allocation Tools.* The Scientific Press, Redwood City, CA.

Sharpe, William F. and Gordon Alexander (1990) *Investments,* 4th Edition, Englewood Cliffs, NJ, Prentice Hall.

Sharpe, William F. and Lawrence G. Tint (1990) Liabilities - a new approach. *Journal of Portfolio Management 17:* 4-10.

Shaw, Julian, Edward O. Thorp and William T. Ziemba (1990) Convergence to efficiency of the Nikkei put warrant market of 1989 and 1990. Mimeo, University of British Columbia, Vancouver, Canada.

Shoken Toshishintatu Kyokai (1989) *Investment Trusts in Japan, 1989.* Tokyo Shoken Kaikan, Nihonbashi Kayaba-cho 1-5-8, Chu-ku, Tokyo.

Sick, Gordon and William T. Ziemba (1991) The turn of the year effect in U.S. futures markets. Working Paper, University of British Columbia, Vancouver, Canada.

Singapore Monetary Exchange (1985, 1990) Nikkei Stock Average Futures, Pamphlet

Smirlock, Michael and Laura Starks (1986) Day of the week effects in stock returns: some intraday evidence. *Journal of Financial Economics* 17: 197-210.

Solnik, Bruno (1988) *International Investments.* Reading Mass: Addison-Wesley.

Solnik, Bruno (1989) Optimal currency hedge ratios: the influence of the interest rate differential, in Rhee and Chang (1989)

Solnik, Bruno and B. Noetzlin (1982) Optimal international asset allocation. *Journal of Portfolio Management 9:* 11-21.

Stoll, Hans R. and Robert E. Whaley (1986) Expiration day effects of index options and futures. New York University Salomon Brothers Center Monograph, NY.

Stone, Douglas and William T. Ziemba (1990) Land and stock prices in Japan. Mimeo, University of British Columbia, Vancouver, Canada and Frank Russell Company, Tacoma Washington.

Suzuki, Yoshio (1988) *The Japanese Financial System.* Oxford University Press, Oxford.

Svensson, L.E.O. (1988) Portfolio choice and asset pricing with non-traded assets. Working Paper, Institute for International Economic Studies, University of Stockholm.

Takagi, Shinji (1987) Transactions costs and the term structure of interest rates in the OTC bond market in Japan. *Journal of Money, Credit and Banking 19:* 515-27.

Takagi, Keizo (1989) The rise of land prices in Japan: the determination mechanism and the effect of taxation system. *Bank of Japan Monetary and Economic Studies 7:* 93-139.

Taylor, James (1985) *Shadows of the Rising Sun*. Charles E. Tuttle Co, Tokyo.

Thomas, L. (1990) *The Currency Hedging Debate*. IFR Publishing, London.

Thompson, Rex (1978) The information content of discounts and premiums on closed-end fund shares. *Journal of Financial Economics 6*: 151-186.

Thurow, Lester (1985) *The Zero Sum Solution*. Simon and Schuster, NY.

Thurow, Lester (1988) America's economy: a formula for recovery, *Financial Executive*, May-June.

Todd, Russel G. (1988) Mutual funds feeling currency shifts. *Asian Wall Street Journal*, September 23-24, 1988.

Tokyo Stock Exchange (1990) *1989 Fact Book*. 2-1 Nihombashi-Kobuto-cho, Chuo-ku, Tokyo 103.

Toyo Keizai Shimposha (1990) *Japan Company Handbook, First and Second Sections*. various issues updated quarterly.

Tse, Y. K. (1991) Price and volume in the Tokyo Stock Exchange: an exploratory study in Ziemba, Bailey and Hamao (1991).

Ueda, Kazuo (1990) Are Japanse stock prices too high? Mimeo, University of Tokyo.

Vander Cruyssen, Bruno and William T. Ziemba (1991) The turn of the year effect in the futures markets. *Interfaces*, forthcoming.

Viner, Aron (1979) *Japan as Number One*. Harvard University Press, Cambridge, Mass.

Viner, Aron (1987) *Inside Japanese Financial Markets*. Dow Jones-Irwin, Homewood, Illinois and *The Japan Times*.

Viner, Aron (1988) *The Emerging Power of Japanese Money*. Dow Jones-Irwin, Homewood, Illinois and *The Japan Times*.

Van Slyke, Richard (1989) Financial services: Japan's next conquest. *New York Times*, Apr 6.

Von Wolferen, Karel (1989) *The Emergence of Japanese Power*. MacMillan, London.

Williams, Joseph (1987) Financial anomalies under rational expectations: a theory of the annual size and related effects. Working Paper, New York University, NY.

Yamaichi Securities Co., Ltd (1990) *The Japanese Stock Market*, Tokyo.

Yonezawa, Y. and F. Kon-ya (1982) The Japanese Market and the Economic Environment. *Journal of Portfolio Mangement 9:* 36-45.

Ziemba, William T. (1989) Seasonality effects in Japanese futures markets, in Rhee and Chang (1989).

Ziemba, William T. (1990a) A Test of Miller's Weekend Hypothesis for the Japanese Stock Market, Journal of Portfolio Management, in press.

Ziemba, William T. (1990b) Cumulative effects of fundamental variables on the Tokyo Stock Exchange: 1979-89. Working paper, University of British Columbia, Vancouver, Canada. Shortened version in *Investing*, February, 1991.

Ziemba, William T. (1990c) Some tests of plausible causes for anomalous behavior in Japanese security markets. Working paper, University of British Columbia, Vancouver, Canada.

Ziemba, William T. (1991a) Japanese security market regularities: monthly, turn of the month and year, holiday and Golden Week effects, *Japan and the World Economy*, in press.

Ziemba, William T. (1991b) The chicken or the egg: land and stock prices in Japan, in Ziemba, Bailey and Hamao (1991).

Ziemba, William T. (1991c) The growth in the Japanese stock market, 1949-90 and prospects for the future. *Management and Decision Economics 12:* 183-195.

Ziemba, William T. (1991d) Currency hedging strategies for U.S. investment in Japan and Japanese investment in the U.S., in S. Zenios, ed., *Computational Methods in Finance*, Cambridge University Press, 1991.

Ziemba, William T. (1991e) *Strategies for Making and Keeping Excess Profits in the Stock Market*. William Morrow, NY.

Ziemba William T., Abdulkadir Akatay and Sandra L. Schwartz (1979) *Turkish Flat Weaves*. Scorpion Publications, London.

Ziemba, William T., Warren Bailey and Yasushi Hamao, eds (1991) *Japanese Financial Market Research.*, North Holland.

Ziemba, William T. and Donald B. Hausch (1987) *Dr. Z's Beat the Racetrack*. New York, William Morrow.

Ziemba, William T. and Sandra L. Schwartz (1991) *Power Japan: How and Why the Japanese Economy Works*, Probus Publishing, Chicago.

Ziemba, William T. and Sandra L. Schwartz (1992) *Trading Japan: The Portfolio Managers Guide to Futures, Options, and Derivative Security Markets.* Probus Publishing, Chicago.

Zweig, Martin (1986) *Winning on Wall Street.* Warner Books, NY.

INDEX

OTHER JAPAN TITLES
FROM PROBUS

Unlocking Japan's Markets: Seizing Marketing and Distribution Opportunities in Today's Japan, Michael R. Czinkota & Jon Woronoff

Japan Inc.: Global Strategies of Japanese Trading Corporations, Max Eli

The Pacific Rim Futures and Options Markets: A Comprehensive, Country-by-Country Reference to the World's Fastest-Growing Financial Markets, Keith K.H. Park & Steven A. Schoenfeld

The Japanese Bond Markets: An Overview & Analysis, ed. Frank J. Fabozzi

FORTHCOMING JAPAN TITLES
FROM PROBUS

Power Japan: How and Why the Japanese Economy Works, William T. Ziemba & Sandra L. Schwartz (Spring 1992)

Venture Japan: How Growing Companies Worldwide Can Tap into the Japanese Venture Capital Markets, James W. Borton (Fall 1991)

The Japanese Futures, Options, and Warrants Markets: Structure, Performance and Opportunities, William T. Ziemba and Sandra L. Schwartz (Spring 1992)

Japan: Economic/Demographic Information

Geographic area:	145,856 sq. miles
Topography:	Four main islands—Honshu (mainland), Hokkaido, Kyushu and Shikoku
Government type:	Parliamentary democracy
Capital:	Tokyo
Population:	123,231,000
Population density:	844 per sq. mile, 76.7% urban
Agricultural products:	Rice, vegetables, fruits and sugar
Industrial products:	Metals, chemicals, textiles and electronics
Natural resources:	Fish, oil, natural gas, negligible amount of mineral resources
Literacy:	99%
Defense:	Less than 1% GNP
National budget:	$470 billion
Balance of payments:	+ $85 billion
Inflation:	0.7%
Gross National Product:	$2.1 trillion
Gross Domestic Product:	$1.6 trillion
International reserves: (less gold)	$98 billion
Gold reserves:	24.2 million fine troy ounces
Major imports:	Fuels, machinery, manufactured goods, raw materials and foodstuffs
Imports:	$187 billion
U.S.	20%
Middle East	26%
Southeast Asia	22%
European Community	6%
Major Exports:	Machinery, electrical equipment, motor vehicles, chemicals and manufactured goods
Exports:	$264 billion
U.S.	37%
Southeast Asia	23%
European Community	12%
Labor Profile:	
Agriculture, Forestry, Fishing	8.8%
Manufacturing	25.02%
Transport./Communications	5.91%
Construction	9.13%
Other	51.17%